THE
Adams-Jefferson
LETTERS

The Omohundro Institute of
Early American History and Culture
is sponsored jointly by the College of
William and Mary and Colonial Williamsburg,
Incorporated. Publication of this book
has been assisted by a grant from
the Lilly Endowment, Inc.

THE
Adams-Jefferson
LETTERS

*The Complete Correspondence
Between Thomas Jefferson
and Abigail and John Adams*

*

EDITED BY
LESTER J. CAPPON

PUBLISHED FOR
*The Omohundro Institute of Early American History
and Culture at Williamsburg, Virginia*
by The University of North Carolina Press
Chapel Hill and London

The paper in this book meets the guidelines for permanence and durability
of the Committee on Production Guidelines for Book Longevity of the
Council on Library Resources.

Printed in the United States of America

cloth   12   11   10   09   08   8   7   6   5   4
paper   12   11   10   09   08   18   17   16   15   14

Library of Congress Cataloging-in-Publication Data

Adams, John, 1735–1826.
    The Adams-Jefferson letters: the complete correspondence between
Thomas Jefferson and Abigail and John Adams / edited by Lester J.
Cappon.
      p.   cm.
    Reprint. Originally published: 1959.
    Includes index.
    ISBN-13: 978-0-8078-1807-7 (cloth : alk. paper)
    ISBN-10: 0-8078-1807-0 (cloth : alk. paper)
    ISBN-13: 978-0-8078-4230-0 (pbk.: alk. paper)

    ISBN-10: 0-8078-4230-3 (pbk.: alk. paper)
    1. Adams, John, 1735–1826—Correspondence.   2. Jefferson, Thomas,
1743–1826—Correspondence.   3. Adams, Abigail, 1744–1818—
Correspondence.   4. Presidents—United States—Correspondence.
5. Presidents—United States—Wives—Correspondence.   I. Jefferson,
Thomas, 1743–1826.   II. Adams, Abigail, 1744–1818.   III. Cappon,
Lester J., 1900–   .   IV. Omohundro Institute of Early American History
and Culture (Williamsburg, Va.)   V. Title.
E322.A4 1988   88-14258
973.4′4′0924—dc19   CIP

For

DOROTHY BERNET CAPPON
"with every sentiment of tenderness,
esteem, and admiration"

CONTENTS

vii

3. *"As We are poor We ought to be Œconomists"* . . . 72

September 1785–February 1786

✳ 1785 ✳

✳ 1786 ✳

* 1787 *

5. *"The first principle of a good government"* 163

January–October 1787

* 1787 *

6. *"On ... Guard against the immeasurable avarice of Amsterdam"* 205

November 1787–May 1789

✳ 1787 ✳

✳ 1788 ✳

✳ 1789 ✳

✳ 1790 ✳

✳ 1791 ✳

✳ 1793 ✳

✳ 1794 ✳

❊   1795   ❊

❊   1796   ❊

❊   1801   ❊

❊   1804   ❊

10. *"Belief . . . the assent of the mind to an intelligible proposition"* 341

June–December 1813

✳ 1813 ✳

❋ 1824 ❋

❋ 1825 ❋

❋ 1826 ❋

PREFACE

NO CORRESPONDENCE in American history is more quotable or more readily recognized for its historical significance than that of John Adams and Thomas Jefferson. Yet, only now, a century and a third after their deaths in 1826, is their exchange of letters presented in full. Publication was first anticipated in their lifetime but never encouraged by them. During the political controversies which cast a long shadow over their public careers, they suffered embarrassment from the unauthorized printing of occasional letters written in confidence. The years of retirement, they hoped, would provide a partial escape from the virulence of party strife and the publicity of high office. But statesmen, even in retirement, still belong to the public, as Jefferson learned from personal experience. He concluded in 1815 that his correspondence with Adams had been observed in the post offices, because a printer "has had the effrontery to propose to me the letting him publish it. These people think they have a right to everything however secret or sacred." [1]

If idle curiosity or selfish motives often aroused the momentary interest of the public, the intelligent citizen had some appreciation, however limited, of the writings of these statesmen as records of historical events. Adams and Jefferson, who lived long enough to acquire perspective on their own times, had become historical figures to the younger generation. As actors on the Revolutionary stage, they were asked innumerable questions about that heroic period, scarcely a half-century removed, which had already acquired the aura of history

1. TJ to JA, Aug. 10, 1815, June 1, 1822, below, 453, 578.

in the minds of the American people. The two venerable patriots themselves were well aware of their role as "Argonauts" [2] to be remembered by posterity. Adams best expressed the point when he hoped for publication of all of Jefferson's letters "in volumes." Even though some letters might "not always appear Orthodox," he wrote, "they will exhibit a Mass of Taste, Sense, Literature and Science, presented in a sweet simplicity and a neat elegance of Stile, which will be read with delight in future ages." [3] This is explanation enough for Adams's saving all he had received. Jefferson too preserved his great accumulation of correspondence, although he agreed that "an hour of conversation would be worth a volume of letters." [4] It is the recipients' copies, originally filed at Quincy and Monticello, that provide the basis for the present edition.

"Posterity," asserted Adams, who seemed more willing than Jefferson to designate their papers public property, "would ... know on what kind terms they lived"; [5] but during the course of a century this information was derived only piecemeal from successive editions of their letters, from Henry Randall's discursive account of Jefferson's life and times and friendship with Adams, [6] and, as a centennial commemoration, from Paul Wilstach's selection from their correspondence of 1812-26. [7] Actually, many of the letters exchanged by Adams and Jefferson have been in the public domain a long time, although they are scattered throughout their published writings rather than assembled as the integrated correspondence of both. During the nineteenth century a small percentage of Jefferson's letters appeared in the writings edited soon after his death by his grandson Thomas Jefferson Randolph, by Henry A. Washington in the 1850's, and by Paul Leicester Ford in the 1890's, the last being the most reliable in respect to texts. The sole edition of Adams's *Works*, carefully prepared by his grandson Charles Francis Adams from the manuscripts in the family's custody, was published in the early 1850's. Soon after the turn of the century came the Lipscomb and Bergh edition of Jef-

2. TJ to JA, March 25, 1826, below, 613.
3. JA to TJ, July 12, 1822, below, 582.
4. TJ to JA, April 8, 1816, below, 467.
5. H. A. S. Dearborn to TJ, Nov. 24, 1823, Jefferson Papers, Library of Congress, quoting JA.
6. Henry S. Randall, *The Life of Thomas Jefferson* (N. Y., 1858), III, Chaps. IX-XIII.
7. Paul Wilstach, ed., *Correspondence of John Adams and Thomas Jefferson 1812-1826* (Indianapolis, [1925]). This selection is only a representative sampling.

ferson's *Writings*, more extensive but less authoritative than Ford. All of these were based largely, if not exclusively, upon retained copies (loose or in letter-books, in polygraph or letter-press) rather than upon the recipients' copies which have prime value for research. Until the planning in the mid-1940's of the Princeton edition of *The Papers of Thomas Jefferson* by Julian P. Boyd, no one had dealt with the problem of evaluating for publication the total *correspondence*—what Jefferson read in his mail as well as what he wrote in his own letters.

The richness of the Adams-Jefferson correspondence can be most fully appreciated by following the letters in chronological sequence. Only then can the reader sense the mental vigor of the two men and exclaim with Adams, "So many Subjects crowd upon me that I know not, with which to begin." [8] During their years in public office they gave close attention to the daily problems that pressed upon them, with occasional reflections revealing the statesmanship behind their decisions. Later, as elder statesmen in retirement, they sat in judgment on the world which had passed through two revolutions, on their country which had won independence and confirmed it, and on themselves; and they did so with an open-mindedness and a feeling of conviction that subsequent generations cannot fail to admire.

The present edition began as one of the early projects of the Institute of Early American History and Culture. The plan for complete coverage of the correspondence, first developed in 1948 by Carl Bridenbaugh, then director of the Institute, received cordial support from the editors of the Jefferson Papers at Princeton. They had already established in their offices a photo-print file of the Jefferson Papers in the Library of Congress. They had also secured permission from the Adams Manuscript Trust to make similar copies of its Adams-Jefferson manuscripts and to transmit the microfilm to the Library of Congress.[9] In October 1948 the Trust granted the Institute permission to publish the pertinent letters from the Adams Family Papers.

The following January, Donald H. Mugridge, on leave from the Library of Congress, undertook the editorship, supported by a grant

8. JA to TJ, July 9, 1813, below, 350.
9. Lyman H. Butterfield, "The Jefferson-Adams Correspondence in the Adams Manuscript Trust," Lib. Cong. *Quarterly Journal of Current Acquisitions*, 5, no. 2 (Feb. 1948), 3-6.

from the Rockefeller Foundation to the Institute. Mr. Mugridge assembled the texts and proofread them, wrote headnotes for individual documents or groups of documents, and supplied detailed annotation. By mid-1950 he had completed the editorial work for the first period, 1777-1801, but the funds were exhausted.

In 1951 Lyman H. Butterfield, second director of the Institute and formerly on the staff of *The Papers of Thomas Jefferson,* took over the work and revised the plan of operation to produce an edition for the general reader. Assisted by Mrs. Stella D. Neiman, he proceeded with the editing of the letters in the second period, 1812-26, but administrative duties diverted him and the task remained unfinished when he left the Institute in 1954 to become editor of the Adams Papers.[10]

When I assumed the editorial responsibility in 1956, at the urging of my colleagues, James Morton Smith and Lawrence W. Towner, I reviewed the existing plan in relation to content and presentation. Without doubt the edition ought to be as complete as possible. The prospect of attaining that objective was better than ever before because of the intensive search by Mr. Boyd and his associates for Jefferson material and because of similar work by Mr. Butterfield and his editorial staff on the Adams Papers. Since the letters between Abigail Adams and Jefferson complement perfectly the correspondence of the two statesmen, it seemed to me that they should be included for their personal charm and tang as well as for their subject matter. Moreover, Mrs. Adams played an influential part in the delayed reconciliation between her husband and Jefferson during 1801-12.

It seemed desirable also to simplify the editorial process by eliminating headnotes for individual documents, by reducing the annotation, by presenting the letters chronologically in a series of chapters, each with an introductory essay, and by providing a general introduction on the historical background of the correspondence. To streamline the scholarly trappings of an edition designed primarily for the general reader is more compelling now than it was in 1948.

10. A comprehensive edition of the Adams Papers sponsored by the Massachusetts Historical Society, with editorial funds provided by Time, Inc., on behalf of *Life,* is in course of publication under Mr. Butterfield's editorship by The Belknap Press of Harvard University Press. Though a microfilm edition of the corpus of the papers is available for research purposes, the manuscripts themselves are closed to inspection during the course of editorial work.

The first volume of the monumental *Papers of Thomas Jefferson* was published in 1950; fifteen more volumes have appeared, and the scholar will turn increasingly to this series, rich in annotation and historical criticism. Readers of the present edition will observe that it leans heavily on the *Papers* for basic documentation to 1789. The meticulous scholarship of Mr. Boyd and his associates can only be fully appreciated by working closely with these superb volumes. Furthermore, the accuracy of the texts in the Boyd edition made it possible to use photocopies of them for printer's copy, which were proofread against the original manuscripts (in microfilm or microprint). Grateful acknowledgment is expressed here to the Princeton University Press for permission to make those photocopies.

Publication of *The Papers of Thomas Jefferson* has affected my editorial procedure in other ways. The descriptive data on each document in the *Papers* provide sufficient reason for omitting addresses and endorsements (with a few exceptions) and the location of each manuscript. Decoded passages have been copied as rendered in the *Papers* and printed in italics. The ampersand is changed to *and* (or to the Latin *et* in the abbreviation, *etc.*), except in the names of firms. Obvious slips of the pen are corrected silently. During the last eight years of his life Adams's palsied hands forced him to dictate his letters to amanuenses in his household. He could not see well enough to correct their errors, many of them the result of ignorance, and it would be misleading to retain them. Capitalization in the original manuscripts has been followed, but the first word of the sentence is capitalized despite Jefferson's customary use of lower case. Punctuation likewise follows the original manuscript unless it obscures the meaning; and excessive punctuation, characteristic of Adams, is usually retained in order to convey the style of the original as much as possible. Abbreviated words are not expanded, the full word being supplied only to avoid ambiguity or misunderstanding. So, too, with erratic spelling, common in the eighteenth century, except when clarification demands the modern equivalent; but the Latin word, that favourite [*sic*] of the pedant, is shunned almost to exclusion. The orthography and other devices of communication of the eighteenth century are not so different from our own that we are justified in sacrificing something of the spirit of that era for the sake of modernization as the comfortable road to learning.

Personal names are identified in the index, thus reducing the

number of footnotes very considerably. The correspondents are referred to as AA, JA, and TJ. After the first citation of a source or
secondary work, subsequent references are by the author's or editor's
name and short title. Since numerous citations are made to the collected writings of Adams and Jefferson, the several editions are listed
here in chronological order of publication for the reader's convenience:

Thomas Jefferson Randolph, ed., *Memoir, Correspondence, and
Miscellanies, from the Papers of Thomas Jefferson*. 4 vols. Charlottesville, Va., 1829.

Charles Francis Adams, ed., *The Works of John Adams ... with a
Life of the Author, Notes and Illustrations*. 10 vols. Boston, 1850-56.

H[enry] A. Washington, ed., *The Writings of Thomas Jefferson
... from the Original Manuscripts, deposited in the Department of
State*. ... 9 vols. Washington, D.C., 1853-54.

Paul Leicester Ford, ed., *The Writings of Thomas Jefferson*.
10 vols. New York and London, 1892-99.

Andrew A. Lipscomb and Albert Ellery Bergh, eds., *The Writings
of Thomas Jefferson*. Library Edition ... Issued under the Auspices
of the Thomas Jefferson Memorial Association. 20 vols. Washington, D.C., 1903-4.

Julian P. Boyd, and others, eds., *The Papers of Thomas Jefferson*.
Princeton, 1950– (in progress).

The present edition of the Adams-Jefferson correspondence would
have been impossible without the generous co-operation of the two
research libraries containing the vast majority of the original manuscripts: the Library of Congress and the Massachusetts Historical
Society. A decade ago the Adams Family Papers, deposited in the
Society in 1905, were still the property of the Adams Manuscript
Trust, whose officers kindly granted permission to the Institute to
publish the Adams-Jefferson material. The late Stewart Mitchell, then
director of the Society, played an important role in this negotiation.
In 1956 the Trust deeded the Adams Papers to the Society. While
the Jefferson Papers in the Library of Congress have long been open
to investigators, its microfilm copy of that vast collection, originally
made for use by the editors of *The Papers of Thomas Jefferson*,
accrued to the benefit of the Institute as well. But it was the "control
file" of the Jefferson office at Princeton that provided the best check-
list of extant manuscripts.

The following analysis of the total correspondence is of considerable interest:

NUMBER OF LETTERS

1777-1801		*1785-1804*	
JA to TJ	80	AA to TJ	24
TJ to JA	91	TJ to AA	21
	171		45

1812-1826		*1813-1817*	
JA to TJ	109	AA to TJ	3
TJ to JA	49	TJ to AA	3
	158		6

Grand Total: 380

The Institute is indebted to the Rockefeller Foundation for the grant which made possible the editorial work of Donald H. Mugridge. His careful research spared me countless hours in a schedule allowing too little time for collateral research. Although the headnotes prepared by Mr. Mugridge were discarded in the final plan for this edition, some of the information has been used profitably in the condensed annotations to the text. During the period in which Mr. Butterfield worked on the correspondence, he as director of the Institute and I as its editor of publications conferred from time to time on editorial problems. His sound judgment and previous experience as a historical editor bore fruit then and later in many intangible ways that are inherent in any scholarly undertaking, and it was always a pleasure to work with him. His revised plan was revised in turn by me, and I must bear the responsibility for the final organization and presentation of the material. That includes also the final proof-reading of all texts against the manuscripts.

I express my thanks to Francis L. Berkeley, Jr., and Robert E. Stocking of the University of Virginia Library's Manuscript Division for their never-failing co-operation in making its rich resources readily accessible. I am also grateful to Mrs. Stella D. Neiman for her reference work on the later part of the correspondence and to Professor Talbot R. Selby of the College of William and Mary for supplying the translation of Greek and Latin quotations in the text. To Frederick

A. Hetzel, Diane Smith Leland, and Elizabeth Duncan Brown of the Institute staff, who relieved me of pressing duties at critical moments, I express my gratitude. I have indicated my indebtedness to my wife in the dedication, which quotes a letter from John Adams to Abigail Adams.[11]

The role of the administrator, even on a small scale, seems ever at odds with time for research and productive scholarship. I can conclude these acknowledgments only by paying tribute to the Institute's editor of books, James Morton Smith, and to the editor of the *William and Mary Quarterly*, Lawrence W. Towner. It was they who urged me to appropriate the time necessary to edit and publish the Adams-Jefferson correspondence, a task I was longing to undertake. I am deeply appreciative of their continuous concern with the Institute program and its long-range objectives. As editor Mr. Smith has been closely involved in this documentary project, keeping a watchful eye on the ever-pressing time schedule, reviewing the annotation, and criticizing essays and notes with a light voice and a sharp pencil. He has been indispensable in making this edition a reality. That is not a minor consideration when our greatest editor of Jefferson's works points out (Boyd, II, 19*n.*) that the Adams-Jefferson correspondence "remains unrivaled, in the United States at least, for its revelation of the writers' minds and characters, its literary distinction, and its historical importance."

L. J. C.

11. May 17, 1776, Charles Francis Adams, ed., *Familiar Letters of John Adams and His Wife Abigail Adams, During the Revolution* (N. Y., 1876), 175.

INTRODUCTION

"Prospect of an immortality in the memories of all the worthy"

FANEUIL HALL, the "Cradle of Liberty," attracted a large crowd of Bostonians on August 2, 1826. The City Council had invited Daniel Webster, well known for his oratory, to deliver the address. It was a day of commemoration rather than of mourning, in recognition of the recent deaths of John Adams and Thomas Jefferson on July 4. The fiftieth anniversary of American independence had been celebrated in this same hall, as it was in countless others throughout the nation. In near-by Quincy, the venerable Adams had been unable to accept the invitation of his fellow citizens to be the guest of honor, and they learned of his death as they were leaving the Quincy town hall.[1]

The speaker was well chosen for the occasion in Boston a month later. A child of the Confederation period, Webster had familiarized himself with the history of the American Revolution in the course of his wide reading; and he could speak on notable events of the past quarter-century from first-hand knowledge. An Adams Federalist, he had held both Jefferson and Adams in great respect; indeed he had been Jefferson's guest at Monticello only a year and a half earlier.[2] His discourse in Faneuil Hall had substance as well as the

---

1. Daniel Webster, *A Discourse in Commemoration of the Lives and Services of John Adams and Thomas Jefferson, delivered in Faneuil Hall, Boston, August 2, 1826* (Boston, 1826), [3]; JA to John Whitney, Chairman of the Committee of Arrangements for celebrating the approaching anniversary of the fourth of July, in the Town of Quincy, June 7, 1826, Charles Francis Adams, ed., *The Works of John Adams*, 10 vols. (Boston, 1850-56), X, 416-17. Hereafter cited as *Works*.

2. Fletcher Webster, ed., *The Private Correspondence of Daniel Webster* (Boston, 1857), I, 361.

characteristic flowing periods that must have captivated his audience, and it struck a significant historical note in evaluating the lives of Adams and Jefferson.

No two men now live, fellow-citizens, perhaps it may be doubted, whether any two men have ever lived, in one age, who, more than those we now commemorate, have impressed their own sentiments, in regard to politics and government, on mankind, infused their own opinions more deeply into the opinions of others, or given a more lasting direction to the current of human thought. Their work doth not perish with them. . . . No age will come, in which the American Revolution will appear less than it is, one of the greatest events in human history. No age will come, in which it will cease to be seen and felt, on either continent, that a mighty step, a great advance, not only in American affairs, but in human affairs, was made on the 4th of July 1776.[3]

In citing the Revolution as an episode of world-wide significance, Webster inevitably found cause for reflection in the aged patriots' passing from the earthly scene on this fiftieth anniversary. "May not such events," he asked, "raise the suggestion that they are not undesigned, and that Heaven does so order things, as sometimes to attract strongly the attention, and excite the thoughts of men?"[4] Webster reflected, of course, the romanticism of his own generation and indulged in mysticism that would have been sharply confuted by Adams and Jefferson as reasonable men. In that year of jubilee, 1826, which occasioned a great outburst of patriotism, Webster was also expressing the feeling of nationalism of the American people. Their Revolution had been a noble experiment, a notable success in establishing the new nation and in inspiring an unmistakable air of confidence in the future. They were the heirs of an age of progress to which their fathers and grandfathers of the eighteenth century had attested. Webster's evaluation of the American Revolution, however exaggerated its emotional overtones may seem, reflected their outlook and has been confirmed by the judgment of subsequent generations.

If Webster had had access to the correspondence of Adams and Jefferson, he could have found no more conclusive contemporary support of his judgment concerning the Revolution. As political

3. Webster, *Discourse*, 9-10.
4. *Ibid.*, 13.

philosophers the two statesmen had a keen sense of perspective and
a consciousness of great events in the making. From their reading of
English and Continental philosophers, whose works were common
property of eighteenth-century intellectuals, they put theory into
practice in government and then reassessed theory in the light of their
own experiments. What would make the rebellion of 1775-76 (as the
British referred to it) a successful revolution beyond confirmation of
independence by the victory at Yorktown? To what degree were
the basic principles of republican government workable under American conditions, in the several states and in a federal government?
Questions such as these were asked and partially answered as Adams
and Jefferson corresponded year after year, never casting doubt on
the momentous decision of 1776 but never believing that achieve-
ments could be assured without eternal vigilance. Long before they
had retired from public life, they fully understood the significance
of their own contributions to the Revolution, and on several occasions one or the other displayed some jealousy of his claims in very
human fashion. It is obvious that the history of the Revolution and
the early federal period of the Republic could not be written ade-
quately without attention to the work of Jefferson and Adams. They
were aware of this fact, perhaps a bit egotistically, but with a profound sense of history.

If the correspondence of Adams and Jefferson embodied no other
theme than the vicissitudes of their friendship, it would meet the test
as an appealing record of human nature. The contribution each made
to this relationship becomes clearer by a study of their characters and
personalities. Jefferson is the more difficult to approach. His contemporaries, it seems clear, did break through his reserve into easy-
flowing conversation. Although he did not lack a sense of humor, he
displayed it sparingly in his letters, and he kept no diary which might
reveal his character on more intimate terms. Thus history is afforded
a half-satisfying record that thwarts our better understanding of a
statesman who wrote almost incessantly, but seldom in a personal
vein. Perhaps Jefferson was as congenial with John Adams as anyone
outside his family; yet even to Adams, Jefferson's expressions of devotion were infrequent. He never wrote with less restraint than when
he offered congratulations on Adams's election to the vice-presidency:

"No man on earth pays more cordial homage to your worth nor wishes more fervently your happiness. Tho' I detest the appearance even of flattery, I cannot always suppress the effusions of my heart." [5]

While Jefferson did not shun controversy when a basic principle was involved, he had no ambition and no heart for personal diatribe. In his desire to live in harmony with his associates and friends he preferred to avoid argument and spare their feelings even when self-defense was justified. He put a high premium on privacy of thought and action. In the classical tradition the hearth of Monticello was his sanctum and no outsider penetrated the inner circle of the family; yet in the same tradition, hospitality was a natural art practiced on Jefferson's mountain top and enjoyed by countless visitors as well as invited guests. The private rights of the individual citizen and his valuation of privacy are complementary factors in Jefferson's desire to perpetuate his republican agrarian society. He was too modest to think of himself as the "squire of Monticello," but that title indicates his social position in the society of Albemarle County along with his feeling of responsibility for the public welfare. It also suggests something of the essence of Jeffersonian republicanism.

The contrast between the tall, angular Jefferson and the chubby, rotund Adams must have been striking whenever they were seen together. Even to a casual acquaintance the reserve of the Virginian undoubtedly accentuated the air of cordiality of the New Englander. "Adams has a heart formed for friendship, and susceptible of its finest feelings," declared the loyalist Jonathan Sewall, who was highly gratified by the hearty greeting which Adams gave him in London after the Revolutionary War.[6] Under the circumstances Adams, "humane, generous, and open," could hardly have received a finer compliment. With his good nature went a keen sense of humor, an eye for the ridiculous and the incongruous, and a willingness to poke fun at himself. When discussing religion with Jefferson he recalled that while at Harvard he had been "a mighty Metaphis[ic]ian"; and how, a few years later, when he thought he was in ill health, Dr. Hersey of Hingham looked him over and prescribed as follows: "Persevere, and as

5. TJ to JA, May 10, 1789, below, 238. TJ referred to the office as "the Presidency of the Senate."
6. C. F. Adams, "Life of John Adams," *Works*, I, 57n.

sure as there is a God in Heaven you will recover." [7] Adams found
ceremonious interviews with the Tripolitan ambassador in London
highly amusing and his vanity was touched by the ambassador's secretary who so admired the American's ability to match the Tripolitan's
coffee-sipping and tobacco-whiffing that he exclaimed in ecstasy,
"Monsieur votes etes un Turk." [8]

Adams's warm nature did not always make for cordial feelings; it
often led to surges of sudden anger, for he felt deeply toward those
he loved and those he despised. His outbursts of temper, antagonizing
his opponents and inflicting injury often out of proportion to the of-
fense, have unfortunately distorted the historical record concerning
his character; his irascibility has overshadowed his kindliness. In retaliation Adams's political enemies sought to damage his reputation
and succeeded in large measure. He never forgave Alexander Hamilton
and Timothy Pickering for their personal and political offenses. Yet
he was no less unselfish than Jefferson concerning the great issues for
which they contended. The self-discipline in his Puritan training came
to his aid on many an occasion in choosing between duty and his own
pleasure, and he was willing to endure long periods of separation from
his family in the service of his country. At the age of twenty-three,
when Adams was considering the practice of law, Jeremiah Gridley,
father of the Boston bar, gave him a piece of advice: "pursue the study
of the law, rather than the gain of it." In taking account of seventeen
years' practice, Adams concluded that "no lawyer in America ever did
so much business as I did afterwards, . . . for so little profit." [9] Unconsciously, perhaps, he applied the principle behind this advice to
other phases of his career. If virtue was indispensable to good government, as he maintained, so it must be to the best citizenship which
Adams exemplified in public service and private life.

The early political and diplomatic careers of Adams and Jefferson
are sketched in Chapter 1. As men of principle they doubtless found
satisfaction in a friendship that responded to their dissimilar tempera-
ments. In the Continental Congress of 1775 they discovered they could
work effectively together, a conclusion borne out during their diplomatic service. When Jefferson expected to join the American peace
commissioners, Adams, Jay, and Franklin, in Paris in 1783, he recalled

7. JA to TJ, Sept. 14, 1813, below, 374.
8. JA to TJ, Feb. 17, 1786, below, 121.
9. JA, "Diary" and "Autobiography," *Works*, II, 45-56.

Adams's strong prejudices—his dislike of both Jay and Franklin, of both the French and the English—but he recognized his honesty and integrity.[10] Since Adams's dislike of all parties and all men might balance his prejudices, Jefferson anticipated constructive results, and certainly this prediction proved true during the five years of their joint efforts. Before Jefferson's arrival in Paris, Adams referred to him as "an old Friend . . . with whom I have often had occasion to labour at many a knotty Problem." Other letters contain the implication that he would be a great improvement over Franklin, who as elder diplomat always dominated the scene [11] and was too much of a Francophile in thought and action to please Adams. Since he expected Jefferson to succeed Franklin at the Court of Versailles, Adams, who was going to the Court of St. James, would be "happy in a Correspondence of Friendship, Confidence, and Affection." [12]

In their collaboration abroad, Adams was the senior diplomat in both age and experience, a factor of some weight in their relationship. Although Jefferson often deferred to the judgment of his colleague, he did so without suppressing his own opinions. If the elder man bespoke a paternal attitude at times, the younger did not record it.[13] He was conscious of Adams's vanity and occasional irritableness, but those shortcomings could be overlooked amid the larger issues at stake. After working personally with Adams seven months in France and seven weeks in England and corresponding regularly, Jefferson developed the highest respect for him as a seasoned diplomat: profound in his views, accurate in his judgments, and disinterested in personal gain. He could hardly have spoken more from the heart when he wrote Madison that Adams "is so amiable, . . . I pronounce you will love him if ever you become acquainted with him." [14]

In the Adams-Jefferson friendship Abigail Adams played both a happy and an unhappy role, and her correspondence with Jefferson is

10. TJ to Madison, Feb. 14, 1783, Julian P. Boyd, and others, eds., *The Papers of Thomas Jefferson* (Princeton, 1950–), VI, 241. Hereafter cited as Boyd.

11. JA to James Warren, Aug. 27, 1784, and JA to Elbridge Gerry, Dec. 12, 1784, Boyd, VII, 382n.

12. JA to Richard Cranch, April 27, 1785, *ibid.*, 652n.

13. A quarter-century later Adams remarked that "Jefferson was but a boy to me." JA to Benjamin Rush, 1809, quoted in Saul K. Padover, ed., *The Complete Jefferson . . .* (N. Y., [1943]), 890n.

14. TJ to Madison, Jan. 30, 1787, Boyd, XI, 94-95.

an integral part of the record. Arriving in France about the same time in August 1784, she and Jefferson seem to have discovered almost at once that they were kindred spirits. For, whatever Mr. Adams may have told his wife in advance about the forty-year-old Virginian, her womanly thoughtfulness strengthened the bond between him and the Adams household. Knowing of his wife's death two years earlier, Mrs. Adams could appreciate his need for solicitation rather than sympathy. She was much concerned about his prolonged illness in the fall of 1784.[15] Although he lived in Paris, he was apparently a frequent and welcome visitor at the Adams residence in Auteuil, the pleasant suburb near the Bois de Boulogne, and he became strongly attached to young John Quincy, then in his late teens.[16]

The removal of Adams and his family to London in the spring of 1785, on his appointment as first American minister to Britain, ended this pleasant interlude. It also initiated the frequent exchange of letters between Mrs. Adams and the American minister to France which reveal best their high regard and admiration for each other. The Adamses left with great reluctance to take up their residence in the English metropolis. Disliking city life, they felt certain they would dislike the English too, and their anticipation was confirmed on both points.[17] They found the former enemies of America still hostile and unwilling to negotiate constructively on behalf of Anglo-American relations. Mrs. Adams, who could speak as sharply and critically as her husband and sometimes more pungently, gave vent to her ire against a certain newspaper account which she branded as "false—if it was not too rough a term for a Lady to use, I would say false as Hell, but I will substitute, one not less expressive and say, false as the English."[18] Again, in 1787 her mercurial emotions responded to the defiance of government in Massachusetts during Shays's Rebellion. She said some harsh words concerning conditions and events of which she was only partially informed, and Jefferson frankly expressed his disagreement.[19]

15. AA to Mrs. Cranch, Dec. 9, 1784, Charles Francis Adams, ed., *Letters of Mrs. Adams, the Wife of John Adams* (Boston, 1841) II, 62.
16. Samuel F. Bemis, *John Quincy Adams and the Foundations of American Foreign Policy* (N. Y., 1950), 14.
17. AA to Mrs. Cranch, June 24, 1785, *ibid.*, 96-99.
18. AA to TJ, Oct. 19, 1785, below, 84.
19. See Chap. 5, below, *passim.*

His respect for Mrs. Adams as a woman of taste and versatility heightened the pleasure of his correspondence with her. She was keenly interested in the world about her, as he always was, and she was essentially an intellectual, having surmounted most of the barriers confronting those women of the eighteenth century who had the talent and the ambition to become more than ornaments of fashion.[20] Mentally and emotionally she complemented her husband's capacities for accomplishment; her portraits suggest a firmness of decision that he could only have admired as a decisive person himself. Both were positive personalities, sometimes too incontestably right to be pleasing to others who under more congenial circumstances would have conceded the point at issue.

But much of Jefferson's enjoyment of Mrs. Adams came about through her feminine sensitiveness and intuition, her thoughtfulness and insight. Soon after her arrival in London she wrote him about the journey. How characteristic of Mrs. Adams, he must have thought, to find herself in a situation on board the Dover pacquet in which she was given two songbirds "by a young Gentleman whom we had received on Board with us, and who being excessively sick I admitted into the cabin, in gratitude for which he insisted upon my accepting a pair of his Birds." Her own little bird was too frightened to take along from Paris, but as these "had been used to travelling I brought them here [to London] in safety, for which they hourly repay me by their melodious notes." [21] Without hesitation Jefferson turned to Mrs. Adams for little favors, and she to him, as their correspondence flourished between Paris and London. When he made arrangements for his younger daughter Polly to join him in France and learned that she must go via England, he relied on Mrs. Adams to take care of her and send her on to Paris. Polly's visit provided a delightful exchange of letters between Jefferson and Mrs. Adams, and Mr. Adams inserted his own expression of pleasure in a business letter to Jefferson. When the Adamses were making plans for returning to the United States, Jefferson in Paris was especially regretful because "I have considered you while in London as my neighbor." [22]

20. William Cranch, *Memoir of the Life, Character, and Writings of John Adams* (Washington, 1827), 16.
21. AA to TJ, June 6, 1785, below, 28.
22. TJ to AA, Feb. 2, 1788, below, 222.

To what degree Jefferson and the Adamses were neighbors in Philadelphia and Washington during the years 1790-1800 cannot be stated with certainty. Mrs. Adams wrote her sister in April 1790 that "Mr. Jefferson is here [in New York], and adds much to the social circle." [23] He had just arrived to take up his duties as secretary of state. The federal government soon moved to Philadelphia, and, when Congress was not in session, both Jefferson and Adams spent as much time as possible at home. Then for three years, 1794-96, after resigning his secretaryship, Jefferson was out of office. By the time he became vice-president in 1797 animosity was mounting between Federalists and Republicans.

Jeffersonian Republicanism developed in opposition to the centralizing tendencies in President Washington's administration—against Alexander Hamilton and the High Federalists—not against Adams, the Vice President. Nevertheless, as Washington's successor, Adams inherited the Jeffersonian opposition to encroachment on state powers and on individual rights, and by the late 1790's the Republican party was an effective organization marshalling strength for the contest of 1800. As head of the Republican party, Jefferson was leading the opposition. Again he was upholding the rights of the individual, now threatened by the Alien and Sedition Acts, and he resorted to protest by state action in the Kentucky and Virginia Resolutions of 1798. Mrs. Adams lent weight to the rumor that the Republicans were plotting to force the resignation of President Adams by defamation, "and then they will Reign triumphant, *headed by the Man of the People*." [24] There could be little, if any, neighborliness in this state of affairs. In the election of 1800 the Federalist party suffered a greater defeat than President Adams. It was their first defeat as well as his, but the party never recovered from the disaster. He, however, went home to Quincy, relieved to be dissociated from extremists among the Federalists, although he was bitter over his defeat by the Democratic-Republicans. Jefferson could not resist calling this first turnover in American politics a "revolution." To whatever extent Adams attributed his political defeat to Jefferson, Mrs. Adams apparently agreed, confirming her husband's bitterness and resentment and offering nothing to

---

23. AA to Mrs. Mary Smith Cranch, April 3, 1790, Stewart Mitchell, ed., *New Letters of Abigail Adams, 1788-1801* (Boston, 1947), 44.
24. AA to Mrs. Cranch, March 20, 1798, *ibid.*, 147.

alleviate the tension straining their friendship. Indeed, her feeling became more deep-seated, more irreconcilable, than his, to judge from her subsequent brief correspondence with Jefferson.[25]

If, in contrast to the philosophical letters between 1812 and 1826, the Adams-Jefferson correspondence before 1801 sometimes seems overburdened with the prosaic details of whale-oil and tobacco contracts and sparse in reflective comment, one must not overlook the fact that the earlier record portrays men of affairs engaged in the routine daily tasks of diplomacy and politics. Policy and decision are usually obscured by detail. One must allow also for the separation of their letters from those of numerous other correspondents whose ideas and reactions had a bearing on what Adams and Jefferson thought and did. But we have the satisfaction of reading almost all the letters exchanged (and a few not delivered) and thus of following what they learned and acted upon day by day. Their years at foreign courts are most revealing of the bonds of friendship and common purpose.

In the game of diplomacy the diplomat must always consider first the interests of his own country, but he must be well informed on those of the nation to which he is accredited and understand the temperament of its people. In these terms, Jefferson may be called the perfect diplomat in the ideal post. He felt a fine rapport with the French people and they with him. It was not an easy post to fill as successor to Dr. Franklin, the philosopher *par excellence*, a great figure at court, frequenter of the fashionable *salons*, and adored by the populace. Jefferson was too young to succeed Franklin as sage, but he admired French culture, and in philosophical and artistic circles he was recognized as a charming intellectual. Although the Marquis de Lafayette was inclined to exaggeration concerning Americans, his countrymen doubtless agreed with him that "nothing can excell M. Jefferson's abilities, virtues, pleasing temper . . . [as a] great statesman [and] zealous citizen." [26] He was always informing himself about the French people, how they lived, what they bought and sold, how notoriously they were governed. He was circumspect in dealing with royal favorites and politicians, in order to keep within the bounds of

25. See Chaps. 8, 12, below.
26. Louis Gottschalk, ed., *The Letters of Lafayette to Washington, 1777-1799* (N. Y., 1944), 344.

diplomatic propriety. He cultivated Vergennes, the foreign minister, for obvious reasons, and no other acquaintance of influence at court; "on the contrary," he stated, I "have studiously avoided it." [27]

Adams had developed no sympathetic understanding of the French during his diplomatic career before 1785. Their ways were not his ways and, if Dr. Franklin was a thorn in his flesh, his trucking with the French was no incentive to Adams to turn Francophile. Wisely Congress had not appointed him minister to Versailles, but it gave him a more difficult assignment: to fight for position in London on behalf of the young Republic. To be American minister to Great Britain in the 1780's was an unenviable appointment. The former colonists were now outside the British Empire and Mother England was in no mood to make concessions—not even to her own advantage, said Adams. "John Bull dont see it, and if he dont see a Thing at first, you know it is a rule with him ever after wards to swear that it dont exist, even when he does both see it and feel it." [28] Or as Jefferson stated the case, with reference to the advantage of American neutrality to the English: "I never yet found any other general rule for foretelling what they will do, but that of examining what they ought not to do." [29] Adams's job was to negotiate and continue to negotiate, no matter how hopeless and distasteful the task, for a weak nation must grasp at small concessions, though always with due caution. It was an irritating, often a humiliating, experience. He compensated for it somewhat by being aggressively patriotic, encouraged by Mrs. Adams who took "a pride in acknowledging my Country." [30] But Adams's responsibility, like Jefferson's, was to keep the peace and always to avoid foreign entanglements.

Jefferson has been characterized as the practical idealist, whose idealism "was durable enough to survive his introduction to European politics" and whose "sense of practicality remained acute enough to restrain him from attempting the impossible." [31] Adams, his worthy colleague across the Channel, may be characterized as the skeptical

27. TJ to Mme Townsend, Nov. 6, 1787, Boyd, XII, 329.
28. JA to TJ, March 1, 1787, below, 175-76.
29. TJ to JA, Sept. 28, 1787, below, 200.
30. AA to Mrs. Elizabeth Smith Shaw, Sept. 15, 1785, quoted in Dorothy S. Eaton, "Some Letters of Abigail Adams," Lib. Cong. *Quart. Jour. of Acquisitions*, 4, no. 4 (Aug. 1947), 4.
31. Boyd, VII, 466.

realist, whose notable success in securing loans from the hard-headed Dutch merchant-diplomats confirmed his basic point of view.[32] Although Adams did not achieve comparable results in England, he laid the groundwork for his successors. Both he and Jefferson had observed European international politics at close range, which spared them a provincial outlook on world affairs later when, in high office at home, the responsibility for foreign policy was theirs. From his experience in Europe and his knowledge of inter-state rivalry in America, Adams drew the following conclusion:

> I have long been settled in my own opinion, that neither Philosophy, nor Religion, nor Morality, nor Wisdom, nor Interest, will ever govern nations or Parties, against their Vanity, their Pride, their Resentment or Revenge, or their Avarice or Ambition. Nothing but Force and Power and Strength can restrain them.[33]

The reward for the distinguished diplomatic service of Adams and Jefferson was high office in the new government of the United States —the vice-presidency and the secretaryship of state respectively. They had no part in drafting the Constitution, but they hoped for the perpetuation of republican virtues and the maintenance of balanced government under its provisions. The Adamses had not found an inherent love of liberty in Europe. It seemed to be indigenous to America, where, as Mrs. Adams put it, "diligence integrity Genius and Spirit are the true sources of Superiority . . . instead of titles stars and garters."[34] But Adams warned Jefferson that "you and I have been indefatigable Labourers through our Whole Lives for a Cause which will be thrown away in the next generation, upon the Vanity and Foppery of Persons of whom we do not now know the Names perhaps."[35] Adams, who had just written his *Defence of the Constitutions of the United States,* pointed out to his brother-in-law that only the virtue and moderation of the people could assure good government. "I am no enemy to elegance, but I say no man has a right to think of elegance till he has secured substance; nor then, to seek more

32. See Chap. 6, below, 205-7.
33. JA to TJ, Oct. 9, 1787, Boyd, XII, 221.
34. AA to Mrs. Elizabeth Smith Shaw, Oct. 15, 1786, Lib. Cong. *Quart. Jour. of Acquisitions,* 4, no. 4 (Aug. 1947), 4.
35. JA to TJ, Oct. 8, 1787, Boyd, XII, 221.

of it than he can afford." [36] Adams was referring, of course, to conditions in the states.

No one in 1787-88 could conjure up a conception of the virulent ebb and flow of party politics during the next decade at the national level, where virtue seemed no longer virtuous and a government of men threatened to replace a government of laws. The outlines of this struggle have already been traced to indicate the political vicissitudes of Adams and Jefferson. Adams emerged in 1801 a disillusioned and rejected statesman, who could never quite forget the injustice and abuse he had suffered; a decade later he recalled that "I have been disgraced and degraded and I have a right to complain." [37] Jefferson developed from a disinterested public servant into a party leader, enunciating his political philosophy in workable form and demonstrating by the critical events of 1800-1801 and the orderly establishment of the Jeffersonian regime that republican government could survive a change of party rule.

During Jefferson's presidency his correspondence with Adams lapsed, thus causing a significant hiatus in the documentary record. In 1804 a limited attempt at renewal through Mrs. Adams failed.[38] In spite of a series of international incidents and crises during the Napoleonic Wars, involving the maintenance of a precarious American neutrality, Jefferson's party was more firmly entrenched by the end of his second administration in 1809. He had weathered political opposition both within and outside his party, and he had kept the nation at peace. Adams, however, who had observed the course of events from his seclusion in Quincy, saw little difference between his own republicanism, on which he was something of an authority, and Jefferson's as president. To his friend Dr. Benjamin Rush, who was trying to effect a reconciliation between the two former Presidents, Adams wrote with a drop of vitriol on his pen:

1. In the difference between speeches and messages. I was a monarchist because I thought a speech more manly, more respectful to Congress and the nation. Jefferson and Rush preferred messages.

2. I held levees once a week, that all my time might not be wasted by idle visits. Jefferson's whole eight years was a levee.

36. JA to Richard Cranch, Jan. 15, 1787, *Works*, I, 433.
37. JA to TJ, June 30, 1813, below, 348.
38. See Chap. 8, below, 265-68.

3. I dined a large company once or twice a week. Jefferson dined a dozen every day.

4. Jefferson and Rush were for liberty and straight hair. I thought curled hair was as republican as straight.[39]

Now, in 1811, the ex-Presidents were elder statesmen of republicanism.

The reconciliation of Adams and Jefferson in 1812, as related in Chapter 9,[40] brought about a rich and voluminous correspondence that has no counterpart in any other period of American intellectual history. These letters are almost completely divorced in subject matter from those of the earlier period. In retirement the former Presidents, though very much interested in world affairs, gave chief consideration to philosophical questions and let the events of the day pass without their participation. They delved into history and literature for examples to illustrate and reinforce their philosophical commentary. They recalled the more recent past of their own experience and reviewed themselves in company with others of the *dramatis personae* who had appeared on the Revolutionary stage.

It is not surprising that events before 1800 rather than afterward occupied the greater share of their reminiscence and that the critical occurrences of 1776 loomed largest. Adams had the more retentive memory for specific incidents. His manner of recording them in writing suggests the loquaciousness of an entertaining conversationalist. Both he and Jefferson had reason to be proud of their early support of independence, but Adams was more inclined to talk about it. Some of his friends in 1775, he told Jefferson, wondered "that a Man of Forty Years of Age, and of considerable Experience in business, and in life should have been guilty of such an Indiscretion." He could boast that by June 1776 his stand had been vindicated. Justification and vindication were essential to Adams, who felt that history had misused and abused him. "How many Gauntletts am I destined to run?" he complained. "How many Martyrdoms must I suffer?"[41]

The two intellectuals were well matched in mental baggage and in the quality of their formal training. Practice of the law had sharpened their agility of thought and powers of reasoning. More especially they

39. JA to Rush, Dec. 25, 1811, *Works*, X, 11.
40. Below, 283-89.
41. JA to TJ, July 12, 1813, below, 354.

expanded their reading early, beginning with the classics which they could hardly escape in the education of their day and finding stimulus in many subjects of inquiry and speculation. Jefferson, in the universality of his interests and his insatiable curiosity about the world of nature, was the more typical eighteenth-century man of learning. The twentieth-century specialist never ceases to wonder at this Virginian's ceaseless compilation of data which made significant contributions toward a more accurate understanding of man and nature.

Adams's mind ran to moral philosophy rather than natural philosophy—the social sciences and ideology rather than to the natural sciences. This preference is borne out in the subject matter of his correspondence with Jefferson during their years of reflection. While it was broad in range and sharpened with provocative ideas, the absence of certain subjects is significant: the fine arts and architecture, gardening and agriculture, medicine and other "practical sciences," and the physical sciences except in relation to cosmology. In most of these fields Jefferson corresponded at length with other friends and acquaintances, but not with Adams, whose interests lay in law and government, theology and religion, philosophy and the classics.

When Jefferson asked for suggestions concerning the academic program for his proposed university, Adams was not especially helpful when he remarked that education "has so long laboured with a Dropsy, that it is a wonder the Patient has not long since expired. Sciences of all kinds have need of Reform, as much as Religion and Government." [42] He felt no urge to wrestle with the problems of formal education. But Adams was a more profound thinker than Jefferson, more intrigued by the abstract proposition, though not as an end in itself. The Age of Enlightenment demanded scientific proof. Jefferson, the practical philosopher, strove always to put things to work; having grasped the principle, he tried to make the best use of the knowledge acquired and the material objects brought under control. "When I meet with a proposition beyond finite comprehension," he confessed, "I abandon it." [43]

Neither Adams nor Jefferson thought of himself as a literary man, although each devoted a large proportion of his time to reading and writing. "I cannot live without books," declared Jefferson, when he began to acquire another library to replace the one he sold to the

42. JA to TJ, June 19, 1815, below, 444.
43. TJ to JA, March 14, 1820, below, 562.

United States in 1815. The collection he had just disposed of numbered some seven thousand volumes, accumulated during a period of over forty years.[44] During the last decade of his life he assembled approximately nine hundred items (many in sets of several volumes each), which were sold at auction in 1829 to help settle his heavily indebted estate.[45] Books were likewise essential to Adams, who as a young man "procured the best library of law in the State." [46] During his later years he read much more than Jefferson, whose responsibilities in administering his plantations commanded a daily portion of his time. "I wish I owned this Book and 100,000 more that I want every day," remarked the acquisitive Adams in 1817. It pleased him that friends "overwhelm me with Books from all quarters." [47] He kept his old friend in Virginia informed on what he was reading, with a tinge of pride in the quantity of matter he covered. Jefferson was duly impressed but would make no attempt to compete. He was frank in admitting that he was "not fond of reading what is merely abstract, and unapplied immediately to some useful science." [48]

Aside from letter writing, which was almost a daily occupation throughout their lives, leaving a priceless heritage that only today is becoming easily available as a whole, Adams and Jefferson engaged frequently in occasional writings, in response to a specific urge or public need. They were designed for practical purposes and in numerous instances took the form of letters to the newspaper press, often reprinted in pamphlet form. All these comprise a large body of material, including "state papers," composed by Adams and Jefferson in their capacity as public officials. Although Jefferson produced nothing so comprehensive and formidable as Adams's *Defence of the Constitutions of the United States of America*, his *Notes on the State of Virginia* is a classic compendium spiced with the author's philosophical commentary on the practical problems of his native "country." He was a more prolific writer than Adams on a much greater variety of subjects, in keeping with the universality of his interests. In fact, Jefferson was an early exponent of "do it yourself" with the pen. When

44. TJ to JA, June 10, 1815, below, 443; G. S. Hillard, ed., *Life, Letters, and Journals of George Ticknor* (Boston, 1877), I, 35.

45. *Catalogue. President Jefferson's Library ... to be sold at auction ... 1829* (Washington, 1829), 3-14; Randolph G. Adams, *Three Americanists ...* (Philadelphia, 1939), 84-89.

46. JA, "Diary," *Works*, III, 50n.

47. JA to TJ, Dec. 25, 1813, April 19, May 18, 1817, below, 411, 508, 515.

48. TJ to JA, Oct. 14, 1816, below, 491.

a *Manual of Parliamentary Practice* was needed in the United States Senate, he prepared it; when he saw the need for a more convenient system of currency, he wrote *Notes on . . . a Money Unit;* and when he felt that Christians ought to dispense with theological verbiage and inform themselves on the basic principles of their religion, he compiled The Life and Morals of Jesus of Nazareth. These are only a few examples of the versatility and expediency of Jefferson's writing, some for public consumption, others for his personal satisfaction, whether published or unpublished at the time. Those of a confidential nature often provoked vigorous expressions of opinion in their private correspondence.

Religious issues occupied Adams's thoughts much more than Jefferson's, but both men were especially outspoken on the subject. Deploring the lack of free inquiry which still prevailed, Adams condemned the Christian world for conveying the impression that Christianity would not bear examination and criticism.[49] The impact of scientific thought on religious belief was not a novelty in the eighteenth century, nor had the achievement of religious freedom in many places subdued the antagonism between the rationalists and the revelationists. The persistent threat of religious bigotry and the upsurge of the evangelistic spirit in the early nineteenth century were matters of serious concern to Adams and Jefferson, who felt that freedom of the mind must be maintained at all cost.[50] Both regarded religious belief as a very personal and private affair, "known to my god and myself alone," insisted Jefferson. Adams, however, would not be secretive about his religion. He summed it up in the Ten Commandments and the Sermon on the Mount.[51]

In the course of their philosophical correspondence Adams and Jefferson indulged in a good deal of reflection about the revolutionary age through which they had lived so long, of the men and times they had known, and of hopes realized and unfulfilled. They sensed and saw a rapidly changing American nation during and after the War of 1812. Adams's comment on the arrival of a letter from Jefferson within a week's time indicated his consciousness of material improvements altering the lives of the people.[52] New economic issues were

49. JA to TJ, Jan. 23, 1825, below, 607.
50. See introduction to Chap. 10, below, 345.
51. JA to TJ, Nov. 4, 1816, below, 494.
52. JA to TJ, Feb. 3, 1812, below, 293-94.

coming to the fore and westward expansion of population beyond the Mississippi had raised the "black cloud" of slavery, giving serious pause to both elder statesmen.[53]

One might presume to say that they had lived almost too long. They were among the last of their generation, only a few of whom still wore the wig and the cocked hat. "Yours as ever" had replaced "Your most humble and obedient servant" and "Esquire" was becoming a badge of courtesy rather than of gentility. New political parties would soon appear to contend for control in a new age. But in the twilight of the Revolutionary era Adams was still occupied with his books and correspondence and Jefferson was building his university on a new plan. They had contributed stature to the government of the United States and to its position in international affairs. In old age they provided a historical tie between the republicanism of the eighteenth century and the democracy of the nineteenth.

At the age of twenty-five Adams said he had few hopes of fame, but added, "I am not ashamed to own that a prospect of an immortality in the memories of all the worthy, to the end of time, would be a high gratification to my wishes." [54] This achievement by both Adams and "the Sage of Monticello," as he first called Jefferson,[55] was realized in their lifetime and confirmed by the judgment of successive generations. To the audience in Faneuil Hall in 1826, Webster observed that "their fame, indeed, is secure. That is now treasured up beyond the reach of accident . . . for with American liberty it rose, and with American liberty only can it perish."

Although the two statesmen would have been too modest to acknowledge this personal praise, they would have agreed with the substance of Webster's peroration.

It cannot be denied, [Webster declared], but by those who would dispute against the sun, that with America, and in America, a new era commences in human affairs. This era is distinguished by Free Representative Governments, by entire religious liberty, by improved systems of national intercourse, by a newly awakened, and an unconquerable spirit of free inquiry, and by a diffusion of knowledge

53. JA to TJ, Feb. 3, 1821, and TJ to JA, Feb. 21, 1820, Jan. 22, 1821, below, 571, 560, 569.
54. JA to Jonathan Sewall, Feb. 1760, *Works*, I, 52.
55. JA to TJ, Feb. 2, 1817, below, 507.

through the community, such as has been before altogether unknown and unheard of. America, America, our country, fellow-citizens, our own dear and native land, is inseparably connected, fast bound up, in fortune and by fate, with these great interests. If they fall, we fall with them; if they stand, it will be because we have upholden them.[56]

56. Webster, *Discourse*, 58, 61-62.

1

"The great Work of Confederation, draggs heavily on"

* MAY 1777 — OCTOBER 1781 *

JOHN ADAMS and Thomas Jefferson first met in Philadelphia during the summer of 1775 as delegates to the Continental Congress. Adams was thirty-nine, Jefferson thirty-two. Both were lawyers and each had to his credit several years' experience in the lower house of his provincial legislature. The elder, who had represented Massachusetts in the Congress of 1774, quickly became identified as a radical in the conflicting loyalties and emotions of the times. His authorship of the anonymous *Novanglus* letters, printed in January 1775, was not long in doubt, so vigorously did they uphold the rights of the Bay Colony against the oppression of the British government. The younger delegate had exposed himself even earlier to the charge of radicalism in his *Summary View of the Rights of British America*, resolutions which he sent to friends in advance of his attending the Virginia House of Burgesses in 1774. Without asking his permission, they supplied the title, "By a Native, and Member of the House of Burgesses," and had it printed at Williamsburg in August of that year. Within a few months it was reprinted in Philadelphia, again anonymously, thus branding the author, who was easily identified, as one of the revolutionary vanguard even before he took his seat in Congress.[1]

During 1775-76 Jefferson and Adams found themselves on the same side of the debates, impatient with the moderates whose hope for conciliation was stronger than their love of liberty, and they readily took each other's measure. The fledgling from Virginia was impressed by Adams's clarity of argument and forcefulness of phrase, and by his

1. John R. Alden, *The American Revolution* (N. Y., 1954), Chap. III.

I

"sound head on substantial points"; [2] the latter probed the depth of the reticent Jefferson, whose "reputation of a masterly pen" had won considerable recognition.[3]

During May 1776 the movement in Congress on behalf of independence was accelerated in response to the more advanced developments in some of the colonies; and after Richard Henry Lee's resolution of June 7 that "the Congress should declare that these United Colonies are and of right ought to be free and independent states," Adams and Jefferson were appointed to the committee of five, with Benjamin Franklin, Roger Sherman, and Robert R. Livingston, to draft a declaration of independence. To Adams it seemed a foregone conclusion that Jefferson the Virginian, rather than an "obnoxious" New Englander, should write the declaration.[4] There is no uncertainty as to authorship, however much some critics may question its originality. Although Adams hailed Congress's adoption of Lee's resolution for independence on July 2 as "the most memorable epocha in the history of America," [5] Jefferson's Declaration, designed to convince a "candid world" that separation from Great Britain was both just and justifiable, has forever fixed the Fourth of July as the anniversary of American independence.

The association of Adams and Jefferson in the Continental Congress continued until September 2, 1776, when Jefferson left Philadelphia to return to Monticello. During the next five years, however, he spent only intermittent periods of a few weeks or months at home, for he was a conscientious member of the Virginia House of Delegates and served on innumerable committees. His attendance in Congress had deprived him of the opportunity to participate in the revolutionary Convention which established the Commonwealth of Virginia, but he now played an important part in assuring the reality of the Revolution to his own people through the orderly operation of government. Two of those years, 1779-81, were spent as governor, when military necessity often threatened civil rights.[6] Adams's services continued

2. TJ to James Madison, Feb. 14, 1783, Julian P. Boyd, and others, eds., *The Papers of Thomas Jefferson* (Princeton, 1950–), VI, 241. Hereafter cited as Boyd.

3. JA, "Autobiography," Charles Francis Adams, ed., *The Works of John Adams ...* (Boston, 1850-56), II, 511. Hereafter cited as *Works*.

4. *Ibid.*, 514-15.

5. JA to AA, July 3, 1776, *ibid.*, IX, 420.

6. "Itinerary and Chronology of Thomas Jefferson, 1776-1781," Paul Leicester Ford, ed., *The Writings of Thomas Jefferson* (N. Y. and London, 1892-99), II, xxii-xxvii. Hereafter cited as Ford.

on the national stage which, for him, merged with the international early in 1778. He had been a member of the American delegation that met Lord Howe on Staten Island in June 1776 to consider impossible terms of reconciliation with Great Britain. Among his many committee assignments, Adams drafted the credentials of the commissioners to France (originally Franklin, Arthur Lee, and Silas Deane), and in February 1778 he was aboard the frigate *Boston* en route to France to replace Deane. Ten years of diplomatic service were to be interrupted only by his brief stay in Massachusetts in 1779 as a member of its Constitutional Convention.[7]

Though Jefferson and Adams thus viewed the issues of the war years from different vantage points, one as a local legislator and executive, the other as a national legislator and diplomat, they still found themselves in fundamental agreement harking back to their collaboration in Congress. From this background and set of circumstances began their correspondence, on a limited scale: six letters in seven years of war and revolution.[8]

In the opening letters of May 1777 they discussed a crucial need of their time—strength and unity of purpose at home in order to win sympathy and support abroad. It was questionable how long the resolute "join or die" spirit that initiated the conflict could survive the attrition of localism and provincial prejudice. In the protracted winning of the war the Americans left an abundant record of defeatism, promoted by successive armies of occupation and the disintegration of civilian life and loyalties. Despite the untiring efforts of Adams and Jefferson on behalf of independence, it was a distant goal when they began their correspondence in 1777. An undercurrent of discouragement runs through it, in their discussion of requisitioning troops for the Continental Army, financing the war—"Financiers," declared Adams, "we want more than Soldiers"[9]—and regulating trade.

Both men were convinced that confederation was "a great and necessary work," but Jefferson doubted that any implied power should be left open to Congress. He was also concerned about the voting power of the states under the Articles and his proposal for reconciling the differences between the large and the small states anticipated one

7. Worthington C. Ford, "Adams, John," *Dictionary of American Biography*, I, 72-82. Hereafter cited as *DAB*.

8. JA's letter to TJ, Paris, June 23, 1783, delivered by Philip Mazzei in 1784, has not been found. Boyd, VI, 318.

9. JA to TJ, May 26, 1777, below, 6.

of the fundamental issues in the Federal Convention of 1787. Although Adams conceded that the "Work of Confederation, draggs heavily on," he was the more optimistic: "I don't despair of it." [10] But it was four years before the Articles of Confederation were ratified by nine states and went into effect in 1781; and it was three more years before the careers of Jefferson and Adams converged on the diplomatic scene in Europe.

Jefferson to Adams

Williamsburgh May 16. 1777.

DEAR SIR

Matters in our part of the continent are too much in quiet to send you news from hence. Our battalions for the Continental service were some time ago so far filled as rendered the recommendation of a draught from the militia hardly requisite, and the more so as in this country it ever was the most unpopular and impracticable thing that could be attempted. Our people even under the monarchical government had learnt to consider it as the last of all oppressions. I learn from our delegates that the Confederation is again on the carpet. A great and a necessary work, but I fear almost desperate. The point of representation is what most alarms me, as I fear the great and small colonies are bitterly determined not to cede. Will you be so good as to recollect the proposition I formerly made you in private and try if you can work it into some good to save our union? It was that any proposition might be negatived by the representatives of a majority of the people of America, or of a majority of the colonies of America. The former secures the larger the latter the smaller colonies. I have mentioned it to many here. The good whigs I think will so far cede their opinions for the sake of the Union, and others we care little for. The journals of congress not being printed earlier gives more uneasiness than I would ever wish to see produced by any act of that body, from whom alone I know our salvation can proceed. In our assembly even the best affected think it an indignity to freemen to be voted away life and fortune in the dark. Our house have lately written for a M.S. copy of your journals, not meaning to desire a communication of any thing ordered to be kept secret. I wish the regulation of the post office adopted by Congress last September could be put in practice. It was for the riders to

10. JA to TJ, May 26, 1777, below, 5.

travel night and day, and to go their several stages three times a week. The speedy and frequent communication of intelligence is really of great consequence. So many falshoods have been propagated that nothing now is beleived unless coming from Congress or camp. Our people merely for want of intelligence which they may rely on are become lethargick and insensible of the state they are in. Had you ever a leisure moment I should ask a letter from you sometime directed to the care of Mr. Dick, Fredericksburgh: but having nothing to give in return it would be a tax on your charity as well as your time. The esteem I have for you privately, as well as for your public importance will always render assurances of your health and happiness agreeable. I am Dear Sir Your friend and servt:

TH: JEFFERSON

Adams to Jefferson

Philadelphia May 26. 1777

MY DEAR SIR

I had this Morning, the Pleasure of your Favour of the Sixteenth inst, by the Post; and rejoice to learn that your Battallions, were so far fill'd, as to render a Draught from the Militia, unnecessary. It is a dangerous Measure, and only to be adopted in great Extremities, even by popular Governments. Perhaps, in Such Governments Draughts will never be made, but in Cases, when the People themselves see the Necessity of them. Such Draughts are widely different from those made by Monarchs, to carry on Wars, in which the People can see, no Interest of their own nor any other object in View, than the Gratification of the Avarice, Ambition, Caprice, Envy, Revenge, or Vanity of a Single Tyrant. Draughts in the Massachusetts, as they have been there managed, have not been very unpopular, for the Persons draughted are commonly the wealthiest, who become obliged to give large Premiums, to their poorer Neighbours, to take their Places.

The great Work of Confederation, draggs heavily on, but I dont despair of it. The great and Small States must be brought as near together as possible: and I am not without Hopes, that this may be done, to the tolerable Satisfaction of both. Your Suggestion, Sir, that any Proposition may be negatived, by the Representatives of a Majority of the People, or of a Majority of States, shall be attended to, and I will endeavour to get it introduced, if We cannot Succeed in our Wishes for a Representation and a Rule of voting, perfectly equitable, which has no equal, in my Mind.

Nothing gives me, more constant Anxiety, than the Delays, in publishing the Journals. Yet I hope, Gentlemen will have a little Patience with Us.[11] We have had a Committee constantly attending to this very Thing, for a long Time. But we have too many Irons in the Fire, you know for Twenty Hands, which is nearly the whole Number We have had upon an Average Since, last fall. The Committee are now busy, every day in correcting Proof Sheets, So that I hope We Shall Soon do better.

A Committee on the Post office, too, have found, a thousand difficulties. The Post is now very regular, from the North and South, altho it comes but once a Week. It is not easy to get faithfull Riders, to go oftener. The Expence is very high, and the Profits, (so dear is every Thing, and so little Correspondence is carried on, except in franked Letters), will not Support the office. Mr. Hazard is now gone Southward, in the Character of Surveyor of the Post office, and I hope will have as good Success, as he lately had eastward, where he has put the office into good order.

We have no News from Camp, but that the General and Army are in good Spirits, and begin to feel themselves powerfull. We are anxiously waiting for News from abroad, and for my own Part I am apprehensive of some insidious Maneuvre from Great Britain, to deceive Us into Disunion and then to destroy.

We want your Industry and Abilities here extreamly. Financiers, We want more than Soldiers. The worst Enemy, We have now is Poverty, real Poverty in the Shape of exuberant Wealth. Pray come and help Us, to raise the Value of our Money, and lower the Prices of Things. Without this, We cannot carry on the War. With it, We can make it a Diversion.

No poor Mortals were ever more perplexed than We have been, with three Misfortunes at once, any one of which would have been, alone, sufficient to have distressed Us. A Redundancy of the Medium of Exchange. A Diminution of the Quantity, at Markett of the Luxuries, the Conveniences and even the Necessaries of Life, and an Increase of the Demand for all these, occasioned by two large Armies in the Country.

I shall, ever esteam it a Happiness to hear of your Welfare, my dear Sir, and a much greater Still to see you, once more in Congress. Your Country is not yet, quite Secure enough, to excuse your Retreat to the Delights of domestic Life. Yet, for the Soul of me, when I attend to my own Feelings, I cannot blame you. I am, Sir your Friend and most obedient Servant,

JOHN ADAMS

11. In his letter-book JA originally wrote: "Yet, for God's sake, have a little Mercy on Us."

Jefferson to Adams

Albemarle in Virginia. Aug. 21. 1777.

DEAR SIR

Your favor of May 26. came safely to hand. I wish it were in my power to suggest any remedy for the evil you complain of. Tho' did any occur, I should propose it to you with great diffidence after knowing you had thought on the subject yourself. There is indeed a *fact* which may not have come to your knolege, out of which perhaps some little good may be drawn. The borrowing money in Europe (or obtaining credit there for necessaries) has already probably been essayed, and it is supposed with some degree of success. But I expect your applications have as yet been only to France, Holland, or such other states as are of principal note. There is however a smaller power, well disposed to our cause, and, as I am informed, possessed of abilities to assist us in this way. I speak of the Grand Duke of Tuscany. The little states of Italy you know have had long peace and shew no disposition to interrupt that peace shortly. The Grand Duke being somewhat avaritious in his nature has availed himself of the opportunity of collecting and hoarding what money he has been able to gather. I am informed from good authority (an officer [Charles Bellini] who was concerned in the business of his treasury) that about three years ago he had ten millions of crowns lying dead in his coffers. Of this it is thought possible as much might be borrowed as would amount to a million of pounds lawful money. At any rate the attempt might be worth making. Perhaps an application from Dr. Franklin who has some acquaintance in that court might be sufficient. Or, as it might be prudent to sound well before the application, in order to prevent the discredit of a rebuff, perhaps Congress would think it worth while to send a special agent there to negotiate the matter. I think we have a gentleman here [Philip Mazzei] who would do it with dexterity and fidelity. He is a native of that dutchy, well connected there, conversant in courts, of great understanding, and equal zeal in our cause. He came over not long since to introduce the cultivation of vines, olives etc. among us. Should you think the matter worth a further thought, either of the Colo. Lees,[12] to whom he is known, can acquaint you more fully of his character. If the money can be obtained in specie, it may be applied to reduce the quantity of circulating paper, and in such a way as to help

12. Richard Henry Lee (1732-92) and his brother Francis Lightfoot Lee (1734-97), members of the Virginia delegation in Congress.

the credit of that which will remain in circulation. If credit alone can be obtained for the manufactures of the country, it will still help us to clothe our armies or to encrease at market the necessaries our people want.

What upon earth can Howe mean by the manoeuvre he is now practising? There seems to me no object in this country which can either be of utility or reputation to his cause. I hope it will prove of a peice with all the other follies they have committed. The forming a junction with the Northern army up the Hudson's river, or the taking possession of Philadelphia might have been a feather in his cap and given them a little reputation in Europe. The former as being the design with which they came. The latter as being a place of the first reputation abroad and the residence of Congress. Here he may destroy the little hamlet of Williamsburgh, steal a few slaves, and lose half his army among the fens and marshes of our lower country, or by the heats of our climate. I am Dear Sir with the greatest esteem Your friend and servt.,

TH: JEFFERSON

Jefferson to Adams

Wmsbgh. Dec. 17. 1777.

DEAR SIR

Congress will receive by this post our approbation of the Confederation. It passed the house of Delegates on Monday and the Senate on Tuesday last. Tho' our house of delegates is almost wholly of those who are truly zealous, yet there have ever been a few who have endeavored to throw obstructions in our way. Objections to this important instrument came therefore not unexpectedly. The most difficult articles however were surmounted by the spirit of the house, determined to secure if possible the union of the states. One objection only, stuck with them. It was urged that by the 9th. article reserving to congress a power 'of entering into treaties and alliances' with the proviso immediately following that they should not give to foreigners an exemption from such imposts as should be paiable by natives; the congress would have the whole regulation of our trade, and consequently might grant a monopoly of it: and it was intimated that such a measure had been in contemplation; and might be given away by those states, which have no staple, as the price of commercial privileges to them. Some warm members kindled at this idea, and all seemed to be struck with it. The advocates however for the confederation insisted that Congress would have no such power by the confederation: that a power to treat, did not include ex vi termini ["from the force of the expression"] a power to pass away every thing by treaty which might be the subject of a treaty; and consequently no more gave such power over our commerce than over every thing else; that the inference from the proviso was merely an *implication* and that congress were by that instrument to derive no powers by implication or construction, but such only (art. 2) as were *expressly* delegated to them: that by the 2d proviso in the same 9th. clause allowing each legislature to prohibit the exportation of any article to all places, an inference arose in our favor that we might prohibit it to certain places, and consequently to the very place making title to the monopoly: that it appeared Congress themselves did not suppose these words gave them so very ample a power over trade, because in a subsequent part they reserve in express terms a right of regulating our trade with the Indians. This reasoning removed the difficulty and satisfied the house that the instrument would give to congress no such powers. Yet there remains a great anxiety that an article so important should not be laid down in more express terms, and so as to exclude all possible doubt; and a fear that at some future day such a power should be assumed. As I am myself of opinion the instrument gives no such powers, I naturally conclude congress had them not in contemplation, and consequently that they would have no objections to pass an explanatory vote declaring that the Confederation will give them no such powers. If the confirming in their affections an assembly which have ever witnessed the highest respect for congress, would be an object with them, I know nothing which would produce that effect more powerfully than such vote passed before the final ratification of the instrument. Knowing your candour I have taken the liberty of mentioning this subject to you, that if you should think it worthy your attention you may favor it with the assistance of your abilities.

I greatly fear your requisition of money by quarterly paiments will be impracticable here. Our counties are so large that an annual collection is as much as we ever attempted to complete. Our people too are quite unaccustomed to be called on oftener than once a year. We are proceeding to make good our numbers in the feild by a draught. I am Dr. Sir with every sentiment of esteem Your friend and servt.,

TH: JEFFERSON

Adams to Jefferson

Paris June 29. 1778. [i.e., 1780]

MY DEAR SIR

Mr. Mazzei, called on me, last Evening, to let me know that he was this morning at three to Sett off, on his Journey, for Italy. He desired me to write you, that he has communicated to me the Nature of his Errand: but that his Papers being lost, he waits for a Commission and Instructions from you. That being limited to five Per Cent, and more than that being given by the Powers of Europe, and indeed having been offered by other States and even by the Ministers of Congress, he has little hopes of succeeding at so low an Interest. That he shall however endeavour to prepare the Way, in Italy for borrowing, and hopes to be usefull to Virginia and the United States.

I know nothing of this Gentleman, but what I have learned of him here. His great affection for you Mr. Wythe, Mr. Mason, and other choice Spirits in Virginia, recommended him to me. I know not in what Light he Stands in your Part: but here, as far as I have had opportunity to See and hear, he has been usefull to Us. He kept good Company and a good deal of it. He talks a great deal, and was a zealous defender of our Affairs. His Variety of Languages, and his Knowledge of American affairs, gave him advantages which he did not neglect.

What his Success will be in borrowing money, I know not. We are impatient to learn whether Virginia and the other States have adopted the Plan of Finances recommended by Congress on the 18 of March. I think We shall do no great Things at borrowing unless that System or some other, calculated to bring Things to some certain and Steady Standard, Succeeds.

Before this reaches you, you will have learned, the Circumstances of the Insurrections in England,[13] which discover So deep and So general a discontent and distress, that no wonder the Nation Stands gazing at one another, in astonishment, and Horror. To what Extremities their Confusions will proceed, no Man can tell. They Seem unable to unite in any Principle and to have no Confidence in one another. Thus it is, when Truth and Virtue are lost: These Surely, are not the People who ought to have absolute authority over Us. In all Cases whatsoever, this is not the nation which is to bring Us to unconditional Submission.

13. The Gordon Riots broke out in London, June 2-8, 1780.

The Loss of Charlestown has given a rude Shock to our Feelings. I am distressed for our worthy Friends in that Quarter. But the Possession of that Town must weaken and perplex the Ennemy more than Us.

By this Time you know more than I do, of the Destination and the operations of French and Spanish armaments. May they have Success, and give Us Ease and Liberty, if the English will not give Us Peace. I have the Honour to be with an affectionate Respect, Sir your Frnd and Servt.

Jefferson to Benjamin Franklin, to John Adams, and to John Jay

Virginia Oct. 5. 1781.

DEAR SIR

The bearer hereof Colo. James Monroe who served some time as an officer in the American army and as such distinguished himself in the affair of Princetown as well as on other occasions, having resumed his studies, comes to Europe to complete them. Being a citizen of this state, of abilities, merit and fortune, and my particular friend, I take the liberty of making him known to you, that should any circumstances render your patronage and protection as necessary as they would be always agreeable to him, you may be assured they are bestowed on one fully worthy of them.

He will be able to give you a particular detail of American affairs and especially of the prospect we have thro' the aid of our father of France, of making captives of Ld. Cornwallis and his army, of the recovery of Georgia and South Carolina, and the possibility that Charlestown itself will be opened to us. I have the honour to be with the most profound respect & esteem, Your Excellency's Most obedient and most humble servt,

TH: JEFFERSON [14]

14. On the same day TJ wrote to Monroe: "I enclose you three letters, the one directed to Dr. Franklin, the other two for Mr. Jay and Mr. Adams...." However, "a series of disappointments," Monroe informed TJ on May 6, 1782, had prevented him from going to Europe and using the letters.

2

"The Subject of a Treaty of Commerce"

EVEN BEFORE the Declaration of Independence, a major objective of the Continental Congress was the negotiation of treaties of amity and commerce with foreign nations. During the summer of 1776, Congress approved a plan embracing the most-favored-nation principle and the protection of private property from devastation and confiscation in time of war. The "Plan of 1776" became the basis for such negotiation throughout the Confederation period,[1] and Congress promptly dispatched commissioners and agents in quest of commercial conventions. These treaties were among the joint responsibilities of the ministers plenipotentiary, Adams and Jefferson, and therefore occupied a major portion of their deliberations and correspondence.

When Jefferson joined Adams and Franklin in France in 1784, Adams was again the senior member in this partnership of equals (Franklin soon retired because of illness and old age). He had served as commissioner to France in 1777-79 although he arrived too late to participate with Franklin and Arthur Lee in concluding the French alliance and commercial treaty of 1778. In 1780 he returned to France to negotiate with Great Britain as soon as the course of war turned toward peace. In the interim he was appointed minister to the United Dutch Provinces where he signed a treaty of amity and commerce in 1782 and secured the first loan from the Dutch government. These amicable relations, together with his personal acquaintance in

1. Samuel F. Bemis, *The Diplomacy of the American Revolution* (N. Y., 1935), 45-48.

Amsterdam, were to be of great service to the debt-ridden United States six years later.[2] In October 1782 he returned to Paris to serve with Franklin and John Jay in negotiating the formal recognition of American independence by Great Britain. Meanwhile Franklin had negotiated a commercial treaty with Sweden, which was signed in 1783, and conversations for the same purpose were under way in Denmark, Portugal, and Austria.[3]

When Jefferson arrived in France in 1784, therefore, Adams had had nearly seven years' intermittent experience in foreign affairs. As a matter of fact, Jefferson had been appointed commissioner to France almost eight years earlier but had declined to serve; again in June 1781 he declined an appointment as peace commissioner. Following the death of his wife in 1782, however, he accepted when this offer was renewed in November, but Congress suspended the appointment in February 1783 because peace negotiations were nearly complete. Instead, he returned to Congress where he served on the committee which approved the definitive treaty with Great Britain.

In peace as in war, however, the United States needed commercial treaties and on May 7, 1784, Congress named Jefferson as minister plenipotentiary to collaborate with Franklin and Adams. Within a week Jefferson was en route through the northern states, gathering commercial data.[4] Accompanied by his eldest daughter Martha ("Patsy"), he sailed from Boston on July 5 and arrived in Paris on August 6.

Jefferson's appointment, Adams wrote to his old fellow patriot James Warren, "gives me great pleasure. He is an old Friend with whom I have often had occasion to labour at many a knotty Problem, and in whose Abilities and Steadiness I have always found great Cause to confide." [5] Perhaps Jefferson was more circumspect in his anticipation, if we may judge from his observation to Madison a year earlier concerning Adams: "His dislike of all parties, and all men, by balancing his prejudices, may give the same fair play to his reason as would a general benevolence of temper." [6] As they shared the common prob-

2. See below, Chap. 6.
3. Edmund C. Burnett, "Note on American Negotiations for Commercial Treaties," *Amer. Hist. Rev.*, 16 (1910-11), 579-87.
4. "Notes on Commerce of the Northern States," Boyd, VII, 323 ff; Dumas Malone, *Jefferson and His Time* (Boston, 1948–), I, 419-22.
5. Aug. 27, 1784, Boyd, VII, 382*n*.
6. TJ to Madison, Feb. 14, 1783, *ibid.*, VI, 241.

lems of the young Republic under stress of European politics, so their friendship ripened.

Mrs. Adams and young Abigail had sailed for Europe shortly before Jefferson, and Adams met them in London on August 7, after a separation of four years and a half. The next day they set out for Paris.[7] Jefferson had arrived the previous day. Here he renewed his acquaintance with Adams and with Mrs. Adams, whom he had met briefly in Boston, and he often visited them in their commodious house at Auteuil, four miles from the city.[8] During the ensuing nine months the two diplomats developed a heightening respect for each other from the collaboration that was so essential to their country's welfare. When their assignments separated them, Adams's feeling was reflected by his wife, who wrote Jefferson that she was "loth . . . to leave behind me the only person with whom my Companion could associate with perfect freedom, and unreserve." [9] Earlier she had characterized Jefferson as "one of the choice ones of the earth." [10] The pleasure of her association with a "respected Friend" was now projected into their correspondence, to the good fortune of posterity.

In March 1784 Adams had gone to the Netherlands to discuss with the Prussian minister, Baron de Thulemeier, a commercial treaty between the United States and Frederick the Great; by June it was drafted. After Jefferson's arrival with new instructions, it was revised and finally signed in 1785. In negotiations with Portugal, Denmark, and Tuscany, the Prussian treaty served as a model. In a modified form it was applied to Morocco, and parts of it were offered to the British, who displayed an attitude of indifference, if not hostility.[11]

In the spring of 1785, however, the diplomatic approach to British trade was facilitated by a major shift of American ministers abroad. In France, Jefferson was to succeed Franklin, ill and anxious to go home, who could retire at last; in Great Britain, Adams became the first American minister. The news of their diplomatic assignments reached the ministers on May 2, 1785. Later that month the Adamses

---

7. JA, "Diary," Aug. 7, 1784, *Works*, III, 389.

8. Charles Francis Adams, ed., *Letters of Mrs. Adams, the Wife of John Adams* (Boston, 1841), II, 45. Hereafter cited as *Letters of Mrs. Adams*.

9. AA to TJ, June 6, 1785, below, 28.

10. AA to Mrs. Richard Cranch, May 8, 1785, *Letters of Mrs. Adams*, II, 94.

11. Burnett, "Note on American Negotiations . . . ," *Amer. Hist. Rev.*, 16 (1910-11), 579-87; Dorset to the American Commissioners, March 26, 1785, Boyd, VIII, 55-56, 56-59*n*.

moved to London, and on June 1 the former subject of George III was presented to His Majesty at the Court of St. James. The King, Adams reported to John Jay, "was indeed much affected, and I confess I was not less so." [12] But the British were in no mood to deal amicably with their former colonists. While Adams was complaining that "the Britons Alliens Duty is a very burthensome Thing," [13] Jefferson was drafting a proposal for a reciprocal-rights treaty between nations, "believing that a free and unfriendly intercourse between them ... cannot be established on a better footing than that of a mutual adoption by each of the citizens or subjects of the other, insomuch that while those of the one shall be travelling or sojourning with the other, they shall be considered to every intent and purpose as members of the nation where they are, entitled to all the protections, rights and advantages of it's native members. . . ." He suggested to Adams that it be proposed to the courts of London and Versailles, but added, "I know it goes beyond our powers; and beyond the powers of Congress too." [14] Indeed it went beyond the serious comprehension of his generation.

Almost as incomprehensible to the Americans was European acquiescence in the outrageous practices of the Barbary states. Although the nations of western Europe and their West Indian possessions offered the sources of trade most essential to the United States, the Mediterranean countries on ancient trade routes might also do business with America if they were accessible. But it was becoming increasingly difficult to approach the piratical states through the good offices of France or Spain, or by more direct means. Congress allowed its ministers a large measure of leeway as to personnel and procedure,[15] and American diplomats took the initiative without hesitation, but it was slow business at best, and unrewarding. This drama would unfold more relentlessly in 1786.

12. June 2, 1785, *Works,* VIII, 257-58.
13. JA to TJ, July 24, 1785, below, 43.
14. TJ to JA, July 28, 1785, Boyd, VIII, 317-18.
15. John Jay to American Commissioners, March [11], 1785, Boyd, VIII, 19-21.

Jefferson to Adams

Boston June 19. 1784.

DEAR SIR

Supposing that you would receive from Congress a direct communication of the powers given to yourself, Doctr. Franklin and myself, I have deferred from day to day writing to you, in hopes that every day would open to me a certainty of the time and place of my departure for the other side of the Atlantic. Paris being my destination I have thought it best to enquire for a passage to France directly. I have hastened myself on my journey hither in hopes of having the pleasure of attending Mrs. Adams to Paris and of lessening some of the difficulties to which she may be exposed. But after some unexpected delays at Philadelphia and New York I arrived here yesterday and find her engaged for her passage to London and to sail tomorrow. It was therefore too late for her to alter her measures tho' I think she might probably meet with you the sooner could she have taken her passage as I shall on board the French packet from N. York where I had ensured her choice of accomodations, and was promised that the departure of the vessel should be made agreeable to our movements. She goes however in a good ship, well accomodated as merchants' ships generally are and I hope will have soon the pleasure of meeting with you. With respect to our joint agency, our instructions are more special than those formerly sent. These I shall have the pleasure of communicating together with the commissions to yourself and Doctr. Franklin at Paris. My expectation is to sail from New York about the first or second week of the next month. The time of my arrival in Paris will depend on winds and weather: but probably it may be the middle or latter part of August.

We are informed that Congress adjourned on the 3d. of June to meet again at Trenton the 1st. Monday in November, leaving a committee of the states at the helm during their recess. The particulars of affairs here I shall have the pleasure of communicating to you more fully than I can by letter. For the present I will only inform you in general that their aspect is encouraging. I beg you to be assured of the sincere esteem and regard with which I have the honor to be Dear Sir Your most obedient and most humble servt.,

TH: JEFFERSON

Jefferson to Adams

On board the Ceres off Scilly. July 24. 1784.

DR. SIR

When I did myself the honor of writing you on the 19th. Ult. it was my expectation that I should take my passage in the French packet which was to sail the 15th. of this month, and of course that I should not be in Paris till the middle or last of August. It had not then been suggested to me, and being no seaman it did not occur to myself, that even from a London-bound vessel I might get ashore off Ushant or elsewhere on the coast of France. On receiving this information I took my passage with Mr. Tracy in this vessel, leaving Boston the 5th. instant and having had a most favourable run am now as you will see above, and on the lookout for a vessel to take me off. My wish is to land at Brest, Morlaix or elsewhere on that part of the coast, in which, if I succeed, I shall go by the way of L'Orient and Nantes to Paris where I shall probably be a fortnight after the date of this letter. Colo. Humphries, Secretary to the legation, having failed getting to Boston in time, I suppose he will pass in the French packet. However our business need not await him as I am possessed of the papers relative to that. In a situation which hardly admits writing at all, and in hopes of seeing you in Paris as soon as your convenience and that of Mrs. Adams will admit, who I hope is now safe with you, I have the honor to be with the most perfect esteem Dr. Sir Your most obedt and most humble servt,

TH: JEFFERSON

Jefferson to Adams and Franklin

Cul-de-sac Tetebout. Oct. 17. 1784.

Mr. Jefferson's compliments to Mr. Adams and Dr. Franklin, and incloses to them the letter to the D. of Dorset on the separate articles. He also sends one on the general subject and in the general form as had been agreed when they parted last: but thinking that it might be better, by reciting what had been done with Mr. Hartley [16] to keep the ground we

16. Hartley, advocate of conciliation with America, met only once with the American commissioners for commercial treaties before being recalled.

have gained, and not to admit that we misplaced our overtures, by taking no notice of them, he submits to the gentlemen a second draught, copied from the first as to the recital of the powers but varied in the latter paragraph. They will be so good as to take their choice of the two forms and having signed the one they prefer Mr. J. will add his signature to the same. P.S. He is ready at any moment to concur in a letter or letters on the subject of the man in the inquisition.[17]

Jefferson to Adams and Franklin

Mar. 1. 1785

Mr. Jefferson's compliments to Mr. Adams and Doctr. Franklin and sends them his notes on the treaty with Prussia. He prays Mr. Adams, when he shall have perused them to send them to Dr. Franklin and proposes to meet them on the subject at Passy on Thursday [March 3] at 12. o'clock. He sends the Prussian propositions, Mr. Adams's and Dr. Franklin's notes, and the former project and observations which were in the hands of Colo. Humphreys.[18]

Adams to Franklin and Jefferson

Auteuil March 20. 1785

GENTLEMEN

According to your desire I went early this morning to Versailles and finding the Ct. de Vergennes unembarrassed with company, and only attended by his private Secretaries, I soon obtained the honor of a conference, in which I told him that my colleagues were very sorry that

17. Blair McClenachan of Philadelphia, arrested in London on a charge of debt. Boyd, VII, 444n.

18. Negotiations for a commercial treaty with Prussia were begun at The Hague in February 1784 between Adams and Friedrich Wilhelm von Thulemeier, Frederick the Great's perennial ambassador to the Netherlands. Modifications in the model Swedish-American treaty of 1783, proposed by Franklin and John Jay, constituted the "former project" of the present note. On November 10, 1784, JA, TJ, and Franklin had sent Thulemeier a "counter project," which as amended was ready for signature on March 14, 1785. *Diplomatic Correspondence of the United States, 1783-1789* (Washington, 1837), I, 520-29, 554-60; Boyd, VIII, 26-33; and subsequent letters, below.

indisposition necessarily prevented their paying their respects to him in person, and obliged them to request me alone to wait on him and ask his advice upon a thorny question we had with the Barbary Powers. He asked what it was and I put into his hand all the letters upon the subject in french, spanish, italian and english—all of which he read very attentively and observed that it was obvious what was wanted and what had piqued the Emperor of Morocco, viz, that Congress had not written to him nor sent him a consul with the customary presents, for that he was the most interested man in the world and the most greedy of money. He asked whether we had written to Congress and obtained their instructions. I answered that we had full powers to treat with Morocco, Algiers, Tunis, Tripoli and the rest, but that it was impossible for us to go there and that we had not a power of substitution. He said then we should write to the Emperor. I asked if he would do us the favour to convey a letter for us through the french consul? He said he could not do this himself, because it was not in his department, but if we would make an office of it he would communicate it to the Marquis de Castries and return us his answer.

I told him that in looking over the treaties between the several christian Powers and the Barbary States, we found that the treaty between the crown of France and Algiers of the 25 April 1684 was expired or near expiring, and we were desirous of knowing, if the question was not indiscreet, whether it had been renewed. He smiled upon this and said, it was true their treaty was upon the point of expiring, but he could not tell me whether it were renewed, as it was not in his department, but if we would insert this inquiry in our office he would endeavour to obtain the Marshall de Castries' Answer.

I told him, that in order to lay before Congress all the information we could, and to enable them to judge the better what orders to give us or what other course to take we had obtained authentic information from Mr. Bisdom and Mr. Vanderhope, concerning the presents annually given by their high Mightinesses and that we should be very glad to know (if it was not improper) what was the annual amount of the presents made by his Majesty to each of those States, and in what articles they consisted. He said the King never sent them any naval or military stores, but he sent them glasses and other things of value, but that as it was not in his department he could not give me particular information, but that we might put this into our office with the other things.

I asked if there was not a considerable trade and frequent intercourse between some ports of this Kingdom and the coast of Barbary. He said there was from Marseilles and the other ports upon the Mediterranean: but he thought if we had presents to send it would be more convenient to send them from Cadiz.

I then asked the favour of his advice whether in our letter to the Emperor of Morocco we should leave it to his option to send a Minister here to treat with us, or to wait until we could write to Congress and recommend it to them to send a consul. He said he would by no means advise us to invite the Emperor to send a Minister here to treat with us because we must maintain him here and bear all the expences of his voyages and journeys which would be much more costly than for Congress to send a Consul.

But the Comte concluded the whole conference by observing that every thing relative to this business was out of his department, and that we must state to him in writing all we desired to know or to have done, and he would convey it to the Minister of Marine, and communicate to us his answer, and that we might depend upon it that whenever we thought proper to make any office to him it should be carefully attended to.

He added very particular enquiries concerning the health of Dr. Franklin and Mr. Jefferson which I answered to the best of my knowledge and took my leave. With great respect I have the honor to be Gentlemen Your most obedient and Most humble Servt.,

JOHN ADAMS

Adams to Jefferson

Auteuil May. 19. 1785

DEAR SIR

Messieurs Wilhem and Jan Willink, Nicholas and Jacob Vanstaphorst and De la Lande and Fynje of Amsterdam, have lodged in the Hands of Messrs. Van den Yvers Bankers in Paris one Thousand Pounds Sterling for the Purpose of paying for certain Medals and Swords which Coll. Humphreys has orders to cause to be made for the United States. This is therefore to authorize and to request you to draw upon Messrs. Van den Yvers in favour of Coll. Humphreys, for Cash to pay for those Medals and Swords as they shall be made, not to exceed however the Said Sum of one Thousand Pounds Sterling. With great esteem I have the Honour to be, dear Sir, your affectionate Colleague and most obedient Servant,

JOHN ADAMS

Adams to Jefferson

Montreuil sur mer May 22. 1785

MY DEAR SIR

We left Auteuil the 20th. afternoon and have made easy Journeys. Indeed We could not have done otherwise, because the Posthorses were engaged, by the unusual Number of Travellers, in such Numbers that We have been sometimes obliged to wait. The Country is an heap of Ashes. Grass is scarcely to be seen and all sorts of Grain is short, thin, pale and feeble while the Flax is quite dead. You see indeed more green Things than in some of our sharp Drouths in America, but as the Heat of this Clymate is not sufficient to destroy vegetation so effectually as with Us, it is not enough neither to produce so rapid a Revivication of the Universe, upon the Return of Rains, so that their Prospects are more melancholly than ours upon such Occasions. I pity this People from my soul. There is at this Moment as little appearance of a change of Weather as ever.

Tomorrow We shall reach Calais, but I cannot calculate how long it will take Us to cross the Channel. I allow two days from Dover to London as I am determined to be in a hurry about nothing from the Beginning to the End of this Adventure. It is best to give myself as well as others time to think.

The Ladies [19] join in respects to you and Mr. Humphreys and Mr. Williamos, the Marquis [20] and his Lady and all other Friends. Be so good as to inform me, if you learn any Thing of the sailing of the Packet, and of the Health of my Boy.[21] I thank you kindly for your Book.[22] It is our Meditation all the Day long. I cannot now say much about it, but I think it will do its Author and his Country great Honour. The Passages upon slavery, are worth Diamonds. They will have more effect than Volumes written by mere Philosophers. The Ladies say you should have mentioned West and Copeley at least among your American Genius's, because they think them the greatest Painters of the Age. Madam[e says] I have not expressed her sentiments politely enough. It should run thus: The Ladies desire that in the next Edition you would insert West and Copeley etc.

19. AA and her daughter Abigail, twenty years old.
20. The Marquis de Lafayette.
21. John Quincy Adams, eighteen years old, en route to the United States to study at Harvard College.
22. *Notes on the State of Virginia*, privately printed, 200 copies, Paris, May 1785, for distribution to TJ's friends.

The melancholly Face of Nature, added to the dull political Prospect before us, on the other side of the Channell, coming upon the Back of our natural Regretts at parting with our Son and our fine summer situation at Auteuil, and all our Friends in and about Paris, make the Journey rather triste, but we have passed through scenes bien plus triste encore. Adieu.

J. ADAMS

Adams to Jefferson

Dessin's Calais May 23. 1785. Monday.

DEAR SIR

We are just arrived, covered with Dust, and we have hired our Boat, to go over tomorrow at ten. No green Peas, no Sallad, no Vegetables to be had upon the Road, and the Sky is still as clear dry and cold as ever. The Flocks of Sheep and herds of Cattle, through the Country, Stalk about the Fields like Droves of Walking Skeletons. The Sheep are pastured chiefly I think in the plowed grounds, upon the Fibres as I suppose of the Roots of Grass turn'd up by the Plow.

From a motive of Humanity I wish that our Country may have plenti-full Rains, and our Husbandmen Industry, that they may Supply the Wants of their Suffering Fellow Creatures in Europe. You see I have nothing so mean as a selfish or even a patriotic Wish in all this. But from the same regard to Europe and her worthy Colonists in the West Indies, I hope that these rainless, heatless Heavens will convince them that it is abundantly for their good that We should bring and carry freely, our Flour, Wheat, Corn, Rice, Flesh, and Fish for their Soulagement. Yours affectionately,

J. ADAMS

The Ladies Compliments of course.

Jefferson to Adams

Paris May 25. 1785.

DEAR SIR

Your letter of the 22d. from Montreuil sur mer is put into my hands this moment, and having received information of your son, and two American gentlemen being to set out for London tomorrow morning, I seize a moment to inform you that he had arrived well at l'Orient and was well on the 20th. when the packet was still detained by contrary winds. Mr. Barclay, who is arrived, had also seen him. Be so good as to inform the ladies that Mrs. Hayes is arrived. I have not yet seen her, but am this moment going to perform that duty. I fear the ladies have had a more triste journey than we had calculated on. The poverty of the country and distress of the drought would of course produce this effect. I am the more convinced of this as you say they have found amusement in my notes. They presented themselves to their notice under fortunate circumstances. I am happy if you find any thing in them worthy your approbation. But my country will probably estimate them differently. A foreknowlege of this has retarded my communicating them to my friends two years. But enough of them. The departure of your family has left me in the dumps. My afternoons hang heavily on me. I go sometimes to Passy and Mont Parnasse. When they are gone too I shall be ready for the dark and narrow house of Ossian. We attended the Queen's entrance yesterday, but lost the sight of her. You can calculate, and without many figures, the extent of this mortification to me. To render it more complete I had placed myself and my daughter in my carriage very finely before the Palais Bourbon to see the illuminations of the Garde meubles which are to cost the king of Spain two or three thousand guineas. But they sent a parcel of souldiers to drive us all away. We submitted without making battle; I carried my daughter to the Abbaye and came home to bed myself. I have now given you all the news of Paris as far as I know it and after recommending myself to the friendly recollection of the ladies I conclude with assurances of the esteem with which I have the honour to be dear Sir Your affectionate friend and servt.,

Th: Jefferson

P.S. Send me your address au plutot.

Adams to Jefferson

London May 27. 1785

Dear Sir

I arrived yesterday and have made my visit to day, and been very politely received by the Marquis [of Carmarthen], but of this more hereafter. This is devoted to a smaller subject.

Upon Enquiry I find that I cannot be exempted from paying duties upon my Wines, because no foreign Minister is, except for a less quantity than I have of the best qualities in my Cellar at the Hague, so that I must stop all that I have in France if I can. To pay Six or Eight Shillings Sterling a Bottle upon the Small Wines I packed at Auteuil would be folly. I must beg you then if possible to stop it all except one Case of Madeira and Frontenac together. Let me beg you too to write to Mr. Garvey and stop the order for five hundred Bottles of Bourdeaux. All my other Things may be sent on to me, as proposed.

Coll. Smith has Letters for you, but waits a private Hand. He Sends his Respects to you and Coll. Humphreys. If my Things are gone and cannot be stopped I must pay the Impost, heavy as it is. I am sorry to give you this Trouble but I beg you to take the Wine, at any Price you please. Let your own Maitre D'Hotel judge, or accept it as a present or sell it at Vendue, i.e. let Petit dispose of it as he will give you an Account of proceeds and give me credit, and then order me to pay Stockdale or any Body here for you to the amount. My Esteem, and Regards as due. Yours affectionately

JOHN ADAMS

Adams to Jefferson

Bath Hotel London May 27. 1785

DEAR SIR

I found that either the Duke of Dorsetts Letter to the Premier had produced an order at Dover or that his Graces Letter to the Custom House Office had as good an effect, for I was allowed to pass without Molestation, and indeed received Marks of particular Respect.

We arrived yesterday 26. in the afternoon, and as Fortune would have it Coll. Smith arrived the Night before 25. We soon met. I wrote a Card to the Marquis of Carmarthen, at Nine at Night, acquainting his Lordship of my Arrival and desiring an Hour to wait on him. This Morning I had an Answer, that his Lordship would be glad to see me at one at his House, or at four at his office, as I chose. I replyed that I would have the Honour to wait on him at one.

Coll. Smith went with me, we were admitted in an Instant, and politely received. I laid before him my Commission, and left him a Copy. Coll. Smith did the same with his. I consulted his Lordship about the Ettiquette of my Letter of Credence, and he gave me the same Answers as the Comte de Vergennes gave you. His Lordship then said that on Wednesday next after the Levee, I should be presented to his Majesty in his Closett, and there deliver my Letter of Credence, and that on the next Levee **Day** Coll. Smith would be presented. This he said was according to the **usage.**

I have since seen the Dutch Minister,[23] who enquired of every particular step by step, and then said that I was received precisely upon the same Footing with all the other Ministers. I learned from the Dutch Minister too another Particular which gave me Pleasure, vizt that the usage here is directly contrary to that in Holland and France. Here the new Minister receives the first Visit, from all the foreign Ministers, whereas in France and Holland the new Minister makes the first Visit to all the foreign Ministers and notifies formally to them his Reception. This saves me from an Embarrassment, and We shall now see who will and who will not. We shall see what will be done by Imperial Ministers, etc. With the most cordial Esteem I have the Honour to be, Sir, your most obedient and most humble Servant,

JOHN ADAMS

Adams to Franklin and Jefferson

Bath Hotel May 29. 1785. Westminster

GENTLEMEN

Our Secretary of State for foreign affairs, in a Letter of 13. Ap. informs me, that he wrote Us a Letter by Capt. Lamb dated 11. March, inclosing a Variety of Papers respecting the Treaties we are directed to negotiate and conclude with the Barbary Powers.

Inclosed is a Copy of a Resolution of Congress of 14. Feb. 1785,[24] inclosed to me, in the Secretary's Letter. I know nothing of Capt. Lambs Arrival or of the Dispatches by him.

On the 26. I communicated to Lord Carmarthen my Credentials, and left him Copies, as we have done upon former occasions in France, and am to have my Audience of the King in his Closet as the Secretary of State informs me, next Wednesday. I have the Honour to be, very respectfully, Gentlemen, your most obedient and most humble Servant,

JOHN ADAMS

23. Baron D. W. van Lynden, like Adams, was a "complete . . . cypher" at the Court of St. James, as JA wrote to John Jay, Dec. 3, 1785, *Works*, VIII, 352.

24. "Resolved that the Ministers of the United States who are directed to form Treaties with the Emperor of Morocco, and the Regencies of Algiers, Tunis, and Tripoly, be empowered to apply so much of the money borrowed in Holland, or any other money in Europe belonging to the United States . . . not exceeding Eighty Thousand Dollars." Full text in Boyd, VIII, 19-20.

Jefferson to Adams

Paris June 2. 1785.

DEAR SIR

Your favours of May 23. and the two of May 27. came safely to hand, the first being open. That of the 22d. from Montreuil sur mer had been received and answered on the 25th.

The day before the receipt of the letters of the 27th. we had had your cases brought to the barrier of Paris in order to get the proper officer to go that far to plumb them. From there they were put on board the boat for Rouen and their portage paid. In the instant of receiving your letter I sent Petit off to try to stop them if not gone. The boat was just departing and they declared it impossible to reland them: and that could it be done, a new passport from the C. de Vergennes would be necessary for the part not landed. I now forward your letter to Mr. Garvey, countermanding your order of the wine from him, and praying him to retain all the cases of wine now sent except that which has the Madeira and Frontignac, till he shall receive your orders. These therefore you will be so good as to send him as soon as convenient. I was very sorry we could not stop the wine. It would have suited me perfectly to have taken it either at the prices it cost you, if known to Petit, or if not known, then at such prices as he and Marc should have estimated it at: and this would have saved you trouble. I inclose you Petit's note of disbursements which I immediately repaid him. You will know the exchange between London and Paris, which is considerably in favor of the former. Make the allowance for that and either retain the money in your own hands or put it into Stockdale's as most convenient. Can you take the trouble of ordering me the two best of the London papers (that is to say one of each party) and by any channel which will save me postage and the search of government?

The inclosed letter to Miss Adams is from a young gentleman [25] of her acquaintance who has a very sincere and high affection for her. When you transferred to her the commission of Secretary, I well hoped the pleasure of her being the intermediate of our communications: but I did not flatter myself with the further one of becoming the confident between herself and persons of the foregoing description. The following paragraphs are for her eye only. Be so good therefore as to deliver over the letter to her. The cypher I suppose to be in her custody.

25. John Quincy Adams, according to TJ's Summary Journal of Letters.

By a dutch Courier which went yesterday we sent an answer to Baron Thulemyer. It contained what we had agreed on when you were here. That is to say we closed and expressing our doubts that it might not suit him to come here, we propose[d] that every one should sign separately puting the date and place of his Signature. We mean to sign here, send it by some confidential Person to you and that he shall carry it on to the Baron, deliver it to him and receive in *exchange the copy signd by him.*

Our answer to Tuscany is copying. It is *precisly what we had agreed when you were with us.*[26] Be so good as to present my highest esteem to the ladies and to be assured of the sincerity with which I am Dear Sir Your friend and servt.,

TH: JEFFERSON

P.S. *My visits have been all returned save by the Portuguese* [ambassador] *who I imagine has* [neglect]*ed* [others?].

Adams to Jefferson

Bath Hotel Westminster June 3. 1785

SIR

I have now the Honour to inform you, that having shewn my Commission to the Right Honourable the Marquis of Carmarthen, and left an authenticated Copy together with a Copy of my Letter of Credence to the King according to the usage, I had the Honour on the first of this Month to be introduced by his Lordship to his Majesty, in his Closet with all the Ceremonies and Formalities, practised on such occasions, with other foreign Ministers, where I delivered to his Majesty, my Letter of Credence from the United States of America, as their Minister Plenipotentiary to the Court of Great Britain. The Mission was treated by his Majesty with all the Respect, and the Person with all the Kindness, which could have been expected or reasonably desired, and with much more, I confess, than was in fact expected by me.[27]

Coll. Smith, has also shewn his Commission as Secretary of Legation, to the Secretary of State and left an authenticated Copy, and is to be presented to the King on the next Levee Day. The Time is not yet fixed for my Introduction to the Queen, but having received an Invitation to dine with the Secretary of State, on Saturday the fourth of this Month, being

---

26. Italicized passages were decoded by young Abigail Adams.
27. JA described his audiences with George III and with Queen Charlotte in greatest detail to John Jay, *Works,* VIII, 255-59, 265-66; also Boyd, VIII, 526.

the Anniversary of his Majestys Birth, I must go to Court again on that Day. With great Respect, I have the Honour to be, Sir your most obedient and most humble servant,

JOHN ADAMS

Abigail Adams to Jefferson, with Enclosure

London Bath Hotel Westminster
June 6. 1785

DEAR SIR

Mr. Adams has already written you that we arrived in London upon the 27 of May.[28] We journey'd slowly and sometimes silently. I think I have somewhere met with the observation that nobody ever leaves paris but with a degree of tristeness. I own I was loth to leave my garden because I did not expect to find its place supplied. I was still more loth on account of the increasing pleasure, and intimacy which a longer acquaintance with a respected Friend promised, to leave behind me the only person with whom my Companion could associate with perfect freedom, and unreserve: and whose place he had no reason to expect supplied in the Land to which he is destinied.

At leaving Auteuil our domesticks surrounded our Carriage and in tears took leave of us, which gave us that painfull kind of pleasure, which arises from a consciousness, that the good will of our dependants is not misplaced.

My little Bird I was obliged, after taking it into the Carriage to resign to my parisian chamber maid, or the poor thing would have fluttered itself to Death. I mourned its loss, but its place was happily supplied by a present of two others which were given me on board the Dover pacquet, by a young Gentleman whom we had received on Board with us, and who being excessively sick I admitted into the cabin, in gratitude for which he insisted upon my accepting a pair of his Birds. As they had been used to travelling I brought them here in safety, for which they hourly repay me by their melodious notes. When we arrived we went to our old Lodgings at the Adelphia, but could not be received as it was full, and almost every other hotel in the city. From thence we came to the Bath Hotel where we at present are, and where Mr. Storer had partly engaged Lodgings for us, tho he thought we should have objections upon account of the Noise, and the constant assemblage of carriages round it, but it was no time for choice, as the sitting of parliament, the Birth Day of the King, and the celebration of Handles Musick had drawn together such a Number of people as all-

28. They arrived on May 26, according to JA's letter of May 27.

ready to increase the price of Lodgings near double. We did not however hesitate at keeping them, tho the four rooms which we occupy costs a third more than our House and Garden Stables etc. did at Auteuil. I had lived so quietly in that calm retreat, that the Noise and bustle of this proud city almost turnd my Brain for the first two or three Days. The figure which this city makes in respect to Equipages is vastly superiour to Paris, and gives one the Idea of superiour wealth and grandeur. I have seen few carriages in paris and no horses superiour to what are used here for Hackneys. My time has been much taken up since my arrival in looking out for a House. I could find many which would suit in all respects but the price, but none realy fit to occupy under 240 £. 250. besides the taxes, which are serious matters here. At last I found one in Grovenor Square which we have engaged.

Mr. Adams has written you an account of his reception at Court, which has been as gracious and as agreeable as the reception given to the Ministers of any other foreign powers. Tomorrow he is to be presented to the Queen.

Mr. Smith appears to be a modest worthy man, if I may judge from so short an acquaintance. I think we shall have much pleasure in our connection with him. All the Foreign Ministers and the Secretaries of Embassies have made their visits here, as well as some English Earls and Lords. Nothing as yet has discovered any acrimony. Whilst the Coals are cover'd the blaize will not burst, but the first wind which blows them into action will I expect envelop all in flames. If the actors pass the ordeal without being burnt they may be considerd in future of the Asbestos kind. Whilst I am writing the papers of this day are handed me. From the publick Advertiser I extract the following. "Yesterday morning a messenger was sent from Mr. Pitt to Mr. Adams the American plenipotentiary with notice to suspend for the present their intended interview" (absolutely false). From the same paper:

"An Ambassador from America! Good heavens what a sound! The Gazette surely never announced any thing so extraordinary before, nor once on a day so little expected. This will be such a phœnomenon in the Corps Diplomatique that tis hard to say which can excite indignation most, the insolence of those who appoint the Character, or the meanness of those who receive it. Such a thing could never have happened in any former Administration, not even that of Lord North. It was reserved like some other Humiliating circumstances to take place

> Sub Jove, sed Jove nondum
> Barbato _____." [29]

29. "Under Jove, but Jove not yet barbaric."

From the morning post and daily advertiser it is said that "Mr. Adams the Minister plenipotentiary from America is extremly desirious of visiting Lord North whom he Regards as one of the best Friends the Americans ever had." Thus you see sir the beginning squibs.

I went last week to hear the musick in Westminster Abbey. The Messiah was performd. It was sublime beyond description. I most sincerely wisht for your presence as your favorite passion would have received the highest gratification. I should have sometimes fancied myself amongst a higher order of Beings; if it had not been for a very troublesome female, who was unfortunately seated behind me; and whose volubility not all the powers of Musick could still.

I thank you sir for the information respecting my son from whom we received Letters. He desires to be remembered to you, to Col. Humphries and to Mr. Williamos. My Daughter also joins in the same request. We present our Love to Miss Jefferson and compliments to Mr. Short. I suppose Madam de la Fayette is gone from paris. If she is not, be so good sir as to present my respects to her. I design writing her very soon. I have to apoligize for thus freely scribling to you. I will not deny that there may be a little vanity in the hope of being honourd with a line from you. Having heard you upon some occasions express a desire to hear from your Friends, even the Minutia respecting their Situation, I have ventured to class myself in that number and to subscribe myself, Sir, your Friend and Humble Servant,

A. ADAMS

ENCLOSURE

The publick Advertiser—

"Yesterday Lord George Gordon had the Honour of a long conference with his Excellency John Adams (honest John Adams), the Ambassador of America, at the hotel of Mons. de Lynden Envoye extrordinaire de Leur Hautes puissances."

This is true, and I suppose inserted by his Lordship who is as wild and as enthusiastic as when he headed the mob. His Lordship came here but not finding Mr. Adams at home was determind to see him, and accordingly followed him to the Dutch Ministers. The conversation was curious, and pretty much in the Stile of Mrs. Wright with whom his Lordship has frequent conferences.

An other paragraph from the same paper—"Amongst the various personages who drew the attention of the drawing-room on Saturday last, Mr. Adams, minister plenipotentiary from the States of America was not the least noticed. From this gentleman the Eye of Majesty and the Court glanced on Lord _____; to whose united Labours this Country stands indebted for the loss of a large territory and a divided and interrupted Commerce."

Adams to Jefferson

Bath Hotel Westminster June 7. 1785.

DEAR SIR

I have received yours of 25. May, and thank you for the News of my Son, and for the News of Paris. I wished to have seen the Queens Entrance into Paris, but I saw the Queen of England on Saturday, the Kings Birth day, in all her Glory. It is paying very dear to be a King or Queen to pass One such a day in a year. To be obliged to enter into Conversation with four or five hundred, or four or five Thousand People of both Sexes, in one day and to find Small Talk enough for the Purpose, adapted to the Taste and Character of every one, is a Task which would be out of all Proportion to my Forces of Mind or Body. The K and Q. speak to every Body. I stood next to the Spanish Minister [Don Bernardo del Campo], with whom his Majesty conversed in good French, for half or Quarter of an Hour, and I did not loose any Part of the discourse, and he said several, clever Things enough. One was Je suis convaincu que le plus grand Ennemy du Bien, est le mieux. You would have applied it as I did, to the Croud of Gentlemen present who had advised his Majesty, to renounce the Bien for the Mieux in America, and I believe he too had that Instance in his mind. Thursday I must be presented to the Queen, who I hope will say as many pretty Things to me, as the K. did.

You would die of Ennui here, for these Ceremonies are more numerous and continue much longer here than at Versailles.

I find I shall be accablé with Business and Ceremony together, and I miss my fine walks and pure Air at Auteuil. The Smoke and Damp of this City is ominous to me. London boasts of its Trottoir, but there is a space between it and the Houses through which all the Air from Kitchens, Cellars, Stables and Servants Appartements ascends into the Street and pours directly on the Passenger on Foot. Such Whiffs and puffs assault you every few Steps as are enough to breed the Plague if they do not Suffocate you on the Spot.

For Mercy Sake stop all my Wine but the Bourdeaux and Madeira, and Frontenac. And stop my order to Rouen for 500 Additional Bottles. I shall be ruined, for each Minister is not permitted to import more than 5 or 600 Bottles which will not more than cover what I have at the Hague which is very rich wine and my Madeira Frontenac and Bourdeaux at Auteuil. Petit will do the Business. Regards to Coll. Humphreys and Mr. Williamos. Adieu.

JOHN ADAMS

Franklin and Jefferson to Adams

Passy June 15, 1785.

SIR

Among the instructions given to the Ministers of the United States for treating with foreign powers, was one of the 11th. of May 1784. relative to an individual of the name of John Baptist Pecquet. It contains an acknowlegement on the part of Congress of his merits and sufferings by friendly services rendered to great numbers of American seamen carried prisoners into Lisbon, and refers to us the delivering him these acknowlegements in honourable terms and the making him such gratification as may indemnify his losses and properly reward his zeal. This person is now in Paris and asks whatever return is intended for him. Being in immediate want of money he has been furnished with ten guineas. He expressed desires of some appointment either for himself or son at Lisbon, but has been told that none such are in our gift, and that nothing more could be done for him in that line than to mention to Congress that his services will merit their recollection, if they should make any appointment there analogous to his talents. He sais his expences in the relief of our prisoners have been upwards of fifty Moidores. Supposing that, as he is poor, a pecuniary gratification will be most useful to him, we propose, in addition to what he had received, to give him a hundred and fifty guineas or perhaps 4000. livres, and to write a joint letter to him expressing the sense Congress entertain of his services. We pray you to give us your sentiments on this subject by return of the first post, as he is waiting here, and we wish the aid of your [coun]sels therein. We are to acknowlege the receipt of your letter of June 3. 1785 informing us of your reception at the court of London.

Adams to Franklin and Jefferson

Bath Hotel Westminster June 20. 1785.

GENTLEMEN

Let me request of you, to turn your Attention as soon as possible to the Subject of a Treaty of Commerce between the United States of America and Great Britain, and transmit to me, a Project that you would advise me to propose in the first Instance. For my own Part I like the Plan agreed on with Prussia so well, that I must request you to send me a Copy of it, and with such Changes as you may advise me to adopt I should be for proposing that. With great Respect etc.

Adams to Franklin and Jefferson

Westminster June 20. 1785

GENTLEMEN

I have just received your Favour of the 15 and have the Honour to agree entirely with you in sentiment respecting Gratification to be given to Mr. John Baptist Pecquet and the Letter to be written to him. I have the Honour etc.

Jefferson to Abigail Adams

Paris June 21. 1785

DEAR MADAM

I have received duly the honor of your letter, and am now to return you thanks for your condescension in having taken the first step for settling a correspondence which I so much desired; for I now consider it as *settled* and proceed accordingly. I have always found it best to remove obstacles first. I will do so therefore in the present case by telling you that I consider your boasts of the splendour of your city and of it's superb hackney coaches as a flout, and declaring that I would not give the polite, self-denying, feeling, hospitable, goodhumoured people of this country and their amability in every point of view, (tho' it must be confessed our streets are somewhat dirty, and our fiacres rather indifferent) for ten such races of rich, proud, hectoring, swearing, squibbing, carnivorous animals as those among whom you are; and that I do love this *people* with all my heart, and think that with a better religion and a better form of government and their present governors their condition and country would be most enviable. I pray you to observe that I have used the term *people* and that this is a noun of the masculine as well as feminine gender. I must add too that we are about reforming our fiacres, and that I expect soon an Ordonance that all their drivers shall wear breeches unless any difficulty should arise whether this is a subject for the police or for the general legislation of the country, to take care of. We have lately had an incident of some consequence, as it shews a spirit of treason, and audaciousness which was hardly thought to exist in this country. Some eight or ten years ago a Chevalier _____ was sent on a message of state to the princess of _____ of _____ of (before I proceed an inch further I must confess my profound stupidity; for tho' I have heard this story told fifty times in all it's circumstances, I declare I am unable to recollect the name of the ambassador, the name of the princess, and the nation he was sent to; I must therefore proceed to tell you the naked story, shorn of all those precious circumstances) some chevalier or other was sent on some business or other to some princess or other. Not succeeding in his negociation, he wrote on his return the following song.[30]

Ennivré du brillant poste
Que j'occupe récemment,
Dans une chaise de poste
Je me campe fierement:
Et je vais en ambassade
Au nom de mon souverain
Dire que je suis malade,
Et que lui se porte bien.

Avec une joue enflée
Je debarque tout honteux:
La princesse boursoufflée,
Au lieu d'une, en avoit deux;
Et son altesse sauvage
Sans doute a trouvé mauvais
Que j'eusse sur mon visage
La moitié de ses attraits.

Princesse, le roi mon maitre
M'a pris pour Ambassadeur;
Je viens vous faire connoitre
Quelle est pour vous son ardeur.
Quand vous seriez sous le
    chaume,
Il donneroit, m'a-t-il dit,
La moitié de son royaume
Pour celle de votre lit.

La princesse à son pupitre
Compose un remerciment:
Elle me donne une epitre
Que j'emporte lestement,
Et je m'en vais dans la rue
Fort satisfait d'ajouter
A l'honneur de l'avoir vue
Le plaisir de la quitter.

30. Printed in the *Journal de Paris*, May 31, 1785.

This song run through all companies and was known to every body. A book was afterwards printed, with a regular license, called 'Les quatres saisons litteraires' which being a collection of little things, contained this also, and all the world bought it or might buy it if they would, the government taking no notice of it. It being the office of the Journal de Paris to give an account and criticism of new publications, this book came in turn to be criticised by the redacteur, and he happened to select and print in his journal this song as a specimen of what the collection contained. He was seised in his bed that night and has been never since heard of. Our excellent journal de Paris then is suppressed and this bold traitor has been in jail now three weeks, and for ought any body knows will end his days there. Thus you see, madam, the value of energy in government; our feeble republic would in such a case have probably been wrapt in the flames of war and desolation for want of a power lodged in a single hand to punish summarily those who write songs. The fate of poor Pilatre de Rosiere will have reached you before this does, and with more certainty than we yet know it. This will damp for a while the ardor of the Phaetons of our race who are endeavoring to learn us the way to heaven on wings of our own. I took a trip yesterday to Sannois and commenced an acquaintance with the old Countess d'Hocquetout. I received much pleasure from it and hope it has opened a door of admission for me to the circle of literati with which she is environed. I heard there the Nightingale in all it's perfection: and I do not hesitate to pronounce that in America it would be deemed a bird of the third rank only, our mockingbird, and fox-coloured thrush being unquestionably superior to it. The squibs against Mr. Adams are such as I expected from the polished, mild tempered, truth speaking people he is sent to. It would be ill policy to attempt to answer or refute them. But counter-squibs I think would be good policy. Be pleased to tell him that as I had before ordered his Madeira and Frontignac to be forwarded, and had asked his orders to Mr. Garvey as to the residue, which I doubt not he has given, I was afraid to send another order about the Bourdeaux lest it should produce confusion. In stating my accounts with the United states, I am at a loss whether to charge house rent or not. It has always been allowed to Dr. Franklin. Does Mr. Adams mean to charge this for Auteuil and London? Because if he does, I certainly will, being convinced by experience that my expences here will otherwise exceed my allowance. I ask this information of you, Madam, because I think you know better than Mr. Adams what may be necessary and right for him to do in occasions of this class. I will beg the favor of you to present my respects to Miss Adams. I have no secrets to communicate to her in cypher at this moment, what I write to Mr. Adams being mere commonplace stuff, not meriting a communication to the Secretary. I have the honour to be with the most perfect esteem Dr. Madam Your most obedient and most humble servt.,

TH: JEFFERSON

Jefferson to Adams

Paris June 22. 1785.

DEAR SIR

My last to you was of the 2d. inst. since which I have received yours of the 3d. and 7th. I informed you in mine of the substance of our letter to Baron Thulemeyer. Last night came to hand his acknolegement of the receipt of it. He accedes to the method proposed for signing, and has forwarded our dispatch to the king. I inclose you a copy of our letter to Mr. Jay to go by the packet of this month. It contains a state of our proceedings since the preceding letter which you had signed with us. This contains nothing but what you had concurred with us in, and as Dr. Franklin expects to go early in July for America, it is probable that the future letters must be written by you and myself. I shall therefore take care that you be furnished with copies of every thing which comes to hand on the joint business.

What is become of this Mr. Lambe? I am uneasy at the delay of that business, since we know the ultimate decision of Congress. Dr. Franklin having a copy of the Corps Diplomatique has promised to prepare a draught of a treaty to be offered to the Barbary states; as soon as he has done so we will send it to you for your corrections. We think it will be best to have it in readiness against the arrival of Mr. Lambe on the supposition that he may be addressed to the joint ministers for instructions.

I asked the favour of you in my last to chuse two of the best London papers for me, one for each party. The D. of Dorset has given me leave to have them put under his address, and sent to the office from which his despatches come. (I think he called it Cleveland office, or Cleveland row or by some such name: however I suppose it can easily be known there.) Will Mr. Stockdale undertake to have these papers sent regularly, or is this out of the line of his business? Pray order me also any really good pamphlets which come out from time to time, which he will charge to me. I have the honour to be with sentiments of real respect and affection Dr. Sir Your most obedient and most humble servt.,

TH: JEFFERSON

Jefferson to Abigail Adams

Paris July 7. 1785.

DEAR MADAM

I had the honour of writing you on the 21st. of June, but the letter being full of treason has waited a private conveiance. Since that date there has been received for you at Auteuil a cask of about 60. gallons of wine. I would have examined it's quality and have ventured to decide on it's disposal, but it is in a cask within a cask, and therefore cannot be got at but by operations which would muddy it and disguise it's quality. As you probably know what it is, what it cost, etc. be so good as to give me your orders on the subject and they shall be complied with.

Since my last I can add another chapter to the history of the redacteur of the Journal de Paris. After the paper had been discontinued about three weeks, it appeared again, but announcing in the first sentence a changement de domicile of the redacteur, the English of which is that the redaction of the paper had been taken from the imprisoned culprit, and given to another. Whether the imprisonment of the former has been made to cease, or what will be the last chapter of his history I cannot tell. I love energy in government dearly. It is evident it was become necessary on this occasion, and that a very daring spirit has lately appeared in this country. For notwithstanding the several examples lately made of suppressing the London papers, suppressing the Leyden gazette, imprisoning Beaumarchais, and imprisoning the redacteur of the journal, the author of the Mercure of the last week has had the presumption, speaking of the German newspapers, to say 'car les journaux de ce pays-la ne sont pas forcés de s'en tenir à juger des hemistiches, ou à annoncer des programes academiques.' [31] Probably he is now suffering in a jail the just punishments of his insolent sneer on this mild government, tho' as yet we do not know the fact.

The settlement of the affairs of the Abbé Mably is likely to detain his friends Arnoud and Chalut in Paris the greatest part of the summer. It is a fortunate circumstance for me, as I have much society with them. What mischeif is this which is brewing anew between Faneuil hall and the nation of God-dem-mees? Will that focus of sedition be never extinguished? I apprehend the fire will take thro' all the states and involve us again in the displeasure of our mother country. I have the honour to be with the most perfect esteem Madam Your most obedt. and most humble servt.,

TH: JEFFERSON

31. "For the newspapers of that country are not compelled to rely on verses or to publish academic programs."

Jefferson to Adams

Paris July 7. 1785.

DEAR SIR

This will accompany a joint letter inclosing the draught of a treaty, and my private letter of June 22, which has waited so long for a private conveiance. We daily expect from the Baron Thulemeyer the French column for our treaty with his sovereign. In the mean while two copies are preparing with the English column which Doctr. Franklin wishes to sign before his departure, which will be within four or five days. The French, when received, will be inserted in the blank column of each copy. As the measure of signing at separate times and places is new, we think it necessary to omit no other circumstance of ceremony which can be observed. That of sending it by a person of confidence and invested with a character relative to the object, who shall attest our signature here, yours in London and Baron Thulemeyer's at the Hague, and who shall make the actual exchanges, we think will contribute to supply the departure from the usual form in other instances. For this reason we have agreed to send Mr. Short on this business, to make him a Secretary pro hac vice, and to join Mr. Dumas for the operations of exchange etc. As Dr. Franklin will have left us before Mr. Short's mission will commence, and I have never been concerned in the ceremonials of a treaty, I will thank you for your immediate information as to the papers he should be furnished with from hence. He will repair first to you in London, thence to the Hague, and so return to Paris.—What is become of Mr. Lambe? Supposing he was to call on the Commissioners for instructions, and thinking it best these should be in readiness, Dr. Franklin undertook to consult well the Barbary treaties with other nations, and to prepare a sketch which we should have sent for your correction. He tells me he has consulted those treaties, and made references to the articles proper for us, which however he shall not have time to put into form, but will leave them with me to reduce. As soon as I see them you shall hear from me.—A late conversation with an English gentleman here makes me beleive, what I did not believe before, that his nation think seriously that Congress have no power to form a treaty of commerce. As the explanations of this matter which you and I may separately give may be handed to their minister, it would be well that they should agree. For this reason, as well as for the hope of your shewing me wherein I am wrong, and confirming me where I am right, I will give you my creed on the subject. It is contained in these few principles. By the

Confederation Congress have no power given them in the first instance over the commerce of the states. But they have a power given them of entering into treaties of commerce, and these treaties may cover the whole feild of commerce, with two restrictions only. 1. That the states may impose equal duties on foreigners as natives, and 2. that they may prohibit the exportation or importation of any species of goods whatsoever. When they shall have entered into such treaty the superintendance of it results to them, all the operations of commerce which are protected by it's stipulations, come under their jurisdiction, and the power of the states to thwart them by their separate acts ceases. If Great Britain asks then why she should enter into treaty with us, why not carry on her commerce without treaty? I answer, because till a treaty is made no Consul of hers can be received (his functions being called into existence by a convention only, and the states having abandoned the right of separate agreements and treaties) no protection to her commerce can be given by Congress, no cover to it from those checks and discouragements with which the states will oppress it, acting separately and by fits and starts. That they will act so till a treaty is made, Great Britain has had several proofs, and I am convinced those proofs will become general. It is then to put her commerce with us on systematical ground, and under safe cover, that it behoves Great Britain to enter into treaty. And I own to you that my wish to enter into treaties with the other powers of Europe arises more from a desire of bringing all our commerce under the jurisdiction of Congress, than from any other views. Because, according to my idea, the commerce of the United states with those countries not under treaty with us, is under the jurisdiction of each state separately, but that of the countries which have treated with us is under the jurisdiction of Congress, with the two fundamental restraints only, which I have before noted.—I shall be happy to receive your corrections of these ideas as I have found in the course of our joint services that I think right when I think with you. I am with sincere affection Dear Sir Your friend and servt.,

TH: JEFFERSON

P.S. Monsr. Houdon has agreed to go to America to take the figure of General Washington. In case of his death between his departure from Paris and his return to it we may lose 20,000 livres. I ask the favour of you to enquire what it will cost to ensure that sum, on his life, in London, and to give me as early an answer as possible that I may order the insurance if I think the terms easy enough. He is I beleive between 30 and 35 years of age, healthy enough, and will be absent about 6 months.

Franklin and Jefferson to Adams

Passy July 8. 1785.

SIR

We duly received your letter of the 20th. of June and now in consequence thereof send you a draught of a treaty which we should be willing to have proposed to the court of London. We have taken for our ground work the original draught proposed to Denmark, making such alterations and additions only as had occurred in the course of our negociations with Prussia and Tuscany and which we thought were for the better. These you will find in the 4th. 9th. 13th. and 25th. articles,[32] and are such as met your approbation when we were considering those treaties. Nevertheless we shall be happy to concur with you in any thing better which you may wish to propose either in the original draught or the amendments. Particularly we wish it were possible to convince the British court that it might be for their interest to continue their former bounties on the productions of our country on account of their quality, and of the nature of the returns, which have always been in manufactures and not in money.

We have the honour to be with sentiments of the highest respect Sir Your most obedt. and most humble servts.

Jefferson to Adams

Paris July 11. 1785.

DEAR SIR

Doctr. Franklin sets out this morning for Havre from whence he is to cross over to Cowes there to be taken on board Capt. Truxen's ship bound from London to Philadelphia. The Doctor's baggage will be contained in 150. or 200 boxes etc. We doubt that the laws of England will not permit these things to be removed from one vessel into another; and it must be attended with great difficulty, delay and expence should he be obliged to enter them regularly merely to pass them from one vessel to another. Will you be so good as to interest yourself (if it be necessary) to obtain a passport for these things or other letters which may protect them in the transfer from one vessel to another. The Doctor being extremely engaged in the moment of departure I informed him that Mr. Harrison was setting out for London today and that I would by him sollicit your interference

32. The full text of the proposed treaty is in JA's letter-book; the enclosure, with alterations in the text of articles 4, 9, 13, 22, 24, and 25, is in Boyd, VIII, 274-75.

in this matter. You will judge best whether the orders had better be delivered to capt. Truxent or sent to Cowes. I rather think the last best, as they would put it in his power to land and store them and to discharge the vessel which carries them. Whatever is done should be speedily done. I am with sincere esteem Dr. Sir Your friend and servt.,

TH: JEFFERSON

Adams to Jefferson

Grosvenor Square Westminster, the Corner of
Duke and Brook Streets July 16th. 1785

DEAR SIR

I have been so perplexed with Ceremonials, Visits, Removals and eternal applications from Beggars of one Species and another, besides the real Business of my Department, that I fear I have not answered your favour of the second of June, which I received in Season. I have received from Mr. Garvey all but my wine and have written him to day to forward that and will run the risque of it, as I believe I shall easily obtain an order to receive it without paying duties. Petits Note of Expences [173 f. 8] which you paid, you either omitted to send me or I have lost it in the Confusion of a Removal, so that I must trouble you to send it again.

As to News Papers, I should advise you to apply to the Comte de Vergennes or Mr. Rayneval or Mr. Gennet the Premier Commis of the Bureau des Interpretes, who, I presume will readily order your Gazettes to come with their own, through the same Channel, free of Expence for Postage. The father of the present Mr. Gennet was so good as to oblige me in this way in the year 1780.

I wrote to you and Dr. Franklin on the 20th. of June, requesting you to send me a Project of a Treaty of Commerce with this Court, and proposed that agreed on with Prussia as the Model. Let me beg your answer to this as soon as possible.

The Doctor is to embark at Spithead or the Isle of White, on board of Captain Truckston as he tells me.

The proceedings at Boston make a Sensation here.[33] Yours most affectionately,

JOHN ADAMS

33. The merchants of Boston on April 15 and the mechanics on May 3 pledged themselves to make no purchases of British goods. Navigation acts were passed by the legislatures of Massachusetts and New Hampshire on June 23. Merrill Jensen, *The New Nation: A History of the United States during the Confederation, 1781-1789* (N. Y., 1950), 292-94.

Adams to Jefferson

Grosvenor Square July 18th. 1785

DEAR. SIR

Your favours of June 22d. and July 7 and 11th. are before me. The delay of Mr. Lamb's arrival is unfortunate, but I think with you that the sooner a project of Treaties is prepared the better, and I will give the earliest attention to it whenever you shall send it. I shall go this morning to Stockdale, to talk with him about sending you the News Papers, and Pamphlets through the Channell of Cleveland Row, i.e. Lord Carmarthens office.

I agree with pleasure to the appointment made by the Doctor and you of Mr. Short, to carry the treaty through London to the Hague, and in joining Mr. Dumas with him in making the Exchange. A Letter to him and another to Mr. Dumas signed by you and me, as the Doctor is gone, would be sufficient Authority: But I shall have no objection of giving each of them a more formal Commission under our Hands and seals, to be our Secretaries specially *pro hac Vice.* He must carry our original Commission to shew to the Baron De Thulemeyer and a Copy of it attested by Colo. Humphries to deliver him, and Mr. Dumas and he should see the Prussian Commission and receive an attested Copy of that. I do not think of any other Papers necessary.

I have given to Lord Carmarthen long ago, an Explanation of the power of Congress to form Treaties of Commerce, exactly conformable to that which you gave the English Gentleman, but I did not extend it to the Case of Consuls. He asked me no questions concerning Consuls, and I did not think it proper for me to say any thing on that subject, not having any Instructions. But I am not easy on that head. Mr. Temple talks of going out in three or four weeks, but I am very apprehensive he will meet with the difficulties you foresee.

I will enquire about insuring 20,000 Livres on the Life of Mr. Houdon. I have written to Mr. Frazier, the Under Secretary of State in Lord Carmarthens office, concerning Dr. Franklins Baggage, have stated the Circumstances as you State them to me, and have solicited the necessary Facilities. I hope for a favourable answer. Truxtun is to depart from hence on Thursday, and I will let him know the answer I may have.

I don't like the symptoms. Galloway, Deane, Chalmers, Watson are too much in favor. The Lottery for the Tories,[34] *although perhaps in Part*

34. The British State Lottery of 1785 was authorized by Parliament on recommendation of Prime Minister William Pitt in order to pay loyalist claims without additional taxation.

*inevitable, has been introduced with such pompous demonstrations of af-
fection and approbation as are neither wise, nor honest.* There is too much
attention to the Navy, and there is another step, which allarms my apprehensions. Hanover is joining Prussia against the Views of the two
Imperial Courts at least in Bavaria. Keep this as secret as the grave, but
search it to the botom where you are. *Does this indicate a Doubt Whether
our Business with De Thulemeyer* may be delayed? Does it indicate a
design in the *British Cabinet, to be Neutral* in order to be more *at Leisure
to deal with us?* Can it be a *Secret Understanding between St. James's
and Versailles?* The *disigns* of *ruining, if they can our carrying Trade, and
annihilating all our Navigation, and Seamen is too apparent.*[35] Yours
sincerely,

JOHN ADAMS

Adams to Jefferson

Grosvenor Square July 24th. 1785

DEAR SIR

I have a Letter from the Baron De Thulemeier of the 19th. and a Copy
of his Letter to you of the same date.[36] I hope now in a few Day's to take
Mr. Short by the hand in Grosvenor Square and to put my hand to the
treaty. I think no time should be lost. We will join Mr. Dumas with Mr.
Short in the Exchange if you please.

I applied as you desired, and obtained the interposition of the Lords
Commissioners of the treasury, and the Commissioners of the Customs for
the transhipping of Dr. Franklin's Baggage. We have heared of the
Doctor's arrival at Rouen, but no further.

*The Britons Alliens Duty is a very burthensome Thing, and they may
carry it hereafter as far upon Tobacco, Rice Indigo and twenty other
Things, as they do now upon oil. To obviate this, I think of substituting
the words "natural born Citizens of the United States," and "natural born
subjects of Great Britain," instead of "the most favoured Nation." You
remember We first proposed to offer this to all Nations, but upon my ob-
jecting that the English would make their ships French or Sweedish or
Dutch etc. to avail themselves of it, without agreeing to it, on their Part,*

---

35. Italicized passages were written in code.
36. On July 24, 1785, JA wrote to De Thulemeier, "It is with great Pleasure I learn
that the Articles of the Treaty between his Prussian Majesty and the United States
are all agreed on mutual Satisfaction." Quoted in Boyd, VIII, 311*n*.

we altered it to the footing of "Gentis Amicissimae ["of the most-favored nation"]." But if the English will now agree to it, we shall secure ourselves against many odious Duties, and no ill Consequence can arise. It is true the French Dutch Sweeds and Prussians will of Course claim the Advantage, but as they must in return allow Us the same Advantage, so much the better. Let me know if any Objection occurs to you.[37]

There is a Bill before Parliament to prevent smuggling Tobacco, in which the restrictions are very rigorous, but cannot be effected. Two thirds of the Tobacco consumed in this Kingdom, I am told is Smuggled. How can it be otherwise, when the impost is five times the original Value of the Commodity. If one Pound in five escapes nothing is lost. If two in five, a great profit is made.

The Duty is 16d. pr. pound and tobacco sells for three pence. Yet all applications for lowering the Duty are rejected. Yours most affectionately,

John Adams

Jefferson to Adams

Paris July 28. 1785.

Dear Sir

Your favors of July 16. and 18. came to hand the same day on which I had received Baron Thulemeier's inclosing the ultimate draught for the treaty. As this draught, which was in French, was to be copied into the two instruments which Doctr. Franklin had signed, it is finished this day only. Mr. Short sets out immediately. I have put into his hands a letter of instructions how to conduct himself, which I have signed, leaving a space above for your signature. The two treaties I have signed at the left hand, Dr. Franklin having informed me that the signatures are read backwards. Besides the instructions to Mr. Short I signed also a letter to Mr. Dumas associating him with Mr. Short. These two letters I made out as nearly as I could to your ideas expressed in your letter of the 18th. If any thing more be necessary, be so good as to make a separate instruction for them signed by yourself, to which I will accede. I have not directed Mr. Dumas's letter. I have heretofore directed to him as 'Agent for the U.S. at the Hague' that being the description under which the journals of Congress speak of him. In his last letter to me is this paragraph. 'Mon nom à la Haie est assez connu, surtout au bureau de la poste, pour que mes lettres me

---

37. This paragraph was written in code.

soient rendus exactement, quand il n'y auroit d'autre direction.' [38] From this I conclude that the address I have used is not agreeable, and perhaps may be wrong. Will you be so good as to address the letter to him and to inform me how to address him hereafter? Mr. Short carries also the other papers necessary. His equipment for his journey requiring expences which cannot come into the account of ordinary expences, such as clothes etc. what allowance should be made him? I have supposed somewhere between a guinea a day and 1000 dollars a year which I beleive is the salary of a private secretary. This I mean as over and above his travelling expences. Be so good as to say, and I will give him an order on his return. The danger of robbery has induced me to furnish him with only money enough to carry him to London. You will be so good as to procure him enough to carry him to the Hague and back to Paris.

The Confederation of the K. of Prussia with some members of the Germanic body for the preservation of their constitution, is I think beyond a doubt. The Emperor has certainly complained of it in formal communications at several courts. By what can be collected from diplomatic conversation here I also conclude it tolerably certain that the Elector of Hanover has been invited to accede to the confederation and has done or is doing it. You will have better circumstances however, on the spot, to form a just judgment. Our matters with the first of these powers being now in conclusion, I wish it was so with the elector of Hanover. I conclude from the general expressions in your letter that little may be expected. Mr. Short furnishing so safe a conveyance that the trouble of the cypher may be dispensed with, I will thank you for such details of what has passed as may not be too troublesome to you.

The difficulties of getting books into Paris delayed for some time my receipt of the Corps diplomatique left by Dr. Franklin. Since that we have been engaged with expediting Mr. Short. A huge packet also brought by Mr. Mazzei has added to the causes which have as yet prevented me from examining Dr. Franklin's notes on the Barbary treaty. It shall be one of my first occupations. Still the possibility is too obvious that we may run counter to the instructions of Congress of which Mr. Lambe is said to be the bearer. There is a great impatience in America for these treaties. I am much distressed between this impatience, and the known will of Congress on the one hand, and the incertainty of the details committed to this tardy servant.

The D. of Dorset sets out for London tomorrow. He says he shall be absent two months. Some whisper that he will not return and that Ld. Carmarthen wishes to come here. I am sorry to lose so honest a man as the

38. "My name at the Hague is well enough known, especially at the post office, so that my letters should be delivered punctually, when no other address is given."

Duke. I take the liberty to ask an answer about the insurance of Houdon's life.

Congress is not likely to adjourn this summer. They have passed an ordinance for selling their lands.[39] I have not received it.

What would you think of the inclosed Draught [40] to be proposed to the courts of London and Versailles? I would add Madrid and Lisbon, but that they are still more desperate than the others. I know it goes beyond our powers; and beyond the powers of Congress too. But it is so evidently for the good of all the states that I should not be afraid to risk myself on it if you are of the same opinion. Consider it if you please and give me your thoughts on it by Mr. Short: but I do not communicate it to him nor any other mortal living but yourself. Be pleased to present me in the most friendly terms to the ladies and believe me to be with great esteem Dear Sir Your friend and servant,

TH: JEFFERSON

You say nothing in your letter about your wine at Auteuil. I think I sent you Petit's bill for I do not find it among my papers. It's amount was 173[tt] [livres] 8s.

Jefferson to Adams

Paris July 31. 1785.

DEAR SIR

I was honoured yesterday with yours of the 24th. instant. When the *1st. article* of *our instructions* of May 7. 1784. was *under debate in Congress*, it was *proposed* that *neither party* should make *the other pay* in *their ports greater duties than* they *paid* in the *ports* of the *other*. One *objection* to this was *it's impracticability*, another *that it* would *put it* out *of our power to lay* such *duties* on *alien importation* as might *encourage importation* by *natives. Some members* much *attached* to *English policy* thought such a *distinction* should actually be *established. Some* thought the *power* to do it should be *reserved* in *case any* peculiar circumstances should *call for it*, tho under the present or *perhaps any* probable *circumstances they* did not *think* it would be *good policy* ever to *exercise* it. The

---

39. The Ordinance of May 20, 1785, establishing the public land system of the United States.

40. A draft treaty proposing reciprocal rights for citizens of one nation traveling in another. As Julian P. Boyd asserts, "If successfully carried out, it would have altered the very nature of the union and of the society of nations." First printed in Boyd, VIII, 317-19, 319-20*n*. See also above, 15.

footing gentis amicissimi was therefore *adopted* as you see in the *instruction*. As far as my enquiries enable me to judge *France and Holland* make no *distinction of duties between Aliens and natives. I* also rather believe that the *other states of Europe* make *none, England* excepted, to whom this *policy*, as that of her *navigation act, seems peculiar.* The question then *is, Should* we *disarm ourselves* of the *power to* make this *distinction against all nations* in order to *purchase an exemption* from the *Alien duties* in *England* only; for if we *put her importations* on the *footing of native,* all other *nations with whom we treat will* have a *right to claim the same. I* think we *should, because against other nations* who make no *distinction* in their *ports between us* and their *own subjects,* we ought *not to* make a *distinction in ours.* And *if the English* will *agree* in *like manner to* make nonc, we *should with equal reason abandon* the *right* as against *them.* I think all the *world would gain* by *setting commerce* at perfèct *liberty. I* remember that when we were *digesting* the *general form* of *our treaty* this *proposition* to *put foreigners* and *natives on the same footing* was *considered*: and we were *all three* (*Dr. F.*) as *well as you* and *myself* in *favor. of it. We* finally however *did not admit* it partly from the *objection* you *mention, but* more *still* on account of *our instructions.* But tho' the *English proclamation* had *appeared* in *America* at the time of *framing these instructions* I think it's *effect as to alien duties* had *not yet been experienced* and therefore was *not attended to. If it* had been *noted* in the *debate I am* sure that the *annihilation of our whale trade* would have been *thought too great a price to pay* for the *reservation of* a *barren power* which a *majority of the members* did not propose *ever to exercise tho* they were willing to *retain it. Stipulating equal rights* for *foreigners and natives we* obtain more in *foreign ports than* our *instructions required, and we* only *part* with, in *our own ports,* a *power* of which *sound policy* would *probably* for *ever forbid* the *exercise.* Add to this that *our treaty will be* for a very *short term,* and *if any* evil be *experienced under it,* a *reformation will soon* be in *our power. I am therefore* for *putting* this among *our original propositions* to the *court of London. If it* should *prove* an *insuperable obstacle with them, or if* it should *stand* in the way of *a greater advantage, we* can *but abandon* it in the *course* of the *negociation.*

In my copy of the cypher, on the Alphabetical side, numbers are wanting from '*Denmark*' to '*disc*' inclusive, and from '*gone*' to '*governor*' inclusive. I suppose them to have been omitted in copying. Will you be so good as to send them to me from yours by the first safe conveyance? Compliments to the ladies and to Colo. Smith from Dr. Sir Your friend and servant,[41]

TH: JEFFERSON

41. Italicized passages were written in code.

Adams to Jefferson

Grosvenor Square Augt. 4. 1785.

MY DEAR SIR

Yesterday our Friend Mr. Short arrived. Mr. Dumas had never any Commission from Congress, and therefore can have no Title under the United States. He never had any other Authorization than a Letter from Dr. Franklin and another from the Committee of Secret Correspondence, in the year 1775. I wish he had a regular Commission. I direct my Letters to Monsieur C. W. F. Dumas a la Haye, only. I should advise you to allow Mr. Short a Guinea a day except Sundays, which will amount to something near your Ideas.

Houdons Life may be insured for five Per Cent, two for the Life and three for the Voyage. I mentioned it at Table with several Merchants; they all agreed that it would not be done for less. But Dr. Price, who was present undertook to enquire and inform me. His answer is, that it may be done at an office in Hackney for five Per Cent. He cannot yet say for less, but will endeavour to reduce it a little. You may write to the Doctor to get it done, and he will reduce it, if possible. I will let you know by Mr. Short, how far I have ventured in conformity to the Propositions you inclose, knowing your sentiments before, but I think We had better wait sometime before We propose them any where else.

Mr. Samuel Watson a Citizen of the U. States, and settled at Charlestown S.C. as a Merchant, sailed from thence about two years ago, for the Havannah, and has not been heard of since, till lately a Gentleman from the Havannah has reported that a Mr. Watson from Charlestown was taken in the Bay of Mexico and carried into Carthagena, from thence sent to the Castle of St. Juan, de Ullua la Vera Cruz and afterwards sent to Trascala, where it is supposed he is at present. His Father and numerous Relations are very anxious for his Fate, and earnestly beg that you would interest yourself with the Comte D'Aranda and Mr. Charmichael for his Release, but if that cannot be had in full that you would endeavour to procure his removal to old Spain, that his Friends may hear from him, and gain Intelligence respecting the Property he may have left in Carolina. I have written to Charmichael, and intend to speak to Don Del Campo.

Pray send me the Arrêt against English Manufactures and every other new Arrêt, which may any Way affect the United States. It is confidently given out here that our Vessells are not admitted into the French W. Indias.

Has there been any new Arret, since that of August 1784? [42] ·Can you discover the Cause, of the great Ballance of Exchange in favour of England, from France, Spain, Holland, etc. as well as America? And whether this Appearance of Prosperity will continue? I think that at the Peace, the British Merchants sent their Factors abroad with immense quantities of their Manufactures, the whole Stock they had on hand. These Factors have sold as they could, and bought Remittances especially Bills of Exchange as they could, i.e. very dear, so that the loss on the Exchange is that of the British Merchant, and consequently that this appearance is not so much in favour of England. Spain I expect will follow the Example of France in prohibiting Brit. Manufactures, at least if Del Campo does not make a commercial Treaty with Woodward who is appointed to treat with him. But the Diplomaticks are of opinion nothing will be done with him, nor with Crawford. The two Years expire in January. If Crawford is likely to do any Thing be so good as to let me know it.

The words "Ship and Sailor," still turn the Heads of this People. They grudge to every other People, a single ship and a single seaman. The Consequence of this Envy, in the End, will be the loss of all their own. They seem at present to dread American Ships and Seamen more than any other. Their Jealousy of our Navigation is so strong, that it is odds if it does not stimulate them to hazard their own Revenue. I am, my dear Sir, with Sincere Esteem your Friend,

JOHN ADAMS

Jefferson to Adams

Paris Aug. 6. 1785.

DEAR SIR

I now inclose you a draught of a treaty for the Barbary states,[43] together with the notes Dr. Franklin left me. I have retained a presscopy of this draught, so that by referring to any article, line and word in it you can propose amendments and send them by the post without any body's being able to make much of the main subject. I shall be glad to receive any alterations you may think necessary as soon as convenient, that this matter may be in readiness. I inclose also a letter containing intelligence from

42. The Arrêt of Aug. 30, 1784, established seven free ports in the French West Indies and extended the list of imports permitted in American vessels, with some exceptions. L. C. Wroth and G. L. Annan, eds., *Acts of French Royal Administration ...prior to 1791* (N. Y., 1930), no. 1980.

43. "Draught of a Treaty of Amity and Commerce," printed in Boyd, VIII, 347-53.

Algiers. I know not how far it is to be relied on. My anxiety is extreme indeed as to these treaties. What are we to do? We know that Congress have decided ultimately to treat. We know how far they will go. But unfortunately we know also that a particular person has been charged with instructions for us, these five months who neither comes nor writes to us. What are we to do? It is my opinion that if Mr. Lambe does not come in either of the packets (English or French) now expected, we ought to proceed. I therefore propose to you this term, as the end of our expectations of him, and that if he does not come we send some other person. Dr. Bancroft or Capt. Jones occur to me as the fittest. If we consider the present object only, I think the former would be most proper: but if we look forward to the very probable event of war with those pirates, an important object would be obtained by Capt. Jones's becoming acquainted with their ports, force, tactics etc. Let me know your opinion on this. I have never mentioned it to either, but I suppose either might be induced to go. Present me affectionately to the ladies and Colo. Smith and be assured of the sincerity with which I am Dr. Sir Your friend and servt.,

TH: JEFFERSON

Adams to Jefferson

Grosvenor Square Westminster Aug. 7. 1785

DEAR SIR

As to the Cask of Wine at Auteuil, it is not paid for. If you will pay for it and take it, you will oblige me. By a sample of it, which I tasted it is good Wine, and very, extreamly cheap.

I am happy to find We agree so perfectly in the Change which is made in the Project. The Dye is cast. The Proposal is made. Let them ruminate upon it.

I thought of proposing a Tariff of Duties, that We might pay no more in their Ports than they should pay in ours. But their Taxes are so essential to their Credit, that it is impossible for them to part with any of them, and We should not choose to oblige ourselves to lay on as heavy ones. We are at Liberty to do it, however, when We please.

If the English will not abolish their Aliens Duty, relatively to us, We must establish an Alien Duty in all the United States. An Alien Duty against England alone will not answer the End. She will elude it by employing Dutch, French, Sweedish, or any other ships, and by frenchifying, dutchifying, or Sweedishizing her own Ships. If the English will persevere in excluding our Ships from their West India Islands, Canada, Nova Scotia, and Newfoundland, and in demanding any Alien Duty of us in their Ports within the Realm, and in refusing to amercian built Ships the Priviledges of british built Ships, We must take an higher Ground, a Vantage Ground. We must do more than lay on Alien Duties. We must take measures by which the Increase of Shipping and Seamen will be not only encouraged, but rendered inevitable. We must adopt in all the States the Regulations which were once made in England 5. Ric. 2. c. 3., and ordain that no American Citizen, or Denizen, or alien friend or Ennemy, shall ship any Merchandise out of, or into the United States and navigated with an American Captain and three fourths American Seamen. I should be sorry to adopt a Monopoly. But, driven to the necessity of it, I would not do Business by the Halves. The French deserve it of us as much as the English; for they are as much Ennemies to our Ships and Mariners. Their Navigation Acts are not quite so severe as those of Spain, Portugal and England, as they relate to their Colonies I mean. But they are not much less so. And they discover as strong a Lust to annihilate our navigation as any body.

Or might We modify a little? Might We lay a Duty of ten per Cent on all Goods imported in any but ships built in the United States, without saying any Thing about Seamen?

If We were to prohibit all foreign Vessells from carrying on our Coasting Trade, i.e. from trading from one State to another, and from one Port to another in the same State, We should do Something, for this Commerce will be so considerable as to employ many Ships and many Seamen, of so much the more Value to us as they will be always at home and ready for the Defence of their Country. But if We should only prohibit Importations, except in our own Bottoms or in the Bottoms of the Country or Nation of whose Growth or Production the Merchandises are, We should do nothing effectual against Great Britain. She would desire nothing better than to send her Productions to our Ports in her own Bottoms and bring away ours in return.

I hope the Members of Congress and the Legislatures of the States will study the British Acts of Navigation, and make themselves Masters of their Letter and Spirit, that they may judge how far they can be adopted by us, and indeed whether they are sufficient to do Justice to our Citizens in their Commerce with Great Britain.

There is another Enquiry which I hope our Countrymen will enter upon, and that is, what Articles of our Produce will bear a Duty upon Exportation? All such Duties are paid by the Consumer, and therefore are so much clear gain. Some of our Commodities will not bear any such

Duties; on the contrary, they will require Encouragement by Bounties: But I suspect that Several Articles would bear an handsome Impost.

We shall find our Commerce a complicated Machine and difficult to manage, and I fear We have not many Men, who have turned their Thoughts to it. It must be comprehended by Somebody in its System and in its detail, before it will be regulated as it should be. With great and Sincere Esteem I am dear Sir, your most obedient,

JOHN ADAMS

The Vacancy in your alphabet may be thus filled from points to points inclusive 1506. 970. 331. 504. 1186. 1268. 356. 517. 754. 1085. 269. 148. 205. 1318. 1258. 942. 712. 75. 246. 127. 609. 885. 1461. 837. 1327. and secondly, in like manner 472. 560. 820. 83.—Now give *me* leave. You make use of the number 1672. It has no meaning in my Cypher. Indeed there is a vacancy from 1596 to 1700 inclusive. When you have filled them up as you proposed I should thank you for a Copy by the first safe Conveyance etc.

Jefferson to Adams

Paris Aug. 10. 1785.

DEAR SIR

Your favor of the 4th. inst. came to hand yesterday. I now inclose you the two Arrets against the importation of foreign manufactures into this kingdom. The cause of the balance against this country in favor of England as well as it's amount is not agreed on. No doubt the rage for English manufactures must be a principal cause. The speculators in Exchange say also that those of the circumjacent countries who have a balance in their favor against France remit that balance to England from France. If so it is possible that the English may count this balance twice: that is, in summing their exports to one of those states, and their imports from it, they count the difference once in their favour: then a second time when they sum the remittances of cash they receive from France. There has been no arret relative to our commerce since that of Aug. 1784. and all the late advices from the French West Indies are that they have now in their ports always three times as many vessels as there ever were before, and that the increase is principally from our States. I have now no further fears of that arret's standing it's ground. When it shall become firm I do not think it's extension desperate. But whether the placing it on the firm basis of treaty be practicable is a very different question. As far as it is possible to judge from appearances I conjecture that Crawford will do nothing. I infer this from some things in his conversation, and from an expression of the Count de Vergennes in a conversation with me yesterday. I pressed upon him the importance of opening their ports freely to us in the moment of the oppressions of the English regulations against us and perhaps of the suspension of their commerce. He admitted it but said we had free ingress with our productions. I enumerated them to him and shewed him on what footing they were and how they might be improved. We are to have further conversations on the subject. I am afraid the voiage to Fontaine-bleau will interrupt them. From the enquiries I have made I find I cannot get a very small and indifferent house there for the season (that is, for a month) for less than 100. or 150 guineas. This is nearly the whole salary for the time and would leave nothing to eat. I therefore cannot accompany the court there, but I will endeavor to go occasionally there from Paris. They tell me it is the most favourable scene for business with the Count de Vergennes, because he is then more abstracted from the domestic applications. Count D'Aranda is not yet returned from the waters of Vichy. As soon as he returns I will apply to him in the case of Mr. Watson. I will pray you to insure Houdon's life from the 27th. of last month to his return to Paris. As he was to stay in America a month or two, he will probably be about 6 months absent: but the 3 per cent for the voiage being once paid I suppose they will ensure his life by the month whether his absence be longer or shorter. The sum to be insured is fifteen thousand livres tournois. If it be not necessary to pay the money immediately there is a prospect of exchange becoming more favourable. But whenever it is necessary be so good as to procure it by selling a draught on Mr. Grand which I will take care shall be honoured. Compliments to the ladies and am Dr. Sir Your friend and servt.,

TH: JEFFERSON

Jefferson to Adams

Paris Aug. 17. 1785.

DEAR SIR

I received yesterday your favor of the 7th. *This was 4. days later than* Mr. Short's of the *same date. It had evidently been opened. We must* therefore consider *both governments as possessed of it's contents.* I write you a line at this moment merely to inform you that *Mr. Barclay is willing* to *go to treat with* the *Barbary states if we desire it* and that *this will* not *take him from any employment here.* It will *only retard his voiage to America. Let me know your sentiments hereon.* The number 1672. is an error in the alphabetical side of the cypher. Turn to the numerical side and in the 11th. column and 72d. line you will see the number it should have been and what it was meant to signify. Correct your alphabetical side accordingly if it is wrong as mine was. We are told this morning that the *Cardinal Prince* of *Rohan* is *confined* to *his chamber* under *guard* for *reflections* on the *Queen who was present herself* in *council on his examination,* the first *time she* was ever *there* and the first *instance* of so *high an Ecclesiastical character* under actual *force.* Adieu. Your friend and servt.,[44]

TH: JEFFERSON

Adams to Jefferson

Grosvenor Square August 18. 1785

DEAR SIR

I have received your Favour of the 6. Aug. with the Notes and Project inclosed.

How can we send another Person? We have not in our Full Power authority to Substitute. Will not the Emperor and the Regencies feel their Dignity offended if a Person appears without a Commission from Congress? Do you mean that he should only agree upon the Terms and transmit them to Us to be signed? If you think this Method will do, I have no objection to either of the Persons you mention—nor to Mr. Short. Dr. Bancroft is the greatest Master of the French Language. If We conclude to send either he should take an attested Copy at least of all our Commissions for Africa, and a Letter and Instructions from Us. If there is any Truth in any of the Reports of Captures by the Algerines, Lambes Vessell may be taken by them.

Whoever is sent by us should be instructed to correspond constantly with us, and to send, by whatever conveyance he may find, whether thro' Spain France England Holland or otherwise, Copies of his Letters to us to Congress. He should be instructed farther to make dilligent Inquiry concerning the Productions of those Countries which would answer in America, and those of the United States which might find a Market in Barbary, and to transmit all such Information to Congress as well as to Us.

I have read over the Project with Care. The 17th. Article appears to be carried farther than our Countrymen will at present be willing to go. I presume the three last words of the third Line of this 17. Article must be

44. Italicized passages were written in code.

left out; and in the fourth line, the 7. 8. 9. 10. 11. and 12. Words; and in the Sixth Line the first, Second, third, fourth, and fifth Words.[45]

You have seen by this Time our Massachusetts Navigation Act, and the Reasonings and Dispositions of all the States tend the same Way at present, so that we must conform our Proceedings, as I suppose, to their Views. My Regards to Messrs. Humphreys, Mazzai, Williamos, etc. and believe me ever yours,

JOHN ADAMS

Mr. Short left us on Tuesday. Dr. Bancroft is just come in. This Letter will be delivered to you by Mr. James Smith, a Gentleman of South Carolina, a Relation of Mrs. Adams, whom I beg leave to introduce to you and recommend to your Civilities.

Abigail Adams to Jefferson

London Grosvenor Square August 21 1785

DEAR SIR

The Gentleman who is so kind as to convey this to you is from Carolina, his name is Smith. He is a distant relation of mine, tho I have not the pleasure of much acquaintance with him. He has resided in England some time, and bears a good Character here. Give me leave Sir to introduce him to your notice.

Mr. Short left us last Tuesday for the Hague. I did myself the honour of writing to you by him.

I find by the last papers from New York that Mr. Rutledge is appointed minister at the Hague; in the room of Mr. Livingstone who declined the embassy. There is no mention made of a secretary.

You will probably see our Massachusetts Navigation act before this reaches you; it has struck the hireling scriblers dumb. There has been less abuse against the Americans in the papers since the publication of it; than for a long time before.

Ireland has exerted herself, and Pharoah and his host are overthrown. The Courier of Europe will doubtless give you the debates. The July packet arrived last week, tho she left New York the seventh of July. She brought not a line of publick dispatch. A private Letter or two for Col. Smith, the contents of which we cannot know; as he is absent upon a Tour to Berlin.

I was much disapointed to find that my son had not arrived when the

45. The omissions from Article 17 advised by JA are shown in the text as printed in Boyd, VIII, 350.

packet saild. As the French packet sails sometime after the English, I am not without hopes that I may hear by that, and I will thank you sir to give me the earliest intelligence if she brings any account of the May packet.

Be so good as to present my Regards to Col Humphries. Mr. Short gives us some encouragement to expect him here this Winter. My Love to Miss Jefferson, to whom also my daughter desires to be rememberd. Our good old Friends the Abbes, I would tender my Regards. If I could write French, I would have scribled a line to the Abbe Arnou.

I think Madam Helvetius must be very melancholy now Franklin as she used to call him is gone. It is said here by a Gentleman lately from Philadelphia, that they determine to elect the Doctor president upon his arrival, as Mr. Dickinsons office expires in october.

In my Letter by Mr. Short I had taken the Liberty to request you to procure for me two or 3 articles, and to convey them by Col. Smith who talks of returning by way of Paris. But if he should not visit you, Mr. Smith when he returns will be so good as to take charge of them for me. But this I shall know in the course of a few weeks, and will take measures accordingly. I am sir with Sentiments of Esteem Your Humble Servant,

ABIGAIL ADAMS

Adams to Jefferson

Grosvenor Square Aug. 23. 1785

DEAR SIR

Last night, I received your Favour of the 17. If both Governments are possessed of the Contents of my letter of the 7th. by opening it in the Post Office, much good may those Contents do them. They both know they have deserved it. I hope it will convince them of their Error, and induce them to adopt more liberal Principles toward Us. I am for answering their Utmost Generosity with equal and indeed with greater Generosity. But I would not advise my Country to be the Bubble of her own Nobleness of Sentiment.

The Spirited Conduct of Ireland, I think will assist me, here. The News of the Reception in the Irish Parliament of the 20 Resolutions together with the Efforts in America towards a Navigation Act have raised my Hopes a good deal. But our States must mature their Plan and persevere in it, in order to effect the Work. In time, and with a Steady pursuit of our Purpose, I begin to think We shall prevail.

If Mr. Barclay will undertake the Voyage, I am for looking no farther. We cannot find a Steadier, or more prudent Man. He should look out for some Clerk or Companion who can write French and understands Italian.

When Dr. Price returns from his August Excursion to some Watering Place, I will get him to make the Insurance upon Houdons Life, on the best Terms he can. Adieu. Yours sincerely,

JOHN ADAMS

Jefferson to Abigail Adams

Paris Sep. 4. 1785.

DEAR MADAM

I was honoured with your letter of Aug. 21. by Mr. Smith who arrived here on the 29th. I am sorry you did not repeat the commission you had favoured me with by Mr. Short as the present would have been an excellent opportunity of sending the articles you wished for. As Mr. Short's return may yet be delayed, will you be so good as to write me by post what articles you desired, lest I should not otherwise know in time to send them by either of the Mr. Smiths. The French packet brought me letters from Mr. Jay and Dr. Ramsay only. They were dated July 13. They do not mention the arrival of your son. Dr. Ramsay's letter was on a particular subject, and Mr. Jay's letter was official. He may have arrived therefore, tho these letters do not mention it. However as he did not sail till June, and Westerly winds prevail in the summer I think the 13th. of July was too early to expect him to have arrived. I will certainly transmit you information of his arrival the moment I know it.

We have little new and interesting here. The Queen has determined to wear none but French gauzes hereafter. How many English looms will this put down? You will have seen the affair of the Cardinal de Rohan so well detailed in the Leyden gazette that I need add nothing on that head. The Cardinal is still in the Bastille. It is certain that the Queen has been compromitted without the smallest authority from her: and the probability is that the Cardinal has been duped into it by his mistress Madme. de la Motte. There results from this two consequences not to his honour, that he is a debauchee, and a booby. The Abbés are well. They have been kept in town this summer by the affairs of the Abbé Mably. I have at length procured a house in a situation much more pleasing to me than my present. It is at the grille des champs Elysees, but within the city. It suits me in every circumstance but the price, being dearer than the one I am now in. It has a clever garden to it. I will pray you to present my best respects to Miss Adams and to be assured of the respect and esteem with which I have the honour to be Dear Madam Your most obedient and most humble servt.,

TH: JEFFERSON

Jefferson to Adams

Paris Sep. 4. 1785.

DEAR SIR

On receipt of your favors of Aug. 18. and 23. I conferred with Mr. Barclay on the measures necessary to be taken to set our treaty with the pyratical states into motion through his agency. Supposing that we should begin with the emperor of Marocco, a letter to the emperor and instructions to Mr. Barclay seemed necessary. I have therefore sketched such outlines for these as appear to me to be proper.[46] You will be so good, as to detract, add to, or alter them as you please, to return such as you approve under your signature, to which I will add mine. A person understanding English, French and Italian, and at the same time meriting confidence, was not to be met with here. Colo. Franks understanding the two first languages perfectly, and a little Spanish instead of Italian, occurred to Mr. Barclay as the fittest person he could employ for a Secretary. We think his allowance (exclusive of his travelling expences and his board which will be paid by Mr. Barclay in common with his own) should be between 100 and 150 guineas a year. Fix it where you please between these limits. What is said in the instructions to Mr. Barclay as to his own allowance was proposed by himself. My idea as to the partition of the whole sum to which we are limited (80,000 D.) was that one half of it should be kept in reserve for the Algerines. They certainly possess more than half of the whole power of the Pyratical states. I thought then that Marocco might claim the half of the remainder, that is to say one fourth of the whole. For this reason in the instructions I propose 20,000 D. as the limits of the expences of the Marocco treaty. Be so good as to think of it, and to make it what you please. I should be more disposed to enlarge than abridge it on account of their neighborhood to our Atlantic trade. I did not think that these papers should be trusted through the post office, and therefore, as Colo. Franks is engaged in the business, he comes with

46. "Documents pertaining to the Mission of Barclay and Lamb to the Barbary States," Boyd, VIII, 610-24.

them. Passing by the diligence the whole expence will not exceed 12 or 14 guineas. I suppose we are bound to avail ourselves of the co-operation of France. I will join you therefore in any letter you think proper to write to the Count de Vergennes. Would you think it expedient to write to Mr. Carmichael to interest the interposition of the Spanish court? I will join you in any thing of this kind you will originate. In short be so good as to supply whatever you may think necessary. With respect to the money Mr. Jay's information to you was that it was to be drawn from Holland. It will rest therefore with you to avail Mr. Barclay of that fund either by your draughts, or by a letter of credit to the bankers in his favour to the necessary amount. I imagine the Dutch Consul at Marocco may be rendered an useful character in the remittances of money to Mr. Barclay while at Marocco.

You were apprised, by a letter from Mr. Short, of the delay which had arisen in the execution of the treaty with Prussia.[47] I wrote a separate letter of which I inclose you a copy, hoping it would meet one from you and set them again into motion. I have the honour to be with the highest respect Dear Sir Your most obedient and most humble servt.,

TH: JEFFERSON

Jefferson to Adams

Paris Sep. 4. 1785.

DEAR SIR

Mr. Mazzei, during the war was employed by the state of Virginia to procure them loans of money in Europe. He thinks that in allowing him for his expences they have allowed less than they actually were. You knew him in Paris, and knew of the journies which he made. I would thank you for the best guess you can make of what his expences may have been, according to the stile in which you observed him to live. My object is to have justice done him, if it has not been done, being assured that if the state has failed in this point, it has been from a want of evidence and that they will rectify their error if they find they have committed one. I am with the highest esteem Dr. Sir Your friend and servant,

TH: JEFFERSON

47. De Thulemeier objected to an English column in the treaty, and TJ informed Dumas and Short that "we should agree to consider the French column as the original if the Baron de Thulemeyer thinks himself bound to insist upon it." *Ibid.*, 459.

Jefferson to Adams

Paris Sep. 4. 1785.

DEAR SIR

Since writing my letter of this morning I have seen Mr. Grand and had a conversation with him on the subject of the interest due here. He is pressed on that subject. By a letter he received not long since from the Commissioners of the treasury it seems their intention that he should pay this interest out of the money in Holland, yet they omitted to give him any authority to ask for any of that money. I thought it possible they might have written to you on the subject and told him I would take the liberty of asking whether you had been desired to do any thing. It is a little unfortunate that our credit should be losing ground for default of paiment while money is understood to be lying dead, and sufficient for that purpose. The Commissioners themselves made this reflection in their letter. If you can give us any information on this subject I will thank you. I am with much esteem Dr. Sir Your friend and servt.,

TH: JEFFERSON

Adams to Jefferson

Grosvenor Square Westminster Septr. 4. 1785

DEAR SIR

I have received three Letter[s] of the Tenor and Date of the within. I cannot find in any Gazetteer or geographical Dictionary any Such Place as Roscoff, and I can make nothing of the Story.[48] I hope you have more Skill in Divination.

I have no Letters from Congress, nor any Answer from the Ministry.

Pray what are the Sentiments in France upon the American Acts of Navigation? And what has been the Success of the French Whale Fishery?

48. The case of Lister Asquith of Baltimore, owner of the schooner *William and Catherine*, which put into a Breton port on Aug. 8, 1785, in distress. Since her cargo was exclusively tobacco, it was seized as an illegal entry. Asquith, along with five others on board, was arrested by agents of the Farmers General (the tobacco monopoly) and imprisoned. Asquith appealed to TJ in Paris who applied to Vergennes on their behalf, Nov. 14, 1785. Boyd, VIII, 477-78; IX, 31-38.

How many Ships have they sent out this Year? The Britons have introduced into theirs a Spirit of Gambling, by giving a Bounty of 500 £ to the Ship which has the greatest Success; 400 £ to the next. This will make many Adventurers and give a temporary Activity to the Business: But I rely upon it both the French and English Essays will fall through. My Reason for thinking so is, because the Business in itself is not profitable, and, excepting the four Vessells which may obtain the Bounties, the others upon an Avarage will be loosers. I know that my Countrymen in the best Times, with all their frugality, with all their Skill, and with their particular manner of conducting the Business could but barely live, and the Fishery was valuable to Us, only as a Remittance. The English are Sacrificing the Bread of thousands of their best Manufacturers to the interested Schemes of a very few Individuals and to a narrow Prejudice and a little Jealousy: but I dont believe the Delusion will be durable. Time will Shew, both them and the French, that it is better to buy our Oil and Candles and Fins, and pay for them in Buttons and Ribbons. If they dont discover their Error, We will lay on Duties upon Buttons and Ribbons, equal to the Alien Duties, and grant them out again in Bounties to our Whalemen.

We must not, my Friend, be the Bubbles of our own Liberal Sentiments. If We cannot obtain reciprocal Liberality, We must adopt reciprocal Prohibitions, Exclusions, Monopolies, and Imposts. Our offers have been fair, more than fair. If they are rejected, we must not be the Dupes. With great Esteem, dear Sir, yours,

JOHN ADAMS

Abigail Adams to Jefferson

London Septr. 6 1785

DEAR SIR

I cannot omit by this opportunity acquainting you that on Sunday the August packet arrived in which came Mr. Church and brought us Letters from our son to our no small joy. He arrived the 17 of july after a very tedious passage. He was however in good Health and Spirits. Mr. Adams has at Length received some Letters from the president, from Mr. Jay and a private Letter from Mr. Gerry, together with some newspapers and journals of Congress. The papers contain nothing very material. Mr. Osgood, Mr. Walter Livingston and Mr. Arthur Lee are the commissioners of the Treasury. Mr. Lee was chosen a few days before the sailing of the packet and was just gone from New York. It is said that the commissioners will have a difficult task to bring order out of the confusion in which the late financier left the office. Mr. Rutledge had not accepted his appointment when the gentlemen wrote. Mr. Jay writes that about the 29 of May Lambe sent for the papers from Congress, that they were sent, and that he saild soon after.

They are very anxious in America with respect to the posts,[49] especially since a reinforcement of troops have been sent out. The merchants say that the trade is worth annually 50.000 pounds sterling.

From the present movements here, there is no great prospect of obtaining them by fair means. *The prospect here*, is not the pleasentest in the World. But I must recollect this is to go by the post. Mr. A. is very buisy writing to New York as Mr. Storer is going out in a few days. He desires me to inform you that he would take any dispatches you may have provided you could trust them here. Mr. Storer was formerly private Secretary to Mr. Adams. I will tuck this in one corner of Mr. A's Letter. Yours etc.

Adams to Jefferson

Grosvr. Square 11th. Septemr. 1785.

DEAR SIR

In answer to your enquiry in your letter of the 4th. inst. I can only say that I knew Mr. Matzei at Paris and that he made long journeys. But in what stile he lived and at what expence he travelled I know not. He always made a genteel appearance without any unnecessary show, and kept good Company wherever he went. I observed this in Paris and heard of it in Holland. In Italy it could not be otherwise, for he is well known and esteemed there as I have always heard and particularly within these few days from the Genoese Ambassador and General Paoli; both of whom enquired of me, very respectfully, after Mr. Mazzei, at the Drawing Room, of their own motion. Knowing as you and I do how little way a thousand pounds go, in expences of living, if I were to guess at his expences, altho' he had not a house and train of Servants to maintain, nor a table that I know of, yet, considering the indispensible article of Cloaths, Carriage, Postage and Stationary, as well as the ordinary expences of Apartments, travelling and all the rest, I could not undertake to pay his way for a less Sum. I am, dear Sir, Yrs: etc: etc.

49. The western posts of defense and the fur trade, Detroit, Michilimackinac, Oswego, Niagara, etc., were still occupied by the British, contrary to the peace treaty of 1783. Samuel F. Bemis, *Jay's Treaty: A Study in Commerce and Diplomacy* (N. Y., 1923), 1-20.

Adams to Jefferson

Grosvenor Square Westminster Septr. 11. 1785.

DEAR SIR

In Answer to your Favour of September 4. I am sorry to inform you that I have not received one line from the Commissioners of the Treasury, nor from Congress, nor any of their Ministers, respecting the Interest due in France. It is possible Messieurs Willinks and Van Staphorsts may, or possibly the orders may have been suspended to be sent by the Minister to the Hague, when they can find one who will venture to Europe under the present Regulations.

The System of having no Ministers in Europe has involved our Country in so many Inconveniences that I fancy it will go out of Fashion. It would be well to send Consuls, I think, who, upon Permission to trade, would serve without Salaries, if We cannot afford the salaries of Ministers. I am with great Respect, sir, your Friend and Servant,

JOHN ADAMS

Adams to Jefferson

Grosvenor Square Septr. 15. 1785

DEAR SIR

I have received your Letter of the fourth instant by Colonel Franks, with a Project of a Letter to the Emperor of Morocco, and several other Papers.

I have had this Letter, fairly copied, with very few and very inconsiderable Alterations and have signed it. I have left room enough, at the Beginning, for you to insert, or leave Mr. Barclay to insert, the Emperors Titles and Address, which may be done, with the most certainty in Morocco.

By the Treaty We have with Holland, the States General have agreed, upon Requisition, to second our negotiations in the most favourable manner, by means of their Consuls. I would have prepared a Memorial and Requisition to that Purpose and have sent it to the Hague, But such a Memorial would publish to all the World Mr. Barclays Mission. I Shall wait for your Advice, and if you think proper, I will Still Send a Memorial.

But I am inclined to think We had better wait till We receive from Mr. Barclay in Morocco some account of his Prospects.

The best Argument Mr. Barclay can use, to obtain Treaties upon moderate Terms, is that We have absolutely as yet no Ships in the Mediterranean Sea, and shall have none untill Treaties are made. That our Seamen will not go there, untill Treaties are made. That therefore the Algerines will have no Chance of taking any American Vessells, any where but in the Atlantic, and there they can expect to take but very few, at a vast Expence of Corsairs, and exposed to our Privateers and Frigates.

Treaties of Peace are very unpopular, with the People of Algiers. They say it is taking from them all the Opportunities of making Profits by Prizes for the sake of inriching the Dey by Presents. The Probability then that our Trade would be more beneficial to the People, than the Few Prizes they would have a chance to make, by going at a vast Expence out of the Mediterranean and spreading themselves over the Ocean in quest of our ships, exposed to our Frigates and the Men of War of Portugal, etc. would be the best Reason for the Dey to use with the People. The common Argument is the Bombardments and Depredations with which their Ennemies threaten them by their Fleets and Squadrons, which commonly accompany the Embassy. Mr. Barclay will be very naked in this respect. With great Respect, your most obedient

JOHN ADAMS

Adams to Jefferson

Grosvenor Square Septr. 16. 1785

DEAR [SIR]

At the desire of the Baron De Poellnitz, I do myself the Honour to introduce him to you. This Nobleman you know married a Daughter of the Earl of Bute once the Wife of Earl Piercy. They have lived some time in New York. He goes to France to meet his Lady who arrived there sometime since.

Coll. Franks will leave Us tomorrow. There are abroad so many infamous Fictions concerning the Captures made by the Algeriens, that I still hope the Report of their Advertizing American Vessells and Cargoes for sale, is without a better foundation. With great Esteem Your Friend and Servant,

JOHN ADAMS

Adams to Jefferson

Grosvenor Square 18 Sepr. 1785

DEAR SIR

Inclosed, you have in Confidence some Compliments. Give me in confidence your Opinion of them. Is there any thing said by me which I ought not to have said? Is there any expression exceptionable? Have I compromised myself or the public in any thing? more than ought to be—

The Custom of making a Speech is so settled, that not only, the Secretary of State and the Master of the Ceremonies, but some of the Foreign Ministers, took the pains to inform me it was indispensable; otherwise being sensible of the difficulty of being complaisant enough without being too much, I intended to have delivered my Credentials, without saying more, than that they were Credentials to his Majesty from the United States. Your Friend.

Jefferson to Adams

Sep. 19. 1785. Paris.

Lambe is *arrived. He brings new full powers* to *us* from *Congress* to *appoint persons* to *negotiate with* the *Barbary states*, but *we* are to *sign* the *treaties. Lambe has* not *even* a *recommendation* from *them* to *us*, but it seems clear that *he would* be *approved* by *them. I told him* of *Mr. Barclay's appointment* to *Marocco* and *proposed Algiers* to *him. He agrees. A small alteration* in the *form* of *our dispatches* will be *necessary*, and of *course* another *courier shall* be *dispatched* to *you* on the *return* of *Colo. Franks*, for *your pleasure herein.*[50]

Jefferson to Adams

Paris Sep. 24. 1785.

DEAR SIR

My letter of Sep. 19. written the morning after Mr. Lamb's arrival here, would inform you of that circumstance. I transmit you herewith copies of the papers he brought to us on the subject of the Barbary treaties. You

50. Italicized passages were written in code.

will see by them that Congress has adopted the very plan which we were proposing to pursue. It will now go on under less danger of objection from the other parties. The receipt of these new papers therefore has rendered necessary no change in matter of substance in the dispatches we had prepared. But they render some formal changes necessary. For instance in our letter of credence for Mr. Barclay to the Emperor of Marocco, it becomes improper to enter into those explanations which seemed proper when that letter was drawn; because Congress in their letter enter into that explanation. In the letter to the Ct. de Vergennes it became proper to mention the new full powers received from Congress and which in some measure accord with the idea communicated by him to us from the M. de Castries. These and other formal alterations, which appeared necessary to me, I have made, leaving so much of the original draughts approved and amended by you as were not inconsistent with these alterations. I have therefore had them prepared fair to save you the trouble of copying; yet wherever you chuse to make alterations you will be so good as to make them; taking in that case the trouble of having new fair copies made out.

You will perceive by Mr. Jay's letter that Congress had not thought proper to give Mr. Lamb any appointment. I imagine they apprehended it might interfere with measures actually taken by us. Notwithstanding the perfect freedom which they are pleased to leave to us on his subject, I cannot feel myself clear of that bias which a presumption of their pleasure gives, and ought to give. I presume that Mr. Lamb met their approbation, because of the recommendations he carried from the Governor and state of Connecticut, because of his actual knowlege of the country and people of the states of Barbary, because of the detention of these letters from March to July, which considering their pressing nature would otherwise have been sent by other Americans who in the mean time have come from N. York to Paris; and because too of the information we received by Mr. Jarvis. These reasons are not strong enough to set aside our appointment of Mr. Barclay to Marocco: that I think should go on, as no man could be sent who would enjoy more the confidence of Congress. But they are strong enough to induce me to propose to you the appointment of Lamb to Algiers. He has followed for many years the Barbary trade and seems intimately acquainted with those states. I have not seen enough of him to judge of his abilities. He seems not deficient as far as I can see, and the footing on which he comes must furnish a presumption for what we do not see. We must say the same as to his integrity; we must rely for this on the recommendations he brings, as it is impossible for us to judge of this for ourselves. Yet it will be our duty to use such reasonable cautions as are in our power. Two occur to me. 1. To give him a clerk capable of assisting and attending to his proceedings and who, in case he thought any thing was going amiss, might give us information. 2. Not to give a credit on Van Staphorst and Willinck, but let his draughts be made on yourself, which with the knowlege you will have of his proceedings, will enable you to check them, if you are sensible of any abuse intended. This will give you trouble; but as I have never found you declining trouble when it is necessary, I venture to propose it. I hope it will not expose you to inconvenience as by instructing Lamb to insert in his draughts a proper usance you can in the mean time raise the money for them by drawing on Holland. I must inform you that Mr. Barclay wishes to be put on the same footing with Mr. Lamb as to this article and therefore I return you your letter of Credit on Van Staphorsts & co. As to the 1st. article there is great difficulty. There is no body at Paris fit for the undertaking who would be likely to accept of it. I mean there is no American, for I should be anxious to place a native in the trust. Perhaps you can send us one from London. There is a Mr. Randolph there from New York whom Mr. Barclay thinks might be relied on very firmly for integrity and capacity. He is there for his health: perhaps you can persuade him to go to Algiers in pursuit of it. If you cannot, I really know not what will be done. It is impossible to propose to Bancroft to go in a secondary capacity. Mr. Barclay and myself have thought of Cairnes at l'Orient as a dernier resort. But it is incertain, or rather improbable that he will undertake it. You will be pleased in the first place to consider of my proposition to send Lamb to Algiers, and in the next all the circumstances before detailed as consequences of that. The inclosed letter from Richard O'Bryan furnishes powerful motives for commencing, by some means or other, the treaty with Algiers more immediately than would be done if left on Mr. Barclay. You will perceive by that that two of our vessels with their crews and cargoes have been carried captive into that port. What is to be done as to those poor people? I am for hazarding the supplementory instruction to Lamb which accompanies these papers. Alter it or reject it as you please. You ask what I think of claiming the Dutch interposition. I doubt the fidelity of any interposition too much to desire it sincerely. Our letters to this court heretofore seemed to oblige us to communicate with them on the subject. If you think the Dutch would take amiss our not applying to them, I will join you in the application. Otherwise the fewer are apprised of our proceedings the better. To communicate them to the States of Holland is to communicate them to the whole world.

Mr. Short returned last night and brought the Prussian treaty duly executed in English and French. We may send it to Congress by the Mr. Fitzhughs going from hence. Will you draw and sign a short letter for that purpose? I send you a copy of a letter received from the

M. Fayette. In the present unsettled state of American commerce, I had as lieve avoid all further treaties except with American powers. If Count Merci therefore does not propose the subject to me, I shall not to him, nor do more than decency requires if he does propose it. I am with great esteem Dr. Sir your most obedient humble servt.,

TH: JEFFERSON

Jefferson to Adams

Paris Sep. 24. 1785.

DEAR SIR

I have received your favor of the 18th. inclosing your compliments on your presentation. The sentiments you therein expressed were such as were entertained in America till the Commercial proclamation, and such as would again return were a rational conduct to be adopted by Gr. Britain. I think therefore you by no means comprometted yourself or our country, nor expressed more than it would be our interest to encourage, if they were disposed to meet us. I am pleased however to see the answer of the king. It bears the marks of suddenness and surprize, and as he seems not to have had time for reflection we may suppose he was obliged to find his answer in the real sentiments of his heart, if that heart has any sentiment. I have no doubt however that it contains the real creed of an Englishman, and that the word which he has let escape is the true word of the ænigma, "The moment I see such sentiments as yours prevail and a disposition to give this country *the preference*, I will etc." All this I stedfastly beleive. But the condition is impossible. Our interest calls for a perfect equality in our conduct towards these two nations; but no preferences any where. If however circumstances should ever oblige us to shew a preference, a respect for our character, if we had no better motive, would decide to which it should be given. My letters from members of Congress render it doubtful whether they would not rather that full time should be given for the present disposition of America to mature itself and to produce a permanent improvement in the federal constitution, rather than, by removing the incentive, to prevent the improvement. It is certain that our commerce is in agonies at present, and that these would be relieved by opening the British ports in the W. Indies. It remains to consider whether a temporary continuance under these sufferings would be paid for by the amendment it is likely to produce. However I beleive there is no fear that Great Britain will puzzle us by leaving it in our choice to hasten or delay a treaty.

Is insurance made on Houdon's life? I am uneasy about it, lest we should hear of any accident. As yet there is no reason to doubt their safe passage. If the insurance is not made I will pray you to have it done immediately.

As I have not received any London newspapers as yet I am obliged to ask you what is done as to them, lest the delay should proceed from some obstacle to be removed. There is a Mr. Thompson at Dover who has proposed to me a method of getting them post free: but I have declined resorting to it till I should know in what train the matter is actually. I have the honour to be with the most perfect esteem Dear Sir Your friend and servt,.

TH: JEFFERSON

Jefferson to Abigail Adams

Paris Sep. 25. 1785.

DEAR MADAM

Mr. Short's return the night before last availed me of your favour of Aug. 12. I immediately ordered the shoes you desired which will be ready tomorrow. I am not certain whether this will be in time for the departure of Mr. Barclay or of Colo. Franks, for it is not yet decided which of them goes to London. I have also procured for you three plateaux de dessert with a silvered ballustrade round them, and four figures of Biscuit. The former cost 192^{tt}, the latter 12^{tt} each, making together 240 livres or 10. Louis. The merchant undertakes to send them by the way of Rouen through the hands of Mr. Garvey and to have them delivered in London. There will be some additional expences of packing, transportation and duties here. Those in England I imagine you can save. When I know the amount I will inform you of it, but there will be no occasion to remit it here. With respect to the figures I could only find three of those you named, matched in size. These were Minerva, Diana, and Apollo. I was obliged to add a fourth, unguided by your choice. They offered me a fine Venus; but I thought it out of taste to have two at table at the same time. Paris and Helen were presented. I conceived it would be cruel to remove them from their peculiar shrine. When they shall pass the Atlantic, it will be to sing a requiem over our freedom and happiness. At length a fine Mars was offered, calm, bold, his faulchion not drawn, but ready to be drawn. This will do, thinks I, for the table of the American Minister in

London, where those whom it may concern may look and learn that though Wisdom is our guide, and the Song and Chase our supreme delight, yet we offer adoration to that tutelar god also who rocked the cradle of our birth, who has accepted our infant offerings, and has shewn himself the patron of our rights and avenger of our wrongs. The groupe then was closed, and your party formed. Envy and malice will never be quiet. I hear it already whispered to you that in admitting Minerva to your table I have departed from the principle which made me reject Venus: in plain English that I have paid a just respect to the daughter but failed to the mother. No Madam, my respect to both is sincere. Wisdom, I know, is social. She seeks her fellows. But Beauty is jealous, and illy bears the presence of a rival—but, Allons, let us turn over another leaf, and begin the next chapter. I receive by Mr. Short a budget of London papers. They teem with every horror of which human nature is capable. Assassinations, suicides, thefts, robberies, and, what is worse than assassination, theft, suicide or robbery, the blackest slanders! Indeed the man must be of rock, who can stand all this; to Mr. Adams it will be but one victory the more. It would have illy suited me. I do not love difficulties. I am fond of quiet, willing to do my duty, but irritable by slander and apt to be forced by it to abandon my post. These are weaknesses from which reason and your counsels will preserve Mr. Adams. I fancy it must be the quantity of animal food eaten by the English which renders their character insusceptible of civilisation. I suspect it is in their kitchens and not in their churches that their reformation must be worked, and that Missionaries of that description from hence would avail more than those who should endeavor to tame them by precepts of religion or philosophy. But what do the foolish printers of America mean by retailing all this stuff in our papers? As if it was not enough to be slandered by one's enemies without circulating the slanders among his friends also.

To shew you how willingly I shall ever receive and execute your commissions, I venture to impose one on you. From what I recollect of the diaper and damask we used to import from England I think they were better and cheaper than here. You are well acquainted with those of both countries. If you are of the same opinion I would trouble you to send me two sets of table cloths and napkins for 20 covers each, by Colo. Franks or Mr. Barclay who will bring them to me. But if you think they can be better got here I would rather avoid the trouble this commission will give. I inclose you a specimen of what is offered me at 100. livres for the table cloth and 12 napkins. I suppose that, of the same quality, a table cloth 2. aunes wide and 4. aunes long, and 20 napkins of 1. aune each, would cost 7. guineas.—I shall certainly charge the publick my house rent and court taxes. I shall do more. I shall charge my outfit. Without this I can never get out of debt. I think it will be allowed. Congress is too reasonable to expect, where no imprudent expences are incurred, none but those which are required by a decent respect to the mantle with which they cover the public servants, that such expences should be left as a burthen on our private fortunes. But when writing to you, I fancy myself at Auteuil, and chatter on till the last page of my paper awakes me from my reverie, and tells me it is time to assure you of the sincere respect and esteem with which I have the honour to be Dear Madam your most obedient and most humble servt.,

TH: JEFFERSON

P.S. The cask of wine at Auteuil, I take chearfully. I suppose the seller will apply to me for the price. Otherwise, as I do not know who he is, I shall not be able to find him out.

3

"As We are poor We ought to be Œconomists"

T HE MOST critical diplomatic question confronting Adams and Jefferson was that of trade relations. In a report to Foreign Secretary Jay on October 11, 1785, Jefferson summarized the situation with respect to commercial treaties negotiated by the American commissioners. The treaty with Prussia had been concluded in July; discussions with other nations were in process, but the results were not assured.[1] In bargaining for the trade so desperately needed, the diplomats would have to take as firm a stand as possible. But always the ebb and flow of power politics must be closely watched.

Both Adams and Jefferson knew that the true test of American diplomacy would come in negotiations with Great Britain and France. To Jay, in the same report, Jefferson observed that "England shews no disposition to treat." As for France he thought that even if her ministers should "be able to keep the ground of the arret of August 1784, against the clamours of her merchants, and should they be disposed hereafter to give us more, it is not probable she will bind herself to it by treaty, but keep her regulations dependent on her own will."[2] This proved to be an accurate prediction.

Although the American treaty of amity and commerce with France guaranteed most-favored-nation treatment, discrimination against Americans strained friendly relations between the two countries. Jefferson sought to preserve amicable relations "by approaching the condition of their citizens reciprocally to that of *natives*, as a better

1. TJ to Jay, Oct. 11, 1785, Boyd, VIII, 608.
2. On the Arrêt of Aug. 1784, see above, 49, n. 42.

ground of intercourse than that of *the most favoured nation*." [3] Since the navigation acts of Massachusetts, New Hampshire, and other states affected French trade adversely, Jefferson found them embarrassing; furthermore, it was difficult to explain technicalities of American law that threatened to deny the French heirs of General Edward Oglethorpe their claims in Georgia. [4]

During months of frustrating negotiation as the envoys of a weak Republic, one accomplishment must have reassured Adams and Jefferson as "œconomists." American spermaceti oil and candles were admitted to French markets, though for a limited period. Before the Revolution, this had been a lucrative but highly competitive business, based upon the famous whaling industry of Nantucket and whale-oil distribution by the merchants of Rhode Island and Massachusetts. The product of highest quality was spermaceti oil from the sperm whale, and spermaceti candles, a by-product of great popularity. No nation had competed successfully in this industry with the New Englanders; their merchants had even achieved a sort of trade association to which they adhered for brief periods. [5]

But the whale fishery had been demoralized during the War for Independence and the chief markets in Great Britain and her island colonies had been swept away. In the process of post-war reorganization, confronted by prohibitive British duties on oil, the New Englanders turned to France. [6] In the fall of 1785 Thomas Boylston, a "solid capitalist" of Boston, was endeavoring through diplomatic channels to introduce a cargo of spermaceti oil into France with remission of duties. About the same time Nathaniel Barrett, agent for several Boston merchants, was seeking a general agreement for developing the trade in France. His proposal impressed Jefferson more favorably than Boylston's which was on an individual basis. [7] As a New Englander Adams became enthusiastic over the prospects of illuminating French cities "with our fine White Sperma Coetic Oil, and their Churches and

3. TJ to Vergennes, Nov. 20, 1785, Boyd, IX, 51.
4. TJ to Governor of Georgia, Dec. 22, 1785, *ibid.*, 120-21; TJ to JA, Feb. 7, 1786, below, 118.
5. Jefferson, "Observations on the Whale Fishing," Boyd, XIV, 242-54; James B. Hedges, *The Browns of Providence Plantations: Colonial Years* (Cambridge, 1952), Chap. V.
6. Hedges, *Browns of Providence*, 295-96, 309-10; Louis Gottschalk, *Lafayette between the American and the French Revolution (1783-1789)* (Chicago, 1950), 221.
7. TJ to JA, Nov. 19, Dec. 10, 1785, below, 94, 104-5.

Families with our beautifull Sperma Coeti Candles." [8] Through the good offices of Lafayette, who had direct approach to M. Tourtille Sangrain, sole contractor for public lighting in Paris and other cities, Jefferson negotiated the removal of the duties on spermaceti oil for one year and secured French credit for the Boston merchants to buy the oil and ship it to France.[9]

To secure an equitable arrangement with Britain, however, seemed impossible. Adams hoped that preferences given to the French might force the issue; indeed he went so far as to suggest that "the thirteen States must each pass a Navigation Act," though only against British merchandise.[10] Jefferson preferred to transfer this power to Congress to assure more effective retaliation and perhaps bring about a commercial treaty with America's best pre-war customer.[11] The stubborn stand of the British embittered both ministers, for it challenged the political independence of the United States by means of economic pressure. "In this Country," wrote Mrs. Adams wryly from London, "there is a great want of many French comodities, Good Sense, Good Nature, Political Wisdom and benevolence." [12]

Despite their failure to conclude a commercial treaty with England, Adams and Jefferson could report some progress in their negotiations, in addition to the treaty with Prussia. When Congress commissioned Jefferson in 1784, it authorized a commercial treaty with Austria. Franklin had made an earlier gesture, but the Emperor had been waiting for an American minister to initiate the conversation.[13] During Lafayette's visit to Vienna in September 1785 he assumed the role of unofficial envoy of good will, suggesting "liberal treaties, that would oppen the door to American importations in order to pay for Austrian goods." [14] But the Emperor moved so slowly that the two-year-old commission from Congress expired before a final agreement could be reached.

More promising were Adams's negotiations with the Portuguese envoy extraordinary, the Chevalier de Pinto, in London. At Adams's

8. JA to TJ, Nov. 1, 1785, below, 87; JA to De Thulemeier, July 24, 1785, Boyd, VIII, 311.
9. TJ to JA, Dec. 27, 1785, and JA to TJ, Jan. 19, 1786, below, 111, 116; Gottschalk, Lafayette, 165-67, 205, 208-9, 211. See also below, Chap. 6.
10. JA to TJ, Oct. 3 and 24, 1785, below, 77-78, 86.
11. TJ to JA, Sept. 24, 1785, above, 68; TJ to JA, Nov. 19, 1785, below, 94-95.
12. AA to TJ, Nov. 24, 1785, below, 100.
13. TJ to JA, Jan. 12, 1786, below, 114.
14. Lafayette to TJ, Sept. 4, 1785, Boyd, VIII, 478-79; Gottschalk, Lafayette, 190-91.

request, Jefferson sent a detailed compilation of commodities that could be conveniently exchanged.[15] Portugal's objections to the British Navigation Acts made her more susceptible to American inducements; indeed, if etiquette had not forbidden making the first move, Portugal would have sent a minister to the United States. By March 1786 the project of a treaty was in the making and Jefferson had gone to London to collaborate with Adams on the spot.[16] There they could compare notes on their diplomatic problems.

Adams had already cautioned Jefferson that "We must not, my Friend, be the Bubbles of our own Liberal Sentiments."[17] The evidence is unmistakable that these molders of the new nation's foreign policy early sensed the dangers of European entanglement and sounded the first warning.

Adams to Jefferson

Grosvenor Square Sept. 25. 1785.

Dear Sir

The Bearer of this Letter Mr. Thomas Boylston, is one of the clearest and most Solid Capitalists, that ever raised himself by private Commerce in North America. He Seems to be desirous of assisting us, in introducing the knowledge and use of our white Sperma Cœti Oil, into France. His Judgment and Abilities to carry through whatever he undertakes may be depended on. Let me beg your Attention to him. With great Esteem, I have the Honour to be, Sir your most obedient and most humble Servant,

John Adams

Adams to Jefferson

Grosvenor Square Octr. 2. 1785.

Dear Sir

Coll. Franks arrived Yesterday afternoon, with your Favour of Septr. 24.—I have signed all the Papers as you sent them, not perceiving any

15. TJ to JA, Nov. 27, 1785, below, 100-3.
16. Boyd, IX, 410 ff.
17. JA to TJ, Sept. 4, 1785, above, 61.

Alteration necessary. I am afraid, that our Agent to Algiers going without any military Power will not succeed; as the Danger of having their Town bombarded, or their Vessells taken, is the Principal Argument which the Dey has to use with the People, to reconcile them to a Peace. However We must try the Experiment. I have received a Letter from Mr. Stephen Sayre, dated N. York 25. Aug. inclosing another of 23. of Aug. signed by Messrs. Gerry, King, Hardy, Monroe, and Grayson recommending strongly Mr. Sayre to you and me, to be employed as Agent to Morocco, Algiers and the other Powers, and inclosing another Letter to you, probably to the same Effect. This Letter I now inclose to you. It is but a day or two that these Letters have been received by me. Franks is gone to see if Mr. Randolph [i.e., Randall] can be prevailed on to go. If he cannot, will you join Sayre with Lamb? If you will, insert his Name in the Papers. Mr. Lamb will meet Mr. Sayre at Madrid, where I suppose he now is. But if he is not, Lamb must not wait for him a Moment. I should very readily undertake the Trouble, of having Bills drawn upon me, both by Mr. Barclay and Mr. Lamb, if the good of the Service could be promoted by it. But you are sensible there must be a Loss, in transferring Money, from Amsterdam to London: Yet the Advantage may ballance it.

You are diffident of Interpositions: but it is possible We may carry this too far. I think Mr. Barclay and Mr. Lamb would do well, to visit all the foreign Consulls, every one of whom will I am persuaded, shew them Civilities, and do nothing at all to obstruct their negotiations. They will not dare to do it, without orders, and no Cabinet in Europe I verily believe, would venture to give such orders. It will not be from Governments, that We shall receive opposition. Agents of Insurance offices in London or of Merchants trading in Fish etc. in the Mediterranean, may stimulate the Corsairs by exaggerated Representations of our Wealth and the Riches of our Prizes, but that is all. As nothing can be more hostile to the United States, than any Endeavours to embarrass, obstruct or counteract them in their Endeavours to form Treaties of Peace with the Barbary Powers, I wish you would impress it upon Mr. Barclay and Mr. Lamb, to be attentive to this, and obtain Proofs; and if the Consul or Agent of any foreign Power should be found and proved to do any Thing against Us, that they transmit to Us the earliest account of it with the Evidence. Congress would no doubt order a formal Complaint to be made against him to his Court, and in this way he would be held up publicly to the Execrations of all Mankind, and probably be punished by his Master.

Oct. 5 [i.e., 6] We have prevailed upon John [i.e., Paul] Randal Esqr. to go with Mr. Lamb, so that Sayre I suppose must be out of the Question, especially as We know not that he is arrived in Europe. I should think that much time may be saved, by Mr. Lambs going directly to Marseilles, and from thence over to Algiers but if you think there will be a greater Advantage, in seeing the Algerine Envoy at Madrid, or the Comte de Spilly, if he negotiated the late Treaty for Spain, I shall submit entirely to your better Judgment.

As our Commission authorizes us, I suppose it will be construed that it requires us to constitute the Agents by Writing under our Hands and Seals: I have accordingly made out four Commissions, which if you approve you will sign and seal, as I have done. I have written Letters to Mr. Barclay and Mr. Lamb authorizing them to draw upon me. These Letters you will please to sign, as the signature of both of us will be necessary.[18] You will be so good as to write also to Messrs. Wilhem and Jan Willink and Nicholas & Jacob Vanstaphorst of Amsterdam, giving your Approbation and Consent to their Paying the Bills to be drawn upon me by Barclay and Lamb, otherwise they may think my Authority alone, imperfect. I am Sir your most obedient and humble Servant,

JOHN ADAMS

Adams to Jefferson

Grosvenor Square Octr. 3. 1785

DEAR SIR

You have undoubtedly hit upon, the true Word of the Riddle. Yet there was no riddle, nor any clear meaning. It is impossible for any Country to give to another, more decided Proofs of Preference, than our thoughtless Merchants have since the Peace given to this, in matters of Commerce. He had seen this Preference sufficiently prevail. This alone then could not be his Meaning. If he meant a political Preference, an Alliance, such as Hartley was perpetually harping upon, he will wait till Doomsday, and it will never come. We ought to have no Prefferences nor Partialities. But this must be understood upon Condition, that this Country uses us, as well as France. If she does not, I am for giving France the Preference. I would wait with Patience and give full Time to deliberate, but if finally this Court will not act a reasonable and equitable Part, I would enter into still closer and stronger connections with France, both commercial and political. I would enter into Treaty, that certain French Manufactures should pay in the U.S. but half or a quarter of the Duties

18. Commissions, letters of credence, instructions, etc., to Barclay and Lamb, in Boyd, VIII, 611-17.

imposed upon English. French ships should have priviledges from which English should be excluded, and I would enter into an Alliance, offensive and defensive. But more of this hereafter.

I went out, eight days ago, to Dr. Price to get him to have the Insurance done.

October 5. Dr. Price called upon me this morning, but had unfortunately wholly forgot the Insurance on Heudon's Life. But I gave him an extract of your Letter to me, and promised to pay the Money for the Premium at any Moment. I am afraid that Certificates of Heudons State of Health will be required, and the Noise of Algerine Captures may startle the Insurers. The Doctor However will get it done if he can, and as low as possible.

I went to Stockdale with your Letter. He says he sent some News Papers by Mr. Short and by a Friend since, and will send by Franks. He applied to the office, he says in Cleaveland Row but could not get them sent that way. But he will call on the Duke of Dorsett, and get his Permission. If your Correspondent at Dover [Thomas Thompson] however can convey them to you free of Postage you had better agree with him. But after all your surest way would be to apply to the Comte de Vergennes, or Mr. Gennet, the Premier Comis du Bureau des Interpretes. In any other way your Papers will be liable to frequent Interruptions. I found that the only sure way, in the year 1780, after many fruitless Projects and Endeavours for several months. Yours affectionately,

JOHN ADAMS

Jefferson to Adams

Paris Oct. 5. 1785.

SIR

The Chevalier Dolomieu of the order of Malta, who served in the army of Count Rochambeau in America being to pass into England, I take the liberty of introducing him to you. An acquaintance with him in America enables me to assure you of his merit; his politeness and good understanding will of themselves recommend him to your esteem. I have the honour to be with the highest respect Sir Your most obedient and most humble servt.,

TH: JEFFERSON

Abigail Adams to Jefferson

London October 7th. 17[85]

DEAR SIR

Your very polite favour was handed me by Colo. Franks. I am much obliged to you for the execution of the several commissions I troubled you with. Be assured sir that I felt myself Honourd by your commands, tho I have only in part executed them. For I could not find at any store table Cloths of the dimensions you directed. The width is as you wisht, but they assure me that four yds. and three quarters are the largest size ever used here which will cover a table for 18 persons. To these Cloths there are only 18 Napkins, and to the smaller size only twelve. I was the more ready to credit what they said, knowing that I had been obliged to have a set of tables made on purpose for me in order to dine 16 or 18 persons. These rooms in general are not calculated to hold more and it is only upon extraordinary occasions that you meet with that number at the tables here. The Marquis of Carmarthan who occasionally dines the Foreign ministers, and has a House furn[ishe]d him by his Majesty, cannot entertain more than 15 at once, and upon their Majesties Birth days, he is obliged to dine his company at his Fathers the Duke of Leeds's. The person where I bought the Cloth offerd to have any size made, that I wisht for, and agreed to take eight pounds ten shillings for 20 Napkins and a cloth 5 yds. long. I gave Seven for this which I send, and shall wait your further directions. I took the precaution of having them made and marked to Secure them against the custom House, and hope they will meet your approbation. I think them finer than the pattern, but it is difficult judging by so small a Scrap. I have also bought you two pairs of Nut crackers for which I gave four Shillings. We [find them so?] convenient that I thought they would be equally so to [you. The]re is the article of Irish linen which is much Superiour here to any that is to be had in France, and cheeper I think. If you have occasion for any you will be so good as to let me know. It cannot easily pass without being made. But that could be easily done. Only by sending a measure, at the rate of 3 Shilling and six pence per yd. by the peice, the best is to be had. As we are still in your debt, the remainder of the money shall be remitted you or expended here as you direct. Mr. Adams supposed there might be something of a balance due to him in the settlement of a private account with Mr. Barclay, which he has orderd paid to you. He will also pay the money here for the insurence of Mr. Hudons Life, by which means what ever remains due to you can be easily settled.

Haveing finishd the article of Business, I am totally foild at that of Compliment. Sure the air of France, conspired with the Native politeness and Complasance of the writer to usher into the World Such an assemblage of fine things. I shall value the warrior Deity the more for having been your choise, and he cannot fail being in taste in a Nation which has given us such proofs of their Hostility; forgiveness of injuries is no part of their Character, and scarcly a day passes without a Boxing match; even in this Square which is calld the polite and Court end of the city, my feelings have been repeatedly shock'd to see Lads not more than ten years old striped and fighting untill the Blood flow'd from every part, enclosed by a circle who were claping and applauding the conquerer, stimulating them to continue the fight, and forceing every person from the circle who attempted to prevent it. Bred up with such tempers and principals, who can wonder at the licentiousness of their Manners, and the abuse of their pens. Their arrows do not wound, they rebound and fall harmless [...] but amidst their boasted freedom of the press, one must bribe [...] to get a paragraph inserted in favour of America, or her Friends. Our Country has no money to spair for such purposes; and must rest upon her own virtue and magnimimity. So we may too late convince this Nation that the Treasure which they knew not how to value, has irrecoverably past into the possession of those who were possesst of more policy and wisdom.

I wish I might flatter myself with the hope of seeing you here this winter. You would find a most cordial welcome from your American Friends, as well as from some very distinguishd literary Characters of this Nation.

My best regards to Miss Jefferson, to Col. Humphries, to Mr. Short, or any other Friends or acquaintance who may inquire after Your Friend and humble Servant,

A ADAMS

My daughter presents her respectfull regards to you and compliments to the rest of the Gentlemen.

Jefferson to Abigail Adams

Paris Oct. 11. 1785.

DEAR MADAM

Your favor of the 7th. was put into my hands the last night and as I received at the same time dispatches from Mr. Adams which occasion a great deal to be done for Congress to be sent by the Mr. Fitzhughs who set out tomorrow morning for Philadelphia as Mr. Preston the bearer of this does for London, I have only time to thank you for your kind attention to my commission and your offer of new service. Your information as to the shirt linen draws a new scene of trouble on you. You had better have held your tongue about it: but as it is, you must submit to what cannot now be prevented and take better care hereafter. You will think it some apology for my asking you to order me a dozen shirts of the quality of the one sent, when I assure you they made me pay for it here 10 livres and a half the aune, which is at the rate of 6/6 sterl. the yard. I will pray you to chuse me linen as nearly as possible of the same quality because it will enable me to judge of the comparative prices of the two countries. There will probably be Americans coming over from London here in the course of the winter who will be so kind as to bring the shirts to me, which being ready made will escape the custom houses. I will not add to your trouble that of a long apology. You shall find it in the readiness and zeal with which I shall always serve you. But I find that with your friends you are a very bad accountant, for after purchasing the table linen, and mentioning the insurance money on Houdon's life, you talk of what will still remain due to me. The truth is that without this new commission I should have been enormously in your debt. My present hurry does not permit me to state the particulars, but I will prove it to you by the first opportunity. And as to the balance which will be due from me to Mr. Adams should he have no occasion of laying it out here immediately I will transmit it by some safe hand. I have not yet seen the table linen you were so kind as to buy for me, but I am sure it is good. The merchant here promises to shew me some of a new supply he has, which will enable me to judge somewhat of the two manufactures and prices. The difference must be considerable tho' to induce me to trouble you. Be so good as to present my respects to Miss Adams and to accept assurances of the esteem and respect with which I have the honour to be Dear Madam Your most obedient and most humble servt.,

TH: JEFFERSON

Jefferson to Adams

Paris Oct. 11. 1785.

DEAR SIR

Colo. Franks and Mr. Randolph [i.e., Randall] arrived last night. This enables me to send copies of all the Barbary papers to Congress by the Mr. Fitzhughs, together with the Prussian treaty. They wait till tomorrow for this purpose.

Considering the treaty with Portugal as among the most important to the U.S. I some time ago took occasion at Versailles to ask the Portuguese Ambassador [de Sousa Coutinho] if he had yet received an answer from his court on the subject of our treaty. He said not, but that he would write again. His Secretaire d'Ambassade called on me two days ago and translated into French as follows a paragraph of a letter from his minister to the Ambassador. 'Relativement à ce que V. E. nous a fait part de ce qu'elle avoit parlé avec le ministre de l'Amerique, cette puissance doit etre dejà persuadée par d'effets la maniere dont ses vaisseaux ont eté accueillis içi: et par consequence sa majesté auroit beaucoup de satisfaction à entretenir une parfaite harmonie et bonne correspondence *entre* [19] les memes etats unis. Mais il seroit à propos de commencer par la nomination reciproque des deux parties des personnes qui, au moins avec la caractere d'Agens, informeroient reciproquement leurs constituents de ce qui pourroit conduire à la connoissance des interets des deux nations sans prejudice de l'un ou de l'autre. C'est le premier pas qu'il paroit convenable de donner pour conduire à la fin proposée.' [20] By this I suppose they will prefer proceeding as Spain has done,[21] and that we may consider it as definitive of our commission to them. I communicate it to Congress that they may take such other measures for leading on a negotiation as they may think proper.

You know that the 3d. article of instructions of Oct. 29. 1783. to the Ministers for negotiating peace, directed them to negociate the claim for the prizes taken by the Alliance and sent in to Bergen, but delivered up by the court of Denmark: [22] you recollect also that this has been deferred in order to be taken up with the general negotiation for an alliance. Capt.

19. TJ interpreted this word in a marginal note: "qu. *avec*.," as he did also in his letter to Jay, Oct. 11, quoting this French translation. Boyd, VIII, 604, 609. This was consistent with TJ's desire, expressed to JA on July 7, "of bringing all our commerce under the jurisdiction of Congress."

20. "With respect to what Your Excellency has told us of the discussion with the American minister, that power should already be convinced by the facts, the manner in which its vessels have been received here, and that consequently Her Majesty would take great satisfaction in maintaining perfect harmony and good correspondence *with* the United States. But it would be proper to begin with the reciprocal nomination by the two parties of persons who, at least in the character of agents, would each inform their principals what could lead to a knowledge of the interests of the two nations without prejudice to either. This is the first step it would seem fitting to take in order to lead to the end proposed."

21. Don Diego de Gardoqui had been commissioned as Spanish chargé d'affaires in the United States, Sept. 27, 1784; his opposite number in Spain was William Carmichael.

22. The American frigate *Alliance*, accompanying the *Bonhomme Richard*, Captain John Paul Jones, had captured two British privateers during the famous voyage of 1779. Lincoln Lorenz, *John Paul Jones* (Annapolis, 1943), 278-79. See JA to TJ, Nov. 4, 1785, and TJ to JA, Nov. 19, 1785, below, 88-89, 96-97.

Jones desiring to go to America proposed to me that he should leave the sollicitation of this matter in the hands of Doctor Bancroft, and to ask you to negotiate it through the minister of Denmark at London. The delay of Baron Waltersdorf [23] is one reason for this. Your better acquaintance with the subject is a second. The Danish minister here being absent is a third: and a fourth and more conclusive one is that, having never acted as one of the commissioners for negotiating the peace I feel an impropriety in meddling with it at all, and much more to become the principal agent. I therefore told Capt. Jones I would sollicit your care of this business. I beleive he writes to you on the subject. Mr. Barclay sets out in two or three days. Lamb will follow as soon as the papers can be got from this ministry. Having no news, I shall only add assurances of the esteem with which I am Dear Sir Your friend and servant,

TH: JEFFERSON

Jefferson to Adams

Paris Oct. 18. 1785.

DEAR SIR

Your letter of the 10th. came safely to hand and I delivered the one therein inclosed to Mr. Grand. It was a duplicate of one he had before received. You will have heard of the safe arrival of Doctr. Franklin in America. Strange we do not hear of that of Otto and Doradour. If you know of the safe arrival of the packet in which they went, pray communicate it to me, as Madame de Doradour, who is ill in Auvergne, is greatly uneasy for her husband. Our dispatches to the Westward are all gone. Those to the Southward will go this week. This goes by post which will account for it's laconicism. I must however add my respects to the ladies and assurances to yourself of the esteem with which I am Dear Sir Your most obedient humble servt.,

TH: JEFFERSON

23. De Walterstorff had discussed a Danish treaty of amity and commerce with the American commissioners in Paris and took a draft treaty to Denmark in Feb. 1785, but no agreement was reached. American Commissioners to President of Congress, Feb. [9], 1785, Boyd, VII, 646-47; TJ to John Jay, May 12, 1786, *ibid.*, IX, 514-15.

Abigail Adams to Jefferson

London October 19 1785

DEAR SIR

Mr. Fox a young gentleman from Philadelphia who came recommended by Dr. Rush to Mr. Adams, will have the Honour of delivering you this Letter. We requested him to call upon Mr. Stockdale for your papers etc.

Mr. Adams is unwell, and will not be able to write you by this opportunity. I am to acquaint you sir that Dr. Price has transacted the business respecting Mr. Hudon. The Money is paid, but the policy is not quite ready but the Doctor has promised that it shall be sent in a few days, when it will be forwarded to you.

In your English papers you will find an extract of a Letter from Nova Scotia, representing the abuse said to be received by a Captain Stanhope at Boston, the commander of the Mercury. The account is as false—if it was not too rough a term for a Lady to use, I would say false as Hell, but I will substitute, one not less expresive and say, false as the English.

The real fact is this. One Jesse Dumbar, a native of Massachusetts, and an inhabitant of a Town near Boston and one Isaac Lorthrope were during the War taken prisoners and from one ship to an other were finally turnd over to this Captain Stanhope, commander of the Mercury, who abused him and the rest of the prisoners, frequently whiping them and calling them Rebels. The ship going to Antigua to refit, he put all the prisoners into Jail and orderd poor Jesse a dozen lashes for refusing duty on Board his ship. This Mr. Dumbar felt as an indignity and contrary to the Law of Nations. Peace soon taking place Jesse returnd Home, but when Stanhope came to Boston, it quickened Jesses remembrance and he with his fellow sufferer went to Boston and according to his deposition, hearing that Captain Stanhope was walking in the Mall, he went theither at noon day and going up to the Captain asked him if he knew him, and rememberd whiping him on Board his Ship. Having no weapon in his hand, he struck at him with his fist, upon which Captain Stanhope stept back and drew his sword. The people immediately interposed and gaurded Stanhope to Mr. Mortens door, Dumbar and his comrade following him, and at Mr. Mortens door he again attempted to seize him, but then the high sheriff interposed and prevented further mischief, after which they all went to their several homes. This Mr. Stanhope calls assassination and complains that the *News papers* abuse him. He wrote a Letter to the Govenour demanding protection. The Govenour replied by telling him that if he had been injured the Law was open to him and would redress him upon which he wrote a very impudent abusive Letter to Mr. Bowdoin, so much so that Mr. Bowdoin thought proper to lay the whole correspondence before Congress, and Congress past some resolves in consequence and have transmitted them with copies of the Letters to be laid before Mr. Stanhopes master.

Dumbars Deposition was comunicated in a private Letter by Mr. Bowdoin himself to Mr. Adams, so that no publick use can be made of it, but the Govenour was sensible that without it the Truth would not be known.[24]

Is Col. Smith in Paris? Or have we lost him? Or is he so mortified at the king of Prussias refusing him admittance to his Reviews, that he cannot shew himself here again? This is an other English Truth, which they are industriously Circulating. I have had, however, the pleasure of contradicting the story in the most positive terms, as Col. Smith had enclosed us the copy of his own Letter and the answer of his Majesty, which was written with his own hand. How mean and contemptable does this Nation render itself?

Col. Franks I hope had the good fortune to carry your things safely to you, and that they will prove so agreeable as to induce you to honour again with your commands Your Friend and Humble Servant,

Abigail Adams

Compliments to the Gentlemen of your family and love to Miss Jefferson. Mr. Rutledge has refused going to Holland. I fancy foreign embassies upon the present terms are no very tempting objects.

Adams to Jefferson

Grosvenor Square Octr. 24. 1785

Dear Sir

Mr. Preston arrived here, two days ago, but had lost his Letters. I hope he had none of Consequence. He dont remember he had any for me. He tells me from you, that the Doctor is arrived at Philadelphia which I am glad to hear, and those oracles of Truth the English Newspapers tell us, he had an honourable Reception, which I should not however have doubted, if I had not any such respectable Authority for it.

24. TJ's account of the Stanhope affair is in Boyd, IX, 4-7.

The Insurance is made upon Houdons Life for Six Months from the 12 of October. I have paid Thirty two Pounds Eleven shillings Præmium and Charges, which you will please to give me Credit for. I could not persuade them to look back, as they say, they never ensure but for the future and from the date of the Policy. I suppose it will be safest to keep the Receipt and Policy here, for fear of Accidents.

I begin to be uneasy about our Funds. The Draughts upon Willinks & Co. and the Expences of the Negotiations in Barbary, will exhaust the little that remains, and unless We have fresh supplies, We shall all be obliged to embark, in the first ships We can find before next March, for Want of bread. I hope you will press this subject in your Letters to America. Rutledge declines,[25] and you will not wonder at it. I dont believe Congress will find any other Man, who will venture abroad upon the present Plan. The Doctor was lucky to get out of the Scrape, in Season. You and I shall soon wish ourselves at home too.

I have a Letter from Thulemeier, that he has received from the King [of Prussia] a Ratification of the Treaty, and is ready to exchange it. I hope you will request of Congress a prompt Ratification on their Part, that one affair at least may be finished. I see no comfortable hopes here. We hold Conferences upon Conferences, but the Ministers either have no Plan or they button it up, closer than their Waistcoats. The thirteen States must each pass a Navigation Act, and heavy Duties upon all British Merchandizes, so as to give a clear Advantage to their own and the Manufactures of France and Germany, Prussia and Russia, or we shall be a long time weak and poor.

This will be delivered you by Dr. Rodgers a Son of Dr. Rodgers of New York a young Gentleman of Merit. I am Sir with the greatest Esteem your Friend and Sert.,

JOHN ADAMS

Abigail Adams to Jefferson

London october 25 1785

SIR

I should not so soon have ventured to interrupt your more important avocations by an other Scrible, having writen you a few Days since, if it was not to inform you of the loss of your Letters by Mr. Preston. He says that when he landed at Dover, he was very sick, and that he could not accompany his trunk to the custom House, into which for *Security* he had

25. John Rutledge declined to serve as minister to the United Dutch Provinces.

put his Letters. But upon his arrival here he found he had lost them; so that unless your Letter should contain any thing for the English newspapers I fear I shall never know its contents. The gentleman deliverd me a little bundle, by the contents of which I conjecture What you design, but must request you to repeat your orders by the first opportunity, that I may have the pleasure of punctually fulfilling them.

A Dr. Rogers from America will convey this to you with the Newspapers in which you will see the Letters I mentiond in my last between Governour Bowdoin and Captain Stanhope. Lord George Gordon appears to interest himself in behalf of his American Friends, as he stiles them, but neither his Lordships Friendship or enmity are to be coveted.

Mr. Adams writes you by this opportunity. I have directed a Letter to Mr. Williamos to be left in your care. Am very sorry to hear of his ill state of Health.

We hear nothing yet of Col. Smith, know not where he is, as we find by the Gentlemen last arrived that he is not at Paris. I am sir with Sentiments of respect and esteem Your etc,

AA

Adams to Jefferson

Grosvenor Square Nov. 1. 1785.

Dear Sir

Your Favour of the 18th. did not reach me, till last night. I am glad the Doctor has arrived safe and in so good health, and would fain hope he may contribute to compose the jarring Parties in Pensilvania, as well as assist in improving the Union of the States. Mrs. Rucker has a Letter from her Sister at New York, which mentions the Arrival of Mr. Otto, so that I think Madame la Comtess de Doradour may be satisfied that the Comte her Husband is arrived.

I have been told that the Court of France has contracted with an House at Nantes for supplying their Navy, with American Masts. As this is an affair somewhat interesting, to Great Britain as well as to France and the United States, I should be obliged to you for the Particulars. I wish the Report may be true, and that it may be soon followed by Arrangements for illuminating their Cities with our fine White Sperma Cœti Oil, and their Churches and Families with our beautifull Sperma Cœti Candles. Pray what is the Reason that the Virginians dont learn to sort their Tobacco at home, that they may be able to furnish the French with such Parts of their Produce as are adapted to that Markett, without obliging the Farmers general to think of going to Holland, or coming to England to purchase them. There is a considerable Loss to our Country, in Freight, Insurance, Commissions and Profits, arising from this indirect Commerce and you know as We are poor We ought to be Œconomists: but if we were rich it would not be wise nor honourable to give away our Wealth without Consideration and Judgment.

General Arnold is gone out to Hallifax, with a Vessell and Cargo, of his own, upon what kind of Speculation I know not. Some say that not associating with British Officers, not being able to bear a Life of Inactivity, and having a young Family to provide for, he is gone to seek his Fortune. Whether it is a political Maneuvre or not, I wish that Mr. Deane, Mr. Irvin, Mr. Chalmers and Mr. Smith, were gone with him. The Doctrine of these Gentlemen is that this Country and her Commerce are so essential to the U. States that they cannot exist without them, and that the States can never unite in any measures of Retaliation, nor in any Plan to encourage their own Navigation Acts, and they find Persons enough who have an ardent Passion to believe what is so conformable to their Wishes. If our Country is so situated that she must consent that G. Britain shall carry all our own Produce, to the West India Islands, to Canada, to Nova Scotia, to Newfoundland and to Europe too, We must be humble. When We are willing they should carry half our own Produce, it is not very modest for them to insist upon carrying all.

It is reported that the Ariel has been sent out, express, since the News of the Hurricane, to carry orders for admitting American Vessells to the English West India Islands: but for what time and under what restrictions I know not.

Captain Bell arrived at Philadelphia, on the 14. Sept. the same day with Dr. F. and is said to have made a good Voyage. This is the third Ship from India, and Insurance is making here upon four oth[er ships bo]und the same Way. The former could not be insured under tw[elve Per] Cent. These are done at Seven. My dear Sir Adieu,

JOHN ADAMS

Adams to Jefferson

Grosvenor Square Nov. 4. 1785

DEAR SIR

Mr. Preston has at last found and sent me your Letter. Dr. Bancroft spoke to me, about Commodore Jones's Demand upon Denmark: but upon looking into the Papers we found that the Commodore is recommended by Congress wholly to the Minister at the Court of Versailles, so that We were apprehensive our Powers would be disputed. The Danish Minister however was not here; I offered to go with Dr. Bancroft to the Charge D'Affairs, and speak to him upon the Subject. But the Doctor thought it would be safest to follow the Intentions of Congress, and write to Jones to request you to speak to the Chargé D'Affairs of Denmark at Paris. I know nothing of the subject more than you. The offer of 10,000 £ was made to Dr. Franklin alone. All that you or I can do is to speak or write to the Minister or Chargé D'Affairs and receive his Answer. The Surrender of the Prizes to the English was an Injury to Jones and his People and to the U. States and ought to be repaired.

Will you be so good as to send me the Ordonnance du Roi of 18 Sept., establishing Bounties upon Salt Fish of the French Fisheries and Imposts upon foreign Fish in the Marketts of the French Islands and in Spain, Portugal and Italy?

The Portuguese Minister told me yesterday that his Court did not choose to treat in France, but I have learned from another Quarter that he has written for and expects full Power to treat here. This you will keep to yourself. As soon as any Proposals are made to me, I will send them to you. But I am every day more and more sensible, We must confine our Exports to our own ships, and therefore shall be afraid to let any more foreign ships into our Ports, without a rich equivalent for it. We must encourage our Manufactures too. All foreign nations are taking an ungenerous Advantage of our Symplicity and philosophical Liberality. We must take heed.

I dont doubt that all the Courts of Europe would join my Friends the Abbes,[26] in their Prayer that We may be perpetually poor, not indeed like them with a desire that We may be perpetually virtuous, but that Europeans may have all the Profit of American Labour.—Our Countrymen I fancy, have more wit, if they have not so much Wisdom as Philosophers with them or so much Patience under insidious Policy, as Courtiers would be glad to find in them. With the most cordial Esteem, your Friend and Sert.,

JOHN ADAMS

26. Abbé Gabriel Bonnot de Mably, who had died on April 23, 1785; Abbé Chalut and Abbé Arnoux maintained a summer residence at Passy, where JA had been their guest.

Adams to Jefferson

Grosvenor Square November 5th. 1785

DEAR SIR

The Chevalier de Pinto, Envoy Extraordinary and Minister Plenipotentiary, from Portugal, after a long absence by leave of his Court is lately arrived here from Lisbon. Upon several occasions, when I met him at Court and upon visits, he told me that he had orders from his Court to confer with me upon the Project of a Treaty between the United States and Portugal, but he [nev]er descended to Particulars till yesterday, when he called upon me and s[aid] that before he left Lisbon his Court had learned that I was in England and had charged him to enter into conference with me, concerning that Project of a Treaty, which had been transmitted to his Court by the Comt de Lusi [i.e., Sousa]. That the Portuguese Ministry, notwithstanding their high Esteem for their Ambassador in France, knowing that he lived in the Country, and was in distress, did not choose that the Negotiation should be any longer conducted by him, but had committed the Project to their Envoy at the Court of England and had instructed him to assure me that the Court of Lisbon was sincerely desirous of entering into a Treaty of Commerce with the United States of America, a Power with which it was more convenient for Portugal to Trade than any other. But there were some things in the Plan proposed which were inadmissible, particularly the Americans could never be admitted into the Brazils. It was impossible, it was the invariable maxim of their Court to exclude all Nations from those Territories, and having himself served for some years as Governor General of one of the Brazils he knew it was a Policy from which his Court could never upon any Consideration depart, that it was a great compliment to him to be prefered to the Comt de Lusi for the Conduct of such a Negotiation, that he made no Pretentions to such merit, but readily acknowledged the superiority of the Ambassador; but it was the pleasure of his Court and he had no right to dispute it.

I answered, that I had no authority to treat, but in conference with Mr. Jefferson, the Minister Plenipotentiary of the United States at the Court of Versailles; that the full Powers to treat with Portugal, was to Mr. Jefferson and me jointly; that I could conclude nothing without his Concurrence, nor Carry on any Conferences without Communicating them to him; to this I supposed he could have no objection. He said none at all.

His first instruction was he said to confer with me concerning the Mutual Wants and several Productions of our Countries which might be the objects of Commerce. His Countrymen wanted he said Grain.— I asked if they did not want Flour? He said he was not precisely instructed concerning Flour, but they had Mills in Portugal which they wished to employ. I replied that in every Negotiation, I thought there ought to be a mutual Consideration of each others profits and Losses advantages and disadvantages, so that the result might be equitable and give sattisfaction on both sides; that a Commerce founded upon Compacts made upon this Principle would be carried on with more Pleasure, and to better effect; that we had Mills which we wished to employ, as well as Portugal, and Mills as Costly and as Good as those of any Nation. In this respect our pretentions were mutual and equal, but there were other Particulars in which without any benefit to Portugal the loss to the United States would be very great. The Commodity was more difficult to preserve in Grain than in Flour. It was more exposed to the Insect, and to heat both at home and upon the Passage, by which means the loss upon Wheat was much greater than that upon Flour; that it would not be equitable then, for Portugal to receive Wheat to the exclusion of Flour; that this was a point of so much Importance that it would facilitate the Treaty and encourage the Commerce, if his Court should think fit to agree to receive our Flour. He said he had not precise instructions but he would write to his Court particularly upon this Point.— The next article wanted by the Portuguese was Lumber of various sorts, particularly staves for Pipes in large Quantities. They wanted also Shiptimber, Pitch, Tar and turpentime, Pot Ash for their Manufactures of Glass, Iron, Masts Yards and Beausprits, Furrs, Ginseng and above all salt Fish. The Consumption of this article in Portugal he said was immense and he would avow to me that the American salt Fish was prefered to any other on account of its Quality. Here you see said the Chevalier de Pinto is a Catalogue of Articles, which the Portuguese will want in larger or smaller Quantities: now what are the Articles you can take in America in Exchange? It behoves my Nation to inquire what they can supply yours with, otherwise the ballance in your favour may be to ruinous to us. It happens unluckily for Portugal that the Americans have no Occasion for our Principal Commodities which are Tobacco, Rice, Indigo and the Produce of the Brazils.

I replied, that the United States had been used to take Considerable Quantities of Maderia, Lisbon and Port Wines, Fruits, Olive Oil, Salt etc. He asked why we could not take Tea, from Lisbon? They imported from the East large quantities, and very good. The English East India Company had purchased of them this year Teas to the amount of forty thousand Pounds, and he thought they could sell it to us cheaper than we bought it elsewhere. They could supply us likewise with all other East India Goods.

Perhaps we intended to supply ourselves by a direct Trade to India: he was glad to hear that our first Enterprises had succeeded: but if we continued to take any Part of our Consumption from Europe, they could supply us as cheap as any other Nation. Sugar too, the Produce of the Brazils, they could furnish to us of as good quality as English or French and much cheaper. If we should think of Manufactures amongst ourselves they could supply us with Wool of the same quality with the Spanish, and Coton in any quantities we might want. If we made Chocolate, they could sell us Cocoa; indeed they had Woolen Manufactures and could afford us Cloth as good and as cheap as other Nations.

These were things I replied in which the Merchants on both sides should speculate. If the United States should proceed in the Plan already begun of encouraging their own Manufactures, the raw Materials of Wool and Coton would be in demand, and if they persevered in their Measures for encouraging their own Navigation they would want large quantities of Hemp, Sail Cloth etc. from the Baltic, and for what I knew they might find their account in taking sugars, Coton, Cocoa etc. at Lisbon to Carry as remittances to Petersbourg and Stockholm. They might even upon some occasions Purchase Tobacco, Rice and Indigo, for the same markett as well as the Mediterranean, if that scene should be open to our ships. But all these things would depend upon the Facilities given to our Commodities by the Treaty. Nothing would contribute so much to promote the Trade as their receiving our Flour without Duties or Discouragements. Our ready built ships too, were an Article of Importance to us.— He said he did not know that our ready built ships were prohibited. I asked if they could not take our White sperma Ceati oil, to burn in their Lamps or for any other uses. He said no, they had such an abundance of Oil made in the Country of Olives which grew there, that they had no occasion for their own sperma Ceati Oil which they sold to Spain; they had now a very pretty sperma Ceati Whale Fishery which they had learn'd of the New Englanders and Carried on upon the Coast of the Brazils. I asked if they could not take our sperma Ceati Candeles and burn them in their Churches. He said they made some Wax in Portugal and some in the Brazils but he would own to me it was not enough for their Consumption. The surplus they bought in Italy and Barbary at a dear rate.

At length I observed to the Chavelier that Portugal abounded in two articles which would be extremely agreeable and convenient to my Fellow Citizens in which she might allways Ballance Accounts with us to our intire sattisfaction, whether she would take more or less of their Comodities. These were Gold and Silver, than which no kind of Merchandise was in greater demand or had a higher reputation.— The Chavel[ier] thought the taste of his Countrymen so much like ours that they had rather pay us in any thing else.

I added if the Conduct of the Court of St. James should oblige the United States to make a navigation Act their Commerce with Portugal must increase. A Navigation Act? says he, why there is not a Nation in Europe that would suffer a Navigation Act to be made in any other, at this day. The English Navigation Act was made in times of Ignorance When few Nations Cultivated Commerce and no Court but this understood or cared any thing about it. But at present all Courts were attentive to it. For his part if he were Minister in Portugal he would not hesitate to exclude from her Ports the Ships of any Nation that should make such an a[ct].

I replied that I did not mean a Navigation act against any Nation but this: but if the English persevered in inforcing their Act against us, We could do no other than make one against them. The Chavelier said we should be perfectly in the right: the Courts of Europe had a long time cried out against this Act of the English. If it were now to begin, it would not be submitted to. This observation is just, it may be carried further. I dont beleive the British Navigation Act can last long, as least I am persuaded if America has spirit enough, Umbone repellere Umbonem [27]— that all other Nations will soon follow her Example, and the apprehension of this would be alone sufficient, if thinking Beings Governed this Island to induce them to silence America by giving her sattisfaction. But they rely upon our Disunion and think it will be time enough when We shall have shewn them that we can agree.

The Chavelier Concluded the Conference by saying that he would write to his Court for further information and instructions, and as I understood him for full Powers. But before he went away, he said he had Orders from his Court to inquire of me what were the sentiments of Congress upon the Head of Ministers and Consuls, whether they would send a Minister and Consul to Lisbon. His Court had a Mind to send some body to the United States, But Etiquette required that Congress should send in return to Portugal. I answered that in the Project of a Treaty which was in His Possession there was an Article that each Party should have a right to send Consuls, so that when the Treaty was concluded Portugal would be at Liberty to send when she would. As to Ministers I had no instructions, but there could be no doubt that if their Majesties of Portugal thought proper to send an Ambassador of any denomination he would be received by Congress with all the respect due to his Character and his sovereign. He said if there was a treaty there ought to be Ministers. I could not make answer to this particular for want of instructions, but

27. "To ward off the thrust of a shield with one's own shield."

Congress had as yet but few Ministers abroad and indeed they had not found many Gentlemen disposed to quit the delight of their own Families and Connections and the Esteem of their Fellow Citizens for the sake of serving in Europe, and here ended the Conversation. Your Friend,

JOHN ADAMS

Jefferson to Adams

Paris Nov. 19. 1785.

DEAR SIR

I wrote to you on the 11th. of Octob. by Mr. Preston and again on the 18th. of the same month by post. Since that yours of Sep. 25. by Mr. Boylston, Oct. 24. Nov. 1. and Nov. 4. have come safe to hand. I will take up their several subjects in order. Boylston's object was first to dispose of a cargo of sperma ceti oyl which he brought to Havre. A secondary one was to obtain a contract for future supplies. I carried him to the M. de la fayette. As to his first object we are in hopes of getting the duties taken off which will enable him to sell his cargo. This has led to discussions with the ministers which give us a hope that we may get the duties taken off in perpetuum. This done, a most abundant market for our oyl will be opened by this country, and one which will be absolutely dependant on us, for they have little expectation themselves of establishing a succesful whale fishery. Perhaps it is possible they may only take the duties off of those oils which shall be the produce of associated companies of French and American merchants. But as yet nothing certain can be said.

I thank you for the trouble you have taken to obtain insurance on Houdon's life. I place the 32 £-11 s to your credit, and not being able as yet to determine precisely how our accounts stand, I send a sum by Colo. Smith which may draw the scales towards a balance.

The determination of the British cabinet to make no equal treaty with us, confirms me in the opinion expressed in your letter of Oct. 24. that the U.S. must pass a navigation act against Great Britain and load her manufactures with duties so as to give a preference to those of other countries: and I hope our assemblies will wait no longer, but transfer such a power to Congress at the sessions of this fall. I suppose however it will only be against Great Britain, and I think it will be right not to involve other nations in the consequences of her injustice. I take for granted the commercial system wished for by Congress was such an one as should leave commerce on the freest footing possible. This was the plan on which we prepared our general draught for treating with all nations. Of those with whom we were to treat, I ever considered England, France, Spain and Portugal as capitally important; the first two on account of their American possessions, the last for their European as well as American. Spain is treating in America, and probably will give us an advantageous treaty. Portugal shews dispositions to do the same. France does not treat. It is likely enough she will chuse to keep the staff in her own hands. But in the mean time she gave us an access to her W. Indies, which tho' not all we wished was yet extremely valuable to us: this access indeed is much wounded by the late arrets of the 18th. and 25th. of September, which I inclose to you.[28] I consider these as a reprisal for the navigation acts of Massachusets and New Hampshire. The minister has complained to me officially of these acts as a departure from the reciprocity stipulated by the treaty. I have assured him that his complaints shall be communicated to Congress, and in the mean time observed that the example of discriminating between foreigners and natives had been set by the Arret of Aug. 1784. and still more remarkeably by those of Sep. 18. and 25. which in effect are a prohibition of our fish in their islands. However it is better for us that both sides should revise what they have done. I am in hopes this country did not mean these as permanent regulations. Mr. Bingham, lately from Holland, tells me the Dutch are much dissatisfied with those acts. In fact I expect the European nations in general will rise up against an attempt of this kind, and wage a general commercial war against us. They can do too well without all our commodities except tobacco, and we cannot find elsewhere markets for them. The selfishness of England alone will not justify our hazarding a contest of this kind against all Europe. Spain, Portugal, and France have not yet shut their doors against us: it will be time enough when they do to take up the commercial hatchet. I hope therefore those states will repeal their navigation clauses except as against Great Britain and other nations not treating with us.

I have made the enquiries you desire as to American shiptimber for this country. You know they sent some person (whose name was not told us) to America to examine the quality of our masts, spars etc. I think this was young Chaumont's business. They have besides this instructed the officer who superintends their supplies of masts, spars etc. to procure good quantities from our Northern states, but I think they have made no contract: on the contrary that they await the trials projected, but with a determination to look to us for considerable supplies if they find our timber answer. They have on the carpet a contract for live oak from the Southern states.

28. The Arrêt of September 25 dealt with duties on codfish imported into the French West Indies. Wroth and Annan, eds., *Acts of French Royal Administration*, no. 2013.

You ask why the Virginia merchants do not learn to sort their own tobaccoes? They can sort them as well as any merchants whatever. Nothing is better known than the quality of every hogshead of tobacco from the place of it's growth. They know too the particular qualities required in every market. They do not send their tobaccoes therefore to London to be sorted, but to pay their debts: and tho they could send them to other markets and remit the money to London, yet they find it necessary to give their English merchant the benefit of the consignment of their tobacco to him (which is enormously gainful) in order to induce him to continue his indulgence for the balance due.

Is it impossible to persuade our countrymen to make peace with the Nova scotians? I am persuaded nothing is wanting but advances on our part; and that it is in our power to draw off the greatest proportion of that settlement, and thus to free ourselves from rivals who may become of consequence. We are at present co-operating with Gr. Br. whose policy it is to give aliment to that bitter enmity between her states and ours which may secure her against their ever joining us. But would not the existence of a cordial friendship between us and them be the best bridle we could possibly put into the mouth of England?

With respect to the Danish business you will observe that the instructions of Congress, article 3. of Octob. 29. 1783. put it entirely into the hands of the *ministers plenipotentiary of the U.S. of A. at the court of Versailles empowered to negotiate a peace or to any one or more of them.* At that time I did not exist under this description. I had received the permission of Congress to decline coming in the spring preceding that date. On the 1st. day of Nov. 1783. that is to say two days after the date of the instruction to the Commissioners Congress recommended J. P. Jones to the Minister Plenipotentiary of the U.S. at Versailles as agent to sollicit under his direction the paiment of all prizes taken in Europe under his command. But the object under their view at that time was assuredly the money due from the court of Versailles for the prizes taken in the expedition by the Bon homme Richard, the Alliance etc. In this business I have aided him effectually, having obtained a definitive order for paying the money to him, and a considerable proportion being actually paid him. But they could not mean by their resolution of Nov. 1. to take from the Commissioners powers which they had given them two days before. If there could remain a doubt that this whole power has resulted to you, it would be cleared up by the instruction of May. 7. 1784. article 9. which declares 'that these instructions be considered as supplementory to those of Octob. 29. 1783. and not as revoking except where they contradict them.' Which shews they considered the instructions of Octob. 29. 1783. as still in full force. I do not give you the trouble of this discussion to save myself the trouble of the negociation. I should have no objections to this part: but it is to avoid the impropriety of meddling in a matter wherein I am unauthorised to act, and where any thing I should pretend to conclude with the court of Denmark might have the appearance of a deception on them. Should it be in my power to render any service in it, I shall do it with chearfulness, but I repeat it that I think you are the only person authorised.

I received a few days ago the Nuova minuta of Tuscany which Colo. Humphrys will deliver you. I have been so engaged that I have not been able to go over it with any attention. I observe in general that the order of the articles is entirely deranged, and their diction almost totally changed. When you shall have examined it if you will be so good as to send me your observations by post, in cypher, I will communicate with you in the same way and try to mature this matter.

The deaths of the Dukes of Orleans and Praslin will probably reach you through the channel of the public papers before this letter does. Your friends the Abbés are well and always speak of you with affection. Colo. Humphries comes to pass some time in London. My curiosity would render a short trip thither agreeable to me also, but I see no probability of taking it. I will trouble you with my respects to Doctr. Price. Those to Mrs. Adams I witness in a letter to herself. I am with very great esteem Dr. Sir Your most obedient and most humble servt.,

Th: Jefferson

Jefferson to Abigail Adams

Paris Nov. 20. 1785.

Dear Madam

I have been honoured with your two letters of Octob. 19. and 25. by Mr. Fox and Doctor Rodgers since the date of my last. I am to thank you for your state of Stanhope's case. It has enabled me to speak of that transaction with a confidence of which I should otherwise have been deprived by the different state of it in the public papers and the want of information from America. I have even endeavored to get it printed in a public paper to counteract the impressions of the London papers and Mercure de France. I do not yet know however whether it will be admitted.—Your letter to Mr. Williamos I immediately sent to him. The illness which had long confined him, proved in the end to be mortal. He died about ten days ago.

Mr. Adams's letter of the 4th. instant informs me that Mr. Preston had at length found my letter to him. I hope he has also found, or that he will in time find that which I took the liberty of writing to you. It was to pray you to order me a dozen shirts, of exactly the quality of the one sent, to be made in London. I gave for that 10^{tt}-10s the aune, and wished to be able to judge of the comparative prices in the two countries. The several commissions you have been so good as to execute for me, with what Mr. Adams has paid for insuring Houdon's life leave me considerably in your debt. As I shall not get so good an opportunity of making a remittance, as by Colo. Smith, I trouble him with thirty two Louis for you. This I expect may place us in the neighborhood of a balance. What it is exactly I do not know. I will trouble you to give me notice when you receive your plateaux de dessert, because I told the marchand I would not pay him till you had received them; he having undertaken to send them. I give you so much trouble that unless you find some means of employing me for yourself in return I shall retain an unpleasant load on my mind. Indeed I am sensible this balance will always be against me, as I want more from London than you will do from Paris. True generosity therefore will induce you to give me opportunities of returning your obligations.

Business being now got through I congratulate you on the return of Colo. Smith. I congratulate you still more however on the extreme worth of his character, which was so interesting an object in a person connected in office so nearly with your family. I had never before had an opportunity of being acquainted with him. Your knowlege of him will enable you to judge of the advantageous impressions which his head, his heart, and his manners will have made on me.

I begin to feel very sensibly the effect of the derangement of the French packets. My intelligence from America lately has become more defective than it formerly was. The proceedings of Congress and of the assemblies there this winter will be very interesting.

The death of the Duc d'Orleans has darkened much the court and city. All is sable. No doubt this is a perfect representation of their feelings, and particularly of those of the Duc de Chartres to whom an additional revenue of four millions will be a paultry solace for his loss. News from Madrid give much to fear for the life of the only son of the Prince of Asturias.

Colo. Humphries comes to take a view of London. I should be gratified also with such a trip, of which the pleasure of seeing your family would make a great part. But I foresee no circumstances which could justify, much less call for, such an excursion. Be so good as to present my respects to Miss Adams and to be assured yourself of the sincerity of the esteem with which I have the honour to be Dear Madam Your most obedient and most humble servt.,

Th: Jefferson

Abigail Adams to Jefferson

Grosvenor Square Novr. 24th. 1785.

Sir

I hope if the Marquiss de la Fayette is returned to Paris he may be able to give us some account of Colln. Smith for whom we are not a little anxious, having no intelligence from him since the begining of September when he wrote that he should tarry at Berlin till the reviews were over which would be by the 20th. of that month and then should make the utmost expedition to Paris where his stay would be six days or six Hours according to the intelligence he should meet with there from Mr. Adams. Ten weeks have since elapsed and not a Line or Syllable respecting him has come to hand. In all that time we have been daily and hourly expecting his return. We should have been still more anxious, if the Spanish Minister had not informed us that by a Letter which he received from Colln. Miranda early in Septemr. he wrote him that he had some thoughts of going to Vienna. Colln. Miranda's friends are allarmed about him and have been here to inquire if we could give any account of him. We are now daily more and more anxious because we cannot account for Coll. Smiths long absence but by sickness or some disaster, and even then we ought to have heard from him or of him. You will be so good Sir as to give us every information in your Power as soon as may be.

We suppose you have made an excursion to Fontainbleau by our not having heard from you for a long time. Mr. Preston found the Letters he supposed to have been taken out of his Trunk, amongst his Linnen ten days after his arrival. Your orders shall be executed to the best of my abilities.

Inclosed is a Letter which I found a few days ago respecting the Wine which you was so kind as to take. Mr. Adams is uncertain whether he requested you to Pay to Mr. Bonfeild on his order 319 Livres for a Cask of Wine which he procured for him and of which he never received any account untill his arrival here. If Mr. Barclay has not done it Mr. Adams would be obliged to you to pay it for him.

A Vessell arrived this week from New York and brings papers to the 16 of Octr. They contain nothing material. A Letter from Mr. Jay informs us that no Minister was yet appointed to the Hague, but that Mr. Izard and Mr. Madison were in Nomination, that the rage for New States was very prevalent, which he apprehended would have no good effect. He wished the Ministers abroad to bear testimony against it in their Letters to Congress.

In this Country there is a great want of many French comodities, Good Sense, Good Nature, Political Wisdom and benevolence. His Christian Majesty would render essential service to His Britanick Majesty if he would permit Cargoes of this kind to be exported into this Kingdom against the next meeting of Parliament.

The Treaty lately concluded between France and Holland and the Conduct of England with respect to America proves Her absolute deficiency in each Article. Compliments to the Gentlemen of your Family from Sir your Humble Servant,

A ADAMS

Jefferson to Adams

Paris Nov. 27. 1785.

DEAR SIR

Your favor of the 5th. came to hand yesterday, and Colo. Smith and Colo. Humphries (by whom you will receive one of the 19th. from me) being to set out tomorrow, I hasten to answer it. I sincerely rejoice that Portugal is stepping forward in the business of treaty, and that there is a probability that we may at length do something under our commissions which may produce a solid benefit to our constituents. I as much rejoice that it is not to be negociated through the medium of the torpid uninformed machine [29] at first made use of. I conjecture from your relation of the conference with the Chevalier de Pinto that he is well informed and sensible. So much the better. It is one of those cases (perhaps no others exist) where the better the interests of the two parties are understood, the broader will be the bottom on which they will connect them.

To the very judicious observations on the subjects of the conference which were made by you, I have little to add.

1. Flour. It may be observed that we can sell them the flour ready manufactured for much less than the wheat of which it is made. In carrying to them wheat, we carry also the bran, which does not pay it's own freight. In attempting to save and transport wheat to them, much is lost by the weavil, and much spoiled by heat in the hold of the vessel. This loss must be laid on the wheat which gets safe to market, where it is paid by the consumer. Now this is much more than the cost of manufacturing it with us, which would prevent that loss. I suppose the cost of manufacturing does not exceed seven per cent on the value. But the loss by the weavil,

29. Count de Sousa de Coutinho, Portuguese ambassador at Versailles.

and damage on ship board amount to much more. Let them buy of us as much wheat as will make a hundred weight of flour. They will find that they have paid more for the wheat than we should have asked for the flour, besides having lost the labour of their mills in grinding it. The obliging us therefore to carry it to them in the form of wheat, is a useless loss to both parties.

Iron. They will get none from us. We cannot make it in competition with Sweden or any other nation of Europe where labour is so much cheaper.

Wines. The strength of the wines of Portugal will give them always an almost exclusive possession of a country where the summers are so hot as in America. The present demand will be very great if they will enable us to pay for them; but if they consider the extent and rapid population of the United states they must see that the time is not distant when they will not be able to make enough for us, and that it is of great importance to avail themselves of the prejudices already established in favor of their wines and to continue them by facilitating the purchase. Do this and they need not care for the decline of their use in England. They will be independant of that country.

Salt. I do not know where the Northern states supplied themselves with salt, but the Southern ones took great quantities from Portugal.

Cotton and wool. The Southern states will take manufactures of both: the Northern will take both the manufactures and raw materials.

East-India goods of every kind. Philadelphia and New York have begun a trade to the East Indies. Perhaps Boston may follow their example. But their importations will be sold only to the country adjacent to them. For a long time to come the states south of the Delaware will not engage in a direct commerce with the East Indies. They neither have nor will have ships or seamen for their other commerce. Nor will they buy East India goods of the Northern states. Experience shews that the states never bought foreign goods of one another. The reasons are that they would, in so doing, pay double freight and charges, and again that they would have to pay mostly in cash what they could obtain for commodities in Europe. I know that the American merchants have looked with some anxiety to the arrangements to be taken with Portugal in expectation that they could get their E. India articles on better and more convenient terms, and I am of opinion Portugal will come in for a good share of this traffic with the Southern states, if they facilitate our paiments.

Coffee. Can they not furnish us of this article from Brazil?

Sugar. The Brazil sugars are esteemed with us more than any other.

Chocolate. This article when ready made, and also the Cacao becomes so soon rancid, and the difficulties of getting it fresh have been so great in America that it's use has spread but little. The way to increase it's consumption would be to permit it to be brought to us immediately from the country of it's growth. By getting it good in quality, and cheap in price, the superiority of the article both for health and nourishment will soon give it the same preference over tea and coffee in America, which it has in Spain where they can get it by a single voiage, and of course while it is sweet. The use of the sugars, coffee, and cotton of Brazil would also be much extended by a similar indulgence.

Ginger and spices from the Brazils, if they had the advantage of a direct transportation might take place of the same articles from the E. Indies.

Ginseng. We can furnish them with enough to supply their whole demand for the E. Indies.

They should be prepared to expect that in the beginning of this commerce more money will be taken by us, than after a while. The reasons are that our heavy debt to Gr. Britain must be paid before we shall be masters of our own returns, and again that habits of using particular things are produced only by time and practice.

That as little time as possible may be lost in this negociation I will communicate to you at once my sentiments as to the alterations in the draught sent them,[30] which will probably be proposed by them, or which ought to be proposed by us, noting only those articles.

Art. 3. They will probably restrain us to their dominions in Europe. We must expressly include the Azores, Madeiras, and Cape du verd islands some of which are deemed to be in Africa. We should also contend for an access to their possessions in America according to the gradation in the 2d. article of our instructions of May 7. 1784. But if we can obtain it in no one of these forms, I am of opinion we should give it up.

Art. 4. This should be put into the form we gave it in the draught sent you by Doctr. Franklin and myself for Great Britain.[31] I think we had not reformed this article when we sent our draught to Portugal. You know the Confederation renders the reformation absolutely necessary; a circumstance which had escaped us at first.

Art. 9. Add from the British draught the clause about wrecks.

Art. 13. The passage 'Nevertheless etc. to run as in the British draught.

Art. 18. After the word 'accident' insert 'or wanting supplies of provisions or other refreshments,' and again instead of 'take refuge' insert 'come' and after 'of the other' insert 'in any part of the world.' The object of this is to obtain leave for our whaling vessels to refit and refresh on the coast of the Brazils, an object of immense importance to that class of our

---

30. "Project of a Treaty Submitted by the American commissioners," Boyd, IX, 412-21; and "Observations by the Portuguese Minister," *ibid.*, 424-26.
31. *Ibid.*, VIII, 274.

vessels. We must acquiesce under such modifications as they may think necessary for regulating this indulgence, in hopes to lessen them in time, and to get a pied-à-terre in that country.

Art. 19. Can we get this extended to the Brazils? It would be precious in case of a war with Spain.

Art. 23. Between 'places' and 'whose' insert 'and in general all others' as in the British draught.

Art. 24. for 'necessaries' substitute 'comforts.'

Art. 25. add 'but if any such Consuls shall exercise commerce etc. as in the British draught.

We should give to Congress as early notice as possible of the reinstitution of this negociation, because in a letter by a gentleman who sailed from Havre the 10th. inst. I communicated to them the answer of the Portuguese minister through the Ambassador here, which I sent to you. They may in consequence be taking other arrangements which might do injury. The little time which now remains of the continuance of our commissions should also be used with the Chevalr. de Pinto to hasten the movements of his court.

But all these preparations for trade with Portugal will fail in their effect unless the depredations of the Algerines can be prevented. I am far from confiding in the measures taken for this purpose. Very possibly war must be recurred to. Portugal is in war with them. Suppose the Chevalier de Pinto was to be sounded on the subject of an union of force, and even a stipulation for contributing each a certain force to be kept in constant cruize. Such a league once begun, other nations would drop into it one by one. If he should seem to approve it, it might then be suggested to Congress, who, if they should be forced to try the measure of war, would doubtless be glad of such an ally. As the Portuguese negociation should be hastened, I suppose our communications must often be trusted to the post, availing ourselves of the cover of our cypher. I am with sincere esteem Dear Sir Your friend and servt.,

Th: Jefferson

Adams to Jefferson

Grosvenor Square Dec. 2. 1785.

DEAR SIR

Mr. Nathaniel Barrett, a Gentleman of a respectable Family in Boston, of a fair Character and long Experience in Trade, will have the Honour to deliver you this Letter. He comes to France for the express Purpose of negotiating with proper Persons concerning the Proposals of Monsieur Tourtille de Sangrain, relative of Sperma Cœti oil. I beg Leave to recommend him and his Business to your Attention. I mean this however as mere matter of Form, as I know very well, that your Zeal for the Support of our Whale Fishery, would have been Introduction enough for Mr. Barrett to you, without any Interference of mine. With great Respect and Esteem, I have the Honour to be Dear Sir, your most obedient and most humble Servant,

JOHN ADAMS

Jefferson to Adams

Paris Dec. 10. 1785.

DEAR SIR

On the arrival of Mr. Boylston I carried him to the Marquis de la Fayette, and received from him communications of his object. This was to get a remission of the duties on his cargo of oil, and he was willing to propose a future contract. I proposed however to the Marquis, when we were alone, that instead of wasting our efforts on individual applications, we had better take it up on general ground, and, whatever could be obtained, let it be common to all. He concurred with me. As the jealousy of office between ministers does not permit me to apply immediately to the one in whose department this was, the Marquis's agency was used. The result was to put us on the footing of the Hanseatic towns, as to whale oil, and to reduce the duties to 11^{lt}-5s for 520 lb. French, which is very nearly two livres on the English hundred weight, or about a guinea and a half the ton. But the oil must be brought in American or French ships, and the indulgence is limited to one year. However as to this I expressed to Ct. de Vergennes my hopes that it would be continued, and should a doubt arise, I should propose at the proper time to claim it under the treaty on the footing gentis amicissimi. After all, I beleive Mr. Boylston has failed of selling to Sangrain, and, from what I learn, through a little too much hastiness of temper. Perhaps they may yet come together or he may sell to somebody else.

When the general matter was thus arranged, a Mr. Barrett arrived here from Boston with letters of recommendation from Govr. Bowdoin, Cushing and others. His errand was to get the whale business here put on a general bottom, instead of the particular one which had been settled you know the last year for a special company. We told him what was done.

He thinks it will answer, and proposes to settle at L'Orient for conducting the sales of the oil and the returns. I hope therefore that this matter is tolerably well fixed as far as the consumption of this country goes. I know not as yet to what amount that is; but shall endeavor to find out how much they consume, and how much they furnish themselves. I propose to Mr. Barrett that he should induce either his state or individuals to send us a sufficient number of boxes of the Spermaceti candle, to give one to every leading house in Paris, I mean to those who lead the ton: and at the same time to deposit a quantity for sale here and advertize them in the Petites affiches.[32] I have written to Mr. Carmichael to know on what footing the use and introduction of the whale oil is there, or can be placed. I have the honour to be with very sincere esteem Dear Sir Your most obedient humb. servt.,

Th: Jefferson

Jefferson to Abigail Adams

Paris Dec. 11. 1785.

Dear Madam

Expecting Baron Polnitz to call every moment, I have only time to acknolege the receipt of your favor of Nov. 24. and to answer you on the subject of the bill for 319 livres drawn by Mr. Adams in favor of Mr. Bonfeild. I had never heard of it before, and Mr. Barclay calling on me this morning I asked of him if he knew any thing of it. He says that such a bill was presented to him, and he desired them not to send it back but to let it lie till he could write to Mr. Adams. He wrote. Not having Mr. Adams's answer in his pocket he can only say that from that he was discouraged from paying it by Mr. Adams's expressing a doubt whether he had not desired me to pay it. The bill therefore went back without my having ever heard a tittle of it. I told Mr. Barclay I would write immediately to Mr. Bondfeild to send it to me on an assurance that I would pay it on sight. But he desired I would not; that he would immediately see to the paiment of it, and that it would be a convenience to him to be permitted to do it, as he had a balance of Mr. Adams's in his hands. I could have urged the same reason, but he had the regular authority. Between us therefore you may count on the settlement of this matter, and always on me for that of any other with which you will please to entrust

---

32. *Annonces, affiches, et avis divers, ou journal général de France,* an eight-page daily edited by Abbé Aubert. E. Hatin, *Bibliographie de la presse périodique française* (Paris, 1866), 19.

me, and which may give me an opportunity of proving to you the sincere esteem with which I have the honor to be Dear Madam your most obedient humble servt.,

TH: JEFFERSON

Jefferson to Adams

Paris Dec. 11. 1785.

DEAR SIR

Baron Polnitz not going off till to-day enables me to add some information which I receive from Mr. Barclay this morning. You know the immense amount of Beaumarchais' accounts with the U.S.[33] and that Mr. Barclay was authorized to settle them. Beaumarchais had pertinaciously insisted on settling them with Congress. Probably he received from them a denial: for just as Mr. Barclay was about to set out on the journey we destined him Beaumarchais tendered him a settlement. It was thought best not to refuse this, and that it would produce a very short delay. However it becomes long, and Mr. Barclay thinks it will occupy him all this month. The importance of the account, and a belief that nobody can settle it so well as Mr. Barclay, who is intimately acquainted with most of the articles, induce me to think we must yeild to this delay. Be so good as to give me your opinion on this subject. I have the honour to be with very great esteem Dear Sir Your most obedient and most humble servt.,

TH: JEFFERSON

P.S. Pray contrive the inclosed letter to Colo. Monroe. It must not pass through the hands of the English post officers.

Adams to Jefferson

Grosvenor Square Decr. 13. 1785.

DEAR SIR

I have received a Letter from my Friend General Warren of Milton Hill near Boston, acquainting me, that Congress have it in Contemplation to appoint their Ministers Consuls General, or rather to give them Author-

33. For military supplies provided by his firm, Roderique Hortalez & Co., with capital advanced by the kings of France and Spain. Bemis, *Diplomacy of the American Revolution*, 27, 37-39.

ity to appoint Consuls, and that you are to have the nomination of that officer for Lisbon, that his son Winslow Warren, went sometime ago and settled at Lisbon, partly upon some Encouragement of some Members of Congress that he might have that Place, and requesting me to write you upon the Subject.

I sincerely hope, as far as it concerns myself that Congress, instead of giving me the Appointment of any, may do the Business themselves. For there can be no Employment more disagreable than that of weighing Merit, by the Grain and Scruple, because the world very seldom form an opinion of a Man precisely the same with his own, and therefore the Scales will always be objected to, as not justly ballanced. It is worse than the Business of a Portrait Painter, as Men are generally better Satisfied with their own Talents and Virtues, than even with their Faces. I fancy you will not be delighted with this Amusement more than myself, but if we are ordered upon this service, I suppose we must do it. In which Case, I only pray you to remember that Mr. Warren now at Lisbon is a Candidate. I have known him from his Infancy, from his very Cradle. He is an ingenious and as far as I have observed a modest Man. His Education, Connections and Course of Life, having been bred to Trade, has been such that his Qualifications for the Place may be supposed to be as good as any who will probably apply for it, or accept of it. Coll. Otis his Grandfather, the famous James Otis his Unkle, his other Unkles, and his Father, have been to my knowledge, for these five and twenty Years, among the firmest and steadiest supporters of the American Cause. I declare, I dont believe there is one Family upon Earth to which the United States are so much indebted for their Preservation from Thraldom. There was scarcely any Family in New England had such Prospects of Opulence and Power under the Royal Government. They have sacrificed them all. It is true, and I know you will act upon the Maxim, that the Public Good alone is the Criterion, but it is equally true that the public Good requires that such conspicuous and exemplary Services and Sacrifices, should not be neglected, and therefore Considerations of this Sort ever did, and ever will and ever ought in some degree to influence Mankind. I know of no other Candidate. Probably there will be several, and I know you will decide upon the purest Principles and with mature deliberation, and therefore I shall not only acquiesce in but defend your Decision, tho it may be against my young Friend the son of a very old and much beloved one. I am with usual Esteem, dear Sir, your Sincere Friend and very humble Servant,

JOHN ADAMS

Abigail Adams to Jefferson

Grosvenor Square Decemr. 20th. 1785

DEAR SIR

Your favours by Colln. Smith and by the Baron Polintz came safe to hand. As you have justly estimated the Worth and merit of the former, you will easily suppose we were very glad to see him, and equally so to wellcome Colln. Humphryes upon English Ground. I hope his reception here will be as agreeable to him as he expected. He will inform you I dare say that he has seen both the Lions, and His Majesty.

You will find by the publick Papers what favourites we are at Court. The Prince of Wales supping with us, Mr. Adams holding frequent conferences with His Majesty, and yesterday going to Windsor for the same purpose. It is said by some that these are Ministerial manoeuvres to keep up the stocks. A Paragraph of this kind has certainly been attended with that effect. Others say it is to seek out the minds of the People with respect to a Treaty with America, of which if I dared to give my opinion, I should say that some simptoms have lately appeard tending to that point. But this is said in confidence Sir, as I must not betray secrets.

The affair of Capt. Stanhope has been officially taken up and his Conduct much disapproved of by the Lords of the Admirality, as Congress are informed by an official reply to them. Mr. A. has also received an answer to his Demand of the Citizens of the United States sent to the East Indies, "that orders were immediately issued for their discharge." It is not probable that any thing very material will take place till the meeting of Parliament.

The Pacquet arrived last week from New York, in which came Passenger Monsieur Houdon. He returns to Paris the latter End of this week. There were no official Dispatches, and only a private Letter or two to the second of November, but as Mr. A. writes you I will leave Politicks with which I really have no business, and talk of that which more properly belongs to me.

The Commission you honourd me with will be compleat to send by the return of Colln. Humphryes. I received my Plateau safe about ten days since. It is a very good one and I am much obliged by your kind attention to it. The Deities however shewed that they were subject to Humane frailty and got a few Limbs dislocated in their Tour.

If Mr. Barclay will be so good as to settle with Mr. Bonfeild Mr. Adams will be obliged to him. Coll. Smith delivered me the Louis's you sent by him, and when Colln. Humphryes returns I will forward you the account of my stewardship.

Compliments to Mr. Short. We are sorry to hear of his indisposition. I once found great benefit in the Dissorder which he complains of by taking an oz. of Castile soap and a pint of Bristol Beer dividing it into three portions; and takeing it three Mornings, fasting.

I wish you could make it convenient to let Miss Jefferson come and pass a few Months with us here. I do not yet dispair of seeing you in England and in that Case you will certainly bring her with you. I am Sir your most obedient servt.,

A Adams

Adams to Jefferson

Grosvenor Square Decr. 20. 1785

Dear Sir

Mr. Barretts Arrival at Paris, is a lucky Event, and his appoinment by the Merchants in Boston a judicious step; but I am not so clear in the Choice he makes of L'Orient to reside in. Paris, or even Havre, seems to me a better situation, Paris in preference to all others. If Boylstone would Act in concert with him, his Capital would be equal to every Thing which relates to the Business: But he is a Singular Character, irritable, fiery, avaricious, parcimonious, to a degree, that made me always doubtfull whether he would succeed: besides his Age and Ignorance of the Language. It is to be regretted that his Cargo cannot be put into the Hands of Sangrain because it is a great Object, to bring that Gentleman into an Acquaintance with the Qualities of the white Sperma Cœti Oil, and into a Course of Experiments of its Use. The first Point to be gained, is to shew that this Oil, considering all its Properties, may be used in the Reverberes [34] cheaper than the Olive Oil, Neatsfoot Oil, or Linseed Oil, or whatever other Substance goes to the Composition of that with which they now enlighten their Cities. We must engage Œconomy, as an Advocate in our Cause, or we shall finally loose it. The Marquis tells me, the Duty is reduced to 7. Liv. 10.s. the Barrique of 520 Weight. You state it at 11.tt 10.s. I should be glad to be exact in this Information, and to know which is right. But, 11:tt 10s the Barrique, even as you state it, is so much less than 18. £ 3.s Sterling the Ton, the Allien Duty paid here that one would think it must turn all the Trade to France, as I hope it will, and as it certainly will if the French Government encourage the Attempt. If an American Merchant can fix himself at Paris and remain a Man of Business, and not become infected with a Rage for Amusements, he might by correspond-

34. French *reverbère,* a reflecting lamp.

ing with all the great Cities of the Kingdom soon do a great deal, towards introducing an extensive Trade between the United States and the French.

I am extreamly sorry for the Accident, which has retarded Mr. Barclay, but I think with you that We must submit to it, for a reasonable Time. But I hope Mr. Barclay will not suffer himself to be delayed one moment unnecessarily. If any Pretences or Excuses for postponing are contrived, I hope he will break away from them all. It is a horrid Thing, that Business so essential should have been neglected so long.

The Chevr. De Pinto is sick, which will unluckily retard our affair with him. But I will quicken it as soon and as much as I can. With great Esteem I am, dear Sir your most obedient Servant,

JOHN ADAMS

Jefferson to Abigail Adams

Paris Dec. 27. 1785.

DEAR MADAM

I am this day honoured with your favor of the 20th. and an opportunity offering to acknolege it immediately, I do not fail to embrace it. I thank you for the intelligence it contains. You refered me to Mr. Adams for news; but he gives me none; so that I hope you will be so good as to keep that office in your own hands. I get little from any other quarter since the derangement of the French packets.

I condole with you sincerely on the dismemberment of the gods and goddesses, and take some blame to myself for not having detained them for Colo. Smith who would have carried them safely. Can I be instrumental in repairing the loss? I will promise not to trust to a workman another time.

Mr. Short is on the recovery. I will take care to communicate to him your prescription, as soon as he returns from St. Germain's. All your friends here are well. The Abbés always desire me to remind you of them. What shall I do for news to tell you? I scratch my head in vain. Oh! true. The new opera of Penelope by Marmontel and Piccini succeeds. Mademoiselle Renaud, of 16. years of age sings as no body ever sung before. She is far beyond Madme. Mara in her own line of difficult execution. Her sister of 12 years of age will sing as well as she does. Having now emptied my budget I have the honour of presenting my respects to Miss Adams and of assuring you of the sincere esteem with which I have the honour to be Dear Madam Your most obedient and most humble servt.,

TH: JEFFERSON

Jefferson to Adams

Paris Dec. 27. 1785.

DEAR SIR

Your favors of the 13th. and 20th. were put into my hands today. This will be delivered you by Mr. Dalrymple, secretary to the legation of Mr. Craufurd. I do not know whether you were acquainted with him here. He is a young man of learning and candor, and exhibits a phaenomenon I never before met with, that is, a republican born on the North side of the Tweed.

You have been consulted in the case of the Chevalr. de Mezieres nephew to Genl. Oglethorpe, and are understood to have given an opinion derogatory of our treaty with France. I was also consulted, and understood in the same way. I was of opinion the Chevalier had no right to the estate, and as he had determined the treaty gave him a right, I suppose he made the inference for me that the treaty was of no weight. The Count de Vergennes mentioned it to me in such a manner that I found it was necessary to explain the case to him, and shew him that the treaty had nothing to do with it. I inclose you a copy of the explanation I delivered him.[35]

Mr. Boylston sold his cargo to an Agent of Monsieur Sangrain. He got for it 55. livres the hundred weight. I do not think that his being joined to a company here would contribute to it's success. His capital is not wanting. Le Couteux has agreed that the Merchants of Boston sending whale oil here, may draw on him for a certain proportion of money, only giving such a time in their draughts as will admit the actual arrival of the oil into a port of France for his security. Upon these draughts Mr. Barrett is satisfied they will be able to raise money to make their purchases in America.—The duty is 7^{tt}-10 on the barrel of 520 lb. French, and 10. sous on every livre, which raises it to 11^{tt}-5, the sum I mentioned to you. France uses between 5. and 6. millions of pounds weight French, which is between 3. and 4000 tons English. Their own fisheries do not furnish one million and there is no probability of their improving. Sangrain purchases himself upwards of a million. He tells me our oil is better than the Dutch or English, because we make it fresh, whereas they cut up the whale and bring it home to be made, so that it is by that time entered into fermentation. Mr. Barrett says that 50. livres the hundred weight will pay the prime cost and duties and leave a profit of 16. per cent to the merchant. I hope that England will within a year or two be obliged to come here to buy whale oil for her lamps.

35. For TJ's amplification of subjects discussed with Vergennes, see Boyd, IX, 107-10; also *ibid.*, 120-22, on TJ's suggestions to Georgia.

I like as little as you do to have the gift of appointments. I hope Congress will not transfer the appointment of their Consuls to their ministers. But if they do, Portugal is more naturally under the superintendance of the minister at Madrid, and still more naturally under the minister at Lisbon, where it is clear they ought to have one. If all my hopes fail, the letters of Govr. Bowdoin and Cushing, in favor of young Mr. Warren, and your more detailed testimony in his favor, are not likely to be opposed by evidence of equal weight in favor of any other.

I think with you too that it is for the public interest to encourage sacrifices and services by rewarding them, and that they should weigh to a certain point in the decision between candidates.

I am sorry for the illness of the Chevalr. Pinto. I think that treaty important: and the moment to urge it is that of a treaty between France and England.

Lamb, who left this place the 6th. of Nov. was at Madrid the 10th. of this month. Since his departure Mr. Barclay has discovered that no copies of the full powers were furnished to himself, nor of course to Lamb. Colo. Franks has prepared copies which I will endeavor to get to send by this conveiance for your attestation: which you will be so good as to send back by the first safe conveiance and I will forward them. Mr. Barclay and Franks being at this moment at St. Germain's, I am not sure of getting the papers in time to go by Mr. Dalrymple. In that case I will send them by Mr. Bingham.

Be so good as to present me affectionately to Mrs. and Miss Adams, to Colos. Smith and Humphries and accept assurances of the esteem with which I am Dear Sir Your friend and servt.,

TH: JEFFERSON

P.S. Be pleased to forward the inclosed, sealing that to Congress after you have read it.

Jefferson to Adams

Paris Jan. 12. 1786.

SIR

You were here the last year when the interest due to the French officers was paid to them, and were sensible of the good effect it had on the credit and honor of the U.S. A second year's interest is become due. They have presented their demands. There is not money here to pay them, the pittance remaining in Mr. Grand's hands being only sufficient to pay current expences three months longer. The dissatisfaction of these officers is extreme, and their complaints will produce the worst effect.[36] The treasury board has not ordered their paiment, probably because they knew there would not be money. The amount of their demands is about 42,000 livres and Mr. Grand has in his hands but twelve thousand. I have thought it my duty under this emergency to ask you whether you could order that sum for their relief from the funds in Holland? If you can, I am persuaded it will have the best of effects.

The imperial Ambassador took me apart the other day at Count d'Aranda's, and observed to me that Doctr. Franklin about eighteen or twenty months ago had written to him a letter proposing a treaty of commerce between the Emperor and the U.S. that he had communicated it to the Emperor and had answered to Doctor Franklin that they were ready to enter into arrangements for that purpose: but that he had since that received no reply from us. I told him I knew well that Doctor Franklin had written as he mentioned, but that this was the first mention I had ever heard made of any answer to the letter, that on the contrary we had always supposed it was unanswered and had therefore expected the next step from him. He expressed his wonder at this and said he would have the copy of his answer sought for and send it to me. However, he observed that this matter being now understood between us, the two countries might proceed to make the arrangements. I told him the delay had been the more unlucky as our powers were now near expiring. He said he supposed Congress could have no objections to renew them, or perhaps to send some person to Brussels to negotiate the matter there. We remitted all further discussion till he should send me a copy of his letter. He has not yet done it, and I doubt whether he has not forgotten the substance of his letter which probably was no more than an acknowlegement of the receipt of Dr. Franklin's and a promise to transmit it to his court. If he had written one proposing conferences, it could never have got safe to Doctor Franklin. Be this as it will he now makes advances, and I pray you to write me your sentiments immediately as to what is best to be done on our part. I will endeavor to evade an answer till I can hear from you. I have the honor to be with the highest respect and esteem Dear Sir, your most obedient and most humble servant,

Th: Jefferson

36. These were French officers who had served in the Continental Army and held certificates under the Commutation Act of 1783, promising full pay for five years in the form of 6 per cent securities. In 1784 Congress authorized new certificates with interest payable at Mr. Grand's in Paris. On the amount due, about $8,200, the Confederation was defaulting. One of these officers, the Chevalier de Segond, filed a typical complaint with TJ in Jan. 1787, which he forwarded to Secretary Jay. Jensen, *New Nation*, 76-82; TJ to Commissioners of the Treasury, Jan. 26, 1786, Boyd, IX, 227; Segond to TJ, Jan. 17, 1787, *ibid.*, XI, 53.

Jefferson to Adams

Paris. Jan. 12. 1786.

DEAR SIR

I had just closed the preceding letter when M. de Blumendorf the Imperial Secretary of legation called on me with the answer to Doctr. Franklin. It was that of Sep. 28. 1784 which you remember as well as myself, wherein Count Merci informed us the Emperor was disposed to enter into commercial arrangements with us and that he would give orders to the Government of the Austrian Netherlands to take the necessary measures. I observed to M. de Blumendorff that this answer shewed the next step was to come from them. He acknoleged it, but said these orders having been for the Netherlands only, they had waited in expectation of others for comprehending Hungary, Bohemia and the Austrian dominions in general, and that they still expect such instructions. I told him that while they should be expecting them, I would write to you on the subject, as it was necessary for us to act jointly in this business. I think they are desirous of treating, and will urge it. I shall be anxious therefore to receive your sentiments on the subject; and renew the assurances of the esteem with which I am Dear Sir, Your friend and servt.,

TH: JEFFERSON

Adams to Jefferson

Grosvenor Square Jan. 19. 1786

DEAR SIR

I am favoured with yours of 27. Decr. and am obliged to you for what you said to the Count De Vergennes in the Case of the Chevalier De Mezieres. You may always very safely depend upon it, that I never have given and never shall give any opinion against the Letter or Spirit of the Treaty with France. In this Case I have never given any opinion at all. Indeed I have never been consulted. The Marquis De Belgarde, with whom I had a Slight Acquaintance at the Hague, called upon me here after the Death of Gen. Oglethorpe, and desired that Mr. Granville Sharp might call upon me and shew me some Papers relative to the Generals Lands in Georgia and S. Carolina. Mr. Sharpe called accordingly, but shewed me no Papers. I never looked nor enquired into the Case, but advised both to write and send a Power of Attorney to our old Friend Edward Rutledge, who was able to give them the best Advice and Information and all the Assurance which the Law allows in their Claim. The Treaty with France never occurred to me, nor was suggested to me in the Conference, nor did I ever give any opinion on any Question concerning it. I have never written a Line to America about it, nor put pen to Paper. The Supposition that any opinion of yours in private Conversation, or of mine if any such had been given which never was, should influence Courts and Juries in Georgia or Carolina, is ridiculous. The Case, as you state it, indeed appears to be unconnected with the Treaty entirely, and if Sound Sense can remove a Prejudice, what you have said upon it, will put an End to the Jealousy.

Does the Count de Vergennes pretend that the United States of America, are bound by their Treaty with France never to lay a Duty on French Vessells? The Mass. and N.H. Navigation Laws, leave French ships, Subjects and Merchandizes upon the Footing Gentis Amicissimae. And does the Treaty require more?

I have been informed by Richard Jackson Esqr., whose Fame is known in America, that a Question has been referred to a Number of the first Lawyers common and civil, among whom he was one, "Whether the Citizens of the United States born before the Revolution, were still entituled in the British Dominions to the Rights of British Subjects." Their unanimous Determination was that Such as were born before, the Signature of the Definitive Treaty of Peace, are still to be considered as British Subjects, if they claim the rights, in the British Dominions. This Decision was I believe more upon Analogy, and Speculation, than upon any Established Principle or Precedent, since ours is I believe a new Case. How it has been determined in America I know not. But I believe not the same way. However the Lawyers and Judges may determine it, I wish the Assemblies may adopt it as a Rule respecting Estates held before the Seperation since a Generosity of this Kind will be more for their Honour and their Interest, as I conceive than a rigorous Claim of an Escheat however clear in Law.

The Chevalier De Pinto informs me, that he has written to his Court for Explanations upon some Points, and expects an Answer in a few Days. When it arrives he will call upon me. In the mean time, he says his Court is solicitous to send a Minister to America: but that Ettiquette forbids it, unless Congress will agree to send one to Lisbon. They would send a Minister to N. York if Congress would return the Compliment, but if Congress will not send a Minister Plenipotentiary they wish to send a Resident, or even a Chargé des Affaires, but Ettiquette will not permit this unless Congress will send a Resident or Chargé D'Affaires to Portugal.

Is it really expected or intended that Eden shall do more than Crawford did? Pray let me know, if there is any Probability of a Treaty, in Earnest, between France and England?

Mr. Barrett has it seems succeeded very well. And Boylston too. If this last has made thirty Per Cent Profit, I will answer for it, that he alone will prevent the Expiration of our Whale Trade and the Depopulation of Nantuckett. He is an admirable Patriot when thirty per Cent can be made by serving his Country. Our Nantuckett and Cape Codd Men and our Boston Merchants are much to blame for having neglected so long the French Markett for their oil and Fins, and for remaining so long in Ignorance of it.

Perhaps the Difference between our White Sperma Cœti Oil and the Ordinary Train Oil of the Dutch and English is not yet sufficiently known to Mr. Sangrain. The Dutch I believe take no Sperma Cœti Whales, and it is but lately that the English have taken any, and they are able to take them now, only with our Skippers, Oarsmen and Endsmen. These we shall soon get back from them if our States are cunning enough to repeal the Refugee Laws, and if France is wise enough to encourage the Exportation of her own Produce and Manufactures by receiving ours in Payment.

Mr. Voss from Virginia has just now called upon me and shewn me a State of the Debt of that Commonwealth which is very consolatory. It is dated 12. Nov. 1785. and signed B. Stark, H. Randolph and J. Pendleton. The whole Debt at that Period was only 928,031 £: 9s: od. The annual Interest 55,649 £ 15s: 3d. Pension List annually 6,000 £ Officers of Government Ditto 29,729 £. Criminal Prosecution ditto 5,509. Thus it appears that 96,878 £: 15s: 3d. annually will pay the whole Interest of their Debt and all the Charges of Government.

Virginia by this may sing O be joyfull.

On the 19. Nov. The [Virginia] Lower House resolved to invest Congress with full Power to regulate Trade, and in the mean time that all Commerce should cease with the British Colonies in the West Indies and North America, and that all ships of foreign Nations with whom we have not Treaties of Commerce should be prohibited from importing any Thing but the Productions of their own Country. It seems they revoked these Resolutions again, because the House was thin, but with design to take them up in another day. This perhaps may not be done till next year. But it is a strong Symptom of what is coming. Mr. Voss gives a comfortable account of the Trade in Peltries as well as Grain and Tobacco. Every Vessell that arrives brings fresh Comfort, and I fancy our Commerce with the East Indies will be effectually secured by the Reception of Mr. Pitts Bill. Mr. Voss tells me, that the British Debts will not be permitted to be sued for untill the Treaty is complied with, by the English by the Evacuation of the Posts and Payment for the Negroes.[37] Ld. Carmarthen told me yesterday, that he was labouring at an Answer to my Memorial concerning the Posts and that he should compleat it, as soon as he could get all the Information he was looking for concerning the British Debts, for that Complaints had been made by the Creditors here to Ministry. I am glad that I am to have an Answer. For whatever Conditions they may tack to the Surrender of the Posts, We shall find out what is broiling in their Hearts, and by degrees come together. An Answer, though it might be a rough one, would be better than none. But it will not be rough. They will smooth it as much as they can and I shall transmit it to Congress who may again pass the smoothing plain over it. I expect it will end in an Accommodation, but it will take Eighteen months more time to finish it. With great Esteem yours,

John Adams

Adams to Jefferson

Grosvenor Square Jan. 28. 1786

Dear Sir

I have received yours of the 12, but yesterday, and wish it were in my Power to order the Interest due to the French Officers to be paid; but it is not. They must remain unpaid, be the Consequence what it may untill Congress or the Board of Treasury order it. Indeed, I dont know how your Subsistence and mine is to be paid after next month. Mr. Grand will be likely to advance yours, but from whence mine is to come I know not.

I am clearly for treating with the Emperors Ambassador immediately, and even for the Netherlands only, although it would be better to extend it to all the rest of his Dominions. Why will not the Prussian Treaty answer for the Model. I pray you to proceed in the Business, as fast as you please. Treaties commercial with the two Imperial Courts cannot possibly do us any harm that I can conceive.

This Letter goes by Mr. Joy, whom I pray you to attend to a little. He wishes to go to the East Indies, with views of promoting a Trade between the United States and that Country. In great Haste yours forever,

John Adams

37. See AA to TJ, Sept. 6, 1785, above, 61-62, n.49.

Jefferson to Adams

Paris Feb. 7. 1786.

DEAR SIR

I am honored with yours of Jan. 19. Mine of Jan. 12. had not I suppose at that time got to your hands as the receipt of it is unacknoleged. I shall be anxious till I receive your answer to it.

I was perfectly satisfied, before I received your letter, that your opinion had been misunderstood or misrepresented in the case of the Chevalier de Mezieres. Your letter however will enable me to say so with authority. It is proper that it should be known that you had not given the opinion imputed to you, tho' as to the main question it is become useless, Monsieur de Reyneval having assured me that what I had written on that subject had perfectly satisfied the Ct. de Vergennes and himself that this case could never come under the treaty. To evince still further the impropriety of taking up subjects gravely on such imperfect information as this court had, I have this moment received a copy of an act of the Georgia assembly placing the subjects of France as to real estates on the footing of natural citizens and expressly recognizing the treaty. Would you think any thing could be added after this to put this question still further out of doors? A gentleman of Georgia [38] assures me General Oglethorpe did not own a foot of land in the state.—I do not know whether there has been any American determination on the question whether American citizens and British subjects born before the revolution can be aliens to one another? I know there is an opinion of Ld. Coke's in Calvin's case that if England and Scotland should in a course of descent pass to separate kings, those born under the same sovereign during the union would remain natural subjects and not aliens. Common sense urges strong considerations against this, e.g. natural subjects owe allegiance. But we owe none.—Aliens are the subjects of a foreign power. We are subjects of a foreign power.—The king by the treaty acknoleges our independance; how then can we remain natural subjects.—The king's power is by the constitution competent to the making peace, war and treaties. He had therefore authority to relinquish our allegiance by treaty.—But if an act of parliament had been necessary, the parliament passed an act to confirm the treaty, etc. etc. So that it appears to me that in this question fictions of law alone are opposed to sound sense.

38. John McQueen, formerly of Charleston, S. C., who made extensive land purchases in Georgia. W. C. Hartridge, ed., *The Letters of Don Juan McQueen to His Family, 1791-1807* (Columbia, S. C., 1943), xxv-vi.

I am in hopes Congress will send a minister to Lisbon. I know no country with which we are likely to cultivate a more useful commerce. I have pressed this in my private letters.

It is difficult to learn any thing certain here about the French and English treaty. Yet, in general, little is expected to be done between them. I am glad to hear that the Delegates of Virginia had made the vote relative to English commerce, tho they afterwards repealed it. I hope they will come to again. When my last letters came away they were engaged in passing the revisal of their laws, with some small alterations. The bearer of this, Mr. Lyons, is a sensible worthy young physician, son of one of our Judges, and on his return to Virginia. Remember me with affection to Mrs. and Miss Adams, Colos. Smith and Humphreys and be assured of the esteem with which I am Dr. Sir your friend and servant,

Th: Jefferson

Abigail Adams to Jefferson, with Enclosure

London, Grosvenor Square, Feb. 11th, 1786.

Col. Humphries talks of leaving us on Monday. It is with regret, I assure you, Sir, that we part with him. His visit here has given us an opportunity of becoming more acquainted with his real worth and merit, and our friendship for him has risen in proportion to our intimacy. The two American Secretaries of Legation would do honor to their country placed in more distinguished stations. Yet these missions abroad, circumscribed as they are in point of expenses, place the ministers of the United States in the lowest point of view of any envoy from any other Court; and in Europe every being is estimated, and every country valued, in proportion to their show and splendor. In a private station I have not a wish for expensive living, but, whatever my fair countrywomen may think, and I hear they envy my situation, I will most joyfully exchange Europe for America, and my public for a private life. I am really surfeited with Europe, and most heartily long for the rural cottage, the purer and honester manners of my native land, where domestic happiness reigns unrivalled, and virtue and honor go hand in hand. I hope one season more will give us an opportunity of making our escape. At present we are in the situation of Sterne's starling.[39]

39. A caged starling appears in Lawrence Sterne's *Sentimental Journey and the Journal to Eliza*, ed. by Ernest Rhys (Everyman's Library edn.; N. Y., [1926?]), 76-80.

Congress have by the last dispatches informed this Court that they expect them to appoint a minister. It is said (not officially) that Mr. Temple is coldly received, that no Englishman has visited him, and the Americans are not very social with him. But as Colonel Humphries will be able to give you every intelligence, there can be no occasion for my adding any thing further than to acquaint you that I have endeavored to execute your commission agreeably to your directions. Enclosed you will find the memorandum. I purchased a small trunk, which I think you will find useful to you to put the shirts in, as they will not be liable to get rubbed on the journey. If the balance should prove in my favor, I will request you to send me 4 ells of cambric at about 14 livres per ell or 15, a pair of black lace lappets—these are what the ladies wear at court—and 12 ells of black lace at 6 or 7 livres per ell. Some gentleman coming this way will be so kind as to put them in his pocket, and Mrs. Barclay, I dare say, will take the trouble of purchasing them for me; for troubling you with such trifling matters is a little like putting Hercules to the distaff.

My love to Miss Jefferson, and compliments to Mr. Short. Mrs. Siddons is acting again upon the stage, and I hope Colonel Humphries will prevail with you to cross the Channel to see her. Be assured, dear Sir, that nothing would give more pleasure to your friends here than a visit from you, and in that number I claim the honor of subscribing myself.

A. ADAMS

4 pair of shoes for Miss Adams, by the person who made Mrs. A.'s, 2 of satin and 2 of spring silk, without straps, and of the most fashionable colors.

ENCLOSURE

Memorandum of purchases made for TJ reading as follows:

To 2 peices of Irish linen at 4s. pr. yd.	8 £	14s.	od.
To making 12 Shirts at 3s per Shirt	1	16	0
To buttons thread silk	0	3	0
To Washing	0	3	6
A Trunk	1	1	0
	11	17	6

The Louis I parted with at 20 shillings

Adams to Jefferson

Grosvenor Square Feb. 17. 1786.

DEAR SIR

I was sometime in doubt, whether any Notice Should be taken of the Tripoline Ambassador [Abdurrahman]; but receiving Information that he made Enquiries about me, and expressed a Surprise that when the other foreign Ministers had visited him, the American had not; and finding that He was a universal and perpetual Ambassador, it was thought best to call upon him. Last Evening, in making a Tour of other Visits, I Stopped at his Door, intending only to leave a Card, but the Ambassador was announced at Home and ready to receive me. I was received in State. Two great Chairs before the Fire, one of which was destined for me, the other for his Excellency. Two Secretaries of Legation, men of no Small Consequence Standing Upright in the middle of the Room, without daring to Sitt, during the whole time I was there, and whether they are not yet upright upon their Legs I know not. Now commenced the Difficulty. His Excellency Speaks Scarcely a Word of any European Language, except Italian and Lingua Franca, in which, you know I have Small Pretensions. He began soon to ask me Questions about America and her Tobacco, and I was Surprized to find that with a pittance of Italian and a few French Words which he understands, We could so well understand each other. "We make Tobacco in Tripoli," said his Excellency "but it is too Strong. Your American Tobacco is better." By this Time, one of his secretaries or *upper servants* brought two Pipes ready filled and lighted. The longest was offered me; the other to his Excellency. It is long since I took a Pipe but as it would be unpardonable to be wanting in Politeness in so ceremonious an Interview, I took the Pipe with great Complacency, placed the Bowl upon the Carpet, for the Stem was fit for a Walking Cane, and I believe more than two Yards in length, and Smoaked in aweful Pomp, reciprocating Whiff for Whiff, with his Excellency, untill Coffee was brought in. His Excellency took a Cup, after I had taken one, and alternately Sipped at his Coffee and whiffed at his Tobacco, and I wished he would take a Pinch in turn from his Snuff box for Variety; and I followed the Example with Such Exactness and Solemnity that the two secretaries, appeared in Raptures and the superiour of them who speaks a few Words of French cryed out in Extacy, Monsieur votes etes un Turk. —The necessary Civilities being thus compleated, His Excellency began upon Business; asked many Questions about America: the soil Climate

Heat and Cold, etc. and said it was a very great Country. But "Tripoli is at War with it." I was "Sorry to hear that." "Had not heard of any War with Tripoli." "America had done no Injury to Tripoli, committed no Hostility; nor had Tripoli done America any Injury or committed any Hostility against her, that I had heard of." True said His Excellency "but there must be a Treaty of Peace. There could be no Peace without a Treaty. The Turks and Affricans were the souvereigns of the Mediterranean, and there could be no navigation there nor Peace without Treaties of Peace. America must treat as France and England did, and all other Powers. America must treat with Tripoli and then with Constantinople and then with Algiers and Morocco." Here a Secretary brought him some Papers, one of which a Full Power in French from the Pacha, Dey and Regency of Tripoli, as Ambassador, to treat with all the Powers of Europe, and to make what Treaties he pleased and to manage in short all the foreign Affairs of his Country, he delivered me to read. He was ready to treat and make Peace. If I would come tomorrow or next day, or any other day and bring an Interpreter, He would hear and propose Terms, and write to Tripoli and I might write to America, and each Party might accept or refuse them as they should think fit. How long would it be before one could write to Congress and have an Answer? Three months. This was rather too long but he should stay here sometime. When I had read his French Translation of his Full Power He Shewed me the original in his own Language. You perceive that his Excellency was more ready and eager to treat than I was as he probably expected to gain more by the Treaty. I could not see him Tomorrow nor next day but would think of it.

I must now my dear sir beg of you to send me a Copy of the Project of a Treaty sent [to Morocco] by Mr. Barclay and Mr. Lamb, as I had not time to take one, when it was here. You will please to write me your Thoughts and Advice upon this Occasion. This is a Sensible Man, well known to many of the foreign Ministers who have seen him before, in Sweeden, at Vienna, in Denmark etc. He has been so much in Europe that he knows as much of America, as anybody; so that nothing new will be suggested to him or his Constituents by our having Conferences with him. It seems best then to know his Demands. They will be higher I fear, than we can venture.

The King told one of the foreign Ministers in my hearing at the Levee, that the Tripoline Ambassador refused to treat with his Ministers and insisted upon an Audience. But that all he had to say was that Tripoli was at Peace with England and desired to continue so. The King added all he wants is, a Present, and his Expences born to Vienna or Denmark.

The Relation of my Visit is to be sure very inconsistent with the Dignity of your Character and mine, but the Ridicule of it was real and the Drollery inevitable. How can We preserve our Dignity in negotiating with Such Nations? And who but a Petit Maitre would think of Gravity upon such an occasion.[40] With great Esteem your most obedient

JOHN ADAMS

Adams to Jefferson

Grosvenor Square Feb. 21. 1786.

DEAR SIR

I have desired Colonel Smith to go Express to Paris, to intreat you to come here without loss of Time. The Portuguese Minister has received his Instructions from his Court, and we may here together conduct and finish the Negotiation with him, I suppose in three Weeks. But there is another Motive more Important. There is here a Tripolitan Ambassador with whom I have had three Conferences. The Substance of what passed Colonel Smith will explain to you. Your Visit here will be imputed to Curiosity, to take a Look at England and pay your Respects at Court and to the Corps Diplomatick. There is nothing to be done in Europe, of half the Importance of this, and I dare not communicate to Congress what has passed without your Concurrence. What has been already done and expended will be absolutely thrown away and We shall be involved in a universal and horrible War with these Barbary States, which will continue for many Years, unless more is done immediately. I am so impressed and distressed with this affair that I will go to New York or to Algiers or first to one and then to the other, if you think it necessary, rather than it should not be brought to a Conclusion. Somebody must go to N. York, one of Us, or Humphries or Smith in order to perswade Congress of the Necessity of doing more. Then somebody must go to Holland to obtain the means, and then somebody perhaps to Algiers to make Use of them. The Tripolitan might be perswaded to go with him. I refer you to the Bearer for all other Particulars, and have the Honour to be with great Esteem your Friend,

JOHN ADAMS

40. JA sent a more prosaic account of his conference with the Tripolitan minister to Jay, Feb. 17, 1786, *Works*, VIII, 372-73.

Adams to Jefferson

Grosvenor Square Feb. 25. 1786

DEAR SIR

Give me Leave to introduce to you Mr. Samuel Hartley a Relation of the late Minister at Paris. He has Business at Paris which he will explain to you, whether you can be of any Service to him in that or not, your Civilities will be very agreeable to him and oblige Dear Sir your most humble Servant,

JOHN ADAMS

4

"Abate the ardor of those pyrates against us"

IN MARCH 1786 at the request of John Adams, Jefferson visited England on a mission which proved to be fruitless and frustrating diplomatically, though pleasant enough otherwise. The two friends made a tour of English gardens, Jefferson with Thomas Whately's *Observations on Modern Gardening* in hand, Adams with an eye to historic sites and the ostentatious luxury of country estates.[1] Jefferson must also have enjoyed frequent visits in the Adams household, where Colonel William Stephens Smith, secretary of the American legation, would soon take young Abigail as his bride. The Virginian sat for a portrait by Mather Brown and presented it to Adams, who returned the favor two years later when he sent Jefferson his own portrait by Brown.[2]

Not long after his arrival on March 11 Jefferson was presented at court, but the author of the Declaration of Independence met with a cold reception.[3] Later he referred caustically to George III as "truly the American Messias. . . . Twenty long years has he been labouring to drive us to our good."[4] That good, however, did not include an Anglo-American commercial treaty, for the project which the American commissioners submitted to the British ministry met only with delay and indifference.[5]

---

1. "Notes on a Tour of English Gardens," Boyd, IX, 369-73, 374-75*n*.
2. Boyd, XII, xxxvii; see frontispieces of Vols. I and II of the present work.
3. According to C. F. Adams, the King turned his back on both JA and TJ. C. F. Adams, "Life of John Adams," *Works*, I, 420; TJ, "Autobiography," Ford, I, 89.
4. TJ to AA, Aug. 9, 1786, below, 149.
5. TJ to Richard Henry Lee, April 22, 1786, and JA and TJ to John Jay, April 25, 1786, Boyd, IX, 398-99, 406-7.

The treaty with Portugal offered better prospects for success during Jefferson's six-week stay in England. Negotiations were completed with De Pinto, but the Portuguese government, faced with domestic difficulties and shifting allegiances abroad, failed to ratify. Nevertheless, Queen Maria I gave protection a few weeks later to American vessels from Algerine corsairs in the Atlantic.[6]

Perhaps the most intriguing aspect of Adams's and Jefferson's collaboration in London was their negotiations with the Barbary states. In initiating the move a year earlier for dealings with them, the American commissioners had sought the advice of the Comte de Vergennes, French foreign minister, who wisely recommended that they operate through agents sent to those countries rather than invite envoys to France at great expense. He even agreed guardedly to such assistance as he might discreetly provide.[7] Acting on this advice, Adams and Jefferson had dispatched Thomas Barclay, American consul general in France, to Morocco, and John Lamb, merchant and consul in Spain, to Algiers in October 1785.[8] The friendly attitude of the Spanish court, which William Carmichael, American chargé d'affaires, had been cultivating, smoothed Barclay's approach to the Emperor of Morocco in the spring of 1786. Lamb had already arrived in Algiers on March 25; but the outcome of the two missions was success on the one hand and failure on the other.

Thus far, indirect dealings with the Barbary powers had not conveyed realistically to the American commissioners the ruthless tactics that would give affront to their principles of morality. In London, however, they met one of the piratical envoys face to face. Abdurrahman, the Tripolitan ambassador, conferred with Adams in February 1786 before Jefferson's arrival and inspired one of the most amusing letters Adams ever wrote. He admitted unofficially to Jefferson that it was "very inconsistent with the Dignity of your Character and mine, but the Ridicule of it was real and the Drollery inevitable." In fact, Adams was so highly entertained that he seems to have misjudged His Excellency's willingness "to treat and make Peace," although he admitted that the sums demanded might be higher "than we can ven-

6. "Negotiations for a Treaty of Amity and Commerce with Portugal," *ibid.*, 410 ff; JA to TJ, June 29, 1786, Jan. 25, 1787, below, 138, 161-62.

7. JA to Franklin and TJ, March 20, 1785, above, 19-20.

8. "Documents Pertaining to the Mission of Barclay and Lamb to the Barbary States," Boyd, VIII, 610-24; Ray W. Irwin, *The Diplomatic Relations of the United States with the Barbary Powers, 1776-1816* (Chapel Hill, 1931), 26-32.

ture." [9] And so it turned out at the conference of the American commissioners with Abdurrahman in March. Perpetual peace was his objective, but at a price: "30,000 Guineas for his Employers and £3,000 for himself were the lowest terms ... and this must be paid in Cash on the delivery of the treaty signed by his sovereign." [10]

After Jefferson returned to France at the end of April, he resumed his correspondence with Adams, much of it concerned with the Barbary pirates whose measure they had taken in London. In Morocco the friendly overtures of the Emperor dating back to the American Revolution, the good offices of the Spanish government, and Barclay's diplomatic acumen brought about a treaty with most-favored-nation provisions, mutual immunity of citizens from seizure, and exchange of prisoners of war in lieu of enslavement. [11] In contrast to this significant achievement (the treaty was ratified by Congress in July 1786), the Algerian negotiations lagged and the American agent was apparently a Lamb among wolves. The Dey of Algiers, head of the most powerful of the Barbary states, "would not speake of Peace" to Lamb, except on his own terms. He demanded an extortionate price for a treaty and insisted on an additional $59,496 for the release of twenty-one Americans held as prisoners. [12] Although Lamb was evidently a clumsy negotiator and raised false hopes among the prisoners, Adams, who had no high opinion of him, admitted that under the circumstances a better qualified appointee would have accomplished no more. [13] When Barclay suggested that he proceed from Morocco to Algiers to try to work diplomatic persuasion on the Dey, Adams and Jefferson vetoed the proposal, the latter reluctantly. [14]

"Money and fear," Vergennes had warned Jefferson, "are the only two agents at Algiers," [15] but the American ministers could neither offer enough money to the pirates nor make any real threats against them. Faced with the humiliation of their country and outraged by this vaunted lawlessness in an age that talked much of the law of

9. JA to TJ, Feb. 17, 1786, above, 121-22. Congress had appropriated $80,000 for bargaining with *all* the Barbary states.

10. American Commissioners to John Jay, March 28, 1786, Boyd, IX, 358.

11. "Treaty with Morocco," *ibid.*, X, 419-26 and *n*.

12. Lamb to American Commissioners, May 20, 1786, *ibid.*, IX, 549-52; Irwin, *Diplomatic Relations with Barbary Powers*, Chap. III.

13. Richard O'Bryen and Others to TJ, June 8, 1786, Boyd, IX, 614-22; JA to TJ, Jan. 25, 1787, below, 162.

14. JA to TJ, Sept. 11, 1786, and TJ to JA, Sept. 26, 1786, below, 153, 154.

15. TJ to JA, May 30, 1786, below, 132-33.

nations and the rights of citizens, Adams and Jefferson were obliged at least to advise Congress on alternative courses to pursue. Perturbed by the pretensions of the Barbary powers "to make war upon Nations who had done them no Injury," Jefferson recommended retaliatory war against the Algerians as more honorable and cheaper in the long run; [16] indeed, he expressed confidence in a highly improbable confederation with Portugal and Naples to blockade the port of Algiers and effect a just peace. Thus it was Jefferson who advocated the beginning of an American navy. Adams would support it, but he took a more practical view, pointing out that war would have to be conducted "with Vigor" and expressing doubts that Congress would do so in its straitened financial condition. For the present, he concluded, the United States had better pay tribute money to save her Mediterranean trade.[17]

Although Jefferson deferred to Adams's judgment, he proceeded to open negotiations for payments to the Order of Mathurins in France, whose good works for centuries had consisted of collecting and disbursing funds for the release of prisoners from Mediterranean pirates. Here the practical-minded and humanitarian Virginian, fundamentally hostile to the priesthood, turned to one of its orders for help in a desperate situation. But the French Revolution dissolved the Mathurins before they could relieve the prisoners, who had to endure their sufferings until the treaty of 1796 between the United States and Algiers.[18]

The ironical aspect of the Algerine crisis was, of course, the willingness of Europeans to condone piracy on the false assumption that the trade of one nation profited from the destruction of the trade of another. The Barbary states were weak bullies whose strongest support came from the great powers. This support of depredation and extortion, of cruelty and inhumanity, casts a grim reflection on the Age of the Enlightenment and its darker corners.

16. American Commissioners to John Jay, March 28, 1786, Boyd, IX, 358; TJ to JA, July 11, 1786, below, 142-43.

17. JA to TJ, July 31, 1786, below, 146-47.

18. TJ to JA, Jan. 11, 1787, and JA to TJ, Jan. 25, 1787, below, 160, 161-62; TJ to John Jay, Feb. 1, 1787, Boyd, XI, 101-2; Irwin, *Diplomatic Relations with Barbary Powers*, 44-46, 74-75.

Jefferson to Adams

Paris May 11. 1786.

DEAR SIR

I do myself the honour of inclosing to you letters which came to hand last night from Mr. Lamb, Mr. Carmichael and Mr. Barclay. By these you will perceive that our peace is not to be purchased at Algiers but at a price far beyond our powers. What that would be indeed Mr. Lamb does not say, nor probably knows. But as he knew our ultimatum, we are to suppose from his letter that it would be a price infinitely beyond that. A reference to Congress seems hereon to be necessary. Till that can be obtained Mr. Lambe must be idle to Algiers, Carthagena or elsewhere. Would he not be better employed in going to Congress? They would be able to draw from him and Mr. Randall the information necessary to determine what they will do, and if they determine to negotiate, they can reappoint the same, or appoint a new negotiator, according to the opinion they shall form on their examination. I suggest this to you as my first thoughts; an ultimate opinion should not be formed till we see Mr. Randall, who may be shortly expected. In the mean time, should an opportunity occur, favour me with your ideas hereon, that we may be maturing our opinions. I send copies of these three letters to Mr. Jay by the packet which sails from l'Orient the 1st. day of the next month.

On my return to Paris the Imperial ambassador informed me he had received full powers for treating with us. I repeated to him the information that ours would expire the 12th. of this month. He said he supposed Congress would have no objections to renew them, proposed that I should write to them on the subject, and in the mean time desired our project and observed that we might be proceeding to arrange the treaty, so as that it should be ready for signature on the arrival of our powers. I gave him a copy of our project, in which, taking the Danish one for the ground work, I made the alterations noted on the within paper;[19] being such as had occurred and met our approbation during the Prussian, Tuscan and Portuguese negotiations. I write to Congress an information of what has passed, and in the mean time shall take no other step till you favor me with your opinion whether we should proceed to prepare terms according to Count Merci's proposition.

I inclose you a copy of the queries[20] of which I had put an illegible one into your hands when in London.

19. Enclosure printed in Boyd, IX, 507-9 and *n*.
20. Probably the queries respecting American trade with the French colonies, *ibid.*, 134.

I beg to leave to present my most friendly respects to the ladies, and to yourself assurances of the esteem with which I have the honor to be Dear Sir your most obedient and most humble servant,

TH: JEFFERSON

Adams to Jefferson

Grosvenor Square May 16. 1786

MY DEAR FRIEND

Mr. Smith, a Son of the Lady you Saw here, who is a Sister of our old Acquaintances the Rutledges, will deliver you this Letter. He goes to reside Sometime in France. Mr. Jay, in a Letter of the 7. of April, writes me "We are well, 'tho not officially informed, that all the States have granted the Impost to Congress, except New York, in whose Legislature there is a Strong Party, against it." And this is all his Letter contains.

New York, I think must Soon come in. If not, all the Blame of Consequences must rest upon her, and She will find the Burthen of it, heavier than the Impost.

I need not ask your Civilities to our young Countryman, who takes this from my dear Sir your Friend and Sert.,

JOHN ADAMS

Jefferson to Adams

Paris May 17. 1787 [i.e., 1786]

DEAR SIR

This will be handed you by young Monsieur de Tronchin, son to a gentleman of that name here who is minister for the republic of Geneva, resident at this court. The son is now in England as a traveller.[21] He is personally unknown to me; but what I hear of him from others, together with my acquaintance with, and respect for, his father, induces me to recommend him to your notice. I do this the rather as it is proposed that he shall finish his travels by a trip to America, where the father has in contemplation to procure an establishment for some of his family. I have

21. TJ suggested that William Stephens Smith might introduce Tronchin to John Trumbull, the young American painter. *Ibid.*, 545.

the honour to be with the greatest respect and esteem Dr. Sir your most obedient and most humble servt.,

TH: JEFFERSON

Adams to Jefferson

London May 23. 1786

DEAR SIR

I am honoured with yours of the 11th. with the enclosures from Mr. Lamb, Mr. Carmichael and Mr. Barclay. I am not surprized that Mr. Lamb has only discovered that our means are inadequate, without learning the Sum that would be Sufficient. Il faut marchander avec ces Gens la ["One must bargain with those people"]. They must be beaten down as low as possible. But We shall find at last the Terms very dear. The Algerines will never make Peace with us, untill We have Treaties finished with Constantinople, Tunis, Tripoli and Morocco. They always stand out the longest. Mr. Barclay will have no better fortune and I dont believe it worth while for him to wait a Moment to discover what sum will do.

I think with you, that it is best to desire Mr. Lamb immediately to return to Congress, and Mr. Randal too. It is Surprising that neither of them, has given Us more circumstantial Information, and that Mr. Randal has not come on to Paris and London. I think you will do well to write him to come forward without loss of time, and am glad You sent Copies of all the Letters to Mr. Jay. I concur with you entirely in the Propriety of your going on with the Comte de Merci, in the Negotiation and in transmitting to Congress the Plan you may agree upon,[22] that they may Send a new Commission if they judge proper.

I have a Letter from Mr. Randal at Madrid 4. May, but shall not answer it as I wish you to write in behalf of both of Us to return immediately to Paris and London. I have a Letter too from Isaac Stephens at Algiers the 15. of April. He Says the Price is 6000 Dollars for a Master, 4000 for a Mate, and 1500 for each Sailor. The Dey will not abate a 6d., he Says and will not have any Thing to Say about Peace with America. He Says "The People" i.e. the Sailors as I suppose, are carrying Rocks and Timber on their backs for nine miles out of the Country, over sharp Rocks and Mountains, That he has an Iron round his Leg, etc. He begs that We would pay the Money for their Redemption, without sending to Congress, but this is impossible. With great Regard I am sir your affectionate

JOHN ADAMS

22. For a commercial treaty with Emperor Joseph II.

Jefferson to Adams

Paris May 30. 1786.

DEAR SIR

In my letter of the 11th. instant I had the honour of inclosing you copies of letters relative to the Barbary affairs. Others came to hand three days ago, of some of which I now send you copies, and of the others the originals. By these you will perceive that Mr. Randall and Mr. Lamb were at Madrid, that the latter means to return to Alicant and send on a courier to us. Mr. Randall does not repeat that he shall come himself. When either he or the courier arrives we shall have information to decide on. But these papers have strengthened my idea of desiring them to repair to Congress. I am anxious to know your sentiments on this. These papers came in time for me to send copies to Mr. Jay by the packet which will sail from l'Orient the day after tomorrow.

The inclosed paper from the Academy of chirurgery was put into my hands to be forwarded to you. I have the honor to be with sentiments of the most perfect esteem and respect Dear Sir Your most obedient and most humble servt.,

TH: JEFFERSON

P.S. I shall be much obliged to Colo. Smith for a copy of the treaty with Portugal as soon as it is signed. I am of opinion we had better send Luzac a copy as soon as it is signed. What think you?

Jefferson to Adams

Paris May 30. 1786.

DEAR SIR

In my letter of this day I omitted to inform you that according to what we had proposed I have had a long consultation with the Count de Vergennes on the expediency of a Diplomatic mission to Constantinople. His information is that it will cost a great deal of money, as great presents are expected at that court and a great many claim them; and his opinion is that we shall not buy a peace one penny the cheaper at Algiers. He says that those people do indeed acknowlege a kind of vassalage to the Porte and avail themselves of it when there is any thing to be claimed; but regard it not at all when it subjects them to a duty; that money and fear are the two only agents at Algiers. He cited the example of Spain which tho under treaty with the Porte is yet obliged to buy a peace at Algiers at a most enormous price. This is the sum of his information. The Baron de Tott is gone to Flanders for the summer. I am with sincere respect and esteem Dr. Sir Your friend and servt,

TH: JEFFERSON

Adams to Jefferson

Grosvenor Square June 6. 1786

DEAR SIR

Yesterday I received your Favour of 30. May with its Inclosures. You have Since that day no doubt received my answer to yours of the 11th., in which I agreed perfectly with you in the Propriety of Sending Mr. Lamb to Congress without Loss of time. I am content to send Mr. Randal with him but had rather he Should come to you first and then to me, and embark in London after we shall have had opportunity from his Conversation to learn as much as we can.

The Comte de Vergennes is undoubtedly right in his Judgment that Avarice and Fear are the only Agents at Algiers, and that we shall not have Peace with them the cheaper, for having a Treaty with the Sublime Porte. But is he certain we can ever at any Price have Peace, with Algiers, unless we have it previously with Constantinople? And do not the Turks from Constantinople, send Rovers into the Mediterranean? And would not even Treaties of Peace with Tunis, Tripoli, Algiers and Morocco be ineffectual for the Security of our Mediterranean Trade, without a Peace with the Porte? The Porte is at present the Theater of the Politicks of Europe, and commercial Information might be obtained there.

The first Question is, what will it cost us to make Peace with all five of them? Set it if you will at five hundred Thousand Pounds Sterling, tho I doubt not it might be done for Three or perhaps for two.

The Second Question is, what Damage shall we suffer, if we do not treat.

Compute Six or Eight Per Cent Insurance upon all your Exports, and Imports. Compute the total Loss of all the Mediterranean and Levant Trade.

Compute the Loss of half your Trade to Portugal and Spain.

These computations will amount to more than half a Million sterling a year.

The third Question is what will it cost to fight them? I answer, at least half a Million sterling a year without protecting your Trade, and when you leave off fighting you must pay as much Money as it would cost you now for Peace.

The Interest of half a Million Sterling is, even at Six Per Cent, Thirty Thousand Guineas a year. For an Annual Interest of 30,000 £ st. then and perhaps for 15,000 or 10,000, we can have Peace, when a War would sink us annually ten times as much.

But for Gods Sake dont let us amuse our Countrymen with any further Projects of Sounding. We know all about it, as much ever we can know, untill we have the Money to offer. We know if we Send an Ambassador to Constantinople, he must give Presents. How much, the Comte de Vergennes can tell you better than any Man in Europe.

We are fundamentally wrong. The first Thing to be done is for Congress to have a Revenue. Taxes [and] Duties must be laid on by Congress or the Assemblies and appropriated to the Payment of Interest. The Moment this is done we may borrow a Sum adequate to all our Necessities. If it is not done in my Opinion you and I as well as every other Servant of the United States in Europe ought to go home, give up all Points, and let all our Exports and Imports be done in European Bottoms. My Indignation is roused beyond all Patience to see the People in all the United States in a Torpor, and see them a Prey to every Robber, Pirate and Cheat in Europe. Jews and Judaizing Christians are now Scheeming to buy up all our Continental Notes at two or three shillings in a Pound, in order to oblige us to pay them at twenty shillings a Pound. This will be richer Plunder than that of Algerines or Loyds Coffee House. My dear friend Adieu,

JOHN ADAMS

Jefferson to Adams

Paris June 16. 1786.

DEAR SIR

I inclose you the copy of a letter received from Mr. Barclay dated Cadiz May 23. by which you will perceive he was still on this side the Mediterranean. Has Mr. Lamb written to you? I hear nothing from him nor of him, since Mr. Carmichael's information of his arrival in Spain. Mr. Randall gave reason to expect that himself would come on. Yet neither himself nor any letters from him arrive. Perhaps they find conveyances for reporting to you the causes of their delay. I am anxious also to receive your opinion what is best to be done.

The Swedish Ambassador [Baron de Stael-Holstein] asked me some time ago to give him in writing my thoughts on the best method of rendering the island of St. Bartholomew useful in the commerce between Sweden and the U.S. He afterwards pressed this on me every time I saw him till I was obliged to do it. I gave it as my opinion that to render that island most instrumental to the commerce of Sweden and the U.S. and also most useful to Sweden in every other point of view, it should be made a free port without a single restriction. As he has pressed this matter so much, I suspect his court might have instructed him to do it, and might also direct their minister at London to get your opinion on the same point. This latter possibility induced me to trouble you with information of what had passed here.

I observe in the Leyden gazette of June 2. the extract of a letter dated Algiers Apr. 15. which says that on the 10th. of April an American vessel the Clementina Captain Palmer from Philadelphia was carried in there by a cruiser. There being other circumstances mentioned in the same letter relative to our affairs which I know to be true, I am afraid this capture is also true.

The king sets out on the 21st. inst. for Cherburg in order to animate by his notice the operations going on there. The Count d'Artois has lately been there. This is an astonishing effort of human industry. It is believed it will be among the best ports in the world and will contain the whole navy of France. Those threats of invasion on England heretofore made, may become real in a future war, besides the bridle which this fixes in the mouth of the Thames.

Present me affectionately to Mrs. and Miss Adams, assuring them of my friendly and respectful remembrance of them, and how much I regret that I am not of their party in visiting the gardens this summer; and accept yourself assurances of the esteem and regard with which I have the honor to be Dear Sir your most obedient humble servt,

TH: JEFFERSON

Jefferson to Adams

Paris June 23. 1786.

DEAR SIR

I hear of a conveyance which allows me but a moment to write to you. I inclose a copy of a letter from Mr. Lamb. I have written both to him and Mr. Randall agreeable to what we had jointly thought best. The

Courier de l'Europe gives us strange news of armies marching from the U.S. to take the posts from the English. I have received no public letters and not above one or two private ones from America since I had the pleasure of seeing you, so I am in the dark as to all these matters. I have only time left to address heaven with my good wishes for Mrs. Adams and Miss Adams, and to assure you of the sincere esteem with which I have the honour to be Dear Sir your most obedt. and most humble servt,

TH: JEFFERSON

Adams to Jefferson

London June 25. 1786

DEAR SIR

Last night I received yours of the 16. Mr. Lamb has not written to me. Mr. Randal I have expected every day, for a long time, but have nothing from him, but what you transmitted me. My opinion of what is best to be done, which you desire to know is, that Mr. Lamb be desired to embark immediately for New York, and make his Report to Congress and render his account, and that Mr. Randal be desired to come to you first and then to me, unless you think it better for him to embark with Lamb. It would be imprudent in us, as it appears to me to incurr any further Expence, by sending to Constantinople, or to Algiers, Tunis or Tripoli. It will be only so much Cash thrown away, and worse, because it will only increase our Embarrassment, make us and our Country ridiculous, and irritate the Appetite of these Barbarians already too greedy.—I have no News of the Clementine Captain Palmer.

The Sweedish Minister here [Baron de Nolken], has never asked me any Question concerning the Island of St. Bartholomew. I suspect there are not many confidential Communications made to him, from his Court; he has been here 20 or 30 years and has married an English Lady, and is a Fellow of the Royal Society. From these Circumstances he may be thought to be *too well* with the English. This is merely conjecture. Your Advice was the best that could be given.

The Kings Visit to Cherbourg will have a great Effect upon a Nation whose Ruling Passion is a Love of their Sovereign, and the Harbour may and will be of Importance. But the Expectation of an Invasion will do more than a Real one.

Mrs. Adams and *Mrs. Smith* [23] have taken a Tour to Portsmouth. We took Paines Hill in our Way out, and Windsor, in our Return; but the Country in general disappointed us. From Guilford to Portsmouth is an immense Heath. We wished for your Company, which would have added greatly to the Pleasure of the Journey. Pray have you visited the Gardens in France? How do you find them? Equal to the English? With great Regard I am dear Sir your Friend and humble Sert,

JOHN ADAMS

Adams to Jefferson

Grosvenor Square June 26. 1786

DEAR SIR

Sometime Since I received from Gov. Bowdoin some Papers relating to Alexander Gross, with an earnest desire that I would communicate them to the French Ambassador here. I did so and his Excellency was so good as to transmit them to the Comte De Vergennes. Mr. Bartholomy however advised me to write to you upon the Subject, that you might prevent it from being forgotten.

Inclosed is a Letter, which I received yesterday from Griffin Green at Rotterdam, with a Paper inclosed dated Dunkirk 15. June. 1786. relating to this unhappy Man. What can be done for his Relief I know not. Neither the Ransom Money nor the other Charges I Suppose can ever be paid, for Government never is expected to redeem such Hostages and his Relations are not able. If this is the Truth as I suppose it is, it would be better for the French Government and for the Persons interested, to set him at Liberty, than to keep him a Prisoner at Expence. [24]

Let me pray you to minute this affair among your Memorandums to talk of, with the Comte De Vergennes and Mr. Rayneval, when you are at Versailles. They will shew you the Papers, which have been transmitted them through the Comte D'Adhemar.

I wrote you on the 23d. of May ulto. and on the 6th. inst. which Letters I hope you have received. Yours,

JOHN ADAMS

23. Abigail Amelia Adams was married to Colonel William Stephens Smith on June 12, 1786, by the Bishop of St. Asaph. Janet Payne Whitney, *Abigail Adams* (Boston, 1947), 212-13; Edward E. Curtis, "Smith, William Stephens," *DAB*, XVII, 369.

24. The case of the unfortunate American seaman, Alexander Gross, is described in Robert Murdoch to TJ, June 29, 1786, Boyd, X, 79-80.

Adams to Jefferson

London June 29. 1786

DEAR SIR

Inclosed is a Letter to Mr. Lamb and another to Mr. Randall: [25] if you approve them please to Sign them and send them on. Why those Gentlemen have lingered in Spain I know not. I have long expected to hear of their Arrival in Paris. Possibly they wait for orders. If so, the inclosed will answer the End.

The Chev. De Pinto told me on Wednesday that he had orders from his Court to inform me, that the Queen had sent a Squadron to cruise in the Mouth of the Streights, and had given them orders to protect all Vessells belonging to the United States of America, against the Algerines equally with Vessells of her own Subjects. With much Affection yours,

JOHN ADAMS

Adams to Jefferson

London July 3. 1786.

DEAR SIR

Yours of the 23 of June is come to hand, with a Copy of Mr. Lambs of 6 June from Aranjuez.

There is no Intelligence from America of Armies marching to take the Posts from the English. The News was made as I Suppose against the opening of the Three Per Cents, and it had the intended Effect to beat down the Stocks a little.

Altho the Posts are important, the war with the Turks is more So. I lay down a few Simple Propositions.

1. We may at this Time, have a Peace with them, in Spight of all the Intrigues of the English or others to prevent it, for a Sum of Money.

2. We never Shall have Peace, though France, Spain, England and Holland Should use all their Influence in our favour without a Sum of Money.

25. American Commissioners to John Lamb, June 29, July 7, 1786, Boyd, X, 96-97; the letter to Randall was not forwarded because he arrived in Paris on July 2.

3. That neither the Benevolence of France nor the Malevolence of England will be ever able materially to diminish or Increase the Sum.

4. The longer the Negotiation is delayed, the larger will be the Demand.

From these Premisses I conclude it to be wisest for Us to negotiate and pay the necessary Sum, without Loss of Time. Now I desire you and our noble Friend the Marquis to give me your opinion of these four Propositions. Which of them do you deny? or doubt? If you admit them all do you admit the Conclusion? Perhaps you will Say, fight them, though it Should cost Us a great Sum to carry on the war, and although at the End of it we should have more Money to pay as presents. If this is your Sentiment, and you can persuade the Southern States into it, I dare answer for it that all from Pensylvania inclusively northward, would not object. It would be a good occasion to begin a Navy.

At present we are Sacrificing a Million annually to Save one Gift of two hundred Thousand Pounds. This is not good Œconomy. We might at this hour have two hundred ships in the Mediterranean, whose Freight alone would be worth two hundred Thousand Pounds, besides its Influence upon the Price of our Produce. Our Farmers and Planters will find the Price of their Articles Sink very low indeed, if this Peace is not made. The Policy of Christendom has made Cowards of all their Sailors before the Standard of Mahomet. It would be heroical and glorious in Us, to restore Courage to ours. I doubt not we could accomplish it, if we should set about it in earnest. But the Difficulty of bringing our People to agree upon it, has ever discouraged me.

You have Seen Mr. Randall before this no doubt, if he is not fallen Sick on the Road.

This Letter is intended to go by Mr. Fox. The Chev. De Pinto's Courier unfortunately missed a Packet, which delayed him and consequently the Treaty a Month. The Queen his Mistress, as I wrote you a few Days Since, has given orders to her Squadron cruising in the Streights to protect all Vessells belonging to the United States. This is noble and Deserves Thanks. Accept the Sincerest Assurances of Esteem and Affection from dear Sir your most obedient

JOHN ADAMS

Mrs. Adams having read this letter finds it deficient in not having added her best respects to Mr. Jefferson and sincere thanks for his petitions.[26]

26. Postscript in AA's hand.

Jefferson to Adams

Paris July 9. 1786.

DEAR SIR

I wrote you last on the 23d. of May.[27] Your favor of that date did not come to hand till the 19th. of June. In consequence of it I wrote the next day letters to Mr. Lamb and Mr. Randall, copies of which I have now the honour to inclose you. In these you will perceive I had desired Mr. Randall, who was supposed to be at Madrid, to return immediately to Paris and London, and to Mr. Lambe, supposed at Alicant, I recommended the route of Marseilles and Paris, expecting that no direct passage could be had from Alicant to America, and meaning on his arrival here to advise him to proceed by the way of London, that you also might have an opportunity of deriving from him all the information he could give. On the 2d. of July Mr. Randall arrived here and delivered me a letter from Mr. Lambe dated May 20. of which I inclose you a copy, as well as of another of June 5. which had come to hand some time before. Copies of these I have also sent to Mr. Jay. Yours of the 29th. of June by Dr. Bancroft and inclosing a draught of a joint letter to Mr. Lambe, came to hand on the 5th. inst. I immediately signed and forwarded it, as it left him more at liberty as to his route than mine had done. Mr. Randall will deliver you the present and supply the informations heretofore received. I think with you that Congress must begin by getting money. When they have this, it is a matter of calculation whether they will buy a peace, or force one, or do nothing.

I am also to acknolege the receipt of your favors of June 6. 25. and 26. The case of Grosse shall be attended to. I am not certain however whether my appearing in it may not do him harm by giving the captors a hope that our government will redeem their citizen. I have therefore taken measures to find them out and sound them. If nothing can be done privately I will endeavour to interest this government.

Have you no news yet of the treaty with Portugal? Does it hang with that court? My letters from N. York of the 11th. of May inform me that there were then 11. states present and that they should ratify the Prussian treaty immediately. As the time for exchange of ratifications is drawing to a close, tell me what is to be done, and how this exchange is to be made. We may as well have this settled between us before the arrival of the

27. TJ's last letter to JA is dated June 23; JA's letter to which he refers is dated May 23.

ratification, that no time may be lost after that. I learn through the Marechal de Castries that he has information of New York's having ceded the impost in the form desired by Congress, so as to close this business.[28] Corrections in the acts of Maryland, Pennsylvania, etc. will come of course. We have taken up again the affair of whale oil, that they may know in time in America what is to be done in it. I fear we shall not obtain any further abatement of duties; but the last abatement will be continued for three years. The whole duties paiable here are nearly 102 livres on the English ton, which is an atom more than four guineas according to the present exchange.

The monopoly of the purchase of tobacco for this country which had been obtained by Robert Morris had thrown the commerce of that article into agonies. He had been able to reduce the price in America from 40/ to 22/6 lawful the hundred weight, and all other merchants being deprived of that medium of remittance the commerce between America and this country, so far as it depended on that article, which was very capitally too, was absolutely ceasing. An order has been obtained obliging the farmers general to purchase from such other merchants as shall offer, 15,000 hogsheads of tobacco at 34, 36, and 38 livres the hundred according to the quality, and to grant to the sellers in other respects the same terms as they had granted to Robert Morris. As this agreement with Morris is the basis of this order I send you some copies of it [29] which I will thank you to give to any American (not British) merchants in London who may be in that line. During the year this contract has subsisted, Virginia and Maryland have lost 400,000 £ by the reduction of the price of their tobacco.

I am meditating what step to take to provoke a letter from Mrs. Adams, from whom my files inform me I have not received one these hundred years. In the mean time present my affectionate respects to her and be assured of the friendship and esteem with which I have the honour to be Dear Sir Your most obedient and most humble servt.,

Th: Jefferson

28. New York had rejected in effect the impost on May 4, 1786, by placing the collection and disposition of the funds in the hands of her own officers. On Feb. 15, 1787, the Assembly rejected the impost outright. Jensen, *New Nation*, 415-17.

29. Printed in Boyd, IX, 586-88

Jefferson to Adams

Paris July 11. 1786.

DEAR SIR

Our instructions relative to the Barbary states having required us to proceed by way of negotiation to obtain their peace, it became our duty to do this to the best of our power. Whatever might be our private opinions, they were to be suppressed, and the line marked out to us, was to be followed. It has been so honestly, and zealously. It was therefore never material for us to consult together on the best plan of conduct towards these states. I acknolege I very early thought it would be best to effect a peace thro' the medium of war. Tho' it is a question with which we have nothing to do, yet as you propose some discussion of it I shall trouble you with my reasons. Of the 4. positions laid down in your letter of the 3d. instant, I agree to the three first, which are in substance that the good offices of our friends cannot procure us a peace without paying it's price, that they cannot materially lessen that price, and that paying it, we can have the peace in spight of the intrigues of our enemies. As to the 4th. that the longer the negotiation is delayed the larger will be the demand, this will depend on the intermediate captures: if they are many and rich the price may be raised; if few and poor it will be lessened. However if it is decided that we shall buy a peace, I know no reason for delaying the operation, but should rather think it ought to be hastened. But I should prefer the obtaining it by war. 1. Justice is in favor of this opinion. 2. Honor favors it. 3. It will procure us respect in Europe, and respect is a safe-guard to interest. 4. It will arm the federal head with the safest of all the instruments of coercion over their delinquent members and prevent them from using what would be less safe. I think that so far you go with me. But in the next steps we shall differ. 5. I think it least expensive. 6. Equally effectual. I ask a fleet of 150. guns, the one half of which shall be in constant cruise. This fleet built, manned and victualled for 6. months will cost 450,000 £ sterling. It's annual expence is 300 £ sterl. a gun, including every thing: this will be 45,000 £ sterl. a year. I take British experience for the basis of my calculations, tho' we know, from our own experience, that we can do, in this way, for pounds lawful, what costs them pounds sterling. Were we to charge all this to the Algerine war it would amount to little more than we must pay if we buy peace. But as it is proper and necessary that we should establish a small marine force (even were we to buy a peace from the Algerines,) and as that force laid up in our dockyards would cost us half as much annually as if kept in order for service, we have a right to say that only 22,500 £ sterl. per ann. should be charged to the Algerine war. 6. It will be as effectual. To all the mismanagements of Spain and Portugal urged to shew that war against those people is ineffectual, I urge a single fact to prove the contrary where there is any management. About 40. year ago, the Algerines having broke their treaty with France, this court sent Monsr. de Massac with one large and two small frigates, he blockaded the harbour of Algiers three months, and they subscribed to the terms he dictated. If it be admitted however that war, on the fairest prospects, is still exposed to incertainties, I weigh against this the greater incertainty of the duration of a peace bought with money, from such a people, from a Dey 80. years old, and by a nation who, on the hypothesis of buying peace, is to have no power on the sea to enforce an observance of it.

So far I have gone on the supposition that the whole weight of this war would rest on us. But 1. Naples will join us. The character of their naval minister (Acton), his known sentiments with respect to the peace Spain is officiously trying to make for them, and his dispositions against the Algerines give the greatest reason to believe it. 2. Every principle of reason tells us Portugal will join us. I state this as taking for granted, what all seem to believe, that they will not be at peace with Algiers. I suppose then that a Convention might be formed between Portugal, Naples and the U.S. by which the burthen of the war might be quotaed on them according to their respective wealth, and the term of it should be when Algiers should subscribe to a peace with all three on equal terms. This might be left open for other nations to accede to, and many, if not most of the powers of Europe (except France, England, Holland and Spain if her peace be made) would sooner or later enter into the confederacy, for the sake of having their peace with the Pyratical states guarantied by the whole. I suppose that in this case our proportion of force would not be the half of what I first calculated on.

These are the reasons which have influenced my judgment on this question. I give them to you to shew you that I am imposed on by a semblance of reason at least, and not with an expectation of their changing your opinion. You have viewed the subject, I am sure in all it's bearings. You have weighed both questions with all their circumstances. You make the result different from what I do. The same facts impress us differently. This is enough to make me suspect an error in my process of reasoning tho' I am not able to detect it. It is of no consequence; as I have nothing to say in the decision, and am ready to proceed heartily on any other plan which may be adopted, if my agency should be thought useful. With respect to the dispositions of the states I am utterly uninformed. I cannot help thinking however that on a view of all circumstances, they might be united in either of the plans.

Having written this on the receipt of your letter, without knowing of any opportunity of sending it, I know not when it will go: I add nothing therefore on any other subject but assurances of the sincere esteem and respect with which I am Dear Sir your friend and servant,

TH: JEFFERSON

Adams to Jefferson

London July 16. 1786

DEAR SIR

Last night Mr. Randal arrived with yours of the 9th. If the Prussian Treaty arrives to you, I think you will do well to Send Mr. Short with it to the Hague and Exchange it with Thulemeier, and get it printed in a Pamphlet Sending a Sufficient Number to you and to me. If it comes to me and you approve, I will Send Some one or go myself.

The Chevr. De Pinto's Courier unfortunately missed a Packet by one Day, which obliged him to wait a month at Falmouth for another. The Chevalier was greatly chagrined at the Delay. He is much obliged for your Notes, and I Should be more so for another Copy, having Sent mine to my Brother Cranch, who writes me that your Argument in favour of American Genius, would have been much Strengthened, if a Jefferson had been Added to a Washington, a Franklin and a Rittenhouse. I wrote you lately that the Queen of Portugal had ordered her Fleet cruising in the Streights to protect all Vessells belonging to American Citizens equally with those of her own Subjects against the Algerines.

Boylstons Vessell Arrived in Boston, with Sugars, and he expects another Vessell hourly, with which he will go again to France. He desires me, to express his obligations to you and the Marquis, for your former Assistance. Coffin Jones has Sent a Vessell to L'Orient, with another Cargo of oil. The French Government would do well to encourage that Trade. If they do not, it will go elsewhere. It is in vain for French or English to think, that Sperma Cæti oil cannot find a Market but in their Territories. It may find a Market in every City that has dark nights, if any one will do as Boylston did, go and shew the People its qualities by Samples and Experiments. The Trade of America in oil and in any Thing else will labour no longer, than public Paper is to be sold under Par. While a Bit of Paper can be bought for five shillings that is worth twenty, all Capitals will be employed in that Trade, for it is certain there is no other that will yeild four hundred Per Cent Profit, clear of Charges and Risques.

As soon as this lucrative Commerce shall cease We shall see American Capitals employed in sending all where it will find a Market, that is all over Europe if France does not wisely monopolise it as she may, if she will. Inclosed is an oration of Dr. Rush. I am my dear Sir, your most obedient

JOHN ADAMS

Abigail Adams to Jefferson

London july 23. 1786

DEAR SIR

Mr. Trumble will have the honour of delivering this to you. The knowledge you have of him, and his own merit will ensure him a favourable reception. He has requested a Letter from me, and I would not refuse him, as it gives me an opportunity of paying my respects to a Gentleman for whom I entertain the highest esteem, and whose portrait dignifies a part of our room, tho it is but a poor substitute for those pleasures which we enjoy'd some months past.[30]

We console ourselves however by the reflection which tends to mollify our grief for our [depar]ted Friends; that they are gone to a better Country, an[d to a] Society more congenial to the benevolence of their minds.

I Supposed Sir that Col. Smith was your constant correspondent, and that his attention, left me nothing to inform you of. This Country produced nothing agreeable and our own appears to be takeing a Nap, as several vessels have lately arrived without a scrip, from any creature. By one of the papers we learn that Col. Humphries was safely arrived.

Perhaps neither of the Gentlemen may think to acquaint you, that the Lords of the admiralty have orderd home Captain Stanhopes Ship, and calld upon him for a justification of his conduct to Govenour Bowdoin, that having received what he offerd as such, they voted it not only unsatisfactory, but his conduct highly reprehensible. As such they have represented it to his Majesty, and Captain Stanhope will not be permitted to return to that Station again. Thus far we must give them credit.

30. The portrait of TJ by Mather Brown, painted during March-April 1786. See Vol. II, frontispiece, of the present work.

I suppose you must have heard the report respecting Col. Smith—that he has taken my daughter from me, a contrivance between him and the Bishop of St. Asaph. It is true he tenderd me a son as an equivilent and it was no bad offer. But I had three Sons before, and but one daughter. Now I have been thinking of an exchange with you Sir. Suppose you give me Miss Jefferson, and in some [fu]ture day take a Son in lieu of her. I am for Strengthening [the] federal union.

Will you be so good as to let petite apply to my shoe maker for 4 pr. of silke shoes for me. I would have them made with straps, 3 pr. of summer silke and one pr. blew sattin. Col. Trumble will deliver you a guiney for them. Whenever I can be of service to you here, pray do not hessitate to commission me. Be assured you confer a favour upon your Humble Servant,

A ADAMS

Adams to Jefferson

London July 31. 1786

DEAR SIR

I have received the Ratification of the Prussian Treaty, and next Thursday Shall Sett off for the Hague in order to exchange it with the Baron De Thulemeyer.

Your favour of the 11th. instant I have received. There are great and weighty Considerations urged in it in favour of arming against the Algerines, and I confess, if our States could be brought to agree in the Measure, I Should be very willing to resolve upon eternal War with them. But in Such a Case We ought to conduct the War with Vigour, and protect our Trade and People. The Resolution to fight them would raise the Spirits and Courage of our Countrymen immediately, and we might obtain the Glory of finally breaking up these nests of Banditti. But Congress will never, or at least not for years, take any such Resolution, and in the mean time our Trade and Honour suffers beyond Calculation. We ought not to fight them at all, unless we determine to fight them forever.

This thought is I fear, too rugged for our People to bear. To fight them at the Expence of Millions, and make Peace after all by giving more Money and larger Presents than would now procure perpetual Peace Seems not to be Œconomical.—Did Monsieur De Massac carry his Point without making the Presents? Did Louis 14. obtain his Point without making the Presents? Has not France made Presents ever Since? Did any

Nation ever make Peace with any one Barbary State, without making the Presents? Is there one Example of it? I believe not, and fancy you will find that even Massac himself made the Presents.

I agree in opinion of the Wisdom and Necessity of a Navy for other Uses, but am apprehensive it will only make bad worse with the Algerines. I will go all Lengths with you in promoting a Navy, whether to be applied to the Algerines or not. But I think at the Same time We should treat. Your Letter however has made me easier upon this Point.—Nevertheless I think you have rather undercalculated the Force necessary to humble the Algerines. They have now fifty Gun Boats, which being Small objects in Smooth Water, against great Ships in rough Water are very formidable. None of these existed in the time of Monsieur Massac. The Harbour of Algiers too is fortified all round, which it was not in Mr. Massac's time, which renders it more difficult and dangerous to attempt a Blockade.

I know not what dependence is to be had upon Portugal and Naples, in Case of a War with the Barbarians. Perhaps they might assist us in some degree.

Blocking Algiers would not obtain Peace with Morocco Tunis or Tripoli, so that our Commerce would still be exposed.

After all, tho I am glad We have exchanged a Letter upon the subject, I percieve that neither Force nor Money will be applied. Our States are so backward that they will do nothing for some years. If they get Money enough to discharge the Demands upon them in Europe, already incurred, I shall be agreably disappointed. A Disposition Seems rather to prevail among our Citizens to give up all Ideas of Navigation and naval Power, and lay themselves consequently at the Mercy of Foreigners, even for the Price of their Produce. It is their Concern, and We must submit, for your Plan of fighting will no more be adopted than mine of negotiating. This is more humiliating to me, than giving the Presents would be. I have a Letter from Mr. Jay of 7. July, by Packet, containing nothing but an Acknowledgment of the Receipt [of] our Letter of 25. of April.

N. Hampshire and R. Island have suspended their Navigation Acts and Massachusetts now left alone will suspend theirs, so that all will be left to the Convention, whose system, if they form one, will not be compleated, adopted and begin to operate under Several Years.

Congress have received the Answer which you saw, to my Memorial of 30 Nov.[31] and Mr. Ramsay writes me, he is not distressed at it, because it will produce a repeal of all the Laws, against recovering private Debts. With every Sentiment of Friendship I am yours,

JOHN ADAMS

31. "A Memorial from Mr. Adams respecting the Evacuation of the Posts, etc.," Nov. 30, 1785, *Diplomatic Correspondence, 1783-1789*, II, 542-43.

Jefferson to Adams

Paris Aug. 8. 1786.

DEAR SIR

Your favour of July 16. came duly to hand by Mr. Trumbul. With respect to the whale oil, tho' this country has shewn a desire to draw it hither, and for that purpose have reduced the duties to about four guineas on the English ton, yet I do not see a probability of a further reduction at this moment. It has been much pressed, and I expect every day to receive a final determination. Should it not be obtained now we have reason to expect some years hence an abatement of one third, as a promise was given to the people that the imposition of 10. sous per livre should not be renewed at the expiration of the term for which it was laid on, which will be about half a dozen years hence. I inclose you copies of letters received from Mr. Carmichael, O'Brian, and Lamb. Be so good as to say what answer we shall give the last about his settlement.[32] Shall we undertake the settlement? If so, where shall it be done? I will join in any thing you please as to this. Taking for granted, from a message delivered by Mr. Trumbul, that you are now in Holland, I will only add a request to send me some copies of the ratified treaty with Prussia (which will be I hope in both languages,) and assurances of the sincere esteem and respect with which I have the honour to be Dear Sir your most obedt. humble servt.,

TH: JEFFERSON

Jefferson to Abigail Adams

Paris Aug. 9. 1786.

DEAR MADAM

It is an age since I have had the honor of a letter from you, and an age and a half since I presumed to address one to you. I think my last was dated in the reign of king Amri, but under which of his successors you

32. Lamb wrote to TJ from Alicante, Spain, July 18, 1786, that because his "Indisposition" would not permit him to travel further, he must "begg a Settlement of my Reasonable Accounts Since I have been on this Journey...." He also desired to defend himself against accusations by "Gentelmen on my mission ... [who] knowd nothing of my business in Algiers and of Course Could not write the Truth." Boyd, X, 151-52.

wrote, I cannot recollect. Ochosias, Joachar, Manahem or some such hard name. At length it is resumed: I am honoured with your favor of July 23. and I am at this moment writing an answer to it. And first we will dispatch business. The shoes you ordered, will be ready this day and will accompany the present letter. But why send money for them? You know the balance of trade was always against me. You will observe by the inclosed account that it is I who am to export cash always, tho' the sum has been lessened by the bad bargains I have made for you and the good ones you have made for me. This is a gaining trade, and therefore I shall continue it, begging you will send no more money here. Be so good as to correct the inclosed that the errors of that may not add to your losses in this commerce. You were right in conjecturing that both the gentlemen might forget to communicate to me the intelligence about Captn. Stanhope. Mr. Adams's head was full of whale oil, and Colo. Smith's of German politics (—but don't tell them this—) so they left it to you to give me the news. De tout mon coeur, I had rather receive it from you than them. This proposition about the exchange of a son for my daughter puzzles me. I should be very glad to have your son, but I cannot part with my daughter. Thus you see I have such a habit of gaining in trade with you that I always expect it.—We have a blind story here of somebody attempting to assassinate your king. No man upon earth has my prayers for his continuance in life more sincerely than him. He is truly the American Messias. The most precious life that ever god gave, and may god continue it. Twenty long years has he been labouring to drive us to our good, and he labours and will labour still for it if he can be spared. We shall have need of him for twenty more. The Prince of Wales on the throne, Lansdowne and Fox in the ministry, and we are undone! We become chained by our habits to the tails of those who hate and despise us. I repeat it then that my anxieties are all alive for the health and long life of the king. He has not a friend on earth who would lament his loss so much and so long as I should. —Here we have singing, dauncing, laugh, and merriment. No assassinations, no treasons, rebellions nor other dark deeds. When our king goes out, they fall down and kiss the earth where he has trodden: and then they go to kissing one another. And this is the truest wisdom. They have as much happiness in one year as an Englishman in ten.—The presence of the queen's sister enlivens the court. Still more the birth of the princess. There are some little bickerings between the king and his parliament, but they end with a sic volo, sic jubeo ["as I wish, so I rejoice"]. The bottom of my page tells me it is time for me to end with assurances of the affectionate esteem with which I have the honor to be, dear Madam, your most obedient and most humble servant,

TH: JEFFERSON

Mrs. Adams to Th:J.   Dr.

1785. June	2.	To paid Petit	173^{tt} - 8s
Aug.	17.	To pd. Mr. Garvey's bill	96 -16 - 6
Nov.		To cash by Colo. Smith	768 - 0 - 0
1786. Jan.	5.	To pd. Bazin for Surtout de dessert and figures etc.	264 -17 - 6
Feb.	27.	To pd. for shoes for Miss Adams	24 -
Mar.	5.	To pd. for sundries viz.	

12. aunes de dentelle	96.^{tt}	
une paire de barbes	36.	
4. aunes of cambric	92.	
4. do.	60.	284 - 0 - 0

(reckoning 24. livres at 20/ sterl.)   1611 - 2 - 0 being £67- 2- 7 ster

Mar. 9. To balance expences of journey
between Mr. Adams and myself   8- 9- 4½
                                                    75-11-11½

Cr.

1785 Oct.	12.	By pd. insurance on Houdon's life	£32-11s- od
1786 Jan.	10.	By damask table cloth and napkins	7 - 0 - 0
		2. pr. nutcrackers	4 - 0

2 peices Irish linen
@ 4/   £8 -14s
making 12. shirts   1 -16
buttons, thread, silk   3
washing   3 -6
a trunk   1 - 1   11-17 - 6

Apr.	9.	By pd. for 9 yds. of muslin @ 11/	4-19 - 0
	12.	By do. for 21 yds. Chintz @ 5/6	5-15 - 6

By pd. for 25 yds.
linen @ 4/   £5. ⎫
for making 7. shirts   1-6-6 ⎬ for Mr. Short   6- 6 - 6
                                  ⎭
By pd. for altering 12. shirts   6 - 6
Balance   6-11 -11½
                                                    75-11 -11½

Jefferson to Adams

Paris Aug. 13. 1786.

DEAR SIR

The inclosed came to hand this morning. Mr. Carmichael you observe, and Mr. Barclay suppose something may yet be done at Algiers. It remains for us to consider whether the conduct of the Dey of that country leaves any room to hope that any negotiator can succeed without a great addition to the price to which we are confined? And should we think in the negative, yet whether the expences of Mr. Barclay's going there may not be compensated by additional information, by the possibility that he may get at their ultimatum, by the importance of possessing Congress of this ultimatum, that knowing their ground, they may not suspend a decision. Spain having made it's peace with Algiers, we may see whether their interference can count as money, as it has done at Marocco. Hostilities too may possibly be suspended or slackened a while longer. These are all chances on which I acknolege I build very little; yet as nothing weighs against them but the expence of Mr. Barclay's journey, they might be tried. If you are of that opinion, send me the necessary papers for Mr. Barclay ready signed by you, and I will sign them and forward them.— There is lodged in Mr. Grand's hands money enough to support the diplomatic establishment of our country in Europe three months, on which your draughts and Colo. Smith's shall be honoured if you think proper to make them. I am with sincere esteem Dear Sir, your friend and servt.,

TH: JEFFERSON

Jefferson to Adams

Paris Aug. 27. 1786.

DEAR SIR

Your favour of July 31. was lately delivered me. The papers inform me you are at the Hague, and, incertain what stay you may make there, I send this by Mr. Voss who is returning to London by the way of Amsterdam. I inclose you the last letters from Mr. Barclay and Mr. Carmichael, by which we may hope our peace with Marocco is signed, thanks to the good offices of a nation which is honest, if it is not wise.[33] This event with the naval cruises of Portugal will I hope quiet the Atlantic for us. I am informed by authority to be depended on, that insurance is made at Lorient, on American vessels sailing under their own flag, against every event, at the price usually paid for risks of the sea alone. Still however the most important of our marts, the Mediterranean, is shut. I wrote you a proposition to accept Mr. Barclay's offer of going to Algiers. I have no hope of it's making peace; but it may add to our information, abate the ardor of those pyrates against us, and shut the mouths of those who might impute our success at Marocco and failure at Algiers to a judicious appointment to the one place and an injudicious one at the other. Let me hear from you as soon as possible on this, and if you accede to it send me all the necessary

33. Spain, whose foreign minister, Count Floridablanca, had encouraged Barclay and promised to provide him with a letter from the King of Spain to the Emperor of Morocco. Barclay to TJ, March 23, 1786, *ibid.*, IX, 352.

papers ready signed. I inclose you the article 'Etats Unis' of one of the volumes of the Encyclopedie, lately published.[34] The author, M. de Meusnier, was introduced to me by the D. de la Rochefoucault. He asked of me information on the subject of our states, and left with me a number of queries to answer. Knowing the importance of setting to rights a book so universally diffused and which will go down to late ages, I answered his queries as fully as I was able, went into a great many calculations for him, and offered to give further explanations where necessary. He then put his work into my hands. I read it, and was led by that into a still greater number of details by way of correcting what he had at first written,[35] which was indeed a mass of errors and misconceptions from beginning to end. I returned him his work and my details; but he did not communicate it to me after he had corrected it. It has therefore come out with many errors which I would have advised him to correct, and the rather as he was very well disposed. He has still left in a great deal of the Abbé Raynal, that is to say a great deal of falsehood, and he has stated other things on bad information. I am sorry I had not another correction of it. He has paid me for my trouble, in the true coin of his country, most unmerciful compliment. This, with his other errors, I should surely have struck out had he sent me the work, as I expected, before it went to the press. I find in fact that he is happiest of whom the world sais least, good or bad.—I think if I had had a little more warning, my desire to see Holland, as well as to meet again Mrs. Adams and yourself, would have tempted me to take a flying trip there. I wish you may be tempted to take Paris in your return. You will find many very happy to see you here, and none more so than, Dear Sir, your friend and servant,

Th: Jefferson

Adams to Jefferson

Grosvenor Square Septr. 11. 1786.

Dear Sir

On my Return from Holland on the Sixth instant I found your Favours of the 8. and 13. Aug. On my Arrival at the Hague The Exchange of Ratifications was made on the 8. of August with The Baron De Thulemeier, and I had it Printed. It is only in French. Copies shall be Sent you

34. *Encyclopédie Méthodique* (1782-1833).
35. "The Article on the United States in the *Encyclopédie Méthodique*" (including TJ's answers to Démeunier's queries and his observations on Démeunier's manuscript), Boyd, X, 3-65.

as soon as I can find an Opportunity. We were present at Utrecht at the August Ceremony of Swearing in their new Magistrates. In no Instance, of ancient or modern History, have the People ever asserted more unequivocally their own inherent and unalienable Sovereignty.—But whatever Pleasure I might have in enlarging upon this Subject, I must forbear.

The Affair of Oil has taken a turn here. The Whale men both at Greenland and the southward, have been unsuccessful and the Price of Spermacæti Oil, has risen above fifty Pounds a Ton. Boy[l]ston's ship arrived with two or three hundred Ton, and finding he could pay the Duties and make a Profit of five and twenty Per Cent, he sold his Cargo here, instead [of] going again to France as he intended. This Circumstance will oblige the French Court, or the French Merchants or both to take other Measures, or they will loose this Trade. The Price of Oil will rise in Boston, so much that I am afraid Mr. Barrett's Contract must be fullfilled at an immense Loss.

As to Mr. Lambs Settlement, I still think he had better embark forthwith for New York from Spain. If he cannot he may transmit to you and me his Account, and remit to us the Ballance in favour of U.S.

Mr. Barclays Proposal, of going to Tunis and Tripoli, I suppose appears to you as it does to me, from what We learned from the Ambassador from Tripoli in London, to be unnecessary, at least till We hear farther from Congress. It seems to me too, very unlikely that any Benefit will be had from a Journey to Algiers. I wish to see the Treaty with Morocco, and to know the Particulars of that Affair, first. At present I believe We are taken in, and that We shall be plagued with Demands for annual Presents. I confess, I have no Faith in the Supposition that Spanish Interference has counted for Money, or at least that it will pass long for it.

If however you are clearly in favour of sending Mr. Barclay to Algiers, I will make out a Commission, and send it to you, for your Signature, Signed by my self, because I would not set up my own Judgment against yours, Mr. Carmichaels and Mr. Barclays: but I confess, at present I cannot see any Advantage in it, but on the contrary Several Disadvantages. Mr. Randall is gone to Congress, and We may expect their further orders, e'er long. With Sincere Affection I am, dear sir, your Friend and servant,

JOHN ADAMS

Inclosed is a Project of an Answer to Mr. Lamb,[36] if you approve it, you will sign and send it.

J.A.

36. Advising Lamb to "return to Congress for their further instructions as soon as possible, and...to embark from Spain by the first opportunity." American Commissioners to Lamb, [Sept. 26, 1786], *ibid.*, 407.

Jefferson to Adams

Paris Septr. 26th. 1786.

DEAR SIR

My last letter to you was dated the 27th. of August since which I have recieved yours of Sep. 11th. The letter to Mr. Lamb therein inclosed I immediately signed and forwarded. In mine wherein I had the honor of proposing to you the mission of Mr. Barclay to Algiers, I mentioned that my expectations from it were of a subordinate nature only. I very readily therefore recede from it in compliance with your judgment that this mission might do more harm than good. I accordingly wrote to Mr. Barclay that he was at liberty to return to this place, to London or to America, as he should think best. I now inclose you copies of such letters from him, Mr. Lamb and Mr. Carmichael as have come to hand since my last to you. I have had opportunities of making further enquiry as to the premium of insurance at L'Orient for Vessels bound to or from America, and I find that no additional premium is there required on account of the risque of capture by the Barbary States. This fact may be worth mentioning to American merchants in London.

We have been continually endeavoring to obtain a reduction of the duties on American whale oil: the prospect was not flattering. I shall avail myself of the information contained in your letter to press this matter further. Mr. Barrett is arrived here, and the first object for his relief is to obtain a dissolution of his former contract.

I will thank you for some copies of the Prussian treaty by the first opportunity and take the liberty of troubling you to forward the packets of letters which Mr. Smith the bearer of this will have the honor of delivering to you. I beg the favor of you to present my most respectful compliments to Mrs. Adams, and to be assured yourself of the sentiments of sincere esteem and respect with which I have the honor to be dear Sir, Your most obedient and humble Servant,

WSHORT FOR TH. JEFFERSON [37]

37. Letter and signature in Short's hand; TJ had dislocated his right wrist on Sept. 18. L. H. Butterfield, in *Wm. and Mary Quart.*, 3d ser., 5 (1948), 620-21.

Jefferson to Adams

Paris Octr. 23d. 1786

DEAR SIR

Your favor of Sept. the 11th. came to hand in due time and since that I have recieved the copies of the Prussian treaty you were so kind as to send me. I have recieved a short letter from Mr. Barclay dated Cadiz Septr. 25th. only announcing his arrival there and that he should proceed immediately to Madrid. At this latter place he would meet my letter informing him that we did not propose any thing further with the Piratical states at this time. The inclosed extract of a letter from Mr. Carmichael also mentions Mr. Barclay's arrival at Cadiz. A letter from Mr. Carmichael some time ago informed me that a bill had been drawn on him by Mrs. Lamb in America, by order as she said of Mr. Lamb; This gentleman not proposing to proceed either to New-York, London, or Paris to settle his accounts, I desired Mr. Carmichael, if any money remained yet in the hands of Mr. Lamb's banker at Madrid, to obstruct it's going out until he could give us information. His answer was that it was all withdrawn by Mr. Lamb. By some means or other I omitted to mention these circumstances to you at the time. I mention them now to explain the reasons of Mr. Carmichael's touching on that subject in the inclosed. We may now hourly expect from Mr. Barclay a copy of the preliminary treaty with Morocco. Is it your opinion that the definitive one [38] should be executed through his agency, or that of Colo. Franks or of any other person? I beg you to present my most friendly respects to Mrs. Adams and to be assured yourself of the esteem and attachment with which I have the honor to be Sir, your most obedient humble Servant,

TH: JEFFERSON

Jefferson to Adams

Paris Oct. 27. 1786.

DEAR SIR

I formerly had the honour of mentioning to you the measures I had taken to have our commerce with this country put on a better footing; and you know the circumstances which had occasioned the articles of whale oil and tobacco to be first brought forward. Latterly we got the

38. "Treaty with Morocco," text and notes, Boyd, X, 419-27.

committee, which had been established for this purpose, to take up the other articles, and on their report the King and council have come to the decisions explained in the inclosed letter from M. de Calonnes to me. The abandonment of revenues raised on articles of *importation* shews a friendly disposition. I have had thro this business a most zealous, and powerful auxiliary in the M. de La fayette, by whose activity it has been sooner and better done than I could otherwise possibly have expected. Tho you are free to shew the inclosed letter as you please, I would wish it to be kept out of the public papers two or three months. I am Dear Sir your affectionate friend and servant,

TH: JEFFERSON [39]

Adams to Jefferson

Grosvenor Square Nov. 30th. 1786

DEAR SIR

By Dr. Gibbon a young Gentleman of Philadelphia whom I beg Leave to introduce to you, I have the Honour to send you a few more Copies of the Prussian Treaty; and to inclose in this, a Resolution of Congress of September 26. annulling Mr. Lambs Commission and Instructions. Mr. Jay desires me to transmit it to him, and although I hope Mr. Lamb is on his Passage to New York or already arrived there, it is proper to send it along to Mr. Carmichael who will be so good as to convey it, if Mr. Lamb should not be departed. The favour of transmitting it to him let me ask of you.

You ask me in your last Letter my opinion who should be sent to exchange the Treaty with Morocco? I am content that either Mr. Barclay or Mr. Franks should go, or to leave it to Mr. Barclay to go in Person or send Mr. Franks as you shall judge best. But I wonder the Treaty has not arrived, to you.

Dont be allarmed at the late Turbulence in New England.[40] The Massachusetts Assembly had, in its Zeal to get the better of their Debt, laid on a Tax, rather heavier than the People could bear; but all will be well, and this Commotion will terminate in additional Strength to Government.

With great and Sincere Esteem, I have the Honour to be, Sir your most obedient and humble Servant,

JOHN ADAMS

39. Written with TJ's left hand.
40. Shays's Rebellion. See below, Chap. 5.

Jefferson to Abigail Adams

Paris [Nov. 1786]

DEAR MADAM

I am never happier than when I am performing good offices for good people; and the most friendly office one can perform is to make worthy characters acquainted with one another. The good things of this life are scattered so sparingly in our way that we must glean them up as we go. Yourself and Madame de Corny then must avail yourselves of the short time she will remain in London to make each other happy. A good heart and a good head will ensure her a place in your esteem. I have promised it to her: and she has yet a better title, a high respect for your character. I asked her to carry me in her pocket, that I might have the pleasure of bringing you together in person; but on examining the treaty of commerce, she found I should be contraband; that there might be a search—and seizure—and that the case would admit very specially of embarras. So instead of my having the honour of presenting her to you, she will have that of putting this into your hands, and of giving you assurances of her esteem and respect, with which permit me to mingle those of, dear Madam, your most obedient and most humble servant,

TH: JEFFERSON

Jefferson to Adams

Paris Dec. 20. 1786.

DEAR SIR

Colo. Franks will have the honor of delivering you the treaty with the emperor of Marocco, and all it's appendages. You will perceive by Mr. Barclay's letters that it is not necessary that any body should go back to Marocco to exchange ratifications. He sais however that it will be necessary that Fennish receive some testimony that we approve the treaty: and as, by the acts of Congress, our signature is necessary to give validity to it, I have had duplicates of ratification prepared, which I have signed, and now send you. If you approve and sign them send one back to me to be forwarded to Fennish thro' Mr. Carmichael. Perhaps a joint letter should be written to Fennish; if you think so, be so good as to write and sign one and send it with the ratification and I will sign and forward it. The other ratification is to go to Congress. Colo. Franks wishes to proceed with the papers to that body. He should do it I think immediately, as Mr. Jay in a letter to me of Oct. 26. says that Congress have heard thro' the French Chargé des affaires that the treaty was signed, and they wonder they have not heard it from us.

I inclose you a copy of a letter from Mr. Lamb: by which you will perceive he does not propose to quit Alicant. I will forward the resolution of Congress to Mr. Carmichael which was inclosed of yours of Nov. 30. to see if that will move him. As the turn of this resolution admits a construction that Congress may think our original appointment of him censurable, I have, as in justice I ought, in a letter to Mr. Jay, taken on myself the blame of having proposed him to you, if any blame were due. I have inclosed him a copy of my letter to you of Sep. 24. 1785. Mr. Barclay has proposed to go to Alicant to settle Lamb's accounts, and has asked to be strengthened with our authority. If Lamb will obey the resolve of Congress it will be better to let him go and settle his account there. But if he will not go back, perhaps it might not be amiss for Mr. Barclay to have instructions from us to require a settlement, those instructions to be used in that case only. If you think so, be so good as to write a joint letter and send it to me. But this, if done at all, should be done immediately. How much money has Lamb drawn?—I have suggested to Mr. Jay the expediency of putting the Barbary business into Carmichael's hands, or sending some body from America, in consideration of our separate residence and our distance from the scene of negociation.

I had seen, without alarm, accounts of the disturbances in the East. But Mr. Jay's letter on the subject had really affected me. However yours sets me to rights. I can never fear that things will go far wrong where common sense has fair play. I but just begin to use my pen a little with my right hand, but with pain. Recommending myself therefore to the friendship of Mrs. Adams I must conclude here with assurances of the sincere esteem of Dr. Sir your friend and servant,

TH: JEFFERSON

Should a Mr. Maury of Virginia, but now a merchant of Liverpool, present himself to you, I recommend him to your notice as my old school-fellow, and a man of the most solid integrity.

Jefferson to Abigail Adams

Paris Dec. 21. 1786.

DEAR MADAM

An unfortunate dislocation of my right wrist has for three months deprived me of the honor of writing to you. I begin now to use my pen a little, but it is in great pain, and I have no other use of my hand. The swelling has remained obstinately the same for two months past, and the joint, tho I beleive well set, does not become more flexible. I am strongly advised to go to some mineral waters at Aix in Provence, and I have it in contemplation.—I was not alarmed at the humor shewn by your country-men. On the contrary I like to see the people awake and alert. But I received a letter which represented it as more serious than I had thought. Mr. Adams however restores my spirits; I believe him and I thank him for it. The good sense of the people will soon lead them back, if they have erred in a moment of surprize.—My friends write me that they will send my little daughter [41] to me by a Vessel which sails in May for England. I have taken the liberty to tell them that you will be so good as to take her under your wing till I can have notice to send for her, which I shall do express in the moment of my knowing she is arrived. She is about 8. years old, and will be in the care of her nurse, a black woman, to whom she is confided with safety. I knew your goodness too well to scruple the giving this direction before I had asked your permission. I beg you to accept assurances of the constant esteem with which I have the honor to be Dear Madam your most obedient and most humble servt.,

TH: JEFFERSON

Jefferson to Adams

Paris Jan. 11. 1787

DEAR SIR

Mr. Jay, in his last letter to me, observes that they hear nothing further of the treaty with Portugal. I have taken the liberty of telling him that I will write to you on the subject, and that he may expect to hear from you

41. Mary ("Polly") Jefferson (b, Aug. 1, 1778).

on it by the present conveyance. The Chevalier del Pinto being at London, I presume he has, or can inform you why it is delayed on their part. I will thank you also for the information he shall give you.

There is here an order of priests called the Mathurins, the object of whose institution is the begging of alms for the redemption of captives. About 18. months ago they redeemed 300, which cost them about 1500 livres a peice. They have agents residing in the Barbary states, who are constantly employed in searching and contracting for the captives of their nation, and they redeem at a lower price than any other people can. It occurred to me that their agency might be engaged for our prisoners at Algiers. I have had interviews with them, and the last night a long one with the General of the order. They offer their services with all the benignity and cordiality possible. The General told me he could not expect to redeem our prisoners as cheap as their own, but that he would use all the means in his power to do it on the best terms possible, which will be the better as there shall be the less suspicion that he acts for our public. I told him I would write to you on the subject, and speak to him again. What do you think of employing them, limiting them to a certain price, as 300 dollars for instance, or any other sum you think proper? He will write immediately to his instruments there, and in two or three months we can know the event.[42] He will deliver them at Marseilles, Cadiz, or where we please, at our expence. The money remaining of the fund destined to the Barbary business may I suppose be drawn on for this object. Write me your opinion if you please, on this subject, finally, fully, and immediately, that, if you approve the proposition, I may enter into arrangements with the General before my departure for the waters of Aix, which will be about the beginning of February. I have the honour to be with very sincere esteem and respect Dear Sir your most obedient and most humble servt.,

TH: JEFFERSON

Jefferson to Adams

Paris Jan. 19. 1787.

SIR

Colo. Franks having occasion for fifty pounds sterling to enable him to pursue his journey to London and New York, Mr. Grand has furnished him with that sum, for the reimbursement whereof I have drawn on you

42. See TJ to JA, Dec. 31, 1787, below, 220.

in his favor, and have to pray you to honour that draught and to charge it against the fund appropriated to the negociations with Marocco, as expended in that business. I have the honour to be with the most perfect esteem and respect, Sir, Your most obedient and most humble servt.,

TH: JEFFERSON

Adams to Jefferson

Grosvenor Square Jan. 25. 1787

DEAR SIR

I have received your Letters of December 20. and Jan. 11. by Coll. Franks. The whole of the Business shall be dispatched, and Coll. Franks sent to Congress as you propose, as soon as possible. I have prepared a Draught of a joint Letter to Mr. Barclay and signed it, concerning Mr. Lamb, and shall inclose it to you with this. As to the Treaty with Portugal, the Chevalier De Pinto's Courier whom he sent off when you were here, is still in Lisbon. He is a confidential Domestick of De Pinto and calls every day, at the Ministers office in Lisbon but can get no answer. De Pinto is very uneasy, makes apologies when he sees me, but can do no more. He says Mr. De Melo has been sick and the Queen in the Country, and that Falkner could obtain no audience for these Causes till December. —I suppose the Treaty of Commerce between France and England has astonished Portugal, and divided the Court into Parties, so that neither administration can be settled, nor a system adopted relative to Spain France, England or America. Congress are always informed of Facts as soon as they happen, and it is not to be expected that we should write Letters every Day to tell them, that Events have not happened. As to the Reasons why the Treaty is not signed, they know at New York as well as you and I know, or even as De Pinto knows them.

The charitable, the humane, the Christian Mathurins deserve our kindest Thanks, and we should be highly obliged to them if they could discover at what Price, our Countrymen may be redeemed: but I dont think we have Authority to advance the Money without the further orders of Congress. There is no Court, or Government, that redeems its Citizens unless by a Treaty of Peace. This is left to private Connections and benevolent Societies. If Congress redeem these, it will be a Precedent for all others, and although I might in Congress vote for Setting the Precedent, and making it a Rule, Yet I dont think that as Subordinate Ministers We have a Right to do it. The Money remaining, must in February be applied to the Payment of Interest, and We must absolutely come to a full Stop in all Expences relating to Barbary Matters untill further orders of Congress. Lamb has drawn on me for Three thousand two hundred and twelve Pounds, twelve shillings. Mr. Barclay has drawn a great sum, £4020..0..0 according to the Minutes inclosed.

If Congress thought the original appointment of Lamb censurable they had reason. But you and I were not censurable. We found him ready appointed to our hands. I never saw him nor heard of him.—He ever was and still is as indifferent to me, as a Mohawk Indian. But as he came from Congress with their Dispatches of such importance, I supposed it was expected We should appoint him.—There is no harm done.—If Congress had sent the ablest Member of their own Body, at such a Time and under such pecuniary Limitations he would have done no better. With great and sincere Esteem I have the honour to be, dear Sir, your most obedient and most humble Servant,

JOHN ADAMS

5

"The first principle of a good government"

LIFE AND HISTORY are full" of political lessons, too often disregarded, Adams wrote Jefferson in October 1787.[1] On both sides of the Atlantic the world was stirring with great events. The *ancien régime* of France was tottering on the brink of revolution. Vergennes, vigilant defender of the Bourbon monarchy, who at times lent a sympathetic though enigmatic ear to American interests, had died in February. Thus a strategic link had been severed in the diplomatic chain of command accessible to Jefferson. In Philadelphia the Federal Convention was in secret session throughout the summer, debating the political future of the American nation, and news of the momentous results would not reach the diplomats in Europe until November. In Massachusetts the climax and anticlimax of Shays's Rebellion provided the most exciting and sobering information, as well as one of the reasons for John Adams to compose an essay on government that grew into a three-volume work.[2]

The letters exchanged by the Adamses and Jefferson were full of these great events as well as family incidents cherished by all three participants. Adams confessed to Jefferson that the "intimate Correspondence with you . . . is one of the most agreable Events in my Life."[3] Jefferson's friendship with Abigail Adams was a source of reflective contentment for him. In July 1786 he wrote her husband that he hoped "to provoke a letter from Mrs. Adams" from whom, he

1. JA to TJ, Oct. 9, 1787, below, 202.
2. C. F. Adams, "Life of John Adams," *Works*, I, 430-32; Marion L. Starkey, *A Little Rebellion* (N. Y., 1955), *passim*.
3. JA to TJ, March 1, 1787, below, 177.

added, "I have not received one these hundred years."[4] She soon resumed the correspondence of news and banter with Mr. Jefferson. Since Colonel Smith "has taken my daughter from me," she proposed that Jefferson exchange one of his daughters for one of her sons. "I am for Strengthening [the] federal union," she reminded him.[5]

That summer, through his artist friend John Trumbull, Jefferson met Mrs. Maria Cosway and fell in love with her. Born in Italy of an English family, Maria Hadfield, a student of art and music, had contracted a marriage of convenience with the artist Richard Cosway, who was somewhat jealous of his wife's attainments as an artist in her own right. It is not surprising that the forty-three-year-old American widower was vulnerable to the charms of this intellectual and artistic young woman of twenty-seven. Their association, though brief, was delightful, and remembrance of it was sustained in their lifelong, though intermittent, correspondence.[6] A month of frequent companionship was suddenly interrupted by an accident on September 18 which dislocated Jefferson's right wrist, probably during a fence-jumping incident while walking along the Seine with Maria.[7] Although severe pain in the wrist sobered him emotionally and forced him to use his left hand, he felt impelled to write the tender twelve-page letter of October 12 to Maria, then in Antwerp, containing the well known dialogue between the Head and the Heart.[8] The Head had prevailed in the man of reason who seldom allowed his self-discipline to get out of control, but not until the Heart had almost won full sway.

No mention of Maria Cosway occurs in the letters between Jefferson and Mrs. Adams. He did not write to her during the months of attention paid to the charming young artist, nor during his recovery from the physical pain and emotional disturbance he had suffered. At length, on December 21, he sent Mrs. Adams an incomplete explanation: "An unfortunate dislocation of my right wrist has for three months deprived me of the honor of writing to you."[9] The

4. TJ to JA, July 9, 1786, above, 141.
5. AA to TJ, July 23, 1786, above, 146.
6. Malone, *Jefferson*, II, Chap. V; Helen D. Bullock, *My Head and My Heart . . .* (N. Y., 1945).
7. TJ to Maria Cosway, [Oct. 5, 1786], Boyd, X, 431-32 and *n.;* see Chap. 4 above, 154, n. 37.
8. TJ to Maria Cosway, Oct. 12, 1786, Boyd, X, 443-53, 453-54*n.;* Malone, *Jefferson*, II, 73-78.
9. TJ to AA, Dec. 21, 1786, above, 159.

reticence which Jefferson consistently maintained concerning the intimate details of personal and family affairs suggests that his feelings for Maria Cosway were too deeply held to risk expression of them even to Mrs. Adams. Jefferson corresponded with Maria in London, where the Cosways made their home, and during the autumn of 1787, while Maria was visiting in Paris, they saw each other occasionally. She broke their last appointment on the morning of her departure and thus there was no final farewell.[10]

During the winter of 1786-87 Jefferson's thoughts were on his little daughter Polly whom Virginia kinsmen were to send in a vessel bound for England the next spring. He hoped Mrs. Adams would "take her under your wing" until he could send for her, and Mrs. Adams readily consented.[11] When Polly arrived in London in June, she quickly won Mrs. Adams's affection.[12] Since Jefferson had only recently returned from a spring tour of southern France and northern Italy, accumulation of business made it inadvisable for him to defer affairs of state so soon again in order to meet his daughter. After the long voyage from Virginia, Polly expressed disappointment (and Mrs. Adams sympathized with her) that her father had not come for her but instead had sent Petit, his maître d'hôtel, "a man whom she cannot understand."[13] She had become devoted to Mrs. Adams and was reluctant to leave her. "If I must go I will," wept Polly, "but I cannot help crying so pray dont ask me to."[14] On July 15 the faithful Petit delivered her safely to her father in Paris. He expressed his own feeling of gratitude as well as his daughter's in promptly reporting her arrival to Mrs. Adams.[15]

Abigail Adams's personal pleasure was marred by the disturbing news of insurgency in her native state, to which she reacted more violently than did her husband. Adams was inclined at first to minimize it by explaining that the Assembly, "to get the better of their Debt, [had] laid on a Tax, rather heavier than the People could bear; but all will be well. . . ."[16] By late January the news was more alarming

10. Bullock, *My Head and My Heart,* Chap. VI.
11. TJ to AA, Dec. 21, 1786, above, 159; AA to TJ, Jan. 29, 1787, below, 169.
12. AA to TJ, June 26 and 27, 1787, below, 178, 179.
13. AA to TJ, July 6, 1787, below, 183-84.
14. AA to TJ, July 10, 1787, below, 184.
15. TJ to AA, July 16, 1787, below, 188. See Dumas Malone, "Polly Jefferson and Her Father," *Va. Quart. Rev.,* 7 (1931), 81-95.
16. JA to TJ, Nov. 30, 1786, above, 156.

and Mrs. Adams more apprehensive that the rebels would be "sapping
the foundation [of the Commonwealth], and distroying the whole
fabrick at once." [17] If reports of Shays's Rebellion were exaggerated
in Massachusetts, small wonder that the degree of violence and lawlessness was magnified among those who, at a much greater distance,
deplored this challenge to republican government. The cry for paper
money, the stopping of the courts, the demand for repudiation of debts,
the threat of mob rule, agitated Mrs. Adams to a high pitch; but
Jefferson translated the episode into "a little rebellion," "the spirit of
resistance to government . . . so valuable on certain occasions." [18] Although his reply must have shocked Mrs. Adams (she wrote no more
to him on the subject until nine months later), the spirit of resistance
won much needed reforms. If the Massachusetts General Court had
not been so obtuse, it might have spared the state Shays's Rebellion, in
which insurgents and militia faced each other reluctantly and bloodshed was almost accidental, in which mercy was in readiness and pardon not too long forthcoming.[19]

When the first news of the disturbance in Massachusetts reached
London in the fall of 1786, John Adams remarked prophetically,
"This Commotion will terminate in additional Strength to Government." [20] In early October he had begun work on his *Defence of the
Constitutions of the United States*, provoked by a combination of
factors: his omnivorous reading of ancient and modern history; his
admiration for the English constitution and the balanced government
it sustained, in contrast to the highly centralized government of
France, so much praised by most of the *philosophes* of the Enlightenment; and his desire to defend the system of balanced or "mixed" government of the American states. He aimed to refute the philosopher
Turgot's charge that they had slavishly imitated the English brand
from which the Revolution could have freed them.[21] The challenge to
republican government in Massachusetts only made Adams's task the
more urgent. His native Commonwealth had produced one of the
better revolutionary constitutions in terms of separation of powers

17. AA to TJ, Jan. 29, 1787, below, 168.
18. AA to TJ, Jan. 29, 1787, below, 168; TJ to AA, Feb. 22, 1787, below, 173; Boyd,
XI, 175n.
19. Robert J. Taylor, *Western Massachusetts in the Revolution* (Providence, 1954),
Chaps. VII-VIII; Starkey, *A Little Rebellion*, Chaps. XVI-XIX.
20. JA to TJ, Nov. 30, 1786, above, 156.
21. "Preface," by C. F. Adams, *Works*, IV, 273-74.

(he had been its chief author); there were others—Pennsylvania's or Virginia's—that badly needed revising, if not rewriting; but the people, with all the imperfection of man's nature, must recognize the virtues of their government. "The best republics will be virtuous, and have been so," Adams declared; "but we may hazard a conjecture, that the virtues have been the effect of the well ordered constitution, rather than the cause." Such a constitution should decentralize power and set up a proper balance between each of the components—legislature, executive, and judiciary.[22]

Adams's *Defence* was an erudite study of comparative government —of ancient republics and Italian city aristocracies—pointing up the conclusion that "the United States of America have exhibited, perhaps, the first example of governments erected on the simple princi ples of nature," applied in concrete terms of their written constitutions. Since Adams was personally acquainted with most of the framers of these documents, his present purpose was "to lay before the public a specimen of that kind of reading and reasoning which produced the American constitutions." [23]

The first volume of his work proved to be more timely than he anticipated, for copies were circulating in the United States not long before the Federal Convention assembled in June. Jefferson predicted that the book "will do great good in America. It's learning and it's good sense will I hope make it an institute for our politicians, old as well as young." [24] His judgment was confirmed by Benjamin Rush, a member of the Convention, who reported the volume made such an impression that "there is little doubt of our adopting a vigorous and compounded federal legislature." [25]

Composition of the *Defence*, interspersed with Adams's diplomatic responsibilities, was completed in about fifteen months. It was a hasty job, unrevised before publication, and he was apologetic about it. The early commendation he received moved him to disclaim being a great scholar.[26] On receipt of the second volume in September 1787,

22. "Defence of the Constitutions," *Works*, VI, 219; C. F. Adams, "Life of John Adams," *ibid.,* I, 426, 427.

23. "Defence," *Works*, IV, 292, 293-94.

24. TJ to JA, Feb. 23, 1787, below, 174.

25. Rush to Richard Price, June 2, 1787, L. H. Butterfield, ed., *Letters of Benjamin Rush* (Princeton, 1951), I, 418.

26. JA to TJ, March 1, 1787, below, 176; JA to Richard Cranch, Jan. 15, 1787, *Works*, I, 432; Zoltan Haraszti, *John Adams and the Prophets of Progress* (Cambridge, 1952), 46-48, Chap. IX.

Jefferson supported Adams's belief in distribution of powers as "the first principle of a good government." [27] But Adams's own generation refused to recognize him as a creative political scientist.

Abigail Adams to Jefferson

London Janry. 29th. 1787

MY DEAR SIR

I received by Col. Franks your obliging favour and am very sorry to find your wrist still continues lame; I have known very salutary effects produced by the use of British oil upon a spraind joint. I have sent a servant to see if I can procure some. You may rest assured that if it does no good: it will not do any injury.

With regard to the Tumults in my Native state [28] which you inquire about, I wish I could say that report had exagerated them. It is too true Sir that they have been carried to so allarming a Height as to stop the Courts of justice in several Counties. Ignorant, wrestless desperadoes, without conscience or principals, have led a deluded multitude to follow their standard, under pretence of grievances which have no existance but in their immaginations. Some of them were crying out for a paper currency, some for an equal distribution of property, some were for annihilating all debts, others complaning that the Senate was a useless Branch of Government, that the Court of common pleas was unnecessary, and that the sitting of the General Court in Boston was a grievence. By this list you will see the materials which compose this rebellion, and the necessity there is of the wisest and most vigorus measures to quell and suppress it. Instead of that laudible spirit which you approve, which makes a people watchfull over their Liberties and alert in the defence of them, these mobish insurgents are for sapping the foundation, and distroying the whole fabrick at once.—But as these people make only a small part of the state, when compared to the more sensible and judicious, and altho they create a just allarm and give much trouble and uneasiness, I cannot help flattering myself that they will prove sallutary to the state at large, by leading to an investigation of the causes which have produced these commotions. Luxery and extravagance both in furniture and dress had pervaded all orders of our Countrymen and women, and was hastning fast to sap their independance by involving every class of citizens in distress, and accumulating debts upon them which they were unable to discharge.

27. TJ to JA, Sept. 28, 1787, below, 199.
28. Shays's Rebellion.

Vanity was becoming a more powerfull principal than patriotism. The lower order of the community were prest for taxes, and tho possest of landed property they were unable to answer the demand, whilst those who possest money were fearfull of lending, least the mad cry of the mob should force the Legislature upon a measure very different from the touch of Midas.[29]

By the papers I send you, you will see the beneficial effects already produced. An act of the Legislature laying duties of 15 per cent upon many articles of British manufacture and totally prohibiting others—a number of Vollunteers Lawyers physicians and Merchants from Boston made up a party of Light horse commanded by Col. Hitchbourn, Leit. Col. Jackson and Higgenson, and went out in persuit of the insurgents and were fortunate enough to take 3 of their principal Leaders, Shattucks Parker and Page. Shattucks defended himself and was wounded in his knee with a broadsword. He is in Jail in Boston and will no doubt be made an example of.

Your request my dear sir with respect to your Daughter shall be punctually attended to, and you may be assured of every attention in my power towards her.

You will be so kind as to present my Love to Miss Jefferson, compliments to the Marquiss and his Lady. I am really conscience smitten that I have never written to that amiable Lady, whose politeness and attention to me deserved my acknowledgment.

The little balance which you stated in a former Letter in my favour, when an opportunity offers I should like to have in Black Lace at about 8 or 9 Livres pr. Ell. Tho late in the Month, I hope it will not be thought out of season to offer my best wishes for the Health, Long Life and prosperity of yourself and family, or to assure you of the Sincere Esteem and Friendship with which I am Your's etc. etc.,

A. ADAMS

Jefferson to Adams

Paris Feb. 6. 1787

DEAR SIR

Your favors by Colo. Franks have come safely to hand. He will set out from hence the 8th. inst. the packet being to sail from Havre the 10th. I

---

29. In AA's draft of this letter the following paragraph appears at this point: "The disturbances which have taken place have roused from their Lethargy the Supine and the Indolent animated the Brave and taught wisdom to our Rulers." Boyd, XI, 87, n. 7.

inclose you the copy of a letter lately received from Mr. Barclay, and of the paper it inclosed.[30] In a letter from Mr. Carmichael is a postscript dated Dec. 25. in the following words 'since writing the preceding, the Portuguese Ambassador has pressed me to hint that the present moment is favorable to push our treaty with his court.' In the body of the letter he sais 'the Ct. d'Expilly has promised me to continue his attention to our prisoners during his stay at Algiers, and I have also engaged the Consul of Spain who remains there on his return to take care of them. Advances have been made for their support which ought to be refunded.' I suppose that these advances have been made by order of Mr. Lamb, and that, his powers being at an end, it will be incumbent on us to take measures on that subject. The Count de Vergennes is extremely ill. His disease is gouty. We have for some days had hopes it would fix itself decidedly in the foot. It shews itself there at times, as also in the shoulder, the stomach etc. Monsr. de Calonnes is likewise ill: but his complaints are of a rheumatic kind which he has often had before. The illness of these two ministers has occasioned the postponement of the Assembly of the Notables to the 14th. and probably will yet postpone it. Nothing is yet known of the objects of that meeting. I send you a pamphlet giving a summary account of all the meetings of a general nature which have taken place heretofore. The treaty between Russia and this country is certainly concluded; but it's contents are not yet known. I shall set out for the waters of Aix [-en-Provence] on the 15th. instant, so that I am unable to say when and whence I shall have the honour of addressing you again. But I take measures for the conveying to me on my road all letters, so that should any thing extraordinary require it, I can at all times be recalled to Paris in a fortnight. I shall hope to hear from you at times as if I were in Paris. I thank you much for the valuable present of your book.[31] The subject of it is interesting and I am sure it is well treated. I shall take it on my journey that I may have time to study it. You told me once you had had thoughts of writing on the subject of hereditary aristocracy. I wish you would carry it into execution. It would make a proper sequel to the present work. I wish you all possible happiness and have the honour to be with sentiments of sincere esteem and affection, Dear Sir, your most obedient and most humble servant,

TH: JEFFERSON

30. Printed in Boyd, XI, 20-22; see also *ibid.*, 119*n*.
31. JA, *Defence of the Constitutions of the United States* (London, 1787), [Vol. I].

Jefferson to Adams

Paris Feb. 14. 1787

DEAR SIR

As I propose to write you on business by Mr. Cairnes who will set out in a few days for London, the object of the present letter is only to inform you that the Count de Vergennes died yesterday morning and that the Count de Montmorin is appointed his successor: and further to beg the favor of you to forward the inclosed by the first vessel from London. I set out on my journey on Sunday the 18th. I have the honour to be with sentiments of very sincere affection and respect Dear Sir Your most obedient and most humble servt.,

TH: JEFFERSON

Jefferson to Adams

Paris Feb. 20. 1787.

DEAR SIR

I am now to acknoledge the receipt of your favor of Jan. 25. Colo. Franks sailed in the packet of this month from Havre for New York. This arrangement of the packets opens a direct communication between Paris and America, and if we succeed as I expect we shall in getting Honfleur made a freeport, I hope to see that place become the deposit for our Whale oil, rice, tobacco and furs, and that from thence what is not wanted in this country may be distributed to others.   You remember giving me a letter of credit on Messrs. Willink and Staphorst for 1000 guineas to pay for the swords and medals. When the swords were finished I drew on the Vandemjvers [i.e., Vandenyver frères] with whom the money was deposited for 6500 livres to pay for the swords. They paid it. A medal is now finished, and others will very soon be: but these gentlemen say they must have fresh orders. In the mean time the workmen complain. Will you be so good as to draw in favor of Mr. Grand on Willink etc. for the balance of the thousand guineas (which is about the sum that will be necessary) and send the bill to Mr. Grand, who in my absence will negotiate it and pay the workmen. I inclose you Vandemjers answer.   The meeting of the Notables on Thursday and the necessity of paying my court to our new minister will detain me till Friday and perhaps till Tuesday next. Nothing is known yet of the objects of this assembly. I inclose you two new pamphlets relative to it: and will inform you of whatever I can discover relative to it during my stay.

I learn with real pain the resolution you have taken of quitting Europe. Your presence on this side the Atlantic gave me a confidence that if any difficulties should arise within my department, I should always have one to advise with on whose counsels I could rely. I shall now feel bewidowed. I do not wonder at your being tired out by the conduct of the court you are at. But is there not room to do a great deal of good for us in Holland in the department of money? No one can do it so well as yourself. But you have taken your resolution I am sure on mature consideration, and I have nothing to offer therefore but my regrets. If any thing transpires from the Notables before my departure worth communication, you shall yet hear from me. In the mean time believe me to be with sincere esteem and respect Dr. Sir your most obedt. and most humble servt.,

TH: JEFFERSON

Adams to Jefferson

Grosvenor Square Feb. 20. 1787

DEAR SIR

Dr. Gordon who is about publishing his Proposals for printing his History desires a Letter to you.—I told him that he might depend upon your good offices without any Letter, but as no harm will be done by complying with his Desire I beg Leave to introduce him, and to recommend his History to your Patronage in France. With equal affection, Esteem and respect, I have the Honour to be, Sir your most obedient humble Servant,

JOHN ADAMS

Jefferson to Abigail Adams

Paris Feb. 22. 1787.

DEAR MADAM

I am to acknolege the honor of your letter of Jan. 29. and of the papers you were so good as to send me. They were the latest I had seen or have yet seen. They left off too in a critical moment; [32] just at the point where the Malcontents make their submission on condition of pardon, and before the answer of government was known. I hope they pardoned them. The spirit of resistance to government is so valuable on certain occasions, that I wish it to be always kept alive. It will often be exercised when wrong, but better so than not to be exercised at all. I like a little rebellion now and then. It is like a storm in the Atmosphere. It is wonderful that no letter or paper tells us who is president of Congress, tho' there are letters in Paris to the beginning of January. I suppose I shall hear when I come back from my journey, which will be eight months after he will have been chosen. And yet they complain of us for not giving them intelligence. Our Notables assembled to-day, and I hope before the departure of Mr. Cairnes I shall have heard something of their proceedings worth communicating to Mr. Adams. The most remarkeable effect of this convention as yet is the number of puns and bon mots it has generated. I think were they all collected it would make a more voluminous work than the Encyclopedie. This occasion, more than any thing I have seen, convinces me that this nation is incapable of any serious effort but under the word of command. The people at large view every object only as it may furnish puns and bon mots; and I pronounce that a good punster would disarm the whole nation were they ever so seriously disposed to revolt. Indeed, Madam, they are gone. When a measure so capable of doing good as the calling the Notables is treated with so much ridicule, we may conclude the nation desperate, and in charity pray that heaven may send them good kings.— The bridge at the place Louis XV. is begun. The hotel dieu is to be abandoned and new ones to be built. The old houses on the old bridges are in a course of demolition. This is all I know of Paris. We are about to lose the Count d'Aranda, who has desired and obtained his recall. Fernand Nunnez, before destined for London is to come here. The Abbés Arnoux and Chalut are well. The Dutchess Danville somewhat recovered from the loss of her daughter. Mrs. Barrett very homesick, and fancying herself otherwise sick. They will probably remove to Honfleur. This is all our news. I have only to add then that Mr. Cairnes has taken charge of 15. aunes of black lace for you at 9 livres the aune, purchased by Petit and therefore I hope better purchased than some things have been for you; and that I am with sincere esteem Dear Madam your affectionate humble servt.,

TH: JEFFERSON

32. In Shays's Rebellion.

Jefferson to Adams

Paris Feb. 23. 1787

DEAR SIR

The Notables met yesterday. The king opened the assembly with a short speech, wherein he expressed his inclination to consult with them on the affairs of his kingdom, to receive their opinions on the plans he had digested, and to endeavor to imitate the head of his family Henry IV. whose name is so dear to the nation. The speech was affectionate. The Guarde des sceaux [33] spoke about 20 minutes, complimented the Clergy, the Noblesse, the Magistrates and tiers etats. The Comptroller general spoke about an hour. He enumerated the expences necessary to arrange his department when he came to it, he said his returns had been minutely laid before the king, he took a review of the preceding administrations, and more particularly of Mr. Neckar's, he detailed the improvements which had been made, he portrayed the present state of the finances, and sketched the several schemes proposed for their improvement; he spoke on a change in the form of the taxes, the removal of the interior custom houses to the frontiers, provincial administrations and some other objects. The assembly was then divided into Committees. To-day there was to be another grand assembly, the plans more fully explained and referred to the discussion of the Committees. The grand assembly will meet once a week and vote individually.   The propriety of my attending the first audience day of Count Montmorin, which will not be till the 27th. retards my departure till then.

I have read your book with infinite satisfaction and improvement. It will do great good in America. It's learning and it's good sense will I hope make it an institute for our politicians, old as well as young. There is one opinion in it however, which I will ask you to reconsider, because it appears to me not entirely accurate, and not likely to do good. Pa. 362. 'Congress is not a legislative, but a diplomatic assembly.' Separating into parts the whole sovereignty of our states, some of these parts are yeilded to Congress. Upon these I should think them both legislative and executive; and that they would have been judiciary also, had not the Confederation required them for certain purposes to appoint a judiciary. It has accordingly been the decision of our courts that the Confederation is a part of the law of the land, and superior in authority to the ordinary laws, because it cannot be altered by the legislature of any one state. I doubt whether

33. Principal judicial officer of the kingdom of France.

they are at all a diplomatic assembly.   On the first news of this work, there were proposals to translate it. Fearing it might be murdered in that operation, I endeavored to secure a good translator. This is done, and I lend him my copy to translate from.[34] It will be immediately announced to prevent others attempting it. I am with sincere esteem and respect Dear Sir Your most obedt. and most humble servt.,

TH: JEFFERSON

Jefferson to Adams

Paris Feb. 28. 1787.

DEAR SIR

The inclosed letter is come to hand since I had the honour of addressing you last.[35] Will you be so good as to forward a copy to Mr. Jay? The assembly of Notables is held to secrecy, so that little transpires and this floats among so much incertain matter that we know not what can be depended on. 80. millions more of annual revenue and provincial assemblies are the certain objects. The giving to the protestants a civil state will be effected without recurrence to the Notables. I am now in the moment of my departure and have therefore only time to add assurances of the esteem and respect with which I have the honor to be Dear Sir your most obedient humble servt.,

TH: JEFFERSON

Adams to Jefferson

London March 1. 1787

DEAR SIR

I am much obliged to you for your favours of Feb. 20. and 23 by Mr. Carnes, and the curious Pamphlets.

Opening a direct Communication between Paris and America will facilitate the Trade of the two Countries, very much, and the new Treaty between France and England, will promote it still more. John Bull dont

---

34. First French edition published by Buisson: *Defense des constitutions americaines* ... (1792) with "Notes et Observations" by Jacques-Vincent Delacroix; but it is not certain that he was the "good translator" referred to by TJ.

35. Barclay to American Commissioners, Feb. 10, 1787, Boyd, XI, 132-33.

see it, and if he dont see a Thing at first, you know it is a rule with him ever after wards to swear that it dont exist, even when he does both see it and feel it.

I have this moment written to Messrs. Willinks and Vanstaphorsts to remit to you or Mr. Grand in your absence, what remains to be received to make up the Thousand Guineas for the Swords and Medals, you having before drawn for 6500 Livres tournois, as part of them.

My Resolution of Quitting Europe, has been taken upon mature deliberation: but really upon motives of Necessity, as much at least as Choice. —Congress cannot consistent with their own honour and Dignity, renew my Commission to this Court—and I assure you, I should hold it so inconsistent with my own honour and Dignity little as that may be, that if it were possible for Congress to forget theirs I would not forget mine, but send their Commission back to them, unless a Minister were sent from his Britannic Majesty to Congress.

As to a Residence in Holland, that Climate is so destructive to my health, that I could never bear it: and I am sure it would be fatal to her, on whom depends all the satisfaction that I have in Life. No Consideration would tempt me to think of removing to that Country with my Family.

For a Man who has been thirty Years rolling like a stone never three years in the same Place, it is no very pleasant Speculation, to cross the seas with a Family, in a State of Uncertainty what is to be his fate; what reception he shall meet at home; whether he shall set down in private Life to his Plough; or push into turbulent Scenes of Sedition and Tumult; whether be sent to Congress, or a Convention or God knows what.—If it lay in my Power, I would take a Vow, to retire to my little Turnip yard, and never again quit it.—I feel very often a violent disposition to take some Resolution and swear to it. But upon the whole, it is best to preserve my Liberty to do as I please according to Circumstances.

The approbation you express in general of my poor Volume, is a vast consolation to me. It is an hazardous Enterprize, and will be an unpopular Work in America for a long time.—When I am dead, it may be regretted that such Advice was not taken in the season of it.—But as I have made it early in life and all along a Rule to conceal nothing from the People which appeared to me material for their Happiness and Prosperity, however unpopular it might be at the time, or with particular Parties, I am determined not now to begin to flatter popular Prejudices and Party Passions however they may be countenanced by great authorities.

The Opinion you Object to p. 362, "that Congress is not a legislative but a diplomatic assembly" I should wish to have considered as a Problem, rather for Consideration, than as an opinion: and as a Problem too, relative to the Confederation as it now stands, rather than to any other Plan that may be in Contemplation of the States. It is a most difficult Topick, and no Man at a distance can judge of it, so well as those in America. If the Book Should be translated into french, I wish you would insert this, in a Note. You have laid me under great obligation, by taking the trouble to Secure a Good Translator.—If the Thing is worth translating at all, it will not surely bare to loose any Thing by the Translation.—But will not the Government proscribe it?—If I should get well home, and Spend a few Years in Retirement, I shall pursue this subject, somewhat further: but I hope never to be left, again, to publish so hasty a Production as this. A Work upon the Subject you mention, *Nobility in general*, which I once hinted to you a wish to see handled at large would be too extensive and Splendid for my means and Forces. It would require many Books which I have not, and a more critical Knowledge both of ancient and modern Languages than at my Age a Man can aspire to.—There are but two Circumstances, which will be regretted by me, when I leave Europe. One is the oppertunity of Searching any questions of this kind, in any books that may be wanted, and the other will be the Interruption of that intimate Correspondence with you, which is one of the most agreable Events in my Life. There are four or five Persons here, with whom I hold a friendly Intercourse and shall leave with some degree of Pain but I am not at home in this Country. With every affectionate and friendly Sentiment I am and shall be in this world and the future yours,

JOHN ADAMS

Adams to Jefferson

London April 18. 1787

DEAR SIR

Mr. Mortimer the Bearer of this Letter, is a Gentleman of Letters, and although little known to me, is recommended by some of my Friends as a worthy, though unfortunate Man. He is represented to be a Friend to Liberty, and Humanity, and as such I beg leave to introduce him to you, and to ask for him any friendly Advice or Aid you may be able to afford him in his Views, of litterary Employment as a Teacher of Languages, or otherwise. With great Regard I am, my dear Sir always yours,

JOHN ADAMS

Abigail Adams to Jefferson

London june 26 1787

DEAR SIR

I have to congratulate you upon the safe arrival of your Little Daughter [Polly] whom I have only a few moments ago received. She is in fine Health and a Lovely little Girl I am sure from her countanance, but at present every thing is strange to her, and she was very loth to try New Friends for old. She was so much attachd to the Captain and he to her, that it was with no small regret that I seperated her from him, but I dare say I shall reconcile her in a day or two. I tell her that I did not see her sister cry once. She replies that her sister was older and ought to do better, besides she had her pappa with her. I shew her your picture. She says she cannot know it, how should she when she should not know you. A few hours acquaintance and we shall be quite Friends I dare say. I hope we may expect the pleasure of an other visit from you now I have so strong an inducement to tempt you. If you could bring Miss Jefferson with you, it would reconcile her little Sister to the thoughts of taking a journey. It would be proper that some person should be accustomed to her. The old Nurse whom you expected to have attended her, was sick and unable to come. She has a Girl about 15 or 16 with her,[36] the Sister of the Servant you have with you. As I presume you have but just returnd from your late excursion, you will not put yourself to any inconvenience or Hurry in comeing or sending for her. You may rely upon every attention towards her and every care in my power. I have just endeavourd to amuse her by telling her that I would carry her to Sadlers Wells.[37] After describing the amusement to her with an honest simplicity, I had rather says she see captain Ramsey one moment, than all the fun in the World.

I have only time before the post goes, to present my compliments to Mr. Short. Mr. Adams and Mrs. Smith desire to be rememberd to you. Captain Ramsey has brought a Number of Letters. As they may be of importance to you to receive them we have forwarded them by the post. Miss Polly sends her duty to you and Love to her Sister and says she will try to be good and not cry. So she has wiped her eyes and layd down to sleep. Believe me dear Sir affectionately yours etc etc,

A ADAMS

36. Sally Hemings (*b.* 1773).
37. Sadler's Wells in Clerkenwell near London dates back to 1683 as a spa. In the eighteenth century it became an amusement park, with athletic contests, dancing, trained-animal acts, and musical programs. Warwick Wroth and Arthur E. Wroth, *The London Pleasure Gardens of the Eighteenth Century* (London and N. Y., 1896), 43-53.

Abigail Adams to Jefferson

London june 27 1787

Dear Sir

I had the Honour of addressing you yesterday and informing you of the safe arrival of your daughter. She was but just come when I sent of my letter by the post, and the poor little Girl was very unhappy being wholy left to strangers. This however lasted only a few Hours, and Miss is as contented to day as she was misirable yesterday. She is indeed a fine child. I have taken her out to day and purchased her a few articles which she could not well do without and I hope they will meet your approbation. The Girl who is with her is quite a child, and Captain Ramsey is of opinion will be of so little Service that he had better carry her back with him. But of this you will be a judge. She seems fond of the child and appears good naturd.

I sent by yesterdays post a Number of Letters which Captain Ramsey brought with him not knowing of any private hand, but Mr. Trumble has just calld to let me know that a Gentleman sets off for paris tomorrow morning. I have deliverd him two Letters this afternoon received, and requested him to wait that I might inform you how successfull a rival I have been to Captain Ramsey, and you will find it I imagine as difficult to seperate Miss Polly from me as I did to get her from the Captain. She stands by me while I write and asks if I write every day to her pappa? But as I have never had so interesting a subject to him to write upon [...] I hope he will excuse the hasty scrips for the [scanty?] intelligence they contain, and be assured Dear Sir that I am with sentiments of sincere esteem your Humble Servant,

A Adams

Jefferson to Abigail Adams

Paris July 1. 1787.

A thousand thanks to you, my dear Madam, for your kind attention to my little daughter. Her distresses I am sure must have been troublesome to you: but I know your goodness will forgive her, and forgive me too for having brought them on you. Petit now comes for her. By this time she will have learned again to love the hand that feeds and comforts her, and have formed an attachment to you. She will think I am made only to tear her from all her affections. I wish I could have come myself. The pleasure of a visit to yourself and Mr. Adams would have been a great additional inducement. But, just returned from my journey, I have the arrearages of 3. or 4. months all crouded on me at once. I do not presume to write you news from America, because you have it so much fresher and frequenter than I have. I hope all the disturbances of your country are quieted and with little bloodshed. What think you of present appearances in Europe? The Emperor and his subjects? The Dutch and their half king, who would be a whole one? in fine the French and the English? These new friends and allies have hardly had time to sign that treaty which was to cement their love and union like man and wife, before they are shewing their teeth at each other. We are told a fleet of 6. or 12 ships is arming on your side the channel; here they talk of 12 or 20, and a camp of 15,000 men. But I do not think either party in earnest. Both are more laudably intent on arranging their affairs.—Should you have incurred any little expences on account of my daughter or her maid, Petit will be in a condition to repay them. If considerable, he will probably be obliged to refer you to me, and I shall make it my duty to send you a bill immediately for the money. Count Sarsfeild sets out for London four days hence. At dinner the other day at M. de Malesherbe's he was sadly abusing an English dish called Gooseberry tart. I asked him if he had ever tasted the cranberry. He said, no. So I invited him to go and eat cranberries with you. He said that on his arrival in London he would send to you and demander á diner. I hope Mrs. Smith and the little grandson are well. Be so good as to present me respectfully to her. I have desired Colo. Smith to take a bed here on his return. I will take good care of him for her, and keep him out of all harm. I have the honour to be with sentiments of sincere esteem and respect Dear Madam your most obedient and most humble servt.,

TH: JEFFERSON

Jefferson to Adams

Paris July 1. 1787.

DEAR SIR

I returned about three weeks ago from a very useless voiage. Useless, I mean, as to the object which first suggested it, that of trying the effect of the mineral waters of Aix en Provence on my hand. I tried these because recommended among six or eight others as equally beneficial, and because they would place me at the beginning of a tour to the seaports of Marseilles, Bourdeaux, Nantes and Lorient which I had long meditated, in hopes that a knowlege of the places and persons concerned in our commerce and the information to be got from them might enable me sometimes to be useful. I had expected to satisfy myself at Marseilles of the causes of the difference of quality between the rice of Carolina and that of Piedmont which is brought in quantities to Marseilles. Not being able to do it, I made an excursion of three weeks into the rice country beyond the Alps, going through it from Vercelli to Pavia about 60 miles. I found the difference to be, not in the management as had been supposed both here and in Carolina, but in the species of rice, and I hope to enable them in Carolina to begin the Cultivation of the Piedmont rice and carry it on hand in hand with their own that they may supply both qualities, which is absolutely necessary at this market. I had before endeavored to lead the depot of rice from Cowes to Honfleur and hope to get it received there on such terms as may draw that branch of commerce from England to this country. It is an object of 250,000 guineas a year. While passing thro' the towns of Turin, Milan and Genoa, I satisfied myself of the practicability of introducing our whale oil for their consumption and I suppose it would be equally so in the other great cities of that country. I was sorry that I was not authorized to set the matter on foot. The merchants with whom I chose to ask conferences, met me freely, and communicated fully, knowing I was in a public character. I could however only prepare a disposition to meet our oil merchants. On the article of tobacco I was more in possession of my ground, and put matters into a train for inducing their government to draw their tobaccos directly from the U.S. and not as heretofore from G.B. I am now occupied with the new ministry here to put the concluding hand to the new regulations for our commerce with this country, announced in the letter of M. de Calonnes which I sent you last fall. I am in hopes in addition to those, to obtain a suppression of the duties on Tar, pitch, and turpentine, and an extension of the privileges of American *whale* oil, to their *fish* oils in general. I find that the quantity of Codfish oil brought to Lorient is considerable. This being got off hand (which will be in a few days) the chicaneries and vexations of the farmers on the article of tobacco, and their elusions of the order of Bernis,[38] call for the next attention. I have reason to hope good dispositions in the new ministry towards our commerce with this country. Besides endeavoring on all occasions to multiply the points of contact and connection with this country, which I consider as our surest main-stay under every event, I have had it

38. Named for Calonne's chateau, where on May 24, 1786, a meeting of the "American Committee" was held, both Calonne and Vergennes being present, to put Franco-American commerce on a better footing. TJ to JA, July 9, Oct. 27, 1786, above, 141, 155-56; *Diplomatic Correspondence, 1783-1789*, I, 764-65.

much at heart to remove from between us every subject of misunderstanding or irritation. Our debts to the king, to the officers, and the farmers are of this description. The having complied with no part of our engagements in these draws on us a great deal of censure, and occasioned a language in the Assemblées des notables very likely to produce dissatisfaction between us. Dumas being on the spot in Holland, I had asked of him some time ago, in confidence, his opinion on the practicability of transferring these debts from France to Holland, and communicated his answer to Congress, pressing them to get you to go over to Holland and try to effect this business.[39] Your knowlege of the ground and former successes occasioned me to take this liberty without consulting you, because I was sure you would not weigh your personal trouble against public good. I have had no answer from Congress, but hearing of your journey to Holland have hoped that some money operation had led you there. If it related to the debts of this country I would ask a communication of what you think yourself at liberty to communicate, as it might change the form of my answers to the eternal applications I receive. The debt to the officers of France carries an interest of about 2000 guineas, so we may suppose it's principal is between 30. and 40,000. This makes more noise against [us] than all our other debts put together.

I send you the arrets which begin the reformation here, and some other publications respecting America: together with copies of letters received from Obryon and Lambe.[40] It is believed that a naval armament has been ordered at Brest in correspondence with that of England. We know certainly that orders are given to form a camp in the neighborhood of Brabant, and that Count Rochambeau has the command of it. It's amount I cannot assert. Report says 15,000 men. This will derange the plans of oeconomy. I take the liberty of putting under your cover a letter for Mrs. Kinloch of South Carolina, with a packet,[41] and will trouble you to enquire for her and have them delivered. The packet is of great consequence, and therefore referred to her care, as she will know the safe opportunities of conveying it. Should you not be able to find her, and can forward the packet to it's address by any very safe conveiance I will beg you to do it. I have the honour to be with sentiments of the most perfect friendship and esteem Dear Sir your most obedient and most humble servant,

TH: JEFFERSON

39. C. W. F. Dumas to TJ, Jan. 23, 1787, Boyd, XI, 62-65.

40. O'Bryen to TJ, April 28, 1787, and Lamb to TJ, May 20, 1787, *ibid.*, 321-22, 368-69.

41. TJ to Anne Cleland Kinloch, July 1, 1787, with "a small parcel of Piedmont rice, addressed to Mr. [William] Drayton chairman of the committee of the South Carolina society for promoting and improving agriculture." *Ibid.*, 520-21.

Abigail Adams to Jefferson

London july 6 1787

MY DEAR SIR

If I had thought you would so soon have sent for your dear little Girl, I should have been tempted to have kept her arrival here, from you a secret. I am really loth to part with her, and she last evening upon Petit's arrival, was thrown into all her former distresses, and bursting into Tears, told me it would be as hard to leave me as it was her Aunt Epps. She has been so often deceived that she will not quit me a moment least she should be carried away. Nor can I scarcely prevail upon her to see Petit. Tho she says she does not remember you, yet she has been taught to consider you with affection and fondness, and depended upon your comeing for her. She told me this morning, that as she had left all her Friends in virginia to come over the ocean to see you, she did think you would have taken the pains to have come here for her, and not have sent a man whom she cannot understand. I express her own words. I expostulated with her upon the long journey you had been, and the difficulty you had to come and upon the care kindness and attention of Petit, whom I so well knew. But she cannot yet hear me. She is a child of the quickest sensibility, and the maturest understanding, that I have ever met with for her years. She had been 5 weeks at sea, and with men only, so that on the first day of her arrival, she was as rough as a little sailor, and then she been decoyed from the ship, which made her very angry, and no one having any Authority over her; I was apprehensive I should meet with some trouble. But where there are such materials to work upon as I have found in her, there is no danger. She listend to my admonitions, and attended to my advice and in two days, was restored to the amiable lovely Child which her Aunt had formed her. In short she is the favorite of every creature in the House, and I cannot but feel Sir, how many pleasures you must lose by committing her to a convent. Yet situated as you are, you cannot keep her with you. The Girl she has with her, wants more care than the child, and is wholy incapable of looking properly after her, without some superiour to direct her.

As both Miss Jefferson and the maid had cloaths only proper for the sea, I have purchased and made up for them, such things as I should have done had they been my own, to the amount of Eleven or 12 Guineys. The particulars I will send by Petit.

Captain Ramsey has said that he would accompany your daughter to

Paris provided she would not go without him, but this would be putting you to an expence that may perhaps be avoided by Petits staying a few days longer. The greatest difficulty in familiarizing her to him, is on account of the language. I have not the Heart to force her into a Carriage against her will and send her from me almost in a Frenzy; as I know will be the case, unless I can reconcile her to the thoughts of going and I have given her my word that Petit shall stay untill I can hear again from you. Books are her delight, and I have furnishd her out a little library, and she reads to me by the hour with great distinctness, and comments on what she reads with much propriety.

Mrs. Smith desires to be remembered to you, and the little Boy[42] his Grandmama thinks is as fine a Boy as any in the Kingdom. I am my dear sir with Sentiments of Esteem Your Friend and Humble Servant,

A ADAMS

Jefferson to Abigail Adams

Paris July 10. 1787.

DEAR MADAM

This being the day on which, according to my calculation, my daughter would be crossing the channel, I had calculated the course from Dover to Calais and was watching the wind when your favour of the 6th. was put into my hands. That of June 27. had been received four days ago. I perceived that that had happened which I had apprehended, that your goodness had so attached her to you that her separation would become difficult. I had been in hopes that Petit would find means to rival you, and I still hope he will have done it so as that they may be on their way here at present. If she were to stay till she should be willing to come, she would stay till you cease to be kind to her, and that, Madam, is a term for which I cannot wait. Her distress will be in the moment of parting and I am in hopes Petit will soon be able to lessen it.—We are impatient to hear what our federal convention are doing. I have no news from America later than the 27th. of April. Nor is there any thing here worth mentioning. The death of Mr. Saint James and flight of M. de Calonnes are perhaps known to you. A letter of M. de Mirabeau to the K. of Prussia is handed about by the Colporteurs. I will endeavor to find an opportunity of sending it

42. William Steuben Smith (*b.* April 30, 1787), son of Colonel William Stephens Smith and Abigail Adams Smith.

to Mr. Adams.—Your kind advances for my daughter shall be remitted you by Colo. Smith when he returns or some other good opportunity. I have the honor to be with sentiments of gratitude for your goodness and with those of perfect esteem Dr. Madam your most obedt. humble servt.,

TH: JEFFERSON

Abigail Adams to Jefferson, with Enclosure

London july 10th. 1787

DEAR SIR

When I wrote you last I did not know that petit had taken places in the Stage and paid for them. This being the case I have represented it to your little daughter and endeavourd to prevail with her to consent to going at the time appointed. She says if I must go I will, but I cannot help crying so pray dont ask me to. I should have taken great pleasure in presenting her to you here, as you would then have seen her with her most engageing countance. Several lines of an old song frequently occur to me as different objects affect her.

> What she thinks in her Heart
> You may read in her Eyes
> For knowing no art
> She needs no disguise.

I never saw so intelligent a countance in a child before, and the pleasure she has given me is an ample compensation for any little services I have been able to render her. I can easily conceive the earnest desire you must have to embrace so lovely a child after so long a seperation from her. That motive, and my own intention of setting out next week upon a journey into the County of Devonshire, has prevaild with me to consent to parting with her so soon, but most reluctantly I assure you. Her temper, her disposition, her sensibility are all formed to delight. Yet perhaps at your first interview you may find a little roughness but it all subsides in a very little time, and she is soon attached by kindness. I inclose a memorandum of the articles purchased [I have? be]en a little particular, that you might know how I [have dispose]d of the money. If at any time I can be of service in this [respec]t it will give me pleasure. I have desired petit to Buy me 12 Ells of black lace at 8 Livres pr. Ell and 1 dozen of white and one of coulourd Gloves. You will be so good as to place them to my account and Col. Smith will take them when he returns.

As to politicks, to avoid touching so disagreeable a subject, I send you the Boston news papers received by the last vessels.

Mrs. Paridise has just left me and desires to be rememberd to you. She is just upon the eve of departure for virginia. Whether he can be prevaild upon to go on Board altho their passage is taken, and every thing in readiness, is very uncertain. She is determined at all Hazards. He most assuredly will get a Seat in Kings Bench if he stays behind. His affairs are daily worse and worse. Mr. Adams will write you. He has not a portrait that he likes to send you. Mr. Trumble talks of taking one. If he succeeds better than his Brethren, Mr. Adams will ask your acceptance of it. You will be so good as to let me hear from my dear little Girl by the first post after her arrival. My Love to her sister whom I congratulate upon such an acquisition.

I have not been able to find Mrs. Kinlock yet, but hope too. If I should not, Mr. Heyward is going to carolina in a few days and I will send the package by him. All your other Letters were deliverd as directed.

With Sentiments of the highest Esteem I am dear sir your Humble Servant,

A ADAMS

I have received of petit six Louis d'ors. [I do not know] what the exchange is. But the remainder you wi[ll be so good] as to let him purchase me some lace and Gloves with the remainder.

ENCLOSURE

Memorandum of articles by Mrs. Adams for Miss Jefferson and Maid

	£	s	d
Paid for bringing the Trunks from Tower Hill		5	6
Four fine Irish Holland frocks	3	10	
5 yd. white dimity for shirts		15	
4 yd. checked muslin for a frock	1	10	
3 yd. lace Edging to trim it		6	6
To making the frock		5	
3 yd. flannel for under coats		7	6
A Brown Bever Hat and feathers		13	
2 pr. leather Gloves		2	4
5 yd. diaper for arm Cloths		5	10
6 pr. cotton Stockings		13	6
3 yd. blue sash Ribbon		3	
To diaper for pockets linning tape cloth for night caps etc		5	6
To a comb and case, comb Brush, tooth Brush		1	6

For the Maid Servant

12 yds. calico for 2 short Gowns and coats	1	5	6
4 yd half Irish linen for Aprons		7	4
3 pr Stockings		6	
2 yd linning		2	
1 Shawl handkerchief		4	6
paid for washing		6	8

Sterling	10	15	8
	11	16	2[43]

Received Six Louis d'ors of petit.

A ADAMS

Adams to Jefferson

Grosvenor Square July 10, 1787

DEAR SIR

I received with great Pleasure your favour of the first.—Your Excursion I dare answer for it, will be advantageous in many respects to our Country. —The object of mine to Holland was to procure Money, and I had the good fortune to obtain as much as was necessary for the then present Purpose: but it was not in Consequence of any orders from Congress, and therefore I am under some Apprehension for fear my Loan should not be ratified with so much Promptitude as I wish. If Congress ratify my Loan they will be able to pay the 2000 Guineas to the officers you mention, and to pay the Principal Sum too, if they please.—I have no doubt that Congress might borrow Money in Holland to pay off the Debt to France, if the States would lay on a Duty, to pay the Interest.—If you will venture to draw upon Willinks and Van Staphorsts, I Suppose you may have the Money to pay the French officers their Interest. But perhaps you would choose to have a previous order of Congress or the Board of Treasury.

I am extreamly sorry, that you could not come for your Daughter in Person, and that we are obliged to part with her so soon. In my Life I never saw a more charming Child. Accept of my Thanks, for the Pamphlets and Arrets.—Tell Mazzei, he cannot conceive what an Italian I am become.—I read nothing else, and if he writes to me it must be in that Language: but he must remember to make his Letters, so plain, that I can

43. Correction of AA's total is in TJ's hand.

see them. In writing English he is obliged to write so slow that his Characters are visible; but in Italian such is the Rapidity of his Eloquence, that I must get a Solar Microscope, if he is not upon his guard. You too, write Italian, and if you like it, you will oblige me: but I am not yet presumptuous enough to write a Line in any Thing but rugged American. I am, my dear Sir with perfect Friendship yours,

JOHN ADAMS

Jefferson to Abigail Adams

Paris July 16. 1787.

DEAR MADAM

I had the happiness of receiving yesterday my daughter in perfect health. Among the first things she informed me of was her promise to you, that after she should have been here a little while she would go back to pay you a visit of four or five days. She had taken nothing into her calculation but the feelings of her own heart which beat warmly with gratitude to you. She had fared very well on the road, having got into favor with gentlemen and ladies so as to be sometimes on the knee of one sometimes of another. She had totally forgotten her sister, but thought, on seeing me, that she recollected something of me. I am glad to hear that Mr. and Mrs. Paradise are gone or going to America. I should have written to them, but supposed them actually gone. I imagined Mr. Hayward gone long ago. He will be a very excellent opportunity for sending the packet to Mr. Drayton. Petit will execute your commissions this morning, and I will get Mr. Appleton to take charge of them. He sets out for London the day after tomorrow. The king and parliament are at extremities about the stamp act, the latter refusing to register it without seeing accounts etc. M. de Calonne has fled to the Hague. I had a letter from Colo. Smith dated Madrid June 30. He had been detained by the illness of his servant, but he was about setting out for Lisbon.[44] My respects attend his lady and Mr. Adams, and eternal thanks yourself with every sentiment of esteem and regard from Dear Madam your most obedient and most humble servt,

TH: JEFFERSON

44. To present to the Queen of Portugal Congress's letter of thanks for giving protection to American vessels. William Stephens Smith to TJ, June 30, 1787, Boyd, XI, 511-12 and n.

Jefferson to Adams

Paris July 17. 1787.

DEAR SIR

I have been duly honoured with your's of the 10th. inst. and am happy to hear of the success of your journey to Amsterdam. There can be no doubt of it's ratification by Congress. Would to heaven they would authorize you to take measures for transferring the debt of this country to Holland before you leave Europe. Most especially is it necessary to get rid of the debt to the officers. Their connections at court are such as to excite very unfavorable feelings there against us, and some very hard things have been said (particularly in the Assemblée des Notables) on the prospects relative to our debts. The paiment of the interest to the officers would have kept them quiet: but there are two years now due to them. I dare not draw for it without instructions, because in the instances in which I have hitherto ventured to act uninstructed, I have never been able to know whether they have been approved in the private sentiments of the members of Congress, much less by any vote. I have pressed on them the expediency of transferring the French debts to Holland, in order to remove every thing which may excite irritations between us and this nation. I wish it may be done before this ministry may receive ill impressions of us. They are at present very well disposed. I send you by Mr. Appleton some pamphlets and have the honour to be with sentiments of very cordial esteem and respect Dear Sir your affectionate humble servant,

TH: JEFFERSON

Jefferson to Adams

Paris July 23. 1787.

DEAR SIR

Frouillé, the bookseller here who is engaged in having your book translated and printed, understanding that you were about publishing a sequel to it, has engaged me to be the channel of his prayers to you to favor his operation by transmitting hither the sheets of the sequel as they shall be printed; and he will have them translated by the same hand, which is a good one.

It is necessary for me to explain the passage in Mr. Barclay's letter of July 13th.[45] of which he writes me he had sent you a duplicate, wherein

45. Barclay to American Commissioners, *ibid.*, 582-83.

he mentions that I had given him a full dispensation from waiting on you in London. Mr. Barclay was arrested in Bourdeaux for debt and put into prison. The parliament released him after five days on the footing of his being Consul and minister from the U.S. to Marocco. His adversaries applied here to deprive him of his privilege. I spoke on the subject to the minister. He told me that the character of Consul was no protection at all from private arrest, but that he would try to avail him of the other character. I found however that the event might be doubtful, and stated the whole in a letter to Mr. Barclay, observing at the same time that I knew of nothing which rendered it necessary for him to come to *Paris* before his departure for America. He determined therefore to go to America immediately which indeed was his wisest course, as he would have been harrassed immediately by his creditors.—Our funds here have been out some time and Mr. Grand is at the length of his tether in advancing for us. He has refused very small demands for current occasions, and I am not clear he will not refuse my usual one for salary. He has not told me so, but I am a little diffident of it. I shall know in a few days. Whether he does or not, I cannot approve of his protesting small and current calls. Having had nothing to do with any other banker, I cannot say what their practice is: but I suppose it their practice to advance for their customers, when their funds happen to be out, in proportion to the sums which they pass thro' their hands. Mr. Grand is a very sure banker, but a very timid one, and I fear he thinks it possible that he may lose his advances for the United states. Should he reject my draught, would there be any prospect of it's being answered in Holland, merely for my own and Mr. Short's salaries, say 4500 livres a month?—You will have heard that the emperor has put troops into march on account of the disturbances in Brabant. The situation of affairs in Holland you know better than I do. How will they end?—I have the honour to be with sentiments of the most perfect esteem and respect Dear Sir your most obedient and most humble servt.,

TH: JEFFERSON

Jefferson to Adams

Paris July 28. 1787.

DEAR SIR

I take the liberty of troubling you with the inclosed bill of exchange for £46-17-10 sterling, rather than engage Mrs. Smith in so disagreeable a business. It will arrive in time I hope to cover the one drawn by General

Sullivan on Colo. Smith,[46] who certainly ought not to have been involved in the business.—The parliament are obstinately decided against the stamp tax. Their last remonstrance is said to be a master peice of good sense and firmness. We have it from the Imperial Ambassador that his master has marched 45,000 men against his resisting subjects. I have the honour to be with sincere sentiments of esteem and respect Dear Sir Your most obedient and most humble servt.,

TH: JEFFERSON

Adams to Jefferson

Grosvenor Square, London Aug. 25. 1787

DEAR SIR

On my return from an Excursion to Devonshire with my Family, where we have been to fly from the Putrefaction of a Great City in the Summer heat, I had the Pleasure to find your favours of 17. and 23. of July.

A Million of Guilders are borrowed on a new Loan in Holland, and I went over lately to Subscribe the obligations, a Punctillio which the Brokers were pleased to think indispensible, to gratify the Fancies of the Money Lenders. But as I had no fresh Authority from Congress, nor any particular new Instructions, I have been and am Still under Serious Apprehensions of its meeting with obstacles in the way of its Ratification.—If it is ratified, Congress may if they please, pay the Interest and Principal too, out of it, to the French officers.—I presume that if Mr. Grand Should refuse your Usual draughts for your Salary Messrs. Willinks and Vanstaphorsts, will honour them to the amount of yours and Mr. Short's Salaries, without any other Interposition than your Letter. But if they Should make any difficulty, and it Should be in my Power to remove it, you may well Suppose, I shall not be wanting. To be explicit, I will either advise or order the Money to be paid, upon your Draught as may be necessary, So that I pray you to make your Mind perfectly easy on that Score.

46. General John Sullivan of New Hampshire had organized a hunting expedition in March 1787 to obtain specimens of moose, caribou, deer, and elk, at TJ's request, so that he might send them to the naturalist Georges L. Buffon, whose theory of degenerate fauna in America TJ had refuted in his *Notes on the State of Virginia*. The shipment was delayed so long that it was October 1 before TJ could transmit to Buffon "these spoils . . . [that] may have the merit of adding any thing new to the treasures of nature which [have] so fortunately come under your observation, and of which she seems [to] have given you the keys." Sullivan should have submitted his charges directly to TJ. See Sullivan's letters to TJ, in April and May 1787, Boyd, XI, 295-96, 321, 326, 359, 384; and TJ's letters of Sept. 28, Oct. 1, 4, 5, 1787, *ibid.*, XII, 192-93, 194-95, 202, 208-9.

Mr. Barclay, I agree with you, took the wisest Course, when he embarked for America, tho it will lay me under Difficulties in Settling my affairs finally with Congress.

The French Debt, and all the Domestic Debt of the United States might be transferred to Holland, if it were judged necessary or profitable, and the Congress or Convention would take two or three preparatory Steps. All the Perplexities, Confusions and Distresses in America arise not from defects in their Constitutions or Confederation, not from a want of Honour or Virtue, So much as from downright Ignorance of the Nature of Coin, Credit and Circulation.—While an annual Interest of twenty, thirty and even fifty Per Cent, can be made, and a hope of augmenting Capitals in a Proportion of five hundred Per Cent is opened by Speculations in the Stocks, Commerce will not thrive. Such a State of Things would annihilate the Commerce, and overturn the Government too in any nation in Europe.

I will endeavour to Send you a Copy, with this Letter of the Second volume of the Defence etc. If Frouillé the Bookseller has a Mind to translate it he may, but it may not Strike others as it does Americans. Three Editions of the first volume have been printed in America.[47] The Second volume contains three long Courses of Experiments in Political Philosophy, every Tryal was intended and contrived to determine the Question whether Mr. Turgots System would do. The Result you may read. It has cost me a good deal of Trouble and Expence to Search into Italian Rubbish and Ruins. But enough of pure Gold and Marble has been found to reward the Pains. I shall be Suspected of writing Romances to expose Mr. Turgots Theory. But I assure you, it is all genuine History. The vast Subject of Confederations remains: but I have neither head, heart, hands, Eyes, Books, or Time, to engage in it. Besides it ought not to be Such an hasty Performance as the two volumes already ventured before the Public. With perfect Esteem, your Sincere Friend,

JOHN ADAMS

Jefferson to Abigail Adams

Paris Aug. 30. 1787.

DEAR MADAM

I have omitted writing sooner to you in expectation that Colo. Smith would have taken this in his route: but receiving now information from

---

47. The first American editions of JA's *Defence of the Constitutions of the United States*, Vol. I, appeared in Philadelphia and New York in 1787; the third in Boston in 1788. See TJ to JA, Feb. 23, 1787, and JA to TJ, March 1, 1787, above, 174-75, 176-77.

him that he embarks from Lisbon, I avail myself of the opportunity by
Mr. Payne of thanking you for the disbursements you were so kind as to
make for my daughter in London, and of stating to you our accounts as
follows.

	£	s	d
Disbursements of Mrs. Adams as summed up in her state of them	10	15	8
Error in addition to her prejudice	1	0	6
	11	16	2
Cash paid by Petit to Mrs. Adams, viz. 6. Louis d'ors @ 19/6	5	17	
Paid by do. for black lace 75.ᵗᵗ which at the same exchange is	3	1	
Do. for 2. doz. pr. gloves 37ᵗᵗ − 12s	1	10	6
Balance due to Mrs. Adams	1	7	8
	11	16	2

which balance I will beg the favor of Colo. Smith to pay you, and to debit
me with.   I am afraid, by the American papers, that the disturbances in
Massachusets are not yet at an end. Mr. Rucker, who is arrived here, gives
me a terrible account of the luxury of our ladies in the article of dress. He
sais that they begin to be sensible of the excess of it themselves, and to
think a reformation necessary. That proposed is the adoption of a national
dress. I fear however they have not resolution enough for this. I rejoice in
the character of the lady who accompanies the Count de Moustier to
America, and who is calculated to reform these excesses as far as her
example can have weight. Simple beyond example in her dress, tho neat,
hating parade and etiquette, affable, engaging, placid, and withal beautiful, I cannot help hoping a good effect from her example. She is the
Marquise de Brehan, sister in law to the Count de Moustier, who goes
partly on account of a feeble health, but principally for the education of
her son (of 17. years of age) which she hopes to find more masculine there
and less exposed to seduction. The Count de Moustier is of a character
well assorted to this. Nothing niggardly, yet orderly in his affairs, genteel
but plain, loving society upon an easy not a splendid tone, unreserved,
honest, and speaking our language like a native. He goes with excellent
notions and dispositions, and is as likely to give satisfaction as any man
that could have been chosen in France.[48] He is much a whig in the politics
of his own country. I understand there is a possibility that Congress will
remove to Philadelphia.—My daughter talks of you often and much, still

48. On the dissatisfaction caused by the Count de Moustier and the Marquise de
Brehan in the United States, see Malone, *Jefferson*, II, 197-98.

fancies she is to pay you the visit she promised. In the mean time she is very contented in the Convent with her sister. Both join me in compliments to Mrs. Smith and in assurances to yourself of the attachment and respect which I have the honour to proffer for them as well as for, dear Madam, your most obedient and most humble servant,

TH: JEFFERSON

Jefferson to Adams

Paris Aug. 30. 1787.

DEAR SIR

Since your favor of July 10. mine have been of July 17. 23 and 28. The last inclosed a bill of exchange from Mr. Grand on Tessier for £46-17-10 sterl. to answer Genl. Sullivan's bill for that sum. I hope it got safe to hand, tho' I have been anxious about it as it went by post and my letters thro' that channel sometimes miscarry.

From the separation of the Notables to the present moment has been perhaps the most interesting interval ever known in this country. The propositions of the Government, approved by the Notables, were precious to the nation and have been in an honest course of execution, some of them being carried into effect, and others preparing. Above all the establishment of the Provincial assemblies, some of which have begun their sessions, bid fair to be the instrument for circumscribing the power of the crown and raising the people into consideration. The election given to them is what will do this. Tho' the minister who proposed these improvements seems to have meant them as the price of the new supplies, the game has been so played as to secure the improvements to the nation without securing the price. The Notables spoke softly on the subject of the additional supplies, but the parliament took them up roundly, refused to register the edicts for the new taxes, till compelled in a bed of justice [49] and prefered themselves to be transferred to Troyes rather than withdraw their opposition. It is urged principally against the king, that his revenue is 130. millions more than that of his predecessor was, and yet he demands 120. millions further. You will see this well explained in the 'Conference entre un ministre d'etat et un Conseiller au parlement' which I send you with some other small pamphlets. In the mean time all tongues in Paris

49. A court session attended by the king in person or by a prince of the blood as his immediate representative.

(and in France as it is said) have been let loose, and never was a license of speaking against the government exercised in London more freely or more universally. Caracatures, placards, bon mots, have been indulged in by all ranks of people, and I know of no well attested instance of a single punishment. For some time mobs of 10; 20; 30,000 people collected daily, surrounded the parliament house, huzzaed the members, even entered the doors and examined into their conduct, took the horses out of the carriages of those who did well, and drew them home. The government thought it prudent to prevent these, drew some regiments into the neighborhood, multiplied the guards, had the streets constantly patrolled by strong parties, suspended privileged places, forbad all clubs, etc. The mobs have ceased: perhaps this may be partly owing to the absence of parliament. The Count d'Artois, sent to hold a bed of justice in the Cour des Aides,[50] was hissed and hooted without reserve by the populace; the carriage of Madame de (I forget the name) in the queen's livery was stopped by the populace under a belief that it was Madame de Polignac's whom they would have insulted, the queen going to the theater at Versailles with Madame de Polignac was received with a general hiss. The king, long in the habit of drowning his cares in wine, plunges deeper and deeper; the queen cries but sins on. The Count d'Artois is detested, and Monsieur [Louis, Comte de Provence] [51] the general favorite. The Archbishop of Thoulouse is made Ministre principale, a virtuous, patriotic and able character. The Marechal de Castries retired yesterday notwithstanding strong sollicitations to remain in office. The Marechal de Segur retired at the same time, prompted to it by the court. Their successors are not yet known. M. de St. Prist goes Ambassador to Holland in the room of Verac transferred to Switzerland, and the Count de Moustier goes to America in the room of the Chevalier de la Luzerne who has a promise of the first vacancy. These nominations are not yet made formally, but they are decided on and the parties are ordered to prepare for their destination. As it has been long since I have had a confidential conveiance to you, I have brought together the principal facts from the adjournment of the Notables to the present moment which, as you will perceive from their nature, required a confidential conveyance.[52] I have done it the rather because, tho' you will have heard many of them and seen them in the public papers, yet floating in the mass of lies which constitute the atmospheres of London and Paris, you may not have been sure of their truth: and I have mentioned every truth of any consequence to enable you to

50. The Cour des Aides (excises), established in 1543, had jurisdiction in suits relating to tax revenues.
51. The King's eldest brother, later Louis XVIII.
52. Thomas Paine, who was carrying letters to London. Boyd, XII, 69n.

stamp as false the facts pretermitted. I think that in the course of three months the royal authority has lost, and the rights of the nation gained, as much ground, by a revolution of public opinion only, as England gained in all her civil wars under the Stuarts. I rather believe too they will retain the ground gained, because it is defended by the young and the middle aged, in opposition to the old only. The first party increases, and the latter diminishes daily from the course of nature. You may suppose that under this situation, war would be unwelcome to France. She will surely avoid it if not forced by the courts of London and Berlin. If forced, it is probable she will change the system of Europe totally by an alliance with the two empires, to whom nothing would be more desireable. In the event of such a coalition, not only Prussia but the whole European world must receive from them their laws. But France will probably endeavor to preserve the present system if it can be done by sacrifising to a certain degree the pretensions of the patriotic party in Holland. But of all these matters you can judge, in your position, where less secrecy is observed, better than I can. I have news from America as late as July 19. Nothing had then transpired from the Federal convention. I am sorry they began their deliberations by so abominable a precedent as that of tying up the tongues of their members. Nothing can justify this example but the innocence of their intentions, and ignorance of the value of public discussions. I have no doubt that all their other measures will be good and wise. It is really an assembly of demigods. Genl. Washington was of opinion they should not separate till October. I have the honour to be with every sentiment of friendship and respect Dear Sir Your most obedient and most humble servant,

TH: JEFFERSON

Adams to Jefferson

Grosvenor Square Sepr. 6 1787

DEAR SIR

I am Sorry to give you the trouble of this Commission: but I fear it will not be effectually done but by you, and therefore let me beg the favour of you to send for Mr. de La Blancherie and withdraw my Subscription to the Society of whose affairs he has the direction, and put a stop to his sending me the Nouvelles de la Republique des Lettres et Des Arts. He persuaded me at the Hague to Subscribe and paid him a years Subscription. The society continued One year and then ceased and I thought I had done with it forever: but since I have been in England now and then a Bundle of those Gazettes are pourd in upon me. I have no use for them, and sometimes I am put to an enormous expence of Postage. I am now determined at all Events to put a stop to it forever and pray you to take Measures for that purpose by paying him off and taking his Receipt, and by delivering him the inclosed Letter which Contains a Renunciation of my Subscription.

With great Esteem I am etc etc.

P.S. When I subcribed I understood it to be for one year only, and accordingly paid him the four Guineas. But I suppose he will now pretend that I am bound by that Subscription to pay for the Subsequent years. I will not dispute this with him, tho I am not bound in Law or Honour. One year the Society and Paper ceased since which it has been revived two years, or nearly so that he may pretend that I am eight Louis D'ors in Arrear. Pay him this if you please and no more, and I will repay you immediately. But at all Events I will be cleared from all Connection with this Man and his society and Nouvelles for the future.

J A

Abigail Adams to Jefferson

London Septr. 10th

DEAR SIR

Your obliging favours of july and August came safe to Hand. The first was brought during my absence on an excursion into the Country. I was very happy to find by it, that you had received your daughter safe, and that the dear Girl was contented. I never felt so attached to a child in my Life on so short an acquaintance. Tis rare to find one possessd of so strong and lively a sensibility. I hope she will not lose her fine spirits within the walls of a convent, to which I own I have many, perhaps false prejudices.

Mr. Appleton deliverd my Lace and gloves safe. Be so good as to let petit know that I am perfectly satisfied with them. Col. Smith has paid me the balance [which] you say was due to me, and I take your word for it, but [I do] not know how. The Bill which was accepted by Mr. Adams [in] the absence of Col. Smith, I knew would become due, in our absence, and before we could receive your orders. The money was left with Brisler our Servant, who paid it when it was presented. On our return we found the Bill which you had drawn on Mr. Tessier, but upon presenting it he refused to pay it, as he had not received any letter of advise tho it was then more than a month from its date, but he wrote immediatly to Mr. Grand, and by return of the next post, paid it.

With regard to your Harpsicord, Col. Smith who is now returnd, will take measures to have it sent to you. I went once to Mr. Kirkmans to inquire if it was ready. His replie was, that it should be ready in a few days, but [that he had] no orders further than to report when it [was done. I told him] to write you, but he seemd to think he had done all [that was] required of him. The Canister addrest to Mr. Drayton [was] delivered to Mr. Hayward with special directions, and he assured me he would not fail to deliver it.

The ferment and commotions in Massachusetts has brought upon the surface abundance of Rubbish; but still there is some sterling metal in the political crusible. The vote which was carried against an emission of paper money by a large majority in the House, shews that they have a sense of justice; which I hope will prevail in every department of the State. I send a few of our News papers, some of which contain sensible speculations.

To what do all the political motions tend which are agitating France Holland and Germany? Will Liberty finally gain the assendency, or arbitrary power strike her dead.

Is the report true that is circulated here, that Mr. Littlepage has a commission from the King of poland to his most Christian Majesty?!

We have not any thing from Mr. Jay later than 4th of july. There was not any congress then, or expected to be any untill the convention rises at Philadelphia.[53]

Col. Smith I presume will write you all the politicks of the Courts he has visited, and I will not detain you longer than to assure you that I am at all times Your Friend and Humble Servant,

A A

Adams to Jefferson

London Septr. 16, 1787

DEAR SIR

Give me Leave to introduce to you Mr. John Brown Cutting, who will need no other Recommendation, than his own Genius. Let me beg your acceptance, too of a Sett of my Defence etc. and let me know your Opinion of the Second volume, and whether it is worth my while to write a third upon Confederations etc. Yours most Sincerely,

JOHN ADAMS

53. The Federal Convention adjourned Sept. 17, 1787. Max Farrand, ed., *The Records of the Federal Convention of 1787* (rev. edn.; New Haven, 1937), II, 649.

Jefferson to Adams

Paris Sep. 28. 1787.

DEAR SIR

I received your favors by Mr. Cutting, and thank you sincerely for the copy of your book. The departure of a packet-boat, which always gives me full emploiment for some time before, has only permitted me to look into it a little. I judge of it from the first volume which I thought formed to do a great deal of good. The first principle of a good government is certainly a distribution of it's powers into executive, judiciary, and legislative, and a subdivision of the latter into two or three branches. It is a good step gained, when it is proved that the English constitution, acknowleged to be better than all which have proceeded it, is only better in proportion as it has approached nearer to this distribution of powers. From this the last step is easy, to shew by a comparison of our constitutions with that of England, how much more perfect they are. The article of Confederations is surely worthy of your pen. It would form a most interesting addition to shew what have been the nature of the Confederations which have existed hitherto, what were their excellencies and what their defects. A comparison of ours with them would be to the advantage of ours, and would increase the veneration of our countrymen for it. It is a misfortune that they do not sufficiently know the value of their constitutions and how much happier they are rendered by them than any other people on earth by the governments under which they live.—You know all that has happened in the United Netherlands.[54] You know also that our friends Van Staphorsts will be among the most likely to become objects of severity, if any severities should be exercised. Is the money in their hands entirely safe? If it is not, I am sure you have already thought of it. Are we to suppose the game already up, and that the Stadtholder is to be reestablished, perhaps erected into a monarch, without this country lifting a finger in opposition to it? If so, it is a lesson the more for us. In fact what a crowd of lessons do the present miseries of Holland teach us? Never to have an hereditary officer of any sort: never to let a citizen ally himself with kings: never to call in foreign nations to settle domestic differences: never to

54. The Patriot party had curtailed severely the powers of the Stadholder, William V of Orange, and insulted his wife, sister of the King of Prussia. When, in false expectation of help from France, the Patriots refused to make reparation, the Prussian Army under the Duke of Brunswick invaded the Netherlands on September 13 and, with the surrender of Amsterdam on October 10, completed occupation of the country. Petrus Johannes Blok, *History of the People of the Netherlands* (N. Y. and London, 1912), V, 244-53.

suppose that any nation will expose itself to war for us etc. Still I am not without hopes that a good rod is in soak for Prussia, and that England will feel the end of it. It is known to some that Russia made propositions to the emperor and France for acting in concert; that the emperor consents and has disposed four camps of 180,000 men from the limits of Turkey to those of Prussia. This court hesitates, or rather it's premier hesitates; for the queen, Monmorin and Breteuil are for the measure. Should it take place, all may yet come to rights, except for the Turks, who must retire from Europe; and this they must do were France Quixotic enough to undertake to support them. We I hope shall be left free to avail ourselves of the advantages of neutrality: and yet much I fear the English, or rather their stupid king, will force us out of it. For thus I reason. By forcing us into the war against them they will be engaged in an expensive land war as well as a sea war. Common sense dictates therefore that they should let us remain neuter: ergo they will not let us remain neuter. I never yet found any other general rule for foretelling what they will do, but that of examining what they ought not to do.—You will have heard doubtless that M. Lambert is Comptroller general, that the office of Directeur general du tresor royal has been successively refused by Monsr. de la Borde and Monsr. Cabarrus; that the Conte de Brienne, brother of the Archbishop, is minister of war, and the Count de la Luzerne minister of Marine. They have sent for him from his government in the West Indies. The Chevalier de la Luzerne has a promise of the first vacant Embassy. It will be that of London if Adhemar can be otherwise disposed of. The Chevalier might have had that of Holland if he would. The Count de Moustier will sail about the middle of next month. Count d'Aranda leaves us in a few days. His successor is hourly expected.—I have the honor to be with my best respects to Mrs. Adams, and sentiments of perfect esteem and regard to yourself dear Sir your most obedient and most humble servant,

TH: JEFFERSON

P.S. Since writing the above, I learn through a *very* [55] *good* [*channel*] *that this court is deci*[*ded*] *and is ar*[*ran*]*ging with the* [*two empires*]. Perhaps as a proof of this we may soon *see them recall their officers in the* [*Dutch serv*]*ice.*

55. This and subsequent words in italics were written in code. Syllables and words in brackets (supplied) are conjectured readings by the editors of *The Papers of Thomas Jefferson;* Boyd, XIII, 190.

Jefferson to Abigail Adams

Paris Octob. 4. 1787.

DEAR MADAM

By Mr. Cutting I have an opportunity of acknoleging the receipt of your favor of Sep. 10th. inclosing one for my daughter Polly. When she received it she flushed, she whitened, she flushed again, and in short was in such a flutter of joy that she could scarcely open it. This faithful history of her sensibility towards you must stand in lieu of her thanks which she has promised me she will write you herself: but at this moment she is in the convent where she is perfectly happy. By Mr. Cutting you will also receive the 5. aunes of cambric which Colo. Smith desired me to have purchased for you at 12. livres the aune. I am sorry you were put to the trouble of advancing the money for Mr. Sullivan's bill. I thought myself sure that Mr. Grand's bill would reach you in time, and did not know he had omitted to advise Mr. Teissier of it. He is always afraid to give to any body a complete power to call on him for money. Mr. Littlepage is here under a secret commission from the King of Poland. Possibly it may become a permanent one. I thank you for the American newspapers, and am glad to find that good sense is still uppermost in our country. Great events are I think preparing here: and a combination of force likely to take place which will change the face of Europe. Mr. Grenville has been very illy received. The annunciation by Mr. Eden that England was arming, was considered as an insult: after this and the King of Prussia's entrance on the territories of Holland, Mr. Grenville's arrival with conciliatory propositions is qualified with the title of 'une insulte tres gratuite.' I am not certain that the final decision of this country is yet taken. Perhaps the winter may be employed in previous arrangements unless any thing takes place at sea to bring on the rupture sooner. The Count de Gortz told me yesterday that the Prussian troops would retire from Holland the moment the states of Holland should make the expected reparation of the insult to the Princess. May not the scene which is preparing render it necessary for Mr. Adams to defer the return to his own country? I have the honor to be with very sincere sentiments of esteem and respect Dear Madam your most obedient and most humble servant,

TH: JEFFERSON

Adams to Jefferson

Grosvenor Square Oct. 9. 1787

DEAR SIR

I sent you a Copy of my second volume by Mr. Barthelemy the French Chargé here now Minister, with a Letter about Money matters. In your favour of Sept. 28. you dont mention the receipt of them.—I have indeed long thought with Anxiety of our Money in the hands of our Friends, whom you mention, and have taken the best Precaution in my Power, against Accidents. I do not consider the Game as up. But a disgrace has happened, which is not easy to get rid of.—Disgrace is not easily washed out, even with blood. Lessons my dear Sir, are never wanting. Life and History are full. The Loss of Paradise, by eating a forbidden apple, has been many Thousand years a Lesson to Mankind; but not much regarded. Moral Reflections, wise Maxims, religious Terrors, have little Effect upon Nations when they contradict a present Passion, Prejudice, Imagination, Enthusiasm or Caprice. Resolutions never to have an hereditary officer will be kept in America, as religiously as that of the Cincinnati was in the Case of General Greens son.[56] Resolutions never to let a Citizen ally himself with things will be kept untill an Opportunity presents to violate it. If the Duke of Angoleme, or Burgundy, or especially the Dauphin should demand one of your beautiful and most amiable Daughters in Marriage, all America from Georgia to New Hampshire would find their Vanity and Pride, so agreably flattered by it, that all their Sage Maxims would give way; and even our Sober New England Republicans would keep a day of Thanksgiving for it, in their hearts. If General Washington had a Daughter, I firmly believe, she would be demanded in Marriage by one of the Royal Families of France or England, perhaps by both, or if he had a Son he would be invited to come a courting to Europe.—The Resolution not to call in foreign Nations to settle domestic differences will be kept untill a domestic difference of a serious nature shall break out.—I have long been settled in my own opinion, that neither Philosophy, nor Religion, nor Morality, nor Wisdom, nor Interest, will ever govern nations or Parties, against their Vanity, their Pride, their Resentment or Revenge, or

56. Immediately after General Nathanael Greene's funeral at Savannah, June 20, 1786, members of the Georgia Society of the Cincinnati convened and resolved, out of respect to the late general, that his eldest son, George Washington Greene, be admitted to the Society, to take his seat on reaching the age of eighteen. G. W. Greene, *Life of Nathanael Greene* (N. Y., 1871), III, 535-36.

their Avarice or Ambition. Nothing but Force and Power and Strength can restrain them. If Robert Morris should maintain his Fortune to the End, I am convinced that some foreign Families of very high rank will think of Alliances with his Children. If the Pen Family should go to America, and engage in public affairs and obtain the Confidence of the People, you will see Connections courted there. A Troop of Light Horse from Philadelphia meeting Dick Pen in New Jersey, will strike the Imaginations of Princes and Princesses. How few Princes in Europe could obtain a Troop of Light Horse to make them a Compliment of Parade. In short my dear Friend you and I have been indefatigable Labourers through our whole Lives for a Cause which will be thrown away in the next generation, upon the Vanity and Foppery of Persons of whom we do not now know the Names perhaps.—The War that is now breaking out will render our Country, whether she is forced into it, or not, rich, great and powerful in comparison of what she now is, and Riches Grandeur and Power will have the same effect upon American as it has upon European minds. We have seen enough already to be sure of this. A Covent Garden Rake will never be wise enough to take warning from the Claps caught by his Companions. When he comes to be poxed himself he may possibly repent and reform. Yet three out of four of them become even by their own sufferings, more shameless instead of being penitent.

Pardon this freedom. It is not Melancholly: but Experience and believe me without reserve your Friend, O tempora— *oh mores*

JOHN ADAMS.

Adams to Jefferson

London Oct. 28. 1787

DEAR SIR

Mr. Daniel Parker will have the Honour to deliver you this. He is an intelligent American, and well informed as any Man you will see from hence. I beg leave to introduce him to you.

Let me thank you for your late Letter and the important State Papers inclosed with it.

I have ordered to your Address, a dozen Copies of my Boudoir [57] for the Marquis, who desired Mr. Appleton and Mr. Paine to have them sent. I have called it a Defence of the American Constitutions, because it is a

---

57. His pouting room or his study? See Boyd, XII, 293n.

Resistance to an Attack of Turgot. The two volumes are confined to one Point, and if a City is defended from an Attack made on the North Gate, it may be called a Defence of the City, although the other three Gates, the East West and South Gates were so weak, as to have been defenceless, if they had been attacked.—If a Warriour should arise to attack our Constitutions where they are not defencible, I'l not undertake to defend them. Two thirds of our States have made Constitutions, in no respect better than those of the Italian Republicks, and as sure as there is an Heaven and an Earth, if they are not altered they will produce Disorders and Confusion.

I can tell you nothing of Politicks. All the world is astonished at the Secrecy of Mr. Pitt. Great Preparations for War, yet the World can find no Ennemy nor Object. Carmarthen "hopes the Scudd will blow over, and even that the Quarrell between the Port and Russia will be made up. While a Fire is burning in any quarter of Europe, no one can tell when or where it may Spread." The General Understanding is that the U.S. are to be let alone, and they have given general orders to the Navy, to let American Vessells and Seamen alone. They will have their hands full, I believe, and there is little Plunder to be made of Americans, so that we may be quiet,—as long as they will let us.—But our Countrymen will do well to think of the Possibility of Danger and of the means of Defence. A war would cost us more than we have of Cash or Credit, but if we should be attacked we must defend, Money or no Money, Credit or no Credit. Whether John Bull has Command enough of his Passions to see us punctually fulfill our Treaties, as we must do, without being transported with rage, you who know him can tell as well as I.—We know this Gentlemans hasty Temper so well that I think we may very safely wish for the Continuance of Peace, between France and him, even upon Selfish Principles, tho' our Commerce and Navigation would be greatly promoted by a War, if we can keep out of it.

I tremble and agonize for the suffering Patriots in Holland. You may judge to what Lengths the Spight extends against them, by a formal Complaint of their High Mightinesses against Dumas, and a Requisition to me, to employ him no longer but to appoint some other Person in my absence. It is not I am well persuaded as Agent for the United States, but as a Friend of France or of the Patriotic Party against the Statholder, that he has unfortunately incurred this Censure and Displeasure. Yet as Mr. Dumas holds not his Character or Authority from me, I can do nothing, but transmit the Papers to Congress. With great Esteem, I have the honour to be dear Sir, your most obedient Servant,

JOHN ADAMS

6

"On... Guard against the immeasurable avarice of Amsterdam"

IN THE HISTORY of the American Republic as well as in the careers of its two ministers to the courts of western Europe, the years 1788-89 marked the end of an era. This was, in fact, the end of an era in the Western world. In February 1787 Jefferson learned that Adams had requested Congress to relieve him of his office so that he might return home.[1] To Jefferson this was most unwelcome news, for he relied on Adams for advice and felt more confidence in his own diplomatic maneuvers because he respected Adams's judgment and longer experience. At the same time he was sympathetic with Adams's desire to depart, for he did "not wonder at your being tired out by the conduct of the court you are at."[2] Jefferson had diagnosed the case correctly; but, fortunately for him and his country, Adams was not released until the spring of 1788. In the interim he was able to contribute something toward meeting the financial obligations of the United States through his previous connections in Holland.

The American debt to France, incurred during the Revolutionary War, had continued unpaid and now interest payments were in arrears. If, however, the American Republic was a debtor nation, the French monarchy was much worse off, with failing revenues aggravated by a restrictive mercantile policy and an extravagant court. Since the United States was still allied with France, Jefferson was sorely embarrassed by the vociferous complaints of French officers whom Congress had failed to pension for their services in the War for

1. W. S. Smith to TJ, Jan. 29, 1787, Boyd, XI, 91.
2. TJ to JA, Feb. 20, 1787, above, 172.

Independence, though legally and morally bound to do so. This damage to American prestige was more injurious to Jefferson's sensibilities than the shortage of his own salary at the hands of the same impecunious Congress.[3] Nevertheless, the young United States, an expanding nation with vast undeveloped resources, was a good financial risk; and Dutch bankers with money to lend recognized America's need as their opportunity.[4]

In the late spring of 1787, without authorization from Congress but in the face of interest payments due June 1, Adams secured a Dutch loan of $400,000 at 5 per cent and, to please the brokers, he went to Holland to sign the obligations. The bonds were not to be issued until approved by Congress. He believed that the domestic debt of the United States as well as its debt to France might be transferred to Holland, if Congress would only take action; indeed, he maintained that the distress and confusion in America resulted mainly "from downright Ignorance of the Nature of Coin, Credit and Circulation." [5] His proposal for transfer was turned down, although the new 5 per cent loan was approved. In January 1788 the twelve-year loan of 1776, the first obtained from private capital during the war (51,000 florins or $20,400), came due to Fizeau & Company in Holland. Would the Amsterdam bankers provide funds for a new loan to pay off the old debt? "Mr. Van staphorst" (of Van Staphorst & Willinck), Adams assured Jefferson, "will have no objection to an handsome Commission, for paying off, the Debt"; in fact, the moneylenders would probably be satisfied with interest payments until Congress could refinance the loans.[6] Adams proved to be somewhat overoptimistic in his expectation. When the banker Willinck insisted on an order from the Treasury of the United States, Jefferson, "willing to participate with you in any risk," [7] looked to Adams to take the lead in these financial negotiations.

The situation was complicated by the fact that much of the domestic as well as the foreign debt of the United States had been bought up at low rates by speculators, supported by collusion between certain

3. TJ to JA, July 17 and 23, 1787, above, 189-90; see also Boyd, XI, 699-700*n.*, and TJ to Abbé Morellet, Oct. 24, 1787, *ibid.*, XII, 286-87.
4. See P. J. van Winter, *Het Aandeel van den Amsterdamschen Handel aan den Opbouw van het Amerikaansche Gemeenebest* (Hague, 1927).
5. JA to TJ, Aug. 25, 1787, above, 191-92; Jefferson, "Autobiography," Ford, I, 116-17.
6. JA to TJ, Dec. 25, 1787, below, 219.
7. TJ to JA, Dec. 12 and 31, 1787, Jan. 13, 1788, below, 215-16, 220, 221.

Americans and Europeans; and the prospects of improved credit under the new Constitution of the United States, now in process of ratification, encouraged the moneylenders. But European confidence in the American people was more than matched by that of Jefferson who declared that he "had rather trust money in their hands than in that of any government on earth." [8]

With Adams departing shortly for America, the burden of this financial problem would rest solely on his Virginia colleague. Fortunately they were able to join forces for a few days in Amsterdam in March 1788 and negotiate a new loan to meet interest payments and other expenses until the new government could get under way.[9] It was distasteful business dealing with speculators, who took every advantage of their superior bargaining power; yet Adams sensed their respect for American credit: "The Amsterdammers love Money too well, to execute their Threats." [10] The bankers were not genuinely interested in getting subscriptions to the new loan beyond the extent that payment of their own interest charges would be assured; therefore after his return to Paris, Jefferson directed his thoughts to a plan for funding the debt over a period of years, the scheduled payments to be derived from duties on imports. Although he failed to get support for the scheme from the expiring Congress of the Confederation, he did anticipate Hamilton's plan adopted by the Congress of the new government, and Jefferson's proposals, recently discovered among his papers, add another cubit to his stature as a practical student of finance.[11]

Among the perennial commercial problems that occupied the ministers of a trading nation struggling for favorable status, the whale-oil fishery came to the fore again in 1788. Jefferson prepared himself to meet the issue. In seeking to recover the markets lost during the War for Independence,[12] the Nantucket whalers were susceptible to offers from both France and Britain, although they were not inclined to change their nationality. Since the war, the British had made a vigorous effort to capture the oil business, but "les Nantuckois," now in distress,

8. TJ to C. W. F. Dumas, Feb. 9, 1787, Boyd, XI, 128.

9. TJ to John Jay, March 13 and 16, 1788, *ibid.*, XII, 661, 671-73.

10. JA to TJ, Feb. 12, 1788, below, 225.

11. TJ's assessment of the debt problem and his attempt to solve it in the face of prevailing opposition and indifference in America and Europe are forcefully presented by Julian P. Boyd in the editorial note to "Proposals for Funding the Foreign Debt," Boyd, XIV, 190-97; "Jefferson's Plan," [Oct. 1788], *ibid.*, 201-9.

12. See above, Chap. 5.

proved more sensitive to French blandishments than to English. In 1786 the port of Dunkirk was opened to William Rotch of Nantucket and his associates. Then in December 1787 the French allowed an abatement of duties on American oil, an affront to the British who retaliated by providing government premiums for underselling the French markets. When the Dunkirk fishermen raised a loud protest, the French answer was the Arrêt (decree) of September 28, 1788, banning the oil trade with all nations. Since *European* oil had not been specified in the decree, *American* was not excepted. This threat of disaster to American interests stirred Jefferson to action. Within a few weeks he gathered pertinent data and documents and composed his substantial *Observations on the Whale Fishery*. This was followed shortly by a "Report to the Ministry" and the Arrêt of December 7, restoring the privileges of American whale oil.[13] Jefferson had not only scored an important gain for American trade; he had also won an advantage over the British insofar as it could be enforced.[14] And he had produced a valuable historical document on whaling in his *Observations*.

If the specific accomplishments of Jefferson and Adams for the United States were of limited duration, one must remember that the bargaining power of a weak republic held a low rating among kings, except to tip the scales in their own game of diplomacy. How could the American Confederation's hand be strengthened? Its ministers abroad provided the answer on numerous occasions, as Jefferson did in the spring of 1786: "I am in hopes our letters will give a new spi[rit] to the proposition for investing Congress with the regulation of our commerce." [15] It was commercial issues that led delegates from a few states to assemble at Annapolis in September of that year, providing the prelude to the Federal Convention in Philadelphia in 1787.

It seems almost an injustice, an inappropriate course of events, that neither Adams nor Jefferson was a member of the Federal Convention, that "assembly of demigods," as Jefferson called it.[16] He deplored its secret sessions, and though he was attached to "the good, old, and

13. "Documents Concerning the Whale Fishery," editorial note, Boyd, XIV, 217-25; *Observations on the Whale Fishery* [Paris, 1788], anonymous, without title page or imprint, 18 pages, printed by Jacques-Gabriel Clousier, text in *ibid.*, 242-54; "Report to the Ministry," *ibid.*, 256-67; "Arret, 7 December 1788," *ibid.*, 268-69; TJ to JA, Dec. 5, 1788, below, 232-33.
14. TJ to Jay, Jan. 14, 1789, Boyd, XIV, 447; TJ to JA, Jan. 14, 1789, below, 234-35.
15. TJ to William Carmichael, May 5, 1786, Boyd, IX, 449.
16. TJ to JA, Aug. 30, 1787, above, 196.

venerable fabrick," the Articles of Confederation,[17] he later hailed the new Constitution as "unquestionably the wisest ever yet presented to men."[18] At his inaugural in 1797, President Adams pointed out, "I first saw the Constitution of the United States in a foreign country. Irritated by no literary altercation, animated by no public debate, heated by no party animosity, I read it with great satisfaction.... In its general principles and great outlines it was conformable to such a system of government as I had ever most esteemed...."[19] This was written ten years afterward, with the retrospect of eight years' experience in the operation of the government. However, as we have seen,[20] his *Defence of the Constitutions* of the several states had arrived in Philadelphia in time to lend serious weight to the argument on behalf of balanced government for the United States of America.

When Adams first read the Constitution, he feared the aristocracy implicit in the Senate rather more than he did the power of the presidency, although he wanted assurance that the latter was properly separated from the legislative branch.[21] To Jefferson he promptly posed the question of a declaration of rights, and after returning to America he observed that "Amendments to the Constitution, will be expected."[22] While Jefferson maintained that "a bill of rights is what the people are entitled to against every government on earth,"[23] he was noncommittal on the Virginia General Assembly's resolution of November 20, 1788, calling for a second constitutional convention.[24]

As Abigail made preparations for the long anticipated return to Massachusetts, Jefferson wrote her, "I have considered you while in London as my neighbor." When he proposed that they continue their correspondence, she gratefully accepted,[25] but sixteen years were to elapse before it was resumed. The Adamses arrived in Boston aboard the *Lucretia* on June 17, 1788. The following autumn Jefferson requested leave of absence to take his daughters home and to attend to

17. TJ to JA, Nov. 13, 1787, below, 212.
18. TJ to David Humphreys, March 18, 1789, Boyd, XIV, 678.
19. James D. Richardson, ed., *Messages and Papers of the Presidents, 1789-1902* ([Washington?], 1903), I, 229.
20. See above, Chap. 5.
21. JA to TJ, Dec. 6, 1787, March 1, 1789, below, 213-14, 236.
22. JA to TJ, Nov. 10, 1787, March 1, 1789, below, 210, 236.
23. TJ to James Madison, Dec. 20, 1787, Boyd, XII, 440.
24. *Ibid.*, XIV, xxxviii-xxxix, and facing p. 329.
25. TJ to AA, Feb. 2, 1788, and AA to TJ, Feb. 21, 1788, below, 222, 226.

his affairs at Monticello.[26] His departure was to be delayed a year during which he watched with intense interest the first critical events of the French Revolution—the convening of the Estates General, the fall of the Bastille. In the autumn of 1789 he would return permanently to enter the service of the new government as secretary of state, again a colleague of John Adams, first vice-president of the United States.

Adams to Jefferson

London. Nov. 10. 1787

My dear Sir

Mr. Boylston is going to Paris, with a Cargo of Sperma Cæti oil, and will be obliged to you for any assistance or advice you can give him.

I forwarded a few days ago, from Mr. Gerry, a Copy as I suppose of the Result of Convention.—It seems to be admirably calculated to preserve the Union, to increase Affection, and to bring us all to the same mode of thinking. They have adopted the Idea of the Congress at Albany in 1754 of a President to nominate officers and a Council to Consent: [27] but thank heaven they have adopted a third Branch, which that Congress did not. I think that Senates and Assemblies should have nothing to do with executive Power. But still I hope the Constitution will be adopted, and Amendments be made at a more convenient opportunity.

What think you of a Declaration of Rights? [28] Should not such a Thing have preceeded the Model?

People here are Solacing themselves in the Prospect of the Continuance of Peace: and the tryumphant Party in Holland carry a high hand.—I suspect that both are rather too sanguine.—They have very insufficient Grounds for so much Exultation. My worthy old Friends the Patriots in Holland are extreamly to be pittied: and so are their deluded Persecutors. That Country I fear is to be ruined, past all Remedy. I wish that all the good Men had Sense and Spirit enough to go to America. With the usual Sentiments Yours,

John Adams

26. TJ to John Jay, Nov. 19, 1788, Boyd, XIV, 214-16.

27. Under Article 23 of the Albany Plan of Union all civil officers were to be nominated by the Grand Council and approved by the President-General. Albert Henry Smyth, ed., *The Writings of Benjamin Franklin* (N. Y., 1907), III, 224-25.

28. The Massachusetts Constitution of 1780, drafted chiefly by JA, was prefaced by a declaration of rights. F. N. Thorpe, ed., *Federal and State Constitutions, Colonial Charters, and Other Organic Laws* (Washington, 1909), III, 1880-1923.

Jefferson to Adams

Paris Nov. 13. 1787.

DEAR SIR

This will be delivered you by young Mr. Rutledge. Your knowledge of his father will introduce him to your notice. He merits it moreover on his own account.

I am now to acknolege your favors of Oct. 8 and 26. That of August 25. was duly received, nor can I recollect by what accident I was prevented from acknoleging it in mine of Sep. 28. It has been the source of my subsistence hitherto, and must continue to be so till I receive letters on the affairs of money from America. Van Staphorsts & Willinks have answered my draughts.—Your books for M. de la Fayette are received here. I will notify it to him, who is at present with his provincial assembly in Auvergne.

Little is said lately of the progress of the negociations between the courts of Petersburg, Vienna, and Versailles. The distance of the former and the cautious, unassuming character of it's minister here is one cause of delays: a greater one is the greediness and instable character of the emperor. Nor do I think that the Principal here [Brienne] will be easily induced to lend himself to any connection which shall threaten a war within a considerable number of years. His own reign will be that of peace only, in all probability; and were any accident to tumble him down, this country would immediately gird on it's sword and buckler, and trust to occurrences for supplies of money. The wound their honour has sus tained festers in their hearts, and it may be said with truth that the Arch- bishop and a few priests, determined to support his measures because proud to see their order come again into power, are the only advocates for the line of conduct which has been pursued. It is said and believed thro' Paris literally that the Count de Monmorin 'pleuroit comme un enfant ["wept like a child"]' when obliged to sign the counter declaration.[29] Considering the phrase as figurative, I believe it expresses the distress of his heart. Indeed he has made no secret of his individual opinion. In the mean time the Principal goes on with a firm and patriotic spirit, in re- forming the cruel abuses of the government and preparing a new constitu-

29. At Versailles on Oct. 27, 1787, British representatives signed a declaration that Britain would disarm if France gave satisfactory explanation on the Dutch question; Montmorin signed a counter declaration that France had never intended to interfere in the affairs of the Dutch Republic and retained no hostility. This concession further weakened the declining prestige of the kingdom of France. *Annual Register, 1787,* 282-83.

tion which will give to this people as much liberty as they are capable of managing. This I think will be the glory of his administration, because, tho' a good theorist in finance, he is thought to execute badly. They are about to open a loan of 100. millions to supply present wants, and it is said the preface of the Arret will contain a promise of the Convocation of the States general during the ensuing year. 12. or 15. provincial assemblies are already in action, and are going on well; and I think that tho' the nation suffers in reputation, it will gain infinitely in happiness under the present administration. I inclose to Mr. Jay a pamphlet which I will beg of you to forward. I leave it open for your perusal. When you shall have read it, be so good as to stick a wafer in it. It is not yet published, nor will be for some days. This copy has been ceded to me as a favor.

How do you like our new constitution? I confess there are things in it which stagger all my dispositions to subscribe to what such an assembly has proposed. The house of federal representatives will not be adequate to the management of affairs either foreign or federal. Their President seems a bad edition of a Polish king. He may be reelected from 4. years to 4. years for life. Reason and experience prove to us that a chief magistrate, so continuable, is an officer for life. When one or two generations shall have proved that this is an office for life, it becomes on every succession worthy of intrigue, of bribery, of force, and even of foreign interference. It will be of great consequence to France and England to have America governed by a Galloman or Angloman. Once in office, and possessing the military force of the union, without either the aid or check of a council, he would not be easily dethroned, even if the people could be induced to withdraw their votes from him. I wish that at the end of the 4. years they had made him for ever ineligible a second time. Indeed I think all the good of this new constitution might have been couched in three or four new articles to be added to the good, old, and venerable fabrick, which should have been preserved even as a religious relique.— Present me and my daughters affectionately to Mrs. Adams. The younger one continues to speak of her warmly. Accept yourself assurances of the sincere esteem and respect with which I have the honour to be, Dear Sir, your friend and servant,

TH: JEFFERSON

P.S. I am in negociation with de la Blancherie. You shall hear from me when arranged.

Abigail Adams to Jefferson

London Grosvenour Square December 5th 1787.

Mrs. Adams presents her respectfull compliments to Mr. Jefferson and asks the favour of him to permit petit to purchase for her ten Ells of double Florence of any fashionable coulour, orange excepted which is in high vogue here. Mrs. A. excepts green also of which she has enough. Mr. Muchier if in paris will be so kind as to take charge of it, and Mrs. Adams will send the money by Mr. Trumble who will be in paris some time next week.

By Letters this day received from Boston it appears that a convention [30] was agred too by both Houses, and that it is to meet, the second wednesday in Jan'ry.

Mr. King writes that Mr. Jeffersons commission is renewed at the court of France, and Mr. Adams's resignation accepted, so that we shall quit this country as soon in the spring as we can go with safety. Love to the Young Ladies and thank my dear polly for her pretty Letter.

Adams to Jefferson

London Decr. 6. 1787

DEAR SIR

The Project of a new Constitution, has Objections against it, to which I find it difficult to reconcile my self, but I am so unfortunate as to differ somewhat from you in the Articles, according to your last kind Letter.

You are afraid of the one—I, of the few. We agree perfectly that the many should have a full fair and perfect Representation.—You are Apprehensive of Monarchy; I, of Aristocracy. I would therefore have given more Power to the President and less to the Senate. The Nomination and Appointment to all offices I would have given to the President, assisted only by a Privy Council of his own Creation, but not a Vote or Voice would I have given to the Senate or any Senator, unless he were of the Privy Council. Faction and Distraction are the sure and certain Consequence of giving to a Senate a vote in the distribution of offices.

You are apprehensive the President when once chosen, will be chosen again and again as long as he lives. So much the better as it appears to me.

30. The Massachusetts convention to consider ratification of the United States Constitution.

—You are apprehensive of foreign Interference, Intrigue, Influence. So am I.—But, as often as Elections happen, the danger of foreign Influence recurs. The less frequently they happen the less danger.—And if the Same Man may be chosen again, it is probable he will be, and the danger of foreign Influence will be less. Foreigners, seeing little Prospect will have less Courage for Enterprize.

Elections, my dear sir, Elections to offices which are great objects of Ambition, I look at with terror. Experiments of this kind have been so often tryed, and so universally found productive of Horrors, that there is great Reason to dread them.

Mr. Littlepage who will have the Honour to deliver this will tell you all the News. I am, my dear Sir, with great Regard,

JOHN ADAMS

Adams to Jefferson

Grosvenor Square Decr 10. 1787

DEAR SIR

I last night received, the Ratification of my last Loan and the inclosed Resolution of Congress of 18 July last, for the Redemption of Prisoners of Algiers. It is probable You have received it before, but as it is, in your Department to execute it, and possible that you may not have received it, I thought it Safest to transmit it to you, as I have now the honour to do, here inclosed. Mr. Vanberckel, Son of the Minister, is arrived at Falmouth by the Packet, but not yet in London. By him, I expect my Dismission. The American Newspapers, already arrived both from New York and Boston, announce it to have passed in Congress, the 5. of October, and now as we say at Sea, huzza for the new world and farewell to the Old One.

All Europe resounds with Projects for reviving, States and Assemblies, I think: and France is taking the lead.—How such assemblies will mix, with Simple Monarchies, is the question. The Fermentation must terminate in Improvements of various kinds. Superstition, Bigotry, Ignorance, Imposture, Tyranny and Misery must be lessened somewhat.—But I fancy it will be found somewhat difficult, to conduct and regulate these debates. Ex quovis ligno non fit Mercurius.[31] The world will be entertained with noble sentiments and enchanting Eloquence, but will not essential Ideas be sometimes forgotten, in the anxious study of brilliant Phrases? Will

31. "An image of Mercury is not made out of any block of wood."

the Duke of orleans make a Sterling Patriot and a determined son of Liberty? [32] Will he rank with Posterity among the Brutus's and Catos?—Corrections and Reformations and Improvements are much wanted in all the Institutions of Europe Ecclesiastical and civil: but how or when they will be made is not easy to guess.—It would be folly I think to do no more than try over again Experiments, that have been already a million times tryed. Attempts to reconcile Contradictions will not succeed, and to think of Reinstituting Republicks, as absurdly constituted as were the most which the world has seen, would be to revive Confusion and Carnage, which must again End in despotism.—I shall soon be out of the Noise of all these Speculations in Europe leaving behind me however the most fervent good Wishes for the Safety and Prosperity of all who have the Cause of Humanity, Equity, Equality and Liberty at heart. With the tenderest Affection of Friendship, I am and ever shall be my dear Sir Yours,

JOHN ADAMS

Abigail Adams to Jefferson

Grosvenour Square december 12th 1787

Mrs. Adams's compliments to Mr. Jefferson and in addition to her former memorandum she requests half a dozen pr. of mens silk stockings. Mr. Trumble will deliver to Mr. Jefferson four Louis and one Guiney. Mr. parker will be so good as to take charge of them, if no opportunity offers before his return.

Jefferson to Adams

Paris Dec. 12. 1787.

DEAR SIR

In the month of July I received from Fiseaux & co. of Amsterdam a letter notifying me that the principal of their loan to the United states would become due the first day of January. I answered them that I had neither powers nor information on the subject, but would transmit their letter to the Board of treasury. I did so by the packet which sailed from

32. The Duke of Orleans was elected to the French Constitutional Convention and changed his name to Philippe Egalité; and, although he voted for the execution of his cousin Louis XVI in 1792, he himself was guillotined the following year. Leo Gershoy, *The French Revolution and Napoleon* (N. Y., 1933), 230, 276.

Havre Aug. 10. The earliest answer possible would have been by the packet which arrived at Havre three or four days ago. But by her I do not receive the scrip of a pen from any body. This makes me suppose that my letters are committed to Paul Jones who was to sail a week after the departure of the packet: and that possibly he may be the bearer of orders from the treasury to repay Fiseaux' loan with the money you borrowed. But it is also possible he may bring no order on the subject. The slowness with which measures are adopted on our side the water does not permit us to count on punctual answers: but on the contrary renders it necessary for us to suppose in the present case that no orders will arrive in time, and to consider whether any thing, and what should be done? As it may be found expedient to transfer all our foreign debts to Holland by borrowing there, and as it may always be prudent to preserve a good credit in that country because we may [be] forced into wars whether we will or no, I should suppose it very imprudent to suffer our credit to be annihilated by so small a sum as 51,000 guelders. The injury will be greater too in proportion to the smallness of the sum: for they will ask 'How can a people be trusted for large sums who break their faith for such small ones?' You know best what effect it will have on the minds of the money lenders of that country should we fail in this payment. You know best also whether it is practicable and prudent for us to have this debt paid without orders. I refer the matter therefore wholly to your consideration, willing to participate with you in any risk, and any responsability which may arise. I think it one of those cases where it is a duty to risk one's self. You will perceive, by the inclosed, the necessity of an immediate answer, and that if you think any thing can and should be done all the necessary authorities from you should accompany your letter. In the mean time should I receive any orders from the Treasury by P. Jones, I will pursue them, and consider whatever you shall have proposed or done, as *non avenue*. I am with much affection Dear Sir Your most obedient and most humble servt.,

TH: JEFFERSON

Jefferson to Adams

Paris Dec. 16. 1787.

DEAR SIR

I wrote you on the 12th instant, that is to say, by the last post. But as that channel of conveiance is sometimes unfaithful I now inclose you a copy of my letter of that date, and of the one of Fiseaux & co. inclosed in that. I have since received my letters by the packet, but, among them, nothing from the Board of Treasury. Still their orders may be among the dispatches with which Paul Jones is charged for me, who was to sail a week after the packet. If he brings any orders, what you shall have done as I observed in my former letter shall be considered as if not done. On further consideration and consultation the object of my letter seems to increase in importance and to render it indispensible in us to do what we can, even without orders, to save the credit of the U.S. I have conferred with Mr. Jacob Van Staphorst, who is here, on this subject. He thinks the failure would have so ill an effect that it should certainly be prevented, he supposes the progress of your late loan may by this time furnish money in the hands of Willincks and Van Staphorsts to face this demand, and at any rate that these gentlemen will exert themselves to do it. By his advice I wrote to ask of them if I might count on their doing it, provided I forwarded your orders, and I wrote to Fizeaux & Co. what steps I was taking, desired them to confer with Willincks and Van Staphorsts, and to regulate the expectations of our creditors accordingly. The answer of Willincks and Van Staphorsts which I shall receive the 22d. inst. and yours which I hope to receive about the same time will decide what is to be done. Still it will be about the 28th. before Fizeaux can receive it through me, and he sais notice should have been given by the middle of the month.

I see by the American papers that your commission to the United Netherlands continues till the spring. Will you have to go there to take leave? If you do, and will give me notice in time, I will meet you there. In so doing I shall gratify my wish to see you before you leave Europe, to confer with you on some subjects, and become acquainted with our money affairs at Amsterdam, and that ground in general on which it may be rendered necessary, by our various debts, for me sometimes to undertake to act. I am very ignorant of it at present. I am with great and sincere esteem Dr. Sir Your most obedient and mo. humble servt.,

TH: JEFFERSON

Adams to Jefferson

London Decr. 18 1787

DEAR SIR

Last night I received your Letter of the 12. Mr. Jarvis and Commodore Jones are arrived here from New york both charged with large Dispatches for you. Mr. Jarvis Sent his Packet on by Col. Trumbul who departed from hence for Paris last Thursday. Comr. Jones went off a day or two ago, but both will arrive to you before this Letter. The Papers they carry, with a Renovation of your Commission at the Court of Versailles contain I presume orders and Instructions about every Thing in Holland.

As my Dismission from the Service arrived at the Same time, not a word has been said to me. Nevertheless Nil Americanum Alienum,[33] and I have the honour to agree with you in Your opinion of the Propriety of keeping good our Credit in Holland. I should advise therefore that the Interest on Mr. Fizeaux's Loan at least should be paid, and the Creditors requested to wait for their Capitals till further orders can be obtained from Congress. If they will not consent to that, I would pay them Principal and Interest provided there is Money enough in the hands of our Bankers and neither you nor they have received contrary orders. No Authorities from me will be necessary. Your own Letter to Messrs. Willinks and Vanstapherst will be sufficient. But if they make any difficulty, which I cannot conceive for want of any orders from me, I will send them.

You have received Authority to negotiate the Redemption of our unfortunate Countrymen in Algiers. To you therefore I send a Petition which I received from them a few days ago. With the highest Regard, I am Dear Sir your most obedient and most humble Servant,

JOHN ADAMS

N.B.[34] The Letter which Colo. Trumbull will deliver addressed to Count Sarsfield, may be sent to his hotel as the Count is on the point of departure for Paris. On referring to a resolve of Congress of the 11th. of october 1787. I find the interest of the foreign debt and that part of the principal due in 1788. has commanded their attention and I suppose put in proper train for operation. Yours,

J. ADAMS

Adams to Jefferson

London Decr. 25. 1787

DEAR SIR

By the last Post I answered your Letter of the 12, and Yesterday received yours of the 16. Com. Jones has before now delivered you dis-

---

33. "Nothing proper to an American is foreign to me"; a condensed adaptation of Terence: *Homo sum; humani nihil a me alienum puto*—"I am a man, and I regard nothing proper to mankind as foreign to me."
34. Postscript in William Stephens Smith's hand but signed by JA.

patches that will serve no doubt for your direction. Mr. Van staphorst, will have no Objection to an handsome Commission, for paying off, the Debt Mr. Fizeaux mentions: and Mr. Fizeau, will be glad to have it paid off, that the Money Lenders not knowing what to do with their Money may be tempted to put it into his French loan. But I am persuaded the Money Lenders on receiving their Interest would very willingly let the Principal remain, till the arrangements of Congress can discharge it. It will cost the United States Eight Per Cent, to transfer this debt, and four or five thousand Guilders are worth saving.

It would rejoice me in my soul to meet you, before I embark for America. But I am so ill, of an uncommon Cold, the present weather is so formidable and a Journey to Holland in the winter is so cruel, that I am obliged to excuse myself from taking leave in Person of the States general, and shall send a Memorial. The Time for me is short and there are many Things to do, so that I must confine my self to London, but if you could venture over here and see the August Spectacle of Mr. Hastings's Impeachment,[35] you would make us all very happy.

I should advise you, by all means to make a Journey to Holland; but not before the Month of May. A Letter to some of the Corps Diplomatique, will introduce You to them and to Court, and Messrs. Willinks and Vanstaphorsts will shew you Amsterdam, and explain to you Money matters. With Sincere Esteem and affection, I am Dear Sir your most obedient and most humble Servant,

JOHN ADAMS

Jefferson to Adams

Paris Dec. 31. 1787.

DEAR SIR

Mr. Parker furnishes me an opportunity of acknoleging the receipt of your favors of Nov. 10. Dec. 6.[36] 10. 18. and 25. which I avoid doing thro post. The orders on the subject of our captives at Algiers have come to

35. Charged with financial extortions from the natives of India, the late governor-general had been impeached by the House of Commons on April 3, 1787; his trial began the following Feb. and he was finally acquitted in 1795. H. G. Keene, "Hastings, Warren," *Dictionary of National Biography*, XXV, 145.

36. This letter, recorded in Jefferson's Summary Journal of Letters as received on Dec. 17, 1787, has not been found. His summary indicates that Adams was recommending Antoine-Marie Cerisier, French historian and diplomat, who was attached to the French embassy in Holland, where Adams met him in 1780. C. F. Adams, "Life of John Adams," *Works*, I, 330; JA to John Luzac, Dec. 13, 1781, *ibid.*, VII, 492. See also Boyd, XII, 397.

me by the last packet. They are to be kept secret even from the captives themselves, lest a knolege of the interference of government should excite too extravagant demands. The settlement of the prices, in the first instance, is important as a precedent.—Willincks & Van Staphorsts answered that they had money enough to pay the February interest, and our draughts for salary for some time, but that the paiment of Fiseaux' capital would oblige them to advance of their own money: they observed too that the paiment of such a sum without the orders of the treasury would lay them under an unnecessary responsibility. I therefore concluded the business by desiring them to pay the year's interest becoming due tomorrow, and praying Mr. Fiseaux to quiet the lenders with that till I could procure the orders of the Treasury to whom I wrote immediately an account of the whole transaction. I was the better satisfied with this on receiving your letter of the 25th. by which I find it your opinion that our credit may not suffer so materially. The declining the paiment came from the Willincks, the Van Staphorsts having offered to advance their moiety. I inclose you a letter I have received from the Comptroller general and an arret on the subject of our commerce.[37] They are the proof sheets, as, at the moment of writing my letter, I have not yet received the fair ones. But the French column is correct enough to be understood. I would wish them not to be public till they are made so on the other side of the water. —I think the alliance of this court with the two imperial ones is going on well. You will have heard of the Emperor's having attempted to surprise Belgrade and failed in the attempt. This necessarily engages him in the war, and so tends to continue it. I think it settled that this country abandons the Turks.

Mr. Parker takes charge of the 10. aunes of double Florence for Mrs. Adams. The silk stockings are not yet ready. I had ordered them to be made by the hermits of Mont Calvaire [38] who are famous for the excellence and honesty of their work, and prices. They will come by the first good opportunity. Be so good as to present my respects to her, and to be assured of the sincere attachment and respect of Dear Sir your most obedient and most humble servant,

TH: JEFFERSON

37. Wroth and Annan, eds., *Acts of French Royal Administration*, no. 2060.
38. Carthusian monastery where silence was enjoined. TJ rented rooms there beginning in Sept. 1787. Malone, *Jefferson*, II, 137-38.

Jefferson to Adams

Paris Jan. 13. 1788.

DEAR SIR

I informed you in my letter of the 31st. of December of the measures I had taken relative to the reimbursement of the 51,000 gelders to Fizeaux & co. to wit, that I had asked the Willincks and Van Staphorsts to pay the interest, and written to the board of treasury for their orders as to the principal. I inclose you a letter just received from Fizeaux & Co. now Hugguer, Grand & Co. by which you will perceive that they have recieved the interest, but that the creditors will not consent to delay the reimbursement of their capital. I inclose you a copy also of what I now write to the Willincks & Van Staphorsts, and will beg of you to give or refuse your sanction, as you think best, but in a letter sent directly to them, because I find by their letters to Mr. Jac. Van Staphorst, they will not be contented with the indirect authorisation of your former letter to me. Perhaps in any other case, the creditors would have been quieted. But Fizeaux is retired from business and chuses to wind up all his affairs. Probably therefore he has not endeavoured to quiet the creditors; perhaps he may consider their clamours as an useful engine to hasten his extrication from this business. Be that as it may, their clamours, should they be raised, may do us great injury. But of this you are the best judge. I am with great and sincere esteem, Dear Sir, your most obedient and most humble servant,

TH: JEFFERSON

Adams to Jefferson

Grosvenor Square Jan. 31. 1788

DEAR SIR

Permit me to introduce to you my young Friend Mr. Alexander Edwards of South Carolina, a modest and amiable young Gentleman who came particularly recommended to me, and whom I have found by Several Months Acquaintance to merit every Attention and Encouragement. I am, my dear Sir yours most affectionately,

JOHN ADAMS

Jefferson to Abigail Adams, with Enclosure

Paris Feb. 2. 1788

DEAR MADAM

The silk you desired was delivered to Mr. Parker a month ago, on the eve of his departure for England, as he supposed. He went however to Holland. Mr. Valnay is so kind as to take charge of that now, as also of the silk stockings. I doubt whether you may like the stockings on first appearance: but I will answer for their goodness, being woven expressly for me by the Hermits of Mont Calvaire with whom I go and stay sometimes, and am favoured by them. They have the reputation of doing the best work which comes to the Paris market. I inclose you their little note of the weight and price, for they sell by weight. I inclose also a state of our accounts subsequent to the paiment of the small sum by Colo. Smith which balanced our former transactions. You will make such additions and amendments to it as you shall find right. I have not yet been able to find M. de la Blancherie at home, so as to settle Mr. Adams's affair with him; but I will do it in time, and render you an account. There being no news here to communicate to you, be pleased to accept my thanks for the many kind services you have been so good as to render me and your friendly attentions on every occasion. I have considered you while in London as my neighbor, and look forward to the moment of your departure from thence as to an epoch of much regret and concern for me. Insulated and friendless on this side the globe, with such an ocean between me and every thing to which I am attached the days will seem long which are to be counted over before I too am to rejoin my native country. Young poets complain often that life is fleeting and transient. We find in it seasons and situations however which move heavily enough. It will lighten them to me if you will continue to honour me with your correspondence. You will have much to communicate to me, I little which can interest you. Perhaps you can make me useful in the execution of your European commissions. Be assured they will afford me sincere pleasure in the execution. My daughters join me in affectionate Adieus to you. Polly does not cease to speak of you with warmth and gratitude. Heaven send you, madam, a pleasant and safe passage, and a happy meeting with all your friends. But do not let them so entirely engross you as to forget that you have one here who is with the most sincere esteem and attachment Dear Madam your most obedient and most humble servant,

TH: JEFFERSON

ENCLOSURE

Mrs. Adams in acct. with Th: J

	Dr. £	Cr. £ s
1787. Oct. 3. To paid for 5. aunes cambrick sent by Dr. Cutting 60ᵗᵗ	2-10	
By cash to Colo. Smith		2-10
Dec. 19. By cash by Mr. Trumbull 120ᵗᵗ		5
1788. Jan. 9. To pd. Hermits of M. Calvaire 12 pr. silk stockings 168ᵗᵗ		
To pd. for 10. aunes double Florence @ 4ᵗᵗ-15 47-10		
23. To pd. Ct. Sarsfeld for books for Mr. Adams 79		
	294-10 12- 5-5	
Balance in favor of Th: J		7- 5-5
	14-15-5	14-15-5

[Endorsed:] Sent this Balance due to Mr Jefferson by Mr Parker Febry 22 1788 Abigail Adams.

Jefferson to Adams

Paris Feb. 6. 1788.

DEAR SIR

The Commissioners of the treasury have given notice to Willincks and Van Staphorsts that they shall not be able to remit them one shilling till the new government gets into action; and that therefore the sole resource for the paiment of the Dutch interest till that period is in the progress of the last loan. Willincks & V.S. reply that there is not the least probability of raising as much on that loan as will pay the next June interest, and that if that paiment fails one day, it will do an injury to our credit which a very long time will not wipe off. A Mr. Stanitski, one of our brokers, who holds 1,340,000 dollars of our domestic debt offers, if we will pay him one year's interest of that debt, he will have the whole of the loan immediately filled up, that is to say he will procure the sum of 622,840 florins still unsubscribed. His year's interest (deducting from it 10 percent which he will allow for paiment in Europe instead of America) will require 180,000 florins of this money. Messrs. W. & V. S. say that, by this means, they can pay Fiseaux debt, and all the Dutch interest and our current expences here, till June 1789. by which time the new government may be in action. They have proposed this to the commissioners of the treasury, but it is possible that the delay of letters going and coming, with the time necessary between their receiving the answer and procuring the money, may force the decision of this proposition on me at the eleventh hour. I wish therefore to avail myself of your counsel before your departure on this proposition. Your knowlege of the subject enables you to give the best opinion, and your zeal for the public interest, and, I trust, your friendly dispositions towards me will prompt you to assist me with your advice on this question, to wit, if the answer of the Commissioners does not come in time, and there shall appear no other means of raising the June interest, will it be worst to fail in that paiment, or to accept of about 700,000 florins, on the condition of letting 180,000 be applied to the paiment of a year's interest of a part of our domestic debt? Do me the friendship to give me an answer to this as soon as possible and be assured of the sentiments of esteem and respect with which I have the honour to be Dear Sir Your most obedient and most humble servt.,

TH: JEFFERSON

Adams to Jefferson

London Feb. 12. 1788

DEAR SIR

I have received your Letter of the 6th. and had before received the same Information from Amsterdam.

I know not how to express to you, the sense I have of the disingenuity of this Plott. The Difficulty of selling the obligations I believe to be mere Pretence, and indeed the whole appears to me to be a concerted Fiction, in consequence of some Contrivance or Suggestion of Mr. Parker, the great Speculator in American Paper, who, though I love him very well, is too ingenious for me. I feel myself obliged to write this in Confidence to you, and to put you on your Guard against the immeasurable avarice of Amsterdam as well as the ungovernable Rage of Speculation. I feel no Vanity in saying that this Project never would have been suggested, if it had not been known, that I was recalled. If I was to continue in Europe and in office I would go to Amsterdam and open a new Loan with John Hodshon before I would submit to it. The Undertakers are bound in Honour, as I understood it, to furnish the Money on the new Loan. They agreed to this upon Condition that I would go to Amsterdam to sign the Obligations. The Truth is that Messrs. Willinks and Vanstaphorst have been purchasing immense Quantities of American Paper, and they now want to have it acknowledged and paid in Europe. It appears to me totally impossible that you or I should ever agree to it, or approve it, and as far as I can comprehend it is equally impossible for the Board of Treasury or Congress to consent to it. You and I however cannot answer for them: but I think We cannot countenance any hopes that they will ever comply with it. The Continental Certificates and their Interest are to be paid in America at the Treasury of the United States. If a Precedent is set of paying them in Europe, I pretend not to Sufficient foresight to predict the Consequences. They appear however to me to be horrid. If the Interest of one Million Dollars is paid this Year in Europe, you will find the Interest of Ten Millions demanded next year. I am very sorry to be obliged at the moment of my Retirement to give opinions which may be misrepresented and imputed to Motives that my soul despizes: but I cannot advise you by any means to countenance this Project: but it is my Serious Opinion that the Judgment of Congress, or the Board of Treasury, ought to be waited for, at all hazards. If the Brokers, Undertakers and Money lenders will take such Advantages of Us, it is high time to have done with them; pay what is due as fast as we can, but never contract another farthing of Debt with them. If a little Firmness is shewn in adhering to the Resolution of waiting the orders of Congress, it is my opinion, Care will be taken in Amsterdam that our Credit shall not suffer. The Interest of our Commissioners, of the Brokers, Undertakers and Money Lenders, all conspire to induce them to prevent a failure. But in my Judgment a failure had better take Place than this Project. I shall not write with the same frankness to Willinks, but I shall give them my opinion that the Judgment of Congress must be waited for.

My dear Friend farewell. I pity you, in your Situation, dunned and teazed as you will be, all your Philosophy will be wanting to support you. But be not discouraged, I have been constantly vexed with such terrible Complaints and frightened with such long Faces these ten years. Depend upon it, the Amsterdammers love Money too well, to execute their Threats. They expect to gain too much by American Credit to destroy it. I am with Sincere Affection and great Esteem, your Friend and Servant,

JOHN ADAMS

Jefferson to Adams

Paris Feb. 20. 1788

DEAR SIR

I am in hopes daily of receiving a letter from you in answer to my last. The delay of the letters which contained the proposition to the board of treasury takes away all probability of their answering in time, and I foresee that I shall be closely pressed by circumstances on that point. I have settled your matter with de la Blancherie, at the sum you fixed (8 Louis). He demanded 12. but without a shadow of reason I think.

This letter will probably find you near your departure. I am in hopes it will be only a change of service, from helping us here, to help us there. We have so few in our councils acquainted with foreign affairs, that your aid in that department, as well as others will be invaluable. The season of the year makes me fear a very disagreeable passage for Mrs. Adams and yourself, tho we have sometimes fine weather in these months. Nobody will pray more sincerely than myself for your passage, that it may be short, safe and agreeable, that you may have a happy meeting with all your friends, be received by them with the gratitude you have merited at their hands, and placed in such a station as may be honourable to you and useful to them. Adieu, my dear Sir, and accept assurances of the unchangeable esteem and respect with which I am Your friend and servant,

TH: JEFFERSON

Abigail Adams to Jefferson

London Febry. 21 1788.

MY DEAR SIR

In the midst of the Bustle and fatigue of packing, the parade and ceremony of taking leave at Court, and else where, I am informed that Mr. Appleton and Mrs. Parker are to set out for Paris tomorrow morning. I Cannot permit them to go without a few lines to my much Esteemed Friend, to thank him for all his kindness and Friendship towards myself and Family, from the commencement of our acquaintance, and to assure him that the offer he has made of his correspondence, is much too flattering, not to be gratefully accepted.

The florence and stockings were perfectly to my mind, and I am greatly obliged to you sir, for your care and attention about them. I have sent by Mrs. Parker the balance due to you, agreable to your statement, which I believe quite right.

Be so good as to present my regards to the Marquiss de la Fayette and his Lady, and to the Abbés. Assure them that I entertain a gratefull remembrance of all their civilities and politeness during my residence in Paris. To Mr. Short and the young Ladies your daughters say every thing that is affectionate for me, and be assured my dear sir, that I am With the Greatest respect Esteem and regard Your Friend and Humble Servant,

ABIGAIL ADAMS

Abigail Adams to Jefferson

London Febry. 26. 1788

DEAR SIR

Mr. Adams being absent I replie to your Letter this day received, that Mr. Adams has written to you upon the subject you refer to. Our time here is short and pressing. Yet short as it is Mr. Adams is obliged to Set out on fryday for the Hague in order to take leave there. Owing wholly to the neglect of Congress in omitting to send him a Letter of recall, tho he particularly requested it of them, when he desired permission to return, and has several times since repeated the same request. A memorial would then have answerd, but now it cannot be received, and he finds at this late hour that he must cross that most horrid passage twice, and make a rapid journey there and back again as it would be greatly injurious to our credit and affairs to give any reasonable cause of offence. He would be delighted to meet you there. But time is so pressing that he cannot flatter himself with that hope, nor be able to stay a day after he has compleated his buisness. Yet as this Letter may reach you about the day he will leave London you will consider whether there is a possibility of seeing each other at the Hague.

I had sent my arrears to you before Mr. Trumble thought of informing me that it was to be paid to him. The Eight Louis you have since been so kind as to pay for Mr. Adams shall be paid Mr. Trumble.

I thank you my dear sir for all your kind wishes and prayers. Heaven only knows how we are to be disposed of. You have resided long enough abroad to feel and experience how inadequate our allowance is to our decent expences, and that it is wholy impossible for any thing to be saved from it. This our countrymen in general will neither know or feel. I have lived long enough, and seen enough of the world, to check expectations, and to bring my mind to my circumstances, and retiring to our own little farm feeding my poultry and improveing my garden has more charms for my fancy, than residing at the court of Saint James's where I seldom meet with characters so innofensive as my Hens and chickings, or minds so well improved as my garden. Heaven forgive me if I think too hardly of them. I wish they had deserved better at my Hands. Adieu my dear sir and believe me at all times and in all situations your Friend and Humble Servant,

A A

Jefferson to Adams

Paris Mar. 2. 1788. Sunday

DEAR SIR

I received this day a letter from Mrs. Adams of the 26th. ult. informing me you would set out on the 29th. for the Hague. Our affairs at Amsterdam press on my mind like a mountain. I have no information to go on but that of the Willincks and Van Staphorsts, and according to that something seems necessary to be done. I am so anxious to confer with you on this, and to see you and them together, and get some effectual arrangement made in time that I determine to meet you at the Hague. I will set out the moment some repairs are made to my carriage. It is promised me at 3. oclock tomorrow; but probably they will make it night, and that I may not set out till Tuesday morning. In that case I shall be at the Hague Friday night. In the mean time you will perhaps have made all your bows there. I am sensible how irksome this must be to you in the moment of your departure, but it is a great interest of the U.S. which is at stake and I am sure you will sacrifice to that your feelings and your interest. I hope to shake you by the hand within 24. hours after you receive this, and in the mean time am with much esteem and respect Dear Sir Your affectionate friend and humble servt,

TH: JEFFERSON

Adams to Jefferson

The Hague March 17. 1788

His Excellency Mr. Jefferson is requested to pay the within Account.

JOHN ADAMS

[Endorsed by TJ on face:] Mr. Adams's bill of coachire [39]

Jefferson to Adams

Paris Aug. 2. 1788.

DEAR SIR

I have received with a great deal of pleasure the account of your safe arrival and joyful reception at Boston. Mr. Cutting was so kind as to send me a copy of the address of the assembly to you and your answer, which with the other circumstances I have sent to have published in the gazette of Leyden, and in a gazette here. It will serve to shew the people of Europe that those of America are content with their servants, and particularly content with you.

The war with the Turks, Russians, and Austrians goes on. A great victory obtained on the black sea over the Turks as commanded by the Captain Pacha, by the Russians commanded by Admiral Paul Jones will serve to raise the spirits of the two empires. He burnt six ships, among which was the admiral's and vice admiral's, took two, and made between three and four thousand prisoners. The Swedes having hastily armed a fleet of about 16. sail of the line, and marched an army into Finland, the king at the head of it, made us believe they were going to attack the Russians. But when their fleet met with three Russian ships of 100 guns each they saluted and passed them. It is pretty well understood that the expences of this armament are paid by the Turks through the negociations of England. And it would seem as if the king had hired himself to strut only, but not to fight, expecting probably that the former would suffice to divert the Russians from sending their fleet round to the Mediterranean. There are some late symptoms which would indicate that Denmark would

39. TJ was in Amsterdam March 10-30. In TJ's account book under March 21, 1788: "pd Mr. Adams's expences here 83/18 his coach hire to Hague 33/." Jefferson Papers, Lib. Cong.

still be opposed to Sweden though she should shift herself into the opposite scale. The alliance between England, Holland and Prussia is now settled. In the mean time this country is losing all it's allies one by one, without assuring to herself new ones. Prussia, Holland, Turkey, Sweden are pretty certainly got or getting into the English interest, and the alliance of France with the two empires is not yet secured. I am in hopes her internal affairs will be arranged without blood. None has been shed as yet. The nation presses on sufficiently upon the government to force reformations, without forcing them to draw the sword. If they can keep the opposition always exactly at this point, all will end well. Peace or war, they cannot fail now to have the States general, and I think in the course of the following year. They have already obtained the Provincial assemblies as you know, the king has solemnly confessed he cannot lay a new tax without the consent of the States general, and when these assemble they will try to have themselves moulded into a periodical assembly, to form a declaration of rights, and a civil list for the government. The Baron de Breteuil has lately retired from the ministry and been succeeded by M. de Villedeuil. Monsieur de Malesherbes will probably retire. The Marquis de la Fayette with several others have lately received a fillup for having assembled to sign a memorial to the king which had been sent up from Brittany. They took from the Marquis a particular command which he was to have ex[ercised du]ring the months of August and September this year [in the] South of France.[40] Your friends the Abbés are well and always enquire after you. I shall be happy to hear from you from time to time, to learn state news and state politics, for which I will give you in return those of this quarter of the earth. I hope Mrs. Adams is well; I am sure she is happier in her own country than any other. Assure her of my constant friendship and accept assurances of the same from Dear Sir Your most obedt. and most humble servt.

TH: JEFFERSON

P.S. Make freely any use of me here which may be convenient either for yourself or Mrs. Adams.

P.S. Aug. 6. Later accounts inform us there have been two actions between the Russians and Turks. The first was of the gallies etc. on both sides. In this P. Jones, being accidentally present, commanded the right wing. The Russians repulsed the Turks. The second action was of the Russian gallies against the Turkish ships of war. The effect was what is stated in the preceding letter. But the command was solely in the prince

40. On July 12, 1788, Lafayette joined the Breton nobles in Paris in protesting against the decree abolishing the parlements. Shortly afterward he was deprived of his military command under the Duc d'Ayen in Languedoc and Roussillon. Gottschalk, *Lafayette*, 387-91.

of Nassau, P. Jones with his fleet of ships of war being absent. Prince Potemkin immediately got under march for Oczakow, to take advantage of the consternation it was thrown into. The Swedes have commenced hostilities against the Russians, and war against them is consequently declared by the empress.

Jefferson to Adams

Paris Nov. [i.e., Dec.] 5. 1788.

DEAR SIR

I had the pleasure of writing to you on the 2d. of Aug. and of adding a P.S. of Aug. 6. You will have known since that that the interposition of Denmark, as auxilliary to Russia against Sweden, has been suppressed magisterially by England and Prussia. This seemed to prove that these two powers did not mean to enter into the war; that on the contrary they wished seriously to quiet things on the Western side of Europe and let the war of the East go on. A new incident now arises which may still endanger the peace of the West. The Prussian party in Poland having obtained a majority in their confederated diet, have voted the establishment of a council of war independant of the king, and propose to hold a perpetual diet, during which you know the king is as nothing. Russia has formally declared she will consider this as a breach of the constitution settled in 1775. under the guaranty of the three powers; and Prussia has put an army into readiness to march at a moment's warning on the frontiers of Poland. The emperor after a disadvantageous campaign, is secretly trying to obtain peace of the Turks, in which he is sincerely aided by this court, and opposed we may be sure by that of London. We do not know how far the Emperor's plan includes Russia. If these powers obtain their peace of the Turks, they will probably give a rap of the knuckles at least to the K. of Prussia. The lunacy of the king of England will probably place the affairs of that country under a regency; and as regencies are generally pacific, we may expect they will concur with this country in an unwillingness to enter into war.   The internal tranquillity of this country, which had never been so far compromitted as to produce bloodshed, was entirely reestablished by the announcing of the States general early in the next year, the reestablishment of the parliament and substitution of Mr. Neckar in the department of finance instead of the Archbishop of Sens. The parliament which had called for the States general only thro' fear that they could not obtain otherwise their own restoration, being once restored, began to fear those very States general and to prepare cavils at the forms of calling and organising them. The court to debarrass itself of the dispute, referred these to the same Notables who had acted, on a former occasion, with approbation. These Notables, being composed of Clergy, Nobility, members of parliament and some privileged persons of the tiers etat, have shamelessly combined against the rights of the people. The court wished the tiers etat should equal the two other orders by the number of their deputies in the States general, and that they should form one house only. 5 bureaux out of 6. of the Notables have voted that the people shall have only as many members as each of the other orders singly, and that they shall vote by orders: so that the votes of the two houses of clergy and nobles concurring, that of the tiers etat will be over-ruled. For it is not here as in England where each branch has a negative on the other two. The votes of the bureaux are not yet consolidated, but I see no reason to suppose that the separate votes will be changed in the consolidation. But in whatever manner the states shall be formed, they will meet in March probably, or April at furthest, and will obtain without much opposition from the court, or perhaps with none 1. their own periodical convocation: 2. their exclusive right to tax: 3. a transfer of the right, now exercised by usurpation by the parliaments, to register laws and propose previous amendments to them. Thus a change in their con-stitution is, I think, certain: and the life of the present king or the minority of his heir will give time to confirm it.

You recollect well the Arret of Dec. 29. 1787. in favor of our com-merce, and which among other things gave free admission to our whale oils under a duty of about two Louis a ton. In consequence of the English treaty their oils flowed in and overstocked the market. The light duty they were liable to under the treaty, still lessened by false estimates, and aided by the high premiums of the British government enabled them to undersell the French and American oils. This produced an outcry of the Dunkirk fishery. It was proposed to exclude all European oils, which would not infringe the British treaty. I could not but encourage this idea, because it woud give to the French and American fisheries a monopoly of the French market. The Arret was so drawn up. But in the very moment of passing it they struck out the word *European* so that our oils became involved. This I believe was the effect of a single person in the ministry. As soon as it was known to me I wrote to M. de Montmorin and had con-ferences with him and the other ministers. I found it necessary to give them full information on the subject of the whale fishery, of which they knew little but from the partial information of their Dunkirk adventurers. I therefore wrote the Observations [41] (of which I enclose you a printed

41. *Observations on the Whale-Fishery*, Boyd, XIV, 242-54. See TJ to John Jay, Nov. 19, 1788, *ibid.*, 211-16; and editorial note to "Documents Concerning the Whale Fishery," *ibid.*, 217-25.

copy) had them printed to entice them to read them, and particularly developed the expence at which they are carrying on that fishery and at which they must continue it, if they do continue it. This part was more particularly intended for Mr. Neckar, who was quite a stranger to the subject, who has principles of oeconomy, and will enter into calculations. Other subjects are incidentally introduced, tho' little connected with the main question. They had been called for by other circumstances. An immediate order was given for the present admission of our oils, till they could form an arret: and at a conference, the draught of an Arret was communicated to me, which re-established that of Dec. 29.[42] They expressed fears that under cover of our name the Nova Scotia oils would be introduced, and a blank was left in the draught for the means of preventing that. They have since proposed that the certificate of their consul shall accompany the oils to authorize their admission, and this is what they will probably adopt. It was observed that if our states would prohibit all foreign oils from being imported into them, it would be a great safeguard, and an encouragement to them to continue the admission. Still there remains an expression in the Arret that it is provisory only. However we must be contented with it as it is; my hope being that the legislation will be transferred to the national assembly in whose hands it will be more stable, and with whom it will be more difficult to obtain a repeal, should the ministry hereafter desire it. If they could succeed in drawing over as many of our Nantucket men as would supply their demands of oil, we might then fear an exclusion. But the present arret, as soon as it shall be passed, will, I hope, place us in safety till that event, and that event may never happen. I have entered into all these details that you may be enabled to quiet the alarm which must have been raised by the arret of Sep. 28. and assure the adventurers that they may pursue their enterprises as safely as if that had never been passed, and more profitably, because we participate now of a monopolized instead of an open market. The inclosed Observations, tho' printed, have only been given to the ministers, and one or two other confidential persons. You will see that they contain matter which should be kept from the English, and will therefore trust them to the perusal only of such persons as you can confide in. We are greatly indebted to the Marquis de la Fayette for his aid on this as on every other occasion. He has paid the closest attention to it and combated for us with the zeal of a native.

The necessity of reconducting my family to America, and of placing my affairs there under permanent arrangements, has obliged me to ask of Congress a six months absence, to wit from April to November next. I hope therefore to have the pleasure of seeing you there, and particularly

42. "Arret Concerning Whale Oil, 7 December 1788," *ibid.*, 268-69.

that it will be at New York that I shall find you. Be so good as to present my sincere esteem to Mrs. Adams, and beleive me to be with very affectionate attachment Dear Sir Your friend and servt,

TH: JEFFERSON

Adams to Jefferson

Braintree near Boston Jany. 2 1789

MY DEAR FRIEND

Give me leave to introduce to you John Coffin Jones Esqr, an eminent Merchant of Boston and a late Member of the Legislature from that Town. His Character both in public and private Life is much respected, and his Intelligence will enable him to give you a much better account of the general and particular Politicks of this Country than I can. Our Fellow Citizens are in the midst of their Elections for the new Government, which have hitherto in general run very well. For my own Part, I have enjoyed a Luxury for the last Six Months which I have never before tasted for, at least eight and twenty Years, and have looked down upon all you Statesmen, with Sovereign Compassion. The new Government has my best Wishes and most fervent Prayers, for its Success and Prosperity: but whether I shall have any Thing more to do with it, besides praying for it, depends on the future suffrages of Freemen. I am with an affection that can never die, your Friend and Servant,

JOHN ADAMS

Jefferson to Adams

Paris Jan. 14. 1789.

DEAR SIR

I now do myself the pleasure to inclose to you a copy of the Arret explanatory of that of Sep. 28. on the subject of our whale oils. Mr. Necker in a letter to me has renewed the promise of taking off the 10. sous per livre at the end of the next year. But at the same time he observes that whenever the national fishery shall be able to supply their demand for whale oil we must expect a repeal of this Arret, which therefore expresses itself to be *provisory*. However, their navigation being the most expensive in Europe, they are the least likely to succeed in a whale fishery, without encouragements more extravagant than even those they now give: and it remains to be seen whether Mr. Necker will continue to give even the present. I am informed there will be fewer French adventurers the next year than there has been this: so that if there be an apparent increase of their fishery, it will be by drawing over more of our fishermen. It is probable the States-general will obtain a participation in the legislation, which will render their laws more stable, and more to be relied on. Mr. Necker has also promised that if the present Arret should at any time be repealed, there shall be a sufficient space of time allowed for the reception of the oils which shall have been previously embarked. But our principal, if not our only danger of a repeal being brought on, will come from the endeavors of the English to introduce their oils under colour of ours, perhaps even with the assistance of our own merchants. Some effectual means must be adopted to prevent them from getting our real ship papers, and our Consuls in the ports of France must be enabled to detect forged papers: and we must moreover convince this government that we use our utmost endeavors, and with good faith, to prevent the entry of English oils under the license given to us. I would advise our shippers of oil always to get the Certificate of the French consul in their state if it be practicable, because those will admit of the least doubt here. When this cannot be had, they may have recourse to the magistrates of the country, and in this case there should be a certificate under the seal of the state that the magistrate who has certified their oil to be the produce of the American fishery is a magistrate duly appointed and qualified by law, and that his signature is genuine. I presume it is the usage in all the states for the Governor's signature to accompany the great seal.

Oczakow is at length taken. The Russians say they gave the assault with 14,000 men, against 12,000 within the walls, that 7000 of these suffered themselves to be cut to peices before they surrendered, and that themselves lost 3000. The only circumstance to be believed in all this is that Oczakow is taken. Every thing else in Europe is quiet, except the internal affairs of Poland. The Prussian party there gains greater superiority daily. The K. of Prussia however will feel less bold on the probability that England will remain inactive in all things external. This secures to this country leizure for their internal improvements. These go on well. The report of Mr. Necker to the king, which has been published, renews the renunciation of the power of laying a new tax or continuing an old one without consent of the states general, admits they are to appropriate the public monies (and of course how much of it the king may spend), that ministers must be responsible, that the king will concur in fixing the periodical meeting of the states, that he will be ready to consider with them what modifications letters de cachet should be put under, and of the degree of liberty which may be given to the press; and further that all this shall be fixed by a convention so solemn as that his successors shall not be free to infringe it, that is to say that he will concur in a Declaration of rights. Nothing is said however of the States sharing in the legislation, but this will surely be pressed. They have given to the tiers etat a representation in the States equal to both the other orders, and it is probable they will form but one house and vote by persons: but that is not decided. Be so good as to present me affectionately to Mrs. Adams and to be assured yourself of the sincere esteem of dear Sir Your friend and servt.,

TH: JEFFERSON

Adams to Jefferson

Braintree March 1. 1789

DEAR SIR

The inclosed Letter from The Hon. Stephen Higginson Esqr. is upon a Subject of so much Importance, and contains so much Information that I cannot withold it from you. The little Jealousy, Envy or Caprice, that shall deprive our Merchants of the Benefit of Trading to the Isles of France and Bourbon, will only compell them to seek the Ultimate Markets upon the Continent, directly.[43]

In four days, the new Government is to be erected.[44] Washington appears to have an unanimous vote: and there is probably a Plurality if not a Majority in favour of your Friend.—It may be found easier to give Authority, than to yeild Obedience.

Amendments to the Constitution, will be expected, and no doubt discussed. Will you be so good as to look over the Code and write me your Sentiments of Amendments which you think necessary or usefull? That greatest and most necessary of all Amendments, the Seperation of the Executive Power, from the Legislative Seems to be better understood than it once was. Without this our Government is in danger of being a continual struggle between a Junto of Grandees, for the first Chair.

43. Higginson to JA, Boston, Jan. 17, 1789, Boyd, XIV, 599-602. The Isle de France was renamed Mauritius by the British after they got possession in 1815; Bourbon was renamed Réunion by the French in 1848.

44. The new House of Representatives did not secure a quorum until April 1, nor the Senate until April 6; Washington and Adams were inaugurated on April 30. Edward Channing, *A History of the United States* (N. Y., 1905-25), IV, 30, 32.

The Success of the new Plan will depend in the first Place upon a Revenue, to defray the Interest of the foreign and domestic debt. But how to get a Revenue? how to render Smuggling and Evasion Shameful?

You must expect the first Operations will be very Slow.—Mrs. A. and your old Admirer, my Son, desire their respects to you. With unabated respect, Esteem and Affection I am, dear Sir, your Friend and humble sert.,

JOHN ADAMS

Jefferson to Adams

Paris May 10. 1789.

DEAR SIR

Since mine of January 14. yours of Jan. 2. and Mar. 1. have been handed to me; the former by Mr. Jones, whom I am glad to know on your recommendation and to make him the channel of evidencing to you how much I esteem whatever comes from you.

The internal agitations of this country and the inactivity to which England is reduced by the state of imbecillity in which the madness of the King has terminated, will leave the Southwestern parts of Europe in peace for the present year. Denmark will probably continue to furnish only it's stipulated succours to Russia, without engaging in the war as a principal. Perhaps a pacification may be effected between Sweden and Russia: tho at present there is little appearance of it: so that we may expect that the war will go on this year between the two empires, the Turks and Swedes, without extending any further. Even the death of the emperor, should it take place, would hardly withdraw his dominions from the war this summer.

The revolution in this country has gone on hitherto with a quietness, a steadiness, and a progress unexampled. But there is danger of a balk now. The three orders which compose the states general seem likely to stumble at the threshold on the great preliminary question How shall they vote, by orders or persons? If they get well over this question, there will be no difficulty afterwards, there is so general a concurrence in the great points of constitutional reformation. If they do not get over this question (and this seems possible) it cannot be foreseen what issue this matter will take.[45]

45. The first revolutionary acts came on June 17, when the Third Estate declared itself to be the National Assembly; three days later it took the Oath of the Tennis Court and thereby defied Louis XVI.

As yet however, no business being begun, no votes taken, we cannot pronounce with certainty the exact state of parties. This is a summary view of European affairs.

Tho I have not official information of your election to the Presidency of the Senate; yet I have such information as renders it certain. Accept I pray you my sincere congratulations. No man on earth pays more cordial homage to your worth nor wishes more fervently your happiness. Tho' I detest the appearance even of flattery, I cannot always suppress the effusions of my heart.

Present me affectionately to Mrs. Adams, Colo. and Mrs. Smith. I hope to see you all this summer, and to return this fall to my prison; for all Europe would be a prison to me, were it ten times as big. Adieu my dear friend Your affectionate humble servt.,

TH: JEFFERSON

7

"The Age of Experiments in Government"

THE CORRESPONDENCE between Adams and Jefferson during the 1790's provides something less than even a bare outline of their participation in the political events which profoundly affected the development of the United States. The paucity of correspondence may be accounted for during the early years of the decade by their close personal contact in public affairs which made letters unnecessary, during the later years by their political differences.

When Jefferson learned that Adams had been elected vice-president of the United States, he wrote from France in May 1789 to congratulate him and pay "cordial homage." [1] Six months later he returned to Virginia on leave from his diplomatic post to learn that President Washington had appointed him secretary of state. [2] Reunited in New York, the first national capital, the old friends could engage in private conversation rather than letter writing. Although Jefferson was secretary of state for four years, he wrote only two letters to Adams about American foreign policy. The first recalled the disputes of long standing with Great Britain over the northeast boundary of the United States, [3] supposedly settled by the Treaty of 1783. It had been a vexation to Adams in London and remained an issue for more than a half-century. The other letter discussed the Consular Convention of 1788 with France, which the new Senate ratified in 1789. It must have given the secretary of state special satis-

1. TJ to JA, May 10, 1789, above, 238.
2. Malone, *Jefferson*, II, Chap. XIII.
3. TJ to JA, April 20, 1790, below, 244.

faction for he had drafted it as minister to France to replace an earlier text which Secretary John Jay had viewed with suspicion as being pro-French and which the old Congress had finally rejected.[4]

One of the first wedges separating Adams and Jefferson grew out of the inadvertent publication of Jefferson's views about Thomas Paine's *Rights of Man* (1791) as an antidote "against the political heresies which have sprung up among us." [5] Paine's work, a reply to Edmund Burke's hostile *Reflections on the French Revolution*, emphasized in its first installment the relationship between the contemporary insurgency in France and the American Revolution. In the second installment Paine criticized the English constitution as the bulwark of a reactionary government opposing the great revolutionary movements of the era. When Paine fled to France in 1792 to escape trial for sedition in England, he became a storm center of political controversy that raged throughout the decade. His writings had met a cordial response privately from Jefferson, who read a borrowed copy of the *Rights of Man* and returned it with a covering note expressing pleasure that it was to be reprinted. But the printer, without Jefferson's permission, published the note with its comment on "political heresies" (Jefferson confessed to Madison that he had in mind Adams's pro-British newspaper articles, "Discourses on Davila," [6] in support of the British system of government), and thus Jefferson's name was coupled with Paine's in the reprint, which appeared early in May 1791.[7]

A month later, in a series of letters to the Boston *Columbian Centinel*, Publicola attacked the *Rights of Man* and its reputed sponsor. From the style of the letters most readers assumed that Adams was the author.[8] But everyone who "knew" Publicola's identity guessed wrong. He turned out to be twenty-four-year-old John Quincy Adams. Nevertheless, Jefferson's belated explanation of his own position could hardly satisfy the elder Adams.[9] He had already assured Jefferson, however, that "your motives for writing to me, I have not a doubt were the most pure and the most friendly; and I

4. TJ to JA, Nov. 25, 1791, below, 252.
5. TJ to JA, July 17, 1791, below, 246.
6. May 9, 1791, Ford, V, 332.
7. Malone, *Jefferson*, II, Chap. XXI.
8. Samuel F. Bemis, *John Quincy Adams and the Foundations of American Foreign Policy* (N. Y., 1950), 26-28. Hereafter cited as Bemis, *John Quincy Adams*.
9. TJ to JA, Aug. 30, 1791, below, 250-51.

have no suspicion that you will not receive this explanation from me in the same candid Light." [10] Adams had replied out of the kindliness of his heart and the friendship he cherished. Jefferson might better have left further comment on the incident unexpressed, along with the hope "that our friendship will never be suffered to be committed." [11]

When Adams published the first volume of his *Defence of the Constitutions*, he had predicted that it "will be an unpopular Work in America for a long time," [12] and the same could have been said of the "Discourses on Davila." Few works on political theory have ever been popular. It is not a favorite subject for politicians because they are practical men who have already made up their minds. Adams was realistic enough in basing his concept of balanced government upon the dominant self-interest of men which must be controlled for the benefit of society; and he found the best example of its attainment in the structure of the British government. But the "Discourses," like the *Defence*, were hard reading, easily misunderstood, and frequently misinterpreted, whether willfully or innocently. It might almost be said that Adams wrote too much; that he was too intellectual for most of his associates, whether "aristocrats" or "republicans." He protested Jefferson's statement that their differences as to the best form of government were well known to them both: "I do not know what your Idea is of the best form of government." As for himself, he denied ever having had a design "of attempting to introduce a Government of King, Lords and Commons . . . into the United States or . . . any Individual State." [13] Jefferson had not set forth his own ideas in writing for all to read, but privately he had referred to Adams's "apostacy to hereditary monarchy and nobility." [14] He, too, it would seem, had not read Adams's writings carefully.

After Jefferson resigned as secretary of state on December 31, 1793, he lived in uninterrupted retirement at Monticello for three years. Despite their political differences, he and Adams carried on a sporadic exchange, discussing the French Revolution, the surge of European refugees to America in its wake, and the unreadiness of Americans to accept foreign culture transplanted in their own soil. Vice-President

10. JA to TJ, July 29, 1791, below, 250.
11. TJ to JA, Aug. 30, 1791, below, 251.
12. JA to TJ, March 1, 1787, above, 176.
13. JA to TJ, July 29, 1791, below, 249.
14. TJ to Washington, May 8, 1791, Ford, V, 329.

Adams envied Jefferson's rural retirement "out of the hearing of the Din of Politicks and the Rumours of War." [15] In fact, throughout the eleven years, 1790-1800, during eight of which Jefferson held high public office, he spent fully one half of the time at Monticello. The Adamses' periods of relaxation at their home in Quincy could not be so prolonged.

Adams and Jefferson agreed that the United States should avoid embroilment in the European war which had erupted in 1793 between France and England. When war fever in the United States burned intensely against Great Britain the following year, Adams declared that "those who dread Monarchy and Aristocracy and at the same time Advocate War are the most inconsistent of all Men." [16] From his mountain top in Albemarle County, Jefferson expressed the hope that "this ... will be an age of experiments in government ... founded on principles of honesty, not of mere force." His countrymen should continue to engage "in agriculture or the pursuits of honest industry, independant in their circumstances, enlightened as to their rights, and firm in their habits of order and obedience to the laws." "Never," he wrote Adams, "was a finer canvas presented to work on than our countrymen." [17]

But the "Din of Politicks" echoed increasingly through their letters. By 1796 the Republican party, molded by Madison and headed by Jefferson, had emerged as a serious challenge to Federalist supremacy.[18] Jefferson hoped that party strife would not lead to personal estrangement, although he and Adams were rival candidates for the presidency in the election of 1796. Lacking the talents of the politician, Adams possessed the virtues which thoughtful men associated with the ideal of virtuous government and which provided him a substantial political following. It had been more than enough to re-elect him vice-president in 1792 by a comfortable majority over the astute anti-federalist Governor George Clinton of New York. It was still enough in 1796 to elect him president by three electoral votes, even though Hamilton shifted his support to Thomas Pinckney with the hope of defeating Adams.[19]

15. JA to TJ, April 4, 1794, below, 253.
16. JA to TJ, May 11, 1794, below, 255.
17. TJ to JA, Feb. 28, 1796, below, 260.
18. Noble E. Cunningham, *The Jeffersonian Republicans: The Formation of Party Organization* (Chapel Hill, 1957), Chap. V.
19. Edward Stanwood, *A History of the Presidency from 1788 to 1897* (Boston, 1898), Chaps. III-IV.

After this close contest was over but before the results were known, Jefferson wrote a letter, dated December 28, to Adams, deploring the efforts of the politicians and the press to set them at odds and congratulating him on the victory. Jefferson's supposition of Adams's election was correct, his desire sincere. Although he valued highly "the share ... I may have had in the late vote," Jefferson disclaimed any "ambition to govern men." But suppose he had been elected instead of Adams. Had he said too much? Jefferson forwarded the letter unsealed to Congressman Madison for advice. Having received the letter after the news of Adams's election, Madison, exercising the discretion Jefferson had allowed him, decided not to send it.[20] Adams was therefore denied the sincere wishes of Jefferson and the testimony that he "retains still for you the solid esteem of the moments when we were working for our independance" [21]—testimony that might have eased their strained relations during Adams's presidency.

From the spring of 1796 until February 20, 1801, when President Adams advised President-elect Jefferson of horses and carriages available "in the stables of the United States," no letter passed between them. Nor, except on a few occasions, did they confer at the seat of government. As the crisis with France worsened and the insulting XYZ Affair provoked demands for a war of retaliation, Francophobe Federalists and Francophile Republicans indulged in another campaign of invective and scurrility through the newspaper columns. In 1798, amid the hysteria of quasi-war and unreasoning fear of foreigners in the United States, Congress passed the Alien and Sedition Acts, Adams signed them, and Jefferson, in protest and warning, drafted the Kentucky Resolutions and revised Madison's Virginia Resolutions. Both documents were as significant for their protest on behalf of civil liberties as for their defense of state rights;[22] yet, at the same time, Jefferson the politician occasionally aided the hack writer James Thomson Callender in his published abuse of Federalist leaders.[23]

20. TJ to Madison, Jan. 1 and 30, 1797, Ford, VII, 99, 115; Madison to TJ, Jan. 15, 1797, Gaillard Hunt, ed., *The Writings of James Madison* (N. Y., 1900-10), VI, 302-5.
21. TJ to JA, Dec. 28, 1796, below, 263.
22. Adrienne Koch and Harry Ammon, "The Virginia and Kentucky Resolutions: An Episode in Jefferson's and Madison's Defense of Civil Liberties," *Wm. and Mary Quart.*, 3d ser., 5 (1948), 174.
23. Cunningham, *Jeffersonian Republicans*, 169-72. For an adverse account of Jefferson's relations with Callender, see Worthington C. Ford, ed., *Thomas Jefferson and James Thomson Callender, 1798-1802* (Brooklyn, 1897); a more sympathetic appraisal is given in Frank L. Mott, *Jefferson and the Press* (Baton Rouge, 1943), 32-37.

Adams, with magnificent courage, sacrificed his political career by sending a new peace mission to France, thereby frustrating the demand of the High Federalists for all-out war.[24] But he succumbed to his feeling of fear and misgiving concerning the victory of the Jeffersonians in the election of 1800-1 and made innumerable "midnight appointments" of Federalists to office on the eve of Jefferson's accession to the presidency.[25]

Thus ended the first era of American national politics. Thus was suspended the friendship of two of its finest statesmen.

Jefferson to Adams

New York 20th. April 1790.

SIR

Encroachments being made on the Eastern limits of the United States by Settlers under the British Government, pretending that it is the Western and not the Eastern river of the Bay of Passamaquoddy which was designated by the name of St. Croix in the Treaty of Peace with that Nation, I have to beg the favour of you to communicate any facts which your memory or papers may enable you to recollect, and which may indicate the true River the Commissioners on both sides had in their view to establish as the boundary between the two Nations.[26] It will be of some consequence to be informed by what Map they traced the boundary. I have the honor to be with the greatest respect Sir Your most obt. and most hble. Servt.

TH: JEFFERSON

24. Joseph Charles, *The Origins of the American Party System: Three Essays* (Williamsburg, Va., 1956), 62-64.

25. See below, Chap. 8, *passim.*

26. The Treaty of Paris of 1783, of which JA had been one of the American negotiators, placed the northeastern boundary of the United States at the St. Croix River, but opinion differed as to which river the French name referred. For lack of diplomatic relations between the United States and Great Britain, no settlement could be made. In 1798 a joint commission on the boundary concluded that the Schoodic River was the dividing line. A. L. Burt, *The United States, Great Britain, and British North America, 1775-1815* (New Haven, 1940), Chap. V, 163-65. The northeastern boundary was settled by the Webster-Ashburton Treaty of 1842. Samuel F. Bemis, *A Diplomatic History of the United States* (N. Y., 1936), 262-64.

Jefferson to Adams

Philadelphia Nov. 26. 1790.

DEAR SIR

From a letter received from the President Mr. Lear is satisfied he cannot be here to-day and doubts even the possibility of his arrival tomorrow. Of course our expedition of to-day would be certainly fruitless,[27] and is therefore laid aside agreeably to a message I have received from Genl Knox and the attorney Genl [Edmund Randolph]. Yours affectionately and respectfully

TH: JEFFERSON

Jefferson to Adams

TH: JEFFERSON presents his respects to the Vice-president of the U. S. and has the honor to inclose him the copy of a letter from the President,[28] just now received.

Apr. 8. 1791.

Jefferson to Adams

P[h]iladelphia July 17. 1791.

DEAR SIR

I have a dozen times taken up my pen to write to you and as often laid it down again, suspended between opposing considerations. I determine

27. Members of President Washington's cabinet had planned to meet him on his way from Mount Vernon to Philadelphia, somewhere south of the city; but on Nov. 23 he wrote Lear from below Baltimore that the roads were "the most infamous ... that ever were seen.... [We] have no expectation of reaching Baltimore to Night." John C. Fitzpatrick, ed., *The Writings of George Washington* (Washington, 1931-44), XXXI, 159. The President and Mrs. Washington arrived in Philadelphia on Nov. 27. Douglas S. Freeman, *George Washington: A Biography* (N. Y., 1948-57), VI, 286.

28. On April 4 Washington informed his secretaries of state, treasury, and war of his itinerary through the southern states and outlined the conditions on which they should conduct the government during his absence. Fitzpatrick, ed., *Writings of Washington*, XXXI, 272-73.

however to write from a conviction that truth, between candid minds, can never do harm.

The first of Paine's pamphlets on the Rights of man, which came to hand here, belonged to Mr. Beckley. He lent it to Mr. Madison who lent it to me; and while I was reading it Mr. Beckley called on me for it, and, as I had not finished it, he desired me, as soon as I should have done so, to send it to Mr. Jonathan B. Smith, whose brother meant to reprint it. I finished reading it, and, as I had no acquaintance with Mr. Jonathan B. Smith, propriety required that I should explain to him why I, a stranger to him, sent him the pamphlet. I accordingly wrote a note of compliment informing him that I did it at the desire of Mr. Beckley, and, to take off a little of the dryness of the note, I added that I was glad it was to be reprinted here and that something was to be publicly said against the political heresies which had sprung up among us etc.[29] I thought so little of this note that I did not even keep a copy of it: nor ever heard a tittle more of it till, the week following, I was thunderstruck with seeing it come out at the head of the pamphlet. I hoped however it would not attract notice. But I found on my return from a journey of a month that a writer came forward under the signature of Publicola,[30] attacking not only the author and principles of the pamphlet, but myself as it's sponsor, by name. Soon after came hosts of other writers defending the pamphlet and attacking you by name as the writer of Publicola. Thus were our names thrown on the public stage as public antagonists. That you and I differ in our ideas of the best form of government is well known to us both: but we have differed as friends should do, respecting the purity of each other's motives, and confining our difference of opinion to private conversation. And I can declare with truth in the presence of the almighty that nothing was further from my intention or expectation than to have had either my own or your name brought before the public on this occasion. The friendship and confidence which has so long existed between us required this explanation from me, and I know you too well to fear any misconstruction of the motives of it. Some people here who would wish me to be, or to be thought, guilty of improprieties, have suggested that I was Agricola, that I was Brutus etc. etc.[31] I never did in my life, either by myself or by any other, have a sentence of mine inserted in a newspaper without putting my name to it; and I believe I never shall.

While the empress is refusing peace under a mediation unless Oczakow

29. TJ's note to the printer, J. B. Smith, continued as follows: "I have no doubt our citizens will rally a second time round the standard of Common Sense." Ford, V, 354*n*.

30. John Quincy Adams, in the *Columbian Centinel*, Boston, June 1791.

31. Agricola rebutted Publicola in the Boston *Independent Chronicle*, Brutus in the *Columbian Centinel*.

and it's territory be ceded to her, she is offering peace on the perfect statu quo to the Porte, if they will conclude it without a mediation. France has struck a severe blow at our navigation by a difference of duty on tob[acc]o carried in our and their ships, and by taking from foreign built ships the capability of naturalization. She has placed our whale oil on rather a better footing than ever by consolidating the duties into a single one of 6. livres. They amounted before to some sous over that sum. I am told (I know not how truly) that England has prohibited our spermaceti oil altogether, and will prohibit our wheat till the price there is 52/ the quarter, which it is almost never is. We expect hourly to hear the true event of Genl. Scott's expedition.[32] Reports give favorable hopes of it. Be so good as to present my respectful compliments to Mrs. Adams and to accept assurances of the sentiments of sincere esteem and respect with which I am Dear Sir Your friend and servant.

TH: JEFFERSON

Adams to Jefferson

Braintree July 29. 1791.

DEAR SIR

Yesterday, at Boston, I received your friendly Letter of July 17th. with great pleasure. I give full credit to your relation of the manner in which your note was written and prefixed to the Philadelphia edition of Mr. Paines pamphlet on the rights of Man: but the misconduct of the person, who committed this breach of your confidence, by making it publick, whatever were his intentions, has sown the Seeds of more evils, than he can ever attone for. The Pamphlet, with your name, to so striking a recommendation to it, was not only industriously propogated in New York and Boston; but, that the recommendation might be known to every one, was reprinted with great care in the Newspapers, and was generally considered as a direct and open personal attack upon me, by countenancing the false interpretation of my Writings as favouring the Introduction of hereditary Monarchy and Aristocracy into this Country. The Question every where was, What Heresies are intended by the Secre-

32. Brigadier General Charles Scott's expedition against the Indian towns on the Wabash, May-June 1791, accomplished little except to arouse the Indians to greater efforts against General Arthur St. Clair later that year. Beverley W. Bond, Jr., *The Foundations of Ohio*, in Carl Wittke, ed., *The History of the State of Ohio* (Columbus, 1941-44), I, 323-24.

tary of State? The answer in the Newspapers was, The Vice Presidents notions of a Limited Monarchy, an hereditary Government of King and Lords, with only elective commons. Emboldened by these murmurs, soon after appeared the Paragraphs of an unprincipled Libeller in the New Haven Gazette, carefully reprinted in the Papers of New York, Boston and Philadelphia, holding up the Vice President to the ridicule of the World for his meanness, and to their detestation for wishing to subjugate the People to a few Nobles. These were soon followed by a formal Speech of the Lieutenant Governor of Massacuhsetts [Samuel Adams] very solemnly holding up the Idea of hereditary Powers, and cautioning the Publick against them, as if they were at that moment in the most imminent danger of them.[33] These Things were all accompanied with the most marked neglect both of the Governor [John Hancock] and Lieutenant Governor of this State towards me; and alltogether opperated as an Hue and Cry to all my Ennemies and Rivals, to the old constitutional faction of Pensilvania in concert with the late Insurgents of Massachusetts, both of whom consider my Writings as the Cause of their overthrow,[34] to hunt me down like a hare, if they could. In this State of Things, Publicola, who, I suppose, thought that Mr. Paines Pamphlet was made Use of as an Instrument to destroy a Man, for whom he had a regard, [whom] he thought innocent, and in the present moment [o]f some importance to the Publick, came forward.

You declare very explicitly that you never did, by yourself or by any other, have a Sentence of yours, inserted in a Newspaper without your name to it. And I, with equal frankness declare that I never did, either by my self or by any other, have a Sentence of mine inserted in any Newspaper since I left Philadelphia. I neither wrote nor corrected Publicola. The Writer in the Composition of his Pieces followed his own Judgment, Information and discretion, without any assistance from me.

You observe "That You and I differ in our Ideas of the best form of Government is well known to us both." But, my dear Sir, you will give me leave to say, that I do not know this. I know not what your Idea is of the best form of Government. You and I have never had a serious conversation together that I can recollect concerning the nature of Government. The very transient hints that have ever passed between Us have been

33. Samuel Adams's speech to the two houses of the Massachusetts legislature had been preceded by correspondence with JA, Sept.-Nov. 1790, in which they argued about the nature of republican government and popular sovereignty versus a mixed government "of three powers, forming a mutual balance." *Works*, VI, 411-26.

34. JA had condemned the Pennsylvania Constitution of 1776, which was replaced by a new one in 1790, providing for more balanced government; and he had strenuously opposed Shays's Rebellion in Massachusetts. See above, Chap. 5.

jocular and superficial, without ever coming to any explanation. If You suppose that I have or ever had a design or desire, of attempting to introduce a Government of King, Lords and Commons, or in other Words an hereditary Executive, or an hereditary Senate, either into the Government of the United States or that of any Individual State, in this Country, you are wholly mistaken. There is not such a Thought expressed or intimated in any public writing or private Letter of mine, and I may safely challenge all Mankind to produce such a passage and quote the Chapter and Verse. If you have ever put such a Construction on any Thing of mine, I beg you would mention it to me, and I will undertake to convince you, that it has no such meaning. Upon this occasion I will venture to say that my unpolished Writings, although they have been read by a sufficient Number of Persons to have assisted in crushing the Insurrection of the Massachusetts, in the formation of the new Constitutions of Pennsylvania, Georgia and South Carolina, and in procuring the Assent of all the States to the new national Constitution, yet they have not been read by great Numbers. Of the few who have taken the pains to read them, some have misunderstood them and others have willfully misrepresented them, and these misunderstandings and misrepresentations have been made the pretence for overwhelming me with floods and Whirlwinds of tempestuous Abuse, unexampled in the History of this Country.

It is thought by some, that Mr. Hancock's friends are preparing the Way, by my destruction, for his Election to the Place of Vice President, and that of Mr. Samuel Adams to be Governor of this Commonwealth, and then the Stone House Faction [35] will be sure of all the Loaves and Fishes, in the national Government and the State Government as they hope. The Opposers of the present Constitution of Pensilvania, the promoters of Shases Rebellion and County Resolves, and many of the Detesters of the present national Government, will undoubtedly aid them. Many People think too that no small Share of a foreign Influence, in revenge for certain untractable conduct at the Treaty of Peace, is and will be intermingled. The Janizaries of this goodly Combination, among whom are three or four, who hesitate at no falshood, have written all the Impudence and Impertinence which have appeared in the Boston Papers upon this memorable Occasion.

I must own to you that the daring Traits of Ambition and Intrigue, and those unbridled Rivalries which have already appeared, are the most melancholly and alarming Symptoms that I have ever seen in this Country:

35. Hancock's mansion on Beacon Hill was a two-story granite structure. Justin Winsor, ed., *The Memorial History of Boston*... (Boston, 1881-86), III, 201-3; Anson E. Morse, *The Federalist Party in Massachusetts to the Year 1800* (Princeton, 1909), 62-66, 140.

and if they are to be encouraged to proceed in their Course, the sooner I am relieved from the Competition the happier I shall be.

I thank you, Sir very sincerely for writing to me upon this Occasion. It was high time that you and I should come to an explanation with each other. The friendship that has subsisted for fifteen Years between Us without the smallest interruption, and untill this occasion without the slightest Suspicion, ever has been and still is, very dear to my heart. There is no office which I would not resign, rather than give a just occasion to one friend to forsake me. Your motives for writing to me, I have not a doubt were the most pure and the most friendly; and I have no suspicion that you will not receive this explanation from me in the same candid Light.

I thank You Sir for the foreign Intelligence and beg leave to present You with the friendly compliments of Mrs. Adams, as well as the repeated Assurances of the friendship, Esteem and respect of Dear Sir Your most obedient and most humble Servant

JOHN ADAMS

Jefferson to Adams

Philadelphia Aug. 30. 1791.

MY DEAR SIR

I recieved some time ago your favor of July 29. and was happy to find that you saw in it's true point of view the way in which I had been drawn into the scene which must have been so disagreeable to you. The importance which you still seem to allow to my note, and the effect you suppose it to have had tho unintentional in me, induce me to shew you that it really had no effect. Paine's pamphlet, with my note, was published here about the 2d. week in May. Not a word ever appeared in the public papers here on the subject for more than a month; and I am certain not a word on the subject would ever have been said had not a writer, under the name of Publicola, at length undertaken to attack Mr. Paine's principles, which were the principles of the citizens of the U. S. Instantly a host of writers attacked Publicola in support of those principles. He had thought proper to misconstrue a figurative expression in my note; and these writers so far noticed me as to place the expression in it's true light. But this was only an incidental skirmish preliminary to the general engagement, and they would not have thought me worth naming, had not he thought proper to bring me on the scene. His antagonists, very criminally in my opinion presumed you to be Publicola, and on that presumption hazarded a personal attack on you. No person saw with more uneasiness than I did, this unjustifiable assault, and the more so, when I saw it continued after the printer had declared you were not the author. But you will perceive from all this, my dear Sir, that my note contributed nothing to the production of these disagreeable peices. As long as Paine's pamphlet stood on it's own feet, and on my note, it was unnoticed. As soon as Publicola attacked Paine, swarms appeared in his defence. To Publicola then and not in the least degree to my note, this whole contest is to be ascribed and all it's consequences.

You speak of the execrable paragraph in the Connecticut paper. This it is true appeared before Publicola. But it had no more relation to Paine's pamphlet and my note, than to the Alcoran. I am satisfied the writer of it had never seen either; for when I past through Connecticut about the middle of June,[36] not a copy had ever been seen by anybody either in Har[t]ford or New Haven, nor probably in that whole State: and that paragraph was so notoriously the reverse of the disinterestedness of character which you are known to possess by every body who knows your name, that I never heard a person speak of the paragraph but with an indignation in your behalf, which did you entire justice. This paragraph then certainly did not flow from my note, any more than the publications which Publicola produced. Indeed it was impossible that my note should occasion your name to be brought into question; for so far from naming you, I had not even in view any writing which I might suppose to be yours, and the opinions I alluded to were principally those I had heard in common conversation from a sect aiming at the subversion of the present government to bring in their favorite form of a king, lords, and commons.

Thus I hope, my dear Sir, that you will see me to have been as innocent *in effect* as I was in intention. I was brought before the public without my own consent, and from the first moment of seeing the effort of the real aggressor in this business to keep me before the public, I determined that nothing should induce me to put pen to paper in the controversy. The business is now over, and I hope it's effects are over, and that our friendship will never be suffered to be committed, whatever use others may think proper to make of our names.

The event of the King's flight from Paris and his recapture will have struck you with it's importance. It appears I think that the nation is firm within, and it only remains to see whether there will be any movement from without. I confess I have not changed my confidence in the favourable issue of that revolution, because it has always rested on my own

36. During May 17-June 19, 1791, TJ and Madison were on a tour from Philadelphia to New York and Albany, through Vermont and down the Connecticut River, to Hartford (June 8), and back to Philadelphia. Malone, *Jefferson*, II, 359-63.

ocular evidence of the unanimity of the nation, and wisdom of the Patriotic party in the national assembly. The last advices render it probable that the emperor will recommence hostilities against the Porte. It remains to see whether England and Prussia will take a part.

Present me to Mrs. Adams with all the affections I feel for her and be assured of those devoted to yourself by, my dear Sir, your sincere friend and servt.

TH: JEFFERSON

Jefferson to Adams

Philadelphia Nov. 25. 1791.

SIR

Supposing that the first Consular convention agreed on with France, and not ratified by Congress, may explain as well as account for some articles in that which was last agreed on and ratified, I take the liberty of inclosing, for the members of the Senate, copies of the two conventions as they were printed side by side, to shew where they differed.[37] These differences are not as great as were to be wished, but they were all which could be obtained. I have the honour to be with the most profound respect and esteem, Sir, Your most obedient and most humble servt.

TH: JEFFERSON

Jefferson to Adams

Philadelphia Mar. 1. 1793.

SIR

In consequence of the information I received from you on the first Wednesday in January that the lists of votes for President and Vice President were received at the seat of government from all the states except that of Kentucky, I sent a special messenger to the District judge of Kentucky for the list of the votes of that state lodged in his custody, and by the return of the messenger received yesterday the inclosed letter for you,

37. This was the ten-page circular which TJ had printed in Paris in 1788, presenting in parallel columns the texts of the Consular Convention of 1784 (viewed adversely by Secretary Jay in his report of 1785 and not ratified by Congress) and of 1788 (prepared by TJ and Montmorin, the French secretary of foreign affairs). The latter became the first treaty ratified by the Senate of the United States, in 1789. The bill for carrying the convention into effect was enacted into law April 24, 1792. "The Consular Convention of 1788," editorial note, Boyd, XIV, 67-92; the official English text as ratified, *ibid.*, 171-77; Hunter Miller, ed., *Treaties and Other International Acts of the United States* (Washington, 1931), II, 228-41.

which he informs me contains the list.[38] I have only to observe that tho' the term between the first Wednesday of January, and the second Wednesday in February was obviously insufficient at this season for the performance of the journey yet the law made it my indispensable duty to send the messenger. I have the honour to be with the most perfect esteem and respect Sir Your most obedt. and most humble servt.

TH: JEFFERSON

Adams to Jefferson

Philadelphia April 4. 1794

DEAR SIR

The inclosed Volume [39] was lately sent in to me by a Servant. I have since heard that the Author of it is in New York. The Book exhibits a curious Picture of the Government of Berne and is well worth reading.

I congratulate you on the charming Opening of the Spring, and heartily wish I was enjoying of it as you are upon a Plantation,[40] out of the hearing of the Din of Politicks and the Rumours of War. This felicity will not fall to my Share, I fear, before June. I am Sir with great Regard your humble Servant

JOHN ADAMS

Jefferson to Adams

Monticello Apr. 25. 1794.

DEAR SIR

I am to thank you for the book you were so good as to transmit me, as well as the letter covering it, and your felicitations on my present quiet. The difference of my present and past situation is such as to leave me nothing to regret but that my retirement has been postponed four years too long. The principles on which I calculate the value of life are entirely

38. Electoral votes cast for vice-president: JA 77; George Clinton 50; TJ 4; Aaron Burr 1. Washington had been re-elected president unanimously.

39. *Lettres de Jean Jacques Cart à Bernard Demuralt, trésorier du pays de Vaud, sur le droit public de ce pays, et sur les événements actuels* (Paris, 1793), protesting against the oppressive rule of Berne over Vaud and its principal city, Lausanne. French "liberation" in 1798 became a dubious improvement in political status. In 1814 Vaud became a canton in the Swiss Confederation.

40. TJ resigned from the secretaryship of state on Dec. 31, 1793.

in favor of my present course. I return to farming with an ardour which I scarcely knew in my youth, and which has got the better entirely of my love of study. Instead of writing 10. or 12. letters a day, which I have been in the habit of doing as a thing of course, I put off answering my letters now, farmerlike, till a rainy day, and then find it sometimes postponed by other necessary occupations.

The case of the Pays de Vaud is new to me. The claims of both parties are on grounds which I fancy we have taught the world to set little store by. The rights of one generation will scarcely be considered hereafter as depending on the paper transactions of another.[41]

My countrymen are groaning under the insults of Gr. Britain. I hope some means will turn up of reconciling our faith and honour with peace: for I confess to you I have seen enough of one war never to wish to see another. With wishes of every degree of happiness to you both public and private, and with my best respects to Mrs. Adams, I am, Dear Sir your affectionate and humble servt.

TH: JEFFERSON

Adams to Jefferson

Philadelphia May 11. 1794

DEAR SIR

Your favour of the 25th of last month came to my hands Yesterday and I am glad to find you so well pleased with your Retirement. I felt the same delightful Satisfaction after my Return from Europe, and I feel still every Summer upon my little farm all the Ardour, and more than all the Ardor of youth: to such a Degree that I cannot bear the thought of writing or reading, unless it be some trifle to fill up a vacant half hour.

The Case of the Pays de Vaud is curious enough. Dr. Cart the Writer of the Book I sent you is arrived at New York and Mr. Rosset whose Tryal and Sentence for high Treason, for dining at a civic feast and drinking two or three Patriotic Toasts, is mentioned in it, is here at Philadelphia. He has lent me in Manuscript a full account of his Tryal. As much as I have ever detested an Aristocratical Government, I did not believe that the Canton of Berne could have been so tyrannical, till I read his Manuscript.

41. This is a paraphrase of TJ's statement of principle to Madison, "which I suppose to be self evident, '*that the earth belongs in usufruct to the living*': that the dead have neither power or rights over it." TJ to Madison, Sept. 6, 1789, Boyd, XV, 392-97.

I think nevertheless that "the Rights of one Generation of Men must Still depend, in some degree, on the Paper Transactions of another." The Social Compact and the Laws must be reduced to Writing. Obedience to them becomes a national Habit and they cannot be changed but by Revolutions which are costly Things. Men will be too Œconomical of their Blood and Property to have Recourse to them very frequently. This Country is becoming the Asylum of all the ardent Spirits in Europe. The Bishop of Autun and Mr. Beaumez are arrived and Dr. Priestley is expected.

The President has sent Mr. Jay to try if he can find any Way to reconcile our honour with Peace.[42] I have no great Faith in any very brill[i]ant Success: but hope he may have enough to keep Us out of a War. Another War would add two or three hundred Millions of Dollars to our Debt, raise up a many headed and many bellied Monster of an Army to tyrannize over Us, totally dissadjust our present Government, and accellerate the Advent of Monarchy and Aristocracy by at least fifty Years.

Those who dread Monarchy and Aristocracy and at the same time Advocate War are the most inconsistent of all Men.

If I had Your Plantation and your Labourers I should be tempted to follow your Example and get out of the Fumum et Opes Strepitumque Romae ["the smoke, the wealth, the din of Rome"] which I abominate. I am Sir with much Esteem your Friend and Sert

JOHN ADAMS

Adams to Jefferson

Philadelphia Nov. 21. 1794

DEAR SIR

I am desired by our old Acquaintance Mr. D'Ivernois to transmit you the inclosed Papers for your inspection Opinion and Advice. The poor Fellow has been obliged to fly a second time into Banishment. The first time, he was driven out as a Democrat: but it is now, Day about, as they say, in Geneva, and he is compelled to run as an Aristocrat.

Shall We print his History? What shall We do with his Academy?

I have spent my Summer so deliciously in farming that I return to the old Story of Politicks with great Reluctance. The Earth is grateful. You find it so, I dare say. I wish We could both say the Same of its Inhabitants.

42. Chief Justice Jay was commissioned envoy extraordinary to Great Britain on April 19. From his mission resulted the unpopular, pro-British Jay's Treaty of 1794, ratified by the Senate, June 24, 1795. Bemis, *Jay's Treaty*, 197, Chap. XIII.

When will the Crisis of this fever in human Nature be over, and in what State of Health will it be left? Solitudinem faciunt, Libertatem appellant.[43]

Virginia I hope will send Us some good Senators. We grow very thin.[44] I begin to think the Senate scarcely numerous enough for so large a People. But this is not a time for Changes: We must go on as well as we can. Make my Compliments, if you please to your Daughters, whom I had once the Pleasure to see, and for whom I retain much Esteem. I am, Sir, with great Regard, your most obedient

JOHN ADAMS

Adams to Jefferson

Philadelphia Feb. 5. 1795

DEAR SIR

The inclosed Pamphlet and Papers I have received this Week from the Author, with his request to transmit them to you. I have before transmitted in the Course of this Winter, another Packet from the same Writer;[45] but have as yet no answer from you: so that I am uncertain whether you have received it.

Mr. Jays Treaty with Britain is not yet arrived at the Secretary of States Office, though there is some reason to suppose it is arrived at New York.

You will see by the Changes in the Executive Department[46] that the Feelings of Officers are in a Way to introduce Rotations enough, which are not contemplated by the Constitution. Those Republicans who delight in Rotations will be gratified in all Probability, till all the Ablest Men in the Nation are roted out. To me these Things indicate something to be amiss somewhere. If Public Offices are to be made Punishments, will a People be well served? Not long I trow. I am Sir with great Regard your most obedient

JOHN ADAMS

43. An adaptation of Tacitus: "They make a solitude and call it peace." JA substitutes "liberty" for "peace," comparing the mass extermination by French revolutionaries of their allies, on behalf of "liberty, equality, fraternity," with mass extermination by Roman imperialism on behalf of the *pax Romana*.

44. Senators from Virginia were lacking, John Taylor having resigned and James Monroe having accepted the mission to France. Their successors were both Jeffersonians: Henry Tazewell and Stevens Thomson Mason.

45. Probably from François D'Ivernois; see TJ to JA, Feb. 6, 1795, below, 257.

46. Secretary of War Henry Knox was succeeded by Timothy Pickering on Jan. 2, 1795; Secretary of the Treasury Alexander Hamilton by Oliver Wolcott on Feb. 2; Edmund Randolph was secretary of state and William Bradford attorney general. George Gibbs, *Memoirs of the Administrations of Washington and John Adams...* (N. Y., 1846), I, 167, 177.

Jefferson to Adams

Monticello Feb. 6. 1795.

DEAR SIR

The time which has intervened between the receipt of your favor, covering D'Ivernois' letter, and this answer, needs appology. But this will be found in the state of the case. I had received from him a letter similar to that you inclosed. As the adoption of his plan depended on our legislature, and it was then in session, I immediately inclosed it to a member [Wilson Cary Nicholas] with a request that he would sound well the opinions of the leading members, and if he found them disposed to enter into D'Ivernois' views, to make the proposition; but otherwise not to hazard it.[47] It is only three days since I have received from him information of his proceedings. He found it could not prevail. The unprepared state of our youths to receive instruction thro' a foreign language, the expence of the institution, and it's disproportion to the moderate state of our population, were insuperable objections. I delayed myself the honor of acknoleging the receipt of your letter, till I might be able to give you at the same time the result of the proposition it forwarded. I have explained this to M. D'Ivernois in the inclosed letter,[48] which my distance from any sea-port, and the convenience of your position will I hope excuse my committing to your care.

I have found so much tranquility of mind in a total abstraction from every thing political, that it was with some difficulty I could resolve to meddle even in the splendid project of transplanting the academy of Geneva, en masse, to Virginia; and I did it under the usual reserve of *sans tirer en consequence*. In truth I have so much occupation otherwise that I have not time for taking a part in any thing of a public kind, and I therefore leave such with pleasure to those who are to live longer and enjoy their benefits. Tranquility becomes daily more and more the object of my life, and of this I certainly find more in my present pursuits than in those of any other part of my life. I recall however with pleasure the memory of some of the acquaintances I have made in my progress through it, and retain strong wishes for their happiness. I pray you to accept with kindness those which I sincerely entertain for you, and to be assured of the high respect and esteem with which I am Dear Sir Your most obedt. and most humble servt.

TH: JEFFERSON

47. TJ to W. C. Nicholas, Nov. 22, 1794, Ford, VI, 513-15.
48. TJ to D'Ivernois, Feb. 6, 1795, *ibid.*, VII, 2-6.

Jefferson to Adams

Monticello May 27. 95.

DEAR SIR

I inclose you a letter from our friend D'Ivernois according to his request expressed in it. Our geographical distance is insensible still to foreigners. They consider America of the size of a [garden] of which Massachusetts is one square and Virginia another. I know not what may have been your sentiments or measures respecting the transplantation of the science of Geneva to this country. If not more [successful] than mine, the mission of their commissaries will make a bad matter worse. In our state we are already too wise to want instruction either foreign or domestic, and the worst circumstance is that the more ignorant we become the less value we set on science, and the less inclination we shall have to seek it.

We have had a hard winter and backward spring. This injured our wheat so much that it cannot be made a good crop by all the showers of heaven which are now falling down on us exactly as we want them. Our first cutting of clover is not yet begun. Strawberries not ripe till within this fortnight, and every thing backward in proportion. What with my farming and my nail manufactory I have my hands full. I am on horseback half the day, and counting and measuring nails the other half. I am trying potatoes on a large scale as a substitute for Indian corn for feeding animals. This is new in this country, but in this culture we cannot rival you. Present my sincere respects to Mrs. Adams and accept assurances of the respect and attachment of Dear Sir Your most obedt. and most humble servt.

TH: JEFFERSON

Adams to Jefferson

Philadelphia January 31. 1796

DEAR SIR

I have received from our old Acquaintance D'Ivernois the inclosed Volume for you in the Course of the last Week.[49]

49. Francois D'Ivernois, *Des révolutions de France et de Genève* (London, 1795). His plans for transplanting the Geneva Academy to the United States did not materialize.

I consider all Reasoning upon French Affairs of little moment. The Fates must determine hereafter as they have done heretofore. Reasoning has been all lost. Passion, Prejudice, Interest, Necessity has governed and will govern; and a Century must roll away before any permanent and quiet System will be established. An Amelioration of human affairs I hope and believe will be the result, but You and I must look down from the Battlements of Heaven if We ever have the Pleasure of Seeing it.

The Treaty is not arrived [50] and Congress seems averse to engage in Business with Spirit till that is considered.

I envy you the Society of your Farm but another Year and one Month may make me the Object of Envy. Mean time I am, with Esteem and Affection your

JOHN ADAMS

Jefferson to Adams

Monticello Feb. 28. 96.

I am to thank you, my dear Sir, for forwarding Mr. D'Ivernois' book on the French revolution. I recieve every thing with respect which comes from him. But it is on politics, a subject I never loved, and now hate. I will not promise therefore to read it thoroughly. I fear the oligarchical executive of the French will not do. We have always seen a small council get into cabals and quarrels, the more bitter and relentless the fewer they are. We saw this in our committee of the states; [51] and that they were, from their bad passions, incapable of doing the business of their country. I think that for the prompt, clear and consistent action so necessary in an Executive, unity of person is necessary as with us. I am aware of the objection to this, that the office becoming more important may bring on serious discord in elections. In our country I think it will be long first; not within our day; and we may safely trust to the wisdom of our successors the remedies of the evil to arise in theirs. Both experiments however

50. Jay's Treaty. See above, 255, n. 42.

51. Under the Articles of Confederation the only executive authority was granted in Article IX to a "Committee of the States," consisting of one delegate from each state, to function only during recesses of Congress. It lacked sufficient authority to be effective and in Jan. 1784 TJ, who had proposed such a committee as early as 1775, prepared a report to Congress outlining enlarged powers for this peculiar executive body. "Report on the Powers of the Committee of the States," editorial note, Boyd, VI, 516-22.

are now fairly committed, and the result will be seen. Never was a finer canvas presented to work on than our countrymen. All of them engaged in agriculture or the pursuits of honest industry, independant in their circumstances, enlightened as to their rights, and firm in their habits of order and obedience to the laws. This I hope will be the age of experiments in government, and that their basis will be founded on principles of honesty, not of mere force. We have seen no instance of this since the days of the Roman republic, nor do we read of any before that. Either force or corruption has been the principle of every modern government, unless the Dutch perhaps be excepted, and I am not well enough informed to except them absolutely. If ever the morals of a people could be made the basis of their own government, it is our case; and he who could propose to govern such a people by the corruption of their legislature, before he could have one night of quiet sleep, must convince himself that the human soul as well as body is mortal. I am glad to see that whatever grounds of apprehension may have appeared of a wish to govern us otherwise than on principles of reason and honesty, we are getting the better of them. I am sure, from the honesty of your heart, you join me in detestation of the corruption of the English government, and that no man on earth is more incapable than yourself of seeing that copied among us, willingly. I have been among those who have feared the design to introduce it here, and it has been a strong reason with me for wishing there was an ocean of fire between that island and us. But away politics.

I owe a letter to the Auditor [Richard Harrison] on the subject of my accounts while a foreign minister, and he informs me yours hang on the same difficulties with mine. Before the present government there was a usage either practised on or understood which regulated our charges. This government has directed the future by a law. But this is not retrospective, and I cannot conceive why the treasury cannot settle accounts under the old Congress on the principles that body acted on. I shall very shortly write to Mr. Harrison on this subject, and if we cannot have it settled otherwise I suppose we must apply to the legislature. In this I will act in concert with you if you approve of it. Present my very affectionate respects to Mrs. Adams, and be assured that no one more cordially esteems your virtues than Dear Sir Your sincere friend and servt.

TH: JEFFERSON

Adams to Jefferson

Philadelphia April 6. 1796

DEAR SIR

Since my Receipt of your favour of the 28 of February I have call'd on the Auditor and had some Conversation with him and with The Secretary of The Treasury and with The Secretary of State upon the Subject of Accounts and they think that some Regulation may be made by Congress which will reach the Cases without any formal Memorial on our Part and indeed without mentioning Names. The Secretary of The Treasury has it under Consideration: But if they finally determine that they cannot accomplish the object without our Interposition I will join you with all my Heart in an Application to Congress.

D'Ivernois is industrious and clever, but he is in Pay, Pension or Employment of some kind or other under Mr. Pitt, and some of his late Publications have a tang of the Cask from whence he draws his Wine. It is good to read all those Party Pamphlets and believe in none of them.

This is indeed as you say the Age of Experiments in Government. One Tryal has been fairly made in America and France of Nedhams perfect Commonwealth,[52] and at length given up. Holland is trying it again and if Britain should have a Revolution she will try it too. An hundred thousand Dutchmen guillotined or beknifed will convince Holland as soon as five hundred thousand Frenchmen and Women have convinced France. How many Hecatombs must be slaughtered to convince John Bull I cannot calculate.

The Plural Executive in France is a new Attempt borrowed from a conceit of De Mably in his posthumous Dialogue with Lord Stanhope.[53] The Danger of Corruption and Intrigue in Elections is rather multiplied five fold, than diminished by this. And Jealousy, Emulation and Division among them are inevitable.

Corruption in Elections has heretofore destroyed all Elective Governments. What Regulations or Precautions may be devised to prevent it in future, I am content with you to leave to Posterity to consider. You and

52. Marchamont Nedham, *The Excellency of a Free State, or the Right Constitution of a Commonwealth* (London, 1656), reprinted, 1767, ed. by Richard Barron under the auspices of Thomas Hollis. JA used Nedham to exemplify the argument on behalf of a sovereign unicameral democratic legislature in his *Defence of the Constitutions of the United States*, III, Chap. IX.

53. Abbé de Mably, *Des droits et des devoirs du citoyen* (1789), in the form of letters dated in Aug. 1758.

I shall go to the Kingdom of the just or at least shall be released from the Republick of the Unjust, with Hearts pure and hands clean of all Corruption in Elections: so much I firmly believe. Those who shall introduce the foul Fiend on the Stage, after We are gone must exorcise him as they can. With great Esteem and regard I am, Sir your most obedient

JOHN ADAMS

Jefferson to Adams

Monticello Dec. 28. 1796 [54]

DEAR SIR

The public and the public papers have been much occupied lately in placing us in a point of opposition to each other. I trust with confidence that less of it has been felt by ourselves personally. In the retired canton where I am, I learn little of what is passing: pamphlets I see never; papers but a few; and the fewer the happier. Our latest intelligence from Philadelphia at present is of the 16th. inst. but tho' at that date your election to the first magistracy seems not to have been known as a fact, yet with me it has never been doubted. I knew it impossible you should lose a vote North of the Delaware, and even if that of Pensylvania should be against you in the mass, yet that you would get enough South of that to place your succession out of danger.[55] I have never one single moment expected a different issue: and tho' I know I shall not be believed, yet it is not the less true that I have never wished it. My neighbors, as my com-

54. This letter was never received by JA. It was enclosed, unsealed, by TJ in his letter to Madison dated Jan. 1, 1797, with this request: "The papers by the last post [which included Madison's letter of Dec. 19, 1796, to TJ] not rendering it necessary to change anything in the letter I enclose it open for your perusal, not only that you may possess the actual state of dispositions between us, but that if anything should render the delivery of it ineligible in your opinion, you may return it to me." Ford, VII, 99. In his reply of Jan. 15, 1797, Madison said he had decided to suspend delivery of the letter addressed to JA for several cogent reasons; if, after considering them, TJ still felt it was expedient to deliver the letter, it would be done. By this time Madison knew that JA had been elected president. "As you have, no doubt retained a copy of the letter [of Dec. 28] I do not send it back as you request." Hunt, ed., *Writings of Madison*, VI, 302-5. TJ had not retained a copy, but he had prepared a "Statement by memory of a letter written to J. Adams. copy omitted to be retained." Ford, VII, 97-98n.

55. JA received 71 electoral votes, TJ 68, Thomas Pinckney 59. TJ's judgment was correct: JA received the unanimous vote of the 7 states northeast of the Delaware, 1 of Pennsylvania's 15 votes, 3 from Delaware, 7 from Maryland, 1 from Virginia, and 1 from North Carolina.

purgators, could aver that fact, because they see my occupations and my attachment to them. Indeed it is possible that you may be cheated of your succession by a trick worthy the subtlety of your arch-friend [Alexander Hamilton] of New York, who has been able to make of your real friends tools to defeat their and your just wishes. Most probably he will be disappointed as to you; and my inclinations place me out of his reach. I leave to others the sublime delights of riding in the storm, better pleased with sound sleep and a warm birth below, with the society of neighbors, friends and fellow laborers of the earth, than of spies and sycophants. No one then will congratulate you with purer disinterestedness than myself. The share indeed which I may have had in the late vote, I shall still value highly, as an evidence of the share I have in the esteem of my fellow citizens. But while, in this point of view, a few votes less would be little sensible, the difference in the effect of a few more would be very sensible and oppressive to me. I have no ambition to govern men. It is a painful and thankless office. Since the day too on which you signed the treaty of Paris our horizon was never so overcast. I devoutly wish you may be able to shun for us this war by which our agriculture, commerce and credit will be destroyed. If you are, the glory will be all your own; and that your administration may be filled with glory and happiness to yourself and advantage to us is the sincere wish of one who tho', in the course of our voyage thro' life, various little incidents have happened or been contrived to separate us, retains still for you the solid esteem of the moments when we were working for our independance, and sentiments of respect and affectionate attachment.

TH: JEFFERSON

Adams to Jefferson

Washington Feb. 20. 1801

SIR

In order to save you the trouble and Expence of purchasing Horses and Carriages, which will not be necessary, I have to inform you that I shall leave in the stables of the United States seven Horses and two Carriages with Harness and Property of the United States. These may not be suitable for you: but they will certainly save you a considerable Expence as they belong to the studd of the President's Household. I have the honor to be with great respect Sir your most obedient and humble servant,

JOHN ADAMS

Jefferson to Adams

TH: JEFFERSON presents his respects to Mr. Adams and incloses him a letter which came to his hands last night; on reading what is written within the cover, he concluded it to be a private letter, and without opening a single paper within it he folded it up and now has the honor to inclose it to Mr. Adams, with the homage of his high consideration and respect.

Washington Mar. 8. 1801.

Adams to Jefferson

Stony Field,[56] Quincy March 24. 1801.

SIR

I have recd. your favour of March 8 with the Letter inclosed, for which I thank you. Inclosed is a letter to one of your Domesticks Joseph Doughtery.

Had you read the Papers inclosed they might have given you a moment of Melancholly or at least of Sympathy with a mourning Father. They relate wholly to the Funeral of a Son [57] who was once the delight of my Eyes and a darling of my heart, cutt off in the flower of his days, amidst very flattering Prospects by causes which have been the greatest Grief of my heart and the deepest affliction of my Life. It is not possible that any thing of the kind should hapen to you, and I sincerely wish you may never experience any thing in any degree resembling it.

This part of the Union is in a state of perfect Tranquility and I See nothing to obscure your prospect of a quiet and prosperous Administration, which I heartily wish you. With great respect I have the honor to be Sir your most obedient and very humble Servant.

JOHN ADAMS

56. This was the "Old House," acquired by JA in 1787 before his return from Great Britain and first named "Peacefield" by him. Later he referred to it as "Mount Wollaston" and eventually as "Montezillo." [National Park Service], *Adams National Historic Site, Massachusetts* (Washington, 1954); JA's letters, 1812-26, below, Vol. II.

57. Charles Adams (1770-1800), who had married Sarah, one of Colonel William Stephens Smith's sisters. Stewart Mitchell, ed., *New Letters of Abigail Adams, 1788-1801* (Boston, 1947), 261-62.

8

"Faithfull are the wounds of a Friend"

O<small>N</small> A<small>PRIL</small> 17, 1804, Mary Jefferson Eppes died at Monticello at the age of twenty-five. Pressing presidential duties, made heavier by the session of Congress extending through March, required Jefferson's presence in Washington, but he arrived home before his daughter's death.[1] With unaccustomed lack of restraint, he poured forth his grief to the friend of his boyhood, John Page. "Having lost even the half of all I had, my evening prospects now hang on the slender thread of a single life [his daughter Martha Randolph]. Perhaps I may be destined to see even this last chord of parental affection broken!"[2]

It was in this depressed state of mind that he received Mrs. Adams's letter of May 20. Nearly three and a half years of silence between them had elapsed since they last conversed in Washington. In making this friendly gesture, she could not overlook the fact that he was president of the United States and not merely "the private inhabitant of Monticello." Various reasons had withheld her pen "untill the powerfull feelings of my heart, have burst through the restraint" and given expression to her condolence. Mrs. Adams's love for Polly during her girlhood in England and France had, of course, never been forgotten. It had strengthened the bond of friendship, as Mrs. Adams's letters from London testified. And this had made irresistible the urge

---

1. TJ to Mary Jefferson Eppes, Feb. 26, 1804; TJ to John W. Eppes, March 15, 1804, Henry S. Randall, *The Life of Thomas Jefferson* (N. Y., 1858), III, 98-99; TJ to Madison, April 23, 1804, Ford, VIII, 300.
2. TJ to Governor John Page, June 25, 1804, Randall, *Jefferson*, III, 103.

to transmit a letter from "her who once took pleasure in subscribing Herself your Friend." [3]

Jefferson, not overlooking this final clause couched in the past tense, welcomed the opportunity to renew correspondence with Mrs. Adams, but before he replied, he wrote to his bereaved son-in-law, John Wayles Eppes and, with mixed feelings, forwarded her letter. That "the sentiments expressed in it are sincere," Jefferson had no doubt. "Her attachment was constant. Although all of them point to another object directly, yet the expressing them to me is a proof that our friendship is unbroken on her part." [4] The real proof, however, remained to be demonstrated in their ensuing correspondence.

Jefferson explained to Eppes that only one act of John Adams had given him personal displeasure during their long friendship, the "midnight appointments" of Federalists to office by President Adams just before the expiration of his term of office. Now Jefferson made the same point to Mrs. Adams, after expressing regret that circumstances of any kind should have caused estrangement. Having "opened myself to you without reserve," he could only entreat her forgiveness for thus taking advantage of her letter of condolence. [5] In this letter and those that followed, the former friends aired their grievances, dispelled some misunderstanding, and found relief through their frank discussion; but they failed to reach any common ground on which incidents might have been minimized or dismissed in favor of mutual interests of deeper significance, as Jefferson and John Adams might more surely have arrived at under similar circumstances. She could not allow their friendship an unfettered renewal.

The grievances of Mrs. Adams over Jefferson's leniency toward James Callender were answered only partially to her satisfaction. Callender had defamed Adams and his administration with at least the tacit support of Jefferson; after Callender was found guilty under the Sedition Act, President Jefferson released him and remitted his fine. That this was within the executive power could not be denied, and the President also justified the release of Callender—a despicable character who turned against his defender—by a damning of the act under which the journalist had been convicted.

Mrs. Adams's complaint about Jefferson's removal of John Quincy

3. AA to TJ, May 20, 1804, below, 269.
4. TJ to John W. Eppes, June 4, 1804, Randall, *Jefferson*, III, 99-100.
5. TJ to AA, June 13, 1804, below, 271.

Adams as commissioner of bankruptcy involved a mother's pride. When the President explained that Congressional action had terminated the appointment, she accepted his explanation and absolved him of personal unkindness.[6] As for Jefferson's initial objection to the "midnight appointment" of Federalist judges, he omitted further discussion of what he must have regarded as an inadequate explanation by Mrs. Adams.

At the bottom of their disagreements, still irreconcilable, were the political differences of the 1790's, which had produced rival parties and led to the "revolution of 1800." Mrs. Adams had attributed the dissension during President Adams's administration to the opposition party, and Jefferson was the leader of the Republicans whose talk of popular rule made her anxious for the fate of the country. "I feel perhaps too keenly the abuse of party," she wrote to her son Thomas in November 1796.[7] Washington's successor would not enjoy the public confidence and overwhelming support which had never failed the general. In 1798 Mrs. Adams deplored the support by French agents of *the Man of the People*" and she warned that if a heedless Congress did not "give the President a respit, they will have Jefferson sooner than they wish."[8] During this period of political transition, Jefferson was in the anomalous position of being a Republican vice-president in a Federalist administration. In March 1797 after the Republicans refused to co-operate with Adams in organizing a mission to France, Jefferson stated that the President never "consulted me as to any measures of the government."[9] Given all these conflicting conditions, even friendships of long standing were severely tested. And now in 1804 Mrs. Adams reminded Jefferson that when he last visited her in Washington, "you assured me, that if it should lay in your power to serve me or my family, nothing would give you more pleasure."[10] If Jefferson meant what he said, did subsequent acts of his belie his sincerity? The impasse could not be dissolved as long as they viewed it exclusively in political terms. The political wounds of 1800-1 were still sensitive and unhealed.

6. AA to TJ, Oct. 25, 1804, below, 281.
7. AA to Thomas B. Adams, Nov. 8, 1796, *Letters of Mrs. Adams*, II, 231-32; Whitney, *Abigail Adams*, 277.
8. AA to Mrs. Mary Cranch, March 20 and May 20-21, 1798, Mitchell, ed., *New Letters of Abigail Adams*, 147, 178.
9. TJ's "Anas," Ford, I, 273.
10. AA to TJ, Oct. 25, 1804, below, 281.

In his exaltation of freedom of opinion, Jefferson was more earnest than tactful, more virtuous than charitable; and his generalizations to Mrs. Adams on that score were a bit gratuitous. "Both of our political parties, at least the honest portion of them," he declared, "agree conscientiously in the same object, the public good: but they differ essentially in what they deem the means of promoting that good. One side believes it best done by one composition of the governing powers, the other by a different one. One fears most the ignorance of the people: the other the selfishness of rulers independant of them. Which is right, time and experience will prove." [11] And time, in 1804, seemed to run in favor of the Republicans, if Jefferson thought about it in that light. Mrs. Adams, who was never wanting a pointed reply, begged to "be permitted to pause, and ask you whether in your ardent zeal, and desire to rectify the mistakes and abuses as you may consider them, of the former administrations, you are not led into measures still more fatal to the constitution, and more derogatory to your honour, and independence of Character? Pardon me Sir if I say, that I fear you are." [12]

Offering her sincere wishes for his administration, Mrs. Adams proceeded to "close this correspondence." [13] Six years later, when Jefferson sent this correspondence to Dr. Benjamin Rush as evidence of an unsuccessful rapprochement, he regretted the prolonged misunderstanding with Mrs. Adams; but "yielding to an intimation in her last letter, I ceased from further explanation." [14] The lady had had the last word.

Abigail Adams to Jefferson

Quincy May 20th 1804

SIR

Had you been no other than the private inhabitant of Monticello, I should e'er this time have addrest you, with that sympathy, which a recent event has awakend in my Bosom. But reasons of various kinds withheld my pen, untill the powerfull feelings of my heart, have burst through the

11. TJ to AA, Sept. 11, 1804, below, 280.
12. AA to TJ, Oct. 25, 1804, below, 281.
13. *Ibid.*
14. TJ to Rush, Jan. 16, 1811, Ford, IX, 298.

restraint, and called upon me to shed the tear of sorrow over the departed remains, of your beloved and deserving daughter,[15] an event which I most sincerely mourn.

The attachment which I formed for her, when you committed her to my care: upon her arrival in a foreign Land: has remained with me to this hour, and the recent account of her death, which I read in a late paper, brought fresh to my remembrance the strong sensibility she discoverd, tho but a child of nine years of age at having been seperated from her Friends, and country, and brought, as she expressed it, "to a strange land amongst strangers." The tender scene of her seperation from me, rose to my recollection, when she clung around my neck and wet my Bosom with her tears, saying, "O! now I have learnt to Love you, why will they tear me from you" [16]

It has been some time since that I conceived of any event in this Life, which could call forth, feelings of mutual sympathy. But I know how closely entwined around a parents heart, are those chords which bind the filial to the parental Bosom, and when snaped assunder, how agonizing the pangs of seperation.[17]

I have tasted the bitter cup, and bow with reverence, and humility before the great dispenser of it, without whose permission, and over ruling providence, not a sparrow falls to the ground. That you may derive comfort and consolation in this day of your sorrow and affliction, from that only source calculated to heal the wounded heart—a firm belief in the Being: perfections and attributes of God, is the sincere and ardent wish of her, who once took pleasure in subscribing Herself your Friend

ABIGAIL ADAMS

Jefferson to Abigail Adams

Washington June 13.04.

DEAR MADAM

The affectionate sentiments which you have had the goodness to express in your letter of May 20. towards my dear departed daughter, have awakened in me sensibilities natural to the occasion, and recalled your kindnesses to her which I shall ever remember with gratitude and friend-

15. Mary Jefferson Eppes (Mrs. John Wayles Eppes, d. April 17, 1804). Malone, Jefferson, I, 434.
16. See AA to TJ, July 6 and 10, 1787, above, 183-84, 185.
17. Her son, Charles Adams, had died on Nov. 30, 1800.

ship. I can assure you with truth they had made an indelible impression on her mind, and that, to the last, on our meetings after long separations, whether I had heard lately of you, and how you did, were among the earliest of her enquiries. In giving you this assurance I perform a sacred duty for her, and at the same time am thankful for the occasion furnished me of expressing my regret that circumstances should have arisen which have seemed to draw a line of separation between us. The friendship with which you honoured me has ever been valued, and fully reciprocated; and altho' events have been passing which might be trying to some minds, I never believed yours to be of that kind, nor felt that my own was. Neither my estimate of your character, nor the esteem founded in that, have ever been lessened for a single moment, although doubts whether it would be acceptable may have forbidden manifestations of it. Mr. Adams's friendship and mine began at an earlier date. It accompanied us thro' long and important scenes. The different conclusions we had drawn from our political reading and reflections were not permitted to lessen mutual esteem, each party being conscious they were the result of an honest conviction in the other. Like differences of opinion existing among our fellow citizens attached them to the one or the other of us, and produced a rivalship in their minds which did not exist in ours. We never stood in one another's way: for if either had been withdrawn at any time, his favorers would not have gone over to the other, but would have sought for some one of homogeneous opinions. This consideration was sufficient to keep down all jealousy between us, and to guard our friendship from any disturbance by sentiments of rivalship: and I can say with truth that one act of Mr. Adams's life, and one only, ever gave me a moment's personal displeasure. I did consider his last appointments to office as personally unkind.[18] They were from among my most ardent political enemies, from whom no faithful cooperation could ever be expected, and laid me under the embarrasment of acting thro' men whose views were to defeat mine; or to encounter the odium of putting others in their places. It seemed but common justice to leave a successor free to act by instruments of his own choice. If my respect for him did not permit me to ascribe the whole blame to the influence of others, it left something for friendship to forgive, and after brooding over it for some little time, and not always resisting the expression of it, I forgave it cordially, and re-

18. The Judiciary Act, passed Feb. 13, 1801, reduced the membership of the Supreme Court to five, increased the number of district judges, and relieved the Supreme Court justices from traveling the circuit. President Adams appointed Federalists to these new positions, to the discomfiture of his successor. The act was repealed by the Republican Congress of 1802. If the act was partisan in origin, it did provide some needed reforms. Max Farrand, "The Judiciary Act of 1801," *Amer. Hist. Rev.*, 5 (1899-1900), 682-86.

turned to the same state of esteem and respect for him which had so long subsisted. Having come into life a little later than Mr. Adams, his career has preceded mine, as mine is followed by some other, and it will probably be closed at the same distance after him which time originally placed between us. I maintain for him, and shall carry into private life an uniform and high measure of respect and good will, and for yourself a sincere attachment. I have thus, my dear Madam, opened myself to you without reserve, which I have long wished an opportunity of doing; and, without knowing how it will be recieved, I feel relief from being unbosomed. And I have now only to entreat your forgiveness for this transition from a subject of domestic affliction to one which seems of a different aspect. But tho connected with political events, it has been viewed by me most strongly in it's unfortunate bearings on my private friendships. The injury these have sustained has been a heavy price for what has never given me equal pleasure. That you may both be favored with health, tranquility and long life, is the prayer of one who tenders you the assurances of his highest consideration and esteem.

TH: JEFFERSON

Abigail Adams to Jefferson

Quincy July 1st 1804

SIR

Your Letter of June 13th came duly to hand; if it had contained no other sentiments and opinions than those which my Letter of condolence could have excited, and which are expressed in the first page of your reply, our correspondence would have terminated here: but you have been pleased to enter upon some subjects which call for a reply: and as you observe that you have wished for an opportunity to express your sentiments, I have given to them every weight they claim.

"One act of Mr. Adams's Life, and *one* only, you repeat, ever gave me a moments personal displeasure. I did think his last appointments to office personally unkind. They were from among my most ardent political enemies."

As this act I am certain was not intended to give any personal pain or offence, I think it a duty to explain it so far as I then knew his views and designs. The constitution empowers the president to fill up offices as they become vacant. It was in the exercise of this power that appointments were made, and Characters selected whom Mr. Adams considerd, as men faithfull to the constitution and where he personally knew them, such as were capable of fullfilling their duty to their country. This was done by president Washington equally, in the last days of his administration so that not an office remaind vacant for his successor to fill upon his comeing into the office. No offence was given by it, and no personal unkindness thought of. But the different political opinions which have so unhappily divided our Country, must have given rise to the Idea, that personal unkindness was intended. You will please to recollect Sir, that at the time these appointments were made, there was not any certainty that the presidency would devolve upon you,[19] which is an other circumstance to prove that personal unkindness was not meant. No person was ever selected by him from such a motive—and so far was Mr. Adams from indulging such a sentiment, that he had no Idea of the intollerance of party spirit at that time, and I know it was his opinion that if the presidency devolved upon you, except in the appointment of Secretaries, no material Changes would be made. I perfectly agree with you in opinion that those should be Gentlemen in whom the president can repose confidence, possessing opinions, and sentiments corresponding with his own, or if differing from him, that they ought rather to resign their office, than cabal against measures which he may think essential to the honour safety and peace of the Country. Much less should they unite, with any bold, and dareingly ambitious Character, to over rule the Cabinet, or betray the Secrets of it to Friends or foes. The two Gentlemen who held the offices of secretaries,[20] when you became president were not of this Character. They were appointed by your predecessor nearly two years previous to his retirement. They were Gentlemen who had cordially co-opperated with him, and enjoyed the public confidence. Possessing however different political sentiments from those which you were known to have embraced, it was expected that they would, as they did, resign.

I have never felt any enmity towards you Sir for being elected president of the United States. But the instruments made use of, and the means which were practised to effect a change, have my utter abhorrence and detestation, for they were the blackest calumny, and foulest falshoods. I had witnessed enough of the anxiety, and solicitude, the envy jealousy and reproach attendant upon the office as well as the high responsibility of the Station, to be perfectly willing to see a transfer of it. And I can truly say, that at the time of Election, I considerd your pretentions much

19. Since the electoral vote in 1800 was a tie, 73-73, between TJ and Aaron Burr, the election was thrown into the House of Representatives, where on Feb. 17, 1801, on the thirty-sixth ballot TJ was elected president. Cunningham, *Jeffersonian Republicans*, 239, 244. Since JA's appointments were not made until the beginning of March, AA's chronology is in error; therefore her defense of JA fails in part.

20. Benjamin Stoddert, secretary of the navy, 1798-1801; Samuel Dexter, secretary of war, 1800, secretary of the treasury, 1801-2.

superior to his [Mr. Burr's], to whom an equal vote was given. Your experience I venture to affirm has convinced you that it is not a station to be envy'd. If you feel yourself a free man, and can act in all cases, according to your own sentiments, opinions and judgment, you can do more than either of your predecessors could, and are awfully responsible to God and your Country for the measures of your Administration. I rely upon the Friendship you still profess for me, and (I am conscious I have done nothing to forfeit it), to excuse the freedom of this discussion to which you have led with an unreserve, which has taken off the Shackles I should otherways have found myself embarrassed with.—And now Sir I will freely disclose to you what has severed the bonds of former Friendship, and placed you in a light very different from what I once viewd you in.

One of the first acts of your administration was to liberate a wretch [21] who was suffering the just punishment of the Law due to his crimes for writing and publishing the basest libel, the lowest and vilest Slander, which malice could invent, or calumny exhibit against the Character and reputation of your predecessor, of him for whom you profest the highest esteem and Friendship, and whom you certainly knew incapable of such complicated baseness. The remission of Callenders fine was a public approbation of his conduct. Is not the last restraint of vice, a sense of shame, renderd abortive, if abandoned Characters do not excite abhorrence.[22] If the chief Majestrate of a Nation, whose elevated Station places him in a conspicuous light, and renders his every action a concern of general importance, permits his public conduct to be influenced by private resentment, and so far forgets what is due to his Character as to give countanance to a base Calumniater, is he not answerable for the influence which his example has upon the manners and morals of the community?

Untill I read Callenders seventh Letter containing your compliment to him as a writer and your reward of 50 dollars, I could not be made to believe, that such measures could have been resorted to: to stab the fair fame and upright intentions of one, who to use your own Language "was acting from an honest conviction in his own mind that he was right."

21. James Thomson Callender, Scottish immigrant and pamphleteer, began his rabid attacks on the Federalist administration in 1797. After a stint in Philadelphia he moved to Virginia and wrote for the Richmond *Examiner*, a Republican paper. In 1800 Callender published *The Prospect before Us*, attacking the Federalist leaders. For his remarks about JA he was tried under the Sedition Law, fined $200, and sentenced to nine months' imprisonment by Justice Samuel Chase in June 1800. President Jefferson pardoned him in 1801 and remitted his fine. James Morton Smith, *Freedom's Fetters: The Alien and Sedition Laws and American Civil Liberties* (Ithaca, 1956), Chap. XV; Dumas Malone, "Callender, James Thomson," *DAB*, III, 425-26.

22. The most recent article on Callender and TJ is Charles A. Jellison, "That Scoundrel Callender," *Va. Mag. of Hist. and Biog.*, 67 (1959), 295-306.

This Sir I considerd as a personal injury. This was the Sword that cut assunder the Gordian knot, which could not be untied by all the efforts of party Spirit, by rivalship by Jealousy or any other malignant fiend.

The serpent you cherished and warmed, bit the hand that nourished him,[23] and gave you sufficient Specimens of his talents, his gratitude his justice, and his truth. When such vipers are let lose upon Society, all distinction between virtue and vice are levelled, all respect for Character is lost in the overwhelming deluge of calumny—that respect which is a necessary bond in the social union, which gives efficacy to laws, and teaches the subject to obey the Majestrate, and the child to submit to the parent.

There is one other act of your administration which I considerd as personally unkind, and which your own mind will readily suggest to you, but as it neither affected character, or reputation, I forbear to state it.

This Letter is written in confidence—no eye but my own has seen what has passed. Faithfull are the wounds of a Friend. Often have I wished to have seen a different course pursued by you. I bear no malice I cherish no enmity. I would not retaliate if I could—nay more in the true spirit of christian Charity, I would forgive, as I hope to be forgiven. And with that disposition of mind and heart, I subscribe the Name of

ABIGAIL ADAMS

Jefferson to Abigail Adams

Washington July 22.04.

DEAR MADAM

Your favor of the 1st inst. was duly recieved, and I would not again have intruded on you but to rectify certain facts which seem not to have been presented to you under their true aspect. My charities to Callendar are considered as rewards for his calumnies. As early, I think, as 1796, I was told in Philadelphia that Callendar, the author of the Political progress of Britain, was in that city, a fugitive from persecution for having written that book, and in distress.[24] I had read and approved the book: I con-

23. Callender soon turned against TJ, attacked the Republican administration with his vitriolic pen, and propagated scandal concerning TJ's private life. He died in 1803. *DAB*, III, 425-26.

24. Callender's pamphlet, criticizing the British government, had led to his indictment for sedition in Jan. 1793. He did not answer the court summons and so became a fugitive from justice and fled to the United States. *Ibid.*

sidered him as a man of genius, unjustly persecuted. I knew nothing of his private character, and immediately expressed my readiness to contribute to his relief, and to serve him. It was a considerable time after, that, on application from a person who thought of him as I did, I contributed to his relief, and afterwards repeated the contribution. Himself I did not see till long after, nor ever more than two or three times. When he first began to write he told some useful truths in his coarse way; but no body sooner disapproved of his writings than I did, or wished more that he would be silent. My charities to him were no more meant as encouragements to his scurrilities than those I give to the beggar at my door are meant as rewards for the vices of his life, and to make them chargeable to myself. In truth they would have been greater to him had he never written a word after the work for which he fled from Britain. With respect to the calumnies and falsehoods which writers and printers at large published against Mr. Adams, I was as far from stooping to any concern or approbation of them as Mr. Adams was respecting those of Porcupine,[25] Fenno, or Russell, who published volumes against me for every sentence vended by their opponents against Mr. Adams. But I never supposed Mr. Adams had any participation in the atrocities of these editors or their writers. I knew myself incapable of that base warfare, and believed him to be so. On the contrary, whatever I may have thought of the acts of the administration of that day, I have ever borne testimony to Mr. Adams's personal worth, nor was it ever impeached in my presence without a just vindication of it on my part. I never supposed that any person who knew either of us could believe that either meddled in that dirty work.

But another fact is that I 'liberated a wretch who was suffering for a libel against Mr. Adams.' I do not know who was the particular wretch alluded to: but I discharged every person under punishment or prosecution under the Sedition law, because I considered and now consider that law to be a nullity as absolute and as palpable as if Congress had ordered us to fall down and worship a golden image; and that it was as much my duty to arrest it's execution in every stage, as it would have been to have rescued from the fiery furnace those who should have been cast into it for refusing to worship their image. It was accordingly done in every instance, without asking what the offenders had done, or against whom they had offended, but whether the pains they were suffering were inflicted under the pretended Sedition law. It was certainly possible that my motives for contributing to the relief of Callender and liberating sufferers under the Sedition law, might have been to protect, encourage and reward

25. *Porcupine's Gazette* was a Federalist newspaper published in Philadelphia, 1797-99, by William Cobbett.

slander: but they may also have been those which inspire ordinary charities to objects of distress, meritorious or not, or the obligations of an oath to protect the constitution, violated by an unauthorized act of Congress. Which of these were my motives must be decided by a regard to the general tenor of my life. On this I am not afraid to appeal to the nation at large, to posterity, and still less to that being who sees himself our motives, who will judge us from his own knolege of them, and not on the testimony of a Porcupine or Fenno.

You observe there has been one other act of my administration personally unkind, and suppose it will readily suggest itself to me. I declare on my honor, Madam, I have not the least conception what act is alluded to. I never did a single one with an unkind intention.

My sole object in this letter being to place before your attention that the acts imputed to me are either such as are falsely imputed, or as might flow from good as well as bad motives, I shall make no other addition than the assurances of my continued wishes for the health and happiness of yourself and Mr. Adams.

TH: JEFFERSON

Abigail Adams to Jefferson

Quincy August 18th 1804

SIR

Your Letter of July 22d was by some mistake in the post office at Boston sent back as far as New York, so that it did not reach me untill the eleventh of this Month. Candour requires of me a reply. Your statement respecting Callender, (who was the wretch referd to) and your motives for liberating him, wear a different aspect as explaind by you, from the impression which they had made, not only upon my mind, but upon the minds of all those, whom I ever heard speak upon the subject. With regard to the act under which he was punished, different persons entertain different opinions respecting it. It lies not with me to decide upon its validity. That I presume devolved upon the supreem Judges of the Nation: but I have understood that the power which makes a Law, is alone competent to the repeal. If a Chief Majestrate can by his will annul a Law, where is the difference between a republican, and a despotic Government? That some restraint should be laid upon the asassin, who stabs reputation, all civilized Nations have assented to. In no Country has calumny falshood, and revileing stalked abroad more licentiously, than in this. No political

Character has been secure from its attacks, no reputation so fair, as not to be wounded by it, untill truth and falshood lie in one undistinguished heap. If there are no checks to be resorted to in the Laws of the Land, and no reperation to be made to the injured, will not Man become the judge and avenger of his own wrongs, and as in a late instance, the sword and pistol decide the contest? [26] All the Christian and social virtues will be banished the Land. All that makes Life desirable, and softens the ferocious passions of Man will assume a savage deportment, and like Cain of old, every Mans hand will be against his Neighbour. Party spirit is blind malevolent uncandid, ungenerous, unjust and unforgiving. It is equally so under federal as under democratic Banners, yet upon both sides are Characters, who possess honest views, and act from honorable motives, who disdain to be led blindfold, and who tho entertaining different opinions, have for their object the public welfare and happiness. These are the Characters, who abhor calumny and evil speaking, and who will never descend to News paper revileing. And you have done Mr. Adams justice in believing him, incapable of such conduct. He has never written a line in any News paper to which his Name has not been affixed, since he was first elected president of the united States. The writers in the public papers, and their employers are alltogether unknown to him.

I have seen and known that much of the conduct of a public ruler, is liable to be misunderstood, and misrepresented. Party hatred by its deadly poison blinds the Eyes and envenoms the heart. It is fatal to the integrity of the moral Character. It sees not that wisdom dwells with moderation, and that firmness of conduct is seldom united with outrageous voilence [i.e., violence] of sentiment. Thus blame is too often liberally bestowed upon actions, which if fully understood, and candidly judged would merit praise instead of censure. It is only by the general issue of measures producing banefull or benificial effects that they ought to be tested.

You exculpate yourself from any intentional act of unkindness towards any one. I will freely state that which I referd to in my former Letter, and which I could not avoid considering as personal resentment. Soon after my eldest son's return from Europe, he was appointed by the district Judge to an office into which no political concerns enterd, personally known to you, and possessing all the qualifications, you yourself being Judge, which you had designated for office. As soon as congress gave the appointments to the president you removed him.[27] This looked so particularly pointed, that some of your best Friends in Boston, at that time

26. Referring, no doubt, to the duel between Hamilton and Burr, fought on July 11, 1804, in which Hamilton was killed.
27. In his letter of Sept. 11, 1804, to AA, TJ provided a correct and satisfying answer to her complaint. See Bemis, *John Quincy Adams*, 112.

exprest their regret that you had done so. I must do him the Justice to say, that I never heard an expression from him of censure or disrespect towards you in concequence of it. With pleasure I say that he is not a blind follower of any party.

I have written to you with the freedom and unreserve of former Friendship to which I would gladly return could all causes but mere difference of opinion be removed. I wish to lead a tranquil and retired Life under the administration of the Government, disposed to heal the wounds of contention, to cool the rageing fury of party animosity: to soften the Rugged Spirit of resentment, and desirious of seeing my Children and Grand Children, Heirs to that freedom and independance which you and your predesessor, united your efforts to obtain. With these sentiments I reciprocate my sincere wishes for your Health and happiness.

ABIGAIL ADAMS

Jefferson to Abigail Adams

Monticello. Sep 11.04.

Your letter, Madam, of the 18th. of Aug. has been some days recieved, but a press of business has prevented the acknolegement of it. Perhaps indeed I may have already trespassed too far on your attention. With those who wish to think amiss of me, I have learnt to be perfectly indifferent: but where I know a mind to be ingenuous, and to need only truth to set it to rights, I cannot be as passive.

The act of personal unkindness alluded to in your former letter is said in your last to have been the removal of your eldest son from some office to which the judges had appointed him. I conclude then he must have been a Commissioner of bankruptcy, but I declare to you on my honor that this is the first knolege I have ever had that he was so. It may be thought perhaps that I ought to have enquired who were such, before I appointed others, but it is to be observed that the former law permitted the judges to name Commissioners occasionally only for every case as it arose, and not to make them permanent officers. Nobody therefore being in office there could be no removal. The judges you well know have been considered as highly federal; and it was noted that they confined their nominations exclusively to federalists. The legislature, dissatisfied with this, transferred the nomination to the President, and made the offices permanent. The very object in passing the law was that he should correct, not confirm, what was deemed the partiality of the judges. I thought it therefore proper to enquire, not whom they had employed, but whom I ought to appoint to fulfil the intentions of the law. In making these appointments I put in a proportion of federalists equal I believe to the proportion they bear in numbers through the union generally. Had I known that your son had acted, it would have been a real pleasure to me to have preferred him to some who were named in Boston in what were deemed the same line of politics. To this I should have been led by my knolege of his integrity as well as my sincere dispositions towards yourself and Mr. Adams.

You seem to think it devolved on the judges to decide on the validity of the sedition law. But nothing in the constitution has given them a right to decide for the executive, more than to the Executive to decide for them. Both magistracies are equally independant in the sphere of action assigned to them. The judges, believing the law constitutional, had a right to pass a sentence of fine and imprisonment, because that power was placed in their hands by the constitution. But the Executive, believing the law to be unconstitutional, was bound to remit the execution of it; because that power has been confided to him by the constitution. That instrument meant that it's co-ordinate branches should be checks on each other. But the opinion which gives to the judges the right to decide what laws are constitutional, and what not, not only for themselves in their own sphere of action, but for the legislature and executive also in their spheres, would make the judiciary a despotic branch.

Nor does the opinion of the unconstitutionality and consequent nullity of that law remove all restraint from the overwhelming torrent of slander which is confounding all vice and virtue, all truth and falsehood in the US. The power to do that is fully possessed by the several state legislatures. It was reserved to them, and was denied to the general government, by the constitution according to our construction of it. While we deny that Congress have a right to controul the freedom of the press, we have ever asserted the right of the states, and their exclusive right, to do so. They have accordingly, all of them, made provisions for punishing slander, which those who have time and inclination resort to for the vindication of their characters. In general the state laws appear to have made the presses responsible for slander as far as is consistent with their useful freedom. In those states where they do not admit even the truth of allegations to protect the printer, they have gone too far.

The candour manifested in your letter, and which I ever believed you to possess, has alone inspired the desire of calling your attention once more to those circumstances of fact and motive by which I claim to be judged. I hope you will see these intrusions on your time to be, what they really are, proofs of my great respect for you. I tolerate with the utmost latitude the right of others to differ from me in opinion without imputing to them criminality. I know too well the weakness and uncertainty of human reason to wonder at it's different results. Both of our political parties, at least the honest portion of them, agree conscientiously in the same object, the public good: but they differ essentially in what they deem the means of promoting that good. One side believes it best done by one composition of the governing powers, the other by a different one. One fears most the ignorance of the people: the other the selfishness of rulers independant of them. Which is right, time and experience will prove. We think that one side of this experiment has been long enough tried, and proved not to promote the good of the many; and that the other has not been fairly and sufficiently tried. Our opponents think the reverse. With whichever opinion the body of the nation concurs, that must prevail. My anxieties on the subject will never carry me beyond the use of fair and honorable means, of truth and reason: nor have they ever lessened my esteem for moral worth; nor alienated my affections from a single friend who did not first withdraw himself. Wherever this has happened I confess I have not been insensible to it: yet have ever kept myself open to a return of their justice.

I conclude with sincere prayers for your health and happiness that yourself and Mr. Adams may long enjoy the tranquility you desire and merit, and see, in the prosperity of your family, what is the consummation of the last and warmest of human wishes.

TH: JEFFERSON

Abigail Adams to Jefferson

Quincy October 25 1804

SIR

Sickness for three weeks past, has prevented my acknowledging the receipt of your Letter of Sepbr the 11th. When I first addrest you, I little thought of entering into a correspondence with you upon political topicks. I will not however regret it, since it has led to some elucidations and brought on some explanations, which place in a more favourable light occurrences which had wounded me.

Having once entertained for you a respect and esteem, founded upon the Character of an affectionate parent, a kind Master, a candid and benevolent Friend, I could not suffer different political opinions to obliterate them from my mind, and I felt the truth of the observation, that the Heart is long, very long in receiving the conviction that is forced upon it by reason. Affection still lingers in the Bosom, even after esteem has taken its flight. It was not untill after circumstances concured to place you in the light of a rewarder and encourager of a Libeller whom you could not but detest and despise, that I withdrew the esteem I had long entertaind for you. Nor can you wonder Sir that I should consider as personal unkindnesses the instances I have mentiond. I am pleased to find that, which respected my son, all together unfounded. He was as you conjecture appointed a commissioner of Bankrupcy together with Judge Daws, and continued to serve in it, with perfect satisfaction to all parties. At least I never heard the contrary, untill superseded by a new appointment. The Idea sugested, that no one was in office, merely because it was not perminent, and concequently no removal could take place, I cannot consider in any other light, than what the Gentlemen of the Law would term a quible—as such I pass it. Judge Daws was continued, or reappointed which placed Mr. Adams, in a more conspicuous light, as the object of personal resentment. Nor could I upon this occasion refrain calling to mind the last visit you made me at Washington, when in the course of conversation you assured me, that if it should lay in your power to serve me or my family, nothing would give you more pleasure. I will do you the justice to say at this hour: that I believe what you then said, you then meant. With respect to the office it was a small object but the disposition of the remover was considerd by me as the barbed arrow. This however by your declaration, is withdrawn from my mind. With the public it will remain, and here Sir may I be permitted to pause, and ask you whether in your ardent zeal, and desire to rectify the mistakes and abuses as you may consider them, of the former administrations, you are not led into measures still more fatal to the constitution, and more derogatory to your honour, and independence of Character? Pardon me Sir if I say, that I fear you are.

I know from the observations which I have made that there is not a more difficult part devolves upon a chief Majestrate, nor one which subjects him to more reproach, and censure than the appointments to office, and all the patronage which this enviable power gives him, is but a poor compensation for the responsibility to which it subjects him. It would be well however to weigh and consider Characters as it respects their Moral worth and integrity. He who is not true to himself, nor just to others, seeks an office for the benifit of himself, unmindfull of that of his Country.

I cannot agree, in opinion, that the constitution ever meant to withhold from the National Government the power of self defence, or that it could be considerd an infringment of the Liberty of the press, to punish the licentiousness of it.[28]

Time Sir must determine, and posterity will judge with more candour, and impartiality, I hope than the conflicting parties of our day, what measures have best promoted the happiness of the people: what raised them from a state of depression and degradation to wealth, honor, and reputation; what has made them affluent at home, and respected abroad, and to whom ever the tribute is due to them may it be given.

I will not Sir any further intrude upon your time, but close this correspondence, by my sincere wishes, that you may be directed to that path which may terminate in the prosperity and happiness of the people over whom you are placed, by administring the Government with a just and impartial hand. Be assured Sir that no one will more rejoice in your success than

ABIGAIL ADAMS

Quincy Nov. 19. 1804. The whole of this Correspondence was begun and conducted without my Knowledge or Suspicion. Last Evening and this Morning at the desire of Mrs. Adams I read the whole. I have no remarks to make upon it at this time and in this place.

J. ADAMS [29]

28. AA expressed the Federalist argument that freedom of speech and of the press could be defined only by the English common law, and that the First Amendment had not deprived Congress of the power to pass a sedition law. The Republicans argued that the First Amendment "not only rejected the English common law concept of libels against the government but also prohibited Congress from adding any restraint, either by previous restrictions, by subsequent punishment, or by an alteration of jurisdiction or mode of trial." Smith, *Freedom's Fetters*, 136, 140.

29. This note, in JA's hand, appears at the end of the letter-book copy in the Adams Papers.

9

"Whether you or I were right Posterity must judge"

D URING THE SUMMER of 1811 Edward Coles, secretary to President Madison, and his brother John were traveling through the northern states, armed with letters of introduction from the President to various statesmen they hoped to meet. John Adams was of course on their list. Cordially received by Mr. and Mrs. Adams, the Coles brothers found their host in a reminiscent mood and they spent the better part of two days talking with him about the history of the United States and especially his presidential administration. As Adams warmed to the subject, he voiced his grievances against Jefferson and recalled events culminating in the election of 1800 and the last days of the Federalist regime.

Edward Coles, a neighbor of Jefferson in Albemarle County, had heard some of these same incidents retold from a different point of view; in particular he gave Adams the Jefferson version of how the President-elect in 1801 had carefully selected the proper time to call on President Adams before the last session of the Federalist Congress and how the tense emotion at the opening of their conference had given way gradually to amicable conversation. The narrative as retold by Coles was accurate according to Adams's own recollection. He admitted that he had been sensitive about their meeting, but he added, "I never heard before that Mr. Jefferson had given a second thought as to the proper time for making the particular visit described." Adams went on to express admiration for the character of his old friend and strong disapproval of the scurrilous attacks upon him in the newspapers of that day. "I always loved Jefferson," Adams exclaimed, "and still love him." [1]

When Jefferson heard the details of Coles's visit, he was deeply moved. There was one friend to whom he turned without hesitation to unburden himself—the same person to whom, earlier that year, he had sent his correspondence of 1804 with Mrs. Adams. "This is enough for me," he wrote Dr. Benjamin Rush concerning Adams's outburst of affection. "I only needed this knowledge to revive towards him all the affections of the most cordial moments of our lives. . . . I knew him to be always an honest man, often a great one, but sometimes incorrect and precipitate in his judgments; and it is known to those who have ever heard me speak of Mr. Adams, that I have ever done him justice myself, and defended him when assailed by others, with the single exception as to political opinions." [2] Thus in early December 1811 Adams and Jefferson were on the eve of reconciliation, but it had taken two years of well-planned, persistent efforts on the part of their mutual friend Dr. Rush.

Rush, two and a half years younger than Jefferson, was a fellow signer of the Declaration of Independence. Although he won both fame and notoriety through his medical theories and practice, his reputation as a teacher had made Philadelphia the medical center of the nation. He carried on a wide correspondence on scientific and other "philosophical" matters, and like Adams and Jefferson, he had a keen sense of national consciousness. As these friends of his grew older and retired from public life, Rush regarded them increasingly as the personification of the American Republic, of its principles and ideals. The prolonged estrangement of the two former Presidents was to Rush both a personal and a national misfortune. In 1809 he thought he had found a way of healing the breach. [3]

During his stimulating correspondence with Adams on a variety of subjects, Rush had urged him to write a history of his life and times for the enlightenment of the American people, but Adams had rejected the proposal. [4] Now, in October 1809, Rush, assuming a casual

1. TJ to Benjamin Rush, Dec. 5, 1811, Ford, IX, 300*n.*; Edward Coles to Henry S. Randall, May 11, 1857, Randall, *Jefferson*, III, 639-40.

2. TJ to Rush, Dec. 5, 1811, Ford, IX, 300*n*. See above, Chap. 8, 268.

3. L. H. Butterfield has written the best account of "The Dream of Benjamin Rush: The Reconciliation of John Adams and Thomas Jefferson," *Yale Review*, 40 (1950-51), 297-319.

4. Rush to JA, July 11, Aug. 22, 1806, April 1, Aug. 14, 1809, Butterfield, ed., *Letters of Rush*, II, 922, 927, 1000-1, 1013-14.

air, recounted a dream he hoped would come true. He was reading in a history of the United States that the two ex-Presidents had renewed their friendship in November of that year. It had come about through a letter from Adams congratulating Jefferson on his domestic happiness in retirement from public office. With Jefferson's cordial reply their correspondence was resumed and continued during the remainder of their lives; and, according to the dream, "these gentlemen sunk into the grave nearly at the same time...." [5] Adams assured Rush that the dream put him in good spirits, but "it is not History. It may be Prophecy." [6] It was indeed prophetic, but Rush's feeler for reconciliation was rebuffed.

A year later, Rush tried a more direct approach through Jefferson, with an allusion to the "patriotic years" of 1774-76, "your early attachment to Mr. Adams, and his to you." "I have ardently wished a friendly and epistolary intercourse might be revived between you.... Human nature will be a gainer by it. I am sure an advance on your side will be a cordial to the heart of Mr. Adams." [7] It was at this juncture that Jefferson forwarded to Rush his unsatisfactory exchange of letters with Mrs. Adams and professed to "the same good opinion of Mr. Adams which I ever had." (At his wife's request John Adams had already read them in 1804, without comment.) [8] After reviewing the issues between Adams and himself, Jefferson asked Rush to "judge for yourself whether they admit a revival of that friendly intercourse for which you are so kindly solicitous." [9] Rush realized he had failed again, but the reply from Monticello nourished his hope that the way to an accord would yet be found.

When Edward Coles proved to be the accidental messenger of good will in 1811, Rush acted promptly on Jefferson's warm response by quoting at length from it in a letter to Adams and concluding: "And now, my dear friend, permit me again to suggest to you to receive the olive branch which has thus been offered to you by the hand of a man who still loves you. Fellow laborers in erecting the great fabric of American independence! ... embrace—embrace each

5. Rush to JA, Oct. 17, 1809, *ibid.*, 1021-22.
6. JA to Rush, Oct. 25, 1809, *ibid.*, 1023n.
7. Rush to TJ, Jan. 2, 1811, *ibid.*, 1075-76.
8. AA to TJ, Oct. 25, 1804, postscript dated Nov. 19, 1804, above, 282.
9. TJ to Rush, Jan. 16, 1811, Ford, IX, 295-99.

other!" [10] The next day Rush informed Jefferson hopefully of his second effort to revive their friendship.[11]

Undoubtedly Adams had made up his mind about writing to Jefferson when he replied to Rush in a half-comic, half-serious vein and left the issue apparently unresolved. He might keep Rush in doubt a while longer, but the doctor had not tricked him. "I perceive plainly enough, Rush, that you have been teasing Jefferson to write to me, as you did me some time ago to write to him. . . . When there has been no war, there can be no room for negotiations of peace." He and Jefferson were in agreement concerning the Constitution and forms of government in general; they differed on measures of administration and other details. Rush seemed to imply that Adams had considered Jefferson as an enemy. "This is not so; I have always loved him as a friend." Rush's exhortation was so hyper-solemn that Adams "had some inclination to be ludicrous." "But why do you make so much ado about nothing? Of what use can it be for Jefferson and me to exchange letters? . . . Time and chance, however, or possibly design, may produce ere long a letter between us." [12]

Adams carried out his "design" a week later when he informed Jefferson that he was mailing him "two Pieces of Homespun lately produced in this quarter." Wishing Jefferson "many happy New Years," [13] the statesman of Quincy expressed his esteem for the statesman of Monticello and thus opened the second and richer period of their correspondence. The prospect of receiving some homespun from Massachusetts prompted Jefferson to begin his reply with a short essay on domestic manufactures in Virginia, a practical subject of deep concern to a practical-minded man who advocated economic independence to fortify his country's political independence in a world at war. However, this was a letter chiefly of reminiscence, of personal matters rather than public affairs, a letter of "recollections very dear to my mind." Jefferson wrote eagerly and saluted his old friend "with unchanged affections and respect." [14] The next day, to his delight, he received the "homespun"—the two-volumed *Lectures*

10. Rush to JA, Dec. 16, 1811, Butterfield, ed., *Letters of Rush*, II, 1110.
11. Rush to TJ, Dec. 17, 1811, *ibid.*, 1111-12.
12. JA to Rush, Dec. 25, 1811, *Works*, X, 10-12. In a letter to Rush, Aug. 28, 1811, JA had referred, almost inadvertently, to TJ as "my friend." *Ibid.*, IX, 638, 639.
13. JA to TJ, Jan. 1, 1812, below, 290.
14. TJ to JA, Jan. 21, 1812, below, 290-92.

on Rhetoric and Oratory by John Quincy Adams, to whom as a youth in Paris, almost thirty years before, he had become strongly attached.[15]

The correspondence of the two former Presidents was resumed amid the mounting national and international tension which culminated in the War of 1812. The controversies with Great Britain over neutral rights and impressment of American sailors had not changed fundamentally since Jefferson's presidency, but the Republican party had split over the power of the national government vis-à-vis the states, and the Federalists of commercial New England were threatening disunion. "The Union is still to me an Object of as much Anxiety," declared Adams, "as ever Independence was. To this I have sacrificed my Popularity in New England"—and so did his son John Quincy Adams.[16] The elder Adams had never been a party man. He put the interests of the nation first, whether he opposed Federalist Hamilton or Republican Burr. President Jefferson had combatted the Essex Junto of Massachusetts, proponents of a confederacy of the eastern states.[17] In their exchange of letters during the winter and spring of 1812, Adams and Jefferson were in agreement on what they opposed, despite their frank discussion of political differences. At Monticello on June 11 Jefferson was "taking for granted that the doors of Congress will re-open with a Declaration of war."[18] On June 18 Congress reached that decision.

Even in retirement Adams could not view the political scene, currently or in retrospect, with the detachment that Jefferson achieved. Charges of corruption against the Republican Presidents Adams treated with contempt, even though he told Jefferson, "in the Measures of Administration I have neither agreed with you or Madison." As for non-importation, non-intercourse, embargoes, the structure of the judiciary, or the neglect of the Navy, "whether you or I were right Posterity must judge."[19] In the conflict with the Barbary states, Jefferson had been the first to propose a navy,[20] but Adams was the more consistent advocate. And now, with the nation at war, "if only a few Frigates had been ordered to be built!"[21] By May 1813 the little

15. TJ to JA, Jan. 23, 1812, below, 292.
16. JA to TJ, Feb. 3, 1812, below, 295; Bemis, *John Quincy Adams*, Chap. VII.
17. TJ to JA, April 20, 1812, JA to TJ, May 3, 1812, below, 300, 303.
18. TJ to JA, below, 308.
19. JA to TJ, May 1, 1812, 301.
20. See above, Chap. 4, 128, 142.
21. JA to TJ, June 28, 1812, below, 311.

American Navy had won some victories—by the frigates *Constitution* and *United States*, by the sloop-of-war *Wasp*—"which must be more gratifying to you than to most men," wrote Jefferson to Adams. "If I have differed with you on this ground, it was not on the principle, but the time." [22] Luckily time had not run out.

Because Adams was extremely sensitive about his political career, one incident of the past, unexpectedly brought to light, put his renewed friendship with Jefferson to a severe test. In 1798 Adams had addressed the young men of Philadelphia in response to a pledge they made to defend their country in the quasi-war with France. During the course of his remarks, "without wishing to damp the ardor of curiosity, or influence the freedom of inquiry," he predicted that "after the most industrious and impartial researches, the longest liver of you will find no principles, institutions, or systems of education more fit, in general, to be transmitted to your posterity, than those you have received from your ancestors." [23] Writing to Joseph Priestley after the Republicans came into power, Jefferson criticized the Federalist regime for its bigotry and backward look to "the education of our ancestors.... President [Adams] himself declaring that we were never to expect to go beyond them in real Science.'" [24] Jefferson also condemned the Alien Act, passed by the Federalist Congress, as a "Libel on Legislation." When in 1813 Adams read these sharp criticisms in the appendix to the *Memoirs of the Late Reverend Theophilus Lindsey* (1812), the English Unitarian, he demanded ("in the French sense of the word," which softened it to a request) proof and explanation.[25] Paraphrasing Jefferson's words, Adams declaimed, "Oh! Mr. Jefferson! What a wave of Public Opinion has rolled over the Universe?" [26]

Jefferson was greatly embarrassed by the publication, without permission, of his private letters to Priestley. Indictment of the party in power before 1801 was not directed personally at Adams, explained his former adversary. Adams's pithy phrases were too quotable to omit. Nevertheless, argued Jefferson, "you possess, yourself, too much

22. TJ to JA, May 27, 1813, below, 324; see also JA to TJ, June 11, 1813, below, 328-29.
23. "To the Young Men of the City of Philadelphia, the District of Southwark, and the Northern Liberties, Pennsylvania," May 7, 1798, *Works*, IX, 188.
24. TJ to Priestley, March 21, 1801, Ford, VIII, 21-22; quoted in JA to TJ, June 10, 1813, below, 327.
25. JA to TJ, May 29, June 10 and 14, 1813, below, 325-26, 326-27, 329-30.
26. JA to TJ, June 14, 1813, below, 330.

science, not to see how much is still ahead of you, unexplained and unexplored." [27] In accepting these explanations in good grace Adams could not resist giving advice: "Checks and Ballances, Jefferson, however you and your Party may have ridiculed them, are our only Security, for the progress of Mind, as well as the Security of Body." And he had stressed the importance of *general principles* in advising the young men of Philadelphia.[28] Jefferson, however, maintained the philosophical point of view, that "the same political parties which now agitate the U.S. have existed thro' all time" and "that every one takes his side in favor of the many, or of the few...." [29]

Although the veteran statesmen did not succeed in excluding political issues from their letters, they derived most pleasure from discussing scientific, historical, and religious subjects. Each man sought information and speculation from the other in a bombardment of ideas. Discovery of prophets in every era, argued Adams, suggested false prophets who have confounded mankind, whether in Biblical or modern times, whether in international relations or among the Indian tribes.[30] Jefferson needed no prodding to launch into a survey of Indian antiquities; happily he analyzed the historical sources available and commented on conflicting hypotheses. Adams ridiculed the far-fetched analogies drawn by some writers to determine the origin of the American Indians and their language.[31] Jefferson contributed first-hand knowledge of the Indians in Virginia, Adams about those in Massachusetts. They also exchanged historical data and queries on their native colonies. As for religion, both were advocates of freedom of the mind and would not minimize the spiritual tyranny that still threatened where it did not prevail over their own generation.[32]

By the summer of 1813 their accord was re-established, despite a few old wounds exposed and irritated. But their mutual friend who had brought about the rapprochement died on April 19. As Adams and Jefferson mourned Rush's death, they took count of the surviving signers of the Declaration of Independence.[33] Besides themselves, only six were still alive.

27. TJ to JA, June 15, 1813, below, 332.
28. JA to TJ, June 25 and 28, 1813, below, 334, 338-40.
29. TJ to JA, June 27, 1813, below, 335, 337.
30. JA to TJ, Feb. 10, 1812, and TJ to JA, April 20, 1812, below, 297, 298-99.
31. TJ to JA, June 11, 1812, and JA to TJ, June 28, 1812, Jan. 26, 1813, below, 305-8, 308-11.
32. JA to TJ, Feb. 10, 1812, June 25, 1813, below, 297-98, 333-34. See also, Chap. 10.
33. Butterfield, ed., *Letters of Rush*, II, 992; TJ to JA, May 27, 1813, below, 323.

Adams to Jefferson

Quincy January 1st. 1812.

DEAR SIR

As you are a Friend to American Manufactures under proper restrictions, especially Manufactures of the domestic kind, I take the Liberty of sending you by the Post a Packett containing two Pieces of Homespun [34] lately produced in this quarter by One who was honoured in his youth with some of your Attention and much of your kindness.

All of my Family whom you formerly knew are well. My Daughter Smith is here and has successfully gone through a perilous and painful Operation, which detains her here this Winter, from her Husband and her Family at Chenango: [35] where one of the most gallant and skilful Officers of our Revolution is probably destined to spend the rest of his days, not in the Field of Glory, but in the hard Labours of Husbandry.

I wish you Sir many happy New Years and that you may enter the next and many succeeding Years with as animating Prospects for the Public as those at present before Us. I am Sir with a long and sincere Esteem your Friend and Servant

JOHN ADAMS

Jefferson to Adams

Monticello Jan. 21. 1812.

DEAR SIR

I thank you before hand (for they are not yet arrived) for the specimens of homespun you have been so kind as to forward me by post. I doubt not their excellence, knowing how far you are advanced in these things in your quarter. Here we do little in the fine way, but in coarse and midling goods a great deal. Every family in the country is a manu-

34. JA sent TJ a copy of John Quincy Adams's *Lectures on Rhetoric and Oratory*, 2 vols. (Cambridge, [Mass.], 1810), prepared while he was professor at Harvard College, 1806-9. Bemis, *John Quincy Adams*, 132-33.

35. Colonel William Stephens Smith's farm was at Lebanon, Madison County, New York, in the Chenango Valley. In 1812 he was elected to Congress as a Federalist and served from 1813 until his death in 1816. Curtis, "Smith, William Stephens," *DAB*, XVII, 368-69.

factory within itself, and is very generally able to make within itself all the stouter and midling stuffs for it's own cloathing and household use. We consider a sheep for every person in the family as sufficient to clothe it, in addition to the cotton, hemp and flax which we raise ourselves. For fine stuff we shall depend on your Northern manufactures. Of these, that is to say, of company establishments, we have none. We use little machinery. The Spinning Jenny and loom with the flying shuttle can be managed in a family; but nothing more complicated. The economy and thriftiness resulting from our household manufactures are such that they will never again be laid aside; and nothing more salutary for us has ever happened than the British obstructions to our demands for their manufactures. Restore free intercourse when they will, their commerce with us will have totally changed it's form, and the articles we shall in future want from them will not exceed their own consumption of our produce.

A letter from you calls up recollections very dear to my mind. It carries me back to the times when, beset with difficulties and dangers, we were fellow laborers in the same cause, struggling for what is most valuable to man, his right of self-government. Laboring always at the same oar, with some wave ever ahead threatening to overwhelm us and yet passing harmless under our bark, we knew not how, we rode through the storm with heart and hand, and made a happy port. Still we did not expect to be without rubs and difficulties; and we have had them. First the detention of the Western posts: [36] then the coalition of Pilnitz,[37] outlawing our commerce with France, and the British enforcement of the outlawry. In your day French depredations. in mine English, and the Berlin and Milan decrees: now the English orders of council, and the piracies they authorise: when these shall be over, it will be the impressment of our seamen, or something else: and so we have gone on, and so we shall go on, puzzled and prospering beyond example in the history of man. And I do believe we shall continue to growl, [i.e., grow] to multiply and prosper until we exhibit an association, powerful, wise and happy, beyond what has yet been seen by men.   As for France and England, with all their pre-eminence in science, the one is a den of robbers, and the other of pirates. And if science produces no better fruits than tyranny, murder, rapine and destitution of national morality, I would rather wish our country to be ignorant, honest and estimable as our neighboring savages are.

But whither is senile garrulity leading me? Into politics, of which I have taken final leave. I think little of them, and say less. I have given up newspapers in exchange for Tacitus and Thucydides, for Newton and Euclid; and I find myself much the happier. Sometimes indeed I look back to

36. See above, Chap. 2, 62, n. 49, and Bemis, *Jay's Treaty*, 3-20.
37. See R. R. Palmer, *A History of the Modern World* (N. Y., 1952), 364.

former occurrences, in remembrance of our old friends and fellow laborers, who have fallen before us. Of the signers of the Declaration of Independence I see now living not more than half a dozen on your side of the Potomak, and, on this side, myself alone.[38] You and I have been wonderfully spared, and myself with remarkable health, and a considerable activity of body and mind. I am on horseback 3. or 4. hours of every day; visit 3. or 4. times a year a possession I have 90 miles distant,[39] performing the winter journey on horseback. I walk little however; a single mile being too much for me; and I live in the midst of my grandchildren, one of whom has lately promoted me to be a great grandfather.[40] I have heard with pleasure that you also retain good health, and a greater power of exercise in walking than I do. But I would rather have heard this from yourself, and that, writing a letter, like mine, full of egotisms, and of details of your health, your habits, occupations and enjoyments, I should have the pleasure of knowing that, in the race of life, you do not keep, in it's physical decline, the same distance ahead of me which you have done in political honors and atchievements. No circumstances have lessened the interest I feel in these particulars respecting yourself; none have suspended for one moment my sincere esteem for you; and I now salute you with unchanged affections and respect.

TH: JEFFERSON

Jefferson to Adams

Monticello Jan. 23. 12.

DEAR SIR

The messenger who carried my letter of yesterday to the Post-office brought me thence, on his return, the two pieces of homespun which had been separated by the way from your letter of Jan. 1. A little more

38. Ten signers of the Declaration, including JA and TJ, were alive in 1812: Elbridge Gerry (d. 1814) and Robert Treat Paine (d. 1814) of Massachusetts, William Ellery (d. 1820) of Rhode Island, William Floyd (d. 1821) of New York, Benjamin Rush (d. 1813) and George Clymer (d. 1813) of Pennsylvania, Thomas McKean (d. 1817) of Delaware, and Charles Carroll (d. 1832) of Maryland.

39. Poplar Forest, in Bedford County, Va., which TJ had acquired in 1774 from his father-in-law's estate. He built an octagon house there while he was president. Malone, *Jefferson*, I, 441-42; Paul Wilstach, *Jefferson and Monticello* (N. Y., 1925), 159-60.

40. TJ's first great-grandchild was John Warner Bankhead (b. 1810), eldest child of Charles Lewis Bankhead and Mrs. Anne Cary Randolph Bankhead, first-born of Thomas Mann Randolph and Mrs. Martha Jefferson Randolph. Walter L. Zorn, *The Descendants of the Presidents of the United States* (2d rev. edn.; Monroe, Mich., 1955), 32.

sagacity of conjecture in me, as to their appellation, would have saved you the trouble of reading a long dissertation on the state of real homespun in our quarter. The fact stated however will not be unacceptable to you: and the less when it is considered as a specimen only of the general state of our whole country and of it's advance towards an independance of foreign supplies for the necessary manufactures.

Some extracts from these volumes which I had seen in the public papers had prepared me to recieve them with favorable expectations. These have not been disappointed; for I have already penetrated so far into them as to see that they are a mine of learning and taste, and a proof that the author of the inimitable reviews of Ames and Pickering [41] excels in more than one character of writing. The thanks therefore which I had rendered by anticipation only in my letter, I reiterate in this Postscript on a knolege of their high merit, and avail myself of the occasion it furnishes of repeating the assurances of my sincere friendship and respect.

TH: JEFFERSON

Adams to Jefferson

Quincy February 3. 1812

DEAR SIR

Sitting at My Fireside with my Daughter Smith, on the first of February My Servant brought me a Bundle of Letters and Newspapers from the Post Office in this Town: one of the first Letters that struck my Eye had the Post Mark of Milton 23. Jany. 1812. Milton is the next Town to Quincy and the Post Office in it is but three Miles from my House. How could the Letter be so long in coming three miles? Reading the Superscription, I instantly handed the Letter to Mrs. Smith. Is that not Mr. Jeffersons hand? Looking attentively at it, she answered it is very like it. How is it possible a Letter from Mr. Jefferson, could get into the Milton Post office? Opening the Letter I found it, indeed from Monticello in the hand and with the Signature of Mr. Jefferson: but this did not much diminish my Surprize. How is it possible a Letter can come from Mr. Jefferson to me in seven or Eight days? I had no Expectation of an Answer, thinking

41. *American Principles: a Review of the Works of Fisher Ames, compiled by a Number of His Friends* (Boston, 1809). J. Q. Adams's authorship of this anonymous work, originally published in the Boston *Patriot*, April-June 1809, in a series of letters, was well known. Bemis, *John Quincy Adams*, 152-53.

the Distance so great and the Roads so embarrassed under two or three Months. This History would not be worth recording but for the Discovery it made of a Fact, very pleasing to me, vizt. that the Communication between Us is much easier, surer and may be more frequent than I had ever believed or suspected to be possible.

The Material of the Samples of American Manufacture which I sent you was not Wool nor Cotton, nor Silk nor Flax nor Hemp nor Iron nor Wood. They were spun from the Brain of John Quincy Adams and consist in two Volumes of his Lectures on Rhetorick and oratory, delivered when he was Professor of that Science in our University of Cambridge. A Relation of mine, a first Cousin of my ever honoured, beloved and revered Mother, Nicholas Boylston, a rich Merchant of Boston, bequeathed by his Will a Donation for establishing a Professorship, and John Quincy Adams, having in his Veins so much of the Blood of the Founder, was most earnestly solicited to become the first Professor. The Volumes I sent you are the Fruit of his Labour during the short time he held that office. But it ought to be remembered that he attended his Duty as a Senator of the United States during the same Period. It is with some Anxiety submitted to your Judgment.

Your Account of the flourishing State of Manufactures in Families in your Part of the Country is highly delightful to me. I wish the Spirit may spread and prevail through the Union. Within my Memory We were much in the same Way in New England: but in later Times We have run a gadding abroad too much to seek for Eatables, Drinkables and Wearables.

Your Life and mine for almost half a Century have been nearly all of a Piece, resembling in the whole, mine in The Gulph Stream, chaced by three British Frigates, in a Hurricane from the North East and a hideous Tempest of Thunder and Lightning, which cracked our Mainmast, struck three and twenty Men on Deck, wounded four and killed one.[42] I do not remember that my Feelings, during those three days were very different from what they have been for fifty Years.

What an Exchange have you made? Of Newspapers for Newton! Rising from the lower deep of the lowest deep of Dulness and Bathos to the Contemplation of the Heavens and the heavens of Heavens. Oh that I had devoted to Newton and his Fellows that time which I fear has been wasted on Plato and Aristotle, Bacon (Nat) Acherly, Bolin[g]broke, De Lolme, Harrington, Sidney, Hobbes, Plato Redivivus,[43] Marchmont, Nedham,

42. On JA's voyage to France in the *Boston* frigate in Feb. 1778. JA, "Diary," *Works*, III, 98-100.
43. By Henry Nevill, an English republican closely allied with James Harrington. Zera S. Fink, *The Classical Republicans* ... (Evanston, Ill., 1945), 129-32.

with twenty others upon Subjects which Mankind is determined never to Understand, and those who do Understand them are resolved never to practice, or countenance.

Your Memoranda of the past, your Sense of the present and Prospect for the Future seem to be well founded, as far as I see. But the Latter i.e. the Prospect of the Future, will depend on the Union: and how is that Union to be preserved? Concordia Res parvae crescunt, Discordia Maximae dilabuntur.[44] Our Union is an immense Structure. In Russia, I doubt not, a Temple or Pallace might be erected of Wood, Brick or Marble, which should be cemented only with Ice. A sublime and beautiful Building it might be; surpassing St. Sophia, St. Peters, St. Pauls, Notre Dame or St. Genevieve. But the first Week, if not the first day of the *Debacle* would melt all the Cement and Tumble The Glass and Marble, the Gold and Silver, the Timber and the Iron into one promiscuous chaotic or anarchic heap.

I will not at present point out the precise Years Days and Months when; nor the Names of the Men by whom this Union has been put in Jeopardy. Your Recollection can be at no more loss than mine.

Cobbets, Callenders, Peter Markoes, Burrs and Hamiltons may and have passed away. But Conquerors do not so easily disappear. Battles and Victories are irresis[t]able by human Nature. When a Man is once acknowledged by the People in the Army and the Country to be the Author of a Victory, there is no longer any Question. He is undoubtedly a great and good Man. Had Hamilton, [or] Burr obtained a recent Victory, neither You, nor Jay nor I should have stood any Chance against them or either of them more than a Swallow or a Sparrow.

The Union is still to me an Object of as much Anxiety as ever Independence was. To this I have sacrificed my Popularity in New England and yet what Treatment do I still receive from the Randolphs and Sheffeys of Virginia. By the Way are not these Eastern Shore Men? My Senectutal Loquacity has more than retaliated your "Senile Garrulity."

I have read Thucidides and Tacitus, so often, and at such distant Periods of my Life, that elegant, profound and enchanting as is their Style, I am weary of them. When I read them I seem to be only reading the History of my own Times and my own Life. I am heartily weary of both; i.e. of recollecting the History of both: for I am not weary of Living. Whatever a peevish Patriarch might say, I have never yet seen the day in which I could say I have had no Pleasure; or that I have had more Pain than Pleasure.

44. "Small communities grow great through harmony, great ones fall to pieces through discord." Sallust, *Jugurtha*, X.

Gerry, Paine, and J. Adams, R. R. Livingston,[45] B. Rush and George Clymer and yourself, are all that I can recollect, of the Subscribers to Independence who remain. Gerry is acting a decided and a splendid Part. So daring and so hazardous a Part; but at the same time so able and upright, that I say: "God save the Governor:" and "prosper long our noble Governor."

I walk every fair day, sometimes 3 or 4 miles. Ride now and then but very rarely more than ten or fifteen Miles. But I have a Complaint that Nothing but the Ground can cure, that is the Palsy; a kind of Paralytic Affection of the Nerves, which makes my hands tremble, and renders it difficult to write at all and impossible to write well.

I have the Start of you in Age by at least ten Years: but you are advanced to the Rank of a Great Grandfather before me. Of 13 Grand Children I have two, William and John Smith, and three Girls, Caroline Smith, Susanna and Abigail Adams, who might have made me Great Grand Children enough. But they are not likely to employ their Talents very soon. They are all good Boys and Girls however, and are the solace of my Age. I cordially reciprocate your Professions of Esteem and Respect. Madam joins and sends her kind Regards to your Daughter and your Grand Children as well as to yourself.

JOHN ADAMS

P. S. I forgot to remark your Preference to Savage over civilized life. I have Something to say upon that Subject. If I am in an Error, you can set me Right, but by all I know of one or the other I would rather be the poorest Man in France or England, with sound health of Body and Mind, than the proudest King, Sachem or Warriour of any Tribe of Savages in America.

Adams to Jefferson

Quincy Feb. 10 1812

DEAR SIR

I have received with great pleasure your favour of the 23 of January. I suspected that the Sample was left at the Post Office and that you would soon have it. I regret the shabby Condition in which you found it: but it

45. Robert R. Livingston was a member of the committee to draft the Declaration of Independence, but the New York delegation in Congress, for lack of instructions, was excused from voting on its adoption and he was absent when it was signed. Robert C. Hayes, "Livingston, Robert R.," *DAB*, XI, 321.

was the only Copy I had, and I thought it scarcely worth while to wait till I could get a Sett properly bound.

The Dissertation on the State of real homespun was a feast to me, who delight in every Information of that kind. In a moral œconomical and political point of View, it ought to be considered by every American Man Woman and child as a most precious Improvement in the Condition and prosperity of our Country.

Although you and I are weary of Politicks, You may be surprised to find me making a Transition to such a Subject as Prophecies. I find that Virginia produces Prophets, as well as the Indiana Territory. There have been lately sent me from Richmond two Volumes, one written by Nimrod Hewes and the other by Christopher Macpherson; both, upon Prophecies, and neither, ill written. I should apprehend that two such Mulattoes might raise the Devil among the Negroes in that Vicinity: for though they are evidently cracked, they are not much more irrational than Dr. Towers who wrote two ponderous Vollumes, near twenty years ago to prove that The French Revolution was the Commencement of the Millenium, and the decapitation of The King of France but the beginning of a Series, immediately to follow, by which all The Monarchies were to be destroyed and succeeded by universal Republicanism over all Europe; nor than Dr. Priestly who told me soberly, cooly and deliberately that though he knew of Nothing in human Nature or in the History of Mankind to justify the Opinion, Yet he fully believed upon the Authority of Prophecy that the French Nation would establish a free Government and that the King of France who had been executed, was the first of the Ten Horns of the great Beast, and that all the other Nine Monarks were soon to fall off after him; nor than The Reverend Mr. Faber who has lately written a very elegant and learned Volume to prove that Napoleon is Antichrist; nor than our worthy Friend Mr. Joseph Wharton of Philadelphia, who in consequence of great Reading and profound Study has long since settled his opinion, that the City of London is or is to be the Head Quarters of Antichrist; Nor than the Prophet of the Wabash [Tenskwatawa], of whom I want to know more than I do, because I learn that the Indians the Sons of the Forrest are as Superstitious as any of the great learned Men aforesaid, and as firm believers in Witchcraft as all Europe and America were in the Seventeenth Century and as frequently punish Witches by splitting their Sculls with the Tomahawk, after a solemn Tryal and Adjudication by the Sachems and Warriours in Council.

The Crusades were commenced by the Prophets and every Age since, when ever any great Turmoil happens in the World, has produced fresh Prophets. The Continual Refutation of all their Prognostications by Time and Experience has no Effect in extinguishing or damping their Ardor.

I think these Prophecies are not only unphilosophical and inconsistent with the political Safety of States and Nations; but that the most sincere and sober Christians in the World ought upon their own Principles to hold them impious, for nothing is clearer from their Scriptures than that Their Prophecies were not intended to make Us Prophets.

Pardon this strange Vagary. I want only to know something more than I do about the Richmond and Wabash Prophets.

Called to Company and to dinner I have only time to repeat the Assurances of the Friendship and Respect of

JOHN ADAMS

Jefferson to Adams

Monticello Apr. 20. 12.

DEAR SIR

I have it now in my power to send you a piece of homespun in return for that I recieved from you.[46] Not of the fine texture, or delicate character of yours, or, to drop our metaphor, not filled as that was with that display of imagination which constitutes excellence in Belles lettres, but a mere sober, dry and formal piece of Logic. Ornari res ipsa negat.[47] Yet you may have enough left of your old taste for law reading to cast an eye over some of the questions it discusses. At any rate accept it as the offering of esteem and friendship.

You wish to know something of the Richmond and Wabash prophets. Of Nimrod Hewes I never before heard. Christopher Macpherson I have known for 20. years. He is a man of color, brought up as a bookkeeper by a merchant, his master, and afterwards enfranchised. He had understanding enough to post up his ledger from his journal, but not enough to bear up against Hypochondriac affections and the gloomy forebodings they inspire. He became crazy, foggy, his head always in the clouds, and rhapsodising what neither himself nor any one else could understand. I think he told me he had visited you personally while you were in the

---

46. *The Proceedings of the Government of the United States, in maintaining the Public Right to the Beach of the Mississippi, Adjacent to New-Orleans, against the Intrusion of Edward Livingston.* Prepared for the Use of Counsel, by Thomas Jefferson (N. Y., 1812); reprinted in H[enry] A. Washington, ed., *The Writings of Thomas Jefferson* (Washington, D.C., 1853-54), VIII, 503-604. Livingston had acquired alluvial lands in New Orleans as payment for legal fees, but he was dispossessed of them by the United States as sovereign of the soil. He brought action in the federal court in New Orleans to recover damages, without success. William S. Carpenter, "Livingston, Edward," *DAB*, XI, 310.

47. "The subject itself refuses to be embellished."

administration, and wrote you letters, which you have probably forgotten in the mass of the correspondencies of that crazy class, of whose complaints, and terrors, and mysticisms, the several presidents have been the regular depositories. Macpherson was too honest to be molested by anybody, and too inoffensive to be a subject for the Mad-house; altho', I believe, we are told in the old Book that 'every man that is mad, and maketh himself a prophet, thou shouldest put him in prison and in the stocks.'

The Wabash prophet [Tenskwatawa] is a very different character, more rogue than fool, if to be a rogue is not the greatest of all follies. He arose to notice while I was in the administration, and became of course a proper subject of enquiry for me. The enquiry was made with diligence. His declared object was the reformation of his red brethren, and their return to their pristine manner of living. He pretended to be in constant communication with the great spirit, that he was instructed by him to make known to the Indians that they were created by him distinct from the Whites, of different natures, for different purposes, and placed under different circumstances, adapted to their nature and destinies: that they must return from all the ways of the Whites to the habits and opinions of their forefathers. They must not eat the flesh of hogs, of bullocks, of sheep etc. the deer and buffalo having been created for their food; they must not make bread of wheat, but of Indian corn. They must not wear linen nor woollen, but dress like their fathers in the skins and furs of wild animals. They must not drink ardent spirits; and I do not remember whether he extended his inhibitions to the gun and gunpowder, in favor of the bow and arrow. I concluded from all this that he was a visionary, inveloped in the clouds of their antiquities, and vainly endeavoring to lead back his brethren to the fancied beatitudes of their golden age. I thought there was little danger of his making many proselytes from the habits and comforts they had learned from the Whites to the hardships and privations of savagism, and no great harm if he did. We let him go on therefore unmolested. But his followers increased till the English thought him worth corruption, and found him corruptible. I suppose his views were then changed; but his proceedings in consequence of them were after I left the administration, and are therefore unknown to me; nor have I ever been informed what were the particular acts on his part which produced an actual commencement of hostilities on ours.[48] I have no doubt however that his subsequent proceedings are but a chapter apart, like that of [John]

48. Indian resistance, led by Tecumseh and his brother, the Prophet, against American expansion west of Ohio, culminated in the Battle of Tippecanoe, Nov. 7, 1811. Although General William Henry Harrison's "victory" was greatly exaggerated, it did end the possibility of an Indian confederacy. Glenn Tucker, *Poltroons and Patriots*... (N. Y., [1954]), I, Chap. VII.

Henry and L[or]d Liverpool [Robert Jenkinson], in the Book of the Kings of England.

Of this mission of Henry your son had got wind, in the time of the embargo, and communicated it to me. But he had learned nothing of the particular agent, altho', of his workings, the information he had obtained appears now to have been correct. He stated a particular which Henry has not distinctly brought forward, which was that the Eastern States were not to be required to make a formal act of separation from the Union, and to take a part in the war against it; a measure deemed much too strong for their people: but to declare themselves in a state of neutrality, in consideration of which they were to have peace and free commerce, the lure most likely to ensure popular acquiescence. Having no indications of Henry as the intermediate in this negociation of the Essex junto,[49] suspicions fell on Pickering and his nephew Williams in London. If he was wronged in this, the ground of the suspicion is to be found in his known practices and avowed opinions, as of that of his accomplices in the sameness of sentiment and of language with Henry, and subsequently by the fluttering of the wounded pidgeons.

This letter, with what it encloses, has given you enough, I presume, of law and the prophets. I will only add to it therefore the homage of my respects to Mrs. Adams, and to yourself the assurances of affectionate esteem and respect.

TH: JEFFERSON

Adams to Jefferson

Quincy May 1. 1812

DEAR SIR

Yesterday, I received from the Post Office, under an envellope inscribed with your hand, but without any letter, a very learned and ingenious Pamphlet, prepared by you for the Use of your Counsel, in the case of Edward Livingston against you. Mr. Ingersol of Philadelphia, two or three Years ago sent me two large Pamphlets upon the same Subject. Neddy is a naughty lad as well as a saucy one. I have not forgotten his lying Villany in his fictitious fabricated Case of a Jonathan Robbins who never existed. His Suit against you, I hope has convinced you of his Character.

49. A group of the rich and well born of Essex County, Mass., organized in 1778 on behalf of a state constitution; ten years later they supported the United States Constitution. As New England Federalists they bitterly opposed President Jefferson's policies and the War of 1812. Henry Adams, ed., *Documents Relating to New-England Federalism, 1800-1815* (Boston, 1877), 108-14 *passim*, 149, 151, 152, 203, 369, 371.

What has become of his defalcation and plunder of the Publick? I rejoice however that you have been plagued by this fellow; because it has stimulated you to a Research that cannot fail to be of great Use to your Country. You have brought up to the View of the young Generation of Lawyers in our Country Tracts and Regions of legal Information of which they never had dreamed: but which will become, every day more and more necessary for our Courts of Justice to investigate.

Good God! Is a President of U. S. to be Subject to a private Action of every Individual? This will soon introduce the Axiom that a President can do no wrong; or another equally curious that a President can do no right.

I have run over this Pamphlet with great pleasure but must read it with more Attention. I have uniformly treated the Charges of Corruption, which I have read in Newspapers and Pamphlets and heard from the Pulpit against you and Mr. Madison with contempt and Indignation. I believe in the Integrity of both, at least as undoubtingly as in that of Washington. In the Measures of Administration I have neither agreed with you or Mr. Madison. Whether you or I were right Posterity must judge. I have never approved of Non Importations, Non Intercourses, or Embargoes for more than Six Weeks. I never have approved and never can approve of the Repeal of the Taxes, the Repeal of the Judiciary System, or the Neglect of the Navy. You and Mr. Madison had as good a right to your Opinions as I had to mine, and I must acknowledge the Nation was with you. But neither your Authority nor that of the Nation has convinced me. Nor, I am bold to pronounce will convince Posterity.

I wrote you on the third of February and on the 10th. of February but have received no answer, which makes me suspect some Accident in the Post Office or in the transportation of the Mail. The Embargo and the fatal Vote against an Augmentation of the Navy have knock'd out Gerry. Even Henry's dear bought disclosures have operated against the Administration. There is something in this Country too deep for me to sound. The escape of Governor Blount, of Aaron Burr, of John Smith, and now the coldness and Indifference about Henrys Communications, are beyond the reach of my Sagacity. So is the Language of John Randolph and Major Sheffey. What do these ignorant Boys mean by the "Profligacy of John Adams's Administration?" Randolph and Sheffey accuse John Adams of Profligacy!

Our old Friend Clinton is gone, and I suppose has left as many Millions as Washington or Franklin. And yet his Administration has not been profligate.

I am still as I ever have been and ever shall be with great Esteem and regard your Friend and Se[r]vant

JOHN ADAMS

Adams to Jefferson

Quincy. May 3. 1812

DEAR SIR

I wrote you on the first of this Month acknowledging the receipt of your "Proceedings" etc. and now repeat my thanks for it. It is as masterly a pamphlet as ever I have read; and every way worthy of the Mind that composed and the pen which commited it to writing. There is witt and fancy and delicate touches of Satyr enough in it to make it entertaining while the profusion of learning, the close reasoning and accurate Criticism must have required a Patience of Investigation that at your Age is very uncommon.

On the second of the Month your letter of the 20. of April was sent me from the Post Office. How it was seperated from the pamphlet I know not. I thank you for the Account of the Wabash Prophet. Macpherson, parson Austin and Abraham Brown made themselves sufficiently known to me when I was in the Government. They all assumed the Character of Ambassadors extraordinary from The Almighty: but as I required miracles in proof of their Credentials, and they did not perform any, I never gave publick Audience to either of them.

Though I have long acknowledged your Superiority in most branches of Science and Litterature, I little thought of being compelled to confess it in Biblical Knowledge. I had forgotten the custom of putting Prophets in the Stocks, and was obliged to have recourse to the concordance to discover Jer. 29. 26 for your Text, and found at the same time [from] Jer. 20. 2. 3 that Jeremiah himself had been put in the Stocks. It may be thought impiety by many, but I could not help wishing that the ancient practice had been continued down to more modern times and that all the Prophets at least from Peter the Hermit, to Nimrod Hews inclusively, had been confined in the Stocks and prevented from spreading so many delusions and shedding so much blood. Could you believe that the mad rant of Nimrod, which was sent to me by Christopher [Macpherson] with his own and which I lent to a Neigbour in whose house it was seen and read by some Visitors, spread a great deal of terror and a serious Apprehension that one third of the human race would be destroyed on the fourth day of the next month? As my neighbours are far from being remarkably superstitious, I could not have believed what has appeared in experience.

The transition from one set of crazy people to another is not unnatural.

There were two Gentlemen in the Senate of The United States together for several Years, who became very intimate Friends and uncommonly fond of each other. These were Mr. Pickering and Mr. Hillhouse. They were understood by the Circle in Boston, who were in the Confidence of the former, to be perfectly united in Opinion. The latter made no Secret of his Opinion, that an Amputation and a Surgical Operation as he called it, was become necessary and he made a motion in Senate, for an Amendment of the Constitution which was indeed a total Alteration of it to as absurd and as arbitrary an Aristocracy as ever was imagined. This plan he published in a Pamphlet. P.'s friends in Boston at first gave out that he perfectly concurred with H. in this project, and I heard some of them say, that they went along with them throughout. I immediately wrote an Examination of it,[50] and put it into the hands of the Anthologists for publication: but as I had made pretty free with some of their favourites they declined printing it. But that Manuscript or Something else put them so out of conceit of it, that they immediately hushed it into Oblivion. This project of a new constitution, which you must remember, was supposed to be intended for the Arm or the Leg, or the head or the Tail that was to be cut off by the chirurgical operation. I have heard that Mr. P. once on his Journey to the Senate of U. S. carried with him from his friends in Boston a project of a Division by the Potomac, the Delaware or the Hudson, i.e. as far as they could succeed, and communicated it to Gen. Hamilton who could not see his way clear, and to Mr. King, who liked it as little.[51] That there is a Party in New England, encouraged by more or less of kindred Spirits in every State in the Union, who wish to urge the Nation to a War with France and to shelter themselves and their Commerce under the Wings of the British Navy at almost any rate there can be little doubt.

I have long opposed these People in all such Projects: but the national Government by Embargoes, Non importations, Non Intercourses, and above all by the Opposition to any naval Power, have been constantly playing popularity into their hands and the consequence will soon be, if

50. James Hillhouse's pamphlet, *Propositions for Amending the Constitution of the United States* (New Haven, 1810), was examined by John Adams in his "Review of the Propositions for Amending the Constitution submitted by Mr. Hillhouse to the Senate of the United States, in 1808," but the manuscript was not published until 1851, in *Works*, VI, 523-50. The *Propositions* included annual election of representatives, three-year terms for senators, and a one-year term for the president who was to be chosen by lot from the retiring senators.

51. Pickering propagandized for a northern confederacy of the commercial states; a member of the House of Representatives from Massachusetts, he opposed the War of 1812 as destructive of American commerce; and he supported the Hartford Convention of 1814. Adams, ed., *Documents Relating to New-England Federalism*, 147-48, 339 ff., 389 ff., 414; Tucker, *Poltroons and Patriots*, II, Chap. XXXV.

it is not already, that I and my Sons and all my Friends will be hated throughout New England worse than Burr ever was or Bonaparte. If these measures are persisted in, there will be a Convulsion as certainly as there is a Sky over our heads.

My better half charges me to present you her ancient respect and regards with those of your old friend

JOHN ADAMS

Adams to Jefferson

Quincy May 21. 1812

DEAR SIR

Samuel B. Malcom Esqr. is not wholly a Stranger to you. He was three Years in my family in the Character of my private Secretary, and I believe his conduct appeared to you, as it invariably did to me, ingenuous, candid faithful and industrious. His Friends in New York were among the most respectable; his Education was public and his Studies in the Law and introduction to the Bar regular.

Congress has erected a new district of which Utica the place of his residence is the centre, and Mr. Malcom aspires to be the Judge. I believe there is no Objection to his morals, politicks, or legal qualifications. If you could find it consistent to intimate any thing in his favour to Mr. Monroe, or Mr. Madison you would oblige him and me.[52] He possesses a landed Estate, but I suppose, like all other landed Estates that I know, [it] is productive of a very small revenue, after the labour and taxes are paid.

The Embargo and the Vote against any Augmentation of the Navy, more than the Taxes and the Threats or prospect of War, have raised a Storm in Massachusetts and New York which has hurled Gerry out of his Chair and electrified and revolutionised all the subsequent Elections. How far the Hurricane or the Earthquake will extend I know not: but if it should not essentially hazard Mr. Madisons Election I fear it will embarrass if not parrallyze his Administration.

Though Mr. Gerry is not too old for the most arduous Service, he is one of the earliest and oldest Legislators in the Revolution and has devoted himself his fortune and his family in the Service of his Country. I

52. TJ forwarded Malcom's application to President Madison, stating "I barely remember such a person as the secretary of Mr. Adams" and calling him "a strong federalist." TJ to Madison, May 30, 1812, Thomas Jefferson Randolph, ed., Memoir, Correspondence, and Miscellanies, from the Papers of Thomas Jefferson (Charlottesville, Va., 1829), IV, 175.

feel for his Situation; and if he is not in some Way or other supported the strongest Pillar of the present best System will fall and great will be the fall of it. The strongest Pillar I mean on this side of Pensilvania. His failure will dishearten and discourage the cause in this quarter of the Union and do incalculable Injury to the Nation.

In one of your letters you mentioned the confused traditions of Indian Antiquities. Is there any Book that pretends to give any Account of these Traditions, or how can one acquire any idea of them? Have they any order of Priesthood among them, like the Druids, Bards or Minstrells of the Celtic nations etc.?

If I had not lived through the War of 1745, the War of 1755 and the War of 1775, I believe I should be now too anxious for a determined Philosopher on Account of the State of the Nation. But in all dangers and in all Vicissitudes I believe I shall never cease, as I have never ceased to be your Friend

JOHN ADAMS

Jefferson to Adams

Monticello June 11. 1812.

DEAR SIR

By our post preceding that which brought your letter of May 21, I had recieved one from Mr. Malcolm on the same subject with yours, and by the return of the post had stated to the President my recollections of him. But both of your letters were probably too late; as the appointment had been already made, if we may credit the newspapers.

You ask if there is any book that pretends to give any account of the traditions of the Indians, or how one can acquire an idea of them? Some scanty accounts of their traditions, but fuller of their customs and characters are given us by most of the early travellers among them. These you know were chiefly French. Lafitau, among them, and Adair an Englishman, have written on this subject; the former two volumes, the latter one, all in 4to [quarto]. But unluckily Lafitau had in his head a preconcieved theory on the mythology, manners, institutions and government of the antient nations of Europe, Asia, and Africa, and seems to have entered on those of America only to fit them into the same frame, and to draw from them a confirmation of his general theory. He keeps up a perpetual parallel, in all those articles, between the Indians of America, and the antients of the other quarters of the globe. He selects therefore all the facts, and adopts all the falsehoods which favor his theory, and very gravely retails such absurdities as zeal for a theory could alone swallow. He was a man of much classical and scriptural reading, and has rendered his book not un-entertaining. He resided five years among the Northern Indians, as a Missionary, but collects his matter much more from the writings of others, than from his own observation.

Adair too had his kink. He believed all the Indians of America to be descended from the Jews: the same laws, usages; rites and ceremonies, the same sacrifices, priests, prophets, fasts and festivals, almost the same religion, and that they all spoke Hebrew. For altho he writes particularly of the Southern Indians only, the Catawbas, Creeks, Cherokees, Chickasaws and Choctaws, with whom alone he was personally acquainted, yet he generalises whatever he found among them, and brings himself to believe that the hundred languages of America, differing fundamentally every one from every other, as much as Greek from Gothic, have yet all one common prototype. He was a trader, a man of learning, a self-taught Hebraist, a strong religionist, and of as sound a mind as Don Quixot in whatever did not touch his religious chivalry. His book contains a great deal of real instruction on it's subject, only requiring the reader to be constantly on his guard against the wonderful obliquities of his theory.

The scope of your enquiry would scarcely, I suppose, take in the three folio volumes of Latin of De Bry. In these fact and fable are mingled together, without regard to any favorite system. They are less suspicious therefore in their complexion, more original and authentic, than those of Lafitau and Adair. This is a work of great curiosity, extremely rare, so as never to be bought in Europe, but on the breaking up, and selling some antient library. On one of these occasions a bookseller procured me a copy, which, unless you have one, is probably the only one in America.

You ask further, if the Indians have any order of priesthood among them, like the Druids, Bards or Minstrels of the Celtic nations? Adair alone, determined to see what he wished to see in every object, metamorphoses their Conjurers into an order of priests, and describes their sorceries as if they were the great religious ceremonies of the nation. Lafitau calls them by their proper names, Jongleurs, Devins, Sortileges; De Bry praestigiatores, Adair himself sometimes Magi, Archimagi, cunning men, Seers, rain makers, and the modern Indian interpreters, call them Conjurers and Witches. They are persons pretending to have communications with the devil and other evil spirits, to foretel future events, bring down rain, find stolen goods, raise the dead, destroy some, and heal others by enchantment, lay spells etc. And Adair, without departing from his parallel of the Jews and Indians, might have found their counterpart, much more aptly, among the Soothsayers, sorcerers and wizards of the Jews, their Jannes and Jambres, their Simon Magus, witch of Endor, and the young damsel whose sorceries disturbed Paul so much; instead of placing them in a line with their High-priest, their Chief priests, and their magnificent hierarchy generally.   In the solemn ceremonies of the Indians, the persons who direct or officiate, are their chiefs, elders and warriors, in civil ceremonies or in those of war; it is the Head of the Cabin, in their private or particular feasts or ceremonies; and sometimes the Matrons, as in their Corn feasts. And, even here, Adair might have kept up his parallel, with ennobling his Conjurers. For the antient Patriarchs, the Noahs, the Abrahams, Isaacs and Jacobs, and, even after the consecration of Aaron, the Samuels and Elijahs, and we may say further every one for himself, offered sacrifices on the altars. The true line of distinction seems to be, that solemn ceremonies, whether public or private, addressed to the Great Spirit, are conducted by the worthies of the nation, Men, or Matrons, while Conjurers are resorted to only for the invocation of evil spirits. The present state of the several Indian tribes, without any public order of priests, is proof sufficient that they never had such an order. Their steady habits permit no innovations, not even those which the progress of science offers to increase the comforts, enlarge the understanding, and improve the morality of mankind. Indeed so little idea have they of a regular order of priests, that they mistake ours for their Conjurers, and call them by that name.

So much in answer to your enquiries concerning Indians, a people with whom, in the very early part of my life, I was very familiar, and acquired impressions of attachment and commiseration for them which have never been obliterated. Before the revolution they were in the habit of coming often, and in great numbers to the seat of our government, where I was very much with them. I knew much the great Outassete [i.e., Outacity], the warrior and orator of the Cherokees. He was always the guest of my father, on his journeys to and from Williamsburg. I was in his camp when he made his great farewell oration to his people, the evening before his departure for England. The moon was in full splendor, and to her he seemed to address himself in his prayers for his own safety on the voyage, and that of his people during his absence. His sounding voice, distinct articulation, animated action, and the solemn silence of his people at their several fires, filled me with awe and veneration, altho' I did not understand a word he uttered. That nation, consisting now of about 2000. wariors, and the Creeks of about 3000. are far advanced in civilisation. They have good Cabins, inclosed fields, large herds of cattle and hogs, spin and weave their own clothes of cotton, have smiths and other of the most necessary tradesmen, write and read, are on the increase in numbers, and a branch of the Cherokees is now instituting a regular representative government. Some other tribes were advancing in the same line. On those who have made any progress, English seductions will have no effect. But the backward will yeild, and be thrown further back. These will relapse into barbarism and misery, lose numbers by war and want, and we shall be obliged to drive them, with the beasts of the forest into the Stony mountains. They will be conquered however in Canada. The possession of that country secures our women and children for ever from the tomahawk and scalping knife, by removing those who excite them: and for this possession, orders I presume are issued by this time; taking for granted that the doors of Congress will re-open with a Declaration of war. That this may end in indemnity for the past, security for the future, and compleat emancipation from Anglomany, Gallomany, and all the manias of demoralized Europe, and that you may live in health and happiness to see all this, is the sincere prayer of Yours affectionately.

TH: JEFFERSON

Adams to Jefferson

Quincy, June 28 1812

DEAR SIR

I know not what, unless it were the Prophet of Tippacanoe [Tenskwatawa], had turned my Curiosity to inquiries after the metaphisical Science of the Indians, their ecclesiastical Establishments and theological Theories: but your Letter, written with all the Accuracy perspicuity and Elegance of your Youth and middle Age, as it has given me great Satisfaction, deserves my best Thanks.

It has given me Satisfaction, because, while it has furnished me with Information *where* all the Knowledge is to be obtained, that Books afford: it has convinced me that I shall never know much more of the Subject than I do now. As I have never aimed at making any Collection of Books upon this Subject I have none of those you have abridged in so concise a manner. Lafitau, Adair and De Bry were known to me only by Name.

The various Ingenuity which has been displayed in Inventions of hypotheses to account for the original Population of America; and the immensity of learning profusely expended to support them, have appeared to me, for a longer time than I can precisely recollect, what the Physicians call the Litteræ nihil Sanantes.[53] Whether Serpents Teeth were sown here and sprung up Men; whether Men and Women dropped from the Clouds

53. "Writings correcting nothing."

upon this Atlantic Island; whether the Almighty created them here, or whether they immigrated from Europe, are questions of no moment to the present or future happiness of Man. Neither Agriculture, Commerce, Manufactures, Fisheries, Science, Litterature, Taste, Religion, Morals, nor any other good will be promoted, or any Evil averted, by any discoveries that can be made in answer to those questions.

The Opinions of the Indians and their Usages, as they are represented in your obliging letter of the 11. June, appear to me to resemble the Platonizing Philo, or the Philonizing Plato, more than the Genuine System of Judaism.

The philosophy both of Philo and Plato are at least as absurd. It is indeed less intelligible.

Plato borrowed his doctrines from Oriental and Egyptian Philosophers, for he had travelled both in India and Egypt.

The Oriental philosophy, immitated and adopted in part if not the whole by Plato and Philo was

1. One God the good.

2. The Ideas, the thought, the Reason, the Intellect, the Logos, the Ratio, of God.

3. Matter, the Universe, the Production of the Logos, or contemplations of God. This Matter was the Source of Evil.

Perhaps, the three powers of Plato, Philo, the Egyptians and Indians, can not be distinctly made out, from your account of the Indians, but

1. The great Spirit, the good, who is worshiped by the Kings, Sachems and all the great Men in their solem Festivals as the Author, the Parent of Good.

2. The Devil, or the Source of Evil. They are not metaphisicians enough as yet to suppose it, or at least to call it matter, like the Wiseacres of Antiquity, and like Frederic the Great, who has written a very silly Essay on the Origin of Evil, in which he ascribes it all to Matter, as if this was an original discovery of his own.

The Watchmaker has in his head an Idea of the System of a Watch before he makes it. The Mechanician of the Universe had a compleat idea of the Universe before he made it: and this Idea, this Logos, was almighty or at least powerful enough to produce the World, but it must be made of Matter which was eternal. For creation out of Nothing was impossible. And Matter was unmanageable. It would not, and could not be fashioned into any System, without a large mixture of Evil in it; for Matter was essentially evil.

The Indians are not Metaphisicians enough to have discovered This *Idea*, this Logos, this intermediate Power between good and Evil, God and Matter. But of the two Powers The Good and the Evil, they seem to have a full Conviction; and what Son or Daughter of Adam and Eve has not?

This Logos of Plato seems to resemble if it was not the Prototype of the *Ratio and its Progress* of Manilius The Astrologer; of the *Progress of the Mind* of Condorcet; and the Age of Reason of Tom. Payne.

I could make a System too. The seven hundred Thousand Soldiers of Zingis, when the whole or any part of them went to battle, they sett up a howl, which resembled nothing that human Imagination has conceived, unless it be the Supposition that all the Devils in Hell were let loose at once to set up an infernal Scream, which terrified their Ennemies and never failed to obtain them Victory. The Indian Yell resembles this: and therefore America was peopled from Asia.

Another System. The Armies of Zingis, sometimes two or three or four hundred Thousands of them, surrounded a Province in a Circle, and marched towards the Centre, driving all the wild Beasts before them, Lyons, Tigers, Wolves, Bears, and every living thing, terrifying them with their Howls and Yells, their Drums, Trumpetts, etc., till they terrified and tamed enough of them to Victual the whole Army. Therefore the Scotch Highlanders who practice the same thing in miniature, are emigrants from Asia. Therefore the American Indians, who, for anything I know, practice the same custom, are emigrants from Asia or Scotland.

I am weary of contemplating Nations from the lowest and most beastly degradations of human Life, to the highest Refinement of Civilization: I am weary of Philosophers, Theologians, Politicians, and Historians. They are immense Masses of Absurdities, Vices and Lies. Montesquieu had sense enough to say in Jest, that all our Knowledge might be comprehended in twelve Pages in Duodecimo: and, I believe him, in earnest. I could express my Faith in shorter terms. He who loves the Workman and his Work, and does what he can to preserve and improve it, shall be accepted of him.

I also have felt an Interest in the Indians and a Commiseration for them from my Childhood. Aaron Pomham the Priest and Moses Pomham the King of the Punkapaug and Neponsit Tribes, were frequent Visitors at my Fathers house at least seventy Years ago. I have a distinct remembrance of their Forms and Figures. They were very aged, and the tallest and stoutest Indians I have ever seen. The titles of King and Priest, and the names of Moses and Aaron were given them no doubt by our Massachusetts Divines and Statesmen. There was a numerous Family in this Town, whose Wigwam was within a Mile of this House. This Family were frequently at my Fathers house, and I in my boyish Rambles used to call at their Wigwam, where I never failed to be treated with Whortle Berries, Blackberries, Strawberries or Apples, Plumbs, Peaches, etc., for they had planted a variety of fruit Trees about them. But the Girls went out to Service and the Boys to Sea, till not a Soul is left. We scarcely see an

Indian in a year. I remember the Time when Indian Murders, Scalpings, Depredations and conflagrations were as frequent on the Eastern and Northern Frontier of Massachusetts as they are now in Indiana, and spread as much terror. But since the Conquest of Canada, all this has ceased; and I believe with you that another Conquest of Canada will quiet the Indians forever and be as great a Blessing to them as to Us.

The Instance of Aaron Pomham made me suspect that there was an order of Priesthood among them. But according to your Account, the Worship of the good Spirit was performed by the Kings, Sachems, and Warriors, as among the ancient Germans, whose highest Rank of Nobility were Priests. The Worship of the Evil Spirit by the Conjurers, Jongleurs, Praestigiatores.

We have War now in Earnest. I lament the contumacious Spirit that appears about me. But I lament the cause that has given too much Apology for it: the total Neglect and absolute Refusal of all maritime Protection and Defence.

Money, Mariners, and Soldiers would be at the Public Service, if only a few Frigates had been ordered to be built. Without this our Union will be a brittle China Vase, a house of Ice or a Palace of Glass. I am, Sir, with an affectionate Respect, yours.

JOHN ADAMS

Adams to Jefferson

Quincy October 12. 1812

DEAR SIR

I have a Curiosity to learn Something of the Character Life and death of a Gentleman, whose name was Wollaston,[54] who came from England with a Company of a few dozens of Persons in the year 1622, took possession of an height on Massachusetts Bay, built houses there for his People, and after looking about him and not finding the face of Nature smiling enough for him, went to Virginia to seek a better Situation, leaving the Government of his little band, in the hands of Thomas Morton. As I have not found any Account of him after his departure from his little flock, in any History or record of New England, I should be very much obliged to you, for any information you can give me, of any notice that remains of him in Virginia.

54. Little is known about Captain Wollaston beyond William Bradford's *Of Plymouth Plantation, 1620-1647*. See edition by Samuel Eliot Morison (N. Y., 1952), 204-5.

My curiosity has been stimulated by an event of singular Oddity. John Quincy Adams, at Berlin, purchased at an Auction a Volume, containing three Pamphlets bound together; Woods Prospect, Wonder working Providence of Zions Saviour in New England, and "The New English Canaan, or New Canaan, containing an Abstract of New England, composed in three Books; the first Book setting forth the Original of the natives, their manners and customs, together with their tractable nature and love towards the English. The second Book setting forth the natural Endowments of the Country, and what Staple Commodities it yeildeth. The third Book setting forth, what people are planted there, their prosperity, what remarkable accidents have happened since the first planting of it, together with their tenents and practice of their Church.

"Written by Thomas Morton of Cliffords Inne Gentleman, upon ten years knowledge and experiment of the Country." "Printed at Amsterdam by Jacob Frederick Stam, in the Year 1637." The Book is dedicated to The Commissioners of the privy Councell, for the Government of all his Majesties foreign Provinces.

To add a trifle to the whimsical Circumstances attending the A[d]ventures of this Volume, there are a few Words in manuscript on a blank leaf, which, had I seen them in any other place, I should have sworn were in the hand Writing of my Father.

The design of the Writer appears to have been to promote two Objects: 1. to spread the fame and exaggerate the Advantages of New England; 2. to destroy the Characters of the English Inhabitants, and excite the Government to suppress the Puritans, and send over Settlers in their Stead, from among the Royalists and the disciples of Archbishop Laud.

That such a Work had been written, has been known by tradition, and I have enquired for it, more than half a Century: but have never been able to learn that any Copy of it ever was seen in this Country. The Berlin Adventurer is I believe the only one in America.[55] It is possible however that some straggling Copy of it may be in Virginia, and if you have ever seen or heard of it, I shall be obliged to you for the information.

I know not whether you have in your library, extensive and well chosen as it is, any of our New England Histories. If you have and feel any inclination to know any Thing of this Cliffords Inn man, this incendiary instrument of spiritual and temporal domination, you may find it in Neals Hist. New England III., 1. Hutchinson 8. 31., Winthrops Journal 20. 27. 321. 352., 2 Belknaps Biography 332.

He hints at his Objects in his Preface: "I have observed how diverse

55. Morton's *The New English Canaan* was reported extremely rare in 1825 by James Savage, noted antiquarian scholar; he said the only extant copy was JA's. From this copy Charles Francis Adams prepared the 1883 edition (Boston).

Persons not so well affected to the Weal public in mine Opinion, out of respect to their own private ends, have laboured to keep, both the practice of the People there, and the real worth of that eminent Country, concealed from public Knowledge, both which I have abundantly in this discourse laid open."

Sir Christopher Gardiner, Knight, as he calls him, tho he was only a Cavalier of St. Iago de Compostella, a Roman Catholick and another Tool of Archbishop Laud as well as a Companion and fellow labourer in the pious Work of destroying the first Planters of Plymouth and Massachusetts: writes in laudem Authoris, and in the despicable Verse of that Age:

> This Work a matchless mirror is that shows
> The humors of the Seperatists, and those
> So truly personated by thy Pen,
> I was amaz'd to see it.
> Nothing but Opposition, 'gainst the Right
> Of sacred Majesty Men; full of Spight
> Goodness abusing, turning Virtue out
> Of doors, to whipping, Stocking, and full bent
> To plotting mischief 'gainst the innocent
> Burning their Houses, as if ordained by fate
> In Spight of Law to be made ruinate.

Another "In laudem Authoris, by F. C. Armiger" shows the high Church and high State Principles of this group of Laudians and their inveterate hatred of that Opposition to Priestcraft and Kingcraft which animated the first Settlers of New England:

> But that I rather pitty I confesse
> The Practice of their Church, I could expresse
> Myself a Satyrist, whose smarting fanges
> Should strike it with a Palsy, and the Pangs
> Beget a fear, to tempt the Majesty,
> Of those, our mortal Gods, will they defy
> The thundering Jove, like children they desire,
> Such is their Zeal, to sport themselves with fire
> So have I seen an angry fly presume
> To strike a burning taper, and consume
> His feeble Wings. Why in an Air so milde
> Are they so monstrous grown up? and so vilde?
> That Savages can of themselves espy
> Their Errors, brand their names with infamy
> What is their Zeale for blood, like Cyrus thirst
> Will they be over head and ears accurst

> A cruel Way to found a Church On? Noe
> T'is not their Zeal, but fury blinds them so.
> And pricks their malice on, like fire to joyne
> And offer up the Sacrifice of Kain;
> Jonas! thou hast done well, to call these men
> Home, to repentance, with thy painful Pen.

Then comes the Authors prologue in a similar Strain of Panegyrick upon his New English Canaan and of Phillippic against the Inhabitants.

> If Art and Industry should do as much
> As Nature hath for Canaan, not such
> Another place, for benefit and rest
> In all the Universe can be possess'd
> The more We prove it by discovery
> The more delight each Object to the Eye
> Discovers etc.

In page 15 is a high wrought Eulogium of Sir Ferdinand Gorges to whom he ascribes all the Glory of discovering and Settling in fine Country situated in the middle of the Golden mean, the temperate Zone.

Then he discovers the wondrous Wisdom and love of God, in sending his Minister, the plague, among the Indians, to sweepe away by heaps the Savages, and in giving Sir Ferdinando length of days, to see the same performed, after his enterprize was begun, for the propagation of the Church of Christ, i. e., as I understand him, the Church of Archbishop Laud and Sir Ferdinando Gorges.

In Chapter 2. p. 17. He says, "In the Year since the Incarnation of Christ 1622, it was my Chance to be landed in the parts of New England, where I found two Sorts of People, the one Christians, the other Infidels; these I found most full of humanity and more friendly than the other: as shall hereafter be made apparent in due course, by their several Actions from time to time, after my Arrival among them."

In no part of the Work has he said any thing of Mr. Wollaston, his Commander in Chief, to whom he was only second, in command of the Party. But it was of Wollaston I was most interested to enquire. I knew enough of Morton, and was therefore much disappointed in perusing the Book.

The Original Indian Name of the Spot possest by the Party was Passonagesset, but the People of the Company changed it to Mount Wollaston by which Name it has been called to this day. Morton, however, after the departure of his Leader for Virginia, chose to alter the Name, and call it Mare Mount from its Position near the Sea and commanding the prospect of Boston Harbour and Massachusetts Bay. In his 132 page He gives us a History of the Ceremonies instituted by him in honor of this important Nomination. Several Songs were composed to be sung. A Pine Tree, Eighty feet long, was erected with a pair of Bucks Horns nailed on the Top. On May Day this mighty May Pole was drawn to its appointed Place on the Summit of the Hill by the help of Savages males and females, with Sound of Guns Drums, Pistols and other Instruments of Musick. A Barrel of excellent Beer was brewed, and a Case of Bottles, (of Brandy I suppose) with other good Chear, and English Men and Indians Sannups and Squaws, danced and sang and revelled round the Maypole till Bacchus and Venus, I suppose, were satiated. The Seperatists called it an Idol, the Calf of Horeb, Mount Dagon, threatening to make it a woeful mount and not a merry Mount.

It is whimsical that this Book, so long lost, should be brought to me, for this Hill is in my Farm. There are curious Things in it, about the Indians and the Country. If you have any Inclination, I will send you more of them. Yours as Usual

JOHN ADAMS

Jefferson to Adams

Monticello Dec. 28. 12.

DEAR SIR

An absence of 5. or 6. weeks, on a journey I take three or four times a year,[56] must apologize for my late acknolegement of your favor of Oct. 12. After getting thro the mass of business which generally accumulates during my absence, my first attention has been bestowed on the subject of your letter. I turned to the passages you refer to in Hutchinson and Winthrop, and with the aid of their dates, I examined our historians to see if Wollaston's migration to this state was noticed by them. It happens unluckily that Smith and Stith, who alone of them go into minute facts, bring their histories, the former only to 1623, and the latter to 1624. Wollaston's arrival in Massachusets was in 1625, and his removal to this state was 'some time' after. Beverley and Keith, who come lower down, are merely superficial, giving nothing but those general facts which every one knew as well as themselves. If our public records of that date were not among those destroyed by the British on their invasion of this state, they may possibly have noticed Wollaston. What I possessed in this way have

56. To Poplar Forest. See above, 292, n. 39.

been given out to two gentlemen the one engaged in writing our history,[57] the other in collecting our antient laws,[58] so that none of these resources are at present accessible to me. Recollecting that Nathaniel Morton in his New England's Memorial, gives with minuteness the early annals of the colony of New Plimouth, and occasionally interweaves the occurrences of that on Massachusetts bay, I recurred to him, and, under the year 1628, I find he notices both Wollaston and Thomas Morton, and gives with respect to both, some details which are not in Hutchinson or Winthrop. As you do not refer to him, and so possibly may not have his book, I will transcribe from it the entire passage, which will prove at least my desire to gratify your curiosity as far as the materials within my power will enable me.

Extract from Nathaniel Morton's New England's Memorial, pa. 93. to 99. anno 1628.[59] 'Whereas about three years before this time there came over one Captain * Wollaston, a man of considerable parts, and with him 3. or 4. more of some eminency, who brought with them a great many servants, with provisions and other requisites, for to begin a plantation, and pitched themselves in a place within the Massachusetts-bay, which they called afterwards by their Captain's name, Mount Wollaston; which place is since called by the name of Braintry. And amongst others that came with him, there was one Mr. Thomas Morton, who it should seem had some small adventure of his own or other men's amongst them, but had little respect, and was slighted by the meanest servants they kept. They having continued sometime in New England, and not finding things to answer their expectation, nor profit to arise as they looked for, the said Capt. Wollaston takes a great part of the servants, and transports them to Virginia, and disposed of them there, and writes back to one Mr. Rasdale, one of his chief partners (and accounted their merchant) to bring another part of them to Virginia likewise, intending to put them off there, as he had done the rest; and he with the consent of the said Rasdale, appointed

57. Louis H. Girardin, who with Skelton Jones completed the fourth volume of John Daly Burk's *History of Virginia* (Petersburg, Va., 1804-16). Edward A. Wyatt IV, *John Daly Burk, Patriot-Playwright-Historian*, in *Southern Sketches*, ed. by J. D. Eggleston, 1st ser., 7 (1936), 22.

58. William Waller Hening, comp., *The Statutes at Large ... of Virginia*, 13 vols. (Richmond and Philadelphia, 1809-23).

59. Nathaniel Morton, *New Englands Memoriall* (Cambridge, Mass., 1669), based on William Bradford's history of Plymouth Plantation, was eclipsed by the publication of the Bradford manuscript, ed. by Charles Deane (Boston, 1856). The excerpt quoted by TJ is from Bradford, *Of Plymouth Plantation, 1620-1647*, ed. by Morison, 204-10.

* [TJ's note:] This gentleman's name is here occasionally used, and altho' he came over in the year 1625, yet these passages in reference to Morton fell out about this year, and therefore referred to this place.

one whose name was Filcher [i.e., Fitcher] to be his Lieutenant, and to govern the remainder of the plantation, until he or Rasdale should take further order thereabout.

But the aforesaid Morton (having more craft than honesty) having been a petty-fogger at Furnivals-inn; he, in the others absence, watches an opportunity (commons being put hard among them) and got some strong drink and other junkets, and made them a feast, and after they were merry, he began to tell them he would give them good counsel; you see (saith he) that many of your fellows are carried to Virginia, and, if you stay still until Rasodales return, you will also be carried away and sold for slaves with the rest; therefore I would advise you to thrust out Lieutenant Filcher, and I, having a part in the plantation, will recieve you as my partners and consociates, so may you be free from service, and we will converse, plant, trade and live together as equals (or to the like effect). This counsel was easily followed, so they took opportunity, and thrust Lieutenant Filcher out of doors, and would not suffer him to come any more amongst them, but forced him to seek bread to eat, and other necessaries amongst his neighbors, till he would get passage for England. (See the sad effect of want of good government.)

After this they fell to great licentiousness of life, in all prophaneness, and the said Moreton became lord of misrule, and maintained (as it were) a school of atheism, and after they had got some goods into their hands, and got much by trading with the Indians, they spent it as vainly, in quaffing and drinking both wine and strong liquors in great excess (as some have reported) ten pounds worth in a morning, setting up a May-pole, drinking and dancing about it, and frisking about it, like so many fairies, or furies rather, yea and worse practices, as if they had anew revived and celebrated the feast of the Romans goddess Flora, or the beastly practices of the mad Bacchanalians. The said Morton likewise to shew his poetry, composed sundry rythmes and verses, some tending to lasciviousness, and others to the detraction and scandal of some persons names, which he affixed to his idle, or idol May-pole; they changed also the name of their place, and instead of calling it Mount Wolloston, they called it the Merry mount, as if this jollity would have lasted always. But this continued not long, for shortly after that worthy gentleman Mr. John Endicot, who brought over a patent under the broad seal of England for the government of the Massachusetts, visiting those parts, caused that May-pole to be cut down, and rebuked them for their prophaness, and admonished them to look to it that they walked better; so the name was again changed and called Mount Dagon.

Now to maintain this riotous prodigality and profuse expence, the said

Morton thinking himself lawless, and hearing what gain the fishermen made of trading of pieces, powder and shot; he as head of this consortship, began the practice of the same in these parts: and first he taught the Indians how to use them, to charge and discharge 'em, and what proportion of powder to give the piece, according to the size or bigness of the same, and what shot to use for fowl, and what for deer; and having instructed them, he imployed some of them to hunt and fowl for him; so as they became somewhat more active in that imployment than any of the English, by reason of their swiftness of foot, and nimbleness of body, being also quick sighted, and by continual exercise, well knowing the haunt of all sorts of game; so as when they saw the execution that a piece would do, and the benefit that might come by the same, they became very eager after them, and would not stick to give any price they could attain to for them; ac-counting their bows and arrows but baubles in comparison of them.

And here we may take occasion to bewail the mischief which came by this wicked man, and others like unto him; in that notwithstanding laws for the restraint of selling ammunition to the natives, that so far base covetousness prevailed, and doth still prevail, as that the Salvages become amply furnished with guns, powder, shot, rapiers, pistols, and also well skilled in repairing of defective arms: yea some have not spared to tell them how gunpowder is made, and all the materials in it, and that they are to be had in their own land; and would (no doubt, in case they could at-tain to the making of Saltpeter) teach them to make powder; and what mischief may fall out unto the English in these parts thereby, let this pestilent fellow Morton (aforenamed) bear a great part of the blame and guilt of it to future generations. But lest I should hold the reader too long in the relation of the particulars of his vile actings; when as the English that then lived up and down about the Massachusetts, and in other places, percieving the sad consequences of his trading, so as the Indians became furnished with the English arms and ammunition, and expert in the im-proving of them, and fearing they should at one time or another get a blow thereby; and also taking notice, that if he were let alone in his way, they should keep no servants for him, because he would entertain any, how vile soever, sundry of the chief of the stragling plantations met to-gether, and agreed by mutual consent to send to Plimouth, who were then of more strength to join with them, to suppress this mischief: who con-sidering the particulars proposed to them to join together to take some speedy course to prevent (if it might be) the evil that was accrewing towards them; and resolved first to admonish him of his wickedness respecting the premises, laying before him the injury he did to their common safety, and that his acting concerning the same, was against the

King's proclamation: but he insolently persisted on in his way, and said, the king was dead, and his displeasure with him, and threatened them that if they come to molest him, they should look to themselves; so that they saw there was no way but to take him by force: so they resolved to proceed in such a way, and obtained of the Governor of Plimouth, to send Capt. Standish and some other aid with him, to take the sd. Morton by force, the which accordingly was done; but they found him to stand stifly on his defence, having made fast his doors, armed his consorts, set powder and shot ready upon the table; scoffed and scorned at them, and he and his complices being filled with strong drink, were desperate in their way: but he himself coming out of doors to make a shot at Capt. Standish, he stepping to him, put by his piece and took him, and so little hurt was done; and so he was brought prisoner to Plimouth, and continued in durance till an opportunity of sending him for England, which was done at their common charge, and letters also with him, to the honourable council for New England, and returned again into the country in some short time, with less punishment than his demerits deserved (as was apprehended.) The year following he was again apprehended, and sent for England, where he lay a considerable time in Exeter goal: for besides his miscarriage here in New England, he was suspected to have murthered a man that had ventured monies with him, when he came first into New England; and a warrant was sent over from the Lord Chief justice to apprehend him, by virtue whereof, he was by the Governor of Massachusetts sent into England, and for other of his misdemeanours amongst them in that government, they demolished his house, that it might no longer be a roost for such unclean birds. Notwithstanding he got free in England again, and wrote an infamous and scurrilous book against many godly and chief men of the country, full of lies and slanders, and full fraught with prophane calumnies against their names and persons, and the ways of god. But to the intent I may not trouble the reader any more with mentioning of him in this history: in fine sundry years after he came again into the country, and was imprisoned at Boston, for the aforesaid book and other things, but denied sundry things therein, affirming his book was adulterated. And soon after being grown old in wickedness; at last ended his life at Piscataqua. But I fear I have held the reader too long about so unworthy a person, but hope it may be useful to take notice how wickedness was beginning, and would have further proceeded, had it not been prevented timely.'

So far Nathaniel Morton. The copy you have of Thomas Morton's New English Canaan, printed in 1637 by Stam at Amsterdam, was a second edition of that 'infamous and scurrilous book against the godly.'

The 1st. had been printed in 1632 by Charles Green in a 4to [quarto] of 188. pages, and is the one alluded to by N. Morton.[60] Both of them made a part of the American library given by White Kennett in 1713 to the Society for the propagation of the gospel in foreign parts. This society, being a chartered one, still, as I believe, existing, and probably their library also, I suppose that these and the other books of that immense collection, the catalogue of which occupies 275. pages 4to.[61] are still to be found with them. If any research I can hereafter make should ever bring to my knolege any thing more of Wollaston, I shall not fail to communicate it to you. Ever, and affectionately your's

TH: JEFFERSON

Adams to Jefferson

Quincy January 26. 1813.

DEAR SIR

I thank you for your rich present of Dec. 28th. The Pettifogger of Furnivals Inn, or of Cliffords Inn, scarcely deserves the pains you have taken to enquire into his Biography. My Curiosity is selfish, personal and local. The Character of the Miscreant, however, is not wholly contemptible. It marks the Complextion of the Age in which he lived. How many such Characters could You and I enumerate, who in our times have had a similar influence on Society!

The fellow was not wholly destitute of Learning, tho' all he had, was not worth much. I promised you some more Samples of his Erudition. His 2. Chapter is "Of the original of the Natives." Moreton, Nathaniel, the Ancestor of Our Perez, the Husband of Philenia, was mistaken. It was not in 1625 but 1622 that Wollaston and Tom Moreton arrived. All our History and Traditions conspire to confirm the Assertion of the latter in this Chapter, that he arrived in 1622. After a Philipic against the Puri-

60. TJ was mistaken about this early edition. The work was written before the close of 1635 and was first printed in Amsterdam in 1637. It was supposed for years, however, that there was a copy of the book of the imprint and date cited here. For an explanation, see Harvard University Library, *Library Bulletin*, Nos. 9 and 10, 1878-79, 196, 244, and Thomas Morton, *New English Canaan*, ed. by C. F. Adams, 99 ff.

61. [White Kennett], *Bibliothecae Americanae Primordia. An Attempt towards laying the Foundation of an American Library, in Several Books, Papers, and Writings, Humbly given to the Society for the Propagation of the Gospel in Foreign Parts* ...By a Member of the said Society (London, 1713). The collection, however, has been partially dispersed. E. Millicent Sowerby, comp., *Catalogue of the Library of Thomas Jefferson* (Washington, D.C., 1952), I, 217-18.

tans and a Panegiric, on the Indians, he enquires Whence the latter proceeded? He finds that they Use "very many Words both of greek and latin; as "En Unimia" to express in earnest, or con amore. "Pascopan, Greedy gut" for "pasco signifies to feed, and Pan is all." "Pasco nantum" quasi "Pasco nondum," "half starved, or not eating as yet." "Equa coge, set it upright" "Mona, an Island," "quasi monon, i. e., alone." "Cos, a Whetstone." "Hame, an instrument to take fish." "Many places retain the name of Ham, as Pantneket, and Matta Pan" "So that it may be thought that these People have, heretofore had the name of Pan, in great reverence, and it may be, have worshipped Pan the great God of the Heathens": "howsoever they do Use no manner of Worship at all now." "It is most likely, descended from People bred towards the Tropick of Cancer, for they retain the memory of some Starrs on that part of the cœlestial globe; as the North Starr, which they call Maske, which in their language signifies, a Bear." "They divide the Winds into Eight parts" "have had some litterature among them, which time hath cancelled" But what traces of it, he perceived, Mr. Morton further saith not. He then reprobates the conjecture, that they came from Tartary over the frozen Sea. "But it may be granted that they might come of the scattered Trojans" "For after that Brutus who was the fourth from Æneas left Latium, upon the conflict had with the Latines etc. this People were dispersed etc. but by reason of their conversation with the Grecians and Latins, had a mixed Language that participated with both." "When Brutus did depart from Latium" etc. "being put to Sea, might encounter a Storm, that would carry them out of Sight of Land and then they might sayle, God knoweth Whither; and so might put upon this coast as well as any other." "Compass, I believe they had none; Sayles they might have." For "Daedalus had Sayles, and Icarus his Son had Sayles" etc. "oars, without question" etc. "For the Use of Compass there is no mention, at that time, About Saul's time, the first King of Israel." "Yet the Loadstone and Compasse, were known in Solomons time etc." "for he sent Ships to fetch the Gold of Ophir." "It is held by Cosmographers to be three Years Voyage from Hierusalem to Ophir." "And it is conceived that such a Voyage could not have been performed, without the Help of the Loadstone and Compass." "Therefore, since I have had the Approbation of Sir Christopher Gardiner Knight, an able Gentleman, that lived among them (the Indians) and of David Tompson, a Scottish Gentleman, that likewise was conversant with them; both Scollers and Travellers, that were diligent in taking notice of these Things, as men of good Judgment" etc. "Now I am bold to conclude that the Original of the Natives of New England may be well conjectured to be from the scattered Trojans after such time as Brutus departed from Latium."

Such is the Learning, such the Sagacity, such the critical discriminating Judgment of Thomas Moreton.

I wonder that the *Houra* of Zingis, the Bonaparte of Asia, has never been Urged as a Proof that our Indians are descended from some of his Soldiers or Subjects, or from some of the Nations who learned the Art of War from him when he scattered and drove so many of them, the Lord knows where. The Indian Yell, is said to be the most horrible Sound that human Voices can produce, and the most intimidating to an Enemy. The same is said of the Asiatic Houra. Neither Nations, nor wild Beasts could resist it. Indeed, when Zingis's Army of seven hundred thousand men were drawn up in the Periphery of a circle, of one hundred miles in diameter, and marched from all points to the Centre, driving all the beasts before them with Drums trumpets and all their Instruments of Musick added to their hideous houra, no wonder the brutes were frightened out of all their Strength and ferocity. Nothing can be conceived like it, even in Imagination, unless we suppose all the Beasts and Birds in Noahs Ark sett to roaring, howling, barking, braying, chattering, cackling, and all the Women shrieking and screaming at once. Miltons millions of rebellious Angels, when they "clash'd on their sounding Shields the din of War" could not have produc'd a harsher dissonance or more tremendous Crash. This practise of hunting in Circles is said to be, or to have not long since been, in Use in the Highlands of Scotland. Has any such Usage ever been known among any of our Tribes of Indians?

I will not teaze you, with any more of Morton lore, at present nor of my own. Hereafter I may send a little more from him,[62] with repeated Assurances of the regard of your old Friend

JOHN ADAMS

62. In an incomplete draft of a letter, JA to TJ, Quincy, Feb. 2, 1813, JA gave "some Account of Tom Moreton's New Canaan, which is infinitely more entertaining and instructive to me, than our Friend Condorcets 'NEW HEAVEN' was almost 30 years ago, or than Swedenborgs 'NEW JERUSALEM' is now. In his Third Chapter is a curious History. Before the English came to New Plymouth, Frenchmen had been here, who had given Some 'distast' to the Natives, who set upon them, killed many, burned their Ship, at Peddocks Island So called in Memory of Leonard Peddock, who first landed there. N.B. This Island is well known, at this day and is called by all of Us *Petticks Island* without knowing why. 'Many wild Anckies haunted there.' Your Researches, in natural History may enable you to say what are Anckies. Unless they be wild Geese, I know no more about them than I do about Yankies. Of these Frenchmen, who came to trade in Beaver, and misbehaved, some were killed and the rest taken Prisoners. These Prisoners, were distributed among Five Sachems, Lords of Several Adjoining Territories, kept for Sport and to fetch Wood and Water. One of these five Frenchmen outliving the rest, learned their Language and rebuked them for their blody deed, saying that God would be angry for it, and in his displeasure destroy them; but the Savages replyed They were *so many that God could not kill them.* . . ."

Jefferson to Adams

Monticello May 27. 13.

Another of our friends of 76. is gone, my dear Sir, another of the Co-signers of the independance of our country. And a better man, than Rush, could not have left us, more benevolent, more learned, of finer genius, or more honest. We too must go; and that ere long. I believe we are under half a dozen at present; I mean the signers of the Declaration. Yourself, Gerry, Carroll, and myself are all I know to be living. I am the only one South of the Patomac. Is Robert Treat Payne, or Floyd living? It is long since I heard of them, and yet I do not recollect to have heard of their deaths.[63]

Moreton's deduction of the origin of our Indians from the fugitive Trojans, stated in your letter of Jan. 26. and his manner of accounting for the sprinckling of their Latin with Greek, is really amusing. Adair makes them talk Hebrew. Reinold Foster derives them from the soldiers sent by Kouli Khan to conquer Japan. Berewood [i.e., Brerewood] from the Tartars, as well as our bears, wolves, foxes etc. which he says 'must of necessity fetch their beginning from Noah's ark, which rested, after the deluge, in Asia, seeing they could not proceed by the course of nature, as the unperfect sort of living creatures do, from putrefaction.' Bernard Romans is of opinion that God created an original man and woman in this part of the globe. Doctr. Barton thinks they are not specifically different from the Persians; but, taking afterwards a broader range, he thinks 'that in all the vast countries of America, there is but one language, nay that it may be proven, or rendered highly probable, that all the languages of the earth bear some affinity together.' This reduces it to a question of definition, in which every one is free to use his own. To wit, what constitutes identity, or difference in two things? (in the common acceptation of *sameness*.) All languages may be called the same, as being all made up of the same primitive sounds, expressed by the letters of the different alphabets. But, in this sense, all things on earth are the same, as consisting of matter. This gives up the useful distribution into genera and species, which we form, arbitrarily indeed, for the relief of our imperfect memories. To aid the question, from whence are our Indian tribes descended? some have gone into their religion, their morals, their manners, customs, habits, and physical forms. By such helps it may be learnedly proved that our trees and plants of every kind are descended from those of Europe; be-

63. See above, 292, n. 38.

cause, like them they have no locomotion, they draw nourishment from the earth, they clothe themselves with leaves in spring, of which they divest themselves in autumn for the sleep of winter etc. Our animals too must be descended from those of Europe, because our wolves eat lambs, our deer are gregarious, our ants hoard etc. But when, for convenience, we distribute languages, according to common understanding, into Classes originally different, as we chuse to consider them, as the Hebrew, the Greek, the Celtic, the Gothic; and these again into genera, or families, as the Icelandic, German, Swedish, Danish, English; and these last into species, or dialects, as English, Scotch, Irish, we then ascribe other meanings to the terms 'same' and 'different.' In some one of these senses, Barton, and Adair, and Foster, and Brerewood, and Moreton, may be right, every one according to his own definition of what constitutes 'identity.' Romans indeed takes a higher stand, and supposes a separate creation. On the same unscriptural ground, he had but to mount one step higher, to suppose no creation at all, but that all things have existed without beginning in time, as they now exist, and may for ever exist, producing and reproducing in a circle, without end. This would very summarily dispose of Mr. Morton's learning, and shew that the question of Indian origin, like many others pushed to a certain height, must recieve the same answer, 'Ignoro.'

You ask if the usage of hunting in circles has ever been known among any of our tribes of Indians? It has been practised by them all; and is to this day, by those still remote from the settlement of the whites. But their numbers not enabling them, like Genghis Kahn's 700,000. to form themselves into circles of 100. miles diameter, they make their circle by firing the leaves fallen on the ground, which gradually forcing the animals to a center, they there slaughter them with arrows, darts, and other missiles. This is called firehunting, and has been practised in this state within my time, by the white inhabitants. This is the most probable cause of the origin and extension of the vast prairies in the Western country, where the grass having been of extraordinary luxuriance, has made a conflagration sufficient to kill even the old, as well as the young timber.

I sincerely congratulate you on the successes of our little navy; which must be more gratifying to you than to most men, as having been the early and constant advocate of wooden walls. If I have differed with you on this ground, it was not on the principle, but the time. Supposing that we cannot build or maintain a navy, which will not immediately fall into the same gulph which has swallowed, not only the minor navies, but even those of the great second rate powers of the sea. Whenever these can be resuscitated, and brought so near to a balance with England that we can turn the scale, then is my epoch for aiming at a navy. In the mean time one competent to keep the Barbary states in order, is necessary; these being the only smaller powers disposed to quarrel with us. But I respect too much the weighty opinions of others to be unyielding on this point, and acquiesce with the prayer 'quod felix faustumque sit ["may this be favorable and auspicious"],' adding ever a sincere one for your health and happiness.

Th. Jefferson

Adams to Jefferson

Quincy May 29. 1813.

Dear Sir

To leave the Pettifogger of Fu[r]nivals Inn, or Cliffords Inn, his Archbishop Laud, and his Chevalier of St. Iago of Compostella, Sir Christopher Gardiner, for the present; Paulo Multo majora canamus.[64]

There has been put into my hands, within a few days a gross Volume in octavo, of 544 Pages, with the Title of "Memoirs of the late reverend Theophilus Lindsey, M. A." including a brief "Analysis of his Works; together with Anecdotes and Letters of eminent Persons, his Friends and Correspondents: also a general View of the progress of the Unitarian doctrine in England and America. By Thomas Belsham, Minister of the Chapel in Essex Street [London, 1812]."

Whether you have seen this Work, I know not. But this I know, the Author, and his Friends ought to have sent you a Copy of it; and therefore I conclude they have.

With Lindsey, Disney, Price, Priestley, Jebb, Kippis etc. and their Connections, whom I could name, I was much Acquainted in London from 1785 to 1788. These Characters, with Cappe, Farmer, and a multitude of others, figure in this Work. The Religion, the Philosophy, the Morality, the Politicks which these People teach, have been Objects of my anxious Attention for more than Three Score Years, as I could demonstrate to you, if I could give you a brief Sketch of my Life. But my Life has been too trifling and my Actions too insignificant for me to write or the Public to read. In my wandering romantic Life, with my incessant Res angusta Domi,[65] and my numerous unfortunate Family, of Children and Grand Children without the honour, which you have attained of being a great grandfather, tho' I have a near prospect of it; it has been impossible for me to pursue such Inquiries with any thing like Learning.

64. "Come let us sing of much greater themes." Virgil, *Eclogues*, IV, 1.
65. "Narrow circumstances at home (poverty)." Juvenal, *Satires*, III, 164; *Multis Satires*, VI, 357.

What may be the Effect, of these "Memoirs" in the U. S. if they should become public I know not; and I will add I care not, for I wish every Subject to be discussed at all Events. The human Mind is awake: Let it not Sleep. Let it however consider. Let it think, Let it pause.

This Work must produce a noise in U. S. Fiat Justitia ["Let justice be done"]. The 12th. Article in the Appendix is "Letters from Dr. Priestley to Mr. Lindsey: and from Thomas Jefferson Esq. President of the United States to Dr. Priestley. p. 525. The first Letter from you is dated March 21. 1801. at Washington. The second April 9. 1803 at Washington.[66] Dr. Priestleys Letter to Mr. Lindsey, containing remarks upon Mr. Jeffersons Letter is dated Northumberland April 23. 1803.

I wish to know, if you have seen this Book. I have much to say on the Subject. And you may depend upon it, I will discuss the Subject with as much Candour, as much Friendship, as much Freedom, as Price, Priestley, Lindsey, Cappe or Farmer ever displayed in their Controversies. I have not time to enlarge at present.

I will only Add, have you seen the Naval History by Mr. Clark,[67] published by Mathew Carey at Philadelphia? I wish I had time and Eyes and fingers to write much to you on this Subject.

I lament the death of my dear Friend of 38 Years, Dr. Benjamin Rush, much the more since I have seen Lindseys Memoirs. I am, with unalterable Esteem and Affection your old Friend

JOHN ADAMS

Adams to Jefferson

Quincy June 10. 1813.

DEAR SIR

In your Letter to Dr. Priestley of March 21. 1801, you ask "What an Effort of Bigotry in politics and religion have We gone through! The barbarians really flattered themselves, they should be able to bring back the times of Vandalism, when ignorance put every thing into the hands of power and priestcraft. All Advances in Science were proscribed as innovations; they pretended to praise and encourage education, but it was to be the education of our ancestors; We were to look backwards, not forwards,

66. Reprinted in Ford, VIII, 21-23, 224-25. See also TJ to Benjamin Rush, April 21, 1803, *ibid.*, 223-24.

67. Benjamin Rush to JA, Feb. 15, March 16, April 10, 1813, Butterfield, ed., *Letters of Rush*, II, 1183, 1190, 1191, concerning Thomas Clark, *Sketches of the Naval History of the United States* ... (Philadelphia, 1813).

for improvement; *the President himself* declaring, in one of his Answers to addresses, that We were never to expect to go beyond them in real Science." [68] I shall stop here. Other parts of this Letter, may hereafter be considered if I can keep the Book long enough: but only four Copies have arrived in Boston, and they have spread terror, as yet, however in secret.

"The President himself declaring, that "We were never to expect to go beyond them in real Science". This Sentence shall be the theme of the present Letter.

I would ask, what President is meant? I remember no such Sentiment in any of Washingtons Answers to addresses. I, myself must have been mean'd. Now I have no recollection of any such Sentiment ever issued from my Pen, or my tongue, or of any such thought in my heart for, at least sixty Years of my past life. I should be obliged to you, for the Words of any Answer of mine, that you have thus misunderstood. A man of 77 or 78 cannot commonly be expected to recollect promptly every passage of his past life, or every trifle he has written. Much less can it be expected of me, to recollect every Expression of every Answer to an Address, when for six months together, I was compelled to answer Addresses of all Sorts from all quarters of the Union. My private Secretary has declared that he has copied fifteen Answers from me in one morning. The greatest Affliction, distress, confusion of my Administration arose from the necessity of receiving and Answering those Addresses. Richard Cromwells Trunk, did not contain so many of the Lives and Fortunes of the English Nati[on] as mine of those in the United States. For the hon[or] of my Country I wish these Addresses and Answers [to be] annihilated. For my own Character and repu[tation I] wish every Word of every Address and every Answer were published.[69]

The Sentiment, that you have attributed to me in your letter to Dr. Priestley I totally disclaim and demand in the French sense of the word demand of you the proof. It is totally incongruous to every principle of my mind and every Sentiment of my heart for Threescore Years at least.

You may expect, many more expostulations from one who has loved and esteemed you for Eight and thirty Years.

JOHN ADAMS

When this Letter was ready to go, I recd your favour of May 27th. came to hand, I can only thank you for it, at present.

68. This letter is reprinted in Ford, VIII, 21-23; for TJ's explanation see TJ to JA, June 15, 1813, below, 331-32.

69. Some words or portions of words, missing at ends of lines in the MS, are supplied by conjecture. For JA's quotation from his address, see JA to TJ, June 28, 1813, below, 339.

Adams to Jefferson

Quincy June 11. 1813

DEAR SIR

I received yesterday your favour of may 27th. I lament with you the loss of Rush. I know of no Character living or dead, who has done more real good in America. Robert Treat Paine still lives, at 83 or 84, alert drol and witty though deaf. Floyd I believe, yet remains. Paine must be very great; Philosopher and Christian; to live under the Afflictions of his Family. Sons and Daughters with Genius and qualities and Connections and prospects the most pleasing, have been signally unfortunate. A Son, whose name was altered, from Thomas to Robert Treat has left a Volume of Prose and Verse, which will attract the Attention of Posterity to his Father, more than his Signature of Independence. It is the History of a Poet, in Genius Excentricity, Irregularity Misfortune and Misery, equal to most in Johnsons Lives.

To your ignoro, I add non curo. I should as soon suppose that the Prodigal Son, in a frolic with one of his Girls made a trip to America in one of Mother Careys Eggshels, and left the fruits of their Amours here, as believe any of the grave hypotheses and solemn reasonings of Philosophers or Divines upon the Subject of the peopling of America. If my Faith in Moses or Noah depended on any of these Speculations, I woul[d] give it up.

I sincerely thank you for your congratulations on the Successes of our Navy. I wish to write you more, than my paralyttic Fingers will justify or tollerate up[on] this Subject. I believe, but am not certain, that you was present in Congress on the 5th. of October 1775, when it appears by the Journal, the first foundation of an American Navy was laid. I wish to know, whether you recollect the Opposition that was made to the Appointment of that Committee, to their report, and to the Adoption [of] the Resolution. Do you retain any recollection of the Speeches of Edward Rutledge, Robert Treat Paine, or any other Member, on that Occasion? [70] It is, to be sure, a question of idle curiosity. But the curiosity is very strong.

I have another Curiosity, more ardent still. I have ever believed that you were the Author of the Essay towards a Navy when you was Secretary of State. I have reason to suspect that Hamilton was averse to that Measure. That you were always for a Navy to compel the Barbary Powers to

70. Adams served on the Navy committee with Silas Deane and John Langdon. See the entry for Oct. 5, 1775, in the *Journals of the Continental Congress, 1774-1789* (Washington, 1905), III, 277-79. For Adams's views on "the true origins and foundations of the American Navy," see his "Autobiography," *Works*, III, 7-12.

peace, I distinctly remember in many of our personal Conversations in Europe; and I have carefully preserved very strong Letters from You full of arguments for such a Navy. If I am mistaken in ascribing to you the measures taken in Washingtons Administration, looking towards a Navy, I wish you to correct my Error.[71] Till that is done I shall sincerely believe myself orthodox. The Mail approaches, and I must cease with Assurances of respect and Esteem

JOHN ADAMS

P. S. We must have a Navy now to command The Lakes, if it costs Us 100 Ships of the Line; whatever becomes of the Ocean.

J. A.

Adams to Jefferson

Quincy June 14. 1813

DEAR SIR

In your Letter to Dr. Priestley of March 21. 1801, you "tender him, the protection of those laws which were made for the wise and good, like him; and disclaim the legitimacy of that Libel on legislation, which, under the form of a Law, was for Sometime placed among them". This Law, I presume was, the Alien Law, as it was called.

As your name is subscribed to that law, as Vice President, and mine as President, I know not why you are not as responsible for it as I am. Neither of Us were concerned in the formation of it. We were then at War with France: French Spies then swarmed in our Cities and in the Country. Some of them were, intollerably, turbulent, impudent and seditious. To check these was the design of this law. Was there ever a Government, which had not Authority to defend itself against Spies in its own Bosom? Spies of an Ennemy at War? This Law was never executed by me, in any Instance.

But what is the conduct of our Government now? Aliens are ordered to report their names and obtain Certificates once a month: and an industrious Scotchman, at this moment industriously labouring in my Garden is

71. In his reply TJ did not comment on the early United States Navy, probably because he overlooked the question among the many that JA had asked him on diverse subjects. When JA reverted to the development of the Navy nine years later (Oct. 15, 1822), TJ replied in considerable detail on Nov. 1. See below, 582-83, 584-85.

TJ had advocated a navy as early as 1786 to bring the Barbary pirates to terms (TJ to JA, July 11, 1786, above, 142), while he was minister to France, and he adhered to this policy as secretary of state. Hamilton also favored a navy. Washington's attitude reflected the agreement in his cabinet. Freeman, *Washington*, VII, 158-59, 346-47, 420.

obliged to walk once a month to Boston, eight miles at least, to renew his Certificate from the Marshall. And a fat organist is ordered into the Country. etc. etc. etc. All this is right. Every Government has by the Law of Nations a right to make prisoners of War, of every Subject of an Enemy.[72] But a War with England differs not from a War with France. The Law of Nations is the same in both.

I cannot write Volumes in a single Sheet: but these Letters of yours require Volumes from me.

"The mighty Wave of public Opinion, which has rolled over!" This is, in your Style, and sometimes in mine, with less precision, and less delicacy. Oh! Mr. Jefferson! What a Wave of public Opinion has rolled over the Universe? By the Universe here, I mean our Globe. I can yet say there is nothing new Under the Sun, in my Sense. The Reformation rolled a Wave of public Opinion over the Globe, as wonderful as this; A War of thirty Years, was necessary to compose this Wave. The Wars of Charlemaigne rolled a Wave. The Crusades rolled a Wave, more mountainous than the French Revolution. Only one hundred Years ago, a Wave was rolled; when Austria England and Holland in Alliance, contended against France, for the dominion or rather the Alliance of Spain.

Had "The Clock run down," I am not so sanguine, as you, that the Consequence would have been as you presume. I was determined in all Events to retire. You and Mr. Madison are indebted to Bayard, for an Evasion of the Contest.[73] Had the voters for Burr, addressed the Nation, I am not sure that your Convention would have decided in your Favour. But what Reflections does this suggest? What Pretensions had Aaron Burr to be President or Vice President?

What "a Wave" has rolled over Christendom for 1500 years? What a Wave has rolled over France for 1500 Years supporting in Power and Glory the Dinasty of Bourbon? What a Wave supported the House of Austria? What a Wave has supported the Dinasty of Mahomet, for 1200 Years? What a Wave supported the House of Hercules, for so many Ages in more remote Antiquity? These waves are not to be slighted. They are less resistable than those in the Gulph Stream in an hurricane. What a Wave has the French Revolution spread? And what a Wave is our Navy of five Frigates raising?

If I can keep this book, "Memoirs of Lindsey," I shall have more to say. Meantime I remain your Friend

JOHN ADAMS

72. During the War of 1812, Congress amended "An act respecting alien enemies," which had been passed during Adams's administration. See *U. S. Stat. at L.*, I, 577-78 (July 6, 1798) and II, 781 (July 6, 1812).

73. For Bayard's role in the election of 1800, see Morton Borden, *The Federalism of James A. Bayard* (N. Y., 1955), Chap. VII.

Jefferson to Adams

Monticello June 15. 13.

Dear Sir

I wrote you a letter on the 27th. of May, which probably would reach
you about the 3d. inst. and on the 9th. I recieved yours of the 29th. of
May. Of Lindsay's Memoirs I had never before heard, and scarcely indeed
of himself. It could not therefore but be unexpected that two letters of
mine should have any thing to do with his life. The name of his editor was
new to me, and certainly presents itself, for the first time, under unfavorable circumstances. Religion, I suppose, is the scope of his book: and
that a writer on that subject should usher himself to the world in the very
act of the grossest abuse of confidence, by publishing private letters which
passed between two friends, with no views to their ever being made public,
is an instance of inconsistency, as well as of infidelity of which I would
rather be the victim than the author. By your kind quotation of the dates
of my two letters I have been enabled to turn to them. They had compleatly evanished from my memory. The last is on the subject of religion,
and by it's publication will gratify the priesthood with new occasion of
repeating their Comminations against me. They wish it to be believed that
he can have no religion who advocates it's freedom. This was not the
doctrine of Priestley, and I honored him for the example of liberality he
set to his order. The first letter is political. It recalls to our recollection the
gloomy transactions of the times, the doctrines they witnessed, and the
sensibilities they excited. It was a confidential communication of reflections on these from one friend to another, deposited in his bosom, and
never meant to trouble the public mind. Whether the character of the
times is justly portrayed or not, posterity will decide. But on one feature
of them they can never decide, the sensations excited in free yet firm
minds, by the terrorism of the day. None can concieve who did not witness them, and they were felt by one party only. This letter exhibits their
side of the medal. The Federalists no doubt have presented the other, in
their private correspondences, as well as open action. If these correspondencies should ever be laid open to the public eye, they will probably be
found not models of comity towards their adversaries. The readers of my
letter should be cautioned not to confine it's view to this country alone.
England and it's alarmists were equally under consideration. Still less
must they consider it as looking personally towards you. You happen
indeed to be quoted because you happened to express, more pithily than

had been done by themselves, one of the mottos of the party. This was in your answer to the address of the young men of Philadelphia. [See Selection of patriotic addresses. pa. 198.] [74] One of the questions you know on which our parties took different sides, was on the improvability of the human mind, in science, in ethics, in government etc. Those who advocated reformation of institutions, pari passu, with the progress of science, maintained that no definite limits could be assigned to that progress. The enemies of reform, on the other hand, denied improvement, and advocated steady adherence to the principles, practices and institutions of our fathers, which they represented as the consummation of wisdom, and akmé of excellence, beyond which the human mind could never advance. Altho' in the passage of your answer alluded to, you expressly disclaim the wish to influence the freedom of enquiry, you predict that that will produce nothing more worthy of transmission to posterity, than the principles, institutions, and systems of education recieved from their ancestors. I do not consider this as your deliberate opinion. You possess, yourself, too much science, not to see how much is still ahead of you, unexplained and unexplored. Your own consciousness must place you as far before our ancestors, as in the rear of our posterity. I consider it as an expression lent to the prejudices of your friends; and altho' I happened to cite it from you, the whole letter shews I had them only in view. In truth, my dear Sir, we were far from considering you as the author of all the measures we blamed. They were placed under the protection of your name, but we were satisfied they wanted much of your approbation. We ascribed them to their real authors, the Pickerings, the Wolcotts, the Tracys, the Sedgwicks, et id genus omne ["and all of their kind"], with whom we supposed you in a state of Duresse. I well remember a conversation with you, in the morning of the day on which you nominated to the Senate a substitute for Pickering, in which you expressed a just impatience under 'the legacy of Secretaries which Gen. Washington had left you' and whom you seemed therefore to consider as under public protection. Many other incidents shewed how differently you would have acted with less impassioned advisers; and subsequent events have proved that your minds were not together. You would do me great injustice therefore by taking to yourself what was intended for men who were then your secret, as they are now your open enemies. Should you write on the subject, as you propose, I am sure we shall see you place yourself farther from them than from us.

As to myself, I shall take no part in any discussions. I leave others to judge of what I have done, and to give me exactly that place which they shall think I have occupied. Marshall has written libels on one side; others, I suppose, will be written on the other side; and the world will sift both,

74. TJ's note.

and separate the truth as well as they can. I should see with reluctance the passions of that day rekindled in this, while so many of the actors are living, and all are too near the scene not to participate in sympathies with them. About facts, you and I cannot differ; because truth is our mutual guide. And if any opinions you may express should be different from mine, I shall recieve them with the liberality and indulgence which I ask for my own, and still cherish with warmth the sentiments of affectionate respect of which I can with so much truth tender you the assurance.

TH: JEFFERSON

Adams to Jefferson

Quincy June 25. 1813

DEAR SIR

Your favour of the 15th came to me Yesterday, and it is a pleasure to discover that We are only 9 days apart.

Be not surprised or alarmed. Lindsays Memoirs will do no harm to you or me. You have right and reason to feel and to resent the breach of Confidence. I have had enough of the same kind of Treachery and Perfidy practiced upon me, to know how to sympathize with you. I will agree with you, in unquallified censure of such Abuses. They are the worst Species of Tyrany over private Judgment and free Enquiry. They suppress the free communication of Soul to Soul.

There are critical moments, when Faction, whether in Church or State, will stick at nothing. Confidence of Friendship the most sacred, is but a cobweb tie. How few! Oh how few are the exceptions! I could name many Cases of the rule, but will mention but one. Do you remember Tenche Coxe?

You must have misunderstood me, when you understood that I "proposed to write on the Subject," if you meant, to the Public. I have written enough and too much. I have no thought, in this correspondence, but to satisfy you and myself. If our Letters should be shewn to a friend or two, in confidence; and if that confidence should be betrayed: your Letters will do you no dishonour. As to mine I care not a farthing. My Reputation has been so much the Sport of the public for fifty Years, and will be with Posterity, that I hold it, a bubble, a Gossameur, that idles in the wanton Summers Air. Now for your Letter.

During the three Years, that I resided in England, I was somewhat acquainted with Lindsay, Disnay, Farmer, Price, Priestley, Kippis, Jebb, Vaughans, Bridgen, Brand Hollis, etc. etc. etc., even Dr. Towers was not personally unknown to me. A Belsham was once introduced to me, probably the Author of Lindsays Memoirs. I had much conversation with him. Whether he is a Brother of Belsham the Historian, I know not. Lindsay was a singular Character, unless Jebb was his parrallel. Unitarianism and Biblical Criticism were the great Characteristicks of them all. All were learned, scientific, and moral. Lindsay was an heroic Christian Philosopher. All professed Friendship for America, and these were almost all, who pretended to any such Thing.

I wish You could live a Year in Boston, hear their Divines, read their publications, especially the Repository. You would see how spiritual Tyranny and ecclesiastical Domination are beginning in our Country: at least struggling for birth.

Now, for your political Letter. No, I have not done with spiritual Pride, in high places and in low. I would trust these liberal Christians in London and in Boston, with Power, just as soon as I would Calvin or Cardinal Lorrain; just as soon as I would the Quakers of Pensylvania; just as soon as I would Methodists or Moravians; just as soon as I would Rochefoucault and Condorcet; just as soon as I would the Œconomists of France; just as soon as I would Bolingbroke and Voltaire, Hume and Gibbon; nay just as soon as I would Robespierre or Brissot. I can go no higher, unless I add the League and the Fronde in France, or Charles the first and Archbishop Laud in England and Ireland.

Let me say, however, by the Way, that I fully believe, that Priestley is only guilty of an indiscretion, very pardonable, in this thing. Lindsay is perfectly innocent. Belsham has done the wrong. I cannot but contrast his Conduct with that of Disney, who found among the Papers of Brand Hollis Letters from me and my Wife, which We had both forgotten. He wrote to Us and asked leave to publish them. Neither of Us recollected a Word of them for We had no Copies. We both left to his discretion to publish what he pleased and he has done it. I expected much more nonsense and extravagance in mine than appears, for I wrote to Hollis without reserve.

Checks and Ballances, Jefferson, however you and your Party may have ridiculed them, are our only Security, for the progress of Mind, as well as the Security of Body. Every Species of these Christians would persecute Deists, as soon as either Sect would persecute another, if it had unchecked and unballanced Power. Nay, the Deists would persecute Christians, and Atheists would persecute Deists, with as unrelenting Cruelty, as any Christians would persecute them or one another. Know thyself, human Nature!

I am not sure, that I am yet ready to return to Politicks.

Upon the whole, I think this is enough for one Letter. Politicks shall be adjourned to a future day. Not a very distant one, however.

JOHN ADAMS

Jefferson to Adams

῎Ιδαν ἐς πολύδενδρον ἀνὴρ ὑλητόμος ἐλθὼν
Παπταίνει, παρέοντος ἄδην, ποθεν ἄρξεται ἔργῳ·
Τί πρᾶτον καταλεξῶ; ἐπεὶ πάρα μυρία εἰπῆν. [75]

Monticello June 27. 13.

And I too, my dear Sir, like the wood-cutter of Ida, should doubt where to begin, were I to enter the forest of opinions, discussions, and contentions which have occurred in our day. I should exclaim with Theocritus, Τί πρᾶτον καταλεξῶ; ἐπεὶ πάρα μυρία ειπῆν. [76] But I shall **not do it.** The summum bonum with me is now truly Epicurean, ease of body and tranquility of mind; and to these I wish to consign my remaining days. Men have differed in opinion, and been divided into parties by these opinions, from the first origin of societies; and in all governments where they have been permitted freely to think and to speak. The same political parties which now agitate the U.S. have existed thro' all time. Whether the power of the people, or that of the ἄριστοι ["aristocrats"] should prevail, were questions which kept the states of Greece and Rome in eternal convulsions; as they now schismatize every people whose minds and mouths are not shut up by the gag of a despot. And in fact the terms of whig and tory belong to natural, as well as to civil history. They denote the temper and constitution of mind of different individuals. To come to our own country, and to the times when you and I became first acquainted, we well remember the violent parties which agitated the old Congress, and their bitter contests. There you and I were together, and the Jays, and the Dickinsons, and other anti-independants were arrayed against us. They cherished the monarchy of England; and we the rights of our countrymen. When our present government was in the mew, passing from Confederation to Union, how bitter was the schism between

75. "A woodcutter, having come onto heavily wooded Ida, looked all around, doubtful at first where he should begin his task. 'What first shall I gather?' he said, gazing at the thousands of trees." Theocritus 17.9.

76. " 'What first shall I gather?' he said, gazing at the thousands of trees."

the Feds and Antis. Here you and I were together again. For altho' for a moment, separated by the Atlantic from the scene of action, I favored the opinion that nine states should confirm the constitution, in order to secure it, and the others hold off, until certain amendments, deemed favorable to freedom, should be made, I rallied in the first instant to the wiser proposition of Massachusets, that all should confirm, and then all instruct their delegates to urge those amendments. The amendments were made, and all were reconciled to the government. But as soon as it was put into motion, the line of division was again drawn, we broke into two parties, each wishing to give a different direction to the government; the one to strengthen the most popular branch, the other the more permanent branches, and to extend their permanence. Here you and I separated for the first time: and as we had been longer than most others on the public theatre, and our names therefore were more familiar to our countrymen, the party which considered you as thinking with them, placed your name at their head; the other, for the same reason, selected mine. But neither decency nor inclination permitted us to become the advocates of ourselves, or to take part personally in the violent contests which followed. We suffered ourselves, as you so well expressed it, to be the passive subjects of public discussion. And these discussions, whether relating to men, measures, or opinions, were conducted by the parties with an animosity, a bitterness, and an indecency, which had never been exceeded. All the resources of reason, and of wrath, were exhausted by each party in support of it's own, and to prostrate the adversary opinions. One was upbraided with recieving the Antifederalists, the other the old tories and refugees into their bosom. Of this acrimony the public papers of the day exhibit ample testimony in the debates of Congress, of state legislatures, of stump-orators, in addresses, answers, and newspaper essays. And to these without question may be added the private correspondences of individuals; and the less guarded in these, because not meant for the public eye, not restrained by the respect due to that; but poured forth from the overflowings of the heart into the bosom of a friend, as a momentary easement of our feelings. In this way, and in answers to addresses, you and I could indulge ourselves. We have probably done it, sometimes with warmth, often with prejudice, but always, as we believed, adhering to truth. I have not examined my letters of that day. I have no stomach to revive the memory of it's feelings. But one of these letters, it seems, has got before the public, by accident and infidelity, by the death of one friend to whom it was written, and of his friend to whom it was communicated, and by the malice and treachery of a third person, of whom I had never before heard, merely to make mischief, and in the same Satanic spirit, in which the same enemy had intercepted and published, in 1776, your letter animadverting on Dickinson's character.[77] How it happened that I quoted you in my letter to Dr. Priestly, and for whom, and not for yourself, the strictures were meant, has been explained to you in my letter of the 15th. which had been committed to the post 8. days before I received yours of the 10th. 11th. and 14th. That gave you the reference which these asked to the particular answer alluded to in the one to Priestley.

The renewal of these old discussions, my friend, would be equally useless and irksome. To the volumes then written on these subjects, human ingenuity can add nothing new: and the rather, as lapse of time has obliterated many of the facts. And shall you and I, my dear Sir, like Priam of old, gird on the 'arma, diu desueta, trementibus aevo humeris ["arms, long unused, upon the trembling shoulders of an old man"]'? Shall we, at our age, become the Athletae of party, and exhibit ourselves, as gladiators, in the Arena of the newspapers? Nothing in the universe could induce me to it. My mind has been long fixed to bow to the judgment of the world, who will judge me by my acts, and will never take counsel from me as to what that judgment shall be. If your objects and opinions have been misunderstood, if the measures and principles of others have been wrongfully imputed to you, as I believe they have been, that you should leave an explanation of them, would be an act of justice to yourself. I will add that it has been hoped you would leave such explanations as would place every saddle on it's right horse, and replace on the shoulders of others the burthens they shifted on yours.

But all this, my friend, is offered, merely for your consideration and judgment; without presuming to anticipate what you alone are qualified to decide for yourself. I mean to express my own purpose only, and the reflections which have led to it. To me then it appears that there have been differences of opinion, and party differences, from the first establishment of governments, to the present day; and on the same question which now divides our own country: that these will continue thro' all future time: that every one takes his side in favor of the many, or of the few, according to his constitution, and the circumstances in which he is placed: that opinions, which are equally honest on both sides, should not affect personal esteem, or social intercourse: that as *we* judge between the Claudii

77. JA to General James Warren, president of the Massachusetts Provincial Congress, July 24, 1775. While he was a member of the Continental Congress, JA, disgusted with John Dickinson's desire for reconciliation with Great Britain, referred to him in this letter, though not by name, as "a certain great fortune and piddling genius, whose fame has been trumpeted so loudly." The carrier of the letter was captured by the British and it was promptly published in Boston by General Gage and soon circulated in the colonies and in England. Although JA lost Dickinson's friendship, he felt that the letter helped the cause of independence. JA, "Diary," *Works*, II, 411-12; John Quincy Adams and Charles Francis Adams, *The Life of John Adams* (Philadelphia, 1871), I, 249-52.

and the Gracchi, the Wentworths and the Hampdens of past ages, so, of those among us whose names may happen to be remembered for awhile, the next generations will judge, favorably or unfavorably, according to the complexion of individual minds, and the side they shall themselves have taken: that nothing new can be added by you or me to what has been said by others, and will be said in every age, in support of the conflicting opinions on government: and that wisdom and duty dictate an humble resignation to the verdict of our future peers. In doing this myself, I shall certainly not suffer moot questions to affect the sentiments of sincere friendship and respect, consecrated to you by so long a course of time, and of which I now repeat sincere assurances.

TH: JEFFERSON

Adams to Jefferson

Quincy June 28th. 1813

DEAR SIR

It is very true, that "the denunciations of the Priesthood are fulminated against every Advocate for a compleat Freedom of Religion. Comminations, I believe, would be plenteously pronounced, by even the most liberal of them, against Atheism, Deism; against every Man who disbelieved or doubted the Resurrection of Jesus or the Miracles of the New Testament. Priestley himself would denounce the man who should deny The Apocalyps, or the Prophecies of Daniel. Priestley and Lindsay both have denounced as Idolaters and Blasphemers, all the Trinitarians and even the Arrians. Poor weak Man, when will thy Perfection arrive? Perfectibility, I shall not deny: for a greater Character than Priestley or Godwin has said, "Be ye perfect" etc. For my part, I cannot deal damnation round the land on all I judge the Foes of God or Man. But I did not intend to say a Word on this Subject, in this Letter. As much of it as you please hereafter: but let me now return to Politicks.

With some difficulty I have hunted up, or down, "the Address of the Young men of the City of Philadelphia, the District of South wark, and the Northern Liberties:" and the Answer.

The Addressers say, "Actuated by *the same principles* on which our forefathers atchieved their independence, the recent Attempts of a foreign Power to derogate from the dignity and rights of our country, awaken our liveliest Sensibility, and our strongest indignation." Huzza, my brave Boys! Could Thomas Jefferson or John Adams hear these Words, with insensibility, and without Emotion? These Boys afterwards add "We regard our Liberty and Independence, as the richest portion given Us by our Ancestors." And, who were these Ancestors? Among them were Thomas Jefferson and John Adams. And I very cooly believe that no two Men among those Ancestors did more towards it than those two. Could either hear this like Statues? If, one hundred Years hence, Your Letters and mine should see the light, I hope the Reader will hunt up this Address and read it all: and remember that We were then engaged or on the point of engaging in a War with France. I shall not repeat the Answer, till We come to the paragraph upon which you cr[i]ticised to Dr. Priestley though every Word of it is true and I now rejoice to see it recorded; and though I had wholly forgotten it.

The Paragraph is "Science and Morals are the great Pillars on which this Country has been raised to its present population, Oppulence and prosperity, and these alone, can advance, support and preserve it." "Without wishing to damp the Ardor of curiosity, or influence the freedom of inquiry, I will hazard a prediction, that after the most industrious and impartial Researches, the longest liver of you all, will find no Principles, Institutions, or Systems of Education, more fit, IN GENERAL to be transmitted to your Posterity, than those you have received from you[r] Ancestors." [78]

Now, compare the paragraph in the Answer, with the paragraph in the Address, as both are quoted above: and see if We can find the Extent and the limits of the meaning of both.

Who composed that Army of fine young Fellows that was then before my Eyes? There were among them, Roman Catholicks, English Episcopalians, Scotch and American Presbyterians, Methodists, Moravians, Anababtists, German Lutherans, German Calvinists Universalists, Arians, Priestleyans, Socinians, Independents, Congregationalists, Horse Protestants and House Protestants, Deists and Atheists; and "Protestans qui ne croyent rien ["Protestants who believe nothing"]." Very few however of several of these Species. Never the less all Educated in the *general Principles* of Christianity: and the general Principles of English and American Liberty.

Could my Answer be understood, by any candid Reader or Hearer, to recommend, to all the others, the general Principles, Institutions or Systems of Education of the Roman Catholicks? Or those of the Quakers? Or those of the Presbyterians? Or those of the Menonists? Or those of the Methodists? or those of the Moravians? Or those of the Universalists? or those of the Philosophers? No.

The *general Principles,* on which the Fathers Atchieved Independence,

78. *Works,* IX, 188.

were the only Principles in which that beautiful Assembly of young Gentlemen could Unite, and these Principles only could be intended by them in their Address, or by me in my Answer. And what were these *general Principles?* I answer, the general Principles of Christianity, in which all those Sects were United: And the *general Principles* of English and American Liberty, in which all those young Men United, and which had United all Parties in America, in Majorities sufficient to assert and maintain her Independence.

Now I will avow, that I then believed, and now believe, that those general Principles of Christianity, are as eternal and immutable, as the Existence and Attributes of God; and that those Principles of Liberty, are as unalterable as human Nature and our terrestrial, mundane System. I could therefore safely say, consistently with all my then and present Information, that I believed they would never make Discoveries in contradiction to these *general Principles*. In favour of these *general Principles* in Phylosophy, Religion and Government, I could fill Sheets of quotations from Frederick of Prussia, from Hume, Gibbon, Bolingbroke, Reausseau and Voltaire, as well as Neuton and Locke: not to mention thousands of Divines and Philosophers of inferiour Fame.

I might have flattered myself that my Sentiments were sufficiently known to have protected me against Suspicions of narrow thoughts, contrasted Sentiments, biggotted, enthusiastic or superstitious Principles civil political philosophical, or ecclesiastical. The first Sentence of the Preface to my Defence of the Constitutions, Vol. 1, printed in 1787, is in these Words: "The Arts and Sciences, in general, during the three or four last centuries, have had a regular course of *progressive* improvement. The Inventions in Mechanic Arts, the discoveries in natural Philosophy, navigation and commerce, and the Advancement of civilization and humanity, have occasioned Changes in the condition of the World and the human Character, which would have astonished the most refined Nations of Antiquity." etc.[79] I will quote no farther; but request you to read again that whole page, and then say whether the Writer of it could be suspected of recommending to Youth, "to look backward, instead of forward" for instruction and Improvement.

This Letter is already too long. In my next I shall consider "The Terrorism of the day." Meantime, I am as ever, your Friend

JOHN ADAMS

79. *Ibid.,* IV, 283.

10

"Belief... the assent of the mind to an intelligible proposition"

✳ JUNE 1813 – DECEMBER 1813 ✳

I HAVE GIVEN UP NEWSPAPERS," Jefferson informed Adams on the resumption of their correspondence in 1812, "in exchange for Tactitus and Thucydides, for Newton and Euclid." Adams, with his New England background, found most pleasure in "Theological and Ecclesiastical Instructors." [1] The major interest of Jefferson in historical and scientific questions, of Adams in theological and religious, is characteristic of each, as their wide-ranging minds were characteristic of the Enlightenment. The intensive reading and worldly experience of each enriched the reflections of the other. Much of that experience had been in politics, which Jefferson had gladly abandoned but which Adams followed more closely through his son John Quincy. Both of the veteran statesmen were very much aware of current developments in the world at large, but they could view them with greater detachment as their years of retirement lengthened.

In 1813 events of great import for the future of republican government could hardly be ignored. In America a war of uncertain outcome was testing the nation's ability to maintain independence and the union of the states. As Adams recalled past political crises in his life and took stock of the current threats of disunion, he found "more real Terrorism in New England than there ever was in Virginia," [2] when the Kentucky and Virginia Resolutions of 1798 had stirred the South. In Europe, Napoleon's ambition and appetite for power, an outcome of the French Revolution, in Adams's judgment, had en-

1. TJ to JA, Jan. 21, 1812, above, 291; JA to TJ, July 18, 1813, below, 362.
2. JA to TJ, June 30, 1813, below, 348.

veloped the Continent in flames for a decade and the final result was still in doubt. How different the outcome of the American Revolution!

When the two diplomats were colleagues in Europe before the collapse of the *ancien régime*, Jefferson had encouraged Adams in his desire to compose a treatise on aristocracy. This became Adams's medium for developing his concept of balanced government in which aristocracy played a significant but often misunderstood role. "I ... have been writing Upon that Subject ever since," he declared, quoting the ancient Greek poets to re-enforce his position: " 'Nobility in Men is worth as much as it is in Horses Asses or Rams, but the meanest blooded Puppy, in the World, if he gets a little money, is as good a man as the best of them.' Yet Birth and Wealth together," according to Adams, "have prevailed over Virtue and Talents in all ages." [3] The French Revolution and the course of events in the American Republic had supplied fresh clinical data for his thesis.

As memories of vital issues of the past and present flooded his mind, Adams wrote a series of letters in close succession, reviewing the occasion for composing his *Defence of the Constitutions* and elaborating on his theory of balanced government.[4] The existence of the "well born" in every society, the real meaning of "Gentleman," could not be ignored or discarded; but aristocracy might be controlled. "The five Pillars of Aristocracy, are Beauty, Wealth, Birth, Genius and Virtues." What chance, asked Adams, had Talents (Genius) and Virtues in competition with the first three attributes? [5]

This question called forth one of Jefferson's most famous letters—his essay on natural and artificial aristocracy and the form of government "which provides the most effectually for a pure selection of these natural aristoi into the offices of the government." [6] It provoked, in turn, Adams's counterpart on the natural aristocracy, asking what talents, physical or intellectual, material or moral, might not assert influence in society and eventually dominate it.[7] Jefferson, the optimist, had confidence in the ability of citizens of a republic to "elect the real good and wise," to separate "the aristoi from the pseudo-aristoi." He cited what the revolution in Virginia had accomplished,

3. JA to TJ, July 9, 1813, below, 351, 352.
4. JA to TJ, July 9, 13, and 15, 1813, below, 350-52, 354-56, 357-58.
5. JA to TJ, Aug. [14?], Sept. 2, 1813, below, 365-66, 371.
6. TJ to JA, Oct. 28, 1813, below, 389.
7. JA to TJ, Nov. 15, 1813, below, 398.

what his proposed system of public education might further attain, and what the American example, along with the liberating influence of science, had already meant to European peoples. Adams, skeptical of man as a rational creature, found no assurance that the natural aristocracy, established by law and honor, would not also secure legal sanction as an hereditary class, succumb to political corruption, and become a venal artificial aristocracy. To Adams such an aristocracy was "a subtle Venom that diffuses itself unseen," "a Phœnix that rises again out of its own Ashes." He would "chain it . . . and place . . . on each side of it" "a Watchful Centinel," consisting of the co-ordinate branches of his balanced government.[8] Although Jefferson's remedy of free elections prevailed as political democracy became unrestricted, Adams's argument that economic and social conditions affect political functions became more widely accepted by later generations.

The two statesmen were neither seeking controversy nor avoiding it, for they agreed that "we ought not to die before we have explained ourselves to each other." [9] With the historical perspective of the revolutionary era, their philosophical discussions ran as easily to religion as to government and from the one subject to the other and back again. Both thought that corruption in government had its parallel in the hierarchies established in the name of religion; dogmatic assertions in a maze of fine-spun theological argument overpowered men's minds and obscured fundamental principles. Although they agreed that complete freedom of religion was an inviolable principle, they discussed religious issues chiefly within the framework of the prevailing faith and subscribed to the fundamentals of Jesus's teachings, "the most sublime and benevolent code of morals which has ever been offered to man." [10]

While Adams was the tireless reader of theological works, it was Jefferson with his scientific bent who sought to organize and systematize his thoughts on religion. Not that he expected to write a treatise on the subject—his friend Dr. Joseph Priestley had provided that—but the corruptions of Christianity ought to be refuted. "I am a Christian," he confessed to Rush, "in the only sense he [Jesus] wished any one to be; sincerely attached to his doctrines, in preference to all others;

8. JA to TJ, Dec. 19, 1813, below, 409.
9. JA to TJ, July 15, 1813, and TJ to JA, Oct. 28, 1813, below, 358, 391.
10. JA to TJ, July 16, 1813, and TJ to JA, Oct. 12, 1813, below, 359-60, 383-86.

ascribing to himself every *human* excellence; and believing he never claimed any other." [11] Shortly before, Jefferson had received a copy of Priestley's *Socrates and Jesus Compared*. To the author he confided the outline (quoted in Adams's letter of July 16, 1813) of the "Christian system" as compared with the precepts of the ancient philosophers and those of the Jews. [12] With this outline in mind Jefferson prepared a more detailed, though still brief, Syllabus of an Estimate of the Merit of the Doctrines of Jesus, Compared with Those of Others. [13]

In 1813 Jefferson sent his Syllabus to Adams. It was not concerned with the divinity of Christ, but the implication of unbelief was clear. Since Jesus himself left no written words, "the committing to writing of his life and doctrines fell on the most unlettered and ignorant men," recording from memory long after the events. Only fragments of what he said were handed down, perverted or disfigured by the corruptions of "schismatising followers" or willfully destroyed by bigots for the same purpose. Jefferson advised going back to the "simple evangelists" and selecting "the very words only of Jesus," as he had already done in compiling The Philosophy of Jesus of Nazareth. [14] Adams noted with approval Jefferson's conclusions concerning the moral and ethical doctrines of Jesus, including his confirmation of the deism of the Jews—"their belief of one only God." [15] Jefferson's comparative study provided a firm relativist approach to combat the absolutism characteristic of most theologians of the period: let historical criticism be applied to Christianity in the same spirit that religious freedom is desired by all men. Adams had found the essence of Christian devotion and piety in the Greek exhortation (as Adams rendered it): "It is our duty and our privilege to address the Throne of thy grace." [16] Jefferson agreed with Adams's "outline of the theism of the three religions when you say that the principle of the Hebrew was the fear, of the Gentile the honor, and of the Christian the love of God." [17]

But Adams and Jefferson were unmistakable vestiges of the vanished Age of Enlightenment, nurturer of revolution, victim of war. Jeffer-

11. TJ to Rush, April 21, 1803, Ford, VIII, 223*n*.
12. TJ to Priestley, April 9, 1803, *ibid.*, 224-25*n*.
13. "Syllabus of an Estimate of the Merit of the Doctrines of Jesus, Compared with Those of Others," *ibid.*, 223-28.
14. See below, 384, n. 71.
15. "Syllabus," Ford, VIII, 228.
16. JA to TJ, [Oct. 4], 1813, below, 380.
17. TJ to JA, Oct. 12, 1813, and JA to TJ, Sept. 22, 1813, below, 385, 380.

son, always reticent about his own religion, observed that "if thinking men would have the courage to think for themselves, and to speak what they think, it would be found they do not differ in religious opinions, as much as is supposed." [18] "The Life and Morals of Jesus of Nazareth" were his guide. And belief he supposed "to be the assent of the mind to an intelligible proposition." [19] For Adams, whose testimony derived strength from its spontaneity, "The love of God and his Creation, delight, Joy, Tryumph, Exultation in my own existence, ... are my religion." "Ask me not, then, whether I am a Catholic or Protestant, Calvinist or Arminian. As far as they are Christians, I wish to be a fellow-disciple with them all." [20]

In religion as in the science of politics the two retired statesmen could turn philosophers without effort. But their frank discussion of religion, it should be remembered, was confined to their private correspondence. Their sharp condemnation of the priestcraft, their ridicule of the mystical Trinity as untenable by rational men, and their use of historical criticism to distinguish fact from "revelation" would have raised public furor. Under the aegis of the Enlightenment, freedom of thought won least recognition in the field of religion and theology. To Adams and Jefferson the achievement of religious freedom in most of the states during the Revolution and the adoption of the First Amendment to the Constitution of the United States had done more, they hoped, than establish a grudging toleration. They insisted on the ultimate truth "that Almighty God hath created the mind free." [21]

By the second decade of the nineteenth century the conservative reaction to rational religion was well advanced in America. Resurgent evangelism was spawning such organizations as the American Tract Society (1814) and the American Bible Society (1816) [22] to propagate the gospel by prescription rather than by exchange of opinions. Adams and Jefferson would have to find what encouragement they could in the substantial minority of free thinkers who provided the nucleus for a countervailing growth of liberal thought.

18. TJ to JA, Aug. 22, 1813, below, 368.
19. *Ibid.*
20. JA to TJ, Sept. 14, 1813, below, 374; JA to Benjamin Rush, Jan. 21, 1810, *Works*, IX, 627.
21. Preamble to TJ's "Act for establishing Religious Freedom," passed by the General Assembly of Virginia in 1786, Jefferson's *Notes on the State of Virginia*, ed. by William Peden (Chapel Hill, 1955), 223.
22. JA to TJ, Nov. 4, 1816, and TJ to JA, Nov. 25, 1816, below, 493-94, 496.

Adams to Jefferson

Quincy June 30th. 1813

DEAR SIR

Before I proceed to the Order of the day, which is the terrorism of a former day: I beg leave to correct an Idea that some readers may infer from an expression in one of your Letters. No sentiment or expression in any of my Answers to Addresses were obtruded or insinuated by any Person about me. Every one of them was written with my own hand. I alone am responsable for all the Mistakes and Errors in them. To have called Council to deliberate upon such a Mass of [writings] would have taken all the time; and the Business of the State must have been suspended. It is true, I was sufficiently plagued by Ps. and Ts. and Ss.[23] These however, were but Puppets danced upon the Wires of two Jugglers behind the Scene: and these Jugglers were Hamilton and Washington. How you stare at the name of Washington! But to return, *for the present* to

"The Sensations excited, in free yet firm Minds by the Terrorism of the day." You say, "none can conceive them who did not witness them, and they were felt by one party only".

Upon this Subject I despair of making myself understood by Posterity, by the present Age, and even by you. To collect and arrange the documents illustrative of it, would require as many Lives as those of a Cat. You never felt the Terrorism of Chaises Rebellion in Massachusetts.[24] I believe You never felt the Terrorism of Gallatins Insurrection in Pensilvania:[25] You certainly never reallized the Terrorism of Fries's,[26] most outragious Riot and Rescue, as I call it, Treason, Rebellion as the World and great Judges and two Juries pronounced it. You certainly never felt the Terrorism, excited by Genet, in 1793, when ten thousand People in the Streets of Philadelphia, day after day, threatened to drag Washington

23. I.e., "the Pickerings, ... the Tracys, the Sedgwicks." TJ to JA, June 15, 1813, above, 331.

24. On Shays's Rebellion see above, Chap. 5.

25. As representative in Congress from western Pennsylvania, Albert Gallatin led the opposition to Hamilton's whiskey tax in 1792, but he was also opposed to violence and his peace policy won out in the Whiskey Rebellion of 1794. Henry Adams, *The Life of Albert Gallatin* (Philadelphia, 1880), 88-89, 123-40.

26. Fries Rebellion occurred in Bucks and Northampton counties, Pa., in 1799. Farmers, led by John Fries, gave armed resistance to a federal tax on land and houses, and women poured scalding water on the assessors. The rebellion was put down by federal troops; Fries was tried for treason and sentenced to be hanged, but President John Adams pardoned him. W. W. H. Davis, *The Fries Rebellion* (Doylestown, Pa., 1899).

out of his House, and effect a Revolution in the Government, or compell it to declare War in favour of the French Revolution, and against England. The coolest and the firmest Minds, even among the Quakers in Philadelphia, have given their Opinions to me, that nothing but the Yellow Fever, which removed Dr. Hutchinson and Jonathan Dickenson Sargent from this World, could have saved the United States from a total Revolution of Government. I have no doubt You was fast asleep in philosophical Tranquility, when ten thousand People, and perhaps many more, were parading the Streets of Philadelphia, on the Evening of my Fast Day; [27] When even Governor Mifflin himself, thought it his Duty to order a Patrol of Horse And Foot to preserve the peace; when Markett Street was as full as Men could stand by one another, and even before my Door; when some of my Domesticks in Phrenzy, determined to sacrifice their Lives in my defence; when all were ready to make a desperate Salley among the multitude, and others were with difficulty and danger dragged back by the others; when I myself judged it prudent and necessary to order Chests of Arms from the War Office to be brought through bye Lanes and back Doors: determined to defend my House at the Expence of my Life, and the Lives of the few, very few Domesticks and Friends within it. What think you of Terrorism, Mr. Jefferson? Shall I investigate the Causes, the Motives, the Incentives to these Terrorisms? Shall I remind you of Phillip Freneau, of Loyd? of Ned Church? of Peter Markoe[?] of Andrew Brown? of Duane? of Callender? of Tom Paine? of Greenleaf, of Cheetham, of Tennison at New York? of Benjamin Austin at Boston? [28] But above all; shall I request you, to collect the circular Letters from Members of Congress in the middle and southern States to their Constituents? I would give all I am worth for a compleat Collection of all those circular Letters. Please to recollect Edward Livingstones motions and Speeches and those of his Associates in the case of Jonathan Robbins.[29]

The real terrors of both Parties have allways been, and now are, The fear that they shall loose the Elections and consequently the Loaves and Fishes; and that their Antagonists will obtain them. Both parties have excited artificial Terrors and if I were summoned as a Witness to say upon Oath, which Party had excited, Machiavillialy, the most terror, and which had really felt the most, I could not give a more sincere Answer, than in the vulgar Style "Put Them in a bagg and shake them, and then see which comes out first."

27. President John Adams proclaimed April 25, 1799, as a fast day, that God "would withhold us from unreasonable discontent, from disunion, faction, sedition, and insurrection...." *Works*, IX, 172-74.

28. All of the foregoing were Republican writers and editors, vehement in their denunciation of the Federalists.

29. See JA to TJ, May 1, 1812, above, 300-1.

Where is the Terrorism, now, my Friend? There is now more real Terrorism in New England than there ever was in Virginia. The Terror of a civil War, a La Vendee, a division of the States etc. etc. etc. How shall We conjure down this damnable Rivalry between Virginia, and Massachusetts? Virginia had recourse to Pensilvania and New York, Massachusetts has now recourse to New York. They have almost got New Jersey and Maryland, and they are aiming at Pennsilvania.[30] And all this in the midst of a War with England, when all Europe is in flames.

I will give you a hint or two more, on the Subject of Terrorism. When John Randolph in the House and Stephens Thompson Mason in the Senate were treating me, with the Utmost Contempt, when Ned Livingston was threatening me with Impeachment for the murder of Jonathan Robbins *the native of Danvers in Connecticutt*. When I had certain Information, that the daily Language in an Insurance Office in Boston, was, even from the Mouth of Charles Jarvis, "We must go to Philadelphia, and dragg that John Adams from his Chair."

I tha[n]k God that Terror never Yet seized on my mind. But I have had more excitements to it, from 1761 to this day than any other Man. Name the other if you can. I have been disgraced and degraded and I have a right to complain. But as I always expected it, I have always submitted to it; perhaps often with too much tameness.

The amount of all the Speeches of John Randolph in the House for two or three Years is, that himself and myself, are the only two honest and consistent Men in the United States. Himself, eternally in Opposition to Government, and myself as constantly in favour of it. He is now in Correspondence with his Friend Quincy. What will come of it, let Virginia and Massachusetts Judge. In my next, you may find Something, upon "Correspondencies" Whigg and Tory; Federal and democratic; Virginian and Novanglian; English and French; Jacobinic and despotic, etc.

Mean time, I am as ever Your Friend,

JOHN ADAMS

30. In the election of 1808 Pennsylvania and New York went heavily Republican; in 1812 most of New York, New Jersey, and Maryland voted Federalist, as did certain sections of Pennsylvania. By 1816 all these states were back in the Republican ranks. Charles O. Paullin, *Atlas of the Historical Geography of the United States* (Washington, 1932), pl. 102.

Adams to Jefferson

Quincy July [3] 1813

DEAR SIR

Correspondences! The Letters of Bernard and Hutchinson, and Oliver and Paxton etc. were detected and exposed before The Revolution. There are I doubt not, thousands of Letters, now in being, but still concealed, (from their Party to their Friends,) which will, one day see the light. I have wondered for more than thirty Years that so few have appeared: and have constantly expected that a Tory History of the Rise and progress of the Revolution would appear. And wished it. I would give more for it than for Marshall, Gordon, Ramsay and all the rest. Private Letters of all Parties will be found analogous to the Newspapers Pamph[l]ets and Historians of the Times. Gordon's and Marshall's Histories were written to make money: and fashioned and finished, to sell high in the London Market. I should expect to find more Truth in a History written by Hutchinson, Oliver or Sewell. And I doubt not, such Histories will one day appear. Marshall's is a Mausolaeum, 100 feet square at the base, and 200 feet high. It will be as durable, as the monuments of the Washington benevolent Societies. Your Character in History may be easily foreseen. Your Administration, will be quoted by Philosophers, as a model, of profound Wisdom; by Politicians, as weak, superficial and short sighted. Mine, like Popes Woman [31] will have no Character at all. The impious Idolatry to Washington, destroyed all Character. His Legacy of Ministers, was not the worst part of the Tradgedy. Though by his own express confession to me, and by Pickerings confession to the World, in his Letters to Sullivan: two of them, at least were fastened upon him by Necessity, because he could get no other. The Truth is, Hamiltons Influence over him was so well known, that no Man fit for the Office of State or War would accept either. He was driven to the Necessity of appointing such as would accept. And this necessity was, in my Opinion the real Cause of his retirement from office: for you may depend upon it, that retirement was not voluntary.[32]

My Friend! You and I have passed our Lives, in serious Times. I know

31. "Most Women have no Characters at all." See "Of the Characters of Women: an Epistle to a Lady," F. W. Bateson, ed., *Alexander Pope, Epistles to Several Persons (Moral Essays)*, (London and New Haven, 1951), 45.

32. President Washington made it a practice to consult his cabinet, but following TJ's resignation as secretary of state, Hamilton was Washington's chief adviser, even after he left the cabinet. The best account of these official and personal relationships is in Charles, *Origins of the American Party System*, Chaps. I-II.

not whether We have ever seen any moments more serious than the present. The Northern States are now retaliating, upon the Southern States, their conduct from 1797 to 1800. It is a mortification to me, to see how servile Mimicks they are. Their Newspapers, Pamphlets, hand Bills, and their Legislative Proceedings, are copied from the Examples sett them, especially by Virginia and Kentucky. I know not which Party has the most unblushing Front, the most lying Tongue, or the most impudent and insolent not to say the most seditious and rebellious Pen.

If you desire explanations on any of the Points in this Letter you shall have them. This Correspondence I hope will be concealed as long as Hutchinsons and Olivers. But I should have no personal Objection to the Publication of it in the national Intelligencer. I am, and shall be for Life Your Friend

JOHN ADAMS

Adams to Jefferson

Quincy July 9 1813

Lord! Lord! What can I do, with so much Greek? When I was of your Age, young Man, i. e. 7 or 8 or 9 Years ago I felt, a kind of pang of Affection, for one of the flames of my Youth, and again paid my Addresses to Isocrates and Dionissius Hallicarnassensis etc. etc. etc. I collected all my Lexicons and Grammers and sat down to περι συνθεσεως ονοματων[33] etc. In this Way I amused myself for sometime: but I found, that if I looked a Word to day, in less than a Week I had to look it again. It was to little better purpose, than writing Letters on a pail of Water.

Whenever I sett down to write to you, I am precisely in the Situation of the Wood Cutter on Mount Ida: I can not see Wood for Trees. So many Subjects crowd upon me that I know not, with which to begin. But I will begin, at random with Belsham,[34] who is, as I have no doubt, a Man of merit. He had no malice against you, nor any thought of doing mischief: nor has he done any, though he has been imprudent. The Truth is the Dissenters of all Denominations in England and especially the Unitarians, are cowed, as We used to say at Colledge. They are ridiculed, insulted, persecuted. They can scarcely hold their heads above water. They catch at Straws and Shadows to avoid drowning. Priestley sent your Letter to Linsay, and Belsham printed it from the

33. "Concerning the treatment of words." Dion. Hal. wrote a treatise by this name on composition.
34. See JA to TJ, May 29, June 25, 1813, above, 325, 334.

same motive, i.e., to derive some countenance from the Name of Jefferson. Nor has it done harm here. Priestley says to Linsay "You see he is almost one of Us, and He hopes will soon be altogether such as We are." Even in our New England I have heard a high Federal Divine say, your Letters had increased his respect for you.

"The same political parties which now agitate U. S. have existed through all time." Precisely. And this is precisely the complaint in the preface to the first volume of my defence. While all other Sciences have advanced, that of Government is at a stand; little better understood; little better practiced now than 3 or 4 thousand Years ago. What is the Reason? I say Parties and Factions will not suffer, or permit Improvements to be made. As soon as one Man hints at an improvement his Rival opposes it. No sooner has one Party discovered or invented an Amelioration of the Condition of Man or the order of Society, than the opposite Party, belies it, misconstrues it, misrepresents it, ridicules it, insults it, and persecutes it. Records are destroyed. Histories are annihilated or interpolated, or prohibited sometimes by Popes, sometimes by Emperors, sometimes by Aristocratical and sometimes by democratical Assemblies and sometimes by Mobs.

Aristotle wrote the History and description of Eighteen hundred Republicks, which existed before his time. Cicero wrote two Volumes of discour[s]es on Government, which, perhaps were worth all the rest of his Works. The Works of Livy and Tacitus etc that are lost, would be more interesting than all that remain. Fifty Gospells have been destroyed, and where are St. Lukes World of Books that had been written? If you ask my Opinion, who has committed all the havoc? I will answer you candidly; Ecclesiastical and Imperial Despotism has done it, to conceal their Frauds.

Why are the Histories of all Nations, more ancient than the Chr[is]tian Æra, lost? Who destroyed the Alexandrian Library? I believe that Christian Priests, Jewish Rabbies Grecian Sages and Roman Emperors had as great a hand in it as Turks and Mahomitans.

Democrats, Rebells and Jacobins, when they possessed a momentary Power, have shewn a disposition, both to destroy and to forge Records, as vandalical, as Priests and Despots. Such has been and such is the World We live in.

I recollect, near 30 years ago to have said car[e]lesly to You, that I wished I could find time and means to write something upon Aristocracy.[35] You seized upon the Idea, and encouraged me to do it, with all that friendly warmth that is natural and habitual to you. I soon began, and have been writing Upon that Subject ever since. I have been so un-

35. See TJ to JA, Feb. 6, 1787, and JA to TJ, March 1, 1787, above, 170, 177.

fortunate as never to be able to make myself understood. Your "ἄριστοι ["aristocrats"]" are the most difficult Animals to manage, of anything in the whole Theory and practice of Government. They will not suffer themselves to be governed. They not only exert all their own Subtilty Industry and courage, but they employ the Commonalty, to knock to pieces every Plan and Model that the most honest Architects in Legislation can invent to keep them within bounds. Both Patricians and Plebeians are as furious as the Workmen in England to demolish labour-saving Machinery.

But who are these "ἄριστοι"? Who shall judge? Who shall select these choice Spirits from the rest of the Congregation? Themselves? We must first find out and determine who themselves are. Shall the congregation choose? Ask Xenophon. Perhaps hereafter I may quote you Greek. Too much in a hurry at present, english must suffice. Xenophon says that the ecclesia, always chooses the worst Men they can find, because none others will do their dirty work.[36] This wicked Motive is worse than Birth or Wealth. Here I want to quote Greek again. But the day before I received your Letter of June 27. I gave the Book to George Washington Adams [37] going to the Accadamy at Hingham. The Title is ΗΘΙΚΗ ΠΟΙΗΣΙΣ a Collection of Moral Sentences from all the most Ancien[t] Greek Poets.[38] In one of the oldest of them I read in greek that I cannot repeat, a couplet the Sense of which was

"Nobility in Men is worth as much as it is in Horses Asses or Rams: but the meanest blooded Puppy, in the World, if he gets a little money, is as good a man as the best of them." Yet Birth and Wealth together have prevailed over Virtue and Talents in all ages. The Many, will acknowledge no other "ἄριστοι". Your Experience of this Truth, will not much differ from that of your old Friend

JOHN ADAMS

Adams to Jefferson

Quincy July 12. 1813

DEAR SIR

I forgot in my last to remark a very trifling Inaccuracy in yours of June 27th. The Letter intercepted in Hichbournes Trunk [39] which was reported to glance at Mr. Dickenson, was not in 1776. It was in the month

36. This statement was attributed to Xenophon in JA's time, but it was later recognized as from the unknown author of *Treatise of the Old Oligarch*.

37. JA's grandson, the son of John Quincy Adams, who died in 1829. Bemis, *John Quincy Adams*, 276.

38. "Moralia ex Poetis," compiler unknown.

39. See above, Chap. 9, 337, n. 77.

of June 1775. Had it been June 1776, the English would not have printed it. The Nation had then too maturely reflected on the necessity of Independence, and was too ripe and too hot for a Proclamation of it. Neither Mr. Dickenson, nor any of his Friends would have dared to express the smallest resentment of it, out of their own gloomy circles. The Penns the Allens the Chews and the Willings, in other Words the Proprietary Gentlemen of Pensilvania, I mean those of them who had not ran away to the English, would have been silent. The Quakers, instead of producing my Letters and reading and recording them in their General Meeting, and holding me up to the detestation of their whole Society as the most odious of Men aiming, or at least having in contemplation the Possibility of Independence in any case whatsoever, would have concealed and dissimulated their hypocritical cant. The Pembertons, (even Israel,) the Drinkers, the Shoemakers and all the rest would have been silent. The Spirit would not have moved one of them to open his Lips.[40]

In June 1776 my Friends would not have put on long faces and lamented my imprudence. None of them would have wondered, as some of them did in 1775, that a Man of Forty Years of Age, and of considerable Experience in business, and in life should have been guilty of such an Indiscretion. Others would not have said "it was a premature declaration of Independence," and Joseph Reed, soon afterwards private Secretary of General Washington, and after that Governor of Pennsylvania, would not have said to me, as he did, "I look upon the Interception and publication of that Letter, as an Act of the Providence of God, to excite the Attention of the people to their real Situation, and to shew them, what they must come to."

You say, "it has been hoped, I would leave such explanations as would place every Saddle on its right Horse, and replace on the Shoulders of others, the burthens they shifted on yours."

Hoped! by whom? They know not what they hope! I have already "replaced on the Shoulders of Franklin, burthens he shifted on mine.["] [41]

40. The attitude in Pennsylvania toward revolution and independence changed considerably during 1775-76. By the beginning of 1776 opposition to the king and abrogation of the colonial charter were getting increasing support, although internal disputes complicated the problem of independence. Many Quakers were disowned by the meetings for joining the Revolutionary movement and as late as June 1776 that sect officially opposed war with England and abrogation of the charter. Charles J. Stille, *The Life and Times of John Dickinson, 1732-1808* (Philadelphia, 1891), 169 ff.; Isaac Sharpless, *A History of Quaker Government in Pennsylvania* (Philadelphia, 1900), II, Chap. VI.

41. Disagreement and ill feeling developed between JA and Franklin on three occasions in France: in 1778-79 when they were commissioners to negotiate a loan; in 1780 when there seemed some prospect of negotiating a peace treaty; and in 1782-83 during the negotiation of the peace treaty, when Franklin disapproved the desire of JA and John Jay to make a separate peace with France.

Shall I "replace on the shoulders of WASHINGTON the burthens that a bastard Bratt of a Scotch Pedlar placed on his Shoulders, and he shifted on mine? ["] [42]

How many Gauntletts am I destined to run? How many Martyrdoms must I suffer?

Be they more or less, I have enjoyed a happy Life, and I would not exchange Life, Character or Fortune with any of them.

There are few Men now living, if any, who know more of me than you do. Yet you know but little of the Life I have led, the hazards I have run, or the "light Afflictions for a moment" I have endured.

I will conclude this grave solemn Letter with a merry Story: but as true as it is diverting.

In my Youth I was acquainted with one of our New England Nobility, Representative, Counsellor, Colonel, Judge, John Chandler of Worcester, of whom I could tell you twenty, humerous and instructive Anecdotes. He was a good, tho a rapid and free Character. He had great Influence in our Legislature. Upon some Occasion there was a complaint against him As a Justice of the Peace in the County of Worcester. He arrived in Boston and the Counsell sent for him, and interrogated him and threatened him. When he came down from the Counsell Chamber, one of his Brother Representatives asked him, "what can the matter be?" "God damn them," said Chandler, "they talk of uncreating their Creator."

If you do not understand this, and wish an explanation, You shall have it. Not to say too much at once.

JOHN ADAMS

Adams to Jefferson

Quincy July 13th. 1813

DEAR SIR

Let me allude, to one circumstance more, in one of your Letters to me, before I touch upon the Subject of Religion in your Letters to Priestley.

The first time, that you and I differed in Opinion on any material

42. Alexander Hamilton, who during the war fever against France, 1798-99, inveigled Washington into demanding that Hamilton be appointed second in command; if President Adams did not comply, Washington would resign as commander-in-chief. Stephen G. Kurtz, *The Presidency of John Adams: The Collapse of Federalism, 1795-1800* (Philadelphia, 1957), 325-27; Charles, *Origins of American Party System,* 48-49.

Question; was after your Arrival from Europe; and that point was the french Revolution.

You was well persuaded in your own mind that the Nation would succeed in establishing a free Republican Government: I was as well persuaded, in mine, that a project of such a Government, over five and twenty millions people, when four and twenty millions and five hundred thousands of them could neither write nor read: was as unnatural irrational and impracticable; as it would be over the Elephants Lions Tigers Panthers Wolves and Bears in the Royal Menagerie, at Versailles. Napoleon has lately invented a Word, which perfectly expresses my Opinion at that time and ever since. He calls the Project Ideology. And John Randolph, tho he was 14 years ago, as wild an Enthusiast for Equality and Fraternity, as any of them; appears to be now a regenerated Proselite to Napoleons Opinion and mine, that it was all madness.

The Greeks in their Allegorical Style said that the two Ladies Αριστοκρατια ["Aristocracy"] and δημοκ[ρ]ατια ["democracy"], always in a quarrel, disturbed every neighbourhood with their brawls. It is a fine Observation of yours that "Whig and Torey belong to Natural History." Inequalities of Mind and Body are so established by God Almighty in his constitution of Human Nature that no Art or policy can ever plain them down to a Level. I have never read Reasoning more absurd, Sophistry more gross, in proof of the Athanasian Creed,[43] or Transubstantiation, than the subtle labours of Helvetius and Rousseau to demonstrate the natural Equality of Mankind. Jus cuique ["Justice for everyone"]; the golden rule; do as you would be done by; Is all the Equality that can be supported or defended by reason, or reconciled to common Sense.

It is very true, as you justly observe, I can say nothing new on this or any other Subject of Government. But when La Fayette harrangued You and me, and John Quincy Adams, through a whole evening in your Hotel in the Cul de Sac, at Paris; and develloped the plans then in Operation to reform France: though I was as silent as you was, I then thought I could say something new to him. In plain Truth I was astonished at the Grossness of his Ignorance of Gover[n]ment and History, as I had been for Years before at that of Turgot, Rochefaucault, Condorcet and Franklin. This gross Ideology of them all, first suggested to me the thought and the inclination which I afterwards hinted to you in London, of writing Something upon Aristocracy. I was restrained for years by many fearful considerations. Who and what was I? A Man of no name or consideration in Europe. The manual Exercise of Writing was painful and distressing to

43. The belief in the Trinity, upheld by Athanasius, later Bishop of Alexandria, against Arius at the Council of Nicaea in 325, the first ecumenical council of the Christian Church.

me, almost like a blow, on the elbow or the knee; my Style was habitually negligent, unstudied, unpolished; I should make Enemies of all the French Patriots, the Dutch Patriots, the English Republicans, Dissenters, Reformers, call them what you will; and what came nearer home to my bosom than all the rest, I knew, I should give offence to many, if not all of my best Friends in America, and very probably destroy all the little Popularity I ever had, in a Country where Popularity had more Omnipotence than the British Parliament assumed. Where should I get the necessary Books? What Printer or Bookseller would undertake to print such hazardous Writings?

But when the French Assembly of Notables met, and I saw that Turgots "Government in one Centre and that Center the Nation" a Sentence as misterious or as contradictory as the Athanasian Creed, was about to take place; and when I saw that Shaises Rebellion was breaking out in Massachusetts, and when I saw that even my obscure Name was often quoted in France as an Advocate for simple Democracy; when I saw that the Sympathies in America had caught the French flame: I was determined to wash my own hands as clean as I could of all this foulness. I had then strong forebodings that I was sacrificing all the honours and Emoluments of this Life; and so it has happened: but not in so great a degree as I apprehended.

In Truth my "defence of the Constitutions" and "Discourses on Davila," [44] laid the foundation of that immense Unpopula[ri]ty, which fell like the Tower of Siloam upon me. Your steady defence of democratical Principles, and your invariable favourable Opinion of the french Revolution laid the foundation of your Unbounded Popularity.

Sic transit Gloria Mundi.

Now, I will forfeit my Life, if you can find one Sentence in my Defence of the Constitutions, or the Discourses on Davila, which by a fair construction, can favour the introduction of hereditary Monarchy or Aristocracy into America.

They were all written to support and strengthen the Constitutions of the United States.

The Woodcutter on Ida, though he was puzzled to find a Tree to chop, at first, I presume knew how to leave off, when he was weary; But I never know when to cease, when I begin to write to you

JOHN ADAMS

44. See above, Chap. 7.

Adams to Jefferson

Quincy July 15th 1813

Never mind it, my dear Sir, if I write four Letters to your one; your one is worth more than my four.

It is true that I can say and have said nothing new on the Subject of Government. Yet I did say in my Defence and in my Discourses on Davila, though in an uncouth Style, what was new to Lock, to Harrington, to Milton, to Hume to Montesquieu to Reauseau, to Turgot, Condorcet, to Rochefaucault, to Price to Franklin and to yourself; and at that time to almost all Europe and America. I can prove all this by indisputable Authorities and documents. Writings on Government had been not only neglected, but discountenanced and discouraged, through out all Europe, from the Restoration of Charles the Second in England, till the french Revolution commenced. The English Commonwealth, the Fate of Charles 1st, and the military despotism of Cromwell had sickened Mankind with disquisitions on Government to such a degree, that there was scarcely a Man in Europe who had looked into the Subject. David Hume had made himself, so fashionable with the Aid of the Court and Clergy, A theist as they call'd him, and by his elegant Lies against the Republicans and gaudy daubings of the Courtiers, that he had nearly laughed into contempt Rapin Sydney and even Lock. It was ridiculous and even criminal in almost all Europe to speak of Constitutions, or Writers upon the Principles or the Fabricks of them. In this state of Things my poor, unprotected, un-patronised Books appeared; and met with a Fate, not quite so cruel as I had anticipated. They were At last how[ev]er overborne by Misrepresentations and will perish in Obscurity, though they have been translated into German as well as french. The three Emperors of Europe, the Prince Regents, and all the ruling Powers would no more countenanc[e] or tolerate such Writings, than the Pope, the Emperor of Haiti, Ben. Austin or Tom Paine.

The Nations of Europe, appeared to me, when I was among them, from the begining of 1778, to 1785 i.e. to the commencement of the Troubles in France, to be advancing by slow but sure Steps towards an Amelioration of the condition of Man, in Religion and Government, in Liberty, Equality, Fraternity Knowledge Civilization and Humanity. The French Revolution I dreaded; because I was sure it would, not only arrest the progress of Improvement, but give it a retrograde course, for at least a Century, if not many Centuries. The French Patriots Appeared to me like young

Schollars from a Colledge or Sailors flushed with recent pay or prize Money, mounted on wild Horses, lashing and speerring, till they would kill the Horses and break their own Necks.

Let me now ask you, very seriously my Friend, Where are now in 1813, the Perfection and perfectability of human Nature? Where is now, the progress of the human Mind? Where is the Amelioration of Society? Where the Augmentations of human Comforts? Where the diminutions of human Pains and Miseries? I know not whether the last day of Dr. Young can exhibit; to a Mind unstaid by Phylosophy and Religion, for I hold there can be no Philosophy without Religion; more terrors than the present State of the World.

When? Where? and how? is the present Chaos to be arranged into Order?

There is not, there cannot be, a greater Abuse of Words than to call the Writings of Calender, Paine, Austin and Lowell [45] or the Speeches of Ned. Livingston and John Randolph, Public Discussions. The Ravings and Rantings of Bedlam, merit the Character as well; and yet Joel Barlow [46] was about to record Tom Paine as the great Author of the American Revolution! If he was; I desire that my name may be blotted out forever, from its Records.

You and I ought not to die, before We have explained ourselves to each other.

I shall come to the Subject of Religion, by and by. Your Friend

JOHN ADAMS

I have been looking for some time for a space in my good Husbands Letters to add the regards of an old Friend, which are still cherished and preserved through all the changes and v[ic]issitudes which have taken place since we first became acquainted, and will I trust remain as long as

A ADAMS

45. John Lowell's *The Antigallican; or The Lover of His Own Country* (Philadelphia, 1797), includes "extracts from letters written during the late war by a person [John Adams] in a high official station abroad."

46. Barlow, one of the original "Hartford Wits," developed from a Federalist into a liberal democrat and was made a citizen of France. His *Advice to the Privileged Orders* (London, 1792) presents the theory of the responsibility of the state. After living abroad for more than a decade, he returned to the United States in 1805. He worked on a history of the United States for TJ, but it was never completed.

Adams to Jefferson

Quincy July 16. 1813

DEAR SIR

Your Letters to Priestley, have encreased my Grief if that were possible, for the loss of Rush. Had he lived, I would have stimulated him to insist on your promise to him to write him on the Subject of Religion. Your Plan, I admire.

In your Letter to Priestley of March 21. 1801, dated at Washington you call "The Christian Philosophy, the most sublime and benevolent, but the most perverted System that ever shone on Man." [47] That it is the most sublime and benevolent, I agree. But whether it has been more perverted than that of Mosse, of Confucius, of Zoroaster, of Sanchoniathan of Numa, of Mahomet of the Druids, of the Hindoos etc. etc. etc. I cannot as yet determine; because I am not sufficiently acquainted with those Systems or the History of their Effects to form a decisive Opinion of the result of the Comparison.

In your Letter dated Washington April 9. 1803, You say "In consequence of some conversations with Dr. Rush in the Years 1798-99, I had promised some day to write him a Letter giving him my View of the Christian System. I have reflected often on it since, and even sketched the Outlines in my own mind. I should first take a general View of the moral doctrines of the most remarkable of the ancient Philosophers, of whose Ethicks We have sufficient information to make an estimate; say of Pythagoras, Epicurus, Epictetus Socrates, Cicero, Seneca, Antoninus. I should do justice to the branches of Morality they have treated well, but point out the importance of those in which they are deficient. I should then take a view of the Deism and Ethicks of the Jews, and shew in what a degraded State they were, and the necessity they presented of a reformation. I should proceed to a view of the Life, Character, and doctrines of Jesus, who sensible of the incorrectness of their Ideas of the Deity, and of morality, and endeavoured to bring them to the Principles of a pure Deism, and juster Notions of the Attributes of God; to reform their moral doctrines to the Standard of reason, justice and Philanthropy and to inculcate the belief of a future State. This View would purposely omit the question of his Divinity, and even of his Inspiration. To do him Justice, it would be necessary to remark the disadvantages his doctrines have to encounter, not having been committed to Writing by himself, but by the

47. Ford, VIII, 21-22.

most unlettered of Men, by memory, long after they had heard them from him, when much was forgotten, much misunderstood, and presented in very paradoxical Shapes. Yet such are the fragments remaining, as to show a master workman, and that his System of Morality was the most benevolent and sublime, probably that has been ever taught, and more perfect than those of any of the ancient Philosophers. His Character and Doctrines, have received still greater injury from those who pretend to be his special Disciples, and who have disfigured and sophisticated his Actions and precepts from views of personal interest, so as to induce the unthinking part of Mankind, to throw off the whole System in disgust, and to pass sentence, as an Impostor, on the most innocent, the most benevolent, the most eloquent and sublime Character, that ever has been exhibited to Man. This is the Outline."! [48]

"Sancte Socrate! Ora pro nobis ["Holy Socrates! Pray for us"]."! Erasmus. Priestley in his Letter to Lindssey inclosing a Copy of your letter to him says "He is generally considered as an Unbeliever: if so, however, he cannot be far from Us, and I hope in the Way to be not only almost, but altogether what We are. He now attends publick worship very regularly, and his moral Conduct was never impeached."

Now, I see not, but you are as good a Christian as Priestley and Lindsey. Piety and Morality were the End and Object of the Christian System according to them, and according to You. They believed in the Resurrection of Jesus, in his Miracles, and in his inspiration: but what inspiration? Not all that is recorded in the New Testament, nor the old. They have not yet told Us, how much they believe, nor how much, they doubt or disbelieve. They have not told Us, how much Allegory how much Parable, they find, nor how they explain them all, in the old Testament or the new.

John Quincy Adams, has written for Years, to his two Sons, Boys of 10 and 12, a Series of Letters, in which he pursues a plan more extensive than yours, but agreeing in most of the essential points. I wish these Letters could be preserved in the Bosoms of his Boys: but Women and Priests will get them: and I expect, if he makes a peace he will be obliged to retire like a Jay [49] to study Prophecies to the End of his Life.

I have more to say, upon this Subject of Religion.

JOHN ADAMS

48. *Ibid.*, 224-25.
49. After his retirement from public life, following his governorship of New York, 1795-1800, John Jay became increasingly interested in religious and church activities and became president of the American Bible Society in 1821. Samuel F. Bemis, "Jay, John," *DAB*, X, 9.

Adams to Jefferson

Quincy. July 18th. 1813

DEAR SIR

I have more to say, on Religion. For more than sixty Years I have been attentive to this great Subject. Controversies, between Calvinists and Arminians, Trinitarians and Uniterians, Deists and Christians, Atheists and both, have attracted my Attention, whenever the singular Life I have lead would admit, to all these questions. The History of this little Village of Quincy, if it were worth recording would explain to you, how this happened. I think, I can now say I have read away Bigotry, if not Enthusiasm.

What does Priestly mean, by an Unbeliever? When he applies it to you? How much did he "unbelieve," himself? Gibbon had him right, when he denominated his Creed, "Scanty." We are to understand, no doubt, that he believed The Resurrection of Jesus, some of his Miracles. His Inspiration, but in what degree? He did not believe in the Inspiration of the Writings that contain his History. Yet he believed in the Apocalyptic Beast, and he believed as much as he pleased in the Writings of Daniel and John. This great, excellent and extraordinary Man, whom I sincerely loved esteemed and respected, was really a Phenomenon; a Comet in the System, like Voltaire Bolingbroke and Hume. Had Bolingbroke or Voltaire taken him in hand, what would they have made of him and his Creed?

I do not believe you have read much of Priestleys "Corruptions of Christianity." His History of early Opinions of Jesus Christ. His Predestination, his No Soul System or his Controversy with Horseley.[50]

I have been a diligent Student for many Years in Books whose Titles you have never seen. In Priestleys and Lindsay Writings; in Farmer, Cappe, in Tuckers or Edwards Searches, Light of Nature pursued; in Edwards and Hopkins, and lately in Ezra Styles Ely; his reverend and learned Panegyrists and his elegant and spirited Opponents. I am not wholly uninformed of the Controversies in Germany and the learned Researches of Universities and Professors; in which the Sanctity of the Bible and the

50. Priestley's best known theological work was *History of the Corruptions of Christianity* (London, 1782). His four-volume *History of Early Opinions Concerning Jesus Christ* (London, 1786), rejecting the doctrine of the infallibility of Christ, "has brought me more antagonists," he wrote, "and I now write a pamphlet annually in defence of the Unitarian doctrine against all my opponents." *Memoirs of the Rev. Joseph Priestley to the Year 1795.* Written by Himself with a Continuation, to the Time of His Decease, by His Son, Joseph Priestley (Reprinted from the American edn.; London, 1809), 88.

Inspiration of its Authors are taken for granted or waived; or admitted, or not denied. I have also read Condorcets Progress of the human mind.

Now, what is all this to you? No more, than if I should tell you that I read Dr. Clark and Dr. Waterland and Emlyn, and Lelands View or Review of the Deistical Writers more than fifty Years ago, which is a litteral Truth.

I blame you not for reading Euclid and Newton, Thucidides and Theocritus: for I believe you will find as much entertainment and Instruction in them as I have found, in my Theological and Ecclesiastical Instructors: Or even as I have found in a profound Investigation of the Life Writings and Doctrines of Erastus, whose Disciples were Milton, Harrington, Selden, St. John, the Chief Justice, Father of Bolingbroke, and others the choicest Spirits of their Age: or in La Harpes History of the Philosophy of the 18th Century, or in Van der Kemps vast Map of the Causes of the Revolutionary Spirit, in the same and preceeding Centuries. These Things are to me, at present, the Marbles and Nine Pins of old Age: I will not say the Beads and Prayer Books.

I Agree with you, as far as you go. Most cordially and I think solidly. How much farther I go, how much more I believe than You, I may explain in a future Letter.

Thus much I will say at present, I have found so many difficulties, that I am not astonished at your stopping where you are. And so far from sentencing you to Perdition, I hope soon to meet you in another Country.

JOHN ADAMS

Adams to Jefferson

Quincy, July 22, 1813

DEAR SIR

Dr. Priestley, in a letter to Mr. Lindsay Northumberland Nov. 4. 1803 says

"As you were pleased with my comparison of Socrates and Jesus, I have begun to carry the same comparison to all the heathen Moralists, and I have all the books that I want for the purpose, except Simplicius and Arrian on Epictetus, and them I hope to get from a Library in Philadelphia: lest however I should fail there, I wish you or Mr. Belsham would procure and send them from London. While I am capable of any thing I can not be idle, and I do not know that I can do any thing better. This too is an Undertaking that Mr. Jefferson recommends to me."

In another Letter dated Northumberland Jan. 16. 1804 Dr. Priestley says to Mr. Lindsey "I have now finished and transcribed for the Press, my comparison of the Grecian Philosophers, with those of Revelation, and with more ease and more to my own Satisfaction, than I expected. They who liked my pamphlet entitled "Socrates and Jesus compared," will not, I flatter myself dislike this work. It has the same Object and completes the Scheme. It has increased my own sense of the unspeakable value of Revelation, and must, I think, that of every person, who will give due attention to the Subject". I have now given You all that relates to yourself in Priestleys Letters.

This was possibly and not improbably, the last Letter this great, this learned, indefatigable, most excellent and extraordinary Man, ever wrote: for on the fourth of February 1804, he was released from his labours and Sufferings. Peace, Rest, Joy and Glory to his Soul! For I believe he had one; and one of the greatest.

I regret; oh how, I lament, that he did not live, to publish this Work! It must exist in Manuscript. Cooper must know Something of it. Can you learn from him where it is, and get it printed? I hope you will still perform your promise to Dr. Rush.

If Priestley had lived, I should certainly have corresponded with him. His Friend Cooper, who unfortunately for him and me, and you, had as fatal an influence over him as Hamilton had over Washington; and whose rash hot head led Priestley into all his Misfortunes and most [of] his Errors in Conduct, could not have prevented explanations between Priestley and me.

I should propose to him a thousand, a million Questions. And no M[an] was more capable or better disposed to answer them candidly than Dr. Priestley. Scarcely any thing that has happened to me, in my curious Life has made a deeper Impression upon me, than that such a learned ingenious scientific and talented Madcap as Cooper, could have had influence enough to make Priestley my Enemy.

I will not yet, communicate to you, more than a Specimen, of the Questions I would have asked Priestley.

One is, learned and scientific Sir! You have written largely about matter and Spirit, and have concluded, there is no human Soul. Will you please to inform me, what matter is? and what Spirit is? Unless We know the meaning of Words, We cannot reason in, or about Words. I shall never send you all my Questions that I would put to Priestley; because they are innumerable: but I may hereafter send you two or three. I am in perfect Charity Your old Friend

JOHN ADAMS

Adams to Jefferson

Quincy Aug. 9 13.

I believe I told you in my last, that I had given you all in Lindseys Memoirs, that interested you. But I was mistaken. In Priestleys Letter to Lindsey Decr. 19. 1803, I find this Paragraph

"With the Work I am now composing I go on much faster and better than I expected; so that in two or three months, if my health continue as it now is, I hope to have it ready for the Press; though I shall hardly proceed to print it, till We have dispatched the Notes. It is upon the same plan with that of Socrates and Jesus compared, considering all the more distinguished of the Grecian Sects of Philosophy, till the establishment of Christianity in the Roman Empire. If you liked that Pamphlet, I flatter myself you will like this. I hope it is calculated to show, in a peculiarly striking Light, the great Advantage of Revelation, and that it will make an impression on candid Unbelievers, if they will read. But I find few that will trouble themselves to read any thing, on the Subject; which considering the great magnitude and interesting nature of the Subject, is a proof of a very improper State of mind unworthy of a rational Being."

I send you this extract for several reasons. 1st. because you sett him upon this Work. 2dly. because I wish you to endeavour to bring it to light and get it printed. 3ly. Because I wish it may stimulate You, to pursue Your own plan which you promised to Dr. Rush.[51] I have not seen any Work which expressly compares the Morality of the old Testament with that of the New in all their Branches: nor either with that of the ancient Philosop[h]ers. Comparisons with the Chinese, the East Indians, the Affricans, the West Indians etc would be more difficult; with more ancient Nations, impossible. The Documents are destroyed.

JOHN ADAMS

51. TJ's Syllabus of the Doctrine of Jesus. See TJ to JA, Aug. 22, 1813, below, 369, n. 58.

Adams to Jefferson

Quincy   August   [14?]   1813

κριοὺς μὲν καὶ ὄνους διζήμεθα, Κύρνε, καὶ ἵππους
εὐγενέας· καί τις βούλεται ἐξ ἀγαθῶν
κτήσασθαι. γῆμαι δὲ κακὴν κακοῦ οὐ μελεδαίνει
ἐσθλὸς ἀνήρ, ἤν οἱ χρήματα πολλὰ διδῷ.

Behold my translation

"My Friend Curnis, When We want to purchace, Horses, Asses or Rams, We inquire for the Wellborn. And every one wishes to procure, from the good Breeds. A good Man, does not care to marry a Shrew, the Daughter of a Shrew; unless They give him, a great deal of Money with her."

What think you, of my translation? Compare it with that of Grotius, and tell me, which, is nearest to the Original in letter and in Spirit.
Grotius renders it

> Nobilitas asinis et equis simul, arietibusque
> Dat pretium: nec de semine degeneri
> Admissura placet. sed pravæ e Sanguine pravo,
> Si dos sit, præsto est optima conditio.

This flower of Greek Poetry, is extracted, from the

ΘΕΟΓΝΙΔΟΣ ΜΕΓΑΡΕΩΣ ΠΑΡΑΙΝΕΣΕΙΣ [52]

Theognis lived five hundred and forty four Years before Jesus Christ. Has Science or Morals, or Philosophy or Criticism or Christianity, advanced or improved, or enlightened Mankind upon this Subject, and shewn them, that the Idea of the "Well born" is a prejudice, a Phantasm, a Point no point, a Gape Fly away, a dream? I say it is the Ordonance of God Almighty, in the Constitution of human nature, and wrought into the Fabrick of the Universe. Philosophers and Politicians, may nibble and quibble, but they never will get rid of it. Their only resource is, to controul it. Wealth is another Monster to be subdued. Hercules could not subdue both or either. To subdue them by regular approaches by a regular Seige, and strong fortifications, was my Object in writing on Aristocracy, as I proposed to you in Grovenor Square.

If you deny any one of these Positions, I will prove them to demonstration by Examples drawn from your own Virginia, and from every other

---

52. "Works of Theognis."

State in the Union, and from the History of every Nation civilized and savage, from all We know of the time of the Creation of the World.

Whence is the derivation of the Words Generous, Generously, Generosity etc? Johnson says "Generous. a. Generosus Latin, Not of mean Birth; of good extraction. Noble of mind. Magnanimous, Open of Heart Liberal, munificent. Strong, vigorous." And he might have added, Couragious, heroic, patriotic.

Littleton happens to be at hand. Generosus— εὐγενὴς, γενναῖος Nobilis, ex præclaro genere ortus: qui a genere non deflectit.
Born of a noble Race, a Gentleman born. See his Examples.[53]

What is the Origin of the Word Gentleman?

It would be a curious critical Speculation for a learned Idler to pursue this Idea, through all Languages.

We may call this Sentiment a prejudice, because We can give what names We please, to such things as We please; but in my Opinion it is a part of the Natural History of Man: and Politicians and Philosophers may as well project to make The Animal live with out Bones or Blood, as Society can pretend to establish, a free Government without Attention to it.

Quincy August 16. 1813. I can proceed no farther, with this Letter, as I intended.

Your Friend, my only Daughter,[54] expired, Yesterday Morning in the Arms of Her Husband her Son, her Daughter, her Father and Mother, her Husbands two Sisters and two of her Nieces, in the 49th. Year of her Age, 46 of which She was the healthiest and firmest of Us all: Since which, She has been a monument to Suffering and to Patience.

JOHN ADAMS

Jefferson to Abigail Adams

Monticello Aug. 22.13.

DEAR MADAM

A kind note at the foot of Mr. Adams's letter of July 15. reminds me of the duty of saluting you with friendship and respect; a duty long suspended by the unremitting labors of public engagement, and which ought to have been sooner revived, since I am become proprietor of my own time. And yet so it is, that in no course of life have I been ever more closely pressed by business than in the present. Much of this proceeds

53. Adam Littleton, *A Latin Dictionary in Four Parts* (London, 1703).
54. Mrs. William Stephens (Abigail Adams) Smith.

from my own affairs; much from the calls of others; leaving little time for indulgence in my greatest of all amusements, reading. Doctr. Franklin used to say that when he was young, and had time to read, he had not books; and now when he had become old and had books, he had no time. Perhaps it is that, when habit has strengthed our sense of duties, they leave no time for other things; but when young, we neglect them, and this gives us time for any thing. However I will now take time to ask you how you do, how you have done? and to express the interest I take in whatever affects your happiness. I have been concerned to learn that, at one time you suffered much and long from rheumatism, and I can sympathise with you the more feelingly, as I have had more of it myself latterly than at any former period; and can form a truer idea of what it is in it's higher degrees. Excepting for this, I have enjoyed general health; for I do not consider as a want of health the gradual decline and increasing debility which are the natural diathesis of age. This last comes on me fast. I am not able to walk much; tho' I still ride without fatigue; and take long and frequent journies to a distant possession.[55]

I have compared notes with Mr. Adams on the score of progeny, and find I am ahead of him, and think I am in a fair way to keep so. I have 10½ grandchildren, and 2 ¾ great-grand-children; and these fractions will ere long become units. I was glad to learn from Mr. Adams that you have a grandson far enough advanced in age and acquirements to be reading Greek. These young scions give us comfortable cares, when we cease to care about ourselves. Under all circumstances of health or sickness, of blessing or affliction, I tender you assurances of my sincere affection and respect; and my prayers that the hand of time and of providence may press lightly on you, till your own wishes shall withdraw you from all mortal feeling.

TH: JEFFERSON

Jefferson to Adams

Monticello Aug. 22. 13.

DEAR SIR

Since my letter of June 27. I am in your debt for many; all of which I have read with infinite delight. They open a wide field for reflection; and offer subjects enough to occupy the mind and the pen indefinitely. I must follow the good example you have set; and when I have not time to take up every subject, take up a single one.

Your approbation of my outline to Dr. Priestly is a great gratification

55. Poplar Forest, in Bedford County, Va.

to me; and I very much suspect that if thinking men would have the courage to think for themselves, and to speak what they think, it would be found they do not differ in religious opinions, as much as is supposed. I remember to have heard Dr. Priestly say that if all England would candidly examine themselves, and confess, they would find that Unitarianism was really the religion of all: and I observe a bill is now depending in parliament for the relief of Anti-Trinitarians. It is too late in the day for men of sincerity to pretend they believe in the Platonic mysticisms that three are one, and one is three; and yet the one is not three, and the three are not one: to divide mankind by a single letter into ὁμοουsians and ὁμοιουsians ["consubstantialists and like-substantialists"]. But this constitutes the craft, the power and the profit of the priests. Sweep away their gossamer fabrics of factitious religion, and they would catch no more flies. We should all then, like the quakers, live without an order of priests, moralise for ourselves, follow the oracle of conscience, and say nothing about what no man can understand, nor therefore believe; for I suppose belief to be the assent of the mind to an intelligible proposition.

It is with great pleasure I can inform you that Priestly finished the comparative view of the doctrines of the Philosophers of antiquity, and of Jesus, before his death; and that it was printed soon after; [56] and, with still greater pleasure, that I can have a copy of his work forwarded from Philadelphia, by a correspondent there, and presented for your acceptance, by the same mail which carries you this, or very soon after. The branch of the work which the title announces is executed with learning and candor, as was every thing Priestly wrote: but perhaps a little hastily; for he felt himself pressed by the hand of death. The Abbé Batteux had in fact laid the foundation of this part, in his Causes premieres; with which he has given us the originals of Ocellus, and Timaeus, who first committed the doctrines of Pythagoras to writing; [57] and Enfield, to whom the Doctor refers, had done it more copiously. But he has omitted the important branch, which in your letter of Aug. 9. you say you have never seen executed, a comparison of the morality of the old testament with that of the new. And yet no two things were ever more unlike. I ought not to have asked him to give it. He dared not. He would have been eaten alive by his intolerant brethren, the Cannibal priests. And yet this was really the most interesting branch of the work.

Very soon after my letter to Doctr. Priestley, the subject being still in

56. *The Doctrines of Heathen Philosophy Compared with Those of Revelation* (Northumberland, Pa., 1804).

57. The works attributed to Ocellus and Timaeus in the eighteenth century are now thought by classical scholars to be spurious and were suspect by the mid-nineteenth century. Anthon's *Classical Dictionary* (N. Y., 1867); *Oxford Classical Dictionary* (Oxford, 1949).

my mind, I had leisure, during an abstraction from business, for a day or two while on the road, to think a little more on it, and to sketch more fully than I had done to him, a Syllabus of the matter which I thought should enter into the work. I wrote it to Dr. Rush; and there ended all my labor on the subject; himself and Dr. Priestley being the only depositories of my secret.[58] The fate of my letter to Priestley, after his death, was a warning to me on that of Dr. Rush; and at my request his family was so kind as to quiet me by returning my original letter and Syllabus. By this you will be sensible how much interest I take in keeping myself clear of religious disputes before the public, and especially of seeing my Syllabus disembowelled by the Aruspices of the modern Paganism. Yet I enclose it *to you* with entire confidence, free to be perused by yourself and Mrs. Adams, but by no one else; and to be returned to me.

You are right in supposing, in one of yours, that I had not read much of Priestley's Predestination, his No-soul system, or his controversy with Horsley. But I have read his Corruptions of Christianity, and Early opinions of Jesus, over and over again; and I rest on them, and on Middleton's writings, especially his letters from Rome, and to Waterland, as the basis of my own faith. These writings have never been answered, nor can be answered, by quoting historical proofs, as they have done. For these facts therefore I cling to their learning, so much superior to my own.

I now fly off in a tangent to another subject. Marshal, in the 1st. vol. of his history, C. 3, pa. 180. ascribes the petition to the king of 1774. (1 Journ. Congr. 67.) to the pen of Richard Henry Lee.[59] I think myself certain it was not written by him, as well from what I recollect to have heard, as from the internal evidence of style. His was loose, vague, frothy, rhetorical. He was a poorer writer than his brother Arthur; and Arthur's standing may be seen in his Monitor's letters, to ensure the sale of which they took the precaution of tacking to them a new edition of the Farmer's

58. During the evenings of 1798-99 in Philadelphia TJ and Dr. Rush sometimes discussed the Christian religion, and TJ promised to set forth his views, one day or other. In August 1800 Rush reminded TJ of his promise, but the pressure of public duties interfered. Then, in April 1803 during a short visit to Monticello, TJ received a copy of Dr. Priestley's *Socrates and Jesus Compared* from the author. This moved TJ that same month to write his Syllabus of an Estimate of the Merit of the Doctrines of Jesus, Compared with Those of Others, which he sent in confidence to Rush. These views, TJ stated, "are the result of a life of inquiry and reflection, and very different from that anti-Christian system imputed to me by those who know nothing of my opinions." Rush to TJ, Aug. 22, 1800, May 5, 1803, Butterfield, ed., *Letters of Rush*, II, 820, 864n.; TJ to Priestley, April 9, 1803, and TJ to Rush, April 21, 1803, and "Syllabus," Ford, VIII, 223-28.

59. John Marshall, *The Life of George Washington*, 5 vols. (Philadelphia, 1804-7). John Dickinson, citing the Journals of Congress to prove his authorship, so informed Marshall, and his claim is generally accepted. Stille, *Dickinson*, 143n.; Edmund C. Burnett, *The Continental Congress* (N. Y., 1941), 51.

letters; like Mezentius who 'mortua jungebat corpora vivis ["bound dead bodies to the living"].' You were of the committee, and can tell me who wrote this petition: and who wrote the Address to the inhabitants of the colonies ib. 45.[60]

Of the papers of July 1775 I recollect well that Mr. Dickinson drew the petition to the king, ib. 149.[61] I think Robt. R. Livingston drew the address to the Inhabitants of Great Britain. ib. 152. Am I right in this? [62] And who drew the Address to the people of Ireland, ib. 180.? [63] On these questions, I ask of your memory to help mine. Ever and affectionately your's.

TH: JEFFERSON

P.S. Miss Lomax, daughter of one of our friends of 1776, lately dead, now here on a visit, asks permission to consign to you a memorial of the family respect for you: not done with the pencil, the burine or the chissel, but with the only instrument habitual to her, the humble scissars. You will find it inclosed.

Adams to Jefferson

Quincy Sept. 2. 1813

Οὐδὲ γυνὴ κακοῦ ανδρὸς ἀναίνεται εἶναι ἄκοιτις
Πλουσίου, ἀλλ' ἀφνεὸν βούλεται ἀντ' ἀγαθοῦ.
Χρήματα γὰρ τιμῶσι· καὶ εκ κακοῦ ἐσθλὸς ἔγημε
Καὶ κακὸς ἐξ ἀγαθοῦ· πλοῦτος ἔμιξ γένος.

Grotius renders this into latin, thus.

> Nec dedignatur ditemque malumque maritum
>   femina: divitiæ præ probitate placent.
> In pretio pretium est: genus et prænobile, vili,
>   Obscurum claro, miscet avaritia.

I should render the Greek into English thus.

60. Written by Richard Henry Lee. Worthington C. Ford, ed., *Journals of the Continental Congress, 1774-1789* (Washington, 1904-37), I, 62n., 90n.
61. This was Dickinson's last opportunity to try reconciliation. TJ, "Autobiography," Ford, I, 17; Burnett, *Continental Congress*, 85.
62. Livingston's authorship cannot be proved, although he was a member of the committee to draft the address, which JA thought was puerile, juvenile, and petty. Ford, ed., *Journals of Continental Congress*, II, 80; Lynn Montross, *The Reluctant Rebels* (N. Y., 1950), 82.
63. This address was prepared by a committee composed of James Duane, William Livingston, John Adams, and Samuel Adams. Ford, ed., *Journals of Continental Congress*, II, 80.

Nor does a Woman disdain to be the Wife of a bad rich Man. But She prefers a Man of Property before a good Man. For Riches are honoured; and a good Man marries from a bad Family, and a bad Man from a good one. Wealth mingles all races.

Now please to tell me, whether my translation has not hit the Sense of Theognis, as exactly as that of Grotius.

Tell me also, whether Poet, Orator, Historian or Philosopher can paint the Picture of every City, County or State in our pure, uncorrupted, unadulterated, uncontaminated federal Republick; or in France England Holland, and all the rest of Chri[s]tendom or Mahometanism, in more precise Lines or Colures.?

Another translation of the whole Passage of Theognis.

Arietes quidem et Asinos quaerimus, Cyrne, et Equos
Generosos, et quisque vult ex bonis,:
Admittere: ducero autem malam (filiam) mali non renuit
Generosus Vir, Si ei pecunias multas dederit.
Nulla (femina) mali viri recusat esse Uxor
Divitis; Sed divitem vult pro bono
Opes quidem æstimant, et ex malo (natam) bonus ducet
Et malus ex bono ortam. Divitiæ mixent genus.[64]

Now, my Friend, who are the ἄριστοι ["aristocrats"]? Philosophy may Answer "The Wise and Good." But the World, Mankind, have by their practice always answered, "the rich the beautiful and well born." And Philosophers themselves in marrying their Children prefer the rich the handsome and the well descended to the wise and good.

What chance have Talents and Virtues in competition, with Wealth and Birth? and Beauty?

Haud facile emergunt, quorum Virtutibus obstant [i.e., obstat]
Res Angusta Domi.

> One truth is clear,; by all the World confess'd
> Slow rises worth, by Poverty oppress'd.

The five Pillars of Aristocracy, are Beauty Wealth, Birth, Genius and Virtues. Any one of the three first, can at any time over bear any one or both of the two last.

Let me ask again, what a Wave of publick Opinion, in favour of Birth has been spread over the Globe, by Abraham, by Hercules, by Mahomet, by Guelphs, Ghibellines, Bourbons, and a miserable Scottish Chief Steuart? By Zingis by, by, by, a million others? And what a Wave will be spread

64. JA earlier quoted the first four lines in his letter of Aug. [14?], 1813; see above, 365. For TJ's quotation from Theognis, see his letter of Oct. 28, 1813, below, 388, 390.

by Napoleon and by Washington? Their remotest Cousins will be sought and will be proud, and will avail themselves of their descent. Call this Principle, Prejudice, Folly Ignorance, Baseness, Slavery, Stupidity, Adulation, Superstition or what you will. I will not contradict you. But the Fact, in natural, moral, political and domestic History I cannot deny or dispute or question.

And is this great Fact in the natural History of Man? This unalterable Principle of Morals, Philosophy, Policy domestic felicity, and dayly Experience from the Creation; to be overlooked, forgotten neglected, or hypocritically waived out of Sight; by a Legislator? By a professed Writer upon civil Government, and upon Constitutions of civil Government?

Thus far I had written, when your favour of Aug. 22 was laid on my table, from the Post Office. I can only say at present that I can pursue this idle Speculation no farther, at least till I have replied to this fresh proof of your friendship and Confidence. Mrs. A. joins in cordial Thanks, with

JOHN ADAMS

You may laugh at the introduction of Beauty, among the Pillars of Aristocracy. But Madame Barry says Le veritable Royauté est la B[e]autee ["true royalty is beauty"], and there is not a more certain Truth. Beauty, Grace, Figure, Attitude, Movement, have in innumerable Instances prevailed over Wealth, Birth, Talents Virtues and every thing else, in Men of the highest rank, greatest Power, and sometimes, the most exalted Genius, greatest Fame, and highest Merit.

Adams to Jefferson

Quincy Sept. 14. 1813

DEAR SIR

I owe you a thousand thanks for your favour of Aug. 22 and its Enclosures, and for Dr. Priestley's "Doctrines of heathen Philosophy compared with those of Revelation". Your Letter to Dr. Rush, and the Syllabus, I return inclosed with this, according to your Injunction; though with great reluctance. May I beg a copy of both? They will do you no harm: me and others much good. I hope you will pursue your plan, for I am confident you will produce a Work much more valuable than Priestleys; tho' that is curious and considering the expiring Powers with which it was written, admirable.

The Bill in Parliament for the relief of Antitrinitarians [65] is a great Event; and will form an Epoch in Ecclesiastical History. The Motion was made by my Friend [William] Smith of Clapham, a Friend of the Belshams. I should be very happy to hear, that the Bill is passed.

The human Understanding is a revelation from its Maker which can never be disputed or doubted. There can be no Scepticism, Pyrrhonism or Incredulity or Infidelity here. No Prophecies, no Miracles are necessary to prove this celestial communication. This revelation has made it certain that two and one make three; and that one is not three; nor can three be one. We can never be so certain of any Prophecy, or the fullfillment of any Prophecy; or of any miracle, or the design of any miracle as We are, from the revelation of nature i.e. natures God that two and two are equal to four. Miracles or Prophecies might frighten Us out of our Witts; might scare us to death; might induce Us to lie; to say that We believe that 2 and 2 make 5. But We should not believe it. We should know the contrary.

Had you and I been forty days with Moses on Mount Sinai and admitted to behold, the divine Shekinah, and there told that one was three and three, one: We might not have had courage to deny it, but We could not have believed it. The thunders and Lightenings and Earthqu[ak]es and the transcendant Splendors and Glories, might have overwhelmed Us with terror and Amazement: but We could not have believed the doctrine. We should be more likely to say in our hearts, whatever We might say with our Lips, This is Chance. There is no God! No Truth. This is all delusion, fiction and a lie: or it is all Chance. But what is Chance? It is motion; it is Action; it is Event; it is Phenomenon, without Cause. Chance is no cause att all. It is nothing. And Nothing has produced all this Pomp and Splendor; and Nothing may produce Our eternal damnation in the flames of Hell fire and Brimstone for what We know, as well as this tremendous Exhibition of Terror and Falshood.

God has infinite Wisdom, goodness and power. He created the Universe. His duration is eternal, a parte Ante, and a parte post. His presence is as extensive as Space. What is Space? an infinite, spherical Vaccuum. He created this Speck of Dirt and the human Species for his glory: and with the deliberate design of making, nine tenths of our Species miserable forever, for his glory. This is the doctrine of Christian Theologians in general: ten to one.

Now, my Friend, can Prophecies, or miracles convince You, or Me, that infinite Benevolence, Wisdom and Power, created and preserves, for

65. The act of 1813 placed Unitarians on an equal basis with other Dissenters by repeal of provisions in the Toleration Act of 1689 which had made denial of the Trinity illegal.

a time, innumerable millions to make them miserable, forever; for his own Glory? Wretch! What is his Glory? Is he ambitious? does he want promotion? Is he vain? tickled with Adulation? Exulting and tryumphing in his Power and the Sweetness of his Vengeance? Pardon me, my Maker, for these Aweful Questions. My Answer to them is always ready: I believe no such Things. My Adoration of the Author of the Universe is too profound and too sincere. The Love of God and his Creation; delight, Joy, Tryumph, Exultation in my own existence, 'tho but an Atom, a Molecule Organique, in the Universe; are my religion. Howl, Snarl, bite, Ye Calvinistick! Ye Athanasian Divines, if You will. Ye will say, I am no Christian: I say Ye are no Christians: and there the Account is ballanced. Yet I believe all the honest men among you, are Christians in my Sense of the Word.

When I was at Colledge I was a mighty Metaphis[ic]ian. At least I thought myself such; and such Men as Lock, Hemenway, and West thought me so too: for We were forever disputing, though in great good humour.

When I was sworn as an Attorney in 1758, in Boston, 'tho I lived in Braintree; I was in a low state of Health; thought in great danger of a Consumption; living on Milk, Vegetable Pudding and Water. Not an Atom of Meat or a drop of Spirit. My next Neighbour, my Cousin my Friend Dr. Savil was my Physician. He was anxious for me, and did not like to take upon himself the sole Responsability of my recovery. He invited me to a ride. I mounted my Horse and rode with him to Hingham, on a visit to Dr. Ezekiel Hersey, a Physician of great fame: who felt my pulse, looked in my Eyes, heard Savil describe my regimen and course of Medicine; and then pronoun[c]ed his Oracle "Persevere, and as sure as there is a God in Heaven you will recover." He was an everlasting Talker, and ran out, into History, Philosophy Metaphysicks, etc and frequently put questions to me, as if he wanted to sound me, and see if there was any thing in me, besides Hectic fever. I was young, and then very bashful; however saucy I may have sometimes been since. I gave him very modest and very diffident Answers. But when he got upon Metaphysicks, I seemed to feel a little bolder, and ventured into some thing like Argument with him. I drove him up, as I thought, into a Corner, from which he could not escape. Sir, it will follow from what you have now advanced, that the Universe, as distinct from God is both infinite and eternal. "Very true, said Dr. Hearsey: Your inference is just; the Consequence is inevitable; and I believe the Universe to be, both eternal and infinite." Here I was brought up! I was defeated. I was not prepared for this Answer. This was 55 Years ago.

When I was in England from 1785, to 1788 I may say, I was intimate with Dr. Price. I had much conversation with him at his own House, at my houses, and at the houses and Tables of many Friends. In some of our most unreserved Conversations, when We have been alone, he has repeatedly said to me "I am inclined to believe that the Universe, is eternal and infinite. It seems to me that an eternal and infinite Effect, must necessarily flow from an eternal and infinite Cause; and an infinite Wisdom Goodness and Power, that could have been induced to produce a Universe in time, must have produced it from eternity." "It seems to me, the Effect must flow from the Cause."

Now, my Friend Jefferson, suppose an eternal self existent Being existing from Eternity, possessed of infinite Wisdom, Goodness and Power, in absolute total Solitude, Six thousand Years ago, conceiving the benevolent project of creating a Universe! I have no more to say, at present.

It has been long, very long a settled opinion in my Mind that there is now, never will be, and never was but one being who can Understand the Universe. And that it is not only vain but wicked for insects to pretend to comprehend it.

JOHN ADAMS

Adams to Jefferson

Quincy Septr. 15. 1813

DEAR SIR

My last Sheet, would not admit an Observation that was material to my design.

Dr. Price was "inclined to think" that infinite Wisdom and Goodness, could not permit infinite Power, to be inactive, from Eternity: but that, an infinite and eternal Universe, must have necessarily flowed from these Attributes.

Plato's System was "Αγαθος ["good"]" was eternal, Self existent etc. His Ideas, his Word, his Reason, his Wisdom, his Goodness, or in one Word, his "Logos," was omnipotent and produced the Universe from all Eternity.

Now! As far as You and I can understand Hersey, Price and Plato, are they not of one Theory? of one mind? What is the difference? I own, an eternal Solitude of a Self existent Being infinitely wise, powerful and good, is to me, altogether incomprehensible, and incredible. I could as soon believe the Athanasian Creed.

You will ask me "What conclusion, I draw from all this?" I answer, I drop into myself, and acknowledge myself to be a Fool. No Mind, but one, can see through, the immeasurable System. It would be Presumption and Impiety in me to dogmatize, on such Subjects. My duties, in my little infinitessimal Circle I can understand and feel. The Duties of à Son, a Brother, a Father, a Neighbour, a Citizen, I can see and feel: But I trust the Ruler with his Skies.

Si quid novisti rectius, istis

Candidus imperti, si non, his Utere mecum.[66]

This World is a mixture of the Sublime and the beautiful, the base and contemptible, the whimsical and ridiculous, (According to our narrow Sense; and triffling Feelings). It is a Riddle and an Enigma. You need not be surprised then, if I should descen[d] from these Heights, to an egregious Trifle. But, first let me say. I asked you in a former Letter, how far advanced We were in the Science of Aristocracy, since Theognis's Stalions Jacks and Rams? Have not Chancellor Livingston and Major General Humphreys introduced an hereditary Aristocracy of Merino Sheep? How shall We get rid of this Aristocracy? It is intailed upon Us forever. And an Aristocracy of Land Jobbers and Stock jobbers, is equally and irremediably entailed upon Us, to endless generations.

Now for the Odd; the whimsical; the frivolous. I had scarcely sealed my last Letter to you, upon Theognis's doctrine of well born, Stallions, Jacks and Rams; when they brought me from the Post Office a Packett, without Post Mark, without Letter, without name date or place. Nicely sealed, was a printed Copy of Eighty or Ninety Pages in large full Octavo,[67] intitled

Section first

Aristocracy. I gravely composed my risible Muscles and read it through. It is, from beginning to End an Attack upon me by name for the doctrines of Aristocracy in my 3 Volumes of "Defence" etc. The Conclusion of the whole is that an Aristocracy of Bank Paper, is as bad as the Nobility of France or England. I, most assuredly will not controvert this point, with this man. Who he is, I cannot conjecture: The Honourable John Taylor of Virginia, of all men living or dead first Occurred to me.

Is it Oberon? Is it queen Mab, that reigns and sports with Us little Beings? I thought my Books as well as myself were forgotten. But behold! I am to become a great Man in my expiring moments. Theognis and Plato,

---

66. "If you know anything better than these maxims, candidly share them; if not, with me adopt these." Horace, *Epistulae*, 1. 6. 67.

67. John Taylor, *An Inquiry into the Principles and Policy of the Government of the United States* ... (Fredericksburg, Va., 1814), first conceived in 1794 as an answer to JA's *Defence of the Constitutions of the United States*. Taylor denied the existence of a "natural aristocracy" and maintained that democracy was endangered by consolidation and the creation of an aristocracy of "paper and patronage." Charles A. Beard, *Economic Origins of Jeffersonian Democracy* (N. Y., 1915), Chap. XI.

and Hersey, and Price and Jefferson and I, must go down to Posterity together; and I know not, upon the whole, where to wish for better company. I wish to add Vanderkemp, who has been here to see me, after an interruption of 24 Years. I could and ought to add many others but the Catalogue would be too long. I am, as ever,

JOHN ADAMS

P. S. Why is Plato associated with Theognis etc? Because no Man ever expressed so much terror of the Power of Birth. His Genius could invent no remedy or precaution against it; but a Community of Wives; a confusion of Families, a total extinction of all Relations of Father, Son and Brother. Did the French Revolutionists contrive much better, against the influence of Birth?

Abigail Adams to Jefferson

Quincy Sepbr 20th 1813

DEAR SIR

Your kind and Friendly Letter found me in great affliction for the loss of my dear and only daughter, Mrs. Smith.

She had been with me only three weeks having undertaken a journey from the State of N. York, desirious once more to see her parents, and to close her days under the paternal roof.

She was accompanied by her son and daughter, who made every exertion to get her here, and gratify which seemed the only remaining wish she had, so helpless and feeble a state as she was in. It is wonderfull how they accomplished it. Two years since, she had an opperation performed for a cancer in her breast. This she supported, with wonderfull fortitude, and we flatterd ourselves that the cure was effectual, but it proved otherways. It soon communicated itself through the whole mass of the Blood, and after severe sufferings, terminated her existance.

You sir, who have been called to seperations of a similar kind, can sympathize with your bereaved Friend. I have the consolation of knowing that the Life of my dear daughter was pure, her conduct in prosperity and adversity, exemplary, her patience and resignation becomeing her religion. You will pardon by [i.e., my] being so minute, the full Heart loves to pour out its sorrows, into the Bosom of sympathizing Friendship.

A lively only daughter of her Mother, lives to console me.

"who in her youth, has all that Age required"
"And with her prudence, all that youth admired"

You called upon me to talk of myself, and I have obeyed the summons from the assurrance you gave me, that you took an interest in what ever affected my happiness.

> "Greif has changed me since you saw me last,
> "And carefull hours, with times deformed hand"
> "hath written strange defections o'er my face"

But altho, time has changed the outward form, and political "Back wounding calumny" for a period interrupted the Friendly intercourse and harmony which subsisted, it is again renewed, purified from the dross.

With this assurance I beg leave to subscribe myself your Friend

ABIGAIL ADAMS

Adams to Jefferson

Quincy Septr. 22 1813

DEAR SIR

Considering all things, I admire Dr. Priestleys last Effort for which I am entirely indebted to you. But as I think it is extreamly imperfect, I beg of you to pursue the investigation, according to your promise to Dr. Rush, and according to your Syllabus. It may be presumptuous in me to denominate any Thing of Dr. Priestley imperfect: but I must avow, that among all the vast Exertions of his Genius, I have never found one, that is not imperfect; and this last is egregiously so. I will instance at present in one Article. I find no notice of Cleanthes: one of whose Sayings alone ought to have commanded his Attention. He compared "Philosophers to Instruments of Musick, which made a Noise, without Understanding it, or themselves." He was ridiculed by his Brother Philosophers, and called "An Ass". He owned, he was the "Ass of Zeno: and the only one whose back and Shoulders were stout enough to carry his Burthens." Why has not Priestley, quoted more from Zeno, and his Disciples? Were they too Christian? though he lived two Centuries and an half before Christ?

If I did not know, it would be sending Coal to Newcastle, I would, with all my dimness of Eyes and trembling of Fingers copy in Greek the Hymn of Cleanthes and request you to compare it, with any Thing of Moses of David of Soloman.

Instead of those ardent oriental Figures, which are so difficult to understand We find that divine Simplicity, which constitutes the Charm of Grecian Eloquence in prose and verse.

Pope had read, if Priestley had not, the

ΚΛΕΑΝΘΟΥΣ ΥΜΝΟΣ ΕΙΣ ΔΙΑ

Κύδιστ' ἀθανάτων, πολυώνυμε, παγκρατὲς αἰεὶ
Ζεῦ, φύσεως ἀρχηγὲ, νόμου μέτα πάντα κυβερνῶν
Χαῖρε.

"Most glorious of immortal beings! though denominated by innumerable names and titles, always omnipotent,! Beginning and End of Nature! governing the Universe by fixed Laws! Blessed be thy name!" What think you, of this translation? Is it too Jewish? or too Christian? Pope did not think it was either: for the first Sentence in his Universal prayer is more Jewish and more christian still. If it is not a litteral translation, it is a close paraphrase, of this Simple Verse of Cleanthes.

> Father of all! in every Age,
> In every clime ador'd
> By Saint by Savage and by Sage
> Johovah, Jove, or Lord.[68]

But it may be said, for it has been said, that Pope, was a Deist and Swift too, as well as Bolingbroke. What will not Men say? But is the Existence, the Omnipotence, the Eternity, the Alpha and Omega, and the Universal Providence of one Supream Being, governing by fixed Laws, asserted by St John in his Gospel, or in the Apocalypse, whether his or not, in clearer or more precise terms?

Can you conjecture, a reason why Grotius has not translated this Hymn? Were Grotius and Priestley both afraid that The Stoicks would appear too much like Unitarian Jews and Christians.

Duport has translated, the Sentence thus

> Magne Pater Divum, cui nomina multa, Sed una
> Omnipotens semper Virtus, tu Jupiter Auctor
> Naturæ, certa qui singula lege gubernas,
> Rex, Salve!

Bougainville, has translated it

> Pere, et Maitre des Dieux, Auteur de la Nature,
> Jupiter, O Sagesse! O loi sublime et pure!
> Unite souveraine a qui tous les mortels
> Sous mille noms divers elevent des Autels;

68. These are the opening lines from Pope's "The Universal Prayer"; Norman Ault and John Butt, eds., *Alexander Pope, Minor Poems* (London and New Haven, 1954), 145.

Je t'adore, nos coeurs te doivent leur homage,
Nous sommes tes enfans, ton ombre, ton image:
Et tout ce qui respire animé par tes mains,
A celébrer ta gloire invite les humains.
Beni sois a jamais!

I am so aukward in Italian, that I am ashamed to quote that Language to you: but Pompeius a Gentleman of Verona, h[as] translated it thus: and you will understand it.

O glorioso fra gli eterni, in guise
Molte nomato, onnipossente ognora,
Tu che, tutto con legge governando,
De la natura sei principio e duce,
Salve, O Giove.

It appears to me, that the great Principle of the Hebrews was the *Fear* of God; that of the Gentiles, *Honour* the Gods, that of Christians, the *Love* of God. Could the quiveration of my nerves and the inflammation of my Eyes be cured and my Age diminished by 20 or 30 Years: I would attend you in these researches, with infinitely more Pleasure, than I would be George the 4th. Napoleone, Alexander, or Madison. But only a few Hours; a few moments remain for Your Old Friend

JOHN ADAMS

Adams to Jefferson

Quincy Sept. [i.e., Oct. 4] 1813

Σὲ γὰρ πάντεσσι θέμις θνητοῖσι προσαυδᾶν

"It is not only permitted but enjoined upon all Mortals to address you". Why should not our Divines translate it
"It is our duty and our priviledge to address the Throne of thy grace and pray for all needed lawfull Blessings temporal and spiritual."
Θεμις was the Goddess of honesty, Justice, Decency, and right; the Wife of Jove, another name for Juno. She presided over all oracles, deliberations and Counsells. She commanded all Mortals to pray to Jupiter, for all lawful Benefits and Blessings.
Now, is not this, (so far forth) the Essence of Christian devotion? Is not this Christian Piety? Is it not an Acknonowledgement [sic] of the

existence of a Supream Being? of his universal Providence? of a righteous Administration of the Government of the Universe? And what can Jews, Christians or Mahometans do more?

Priestley, the heroic Priestley, would not have dared to answer or to ask these questions; tho' he might have answered them, consistently enough with the Spirit of his System.

I regret that Grotius has not translated this Hymn: and cannot account for his Omission of it. Duport translates, the above line, only by "Te nempe licet mortalibus ægris cunctis compellare." Where he finds his ægris ["sick"], I know not. No such Idea, is in the greek. All Mortalls, sick or well, have a right and it is their duty to pray, as far as I can understand the Greek.

Bougainville translates it

["]Et tout ce qui respire animé par tes mains, à celebrer tu gloire, invite les humains. Beni sois a jamais." This translation is Christian with a witness. None but a Jew, a Mahometan or a Christian, could ever have translated that simple line in this manner. Yet the Idea, the Sentiment translated into Christianity is very well: well enough.

The Gentleman of Verona Gironomo Pompei, translates it thus. After Salve O Giove, for "Χαῖρε." "pero che gli nomin tutte, dritto è ben, che a te volgan le parole." Now tell me, what resemblance of the Greek you can find in this Italian Version.

In this manner are the most ancient Greek Theologians rendered and transmitted to our Youth, by the Christians.

Ἐκ σοῦ γὰρ γένος ἐσμὲν, ἰῆς μίμημα λαχόντες
Μοῦνον, ὅσα ζώει τε καὶ ἔρπει θνήτ' ἐπὶ γαῖαν. [69]

I presume is the phrase quoted by Saint Paul, when he says to the Atheneans, "One of your own Poets have said We are all his Offspring." Acts. 17th. 28. "For in him We live and move and have our being; as certain also of your own Poets have said, for We are also his Offspring." "Forasmuch then as We are the Offspring of God, We ought not to think that the Godhead is like unto Silver or Gold, or Stone graven by Mans device." This reasoning is irresistable. For what can be more mad, than to represent the eternal almighty omnipresent Cause and Principle of the Universe, by Statues and Pictures, by Coins or Medals?

Duport renders these two lines by "Omnes tua namque Propago

Nos sumus, æternæ quasi imago vocis et echo
Tantum, quotquot humi spirantes repimus."

69. "For we are of your race, being only a copy of your voice,
How ever many a mortal lives or creeps on the earth."

Bougainville translates them thus

> Nous sommes tes enfans, ton Ombre ton image:
> Et tout ce qui respire animé par tes mains,
> A celebrer ta gloire invite les humains.
> Beni sois a jamais.

Pompei renders them

> Che siam tua Stirpe, e solo noi, fra quanti
> Vivon mortali e muovon su la terra,
> Lo imitar de la voce abbiam sortito.

Moses says, Genesis. 1. 27. ["]God created man in his own image." What then is the difference between Cleanthes and Moses? Are not the Being and Attributes of the Supream Being: The Resemblance, the Image the Shadow of God in the Intelligence, and moral qualities of Man, and the Lawfulness and duty of Prayer, as clear[l]y asserted by Cleanthes as by Moses? And did not the Chaldeans, the Egyptians the Persians the Indians, the Chinese, believe all this, as well as the Jews and Greeks?

Alexander appears to have behaved to the Jews, as Napoleon did to the Mahometans in the Pyramid of Grand Cairo. Ptolomy the greatest of his Generals, and a greater Man than himself was so impressed with what he learned in Judea, that he employed 70 learned Men to translate the Hebrew Scriptures into Greek, nearly 300 Years before Christ. He sent learned Men to collect Books from all Nations and deposited them in the Alexandrian Library. Will any Man make me believe that Caesar that Pompey, that Cicero, that Seneca, that Tacitus, that Dionisius Hallicarnarnassensis, that Plutarch, had never seen nor heard of the Septuagint? Why, might not Cleanthes, have seen the Septuagint? [70] The Curiosity of Pompey to see, the interiour of the temple shews that the System of the Jews, was become an Object of Speculation. It is impossible to believe, that the Septuagint, was unknown and unheard of by Greeks or Romans at that time, at least by the great Generals Orators Historians Phylosophers and Statesmen, who looked through the then known World, for information of every thing. On the other hand how do We know how much Moses Samuel Joshua David Solomon and Esdrass, Daniel Ezekiel, Isaiah and Jeremiah learned in Babilon Egypt and Persia? The Destruction of the Library at Alexandria, is all the Answer We can obtain to these Questions. I believe that Jews Grecians Romans and Christians all conspired, or connived At that Savage Catastrophy.

---

70. C. A. Muses, ed., *The Septuagint Bible . . . in the Translation of Charles Thomson, Secretary of the Continental Congress . . . 1774-1789* (Indian Hills, Colorado, 1954), xviii-xxiv.

I believe Cleanthes to be as good a Christian as Priestley.

But enough of my School Boy criticisms and crude Philosophy, problematical History and heretical Divinity for the present.

JOHN ADAMS

Jefferson to Adams

Monticello Oct. 12. 13.

DEAR SIR

Since mine of Aug. 22. I have recieved your favors of Aug. 16. Sep. 2. 14. 15. and—and Mrs. Adams's of Sep. 20. I now send you, according to your request a copy of the Syllabus. To fill up this skeleton with arteries, with veins, with nerves, muscles and flesh, is really beyond my time and information. Whoever could undertake it would find great aid in Enfield's judicious abridgment of Brucker's history of Philosophy, in which he has reduced 5. or 6. quarto vols. of 1000. pages each of Latin closely printed, to two moderate 8 vos. [octavos] of English, open, type.

To compare the morals of the old, with those of the new testament, would require an attentive study of the former, a search thro' all it's books for it's precepts, and through all it's history for it's practices, and the principles they prove. As commentaries too on these, the philosphy of the Hebrews must be enquired into, their Mishna, their Gemara, Cabhala, Jezirah, Sohar, Cosri, and their Talmud must be examined and understood, in order to do them full justice. Brucker, it should seem, has gone deeply into these Repositories of their ethics, and Enfield, his epitomiser, concludes in these words. 'Ethics were so little studied among the Jews, that, in their whole compilation called the Talmud, there is only one treatise on moral subjects. Their books of Morals chiefly consisted in a minute enumeration of duties. From the law of Moses were deduced 613. precepts, which were divided into two classes, affirmative and negative, 248 in the former, and 365 in the latter. It may serve to give the reader some idea of the low state of moral philosophy among the Jews in the Middle age, to add, that of the 248. affirmative precepts, only 3. were considered as obligatory upon women; and that, in order to obtain salvation, it was judged sufficient to fulfill any one single law in the hour of death; the observance of the rest being deemed necessary, only to increase the felicity of the future life. What a wretched depravity of sentiment and manners must have prevailed before such corrupt maxims could have obtained credit! It is impossible to collect from these writings a consistent series of moral Doctrine.' Enfield, B. 4. chap. 3. It was the reformation of this 'wretched depravity' of morals which Jesus undertook. In extracting the pure principles which he taught, we should have to strip off the artificial vestments in which they have been muffled by priests, who have travestied them into various forms, as instruments of riches and power to them. We must dismiss the Platonists and Plotinists, the Stagyrites and Gamalielites, the Eclectics the Gnostics and Scholastics, their essences and emanations, their Logos and Demi-urgos, Aeons and Daemons male and female, with a long train of Etc. Etc. Etc. or, shall I say at once, of Nonsense. We must reduce our volume to the simple evangelists, select, even from them, the very words only of Jesus, paring off the Amphibologisms into which they have been led by forgetting often, or not understanding, what had fallen from him, by giving their own misconceptions as his dicta, and expressing unintelligibly for others what they had not understood themselves. There will be found remaining the most sublime and benevolent code of morals which has ever been offered to man. I have performed this operation for my own use, by cutting verse by verse out of the printed book, and arranging, the matter which is evidently his, and which is as easily distinguishable as diamonds in a dunghill. The result is an 8vo. [octavo] of 46. pages of pure and unsophisticated doctrines,[71] such as were professed and acted on by the *unlettered* apostles, the Apostolic fathers, and the Christians of the 1st. century. Their Platonising successors indeed, in after times, in order to legitimate the corruptions which they had incorporated into the doctrines of Jesus, found it necessary to disavow the primitive Christians, who had taken their principles from the mouth of Jesus himself, of his Apostles, and the Fathers cotemporary with them. They excommunicated their followers as heretics, branding them with the opprobrious name of Ebionites or Beggars.

For a comparison of the Graecian philosophy with that of Jesus, materials might be largely drawn from the same source. Enfield gives a history, and detailed account of the opinions and principles of the different sects. These relate to

the gods, their natures, grades, places and powers;

the demi-gods and daemons, and their agency with man;

the Universe, it's structure, extent, production and duration;

the origin of things from the elements of fire, water, air and earth;

the human soul, it's essence and derivation;

the summum bonum and finis bonorum; with a thousand idle dreams and

71. The Philosophy of Jesus of Nazareth (text in Randall, *Jefferson*, III, 654-55), which TJ was planning as early as 1804; see TJ to Priestley, Jan. 29, 1804, Ford, VIII, 294, and Rush to TJ, Aug. 29, 1804, Butterfield, ed., *Letters of Rush*, II, 886. In 1819 or later TJ prepared the more elaborate The Life and Morals of Jesus of Nazareth Extracted textually from the Gospels in Greek, Latin French and English. See Introduction by Cyrus Adler to facsimile edn. [Washington, 1904], 12-18.

fancies on these and other subjects the knolege of which is withheld from man, leaving but a short chapter for his moral duties, and the principal section of that given to what he owes himself, to precepts for rendering him impassible, and unassailable by the evils of life, and for preserving his mind in a state of constant serenity.

Such a canvas is too broad for the age of seventy, and especially of one whose chief occupations have been in the practical business of life. We must leave therefore to others, younger and more learned than we are, to prepare this euthanasia for Platonic Christianity, and it's restoration to the primitive simplicity of it's founder. I think you give a just outline of the theism of the three religions when you say that the principle of the Hebrew was the fear, of the Gentile the honor, and of the Christian the love of God.

An expression in your letter of Sep. 14. that 'the human understanding is a revelation from it's maker' gives the best solution, that I believe can be given, of the question, What did Socrates mean by his Daemon? He was too wise to believe, and too honest to pretend that he had real and familiar converse with a superior and invisible being. He probably considered the suggestions of his conscience, or reason, as revelations, or inspirations from the Supreme mind, bestowed, on important occasions, by a special superintending providence.

I acknolege all the merit of the hymn of Cleanthes to Jupiter, which you ascribe to it. It is as highly sublime as a chaste and correct imagination can permit itself to go. Yet in the contemplation of a being so superlative, the hyperbolic flights of the Psalmist may often be followed with approbation, even with rapture; and I have no hesitation in giving him the palm over all the Hymnists of every language, and of every time. Turn to the 148th. psalm, in Brady and Tate's version.[72] Have such conceptions been ever before expressed? Their version of the 15th. psalm is more to be esteemed for it's pithiness, than it's poetry. Even Sternhold,[73] the leaden Sternhold, kindles, in a single instance, with the sublimity of his original, and expresses the majesty of God descending on the earth, in terms not unworthy of the subject.

'The Lord descended from above   And bowed the heav'ns most high;
And underneath his feet he cast   The darkness of the sky.
On Cherubim and Seraphim   Full royally he rode;
And on the wings of mighty winds   Came flying all abroad.[']

Psalm xviii. 9. 10.

72. N. Tate and N. Brady, *A New Version of the Psalms of David, Fitted to the Tunes in Churches* (London, 1696, and later edns.).

73. Thomas Sternhold, J. Hopkins, and others, *The Whole Book of Psalmes Collected into Englysche Meter* (London, 1564, and later edns.).

The Latin versions of this passage by Buchanan and by Johnston,[74] are but mediocres. But the Greek of Duport [75] is worthy of quotation.

Ουρανον αγκλινας κατεβη· ὑπο ποσσι δ' ἐοισιν
Αχλυς αμφι μελαινα χυθη και νυξ ερεβεννη.
Ριμφα ποτᾶτο Χερουβῳ οχευμενος, ωσπερ εφ' ἱππῳ.
῾Ιπτατο δε πτερυγεσσι πολυπλαγκτου ανεμοιο.

The best collection of these psalms is that of the Octagonian dissenters of Liverpool, in their printed Form of prayer; but they are not always the best versions. Indeed bad is the best of the English versions; not a ray of poetical genius having ever been employed on them. And how much depends on this may be seen by comparing Brady and Tate's XVth. psalm with Blacklock's Justum et tenacem propositi virum ["a man just and steadfast of purpose"] of Horace, quoted in Hume's history, Car. 2. ch. 65. A translation of David in this style, or in that of Pompei's Cleanthes, might give us some idea of the merit of the original. The character too of the poetry of these hymns is singular to us. Written in monostichs, each divided into strophe and antistrophe, the sentiment of the 1st. member responded with amplification or antithesis in the second.

On the subject of the Postscript of yours of Aug. 16. and of Mrs. Adams's letter, I am silent. I know the depth of the affliction it has caused, and can sympathise with it the more sensibly, inasmuch as there is no degree of affliction, produced by the loss of those dear to us, which experience has not taught me to estimate. I have ever found time and silence the only medecine, and these but assuage, they never can suppress, the deep-drawn sigh which recollection for ever brings up, until recollection and life are extinguished together. Ever affectionately yours

TH: JEFFERSON

P.S. Your's of Sep—just recieved

74. George Buchanan, ed., *Psalmorum Davidis paraphrasis poetica*, nunc primum edita (Paris, 1566); Arthur Johnston, *Paraphrasis poetica Psalmorium Davidis* (Aberdeen, 1637).

75. James Duport, Δαβιδης Ἐμμετρος, *sive metaphrasis libri Psalmorum Graecis versibus contexta* (London, 1712).

Jefferson to Adams

Monticello Oct. 28. 13.

DEAR SIR

According to the reservation between us, of taking up one of the subjects of our correspondence at a time, I turn to your letters of Aug. 16. and Sep. 2.

The passage you quote from Theognis, I think has an Ethical, rather than a political object. The whole piece is a moral *exhortation,* παραίνεσις, and this passage particularly seems to be a reproof to man, who, while with his domestic animals he is curious to improve the race by employing always the finest male, pays no attention to the improvement of his own race, but intermarries with the vicious, the ugly, or the old, for considerations of wealth or ambition. It is in conformity with the principle adopted afterwards by the Pythagoreans, and expressed by Ocellus in another form. Περι δε τῆς ἐκ τῶν αλληλων ανθρωπων γενεσεως etc.— ουχ ἡδονης ἐνεκα ἡ μιξις. Which, as literally as intelligibility will admit, may be thus translated. 'Concerning the interprocreation of men, how, and of whom it shall be, in a perfect manner, and according to the laws of modesty and sanctity, conjointly, this is what I think right. First to lay it down that we do not commix for the sake of pleasure, but of the procreation of children. For the powers, the organs and desires for coition have not been given by god to man for the sake of pleasure, but for the procreation of the race. For as it were incongruous for a mortal born to partake of divine life, the immortality of the race being taken away, god fulfilled the purpose by making the generations uninterrupted and continuous. This therefore we are especially to lay down as a principle, that coition is not for the sake of pleasure.' But Nature, not trusting to this moral and abstract motive, seems to have provided more securely for the perpetuation of the species by making it the effect of the oestrum implanted in the constitution of both sexes. And not only has the commerce of love been indulged on this unhallowed impulse, but made subservient also to wealth and ambition by marriages without regard to the beauty, the healthiness, the understanding, or virtue of the subject from which we are to breed. The selecting the best male for a Haram of well chosen females also, which Theognis seems to recommend from the example of our sheep and asses, would doubtless improve the human, as it does the brute animal, and produce a race of veritable αριστοι ["aristocrats"]. For experience proves that the moral and physical qualities of man, whether good or evil, are transmissible in a certain degree from father to son. But I suspect that the equal rights of men will rise up against this privileged Solomon, and oblige us to continue acquiescence under the Ἀμαυρωσις γενεος ἀστων ["the degeneration of the race of men"] which Theognis complains of, and to content ourselves with the accidental aristoi produced by the fortuitous concourse of breeders. For I agree with you that there is a natural aristocracy among men. The grounds of this are virtue and talents. Formerly bodily powers gave place among the aristoi. But since the invention of gunpowder has armed the weak as well as the strong with missile death, bodily strength, like beauty, good humor, politeness and other accomplishments, has become but an auxiliary ground of distinction. There is also an artificial aristocracy founded on wealth and birth, without either virtue or talents; for with these it would belong to the first class. The natural aristocracy I consider as the most precious gift of nature for the instruction, the trusts, and government of society. And indeed it would have been inconsistent in creation to have formed man for the social state, and not to have provided virtue and wisdom enough to manage the concerns of the society. May we not even say that that form of government is the best which provides the most effectually for a pure selection of these natural aristoi into the offices of government? The artificial aristocracy is a mischievous ingredient in government, and provision should be made to prevent it's ascendancy. On the question, What is the best provision, you and I differ; but we differ as rational friends, using the free exercise of our own reason, and mutually indulging it's errors. *You* think it best to put the Pseudo-aristoi into a separate chamber of legislation where they may be hindered from doing mischief by their coordinate branches, and where also they may be a protection to wealth against the Agrarian and plundering enterprises of the Majority of the people. I think that to give them power in order to prevent them from doing mischief, is arming them for it, and increasing instead of remedying the evil. For if the coordinate branches can arrest their action, so may they that of the coordinates. Mischief may be done negatively as well as positively. Of this a cabal in the Senate of the U. S. has furnished many proofs. Nor do I believe them necessary to protect the wealthy; because enough of these will find their way into every branch of the legislation to protect themselves. From 15. to 20. legislatures of our own, in action for 30. years past, have proved that no fears of an equalisation of property are to be apprehended from them.

I think the best remedy is exactly that provided by all our constitutions, to leave to the citizens the free election and separation of the aristoi from the pseudo-aristoi, of the wheat from the chaff. In general they will elect the real good and wise. In some instances, wealth may corrupt, and birth blind them; but not in sufficient degree to endanger the society.[76]

It is probable that our difference of opinion may in some measure be produced by a difference of character in those among whom we live. From what I have seen of Massachusets and Connecticut myself, and still more from what I have heard, and the character given of the former by your-self, [vol. 1. pa. 111.] [77] who know them so much better, there seems to be in those two states a traditionary reverence for certain families, which has rendered the offices of the government nearly hereditary in those families. I presume that from an early period of your history, members of these families happening to possess virtue and talents, have honestly exercised them for the good of the people, and by their services have endeared their names to them.

In coupling Connecticut with you, I mean it politically only, not morally. For having made the Bible the Common law of their land they seem to have modelled their morality on the story of Jacob and Laban. But altho' this hereditary succession to office with you may in some degree be founded in real family merit, yet in a much higher degree it has pro-ceeded from your strict alliance of church and state. These families are canonised in the eyes of the people on the common principle 'you tickle me, and I will tickle you.' In Virginia we have nothing of this. Our clergy, before the revolution, having been secured against rivalship by fixed salaries, did not give themselves the trouble of acquiring influence over the people. Of wealth, there were great accumulations in particular families, handed down from generation to generation under the English law of entails. But the only object of ambition for the wealthy was a seat in the king's council. All their court then was paid to the crown and it's crea-tures; and they Philipised in all collisions between the king and people. Hence they were unpopular; and that unpopularity continues attached to their names. A Randolph, a Carter, or a Burwell must have great personal superiority over a common competitor to be elected by the people, even at this day.

At the first session of our legislature after the Declaration of Inde-pendance, we passed a law abolishing entails. And this was followed by one abolishing the privilege of Primogeniture, and dividing the lands of intestates equally among all their children, or other representatives. These laws, drawn by myself, laid the axe to the root of Pseudo-aristocracy. And had another which I prepared been adopted by the legislature, our work

76. The foregoing is TJ's most explicit statement concerning natural aristocracy. Cf. his "Autobiography," Ford, I, 49-50, 68-69.
77. TJ's note, referring to JA's *Defence.*

would have been compleat. It was a Bill for the more general diffusion of learning.[78] This proposed to divide every county into wards of 5. or 6. miles square, like your townships; to establish in each ward a free school for reading, writing and common arithmetic; to provide for the annual selection of the best subjects from these schools who might recieve at the public expence a higher degree of education at a district school; and from these district schools to select a certain number of the most promising subjects to be compleated at an University, where all the useful sciences should be taught. Worth and genius would thus have been sought out from every condition of life, and compleatly prepared by education for defeating the competition of wealth and birth for public trusts.

My proposition had for a further object to impart to these wards those portions of self-government for which they are best qualified, by confiding to them the care of their poor, their roads, police, elections, the nomination of jurors, administration of justice in small cases, elementary exercises of militia, in short, to have made them little republics, with a Warden at the head of each, for all those concerns which, being under their eye, they would better manage than the larger republics of the county or state. A general call of ward-meetings by their Wardens on the same day thro' the state would at any time produce the genuine sense of the people on any required point, and would enable the state to act in mass, as your people have so often done, and with so much effect, by their town meetings. The law for religious freedom,[79] which made a part of this system, having put down the aristocracy of the clergy, and restored to the citizen the freedom of the mind, and those of entails and descents nurturing an equality of condition among them, this on Education would have raised the mass of the people to the high ground of moral respectability necessary to their own safety, and to orderly government; and would have compleated the great object of qualifying them to select the veritable aristoi, for the trusts of government, to the exclusion of the Pseudalists: and the same Theognis who has furnished the epigraphs of your two letters assures us that 'ουδεμιαν πω, Κυρν' αγαθοι πολιν ωλεσαν ανδρες ["Curnis, good men have never harmed any city"]'. Altho' this law has not yet been acted on but in a small and inefficient degree, it is still considered as before the legislature, with other bills of the revised code, not yet taken up, and I have great hope that some patriotic spirit will, at a favorable moment, call it up, and make it the key-stone of the arch of our government.

78. "A Bill for the More General Diffusion of Knowledge," No. 79 in the "Catalogue of Bills Prepared by the Committee of Revisors," Boyd, II, 526-35 and *n*.

79. "An ACT for establishing RELIGIOUS FREEDOM, passed in the Assembly of Virginia in the beginning of the year 1786," in TJ, *Notes on the State of Virginia*, ed. by Peden (1955), 223-25.

With respect to Aristocracy, we should further consider that, before the establishment of the American states, nothing was known to History but the Man of the old world, crouded within limits either small or over-charged, and steeped in the vices which that situation generates. A govern-ment adapted to such men would be one thing; but a very different one that for the Man of these states. Here every one may have land to labor for himself if he chuses; or, preferring the exercise of any other industry, may exact for it such compensation as not only to afford a comfortable subsistence, but wherewith to provide for a cessation from labor in old age. Every one, by his property, or by his satisfactory situation, is inter-ested in the support of law and order. And such men may safely and ad-vantageously reserve to themselves a wholsome controul over their public affairs, and a degree of freedom, which in the hands of the Canaille of the cities of Europe, would be instantly perverted to the demolition and de-struction of every thing public and private. The history of the last 25. years of France, and of the last 40. years in America, nay of it's last 200. years, proves the truth of both parts of this observation.

But even in Europe a change has sensibly taken place in the mind of Man. Science had liberated the ideas of those who read and reflect, and the American example had kindled feelings of right in the people. An insurrection has consequently begun, of science, talents and courage against rank and birth, which have fallen into contempt. It has failed in it's first effort, because the mobs of the cities, the instrument used for it's accomplishment, debased by ignorance, poverty and vice, could not be restrained to rational action. But the world will recover from the panic of this first catastrophe. Science is progressive, and talents and enterprize on the alert. Resort may be had to the people of the country, a more govern-able power from their principles and subordination; and rank, and birth, and tinsel-aristocracy will finally shrink into insignificance, even there. This however we have no right to meddle with. It suffices for us, if the moral and physical condition of our own citizens qualifies them to select the able and good for the direction of their government, with a recurrence of elections at such short periods as will enable them to displace an un-faithful servant before the mischief he meditates may be irremediable.

I have thus stated my opinion on a point on which we differ, not with a view to controversy, for we are both too old to change opinions which are the result of a long life of inquiry and reflection; but on the suggestion of a former letter of yours, that we ought not to die before we have ex-plained ourselves to each other. We acted in perfect harmony thro' a long and perilous contest for our liberty and independance. A constitution has been acquired which, tho neither of us think perfect, yet both consider as competent to render our fellow-citizens the happiest and the securest on whom the sun has ever shone. If we do not think exactly alike as to it's imperfections, it matters little to our country which, after devoting to it long lives of disinterested labor, we have delivered over to our successors in life, who will be able to take care of it, and of themselves.

Of the pamphlet on aristocracy which has been sent to you, or who may be it's author, I have heard nothing but thro' your letter. If the person you suspect [80] it may be known from the quaint, mystical and hyperbolical ideas, involved in affected, new-fangled and pedantic terms, which stamp his writings. Whatever it be, I hope your quiet is not to be affected at this day by the rudeness of intemperance of scribblers; but that you may continue in tranquility to live and to rejoice in the prosperity of our country until it shall be your own wish to take your seat among the Aristoi who have gone before you. Ever and affectionately yours.

TH: JEFFERSON

P.S. Can you assist my memory on the enquiries of my letter of Aug. 22.?

Adams to Jefferson

Quincy November 12. 1813

DEAR SIR

As I owe you more for your Letters of Oct. 12. and 28 than I shall be able to pay, I shall begin with the P.S. to the last.

I am very sorry to say, that I cannot "assist your memory in the Enquiries of your letter of August 22d." I really know not who was the compositor of any one of the Petitions or Addresses you enumerate. Nay farther I am certain I never did know. I was so shallow a polititian, that I was not aware of the importance of those compositions. They all appeared to me, in the circumstances of the Country like childrens play at marbles or push pin, or rather like misses in their teens emulating each other in their pearls, their braceletts their Diamond Pins and brussells lace.

In the Congress of 1774 there was not one member, except Patrick Henry, who appeared to me sensible of the Precipice or rather the Pinnacle on which he stood, and had candour and courage enough to acknowledge it. America is in total Ignorance, or under infinite deception concerning that Assembly. To draw the characters of them all would require a volume and would now be considered as a caracatura print. One third Tories, another Whigs and the rest mongrels.

80. John Taylor of Caroline.

There was a little Aristocracy, among Us, of Talents and Letters. Mr. Dickinson was primus inter pares; the Bell Weather; the leader of the Aristocratical flock. Billy, alias Governor Livingstone, and his Son in law Mr. Jay, were of this priviledged order. The credit of most if not all those compositions was often if not generally given to one or the other of these choice Spirits. Mr. Dickenson however was not on any of the original Committees. He came not into Congress till Oct. 17. He was not appointed till the 15th by his Assembly. [*Journals of Congress, containing Their Proceedings*] Vol. 1. 30. Congress adjourned 27. Oct. though our correct Secretary has not recorded any final Adjournment or dissolution. Mr. Dickenson was in Congress but ten days. The business was all prepared arranged and even in a manner finished before his Arrival.

R. H. Lee was the Chairman of the Committee for preparing "the loyal and dutiful Address to his Majesty." Johnson and Henry were acute Spirits and understood the Controversy very well; though they had not the Advantages of Education like Lee and John Rutledge. The Subject had been near a month under discussion in Congress and most of the materials thrown out there. It underwent another deliberation in committee; after which they made the customary compliment to their Chairman, by requesting him to prepare and report a draught, which was done, and after examination, correction, amelioration or pejoration, as usual reported to Congress. Oct. 3. 4. and 5th were taken up in debating and deliberating on matters proper to be contained in the Address to his Majesty. Vol. 1. 22. October 21. The Address to the King was after debate recommitted and Mr. John Dickenson added to the Committee. The first draught was made and all the essential materials put together by Lee, it might be embellished and seasoned Afterward with some of Mr. Dickenson piety; but I know not that it was. Neat and handsome as the composition is, having never had any confidenc[e] in the Utility of it, I never have thought much about it since it was adopted. Indeed I never bestowed much Attention on any of those Addresses; which were all but repetitions of the same Things: the same facts and Arguments. Dress and ornament rather than Body, Soul or Substance. My thoughts and cares were nearly monopolized by the Theory of our Rights and Wrongs, by measures for the defence of the country; and the means of governing our Selves.
Please to turn over [to see N. B. at end of letter].

I was in a great Error, no doubt, and am ashamed to confess it; for those things were necessary to give Popularity to Our cause both at home and abroad. And to shew my Stupidity in a stronger light the reputation of any one of those compositions, has been a more splendid distinction than any aristocratical Starr or garter, in the Escutchion of every man who has enjoyed it. Very sorry that I cannot give you more Satisfactory information, And more so that I cannot at present give more Attention to your two last excellent Letters I am as Usual affectionately yours

JOHN ADAMS

N.B. I am almost ready to believe that John Taylor of Caroline, or of Hazel Wood Port Royal, Virginia, is the Author of 630 pages of printed Octavo, upon my Books, that I have received. The Style answers every characteristic, that you have intimated.

Within a Week I have received, and looked into his Arator.[81] They must spring from the same brain as Minerva issued from the head of Jove; or rather as Venus rose from the froth of the Sea.

There is however a great deal of good Sense in Arator. And there is some in his "Aristocracy."

Adams to Jefferson

Quincy Nov. 14. 1813

DEAR SIR

Accept my thanks for the comprehensive Syllabus, in your favour of Oct. 12.

The Psalms of David, in Sublimity beauty, pathos and Originality, or in one Word, in poetry, are superiour to all the Odes Hymns and Songs in any language. But I had rather read them in our prose translation, than in any version I have seen. His Morality, however, often shocks me, like Tristram Shandy's execrations.

Blacklocks translation of Horace's "Justum" is admirable; superiour to Addisons. Could David be translated as well; his Superiority would be universally acknowledged. We cannot compare the Sybbiline Poetry. By Virgils Pollio [82] we may conjecture, there was Prophecy as well as Sublimity. Why have those Verses been annihilated? I suspect platonick Christianity, pharisaical Judaism, or machiavilian Politicks, in this case; as in all other cases of the destruction of records and litterary monuments. The Auri sacra fames, et dominandi sæva cupido.[83]

81. *Arator; Being a Series of Agricultural Essays, Practical and Political:* in Sixty-one Numbers. By a Citizen of Virginia (Georgetown, D.C., 1813), explaining Taylor's methods of scientific agriculture.

82. The phrasing of Virgil's Pollio (Fourth Eclogue) parallels that of Isaiah, chapter 11. This similarity, along with its contents, led the early Church fathers to believe that Virgil prophesied the birth of Christ.

83. "The horrible hunger of gold, and the savage lust of power." Virgil, *Aen.,* III, 57.

Among all your researches in Hebrew History and Controversy have you ever met a book, the design of which is to prove, that the ten Commandments, as We have them in our Catechisms and hung up in our Churches, were not the Ten Commandments written by the Finger of God upon tables, delivered to Moses on mount Sinai and broken by him in a passion with Aaron for his golden calf, nor those afterwards engraved by him on Tables of Stone; but a very different Sett of Commandments?

There is such a book by J. W. Goethens Schristen.[84] Berlin 1775-1779. I wish to see this Book.

You will see the Subject and perceive the question in Exodus 20. 1-17. 22-28. chapter 24. 3 etc. ch. 24. 12. ch. 25. 31 ch. 31. 18. ch. 31. 19. ch. 34. 1. ch. 34. 10 etc.

I will make a Covenant with all this People. Observe that which I command this day.

1

Thou shall not adore any other God. Therefore take heed, not to enter into covenant, with the Inhabitants of this country; neither take for your Sons, their daughters in marriage. They would allure thee to the Worship of false Gods. Much less shall you in any place, erect Images.

2

The Feast of unleavened bread, shall thou keep. Seven days, shall thou eat unleavened bread, at the time of the month Abib; to remember that about that time, I delivered thee from Egypt.

3

Every first born of the mother is mine; the male of thine herd, be it Stock or flock. But you shall replace the first born of an Ass with a Sheep. The first born of your Sons shall you *redeem*. No Man shall appear before me with empty hands.

4

Six days shall thou labour: the seventh day, thou shall rest from ploughing and gathering.

84. JA misread the *f* in *Schriften* for a long *s* and took the title for part of the author's name (*Goethens* was a possessive form already obsolescent). One of the earliest collected editions of Goethe's *Writings*, unauthorized by him, was first issued by C. F. Himberg in 3 vols. (Berlin, 1775). A fourth volume (1779) included two tracts on religious subjects, in part an early application of historical criticism to the Old Testament. The derivation of JA's translation of Goethe's selection from Exodus 34: 10-27 has not been determined.

5

The Feast of Weeks shall thou keep, with the firstlings of the Wheat Harvest: and the Feast of Harvesting, at the end of the year.

6

Thrice, in every year, all male persons shall appear before the Lord. Nobody shall invade your Country, as long as you obey this Command.

7

Thou shall not sacrifice the blood of a Sacrifice of mine, upon leavened bread.

8

The Sacrifice of the Passover shall not remain, till the next day.

9

The Firstlings of the produce of your land, thou shall bring to the House of the Lord.

10

Thou shall not boil the kid, while it is yet sucking.

And the Lord spake to Moses: Write these Words; as, after these Words I made with you, and with Israel a Covenant.

I know not whether Goethens translated or abridged from the Hebrew, or whether he used any translation Greek, Latin, or German. But he differs in form and Words, somewhat from our Version. Exod. 34. 10. to 28. The Sense seems to be the same. The Tables were the evidence of the covenant, by which the Almighty attached the People of Israel to himself. By these laws they were seperated from all other nations, and were reminded of the principal Epochas of their History.

When and where originated our Ten Commandments? The Tables and The Ark were lost. Authentic Copies, in few, if any hands; the ten Precepts could not be observed, and were little remembered.

If the Book of Deuteronomy was compiled, during or after the Babilonian Captivity, from Traditions, the Error or Amendment might come in there.

But you must be weary, as I am at present, of Problems, Conjectures, and paradoxes, concerning Hebrew, Grecian and Christian and all other Antiquities; but while We believe that the finis bonorum will be happy, We may leave learned men to this disquisitions and Criticisms.

I admire your Employment, in selecting the Philosophy and Divinity of Jesus and seperating it from all intermixtures. If I had Eyes and Nerves,

I would go through both Testaments and mark all that I understand. To examine the Mishna Gemara Cabbala Jezirah, Sohar Cosri and Talmud of the Hebrews [85] would require the life of Methuselah, and after all, his 969 Years would be wasted to very little purpose. The Dæmon of Hierarchical despotism has been at Work, both with the Mishna and Gemara. In 1238 a French Jew, made a discovery to the Pope (Gregory 9th) of the heresies of the Talmud.[86] The Pope sent 35 Articles of Error, to the Archbishops of France, requiring them to seize the books of the Jews, and burn all that contained any Errors. He wrote in the same terms to the Kings of France, England Arragon, Castile Leon, Navarre and Portugal. In consequence of this Order 20 Cartloads of Hebrew Books were burnt in France: and how many times 20 Cartloads were destroyed in the other Kingdoms? The Talmud of Babylon and that of Jerusalem were composed from 120 to 500 Years after the destruction of Jerusalem. If Lightfoot derived Light from what escaped from Gregorys fury in explaining many passages in the New Testament by comparing the Expressions of the Mishna, with those of the Apostles and Evangelists, how many proofs of the Corruptions of Christianity might We find in the Passages burnt?

JOHN ADAMS

Adams to Jefferson

Quincy November 15.13

DEAR SIR

I cannot appease my melancholly commiseration for our Armies in this furious snow storm in any way so well as by studying your Letter of Oct. 28.

We are now explicitly agreed, in one important point, vizt. That "there is a natural Aristocracy among men; the grounds of which are Virtue and Talents."

You very justly indulge a little merriment upon this solemn subject of Aristocracy. I often laugh at it too, for there is nothing in this laughable world more ridiculous than the management of it by almost all the nations of the Earth. But while We smile, Mankind have reason to say to Us, as the froggs said to the Boys, What is Sport to you is Wounds and death

---

85. The principal literary expressions of the Hebrew religion. The Talmud as the main teaching of Judaism was under attack by the Catholic Church from the thirteenth century on and at times copies by the cartload were burned; hence manuscripts of the Talmud are extremely rare.

86. These burnings were ordered under Pope Innocent IV, not Gregory IX.

to Us. When I consider the weakness, the folly, the Pride, the Vanity, the Selfishness, the Artifice, the low craft and meaning cunning, the want of Principle, the Avarice the unbounded Ambition, the unfeeling Cruelty of a majority of those (in all Nations) who are allowed an aristocratical influence; and on the other hand, the Stupidity with which the more numerous multitude, not only become their Dupes, but even love to be Taken in by their Tricks: I feel a stronger disposition to weep at their destiny, than to laugh at their Folly.

But tho' We have agreed in one point, in Words, it is not yet certain that We are perfectly agreed in Sense. Fashion has introduced an indeterminate Use of the Word "Talents." Education, Wealth, Strength, Beauty, Stature, Birth, Marriage, graceful Attitudes and Motions, Gait, Air, Complexion, Physiognomy, are Talents, as well as Genius and Science and learning. Any one of these Talents, that in fact commands or influences true Votes in Society, gives to the Man who possesses it, the Character of an Aristocrat, in my Sense of the Word.

Pick up, the first 100 men you meet, and make a Republick. Every Man will have an equal Vote. But when deliberations and discussions are opened it will be found that 25, by their Talents, Virtues being equal, will be able to carry 50 Votes. Every one of these 25, is an Aristocrat, in my Sense of the Word; whether he obtains his one Vote in Addition to his own, by his Birth Fortune, Figure, Eloquence, Science, learning, Craft Cunning, or even his Character for good fellowship and a bon vivant.

What gave Sir William Wallace his amazing Aristocratical Superiority? His Strength. What gave Mrs. Clark, her Aristocratical Influence to create Generals Admirals and Bishops? her Beauty. What gave Pompadour and Du Barry the Power of making Cardinals and Popes? their Beauty. You have seen the Palaces of Pompadour and Du Barry: and I have lived for years in the Hotel de Velentinois, with Franklin who had as many Virtues as any of them. In the investigation of the meaning of the Word "Talents" I could write 630 Pages, as pertinent as John Taylors of Hazelwood. But I will select a single Example: for female Aristocrats are nearly as formidable in Society as male.

A daughter of a green Grocer, walks the Streets in London dayly with a baskett of Cabbage, Sprouts, Dandlions and Spinage on her head. She is observed by the Painters to have a beautiful Face, an elegant figure, a graceful Step and a debonair. They hire her to Sitt. She complies, and is painted by forty Artists in a Circle around her. The scientific Sir William Hamilton outbids the Painters, sends her to Schools for a genteel Education and Marries her. This Lady not only causes the Tryumphs of the Nile of Copinhagen and Trafalgar, but seperates Naples from France and finally banishes the King and Queen from Sicilly. Such is the Aristocracy of the natural Talent of Beauty. Millions of Examples might be quoted from History sacred and profane, from Eve, Hannah, Deborah Susanna Abigail, Judith, Ruth, down to Hellen Madame de Maintenon and Mrs. Fitcherbert. For mercy's sake do not compell me to look to our chaste States and Territories, to find Women, one of whom lett go, would, in the Words of Holopherne's Guards "deceive the whole Earth."

The Proverbs of Theognis, like those of Solomon, are Observations on human nature, ordinary life, and civil Society, with moral reflections on the facts. I quoted him as a Witness of the Fact, that there was as much difference in the races of Men as in the breeds of Sheep; and as a sharp reprover and censurer of the sordid mercenary practice of disgracing Birth by preferring gold to it. Surely no authority can be more expressly in point to prove the existence of Inequalities, not of rights, but of moral intellectual and physical inqualities in Families, descents and Generations. If a descent from, pious, virtuous, wealthy litterary or scientific Ancestors is a letter of recommendation, or introduction in a Mans his favour, and enables him to influence only one vote in Addition to his own, he is an Aristocrat, for a democrat can have but one Vote. Aaron Burr had 100,000 Votes from the single Circumstance of his descent from President Burr and President Edwards.

Your commentary on the Proverbs of Theognis reminded me of two solemn Charactors, the one resembling John Bunyan, the other Scarron. The one John Torrey: the other Ben. Franklin. Torrey a Poet, an Enthusiast, a superstitious Bigot, once very gravely asked my Brother Cranch, "whether it would not be better for Mankind, if Children were always begotten from religious motives only"? Would not religion, in this sad case, have as little efficacy in encouraging procreation, as it has now in discouraging it? I should apprehend a decrease of population even in our Country where it increases so rapidly. In 1775 Franklin made a morning Visit, at Mrs. Yards to Sam. Adams and John. He was unusually loquacious. "Man, a rational Creature"! said Franklin. "Come, Let Us suppose a rational Man. Strip him of all his Appetites, especially of his hunger and thirst. He is in his Chamber, engaged in making Experiments, or in pursuing some Problem. He is highly entertained. At this moment a Servant Knocks, "Sir dinner is on Table." "Dinner! Pox! Pough! But what have you for dinner?" Ham and Chickens. "Ham"! "And must I break the chain of my thoughts, to go down and knaw a morsel of a damn'd Hogs Arse"? "Put aside your Ham." "I will dine tomorrow."

Take away Appetite and the present generation would not live a month and no future generation would ever exist. Thus the exalted dignity of human Nature would be annihilated and lost. And in my opinion, the whole loss would be of no more importance, than putting out a Candle, quenching a Torch, or crushing a Firefly, *if in this world only We have hope.*

Your distinction between natural and artificial Aristocracy does not appear to me well founded. Birth and Wealth are conferred on some Men, as imperiously by Nature, as Genius, Strength or Beauty. The Heir is honours and Riches, and power has often no more merit in procuring these Advantages, than he has in obtaining an handsome face or an elegant figure. When Aristocracies, are established by human Laws and honour Wealth and Power are made hereditary by municipal Laws and political Institutions, then I acknowledge artificial Aristocracy to commence: but this never commences, till Corruption in Elections becomes dominant and uncontroulable. But this artificial Aristocracy can never last. The everlasting Envys, Jealousies, Rivalries and quarrells among them, their cruel rapacities upon the poor ignorant People their followers, compell these to sett up Caesar, a Demagogue to be a Monarch and Master, pour mettre chacun a sa place ["to put each one in his place"]. Here you have the origin of all artificial Aristocracy, which is the origin of all Monarchy. And both artificial Aristocracy, and Monarchy, and civil, military, political and hierarchical Despotism, have all grown out of the natural Aristocracy of "Virtues and Talents." We, to be sure, are far remote from this. Many hundred years must roll away before We shall be corrupted. Our pure, virtuous, public spirited federative Republick will last for ever, govern the Globe and introduce the perfection of Man, his perfectability being already proved by Price Priestly, Condorcet Rousseau Diderot and Godwin.

"Mischief has been done by the Senate of U.S." I have known and felt more of this mischief, than Washington, Jefferson and Madison altoge[the]r. But this has been all caused by the constitutional Power of the Senate in Executive Business, which ought to be immediately, totally and eternally abolished.

Your distinction between the aristoi and pseudo aristoi, will not help the matter. I would trust one as soon as the other with unlimited Power. The Law wisely refuses an Oath as a witness in his own cause to the Saint as well as to the Sinner.

No Romance would be more amusing, than the History of your Virginian and our new England Aristocratical Families. Yet even in Rhode Island, where there has been no Clergy, no Church, and I had almost said, no State, and some People say no religion, there has been a constant respect for certain old Families. 57 or 58 years ago, in company with Col. Counsellor, Judge, John Chandler, whom I have quoted before, a Newspaper was brought in. The old Sage asked me to look for the News from Rhode Island and see how the Elections had gone there. I read the List of

Wantons, Watsons, Greens, Whipples, Malbones etc. "I expected as much" said the aged Gentleman, "for I have always been of Opinion, that in the most popular Governments, the Elections will generally go in favour of the most ancient families." To this day when any of these Tribes and We may Add Ellerys, Channings Champlins etc are pleased to fall in with the popular current, they are sure to carry all before them.

You suppose a difference of Opinion between You and me, on the Subject of Aristocracy. I can find none. I dislike and detest hereditary honours, Offices Emoluments established by Law. So do you. I am for ex[c]luding legal hereditary distinctions from the U.S. as long as possible. So are you. I only say that Mankind have not yet discovered any remedy against irresistable Corruption in Elections to Offices of great Power and Profit, but making them hereditary.

But will you say our Elections are pure? Be it so; upon the whole. But do you recollect in history, a more Corrupt Election than that of Aaron Burr to be President, or that of De Witt Clinton last year. By corruption, here I mean a sacrifice of every national Interest and honour, to private and party Objects.

I see the same Spirit in Virginia, that you and I see in Rhode Island and the rest of New England. In New York it is a struggle of Family Feuds. A fewdal Aristocracy. Pensylvania is a contest between German, Irish and old English Families. When Germans and Irish Unite, they give 30,000 majorities. There is virtually a White Rose and a Red Rose a Caesar and a Pompey in every State in this Union and Contests and dissentions will be as lasting. The Rivalry of Bourbons and Noailleses produced the French Revolution, and a similar Competition for Consideration and Influence, exists and prevails in every Village in the World.

Where will terminate the Rabies Agri ["madness for land"]? The Continent will be scattered over with Manors, much larger than Livingstons, Van Ranselaers or Phillips's. Even our Deacon Strong will have a Principality among you Southern Folk. What Inequality of Talents will be produced by these Land Jobbers?

Where tends the Mania for Banks? At my Table in Philadelphia, I once proposed to you to unite in endeavours to obtain an Amendment of the Constitution, prohibiting to the separate States the Power of creating Banks; but giving Congress Authority to establish one Bank, with a branch in each State; the whole limited to Ten Millions of dollars. Whether this Project was wise or unwise, I know not, for I had deliberated little on it then and have never thought it worth thinking much of since. But you spurned the Proposition from you with disdain.

This System of Banks begotten, hatched and brooded by Duer, Robert and Governeur Morris, Hamilton and Washington, I have always considered as a System of national Injustice. A Sacrifice of public and private Interest to a few Aristocratical Friends and Favourites. My scheme could have had no such Effect.

Verres plundered Temples and robbed a few rich Men; but he never made such ravages among private property in general, nor swindled so much out of the pocketts of the poor and the middle Class of People as these Banks have done. No people but this would have borne the Imposition so long. The People of Ireland would not bear Woods half pence. What Inequalities of Talent, have been introduced into this Country by these Aristocratical Banks!

Our Winthrops, Winslows, Bradfords, Saltonstalls, Quincys, Chandlers, Leonards Hutchinsons Olivers, Sewalls etc are precisely in the Situation of your Randolphs, Carters and Burwells, and Harrisons. Some of them unpopular for the part they took in the late revolution, but all respected for their names and connections and whenever they fall in with the popular Sentiments, are preferred, cetoris paribus to all others. When I was young, the Summum Bonum in Massachusetts, was to be worth ten thousand pounds Sterling, ride in a Chariot, be Colonel of a Regiment of Militia and hold a seat in his Majesty's Council. No Mans Imagination aspired to any thing higher beneath the Skies. But these Plumbs, Chariots, Colonelships and counsellorships are recorded and will never be forgotten. No great Accumulations of Land were made by our early Settlers. Mr. Bausoin a French Refugee, made the first great Purchases and your General Dearborne, born under a fortunate Starr is now enjoying a large Portion of the Aristocratical sweets of them.

As I have no Amanuenses but females, and there is so much about generation in this letter that I dare not ask any one of them to copy it, and I cannot copy it myself I must beg of you to return it to me, your old Friend

JOHN ADAMS

Adams to Jefferson

Quincy Decr. 3. 13

DEAR SIR

The Proverbs of the old greek Poets, are as short and pithy as any of Solomon or Franklin. Hesiod has several. His

Αθανατως μεν πρωτα θωες νομω ως διακειται τιμα.

Honour the Gods established by Law. I know not how We can escape Martyrdom, without a discreet Attention to this præcept. You have suffered, and I have suffered more than You, for want of a strict if not a due Observance of this Rule.

There is another Oracle of this Hesiod, which requires a kind of dance upon a tight rope, and a slack rope too, in Philosophy and Theology.

πιστεις δ'ἄρα ὁμῶς κ' απιστιας ὥλεσαν ανδρας.[87]

If believing too little or too much, is so fatal to Mankind what will become of Us all?

In studying the Perfectability of human Nature and its progress towards perfection, in this World, on this Earth, (remember that) I have met many curious things, and interesting Characters.

About three hundred Years ago, There appeared a number of Men of Letters, who appeared to endeavour to believe neither too little, nor too much. They laboured to imitate the Hebrew Archers who could shoot to an hairs breadth. The Pope and his Church believed too much: Luther and his Church believed too little. This little band was headed by three great Scholars, Erasmus, Vives, and Budeus. This Triumvirate is said to have been at the head of the Republick of Letters, in that Age. Had Condorcet been Master of his Subject, I fancy he would have taken more Notice in his History of the progress of Mind, of these Characters. Have you their Writings? I wish I had. I shall confine myself at present to Vives. He wrote Commentaries on the City of God of St. Augustine, some parts of which were censured by the Doctors of the Louvain as too bold and too free. I know not, whether the following passage of the learned Spaniard was among the Sentiments condemned, or not.

"I have been much afflicted," says Vives, "when I have seriously considered, how diligently, and with what exact care, the Actions of Alexander, Hannibal, Scipio Pompey, Caesar and other Commanders: and the Lives of Socrates Plato Aristotle, and other Phylosophers, have been written and fixed in an everlasting Remembrance, so that there is not the least danger they can ever be lost: but then the Acts of the Apostles and Martyrs and Saints of our religion and of the Affairs of the rising and established Church, being involved in much darkness, are almost totally unknown, though they are of so much greater Advantage, than the Lives of the Phylosophers, or great Generals, both as to the improvement of our knowledge and Practice. For, what is written of these holy men, except a very few things is very much corrupted and defaced, with the mixture of many fables; while the Writer, indulging his own humour, doth not tell Us what the Saint did, but what the Historian would have had him done:

87. "Ah, faith and likewise faithlessness have destroyed men."

and the fancy of the Writer dictates the Life and not the truth of things."
And again, Vives says

"There have been men, who have thought it a great piece of Piety, to invent Lies for the sake of religion."

The great Cardinal Barronius too, confesses "There is nothing, which seems so much neglected to this day, as a true and certain Account of the Affairs of the Church, collected with an exact diligence. And that I may speak of the more Ancient, it is very difficult to find any of them, who have published Commentaries on this Subject which have hit the truth in all points."

Canus, too another Spanish Prelate of great name says "I speak it with grief, and not by way of reproach, Laertius has written the lives of the Philosophers, with more care and industry, than the Christians have those of the Saints; Suetonius has represented the Lives of the Caesars with much more truth and sincerity, than the Catholicks have the Affairs, I will not say of the Emperors, but even those of the Martyrs, holy Virgins and Confessors. For they have not concealed the Vices nor the very Suspicions of Vice, in good and commendable Philosophers or Princes, and in the worst of them, they discover the very colours or Appearances of Virtue. But the greatest part of our Writers, either follow the Conduct of their Affections, or industriously fain many things; so that I, for my part am very often both weary and ashamed of them; because I know they have thereby brought nothing of Advantage to the Church of Christ, but very much inconvenience."

Vives and Canus are Moderns, but Arnobius the Converter of Lactantius was ancient. He says "But neither could all that was done be written or arrive at the knowledge of all men. Many of our great Actions being done by obscure Men, and those who had no knowledge of Letters: and if some of them are committed to Letters and Writings; yet even here, by the malice of the Devils, and of men like them, whose great design and Study it is to intercept and ruin this truth, by interpolating, or adding some things to them, or by changing or taking out Words, Syllables, or Letters, they have put a Stop to the Faith of wise Men, and corrupted the truth of things."

Indeed, Mr. Jefferson, what could be invented to debase the ancient Christianism, which Greeks Romans, Hebrews, and Christian Factions, above all the Catholicks, have not fraudulently imposed upon the Publick? Miracles after Miracles have rolled down in Torrents, Wave succeeding Wave, in the Catholic Church from the Council of Nice, and long before, to this day. Aristotle, no doubt, thought his οὔτε πᾶσα πιστευοντες, οὔτε πασιν ἀπιστοῦντες [88] very wise and very profound: but what is its Worth? What Man, Woman or Child, ever believed, every Thing, or nothing?

Oh! that Priestley could live again! and have leisure and means. An Enquirer after Truth, who had neither time nor means might request him to search and research for answers to a few Questions.

1. Have We more than two Witnesses of the Life of Jesus? Mathew and John?
2. Have We one Witness to the Existence of Mathews Gospel in the first Century?
3. Have We one Witness of the Existence of Johns Gospell in the first Century?
4. Have We one Witness of the Existence of Marks Gospell in the first Century?
5. Have We one Witness of the Existence of Lukes Gospell in the first Century?
6. Have We any Witness of the existence of St. Thomas's Gospell, that is the Gospell of the Infancy in the first Century?
7. Have We any Evidence of the Existence of the Acts of the Apostles in the first Century?
8. Have We any Evidence of the Existence of the Supplement to the Acts of the Apostles, Peter and Paul, or Paul and Tecle, in the first Century?

Here I was interrupted, by a new book, Chataubriands Travels in Greece Palestine and Egypt [89] and by a Lung Fever, with which the amiable Companion [of] My Life has been violently And dangerously attacked.

December   13. I have fifty more questions to put to Priestley: but must adjourn them to a future Opportunity.

I have read Chateaubriand, with as much delight, as I ever read Bunyan['s] Pilgrims Progress, Robinson Crusoes Travels or Gullivers; or Whitefields; or Westleys Life; or the Life of St. Francis, St. Anthony or St. Ignatius Loyaula. A Work of infinite Learning, perfectly well written, a Magazine of Information: but an enthusiastic, biggotted, superstitious Roman Catholic throughout. If I were to indulge in jealous criticism and Conjecture, I should suspect, that there had been an Œcuemenical Counsel of Pope Cardinals and Bishops, and that this Traveller has been employed at their expence, to make this tour, to lay a foundation for the resurrection of the Catholic Hierarchy in Europe.

88. "Neither trusting all things nor distrusting all."
89. *Itineraire de Paris à Jerusalem et de Jerusalem à Paris; en allant par la Grèce et revenant par l'Egypte, la Barbarie et l'Espagne*, 3 vols. (Paris, 1811).

Have you read La Harpes Course de Litterature, in 15. Volumes? have you read St. Pierres Studies of Nature?

I am now reading the Controversy between Voltaire and Nonotte.[90]

Our Friend Rush has given Us for his last Legacy, an Analysis of some of the diseases of the Mind. Johnson said We are all more or less mad; and who is or has been more mad than Johnson?

I know of no Philosopher, or Theologian, or Moralist ancient or modern more profound; more infallible than Whitefield, if the Anecdote that I have heard be true.

He began; "Father Abraham"! with his hands and Eyes gracefully directed to the Heavens as I have more than once seen him; "Father Abraham," "who have you there with you"? ["]have you Catholicks?" No. "Have you Protestants". No. "Have you Churchmen". No. "Have you Dissenters". No. "Have you Presbyterians"? No. "Quakers?" No. ["]Anabaptists"? No. "Who have you then?" "Are you alone"? No.

"My Brethren,! You have the Answer to all these questions in the Words of my Text, "He who feareth God and worketh Righteousness, shall be accepted of him."

Allegiance to the Creator and Governor of the Milky Way and the Nebulae, and Benevolence to all his Creatures, is my Religion. Si quid novisti rectius estis [i.e., istis], Candidus imperti.[91] I am as ever

JOHN ADAMS

Adams to Jefferson

Quincy December 19. 1813

DEAR SIR

Ridendo dicere Verum, quid vetat.[92] I must make you and myself merry or melancholly by a little more Phylosophical Speculation about the formidable Subject of Aristocracy.

Not long after General Dearborn's return to Boston from the Army, a violent Alarm was excited and spread in Boston and through the country, by a report at first only secretly whispered in private circles that an Affair of Love was commencing between the General and Madam Bowdoin, the

90. Voltaire's *L'Essai sur les moeurs* (1754-58) versus Nonnette's *Erreurs de Voltaire* (1762), and Voltaire's rebuttal: *Eclaircissements historiques* (1763).
91. "If you know anything better than these maxims, candidly share them." Horace, *Epistulae*, 1. 6. 67.
92. "What forbids a man to speak the truth by joking?" Horace, *Sermones*, 1. 1. 24.

virtuous and amiable relict of my Friend and your Ambassador, James Bowdoin. The Surprise, the astonishment, were universal and the indignation very general. The exclamations were in every mouth. "Impossible!" "It cannot be!" "It is a false report." "It is too bad!" "It is a scandalous fiction!" "It is a malicious Calumny against Mrs. Bowdoin!" "Would that Lady disgrace her Husband?" She was herself a Bowdoin: "Would she degrade her own and her Husbands Name and Blood?" "Would she disgrace the illustrious Name of Bowdoin which has been so long famous in France?" "Would she disgrace her Husband who has been an Ambassador? And her Father in Law, who was her Uncle, and had been Governor?"

This is no exaggeration. I have heard all these exclamations. Have you read Cecilia,[93] or the Scottish Chiefs? [94] Is there any thing in the Character of the Delville Family, or in any of the Scotch Thanes, more outrageously Aristocratical, than these popular Sentiments in this our Democratical Country?

I undertook like a genuine Knight Errant to be the Champion of the Lady: and said some things very shocking to some Companies. To some very grave Ladies I said "Why, Madam, if Mrs. Bowdoins Object is Love and domestic comfort, the General is an healthy, robust and personable Man, which her former Husband was not. If her Object is Ambition, She will advance her Degree and condition by this Alliance; for neither Governors nor Ambassadors nor Earls hold so high a Rank as a Secretary at War and Commander in Chief, of all the Armies of a great Nation. Her Object cannot be Wealth, for She has enough; but if it was, Collectorships and other Offices must have given the General a Competency."

Till very lately the French descent of the Bowdoins has been known to very few and never boasted by any body. But it has been published and proclaimed by Mr. William Jenks, Secretary to the Board of Trustees of Bowdoin Colledge in his Eulogy on Mr. Bowdoin. This Eulogy Mrs. Bowdoin, I presume has sent to You as well as to me. If not, I will send you an extract.

The Race of Baudouins it is true has long been notable in France. The Name I believe is to be found among the Crusaders to Jerusalem, when, no doubt, they were Orthodox Catholicks: but afterwards, in the Crusades against the Albigenses, they were suspected on both Sides. In all the Seiges and in all the battles, there were many Nobles and Cavaliers among the Sectaries. The Counts De Foix, De Comminges, De Besiers, De Bearn, and almost all the Lords who inhabited towards the Pyrennes, were of the Sect, or at least favoured and protected it. The Count de Thoulouse, without de-

93. Fanny Burney, *Cecilia, or Memoirs of an Heiress,* 5 vols. (London, 1782).
94. Jane Porter, *The Scottish Chiefs,* 5 vols. (N. Y., 1810).

claring himself a Manichean (so they called the Albigenses as well as the Waldenses) had for the Sect and for their Preachers a respect which bordered on extravagance, and laid the foundation of all the misfortunes of his princely house. Baudouin, Brother of the Count de Thoulouse, was hanged on a Tree by the Hereticks, notwithstanding the Tenderness of the Family for them, and though he begged for time to confess and receive the Communion.

The Count de Thoulouse (Baudouin) acted a mysterious part. Though he protested his orthodox faith, yet he obstinately protected the Hereticks. He made Promisses, but could not determine to fullfill them. The Pope innocent the third, interrested himself in his favour, and arrested, for some time, the Proceedings of the Legates against him. But he knew not how to take Advantage of these dispositions. Without Firmness, without Wisdom, without Prudence, he could not conquer the secret Inclination he had for Heresy; nor foresee that he was commencing the misfortunes of his Family; nor that the Ambition of the neighbouring Potentate, would soon compleat its destruction. A Miracle, it seems, was wrought for the destruction of this Family. Simon de Monfort with only Eight hundred Men, and One Thousand Fantassins, attacked the Army of the King of Arragon and the Count de Thoulouse, which was of one hundred thousand men, and totally defeated them.

This I learn from Nonotte, the Scourge of Voltaire, whom Voltaire scourges in his turn with a long Catalog of "Sottises." This is however but a ray of the historical Glory of the name. Baudoin the eighth Count of Flanders was Emperor of Constantinople in 1204. Baudouin the 2d. was the last latin Emperor of Constantinople in 1228. A Baudouin was King of Jerusalem in the 12th. Century and Saladin or Noraddin his Enemy said he had not left his equal. The name has been distinguished in Lettres as well as in War and Politicks. A Baudouin was solicited by Henry 3, then Duke of Anjou, to write in Justification of the Massacre of St. Bartholemy. But he was too honest a man. Another Baudouin, who died in 1650 translated all the Classicks and wrote many other Things.

All these litterary, civil, political, millitary, religious, noble, royal and imperial honours are now to be devolved on the Bowdoin Family of Massachusetts. But the name is extinct in the male line. To repair this breach a law of the State has been procured to alter the Name of a Sisters Son from Temple to Bowdoin, and to him the Family Estate is given. Sir John Temple, too, the Father of that Son, has poured a Stream of English noble blood into the mighty river of Bawdoin. A splendid Funeral Sermon of Mr. Gardner has been printed: "On the Death of Elizabeth Lady Temple." The name of Bowdoin is immortalized, by a flourishing University founded by the Family. You have immortalized the Name by making an Ambassador of it, and by making a Cousin another Ambassador.

Do you call this natural or artificial Aristocracy? Aristocracy it is most certainly, for the Name of Bowdoin in this State has more influence than the name of Russell or Howard has in England. So have the names of Livingston and Clinton in New York. We had a General Sterling, but that Title would not satisfy. He must be called Lord Sterling, and his Daughter "Lady Kitty Duer." Our Russell Family wear the Arms, and claim Relation to the Dukes of Bedford. Our Quincys are descended from Saer de Quincy, Marquis of Winchester, who extorted Magna Charta from King John, and whose Signature to that Instrument, "Sayer de Winton," you have seen in the British Musæum and in Blacstones Copy. General Talmadge of Connecticutt is by Law a Member of the British House of Peers. And who knows but We may have Lord and Ladies Yrujo's from Spain and Lord and Ladies Mansfields from Great Britain? Aristocracy, like Waterfowl, dives for Ages and then rises with brighter Plumage. It is a subtle Venom that diffuses itself unseen, over Oceans and Continents, and tryumphs over time. If I could prevent its deleterious influence I would put it all into "The Hole" of Calcutta: [95] but as this is impossible, as it is a Phœnix that rises again out of its own Ashes, I know no better Way than to chain it in a "Hole by itself," and place a Watchfull Centinel on each Side of it.

An hundred other foreign Aristocracies have sown and are sowing their Seeds in this Country: and We have an Abundance of them springing up in this Country not from Virtues and Talents so much as from Banks and Land Jobbing. I am as ever Yours

JOHN ADAMS

Adams to Jefferson

Quincy Decr. 25th. 1813

DEAR SIR

Answer my Letters at Your Leisure. Give yourself no concern. I write as for a refuge and protection against Ennui.

The fundamental Principle of all Phylosophy and all Christianity is "REJOICE ALWAYS IN ALL THINGS. Be thankfull at all times for all good and all that We call evil." Will it not follow, that I ought to rejoice and be

95. The narrow prison into which the Nawab of Bengal threw his European prisoners in July 1756. Most of them perished by suffocation.

thankful that Priestley has lived? Aye! that Voltaire has lived? [96] That Gibbon has lived? That Hume has lived, though a conceited Scotchman? That Bolingbroke has lived, tho' a haughty arrogant supercilious Dogmatist? that Burke and Johnson have lived, though superstitious Slaves or Self deceiving Hypocrites both. Is it not laughable to hear Burke call Bolingbroke a superficial Writer? To hear him ask "Who ever read him through?" Had I been present I would have answered him "I, I, myself, I have read him through, more than fifty Years ago, and more than five times in my Life, and once within five Years past. And in my Opinion the epithat "Superficial" belongs to you and your Friend Johnson more than to him. I might say much more. But I believe Burke and Johnson to have been as political Christians, as Leo 10th.

I return to Priestley, though I have great Complaints against him for personal Injuries and Persecution, at the same time that I forgive it all, and hope and pray that he may be pardoned for it all, above. Dr. Broklesby an intimate Friend and convivial Companion of Johnson told me, that Johnson died in Agonies of Horror of Annihilation, and all the Accounts We have of his death corroborate this Account of Broklesby. Dread of Annihilation! Dread of Nothing? A dread of Nothing I should think would be no dread at all. Can there be any real substantial rational fear of nothing? Were you on your deathbed, and in your last moments informed by demonstration or Revelation that you would cease to think and to feel at your dissolution, should you be terrified? You might be ashamed of yourself for having lived so long, to bear the proud Mans Contumely. You might be ashamed of your Maker, and compare him to a little Girl amusing herself her Brothers and Sisters by blowing Bubbles in Soap Sudds. You might compare him to Boys sporting with Crakers and Rocketts: or to Men employed in making more artificial Fire Works; or to Men and Women at Farces and Operas, or Sadlers Wells Exploits; or to Politicians in their Intrigues; or to Heroes in their Butcheries; or to Popes in their Devilisms. But what should you fear? Nothing. Emori nolo Sed me mortuum esse nihil estimo. [97]

To return to Priestley. You could make a more luminous Book, than his upon "the Doctrines of Heathen Phylosophers compared with those of Revelation." Why has he not given Us a more satisfactory Account of the Pythagorean Philosophy and Theology? He barely names Ocellus, who lived long before Plato. His Treatise of Kings and Monarchy has been destroyed, I conjecture by Platonic Phylosophers, Platonic Jews or Chris-

96. JA's marginal note: "I should have given my Reason for rejoicing in Voltaire etc. It is because I believe they have done more than Even Luther or Calvin, to lower the Tone of that proud Hierarchy that shot itself up above the Clouds, and more to propagate religious Liberty than Calvin or Luther, or even lock [i.e., Locke]."
97. "I have no wish to die, but that I be dead and considered as nothing."

tians, or by fraudulent Republicans or Despots. His Treatise of "The Universe["] has been preserved. He labours to prove the Eternity of the World. The Marquiss D'Argens translated it, in all its noble Simplicity. The Abby Batteux has since given another translation. D'Argens not only explains the Text, but sheds more light upon the antient Systems. His remarks are so many Treatisses, which devellop the concatenation of antient Opinions. The most essential Ideas of the Theology, of the Physics and of the Morality of the antients are clearly explained: and their different Doctrines, compared with one another, and with the modern discoveries. I wish I owned this Book and 100,000 more that I want every day, now when I am almost incapable of making any Use of them. No doubt he informs Us that Pythagoras was a great Traveller.

Priestley barely mentions Timaeus: but it does not appear that he had read him. Why has he not given Us an Account of him and his Book? He was before Plato and gave him the Idea of his Timæus, and much more of his Phylosophy. After his Master he maintained the existence of Matter: that Matter was capable of receiving all sorts of forms: that a moving Power agitatated all the Parts of it: and that an Intelligence directed the moving Power; that this Intelligence produced a regular and harmonious World. This Intelligence had seen a Plan, an *Idea* (Logos) in conformity to which, it wrought, and without which it would not have known what it was about, nor what it wanted to do. This Plan was the *Idea*, Image or Model, which had represented, to the Supream Intelligence, the World before it existed, which had directed it, in its Action upon the moving Power, and which it contemplated in forming the Elements the Bodies and the World. This Model was distinguished from The Intelligence which produced the World as the Architect is from his plans. He divided, The productive Cause of the World into a Spirit, which directed the moving Force, and into an Image, which determined it in the choice of the directions which it gave to the moving Force, and the forms which it gave to matter.

I wonder that Priestley has overlooked this because it is the same Phylosophy with Plato's and would have shewn that the Pythagorean as well as the Platonic Phylosophers probably concurred in the fabrication of the Christian Trinity. Priestley mentions the name of Archytas, but does not appear to have read him; tho he was a Sucessor of Pythagoras, and a great Mathematician, a great Statesman and a great General. John Gram a learned and honourable Dane has given a handsome Edition of his Works with a latin translation, and an ample Account of his Life and Writings. Saleucus The Legislator of Locris and Charondas of Sybaris were Disciples of Pythagoras, and both celebrated to immortality for the Wisdom of their Laws, 500 Years before Christ. Why are those Laws lost?

I say *the Spirit of Party* has destroyed them, civil, political and ecclesiastical Bigotry. Despotical, monarchical Aristocratical and democratical Fury, have all been employed in this Work of destruction of every Thing that could give Us true light and a clear insight of Antiquity. For every One of these Parties, when possessed of Power, or when they have been Undermost and Struggling to get Uppermost, has been equally prone to every Species of fraud and Violence, and Usurpation.

Why has not Priestley mentioned these Legislators? The Preamble to the Laws of Zaleucus, which is all that remains, is as orthodox Christian Theology as Priestleys: and Christian Benevolence and forgiveness of Injuries almost as clearly expressed.

Priestley ought to have done impartial Justice to Philosophy and Phylosophers, Phylosophy which is the result of Reason, is the first, the original Revelation of The Creator to his Creature, Man. When this Revelation is clear and certain, by Intuition or necesary Induction, no subsequent Revelation supported by Prophecies or Miracles can supercede it. Philosophy is not only the love of Wisdom, but the Science of the Universe and its Cause. There is, there was and there will be but one Master of Philosophy in the Universe. Portions of it, in different degrees are revealed to Creatures. Phylosophy looks with an impartial Eye on all terrestrial religions. I have examined all, as well as my narrow Sphere, my streightened means and my busy Life would allow me; and the result is, that the Bible is the best book in the World. It contains more of my little Phylosophy than all the Libraries I have seen: and such Parts of it as I cannot reconcile to my little Phylosophy I postpone for future Investigation.

Priestley ought to have given Us a Sketch of the Religion and Morals of Zoroaster of Sanchoniathon of Confucius, and all the Founders of Religions before Christ, whose superiority, would from such a comparison have appeared the more transcendant.

Priestley ought to have told us, that Pythagoras passed twenty Years, in his Travels in India, in Egypt, in Chaldea, perhaps in Sodom and Gomorrah, Tyre and Sydon. He ought to have told Us that in India he conversed with the Brahmans and read the Shast[r]a,[98] 5000 Years old, written in the Language of the sacred Sanscrists with the elegance and Sentiments of Plato. Where is to be found Theology more orthodox or Phylosophy more profound than in the Introduction to the Shast[r]a? "God is one, creator of all, Universal Sphere, without beginning, without End. God governs all the Creation by a general Providence, resulting from his eternal designs. ——— Search not the Essence and the nature of the Eternal, who

---

98. The shastra, or sastra (treatise), especially that explaining the Vedas, the most ancient sacred literature of the Hindus.

is one; Your research will be vain and presumptuous. It is enough that, day by day, and night by night, You adore his Power, his Wisdom and his Goodness, in his Works." ["]The Eternal willed, in the fullness of time, to communicate of his Essence and of his Splendor, to Beings capable of perceiving it. They as yet existed not. The Eternal Willed, and they were. He created Birma, Vitsnow, and Sib." These Doctrines, sublime if ever there were any sublime, Pythagoras learned in India and taught them to Zaleucus and his other disciples. He there learned also his Metempsychosis, but this never was popular, never made much progress in Greece or Italy, or any other Country besides India and Tartary, the Region of the Grand immortal Lama: And how does this differ, from the Possessions of Demons in Greece and Rome, from the Demon of Socrates from the Worship of Cows and Crocodiles in Egypt and elsewhere. After migrating throw various Animals from Elephants to Serpents according to their behaviour, Souls that at last behaved well became Men and Women, and then if they were good, they went to Heaven. All ended in Heaven if they became virtuous. Who can wonder at the Widow of Malabar. Where is the Lady, who, if he[r] faith were without doubt, that she should go to Heaven with her Husband on the one, or migrate into a Toad or a Waspe on the other, would not lay down on The Pile and set fire to the Fuel? Modifications and disguises of the Metempsichosis had crept into Egypt and Greece and Rome and other Countries. Have you read Farmer on the Dæmons and Possessions of the New Testament?

According to the Shast[r]a, Moisazor, with his Companions rebelled against the Eternal, and were precipitated, down to Ondero, the region of Darkness. Do you know any thing of the Prophecy of Enoch? [99] Can you give me a Comment on the 6th. the 9th. the 14th verses of the Epistle of Jude? [100]

If I am not weary of writing, I am sure you must be of reading such inchoherent rattle. I will not persecute you so severely in future, if I can help it. So farewell

JOHN ADAMS

99. The Book(s) of Enoch, written ca. 170 B.C. to 64 B.C., constitutes an important piece of apocalyptic literature. The Christian Church began to discredit it ca. 300 and it was lost from the ninth century until 1773, when two manuscripts were discovered. They were translated frequently and critical inquiries made into their contents.

100. The Epistle of Jude, verse "6. And the angels which kept not their first estate, but left their own habitation, he hath reserved in everlasting chains, under darkness, unto the judgment of the great day.

"9. Yet Michael the archangel, when contending with the devil, he disputed about the body of Moses, durst not bring against him a railing accusation, but said, The Lord rebuke thee.

"14. And Enoch also, the seventh from Adam, prophesied of these, saying Behold, the Lord cometh with ten thousand of his saints,

"15. To execute judgment upon all. . . ."

11

"The Eighteenth Century...
most honourable to human Nature"

AS PHILOSOPHICAL CITIZENS of the eighteenth century, Adams and Jefferson witnessed the rude shaking and shattering of their world by the Napoleonic Wars. With Europe in turmoil and reactionary forces in the ascendant during the opening decades of the new century, the two American statesmen weighed their own era and found the balance in its favor. In spite of errors and vices, declared Adams, it was "the most honourable to human Nature.... Arts, Sciences useful to Men, ameliorating their condition, were improved, more than in any former equal Period." [1] Jefferson agreed. "I think too we may add, to the great honor of science and the arts, that their natural effect is, by illuminating public opinion, to erect it into a Censor, before which the most exalted tremble for their future, as well as present fame.... You must have observed while in Europe, as I thought I did, that those who administered the governments of the greater powers at least, had a respect to faith, and considered the dignity of their governments as involved in it's integrity." [2]

The American Revolution had become a factor in this civilizing and liberating process, nourishing the revolutionary movement in France which, Jefferson admitted, turned out to be far more bloody than he had expected in 1789. "That same light from our West seems to have spread and illuminated the very engines employed to extinguish it.... The idea of representative government has taken root and growth

1. JA to TJ, Nov. 13, 1815, below, 456.
2. TJ to JA, Jan. 11, 1816, below, 458–59.

among them. . . . Opinion is power, and that opinion will come." [3] Although the science of government had never been much studied, Adams took hope from experiments in constitution-making in America and Europe since 1776 and from the advancement in civil and religious liberties, recalling, no doubt, his own contribution to this great achievement. Realist that he was, however, he could not overlook the low "Morality of Patriotism" that prevailed among nations. All contemporary sovereigns "have acted on the same Principle 'All things were made for my Use.'" Adams scoffed at philosophers and priests in all ages who, expressing belief in the perfectability of human nature, had no respect for Truth.[4]

If Adams and Jefferson agreed that the eighteenth century was an age of progress in science and the arts, including republican government, how did they assess the status of the individual in this class-ridden society? Amid concern over the universal rights of man in the abstract, how well had men in the flesh fared in their pursuit of life, liberty, and happiness? Adams, desiring to get down to specific examples, soon provoked a reply from Jefferson concerning the reliving of his seventy years. "I think with you," Jefferson affirmed, "that it is a good world on the whole, that it has been framed on a principle of benevolence, and more pleasure than pain dealt out to us. . . . How much pain have cost us the evils which have never happened? My temperament is sanguine. I steer my bark with Hope in the head, leaving Fear astern." [5] In contributing toward the good life of his fellow men this philosopher relied on science (accumulated knowledge) to serve practical ends for the benefit of all.

Adams carried the concept a step farther. He was willing to sail in Jefferson's bark because "Hope is all that endures"—the hope of a future and better state. "The Maker of the Universe, the Cause of all Things, whether we call it, *Fate* or *Chance* or *God*, has inspired this Hope. If it is a *Fraud*, We shall never know it." But if death were revealed as eternal extinction, "What would Men say to their Maker? . . . They would reproach him; they would curse him to his Face." [6] To end up with such a conclusion was impossible for Adams. "Why then should We abhor the Word God, and fall in Love with the Word

3. *Ibid.*
4. JA to TJ, July 16, 1814, Feb. 2, 1816, below, 436, 462.
5. JA to TJ, March 2, 1816, and TJ to JA, April 8, 1816, below, 464, 467.
6. JA to TJ, May 3, 1816, below, 471.

Fate?" Such negation was atheism in which Liberty and Spirit and the Universe could have no meaning.[7] Adams rejected this philosophy, which he attributed to Diderot and Voltaire, but found these philosophers no less "restless vain extravagant Animals" than Robespierre and Bonaparte.

As ambassadors who had served in Europe before the storm broke, Adams and Jefferson were intensely interested in Napoleon's meteoric career. During the days of the *ancien régime* they had sought to maintain American neutrality as the cornerstone of foreign policy. While in office President Adams and President Jefferson adhered to this same policy. Personal sympathies aside, they regarded both belligerents as inimical to the United States and they watched for any advantage that the turn of events offered. But their country could not escape the world-wide repercussions of Bonaparte's conquest of the Continent. It precipitated the War of 1812, which brought in its train the threat of disunion by New England's commercial interests, reminding Adams of the Virginia and Kentucky Resolutions of 1798-99. "The Northern States are now retaliating," he exclaimed. "It is a mortification to me, to see how servile Mimicks they are." [8]

How much closer the war seemed to Massachusetts and to Adams than to Virginia and to Jefferson, George Ticknor, a youthful Bostonian of twenty-two, had an unusual opportunity to observe. Seeking a letter of introduction from Adams to Jefferson, he approached Adams through a mutual friend, George Cabot, merchant-banker in the inner circles of New England business interests. At Quincy, in the Adams's parlor, with Mrs. Adams knitting and the awe-struck Ticknor listening, the conversation became a soliloquy by Mr. Adams. He expatiated on the serious condition of the country made worse by the Hartford Convention of malcontents, presided over by Cabot, who, fearful of secession, was providing a moderating influence. Adams was dressed in a tightly buttoned single-breasted coat into which he tried to thrust his hand as his voice became more and more animated. When the buttons did not yield readily, he forced his hand in, exclaiming, "Thank God, thank God! George Cabot's close-buttoned ambition has broke out at last: he wants to be President of New England, sir!" [9]

7. JA to TJ, March 2, 1816, below, 465.
8. JA to TJ, July [3], 1813, above, 350.
9. G. S. Hillard, ed., *Life, Letters, and Journals of George Ticknor* (Boston, 1877), I, 13; JA to TJ, Dec. 11 and 20, 1814, below, 440, 441.

About six weeks later Ticknor was Jefferson's guest at Monticello, along with a fellow Bostonian, Francis C. Gray, and Daniel Webster. In the serene atmosphere of the mountain top they browsed among the seven thousand books which Mr. Jefferson had just sold to the United States—volumes to become the nucleus of a new Library of Congress after the rebuilding of the Capitol which the British had burned. Delighted with his young guests, Jefferson considered Ticknor "the best bibliograph I have met with," [10] and their conversation ranged over many subjects, ancient and modern. Jefferson captivated the young men as he talked freely about the public debt and the expediency of separation of powers in government. And Ticknor recalled an amusing incident concerning the "old philosopher." Late one night Jefferson's grandson brought the newspaper from Charlottesville reporting the defeat of the British by General Jackson in the Battle of New Orleans, but Jefferson, who had gone to bed, was content to wait until morning to read the account.[11]

While the last chapter of the Napoleonic regime was being recorded during the Hundred Days, March to June 1815, Jefferson and Adams from their long-range vantage point expressed mixed feelings about the denouement of the protracted drama. Jefferson had referred to Bonaparte, banished to the island of Elba in 1814, as "the Attila of the age dethroned," a usurper in civil life and no statesman; and Adams castigated him for his vanity, swollen by conquest. Yet these Americans could not forget their long-time foe: was Bonaparte the greater tyrant, they asked, or John Bull, who had never ceased to domineer in the play of power politics? [12]

When Napoleon escaped from Elba and was welcomed back by the French people as deliverer of the nation, Jefferson could rationalize the outcome by saying that the Emperor in his new role was preferable to a Bourbon king. "At least he is defending the cause of his nation," wrote Jefferson, "and that of all mankind, the rights of every people to independance and self-government. . . . We had better take the chance of his word for doing right, than the certainty of the wrong which his adversaries are doing and avowing." Before Jefferson mailed

10. TJ to JA, June 10, 1815, below, 443.
11. Hillard, ed., *Life of Ticknor*, I, 34-38; Francis Calley Gray, *Thomas Jefferson in 1814; being an Account of a Visit to Monticello, Virginia*, ed. by Henry S. Rowe and T. Jefferson Coolidge, Jr. (Boston, 1924), 67-74; Fletcher Webster, ed., *The Private Correspondence of Daniel Webster* (Boston, 1857), I, 304-66.
12. TJ to JA, July 5, 1814, and JA to TJ, July 16, 1814, below, 431, 436.

this letter, he received news of Bonaparte's second abdication. He then added a postscript: "Very well. . . . [The French] have taken the allies at their word, that they had no object in the war but his removal. The nation is now free to give itself a good government, either with or without a Bourbon." [13] Adams hoped that Liberty, Equality, and Fraternity would never again blindly surrender to Ambition, but such was not the prevailing spirit at the Congress of Vienna where reactionary leaders established the peace of 1815. "When," asked Adams, "will the Rights of Mankind, the Liberties and Independence of Nations be respected?" [14]

In passing judgment on the Age of the Enlightenment and the recent cataclysm of Europe, Adams and Jefferson discoursed not only from their own experience but also from a knowledge of history which provided perspective on the near past. They realized that to the younger generation of the early nineteenth century the American Revolution was history in a somewhat different sense from what they as participants regarded it and that the "external facts" which were the sole concern of many of their inquirers fell far short of telling the whole story. These founding fathers were anxious that the American people should profit by a thorough knowledge of the Revolution. An understanding of the origin of the United States would be useful in making them appreciative of republican government. "Who shall write the history of the American revolution? Who can write it?" asked Adams as he found leisure to reflect upon those momentous times.[15] Not John Marshall, whose dull biography of Washington, a "party diatribe," never penetrated the externals. Not the Italian Carlos Botta, who copied too much from other writers, including Marshall. Jefferson had a higher regard for Botta's precision and candor and his "just sense of right in opposition to usurpation"; [16] strangely he overlooked David Ramsay's well-tempered *History of the American Revolution* (1789), although the author had sent him a copy soon after publication.[17] It was disturbing to the reminiscent patriots that young Americans regarded the Revolution and the War for Independence as

13. TJ to JA, Aug. 10[-11], 1815, and TJ to AA, Jan. 11, 1817, below, 454, 503.
14. JA to TJ, Aug. 24, 1815, May 26, 1817, below, 455-56, 517.
15. JA to TJ, July 30, 1815, below, 451.
16. TJ to JA, Aug. 10, 1815, May 5, 1817, below, 452-53, 513 and nn.
17. TJ had read Ramsay's *History of the Revolution of South-Carolina* (Trenton, 1785) and assisted in getting a French translation printed in France. Sowerby, *Catalogue of the Library of Thomas Jefferson*, I, 229-35.

identical. When Adams declared that "the Revolution was in the Minds of the People," he gave the whole problem new perspective.[18] Jefferson thought that it was difficult, if not impossible, to date the beginning of the Revolution,[19] and neither he nor Adams speculated on its termination, perhaps because they still saw evidence of its effects in their declining years.

Emphasis on the philosophical and interpretive aspects of history should not obscure Jefferson's persistent queries concerning authenticity of the sources. He rescued and preserved numerous manuscripts pertaining to colonial and revolutionary Virginia. He saved some unique records of the Continental Congress and he appreciated the basic importance of Madison's Journal of the Federal Convention, although it was inaccessible during Jefferson's lifetime. Adams, too, in his study of the state constitutions pointed out that he was personally acquainted with most of the gentlemen who "had the principal share in the first draughts of these documents," [20] and of course he had access to the texts.

It is understandable, in the light of Jefferson's attention to historical sources, that he reacted vigorously to the news about the purported Mecklenburg Declaration of Independence of 1775, which was belatedly published in 1819. This was both a challenge to the priority of his own great document and a mustering of inconclusive, misdirected evidence to contradict history. His clear-cut refutation won the support of Adams, who at first had been inclined to accept the North Carolina claim; but this was only the beginning of a prolonged controversy that has been revived from time to time for more than a century.[21] In the same spirit of historical criticism Adams reviewed the historiography of the *Acta Sanctorum,* compiled and preserved by the Jesuit Bollandists before their suppression by the papacy and after the restoration of the order in 1813. Adams could not accept as authentic historical research their attempt to discriminate among true, false, and dubious miracles. He could only conclude that the *Lives of the Saints* as ecclesiastical history, when exposed to rational criticism

18. JA to TJ, Aug. 24, 1815, below, 455.
19. TJ to JA, May 17, 1818, and JA to TJ, May 29, 1818, below, 524, 525.
20. "Defence of the Constitutions," *Works,* IV, 293.
21. JA to TJ, June 22, 1819; TJ to JA, July 9, 1819; and JA to TJ, July 21 and 28, 1819, below, 542-46; William H. Hoyt, *The Mecklenburg Declaration of Independence; a Study of Evidence* ... (N. Y. and London, 1907).

and interpretation, was an "enormous Mass of Lies Frauds, Hypocracy and Imposture," and Jefferson agreed.[22]

Close students of history themselves, Adams and Jefferson recognized the significance of the revolutionary age through which they had lived and anticipated its usefulness as history to posterity. They regarded history as a humanistic study through which the recorded deeds of men were assessed in relation to the advancement of society; and they believed that the discoverable truth, when applied by reasonable men, would benefit their contemporaries and offer assurance for the future. As history could scarcely be divorced from philosophy, so its didactic quality strengthened its usefulness. It was likely to be "whig" or "tory," reinforcing the author's prejudices and point of view. Nevertheless, history was a product of reason, not revelation; but impartiality, that chimera of the twentieth-century historian, had not yet joined forces with scientific objectivity.

In the spirit of the Enlightenment, philosophers put the facts to useful purposes for the amelioration of society. In America the prospects of accomplishment seemed best and the Revolution had confirmed that hope through the establishment of republican government. The indoctrination of the heirs of the Enlightenment in the United States is suggested by the advice of Mrs. Adams to her son John Quincy in his early teens, when he was in Holland with his father in 1781:

I would recommend it to you to become acquainted with the history of that country, as in many respects it is similar to the Revolution of your own. Tyranny and oppression were the original causes of the revolt of both countries. It is from a wide and extensive view of mankind that a just and true estimate can be formed of the powers of human nature.[23]

Man and nature, history and philosophy, collaborated in an Age of Reason and Progress.

22. JA to TJ, June 22, 1815, and TJ to JA, Aug. 10, 1815, below, 450, 452. JA also cited the *Acta Sanctorum* as evidence against reactionary theologians by branding it "the most complete History of the Corruptions of Christianity." JA to TJ, Aug. 24, 1815, below, 454-55.

23. AA to J. Q. Adams, May 26, 1781, Charles Francis Adams, ed., *Familiar Letters of John Adams and His Wife Abigail Adams, during the Revolution* (N.Y. and Cambridge, 1876), 395.

Jefferson to Adams

Monticello Jan. 24. 14.

DEAR SIR

I have great need of the indulgence so kindly extended to me in your favor of Dec. 25. of permitting me to answer your friendly letters at my leisure. My frequent and long absences from home are a first cause of tardiness in my correspondence, and a 2d. the accumulation of business during my absence, some of which imperiously commands first attentions. I am now in arrear to you for your letters of Nov. 12. 14. 16. Dec. 3. 19. 25.

I have made some enquiry about Taylor's book,[24] and I learn from a neighbor of his that it has been understood for some time that he was writing a political work. We had not heard of it's publication, nor has it been announced in any of our papers. But this must be the book of 630. pages which you have recieved; and certainly neither the style nor the stuff of the author of Arator can ever be mistaken. In the latter work, as you observe, there are some good things, but so involved in quaint, in far-fetched, affected, mystical conciepts, and flimsy theories, that who can take the trouble of getting at them?

You ask me if I have ever seen the work of J. W. Goethens Schristen? Never. Nor did the question ever occur to me before Where get we the ten commandments? The book indeed gives them to us verbatim. But where did it get them? For itself tells us they were written by the finger of god on tables of stone, which were destroyed by Moses: it specifies those on the 2d. set of tables in different form and substance, but still without saying how the others were recovered. But the whole history of these books is so defective and doubtful that it seems vain to attempt minute enquiry into it: and such tricks have been plaid with their text, and with the texts of other books relating to them, that we have a right, from that cause, to entertain much doubt what parts of them are genuine. In the New testament there is internal evidence that parts of it have proceeded from an extraordinary man; and that other parts are of the fabric of very inferior minds. It is as easy to separate those parts, as to pick out diamonds from dunghills. The matter of the first was such as would be preserved in the memory of the hearers, and handed on by tradition for a long time; the latter such stuff as might be gathered up, for imbedding it, any where, and at any time.

24. Taylor, *An Inquiry into the Government of the United States.*

I have nothing of Vives, or Budaeus, and little of Erasmus. If the familiar histories of the saints, the want of which they regret, would have given us the histories of those tricks which these writers acknolege to have been practised, and of the lies they agree have been invented for the sake of religion, I join them in their regrets. These would be the only parts of their histories worth reading. It is not only the sacred volumes they have thus interpolated, gutted, and falsified, but the works of others relating to them, and even the laws of the land. We have a curious instance of one of these pious frauds in the Laws of Alfred. He composed, you know, from the laws of the Heptarchy, a Digest for the government of the United kingdom, and in his preface to that work he tells us expressly the sources from which he drew it, to wit, the laws of Ina, of Offa and Aethelbert, (not naming the Pentateuch.) But his pious Interpolator, very awkwardly, *premises* to his work four chapters of Exodus (from the 20th. to the 23d.) as a part of the laws of the land; so that Alfred's *preface* is made to stand in the body of the work. Our judges too have lent a ready hand to further these frauds, and have been willing to lay the yoke of their own opinions on the necks of others; to extend the coercions of municipal law to the dogmas of their religion, by declaring that these make a part of the law of the land. In the Year Book 34. H. 6, fo. 38. in Quare impedit,[25] where the question was how far the Common law takes notice of the Ecclesiastical law, Prisot, Chief Justice, in the course of his argument says 'a tiels leis que ils de Seint eglise ont en *ancien scripture*, covient a nous a donner credence; car ces Common ley sur quels touts manners leis sont fondes: et auxy, Sir, nous sumus obliges de conustre lour ley de saint eglise Etc.' [26] Finch begins the business of falsification by mistranslating and mistating the words of Prisot thus 'to such laws of the church as have warrant in *holy scripture* our law giveth credence,' citing the above case and the words of Prisot in the margin, Finch's law. B. 1. c. 3. Here then we find *ancien scripture*, antient writing, translated 'holy scripture.' This, Wingate in 1658. erects into a Maxim of law, in the very words of Finch, but citing Prisot, and not Finch. And Sheppard tit. Religion, in 1675 laying it down in the same words of Finch, quotes the Year Book, Finch and Wingate. Then comes Sr. Matthew Hale, in the case of the King v. Taylor 1 Ventr. 293. 3 Keb. 607. and declares that 'Christianity is parcel of the laws of England.' Citing nobody, and resting it, with his judgment against the

25. Reports of cases in the *Year Book* cover the period from Edward I (1292) to Henry VIII (1536). The reference is to a law of the thirty-fourth year of Henry VI's reign, folio 38. Cases in Quare impedit are actions in English law brought only in the Court of Common Pleas to recover the right of a patron over a church or benefice.

26. "To such laws of the church as have warrant in ancient writing our law giveth credence; for it is the common law on which all laws are based; and also, Sir, we are obliged to recognize the law of the church, etc."

witches,[27] on his own authority, which indeed was sound and good in all cases into which no superstition or bigotry could enter. Thus strengthened, the court in 1728 in the King v. Woolston, would not suffer it to be questioned whether to write against Christianity was punishable at Common law, saying it had been so settled by Hale in Taylor's case. 2 Stra. 834. Wood therefore, 409. without scruple, lays down as a principle that all blasphemy and profaneness are offences at the Common law, and cites Strange. Blackstone, in 1763. repeats in the words of Sr. Matthew Hale that 'Christianity is part of the laws of England,' citing Ventris and Strange ubi supra. And Ld. Mansfield in the case of the Chamberlain of London v. Evans, in 1767. qualifying somewhat the position, says that 'the essential principles of revealed religion are part of the Common law.' [28] Thus we find this string of authorities all hanging by one another on a single hook, a mistranslation by Finch of the words of Prisot, or on nothing. For all quote Prisot, or one another, or nobody. Thus Finch misquotes Prisot; Wingate also, but using Finch's words; Sheppard quotes Prisot, Finch and Wingate; Hale cites nobody; the court in Woolston's case cite Hale; Wood cites Woolston's case; Blackstone that and Hale; and Ld. Mansfield volunteers his own ipse dixit. And who now can question but that the whole Bible and Testament are a part of the Common law? And that Connecticut, in her blue laws, laying it down as a principle that the laws of god should be the laws of their land, except where their own contradicted them, did anything more than express, with a salvo, what the English judges had less cautiously declared without any restriction? And what I dare say our cunning Chief Justice [Marshall] would swear to, and find as many sophisms to twist it out of the general terms of our Declarations of rights, and even the stricter text of the Virginia 'act for the freedom of religion' as he did to twist Burr's neck out of the halter of treason.[29] May we not say then with him who was all candor and benevolence 'Woe unto you, ye lawyers, for ye lade men with burdens grievous to bear.'

27. In King v. Taylor, 1661-62, at the Bury St. Edmonds Assizes two women were tried for witchcraft. In directing the jury Hale stated there was no doubt of the existence of witches as proved by the Bible, the general consent, and acts of Parliament.

28. In this case Mansfield spoke in favor of a Dissenter's not accepting official appointment which required that he take communion in the Anglican Church and excused him from payment of a fine.

29. Aaron Burr was indicted for treason in 1807 in connection with his "conspiracy" in the West and was brought to trial in the United States Circuit Court at Richmond, Va., before Chief Justice John Marshall sitting as circuit judge. The interpretation Marshall gave to the treason clause in the Constitution so restricted the meaning that Burr was acquitted. The trial had its political overtones in the friction between President Jefferson and the Chief Justice. Thomas P. Abernethy, *The Burr Conspiracy* (N.Y., 1954), 227-49.

I think with you that Priestley, in his comparison of the doctrines of Philosophy and of revelation, did not do justice to the undertaking, but he felt himself pressed by the hand of death. Enfield has given us a more distinct account of the ethics of the antient philosophers; but the great work, of which Enfield's is an abridgment, Brucker's history of Philosophy, is the treasure which I would wish to possess, as a book of reference or of special research only, for who could read 6. vol. 4to. [quarto] of 1000 pages each, closely printed, of modern Latin? Your account of D'Argens' Ocellus makes me wish for him also. Ocellus furnishes a fruitful text for a sensible and learned commentator. The Abbé Batteaux', which I have, is a meagre thing.

You surprise me with the account you give of the strength of family distinction still existing in your state. With us it is so totally extinguished that not a spark of it is to be found but lurking in the hearts of some of our old tories. But all bigotries hang to one another; and this in the Eastern states hangs, as I suspect, to that of the priesthood. Here youth, beauty, mind and manners are more valued than a pedigree.

I do not remember the conversation between us which you mention in yours of Nov. 15. on your proposition to vest in Congress the exclusive power of establishing banks. My opposition to it must have been grounded, not on taking the power from the states, but on leaving any vestige of it in existence, even in the hands of Congress; because it would only have been a change of the organ of abuse. I have ever been the enemy of banks; not of those discounting for cash; but of those foisting their own paper into circulation, and thus banishing our cash. My zeal against those institutions was so warm and open at the establishment of the bank of the U.S. that I was derided as a Maniac by the tribe of bank-mongers, who were seeking to filch from the public their swindling, and barren gains. But the errors of that day cannot be recalled. The evils they have engendered are now upon us, and the question is how we are to get out of them? [30] Shall we build an altar to the old paper money of the revolution, which ruined individuals but saved the republic, and burn on that all the bank charters present and future, and their notes with them? For these are to ruin both republic and individuals. This cannot be done. The Mania is too strong. It has siesed by it's delusions and corruptions all the members of our governments, general, special, and individual. Our circulating paper of the last year was estimated at 200. millions of dollars. The new

30. From 1811, when the first Bank of the United States expired, until 1817, when the second Bank of the United States went into operation, all such business was conducted by state banks. Land speculation and the expanding economy during the War of 1812 brought about tremendous inflation, suspension of specie payments by many banks, and the need for a central financial institution. Bray Hammond, *Banks and Politics in America from the Revolution to the Civil War* (Princeton, 1957), 225-50.

banks now petitioned for, to the several legislatures, are for about 60. millions additional capital, and of course 180. millions of additional circulation, nearly doubling that of the last year; and raising the whole mass to near 400. millions, or 40. for 1. of the wholesome amount of circulation for a population of 8. millions circumstanced as we are: and you remember how rapidly our money went down after our 40. for 1. establishment in the revolution. I doubt if the present trash can hold as long. I think the 380. millions must blow all up in the course of the present year; or certainly it will be consummated by the reduplication to take place of course at the legislative meetings of the next winter. Should not prudent men, who possess stock in any monied institution, either draw and hoard the cash, now while they can, or exchange it for canal stock, or such other as being bottomed on immoveable property, will remain unhurt by the crush? I have been endeavoring to persuade a friend in our legislature to try and save this state from the general ruin by timely interference. I propose to him 1. to prohibit instantly all foreign paper. 2. to give our banks 6. months to call in all their 5. Dollar bills (the lowest we allow) another 6. months to call in their 10. D. notes, and 6. months more to call in all below 50. Dollars. This would produce so gradual a diminution of medium as not to shock contracts already made; would leave finally bills of such size as would be called for only in transactions between merchant and merchant, and ensure a metallic circulation for those of the mass of citizens. But it will not be done. You might as well, with the sailors, whistle to the wind, as suggest precautions against having too much money. We must scud then before the gale, and try to hold fast, ourselves, by some plank of the wreck. God send us all a safe deliverance, and to yourself every other species and degree of happiness.

TH: JEFFERSON

P.S. I return your letter of Nov. 15. as it requests: and supposing that the late publication of the life of our good and really great Rittenhouse [31] may not have reached you, I send a copy for your acceptance. Even it's episodes and digressions may add to the amusement it will furnish you. But if the history of the world were written on the same scale, the whole world would not hold it. Rittenhouse, as an astronomer, would stand on a line with any of his time, and as a mechanician he certainly has not been equalled. In this view he was truly great; but, placed along side of Newton, every human character must appear diminutive, and none would have shrunk more feelingly from the painful parallel than the modest and amiable Rittenhouse, whose genius and merit are not the less for this exaggerated comparison of his over zealous biographer.

31. William Barton, *Memoirs of the Life of David Rittenhouse* ... (Philadelphia, 1813).

Adams to Jefferson

Quincy Feb[–March 3] 1814.

DEAR SIR

I was nibbing my pen and brushing my Faculties, to write a polite Letter of Thanks to Mr. Counsellor Barton for his valuable Memoirs of Dr. Rittenhouse though I could not account for his sending it to me, when I received your favour of Jan. 24th. I now most cordially indorse my Thanks over to you. The Book is in the modern American style, an able imitation of Marshalls Washington, though far more entertaining and instructive; a Washington Mausolæum; an Egyptian Pyramid, I shall never read it, any more than Taylors Aristocracy. Mrs. Adams reads it, with great delight, and reads to me, what she finds interresting, and that is indeed the whole Book. I have not time to hear it all.

Writtenhouse was a virtuous and amiable Man; an exquisite Mechanician; Master of the Astronomy known in his time; an expert Mathematician, a patient calculator of Numbers. But We have had a Winthrop an Andrew Oliver a Willard a Webber, his equals and We have a Bowditch his Superior in all these particulars, except the Mechanism. But you know, Phyladelphia is the Heart, the Censorium, the Pineal Gland of U. S. In Politicks, Writtenhouse was a good, simple ignorant well meaning Franklinian Democrat, totally ignorant of the World, as an Anachorite, an honest Dupe of the French Revolution; a mere Instrument of Jonathan Dickinson Sargent, Dr. Hutchinson, Genet and Mifflin. I give him all the Credit of his Planetarium. The Improvement of the Orrery [32] to the Planetarium was an easy, natural thought and nothing was wanting but caculations of Orbits Distrances, and Periods of Revolutions all of which were made to his hands, long before he existed. Patience, Perseverance and Slight of hand is his undoubted Merit and Praise.

I had heard Taylor in Senate, till his Style was so familiar to me that I had not read 3 pages before I suspected the Author. I wrote a Letter to him and he candidly acknowledged that the 650 Pages were sent me, with his consent.[33] I wait with impatience for the Publication and Annunciation of the Work. Arator ought not to have been adulterated with Politicks: but his precept "Gather up the Fragments that nothing be lost" is

32. The Rittenhouse orrery, long lost to view or misplaced, was rediscovered at Princeton University in 1948 and is on display in the library. Howard C. Rice, *The Rittenhouse Orrery; Princeton's Eighteenth-Century Planetarium, 1767-1954* (Princeton, 1954), 62-63.

33. Taylor, *An Inquiry into the Government of the United States.*

of inestimable Value in Agriculture and Horticulture. Every Weed Cob, Husk Stalk ought to be saved for manure.

Your research in the Laws of England, establishing Christianity as the Law of the Land and part of the common Law, are curious and very important. Questions without number will arise in this Country. Religious Controversies, and Ecclesiastical Contests are as common and will be as Sharp as any in civil Politicks foreign, or domestick? In what sense and to what extent the Bible is Law, may give rise to as many doubts and quarrells as any of our civil political military or maritime Laws and will intermix with them all to irritate Factions of every sort. I dare not look beyond my Nose into futurity. Our Money, our Commerce, our Religion, our National and State Constitutions, even our Arts and Sciences, are so many seed Plotts of Division, Faction, Sedition and Rebellion. Every thing is transmuted into an Instrument of Electioneering. Election is the grand Brama, the immortal Lama, I had almost said, the Jaggernaught, for Wives are almost ready to burn upon the Pile and Children to be thrown under the Wheel.

You will perceive, by these figures that I have been looking into Oriental History and Hindoo religion. I have read Voyages and travels and every thing I could collect, and the last is Priestleys "Comparison of the Institutions of Moses, with those of the Hindoos and other ancient Nations," a Work of great labour, and not less haste. I thank him for the labour, and forgive, though I lament the hurry. You would be fatigued to read, and I, just recruiting a little from a longer confinement and indisposition than I have had for 30 Years, have not strength to write many Observations. But I have been disappointed in the principal Points of my Curiosity.

1. I am disappointed, by finding that no just Comparison can be made, because the original Shast[r]a, and the original Vedams are not obtained, or if obtained not yet translated into any European Language.

2. In not finding such Morsells of the Sacred Books as have been translated and published which are more honourable to the original Hindo[o] Religion than any thing he has quoted.

3. In not finding a full devellopement of the History of the Doctrine of the Metempsichosis which orig[i]nated

4. In the History of the Rebellion of innumerable Hosts of Angells in Heaven against the Supream Being, who after some thousands of Years of War conquered them and hurled them down to the Region of total darkness, where they suffered a part of the Punishment of their Crime, and then were mercifully released from Prison permitted to ascend to Earth and migrate into all sorts of Animals, reptiles, Birds Beasts and Men according to their Rank and Chara[c]ter, and even into Vegetables and Minerals, there to serve on probation. If they passed without reproach

their Several gradations they were permitted to become Cows and Men. If as Men they behaved well, i. e. to the satisfaction of the Priests, they were restored to their Original rank and Bliss in Heaven.

5 In not finding the Trinity of Pythagoras and Plato, their contempt of Matter, flesh and blood, their almost Adoration of Fire and Water, their Metempsicosis, and even the prohibition of Beans so evidently derived from India.

6. In not finding the Prophecy of Enoch deduced from India in which the fallen Angels make such a figure.

But you are weary. Priestly has proved the superiority of the Hebrews to the Hindoos, as they Appear in the Gentoo Laws and Institutes of Menu: but the comparison remains to be made with the Shast[r]a.

In his remarks on Mr. Dupuis, p. 342. Priestley says, "The History of the fallen Angels is another Circumstance, on which Mr. Dupuis lays much Stress.["] "According to the Christians," he says, Vol. 1. p. 336, "there was from the beginning, a division among the Angels; some remaining faithful to the light, and others taking the part of Darkness" etc. But this supposed history is not found in the Scriptures. It has only been inferred, from a wrong interpretation of one passage in the 2d. Epistle of Peter, and a corresponding One in that of Jude, as has been shewn by judicious Writers. That there is such a Person as The Devil is no part of my Faith, nor that of many other Christians; nor am I sure that it was the belief of any of the christian Writers. Neither do I believe the doctrine of demoniacal possessions, whether it was believed by the sacred Writers or not; and yet my unbelief in these Articles does not affect my faith in the great facts of which the Evangelists were eye and ear Witnesses. They might not be competent Judges, in the one case, tho perfectly so, with respect to the other."

I will ask Priestley, when I see him, Do you believe those Passages in Peter and Jude to be interpolations? If so, by whom made? and when? and where? and for what End? Was it to support, or found the doctrine of The Fall of Man, Original Sin, the universal Corruption depravation and guilt of human nature and mankind; and the subsequent Incarnation of God to make Attonement and Redemption?   Or do you think that Peter and Jude believed the Book of Enoch to have been written, by the 7th. from Adam, and one of the sacred cannonical Books of the Hebrew Prophets? Peter, 2. Ep. c. 2. v. 4, says "For if God spared not the Angels that sinned, but cast them down to HELL and delivered them into chains of DARKNESS, to be reserved unto Judgment." Jude v. 6th. says "And the Angels which kept not their first Estate, but left their own habitations, he hath reserved in everlasting Chains under darkness, unto the Judgment of the great day. v. 14th.["] "And Enoch also, the 7th. from Adam, prophesied of these Saying, behold the Lord cometh with ten thousands of his Saints, to execute Judgment upon all etc" Priestley says "a wrong Interpretation" has been given to these Texts. I wish he had favoured Us with his right interpretation of them.

In another place. p. 326. Priestley says "There is no Circumstance of which Mr. Dupuis avails himself so much, or repeats so often, both with respect to the Jewish and Christian religions, as the history of *the Fall of Man*, in the beginning of the Book of Genesis. I believe with him, and have maintained in my Writings, that this history is either an Allegory, or founded on uncertain Tradition: that it is an hypothesis to account for the origin of evil, adopted by Moses, which by no means Accounts for the Facts."

March 3d. So far, was written almost a month ago: but Sickness has prevented Progress. I had much more to say about this Work. I shall never be a Disciple of Priestley. He is as absurd inconsistent, credulous and incomprehensible as Athanasius. Read his Letter to The Jews in this Volume. Could a rational Creature write it? Aye! such rational Creatures as Rochefaucault and Condorsett and John Taylor in Politicks, and Towers's, Juricus [Jurieu?] and French Prophets in Theology.

Priestleys Account of the Philosophy and Religion of India appears to me to be much such a Work, as a Man of busy research would produce, who should undertake to describe Christianity from the sixth to the twelfth Century, when a deluge of Wonders overflowed the World; when Miracles were performed and proclaimed from every Convent and Monastry, Hospital, Church Yard, Mountain Valley Cave and Cupola.

There is a Work, which I wish I possessed. It has never crossed the Atlantic. It is entitled Acta Sanctorum, in forty seven Volumes in Folio. It contains the Lives of the Saints. It was compiled in the beginning of the 16th. Century by Bollandus, Henschenius and Papebrock. What would I give to possess in one immense Mass, One Stupendous draught all the Legends, true doubtful and false. These Bollandists dared to discuss some of the Facts and to hint that some of them were doubtful, E. G. Papebrock doubted The Antiquity of the Carmellites from Elias; and whether the Face of J. C. was painted on the Handkerchief of St. Veronique; and whether the Prepuce of the Saviour of the World, which was shewn in the Church at Antwerp, could be proved to be genuine? For these bold Scepticisms he was libelled in Pamphlets and denounced to the Pope and the Inquisition in Spain. The Inquisition condemned him: but the Pope not daring to acquit or condemn him, prohi[bi]ted all Writings, Pro and Con. But as the Physicians cure one disease by exciting Another, as a Fever by a Salivation, this Bull was produced by a new Claim. The Brothers of the

Order of Charity asserted a Descent from Abraham 900 Years anterior to the Carmelites.

A Phylosopher who should write a description of Christianism from the Bollandistic Saints of the sixth or the tenth Century would probably produce a Work tolerably parrallel to Priestleys upon the Hindoos.

JOHN ADAMS

Jefferson to Adams

Monticello May 18.14.

MY DEAR SIR

This will be handed you by Mr. Rives a young gentleman of this state and my neighborhood. He is an eleve of mine in law, of uncommon abilities, learning and worth. When you and I shall be at rest with our friends of 1776, he will be in the zenith of his fame and usefulness. Before entering on his public career he wishes to visit our sister states, and would not conceive he had seen any thing of Massachusets were he not to see the venerable patriot of Braintree. I therefore request your indulgence of his wishes to be presented to you, a favor to which his high esteem for your character will give double value. But his wishes would be but partly gratified were he not presented to Mrs. Adams also. May I then ask this additional favor of you which I shall value the more as it will give him the opportunity which I hope of bringing back to me a favorable report of both your healths. Accept as heretofore the assurances of my affectionate esteem and respect.

TH: JEFFERSON

Jefferson to Adams

Monticello July 5. 14.

DEAR SIR

Since mine of Jan. 24. yours of Mar. 14. was recieved. It was not acknoleged in the short one of May 18. by Mr. Rives, the only object of that having been to enable one of our most promising young men to have the advantage of making his bow to you. I learned with great regret the serious illness mentioned in your letter: and I hope Mr. Rives will be able to tell me you are entirely restored. But our machines have now been running for 70. or 80. years, and we must expect that, worn as they are, here a pivot, there a wheel, now a pinion, next a spring, will be giving way: and however we may tinker them up for awhile, all will at length surcease motion. Our watches, with works of brass and steel, wear out within that period. Shall you and I last to see the course the seven-fold wonders of the times will take? The Attila of the age dethroned, the ruthless destroyer of 10. millions of the human race, whose thirst for blood appeared unquenchable, the great oppressor of the rights and liberties of the world, shut up within the circuit of a little island of the Mediterranean,[34] and dwindled to the condition of an humble and degraded pensioner on the bounty of those he had most injured. How miserably, how meanly, has he closed his inflated career! What a sample of the Bathos will his history present! He should have perished on the swords of his enemies, under the walls of Paris.

> 'Leon piagato a morte Cosi fra l'ire estrema
> Sente mancar la vita, rugge, minaccia, e freme,
> Guarda la sua ferita, Che fa tremar morendo
> Ne s'avilisce ancor. Tal volta il cacciator.'[35]
>   Metast Adriano.

But Bonaparte was a lion in the field only. In civil life a cold-blooded, calculating unprincipled Ursurper, without a virtue, no statesman, knowing nothing of commerce, political economy, or civil government, and supplying ignorance by bold presumption. I had supposed him a great man until his entrance into the Assembly des cinq cens, 18. Brumaire (an. 8.)[36] From that date however I set him down as a great scoundrel only. To the wonders of his rise and fall, we may add that of a Czar of Muscovy dictating, *in Paris*, laws and limits to all the successors of the Caesars,[37] and holding even the balance in which the fortunes of this new world are suspended. I own that, while I rejoice, for the good of mankind, in the deliverance of Europe from the havoc which would have never ceased while Bonaparte should have lived in power, I see with anxiety the tyrant of the ocean remaining in vigor, and even participating in the merit

34. Napoleon was banished to the island of Elba in 1814. He escaped on March 1, 1815, to lead the French armies during the Hundred Days until his final defeat at Waterloo, June 18.

35. "The lion stricken to death Then with his final wrath
    realizes that he is dying, he roars, threatens, and screams,
    and looks at his wounds from which which makes the hunter
    he grows ever weaker and weaker. tremble at him dying."

36. The coup d'état of Nov. 9, 1799, in which Bonaparte drove the legislative Council of 500 of the French Republic (the Directory) from its meeting place and proclaimed the Consulate (headed by three consuls) with himself as First Consul.

37. The "constitutional charter," issued in 1814 by Louis XVIII of the restored Bourbon dynasty, partly at the insistence of Tsar Alexander I.

of crushing his brother tyrant. While the world is thus turned up side down, on which side of it are we? All the strong reasons indeed place us on the side of peace; the interests of the continent, their friendly dispositions, and even the interests of England. Her passions alone are opposed to it. Peace would seem now to be an easy work, the causes of the war being removed. Her orders of council will no doubt be taken care of by the allied powers, and, war ceasing, her impressment of our seamen ceases of course. But I fear there is foundation for the design intimated in the public papers, of demanding a cession of our right in the fisheries.[38] What will Massachusets say to this? I mean her majority, which must be considered as speaking, thro' the organs it has appointed itself, as the Index of it's will. She chose to sacrifice the liberty of our seafaring citizens, in which we were all interested, and with them her obligations to the Co-states; rather than war with England. Will she now sacrifice the fisheries to the same partialities? This question is interesting to her alone: for to the middle, the Southern and Western States they are of no direct concern; of no more than the culture of tobacco, rice and cotton to Massachusets. I am really at a loss to conjecture what our refractory sister will say on this occasion. I know what, as a citizen of the Union, I would say to her. 'Take this question ad referendum. It concerns you alone. If you would rather give up the fisheries than war with England, we give them up. If you had rather fight for them, we will defend your interests to the last drop of our blood, chusing rather to set a good example than follow a bad one.' And I hope she will determine to fight for them. With this however you and I shall have nothing to do; ours being truly the case wherein 'non tali auxilio, nec defensoribus istis Tempus eget.'[39] Quitting this subject therefore I will turn over another leaf.

I am just returned from one of my long absences, having been at my other home for five weeks past. Having more leisure there than here for reading, I amused myself with reading seriously Plato's republic. I am wrong however in calling it amusement, for it was the heaviest task-work I ever went through. I had occasionally before taken up some of his other works, but scarcely ever had patience to go through a whole dialogue. While wading thro' the whimsies, the puerilities, and unintelligible jargon of this work, I laid it down often to ask myself how it could have been that the world should have so long consented to give reputation to such nonsense as this? How the soi-disant Christian world indeed should have

38. No agreement was reached on the Anglo-American fisheries at the peace conference at Ghent in 1814, but the Convention of 1818 allowed Americans to fish off the northern coast of North America and to dry and cure fish on the unsettled shores of Labrador and southern Newfoundland. Bemis, *Diplomatic History of U.S.*, 174-75.
39. "We do not, at this time, want such aid as that, nor such defenders." Virgil, *Aen.*, II, 521.

done it, is a piece of historical curiosity. But how could the Roman good sense do it? And particularly how could Cicero bestow such eulogies on Plato? Altho' Cicero did not wield the dense logic of Demosthenes, yet he was able, learned, laborious, practised in the business of the world, and honest. He could not be the dupe of mere style, of which he was himself the first master in the world. With the Moderns, I think, it is rather a matter of fashion and authority. Education is chiefly in the hands of persons who, from their profession, have an interest in the reputation and the dreams of Plato. They give the tone while at school, and few, in their after-years, have occasion to revise their college opinions. But fashion and authority apart, and bringing Plato to the test of reason, take from him his sophisms, futilities, and incomprehensibilities, and what remains? In truth, he is one of the race of genuine Sophists, who has escaped the oblivion of his brethren, first by the elegance of his diction, but chiefly by the adoption and incorporation of his whimsies into the body of arti-ficial Christianity. His foggy mind, is forever presenting the semblances of objects which, half seen thro' a mist, can be defined neither in form or dimension. Yet this which should have consigned him to early oblivion really procured him immortality of fame and reverence. The Christian priesthood, finding the doctrines of Christ levelled to every understanding, and too plain to need explanation, saw, in the mysticisms of Plato, ma-terials with which they might build up an artificial system which might, from it's indistinctness, admit everlasting controversy, give employment for their order, and introduce it to profit, power and pre-eminence. The doctrines which flowed from the lips of Jesus himself are within the comprehension of a child; but thousands of volumes have not yet explained the Platonisms engrafted on them: and for this obvious reason that non-sense can never be explained. Their purposes however are answered. Plato is canonized; and it is now deemed as impious to question his merits as those of an Apostle of Jesus. He is peculiarly appealed to as an advocate of the immortality of the soul; and yet I will venture to say that were there no better arguments than his in proof of it, not a man in the world would believe it. It is fortunate for us that Platonic republicanism has not obtained the same favor as Platonic Christianity; or we should now have been all living, men, women and children, pell mell together, like beasts of the field or forest. Yet 'Plato is a great Philosopher,' said La Fontaine. But says Fontenelle 'do you find his ideas very clear'? 'Oh no! he is of an obscurity impenetrable.' 'Do you not find him full of contradictions?' 'Certainly,' replied La Fontaine, 'he is but a Sophist.' Yet immediately after, he exclaims again, 'Oh Plato was a great Philosopher.' Socrates had reason indeed to complain of the misrepresentations of Plato; for in truth his dialogues are libels on Socrates.

But why am I dosing you with these Ante-diluvian topics? Because I am glad to have some one to whom they are familiar, and who will not recieve them as if dropped from the moon. Our post-revolutionary youth are born under happier stars than you and I were. They acquire all learning in their mothers' womb, and bring it into the world ready-made. The information of books is no longer necessary; and all knolege which is not innate, is in contempt, or neglect at least. Every folly must run it's round; and so, I suppose, must that of self-learning, and self sufficiency; of rejecting the knolege acquired in past ages, and starting on the new ground of intuition. When sobered by experience I hope our successors will turn their attention to the advantages of education. I mean of education on the broad scale, and not that of the petty *academies*, as they call themselves, which are starting up in every neighborhood, and where one or two men, possessing Latin, and sometimes Greek, a knolege of the globes, and the first six books of Euclid, imagine and communicate this as the sum of science. They commit their pupils to the theatre of the world with just taste enough of learning to be alienated from industrious pursuits, and not enough to do service in the ranks of science. We have some exceptions indeed. I presented one to you lately, and we have some others. But the terms I use are general truths. I hope the necessity will at length be seen of establishing institutions, here as in Europe, where every branch of science, useful at this day, may be taught in it's highest degrees. Have you ever turned your thoughts to the plan of such an institution? I mean to a specification of the particular sciences of real use in human affairs, and how they might be so grouped as to require so many professors only as might bring them within the views of a just but enlightened economy? I should be happy in a communication of your ideas on this problem, either loose or digested. But to avoid my being run away with by another subject, and adding to the length and ennui of the present letter, I will here present to Mrs. Adams and yourself the assurance of my constant and sincere friendship and respect.

TH: JEFFERSON

Adams to Jefferson

Quincy July 16. 1814

DEAR SIR

I recd. this morning your favour of the 5th. and as I can never let a Sheet of your's rest I sit down immediately to acknowledge it.

Whenever Mr. Rives, of whom I have heard nothing, shall arrive he shall receive all the cordial Civilities in my power.

I am sometimes afraid that my "Machine" will not "surcease motion" soon enough; for I dread nothing so much as "dying at top" and expiring like Dean Swift "a driveller and a Show" or like Sam. Adams, a Grief and distress to his Family, a weeping helpless Object of Compassion for Years.

I am bold to say that neither you nor I, will live to see the Course which "the Wonders of the Times" will take. Many Years, and perhaps Centuries must pass, before the current will acquire a settled direction. If the Christian Religion as I understand it, or as you understand it, should maintain its Ground as I believe it will; Yet Platonick Pythagoric, Hindoo, and cabballistical Christianity which is Catholic Christianity, and which has prevailed for 1500 Years, has recd. a mortal Wound of which the Monster must finally die; Yet so strong is his constitution that he may endure for Centuries before he expires. Government has never been much studied by Mankind. But their Attention has been drawn to it, in the latter part of the last Century and the begining of this, more than at any former Period: and the vast Variety of experiments that have been made of Constitutions, in America in France, in Holland, in Geneva in Switzerland, and even in Spain and South America, can never be forgotten. They will be studied, and their immediate and remote Effects, and final Catastrophys noted. The result in time will be Improvements. And I have no doubt that the horrors We have experienced for the last forty Years, will ultimately, terminate in the Advancement of civil and religious Liberty, and Ameliorations, in the condition of Mankind. For I am a Believer, in the probable improvability and Improvement, the Ameliorabi[li]ty and Amelioration in human Affairs: though I never could understand the Doctrine of the Perfectability of the human Mind. This has always appeared to me, like the Phylosophy or Theology of the Gentoos, viz. "that a Brachman by certain Studies for a certain time pursued, and by certain Ceremonies a certain number of times repeated, becomes Omniscient and Almighty."

Our hopes however of sudden tranquility ought not to be too sanguine. Fanaticism and Superstition will still be selfish, subtle, intriguing, and at times furious. Despotism will still struggle for domination; Monarchy will still study to rival nobility in popularity; Aristocracy will continue to envy all above it, and despize and oppress all below it; Democracy will envy all, contend with all, endeavour to pull down all; and when by chance it happens to get the Upper hand for a short time, it will be revengefull bloody and cruel. These and other Elements of Fanaticism and Anarchy will yet for a long time continue a Fermentation, which will excite alarms and require Vigilance.

Napoleon is a Military Fanatic like Achilles, Alexander, Caesar, Mahomet, Zingis Kouli, Charles 12th. etc. The Maxim and Principle of all of them was the same "Jura negat sibi cata [i.e., nata], nihil non arrogat Armis." [40]

But is it strict, to call him An Usurper? Was not his Elevation to the Empire of France as legitimate and authentic a national Act as that of William 3d. or the House of Hanover to the throne of the 3 Kingdoms or as the Election of Washington to the command of our Army or to the Chair of the States.

Human Nature, in no form of it, ever could bear Prosperity. That peculiar tribe of Men, called Conquerors, more remarkably than any other have been swelled with Vanity by any Series of Victories. Napoleon won so many mighty Battles in such quick succession and for so long a time, that it was no Wonder his brain became compleatly intoxicated and his enterprises, rash, extravagant and mad.

Though France is humbled, Britain is not. Though Bona is banished a greater Tyrant and wider Usurper still domineers. John Bull is quite as unfeeling, as unprincipled, more powerful, has shed more blood, than Bona. John by his money his Intrigues and Arms, by exciting Coalition after coalition against him made him what he was, and at last, what he is. How shall the Tyrant of Tyrants, be brought low? Aye! there's the rub. I still think Bona great, at least as any of the Conquerors. "The Wonders of his rise and fall," may be seen in the Life of King Theodore, or Pascall Paoli or Rienzi, or Dyonisius or Mazzionelli, or Jack Cade or Wat Tyler. The only difference is that between miniatures and full length pictures. The Schoolmaster at Corinth, was a greater Man, than the Tyrant of Syracuse; upon the Principle, that he who conquers himself is greater than he who takes a City. Tho' the ferocious Roar of the wounded Lion, may terrify the Hunter with the possibility of another dangerous leap; Bona was shot dead at once, by France. He could no longer roar or struggle growl or paw, he could only gasp the grin of death. I wish that France may not still regret him. But these are Speculations in the Clouds. I agree with you that the Milk of human kindness in the Bourbons is safer for Mankind than the fierce Ambition of Napoleon.

The Autocrator, appears in an imposing Light. Fifty Years ago English Writers, held up terrible Consequences from "thawing out the monstrous northern Snake." If Cossacks and Tartars, and Goths and Vandalls and Hunns and Ripuarians, should get a taste of European Sweets, what may happen? Could Wellingtons or Bonapartes, resist them? The greatest trait of Sagacity, that Alexander has yet exhibited to the World is his Courtship of the United States. But whether this is a mature well digested Policy or

40. "He denies that laws were made for him; he arrogates everything to himself by force of arms." Horace, *Ars Poetica*, 122.

only a transient gleam of thought, still remains to be explained and proved by time.

The "refractory Sister" [Massachusetts] will not give up the Fisheries. Not a Man here dares to hint at so base a thought.

I am very glad you have seriously read Plato: and still more rejoiced to find that your reflections upon him so perfectly harmonize with mine. Some thirty Years ago I took upon me the severe task of going through all his Works. With the help of two Latin Translations, and one English and one French Translation and comparing some of the most remarkable passages with the Greek, I laboured through the tedious toil. My disappointment was very great, my Astonishment was greater and my disgust was shocking. Two Things only did I learn from him. 1. that Franklins Ideas of exempting Husbandmen and Mariners etc. from the depredations of War were borrowed from him. 2. that Sneezing is a cure for the Hickups. Accordingly I have cured myself and all my Friends of that provoking disorder, for thirty Years with a Pinch of Snuff.

Some Parts of some of his Dialogues are entertaining, like the Writings of Rousseau: but his Laws and his Republick from which I expected most, disappointed me most. I could scarcely exclude the suspicion that he intended the latter as a bitter Satyre upon all Republican Government, as Xenophon undoubtedly designed by his Essay on Democracy, to ridicule that Species of Republick. In a late letter to the learned and ingenious Mr. Taylor of Hazelwood, I suggested to him the Project of writing a Novel, in which The Hero should be sent upon his travels through Plato's Republick, and all his Adventures, with his Observations on the principles and Opinions, the Arts and Sciences, the manners Customs and habits of the Citizens should be recorded. Nothing can be conceived more destructive of human happiness; more infallibly contrived to transform Men and Women into Brutes, Yahoos, or Dæmons than a Community of Wives and Property. Yet, in what, are the Writings of Rousseau and Helvetius wiser than those of Plato? "The Man who first fenced a Tobacco Yard, and said this is mine ought instantly to have been put to death" says Rousseau. "The Man who first pronounced the barbarous Word "Dieu," ought to have been immediately destroyed," says Diderot. In short Philosophers antient and modern appear to me as Mad as Hindoos, Mahomitans and Christians. No doubt they would all think me mad; and for any thing I know this globe may be, the bedlam, Le Bicatre [i.e., Bicêtre] of the Universe.

After all; as long as Property exists, it will accumulate in Individuals and Families. As long as Marriage exists, Knowledge, Property and Influence will accumulate in Families. Your and our equal Partition of intestate Estates, instead of preventing will in time augment the Evil, if it is one.

The French Revolutionists saw this, and were so far consistent. When they burned Pedigrees and genealogical Trees, they anni[hi]lated, as far as they could, Marriages, knowing that Marriage, among a thousand other things was an infallible Source of Aristocracy. I repeat it, so sure as the Idea and the existence of PROPERTY is admitted and established in Society, Accumulations of it will be made, the Snow ball will grow as it rolls.

Cicero was educated in the Groves of Academus where the Name and Memory of Plato, were idolized to such a degree, that if he had wholly renounced the Prejudices of his Education his Reputation would have been lessened, if not injured and ruined. In his two Volumes of Discourses on Government We may presume, that he fully examined Plato's Laws and Republick as well as Aristotles Writings on Government. But these have been carefully destroyed; not improbably, with the general Consent of Philosophers, Politicians and Priests. The Loss is as much to be regretted as that of any Production of Antiquity.

Nothing seizes the Attention, of the stareing Animal, so surely, as Paradox, Riddle, Mystery, Invention, discovery, Mystery, Wonder, Temerity.

Plato and his Disciples, from the fourth Century Christians, to Rousseau and Tom Paine, have been fully sensible of this Weakness in Mankind, and have too successfully grounded upon it their Pretensions to Fame. I might indeed, have mentioned Bolingbroke, Hume, Gibbon Voltaire Turgot Helvetius Diderot, Condorcet, Buffon De La Lande and fifty others; all a little cracked! Be to their faults a little blind; to their Virtues ever kind.

Education! Oh Education! The greatest Grief of my heart, and the greatest Affliction of my Life! To my mortification I must confess, that I have never closely thought, or very deliberately reflected upon the Subject, which never occurs to me now, without producing a deep Sigh, an heavy groan and sometimes Tears. My cruel Destiny seperated me from my Children, allmost continually from their Birth to their Manhood. I was compelled to leave them to the ordinary routine of reading writing and Latin School, Accademy and Colledge. John alone was much with me, and he, but occasionally. If I venture to give you any thoughts at all, they must be very crude. I have turned over Locke, Milton, Condilac Rousseau and even Miss. Edgeworth as a bird flies through the Air. The Præcepter,[41] I have thought a good Book. Grammar, Rhetorick, Logic, Ethicks mathematicks, cannot be neglected; Classicks, in spight of our Friend Rush,[42] I must think indispensable. Natural History, Mechanicks,

41. [Robert Dodsley], *The Preceptor: Containing a General Course of Education* ...2 vols. (5th edn.; London, 1764). Listed in *Catalogue of the John Adams Library in the Public Library of the City of Boston* (Boston, 1917).

42. Benjamin Rush advocated dropping Greek and Latin from the school curriculum, except for the few students who would go to college. The vast majority ought to

and experimental Philosophy, Chymistry etc att least their Rudiments, can not be forgotten. Geography Ast[ron]omy, and even History and Chronology, tho' I am myself afflicted with a kind of Pyrrhonism in the two latter, I presume cannot be omitted. Theology I would leave to Ray, Derham, Nicuenteyt and Payley, rather than to Luther Zinzindorph, Sweedenborg Westley, or Whitefield, or Thomas Aquinas or Wollebius.[43] Metaphysics I would leave in the Clouds with the Materialists and Spiritualists, with Leibnits, Berkley Priestley and Edwards, and I might add Hume and Reed, or if permitted to be read, it should be with Romances and Novels. What shall I say of Musick, drawing, fencing, dancing and Gymnastic Exercises? What of Languages Oriental or Occidental? of French Italian German or Russian? of Sanscrit or Chinese?

The Task you have prescribed to me of Grouping these Sciences, or Arts, under Professors, within the Views of an inlightened Economy, is far beyond my forces. Loose indeed and indigested must be all the hints, I can note. Might Gramar, Rhetoric, Logick and Ethicks be under One Professor? Might Mathematicks, Mechanicks, Natural Phylosophy, be under another? Geography and Astro[no]my under a third. Laws and Gover[n]ment, History and Chronology under a fourth. Classicks might require a fifth.

Condelacs course of Study has excellent Parts. Among many Systems of Mathematicks English, French and American, there is none preferable to Besouts Course La Harps Course of Litterature is very valuable.[44]

But I am ashamed to add any thing more to the broken innuendos except Assurances of the continued Friendship of

John Adams

Adams to Jefferson

Quincy Oct 28 1814

Dear Sir

I have great pleasure in giving this Letter to the Gentleman who requests it. The Revd Edward Everett, the successor of Mr. Buckminster

---

take practical subjects; but he did "not reject modern languages as a part of academical education." Butterfield, ed., *Letters of Rush*, I, 524, 531, 605-7.

43. In other words, JA would leave theology to the naturalists rather than to the revealed religionists.

44. See JA to TJ, July 18, Dec. 3, 1813, above, 362, 406.

and Thatcher and Cooper in the politest Congregation in Boston,[45] and probably the first litterary Character of his Age and State, is very desirous of seeing Mr. Jefferson. I hope he will arrive before your Library is translated to Washington.[46]

By the Way I envy you that immortal honour: but I cannot enter into competition with you for my books are not half the number of yours: and moreover, I have Shaftesbury, Bolingbroke, Hume Gibbon and Raynal, as well as Voltaire.

Mr. Everett is respectable in every View; in Family fortune Station Genius Learning and Character. What more ought to be said to Thomas Jefferson by

JOHN ADAMS

Adams to Jefferson

Quincy December 11. 1814

DEAR SIR

The Bearer of this Letter, after an Education at our Cambridge, travelled with J. Q. A. to Russia, spent two Years in looking at parts of Europe, returned to Boston, read Law with one of our first Professors in Boston, is admitted to the Bar, and now Wishes to have the honour of seeing Montecello and paying his respects to President Jefferson. His Name is Francis C. Gray, a Son of our Lt. Governor Gray.

If he can explain to you the incomprehensible Politicks of New England, he can do more than I shall or can pretend to do.

Paine, Lovel and Gerry are gone and I am left alone. Gerry is happy in his Death; for what horrors of Calumny has he not escaped in the Electioneering Campaigne of next Summer? But what is to be the destiny of an amiable Widow and nine Children all as amiable as they are destitute?

JOHN ADAMS

45. The Brattle Street Church.
46. TJ sold his library to the United States in 1815 to form the nucleus of the second Library of Congress after the burning of the Capitol by the British in 1814. Congress paid TJ $23,950, or an average of $3.50 per volume; the titles of the books, arranged under his scheme of classification, were printed in *The Catalogue of the Library of the United States* (Washington, 1815). Randolph G. Adams, *Three Americanists* ... (Philadelphia, 1939), 84-94.

Adams to Jefferson

Quincy December 20. 1814

Dear Sir

The most exalted of our young Genius's in Boston have an Ambition to see Montecello, its Library and its Sage. I lately gave a Line of Introduction to Mr. Everett, our most celebrated Youth: But his Calls at home, forced him back from Washington.

George Ticknor Esquire who will have the Honour to present this to you, has a reputation here, equal to the Character given him in the enclosed Letter from my Nephew, our Athenæum Man,[47] whom you know.

As you are all Heluones Librorum ["gluttons for books"], I think you ought to have a Sympathy for each other.

I gave a Letter to Francis Gray, a Son of our great Merchant and Patriot, which I hope he will have the Honor to present in due time.

The Gentleman recommended to me, to my great regret has not arrived. I hope no Misfortune has befallen him.

Paine, Lovell and Gerry are gone and left alone

John Adams

Jefferson to Adams

Monticello June 10. 15.

Dear Sir

It is long since we have exchanged a letter, and yet what volumes might have been written on the occurrences even of the last three months. In the first place, Peace, God bless it! has returned to put us all again into a course of lawful and laudable pursuits: a new trial of the Bourbons has proved to the world their incompetence to the functions of the station they have occupied: and the recall of the Usurper has clothed him with

47. William Smith Shaw ("Athenaeum Shaw"), whose mother was a sister of Abigail Adams, helped found the Anthology Society in 1805, out of which grew the Boston Athenaeum in 1807. His sobriquet resulted from the enthusiastic support he gave the Athenaeum as librarian to 1822 and secretary to 1823. Josiah Quincy, *The History of the Boston Athenaeum* ... (Cambridge, Mass., 1851), Chaps. I-III, 90-92; biographical section, 22-44.

the semblance of a legitimate Autocrat.[48] If adversity should have taught him wisdom, of which I have little confidence, he may yet render some service to mankind by teaching the antient dynasties that they can be changed for misrule, and by wearing down the maritime power of England to limitable and safe dimensions. But it is not possible he should love us, and of that our commerce had sufficient proofs during his power. Our military atchievements indeed, which he is capable of estimating, may in some degree moderate the effect of his aversions; and he may perhaps fancy that we are to become the natural enemies of England, as England herself has so steadily endeavored to make us and as some of our own over-zealous patriots would be willing to proclaim. And in this view he may admit a cold toleration of some intercourse and commerce between the two nations. He has certainly had time to see the folly of turning the industry of France from the cultures for which nature has so highly endowed her to those of sugar, cotton, tobacco and others which the same creative power has given to other climates: and on the whole, if he can conquer the passions of his tyrannical soul, if he has understanding enough to pursue, from motives of interest, what no moral motives lead him to, the tranquil happiness and prosperity of his country, rather than a ravenous thirst for human blood, his return may become of more advantage than injury to us. And if again some great man could arise in England, who could see and correct the follies of his nation in their conduct as to us, and by exercising justice and comity towards ours bring both into a state of temperate and useful friendship, it is possible we may thus attain the place we ought to occupy between these two nations without being degraded to the condition of mere partisans of either.

A little time will now inform us whether France, within it's proper limits, is big enough for it's ruler, on the one hand, and whether, on the other, the allied powers are either wicked or foolish enough to attempt the forcing on the French a ruler and government which they refuse? Whether they will risk their own thrones to reestablish that of the Bourbons? If this is attempted, and the European world again committed to war, will the jealousy of England at the commerce which neutrality will give us, induce her again to add us to the number of her enemies, rather than see us prosper in the pursuits of peace and industry? And have our commercial citizens merited from their country it's encountering another war to protect their gambling enterprises? That the persons of our citizens shall be safe in freely traversing the ocean, that the transportation of our

48. The Treaty of Ghent ending the war between the United States and Great Britain had been signed on Dec. 24, 1814; Bonaparte's return from Elba to become emperor of the French again had forced the abdication of Louis XVIII. TJ was writing eight days before the Battle of Waterloo where Bonaparte met his final defeat; Louis XVIII then regained the Bourbon throne.

own produce, in our own vessels, to the markets of our choice, and the return to us of the articles we want for our own use shall be unmolested I hold to be fundamental, and that the gauntlet must be for ever hurled at him who questions it. But whether we shall engage in every war of Europe to protect the mere agency of our merchants and shipowners in carrying on the commerce of other nations, even were those merchants and ship owners to take the side of their country in the contest, instead of that of the enemy, is a question of deep and serious consideration, with which however you and I shall have nothing to do; so we will leave it to those whom it will concern.

I thank you for making known to me Mr. Ticknor and Mr. Gray. They are fine young men indeed, and if Massachusets can raise a few more such, it is probable she would be better counselled as to social rights and social duties. Mr. Ticknor is particularly the best bibliograph I have met with, and very kindly and opportunely offered me the means of reprocuring some part of the literary treasures which I have ceded to Congress to replace the devastations of British Vandalism at Washington.[49] I cannot live without books: but fewer will suffice where amusement, and not use, is the only future object. I am about sending him a catalogue to which less than his critical knolege of books would hardly be adequate. Present my high respects to Mrs. Adams, and accept yourself the assurance of my affectionate attachment.

TH: JEFFERSON

Adams to Jefferson

Quincy June 19. 1815

DEAR SIR

Education, which you brought into View in one of your Letters, is a Subject so vast, and the Systems of Writers are so various and so contradictory: that human Life is too short to examine it; and a Man must die before he can learn to bring up his Children. The Phylosophers, Divines, Politicians and Pædagogues, who have published their Theories and Practices in this department, are without number.

49. Ticknor and Gray spent three days at Monticello early in Feb. 1815. TJ was especially impressed with Ticknor, whom he commissioned to buy in Europe certain editions of the classics. After Ticknor's return to America, TJ offered him a professorship at the University of Virginia, but commitments at Harvard necessitated his refusal. Orie W. Long, *Thomas Jefferson and George Ticknor* (Williamstown, Mass., 1933), 11-34.

Your present Inquiries, I presume, are not confined to early Education, perhaps do not comprehend it. The Constitution of a University is your Object, as I understand you. Here also the Subject is infinite. The Science has so long laboured with a Dropsy, that it is a wonder the Patient has not long since expired. Sciences of all kinds have need of Reform, as much as Religion and Government.

I never know what to write to you, because I consider it as sending Coal to Newcastle.

Tallerand Perigord, soon after his Arrival at Philadelphia, presented to me his "Rapport sur l'instruction publique." [50] I presume he presented the same Work to you. This production has some fame and may suggest some Ideas to you.

The Universities in Protestant Germany have at present the Vogue and the Ton in their favour. There is in Print a "Coup-D'Œil sur les Universités, et le mode D'Instruction Publique de L'Allemagne Protestante; en particulier Du Royaume de Westphalie, Par Charles Villers," Correspondant de l'Institut national de France, de la Societé Royale des Sciences de Gœttingue, etc.[51]

There is also in print, "Recueil de recherches sur l'education; memoire qui a concouru, en l'an XI a la Société des Sciences et Arts de Grenoble, sur cette question, Quells sont les moyens de perfectioner l'Education physique et morale des enfans?" ["]Par. J. J. Droüin, employé au ministere des relations exterieures." [52]

If I had not reason to presume that you possess these Pamp[h]lets, I would attempt to give you some Account of them. They will convince you that you have a task difficult and perplexed enough.

The War of the Reformation still continues. The Struggle between different and opposite Systems of Religion and Government has lasted from Huss and Wickliff to Lindsey and Priestly. How many powder Plotts, Bartholomews days, Irish Massacres, Paris Guillotines, how many Charles's and Maurices, Louis's and Williams, Georges and Napoleons, have intervened. And the Philosophers, if We believe Condorcet, have been as arrant Hypocrites as any of them. I am, as ever,

JOHN ADAMS.

50. This "Report on Public Instruction" was made to the National Assembly by the Committee on the Constitution in 1791.
51. "A Look at the Universities, and the Method of Public Instruction of the German Protestant; in Particular of the Kingdom of Westphalia" (Cassel, 1808).
52. "Collection of Researches on Education; a Memoir in the year XI to the Society of Sciences and Arts of Grenoble which has contributed to this Question, What are the Means of perfecting the Physical and Moral Education of Children?" (Paris, An XII [1804]).

Adams to Jefferson

Quincy June 20. 1815

DEAR SIR

The fit of recollection came upon both of Us, so nearly at the same time that I may, sometime or other, begin to think there is some thing in Priestleys and Hartleys vibrations.[53] The day before Yesterday I sent to the Post office a letter to you, and last night I received your kind favour of the 10th.

The question before the human race is, Whether the God of nature shall govern the World by his own laws, or Whether Priests and Kings shall rule it by fictitious Miracles? Or, in other Words, whether Authority is originally in the People? or whether it has descended for 1800 Years in a succession of Popes and Bishops, or brought down from Heaven by the holy Ghost in the form of a Dove, in a Phyal of holy Oil?

Who shall take the side of God and Nature? Brachmans,? Mandarins? Druids? Or Tecumseh and his Brother the Prophet? Or shall We become Disciples of the Phylosophers? And who are the Phylosophers? Frederick? Voltaire? Rousseau? Buffon? Diderot? or Condorcet? These Phylosophers have shewn them selves as incapable of governing mankind, as the Bou[r]bons or the Guelphs.

Condorcet has let the Cat out of the Bag. He has made precious confessions. I regret that I have only an English Translation of his "Outlines of an historical View of the progress of the human Mind." But in pages 247. 248 and 249 you will find it frankly acknowledged that the Phylosophers of the 18th Century, adopted all the Maxims and practiced all the Arts of the Pharisees, the ancient Priests of all Countries, the Jesuits, the Machiavillians etc etc to overthrow the Institutions that such Arts had established. This new Phylosophy, was by his own Account, as insideous, fraudulent hypocritical and cruel, as the old Policy of Priests, Nobles and Kings. When and where were ever found or will be found, Sincerity, Honesty or Veracity in any Sect or Party in Religion Government or Phylosophy? Johnson and Burke were more of Catholicks than Protestants at Heart and Gibbon became an Advocate for the Inquisition. There is no Act of

53. David Hartley, founder of the associationist school of psychology, presented two theories, the doctrine of vibrations (sensation is the result of vibration of particles of nerves) and the doctrine of associations. He pointed out the close relationship between the physiological and the psychical. Under Hartley's influence Priestley modified his traditional Calvinism to "necessarianism." David Hartley, *Observations on Man, His Frame, His Duty, and His Expectations* (London, 1749; reprinted 1801).

Uniformity in the Church or State phylosophick. As many Sects and Systems among them as among Quakers and Baptists.

Bona will not revive Inquisitions Jesuits or Slave Trade for which hebetudes, Bourbons have been driven again into Exile.

We shall get along, with or without War.

I have at last procured the Marquis D'Argens's Ocellus Timaeus [54] and Julian. Three such Volumes I never read. They are a most perfect exemplification of Condorcetts precious Confessions. It is astonishing they have not made more Noise in the World.

Our Athanasians have printed in a Pamphlet in Boston Your Letters and Priestleys from Belshams Lindsey.[55] It will do you no harm. Our Correspondence shall not again be so long interrupted. Affectionately,

JOHN ADAMS

Mrs. Adams thanks Mr. Jefferson for his friendly remembrance of her, and reciprocates to him, a thousand good wishes.[56]

P. S. Tickner and Gray were highly delighted with their Visit; charmed with the whole Family.

Have you read Carnot? Is it not afflicting to see a Man of such large Views so many noble Sentiments and such exalted integrity, groping in the dark for a Remedy? a ballance or a mediator between Independence and Despotism? How shall his "Love of Country," his "Honor" and his "national Spirit" be produced.

I cannot write a hundreth part of what I wish to say to you.

J. A.

Adams to Jefferson

Quincy June 22d. 15

DR. SIR

Can you give me any Information, concerning A. G. Camus? Is he a Chateaubriand? or a Marquis D'Argens? Does he mean to abolish Christianity? or to restore the Inquisition, the Jesuits, the Pope and the Devil?

Within a few days, I have received a thing as unexpected to me as an

54. See JA to TJ, Dec. 25, 1813, above, 411.
55. *American Unitarianism* . . . Compiled, . . . by Rev. Thomas Belsham . . . (Boston, 1815).
56. This sentence is in AA's hand.

Apparition from the dead; "Rapport a L'Institut National, Par A. G. Camus, imprime par Ordre de L'Institut, Pluviose An XI["] [1803].

In page 55 of this report he says

"Certain Pieces which I found in the Chamber of Accounts in Brussells gave me useful indications, concerning the grand Collection of the Bollandists; and conducted me, to make researches into the State of that Work, unfortunately interrupted at this day. It would add to the Institut to propose to Government the means of compleating it; as it has done with Success, for the collection of the historians of France, of diplomas and Ordinances." Permit me, to dwell a few minutes on this important Work. Note. "The Committee of the Institut for proposing and superintending the litterary labours, in the month of Frimaire an XI. wrote to the Minister of the interiour, requesting him to give orders, to the Prefect of the Dyle, and to the Prefect of the two Nethes, to summon the Citizens, Debue, Fonson, Heyten and all others, who had taken any part, in the Sequel of the Work of the Bollandists; to confer with these persons, as well concerning the continuation of this Work, as concerning the cession of the materials destined for the continuation of it; to promise to the Continuators of the Bollandists the support of the french Government, and to render an Account of their Conferences." End of the Note.

"Almost all the History of Europe, and a part of that of the East, from the seventh Century, to the thirteenth, is in the Lives of Personages, to whom have been given the title of *Saints*. Every one may have remarked, that in reading history, there is no event of any importance, in civil order, in which, some Bishop, some Abby, some Monk, or some Saint, did not take a part. It is therefore, a great Service, rendered by the Jesuits, known under the name of the Bollandists, to those who would write History, to have formed the immense Collection, extended to Fifty two Volumes in folio, known under the title of The Acts of the Saints.[57] The Service they have rendered to Litterature, is considerably augmented, by the insertion in their Acts of the Saints, a great number of Diplomas and dissertations, the greatest part of which, are Models of Criticism. There is no man, among the learned, who does not interest himself, in this great collection. My intension is not to recall to your recollection the original Authors or their first labours. We may easily know them, by turning over the leaves

57. After the Bollandists' library was dispersed by the French government in 1794, many of the volumes were lost. When the persecution abated, some of the books were salvaged and restored to the abbey of Tougerloo until 1825. Since there seemed to be no hope of resuming the work, a public sale of the volumes was held and the remainder deposited in the Royal Library of The Hague; the manuscripts were placed in the Library of Bourgogne, Brussels. The Institute of France tried in 1802 without success to induce the former Bollandists to resume the task; but it was re-established in 1836. In addition to the present letter, quoting from Camus, see JA to TJ, Feb. [–March 3], 1814, above, 429-30.

of the Collection, or if We would find the result already written, it is in the historical library of Meusel, T. 1. part 1. p. 306. or in the Manuel of litterary history by Bouginé. T. 2. p. 641. I shall date what I have to say to you, only from the Epoch of the Suppression of the Society of which the Bollandists were Members.

"At that time, three Jesuits were employed in the collection of the Acts of the Saints; to Witt; the Fathers, De Bie, De Bue, and Hubens. The Father Gesquière who had also laboured at the Acts of the Saints, reduced a particular collection intitled Select fragments from belgical Writers, and extracts or Refferences to matters contained in a collection intitled Musæum of Bellarmine. These four Monks inhabited the House of the Jesuits at Antwerp. Independently of the Use of the Library of the Convent, the Bollandists had their particular Library, the most important portion of which was a State of the Lives of the Saints for every day of the Month, with indi[c]ations of the Books in which were found those which were already printed, and the original Manuscripts, or the copies of Manuscripts, which were not yet printed. They frequently quote this particular Collection in their general Collection. The greatest part of the Copies they had assembled were the fruit of a Journey of the Fathers Papebroch and Henshen made to Rome in 1660; They remained there 'till 1662. Papebroch and his Associate brought from Rome, Copies of seven hundred Lives of Saints in greek or in latin. The Citizen La Serna, has in his Library a Copy taken by himself, from the Originals, of the relation of the Journey of Papebroch to Rome, and of the Correspondence of Henshen with his Colleagues. The Relation and the Correspondence are in latin. See Catalogue de La Serna.[58] T. 3. No. 3903.

"After the suppression of the Jesuits, The Commissione[r]s apposed their Seals upon the Library of the Bollandists, as well as on that of the Jesuits of Antwerp. But Mr. Girard, then Secretary of the Accademy of Brussells, who is still living, and who furnished me a part of the documents I use; charged with the Inventory and Sale of the Books, withdrew those of the Bollandists and transported them to Brussells.

"The Academy of Brussells, proposed to continue the Acts of the Saints under its own Name, and for this purpose to admit the four Jesuits into the number of its members. The Father Gesquiere alone consented to this Arrangement. The Other Jesuits obtained of Government, through the intervention of the Bishop of Neustadt, the Assurance, that they might continue their Collection. In Effect, the Empress Maria Theresa approved,

58. Carlos Antonio de La Serna Santander, *Catalogue des livres de la bibliotheque de M. C. de La Serna Santander*...corrected and enlarged, 4 vols. [Brussels, 1803]. La Serna had first published a catalogue of his uncle's library (1792), the richest collection in the Low Countries.

by a decree of the 19th. of June 1778 a plan which was presented to her, for the continuation of the Works, both of the Bollandists and of Gesquiere. This plan is in ample detail. It contains twenty Articles, and would be Useful to consult, if any Persons should resume the Acts of the Saints. The establishment of the Jesuits was fixed in the Abby of Caudenberg at Brussells; the library of the Bollandists was transported to that place; One of the Monks of the Abby, was associated with them; and the Father Hubens being dead, was replaced by Father Berthod, a Benedictin, who died in 1789.

"The Abby of Caudenberg, having been suppressed, the Government Assigned to the Bollandists a place in the ancient Colledge of the Jesuits at Brussells. They there placed their Library and went there to live. There they published the Fifty first Volume of their collection in 1786. the fifth tome of the month of October, printed at Brussells, at the Printing Press, Imperial and Royal, in Types Imperial and Royal (in Typis Caesario regiis). They had then two Associates, and they flattered themselves that the Emperor would continue to furnish the expence of their labours. Nevertheless, in 1788, the establishment of the Bollandists was suppressed, and they even proposed to sell the Stock of the printed Volumes; But, by an Instruction (Avis) of the 6th. December 1788, the Ecclesiastical Commission superceded the Sale, till the result could be known of a Negotiation which the Father De Bie, had commenced with the Abby of Saint Blaise to establish the Authors and transport the Stock of the Work, as well as the materials for its continuation at Saint-Blaise.

"In the meantime, the Abby of Tongerloo, offered the Government, to purchase the Library and the Stock of the Bollandists, and to cause the Work to be continued by the ancient Bollandists with the Monks of Tongerloo associated with them. These propositions were accepted: the Fathers De Bie, De Bue, and Gesquiere removed to Tongerloo; the Monks of Caudenberg refused to follow them, though they had been associated with them. On the Entry of the French Troops into Belgium, the Monks of Tongerloo quitted their Abbay: the Fathers de Bie and Gesquiere retired into Germany where they died; the Father De Bue, retired to the City of Hall, hereto fore Province of Hainault, his native Country. He lives, but is very aged. One of the Monks of Tongerloo, who had been associated with them is the Father Heylen: they were not able to inform me of the place of his residence. Another Monk, associated with the Bollandists of 1780 is the Father Fonson, who resides at Brussells.

"In the midst of these troubles, the Bollandists have caused to be printed the fifty second Volume of the Acts of the Saints, the sixth Volume of the Month of October. The fifty first volume is not common in commerce; because the sale of it, has been interrupted, by the continual Changes of the residence of the Bollandists. The fifty second Volume, or the Sixth of the same month of October, is much more rare. Few Persons know its Existence.

"The Citizen Serna has given me the 296 first pages of the Volume which he believes were printed at Tongerloo. He is persuaded that the Rest of the Volume exists; and he thinks it was at Rome that it was finished. (terminé).

"The Citizen D'Herbouville, Préfect of the department of the two Neths at Antwerp, has made, for about 18 months, Attempts, with the Ancient Bollandists, to engage them, to resume their labours. They have not had Success. Perhaps the present moment, would be the most critical. (opportune), especially if the Government should consent to give to the Bollandists Assurance of their Safety.

"The essential point would be to make sure of the Existence of the Manuscripts which I have indicated; and which by the relation of the Citizen *La Serna*, filled a Body of a Library of about three Toises in Length, and two in breadth. If these Manuscripts still exist, it is easy to terminate, the Acts of the Saints; because We shall have all the necessary Materials. If these Manuscripts are lost, We must despair to see this Collection compleated.

"I have enlarged, a little, in this digression, on the Acts of the Saints, because it is a Work of great importance; and because these documents, which cannot be obtained with any Exactitude but upon the Spots; seem to me to be among the principal Objects, which your Travellers, have to collect, and of which they ought to give you an Account."

Now, my Friend Jefferson! I await your observations on this Morcell. You may think I waste my time and yours. I do not think so. If you will look into the "Nouveau Dictionaire Historique," under the Words Bollandus, Heinshemius and Papebrock you will find more particulars of the Rise and progress of this great Work "The Acts of the Saints."

I shall make only an Observation or two.

1. The Pope never suppressed the Work, and Maria Theresia established it. It therefore, must be Catholick.

2. Notwithstanding the Professions of the Bollandists, to discriminate the true from the false Miracles and the dubious from both; I suspect that the false, will be found the fewest, the dubious the next, and the true the most numerous of all.

3. From all that I have read, of the Legends, of the Lives and Writings of the Saints and even of the Fathers, and of Ecclesiastical History in general: I have no doubt that the Acta Sanctorum is the most enormous Mass of Lies Frauds, Hypocracy and Imposture, that ever was heaped together upon this Globe. If it were impartially consulted it would do

more to open the Eyes of Man kind, than all the Phylosophers of the 18th. Century, who were as great Hypocrites as any of the Phylosophers or Theologians of Antiquity.

JOHN ADAMS

Adams to Jefferson and Thomas McKean

Quincy July 30th 1815

DEAR SIR

Who shall write the history of the American revolution? Who can write it? Who will ever be able to write it?

The most essential documents, the debates and deliberations in Congress from 1774 to 1783 were all in secret, and are now lost forever. Mr. Dickinson printed a speech, which he said he made in Congress against the Declaration of Independence; [59] but it appeared to me very different from that, which you, and I heard. Dr. Witherspoon has published speeches [60] which he wrote beforehand, and delivered Memoriter, as he did his Sermons. But these I believe are the only speeches ever committed to writing. The Orators, while I was in Congress from 1774 to 1778 appeared to me very universally extemporaneous, and I have never heard of any committed to writing before or after delivery.

These questions have been suggested to me, by a review, in the Analectic Magazine, for May 1815, published in Philadelphia, page 385 of the Chevalier Botta's "Storia della Guerra Americana." The Reviewers inform us, that it is the best history of the revolution that ever has been written. This Italian Classick has followed the example, of the Greek and Roman Historians, by composing speeches for his Generals and Orators. The Reviewers have translated, one of Mr R H Lee in favour of the declaration of Independence. A splendid morcell of oratory it is; how faithful, you can judge.

I wish to know your sentiments, and opinions of this publication. Some future Miss Porter, may hereafter, make as shining a romance, of what passed in Congress, while in Conclave, as her Scottish Chiefs. Your friend durante Vitæ.

JOHN ADAMS [61]

59. First published in Carlo Guiseppo Guglielmo Botta, *Storia della guerra Americana* (Paris, 1809); French transl. (Paris, 1812-13).

60. No such speeches were published by Witherspoon, according to Varnum L. Collins, *President Witherspoon* (Princeton, 1925), I, 219-21.

61. McKean replied that Botta "appears to me a vain and presuming character to have attempted such a history" and suggested that perhaps poverty "impelled him." McKean to JA, Nov. 20, 1815, *Works*, X, 177.

Jefferson to Adams

Monticello Aug. 10.[-11] 15.

DEAR SIR

The simultaneous movements in our correspondence have been really remarkable on several occasions. It would seem as if the state of the air, or state of the times, or some other unknown cause produced a sympathetic effect on our mutual recollections. I had sat down to answer your letters of June 19. 20. 22. with pen, ink, and paper before me, when I recieved from our mail that of July 30.

You ask information on the subject of Camus. All I recollect of him is that he was one of the deputies sent to arrest Dumourier at the head of his army, who were however themselves arrested by Dumourier, and long detained as prisoners. I presume therefore he was a Jacobin. You will find his character in the most excellent revolutionary history of Toulongeon: I believe also he may be the same person who has given us a translation of Aristotle's natural history from the Greek into French. Of his report to the National Institute on the subject of the Bollandists your letter gives me the first information. I had supposed them defunct with the society of Jesuits, of which they were: and that their works, altho' above ground, were, from their bulk and insignificance, as effectually entombed on their shelves, as if in the graves of their authors. Fifty two volumes in folio of the Acta Sanctorum, in dog-Latin, would be a formidable enterprize to the most laborious German. I expect, with you, they are the most enormous mass of lies, frauds, hypocrisy and imposture that ever was heaped together on this globe. By what chemical process M. Camus supposed that an Extract of truth could be obtained from such a farrago of falsehood, I must leave to the Chemists and Moralists of the age to divine.

On the subject of the history of the American revolution, you ask Who shall write it? Who can write it? And who ever will be able to write it? Nobody; except merely it's external facts. All it's councils, designs and discussions, having been conducted by Congress with closed doors, and no member, as far as I know, having even made notes of them, these, which are the life and soul of history must for ever be unknown. Botta, as you observe, has put his own speculations and reasonings into the mouths of persons whom he names, but who, you and I know, never made such speeches. In this he has followed the example of the antients, who made their great men deliver long speeches, all of them in the same style, and in that of the author himself. The work is nevertheless a good one, more judicious, more chaste, more classical, and more true than the party diatribe of Marshall. It's greatest fault is in having taken too much from him. I possessed the work, and often recurred to considerable portions of it, altho' I never read it through. But a very judicious and well informed neighbor of mine went thro' it with great attention, and spoke very highly of it. I have said that no member of the old Congress, as far as I knew, made notes of the discussions. I did not know of the speeches you mention of Dickinson and Witherspoon. But on the questions of Independance, and on the two articles of Confederation respecting taxes and voting, I took minutes of the heads of the arguments. On the first I threw all into one mass, without ascribing to the speakers their respective arguments; pretty much in the manner of Hume's summary digests of the reasonings in parliament for and against a measure. On the last, I stated the heads of arguments used by each speaker. But the whole of my notes on the question of independance does not occupy more than 5. pages, such as of this letter: and on the other questions two such sheets. They have never been communicated to any one.[62]

Do you know that there exists in MS. the ablest work of this kind ever yet executed, of the debates of the Constitutional convention of Philadelphia in 1788 [i.e., 1787]? The whole of everything said and done there was taken down by Mr. Madison, with a labor and exactness beyond comprehension.[63]

I presume that our correspondence has been observed at the post offices, and thus has attracted notice. Would you believe that a printer has had the effrontery to propose to me the letting him publish it? These people think they have a right to everything however secret or sacred. I had not before heard of the Boston pamphlet with Priestly's letters and mine.

At length Bonaparte has got on the right side of a question. From the time of his entering the legislative hall to his retreat to Elba, no man has execrated him more than myself. I will not except even the members of the Essex junto; altho' for very different reasons; I, because he was warring against the liberty of his own country, and independance of others; they, because he was the enemy of England, the Pope, and the Inquisition. But at length, and as far as we can judge, he seems to have become the choice

62. "Notes of Proceedings in the Continental Congress" [June 7 to Aug. 1, 1776], Boyd, I, 309-27. Boyd regards TJ's graphic account as "perhaps the best single source of information concerning the movement toward independence and the formation of the Articles of Confederation, not even excepting the similar notes made by John Adams"; *ibid.*, 299. The "Notes" were inserted in TJ's Autobiography some time between 1822 and 1825; *ibid.*, 299-301. TJ had sent a copy to Madison on June 1, 1783; *ibid.*, 327n.

63. First published in Madison's *Papers ... being His Correspondence and Reports of Debates*, ed. by Henry D. Gilpin, 3 vols. (Washington, 1840). The best edition is Farrand, ed., *Records of the Federal Convention of 1787*.

of his nation. At least he is defending the cause of his nation, and that of all mankind, the rights of every people to independance and self-government. He and the allies have now changed sides. They are parcelling out among themselves Poland, Belgium, Saxony, Italy, dictating a ruler and government to France, and looking askance at our republic, the splendid libel on their governments: and he is fighting for the principle of national independance, of which his whole life hitherto has been a continued violation. He has promised a free government to his own country, and to respect the rights of others: and altho' his former conduct inspires little confidence in his promises yet we had better take the chance of his word for doing right, than the certainty of the wrong which his adversaries are doing and avowing. If they succeed, ours is only the boon of the Cyclops to Ulysses, of being the last devoured. Present me affectionately and respectfully to Mrs. Adams, and heaven give you both as much more of life as you wish, and bless it with health and happiness.

TH: JEFFERSON

Aug. 11. P.S. I had finished my letter yesterday, and this morning recieve the news of Bonaparte's second abdication. Very well. For him personally I have no feeling but of reprobation. The representatives of the nation have deposed him. They have taken the allies at their word, that they had no object in the war but his removal. The nation is now free to give itself a good government, either with or without a Bourbon; and France unsubdued will still be a bridle on the enterprises of the combined powers, and a bulwark to others.

Adams to Jefferson

Quincy Aug. 24. 15

DEAR SIR

If I am neither deceived by the little Information I have, or by my Wishes for its truth, I should say that France is the most *Protestant* Country of Europe At this time, though I cannot think it the most *reformed*. In consequence of these Reveries I have imagined that Camus and the Institute, meant, by the revival and continuance of the Acta Sanctorum, to destroy the Pope and the Catholic Church and Hierarchy, de fonde en comble ["from top to bottom"], or in the language of Frederick, Voltaire, D'Alembert etc "ecraser le miserable," "crush the Wretch." This great Work must contain the most complete History of the corruptions of Christianity, that has ever appeared; Priestleys not excepted. And his History of ancient Opinions not excepted.

As to the history of the Revolution, my Ideas may be peculiar, perhaps singular. What do We Mean by the Revolution? The War? That was no part of the Revolution. It was only an Effect and Consequence of it. The Revolution was in the Minds of the People, and this was effected, from 1760 to 1775, in the course of fifteen Years before a drop of blood was drawn at Lexington. The Records of thirteen Legislatures, the Pamp[h]-lets, Newspapers in all the Colonies ought [to] be consulted, during that Period, to ascertain the Steps by which the public Opinion was enlightened and informed concerning the Authority of Parliament over the Colonies. The Congress of 1774, resembled in some respects, tho' I hope not in many, the Counsell of Nice in Ecclesiastical History.[64] It assembled the Priests from the East and the West the North and the South, who compared Notes, engaged in discussions and debates and formed Results by one Vote and by two Votes, which went out to the World as unanimous.

Mr. Madisons Notes of the Convention of 1787 or 1788 are consistent with his indefatigable Character. I shall never see them; but I hope Posterity will.

That our correspondence has been observed is no Wonder; for your hand is more universally known than your face. No Printer has asked me for copies: but it is no Surprize that you have been requested. These Gentry will print whatever will sell: and our Correspondence is thought such an Oddity by both Parties, that the Printers imagine an Edition would soon go off and yeild them a Profit. There has however been no tampering with Your Letters to me. They have all arrived in good Order.

Poor Bonaparte! Poor Devil! What has and what will become of him? Going the Way of King Theodore, Alexander Cæsar, Charles 12th Cro[m]well, Wat Tyler and Jack Cade; i.e. to a bad End. And what will become of Wellington? Envied, hated despized by all the Barons, Earls, Viscounts, Marquis's as an Upstart a Parvenue elevated Over their heads. For these People have no Idea of any Merit, but Birth. Wellington must pass the rest of his days buffetted ridiculed, scorned and insulted by Factions as Marlborough and his Dutchess did. Military Glory dazzles the Eyes of Mankind, and for a time eclipses all Wisdom all Virtue, all Laws humane and divine; and after this it would be Bathos to desend to Services merely civil or political.

Napoleon has imposed Kings Upon Spain Holland Sweeden Westphalia Saxony Naples etc. The combined Emperors and Kings are about to retaliate Upon France, by imposing a King upon her. These are all abominable Examples, detestable Precedents. When will the Rights of Mankind

64. See above, Chap. 9, n. 43.

the Liberties and Independence of Nations be respected? When the Perfectibility of the human Mind shall arrive at Perfection. When the Progress of Manillius's *Ratio* shall have not only

Eripuit Cælo fulmen, Jovisque fulgoves [i.e., fulgores],[65] but made Mankind rational Creatures

It remains to be seen whether The Allies were honest in their Declaration that they were at War only with Napoleon.

Can the French ever be cordially reconciled to the Bourbons again? If not, who can they find for a head? The Infant or one of the Generals? Innumerable difficulties will embarrass either Project. I am as ever

JOHN ADAMS

Adams to Jefferson

Quincy Nov. 13 1815

DEAR SIR

The fund[a]mental Article of my political Creed is, that Despotism, or unlimited Sovereignty, or absolute Power is the same in a Majority of a popular Assembly, an Aristocratical Counsel, an Oligarchical Junto and a single Emperor. Equally arbitrary cruel bloody and in every respect diabolical.

Accordingly arbitrary Power, wherever it has resided, has never failed to destroy all the records Memorials and Histories of former times which it did not like and to corrupt and interpolate such as it was cunning enough to preserve or to tolerate. We cannot therefore say with much confidence, what Knowledge or what Virtues may have prevailed in some former Ages in some quarters of the World.

Nevertheless, according to the few lights that remain to Us, We may say that the Eighteenth Century, notwithstanding all its Errors and Vices has been, of all that are past, the most honourable to human Nature. Knowledge and Virtues were increased and diffused, Arts, Sciences useful to Men, ameliorating their condition, were improved, more than in any former equal Period.

But, what are We to say now? Is the Nineteenth Century to be a Contrast to the Eighteenth? Is it to extinguish all the Lights of its Predecessor? Are the Sorbonne, the Inquisition, the Index expurgatorius, and the Knights Errant of St Ignatius Loyola to be revived and restored to all their salutary Powers of supporting and propagating the mild Spirit of

65. "He snatched the thunderbolt from the sky, and the lightning of Jove."

Christianity? The Proceedings of the Allies and their Congress at Vienna, the Accounts from Spain France etc the Chateaubriands and the Genlis, indicate which Way the Wind blows. The Priests are at their Old Work again. The Protestants are denounced and another St Bartholomew's day, threatened.

This however, will probably, 25 Years hence, be honoured with the Character of "*The effusions of a splenetic mind, rather than as the sober reflections of an unbiassed Understanding.*" I have recd. "Memoirs of the Life of Dr. Price["] by William Morgan F.R.S.[66] In pages 157 and 155 [i.e., 158] Mr. Morgan says. "So well assured was Dr. Price of the establishment of a free Constitution in France, and of the subsequent Overthrow of Despotism throughout Europe as the consequence of it, that he never failed to express his Gratitude to Heaven for having extended his life to the present happy Period in which After sharing the Benefits of one Revolution, he had been spared to be a Witness to two others Revolutions both glorious." But some of his Correspondents were not quite so sanguine in their expectations from the last of these Revolutions; and among these, the late American Ambassador, Mr. John Adams. In a long letter which he wrote to Dr. Price at this time,[67] so far from congratulating him, on the Occasion, he expresses himself in terms of contempt, in regard to the French revolution; and after asking rather too severely what good was to be expected from a Nation of Athei[s]ts, he concludes with foretelling the destru[c]tion of a million of human Beings as the probable consequence of it. These harsh censures and gloomy Predictions were particularly ungratefull to Dr. Price; nor can it be denied that they must have then appeared as *the effusions of a splenetic mind, rather than as the sober reflections of an unbiassed Understanding.*"

I know not what a candid Public will think of this practice of Mr. Morgan after the Example of Mr. Belsham, who finding private Letters in the Cabinet of a great and good Man after his decease, written in the Utmost fre[e]dom and confidence of intimate friendship, by Persons still living, though after the lapse of a quarter of a Century, produces them before the World.[68] Dr. Disney had different Feelings, and a different Judgment. Finding some cursory Letters among the Papers of Mr. Hollis he would not publish them without my consent.[69] In Answer to his request

66. William Morgan, *Memoirs of the Life of the Rev. Richard Price* (London, 1815). In view of Morgan's statement about JA's letter (below), it is ironical that in his preface (p. vi) Morgan said he had used Price's private correspondence sparingly, since he should not "under any circumstances, have thought myself justified in gratifying an idle curiosity by the indiscriminate publication of letters... written in the confidence of private friendship."

67. JA to Price, April 19, 1790, *Works*, IX, 563-65.

68. See JA to TJ, May 29, June 10, 11, 14, and 25, 1813, above, 325-30, 333-34.

69. John Disney, *Memoirs of T. Brand-Hollis* (London, 1808).

I submitted them to his discretion and might have done the same to Mr. Morgan. Indeed had Mr. Morgan published my Letter entire I should not have given him nor myself any concern about it. But as in his Summary he has not done this Letter Justice, I shall give it with all its faults.

Mr. Morgan has been more discrete and complaisant to you than to me. He has mentioned respectfully Your Letters from Paris to Dr. Price, but has given Us none of them.[70] As I would give more for those Letters that [i.e., than] for all the rest of [the] book, I am more angry with him for disappointing me; than for all he says of me and my Letter which, scambling as it is, contains nothing but the sure Words of Prophecy. I am as usual Yours

JOHN ADAMS

Jefferson to Adams

Monticello Jan. 11. 16.

DEAR SIR

Of the last five months I have past four at my other domicil, for such it is in a considerable degree. No letters are forwarded to me there, because the cross post to that place is circuitous and uncertain. During my absence therefore they are accumulating here, and awaiting acknolegments. This has been the fate of your favor of Nov. 13.

I agree with you in all it's eulogies on the 18th. century. It certainly witnessed the sciences and arts, manners and morals, advanced to a higher degree than the world had ever before seen. And might we not go back to the aera of the Borgias, by which time the barbarous ages had reduced national morality to it's lowest point of depravity, and observe that the arts and sciences, rising from that point, advanced gradually thro' all the 16th. 17th. and 18th. centuries, softening and correcting the manners and morals of man? I think too we may add, to the great honor of science and the arts, that their natural effect is, by illuminating public opinion, to erect it into a Censor, before which the most exalted tremble for their future, as well as present fame. With some exceptions only, through the 17th. and 18th. centuries morality occupied an honorable chapter in the political code of nations. You must have observed while in Europe, as I thought I did, that those who administered the governments of the greater

70. Morgan explained that he did not quote TJ because events had either sustained or falsified his predictions about the French Revolution. Morgan, *Memoirs of Price*, 151.

powers at least, had a respect to faith, and considered the dignity of their government as involved in it's integrity. A wound indeed was inflicted on this character of honor in the 18th. century by the partition of Poland.[71] But this was the atrocity of a barbarous government chiefly, in conjunction with a smaller one still scrambling to become great, while one only of those already great, and having character to lose, descended to the baseness of an accomplice in the crime. France, England, Spain shared in it only inasmuch as they stood aloof and permitted it's perpetration. How then has it happened that these nations, France especially and England, so great, so dignified, so distinguished by science and the arts, plunged at once into all the depths of human enormity, threw off suddenly and openly all the restraints of morality, all sensation to character, and unblushingly avowed and acted on the principle that power was right? Can this sudden apostacy from national rectitude be accounted for? The treaty of Pilnitz [72] seems to have begun it, suggested perhaps by the baneful precedent of Poland. Was it from the terror of monarchs, alarmed at the light returning on them from the West, and kindling a Volcano under their thrones? Was it a combination to extinguish that light, and to bring back, as their best auxiliaries, those enumerated by you, the Sorbonne, the Inquisition, the Index expurgatorius, and the knights of Loyola? Whatever it was, the close of the century saw the moral world thrown back again to the age of the Borgias, to the point from which it had departed 300. years before. France, after crushing and punishing the conspiracy of Pilnitz, went herself deeper and deeper into the crimes she had been chastising. I say France, and not Bonaparte; for altho' he was the head and mouth, the nation furnished the hands which executed his enormities. England, altho' in opposition, kept full pace with France, not indeed by the manly force of her own arms, but by oppressing the weak, and bribing the strong. At length the whole choir joined and divided the weaker nations among them. Your prophecies to Dr. Price proved truer than mine; and yet fell short of the fact, for instead of a million, the destruction of 8. or 10. millions of human beings has probably been the effect of these convulsions. I did not, in 89. believe they would have lasted so long, nor have cost so much blood. But altho' your prophecy has proved true so far, I hope it does not preclude a better final result. That same light from our West seems to have spread and illuminated the very engines employed to extinguish it. It has given them a glimmering of their rights and their power. The idea of representative government has taken root and growth among

71. By Austria, Russia, and Prussia in 1773, 1793, and 1795.
72. In Aug. 1791 the Emperor Leopold and Frederick William II of Prussia agreed to take common action against any attack by the French and thus formed the basis for the first coalition against France.

them. Their masters feel it, and are saving themselves by timely offers of this modification of their own powers. Belgium, Prussia, Poland, Lombardy etc. are now offered a representative organization: illusive probably at first, but it will grow into power in the end. Opinion is power, and that opinion will come. Even France will yet attain representative government. You observe it makes the basis of every constitution which has been demanded or offered: of that demanded by their Senate; of that offered by Bonaparte; and of that granted by Louis XVIII. The idea then is rooted, and will be established, altho' rivers of blood may yet flow between them and their object. The allied armies now couching upon them are first to be destroyed, and destroyed they will surely be. A nation united can never be conquered. We have seen what the ignorant bigotted and unarmed Spaniards could do against the disciplined veterans of their invaders. What then may we not expect from the power and character of the French nation? The oppressors may cut off heads after heads, but like those of the Hydra, they multiply at every stroke. The recruits within a nation's own limits are prompt and without number; while those of their invaders from a distance are slow, limited, and must come to an end. I think too we percieve that all these allies do not see the same interest in the annihilation of the power of France. There are certainly some symptoms of foresight in Alexander that France might produce a salutary diversion of force were Austria and Prussia to become her enemies. France too is the natural ally of the Turk, as having no interfering interests, and might be useful in neutralizing and perhaps turning that power on Austria. That a re-acting jealousy too exists with Austria and Prussia I think their late strict alliance indicates; and I should not wonder if Spain should discover a sympathy with them. Italy is so divided as to be nothing. Here then we see new coalitions in embrio which after France shall in turn have suffered a just punishment for her crimes, will not only raise her from the earth on which she is prostrate, but give her an opportunity to establish a government of as much liberty as she can bear, enough to ensure her happiness and prosperity. When insurrection begins, be it where it will, all the partitioned countries will rush to arms, and Europe again become an Arena of gladiators. And what is the definite object they will propose? A restoration certainly of the status quo prius, of the state of possession of 89. I see no other principle on which Europe can ever again settle down in lasting peace. I hope your prophecies will go thus far, as my wishes do, and that they, like the former, will prove to have been the sober dictates of a superior understanding, and a sound calculation of effects from causes well understood. Some future Morgan will then have an opportunity of doing you justice, and of counterbalancing the breach of confidence of which you so justly complain, and in which no one has had more frequent occasion of fellow-feeling than myself. Permit me to place here my affectionate respects to Mrs. Adams, and to add for yourself the assurances of cordial friendship and esteem.

TH: JEFFERSON

Adams to Jefferson

Quincy Feb. 2. 1816

DEAR SIR

I know not what to say of your Letter of the 11th. of Jan. but that it is one of the most consolatory, I ever received.

To trace the Commencement of the Reformation I suspect We must go farther back than Borgia, or even than Huss or Wickliff, and I want the Acta Sanctorum to assist me in this Research. That stupendous Monument of human Hypocricy and Fanaticism the Church of St. Peter at Rome, which was a Century and an Half in Building; excited the Ambition of Leo the tenth, who believed no more of the Christian Religion than Diderot, to finish it: and finding St. Peters Pence insufficient, he deluged all Europe with Indulgences for Sale, and excited Luther to contravert his Authority to grant them. Luther and his Associates and Followers, went less than half way in detecting the Corruptions of Christianity; but they acquired Reverence and Authority among their Followers almost as absolute as that of the Popes had been. To enter into details would be endless. But I agree with you, that the natural Effect of Science and Arts is to erect public opinion into a Censor, which must in some degree be respected by all.

There is no difference of Opinion or Feeling between Us, concerning the Partition of Poland, the intended Partitions of Pilnitz or the more daring Partitions of Vienna.[73]

Your Question "How the Apostacy from National Rectitude can be Accounted for" is too deep and wide for my Capacity to answer. I leave Fisher Ames to dogmatize up[on] the Affairs of Europe and Mankind. I have done too much in this Way. A burned Child dreads the Fire. I can only say at present, that it should seem that human Reason and human Conscience, though I believe there are such things, are not a Match, for human Passions, human Imaginations and human Enthusiasm. You however I believe have hit one Mark, "the Fires the Governments of Europe

73. At the Congress of Vienna, 1814-15.

felt kindling under their Seats": and I will hazard a shot at another, The Priests of all Nations imagined they felt Approaching such Flames as they had so often kindled about the Bodies of honest Men. Priests and Politicians, never before, so suddenly and so unanimously concurred in reestablishing Darkness and Ignorance Superstition and Despotism.

The Morality of Tacitus, is the Morality of Patriotism, and Britain and France have adopted his Creed; i.e. that all things were made for Rome. Jura negat sibi Cata [i.e., nata], nihil non arrogat Armis,[74] said Achilles. Laws were not made for me, said the Regent of France and his Cardinal Minister Du Bois. The Universe was made for me, says Man. Jesus despized and condemned this Patr[i]otism: But what Nation or What Christian has adopted his System? He was, as you say "the most benevolent Being, that ever appeard on Earth." France and England, Bourbons and Bonaparte, and all the Sovereigns at Vienna, have acted on the same Principle "All things were made for my Use." "Lo! Man for mine, replies a Pampered Goose".[75] The Philosophers of the 18th. Century have acted on the same Principle. ["]When it is to combat Evil, 'tis lawful to employ the Devil." [76] Bonus Populus Vult decipi; decipiatur.[77] They have employed the same Fals[e]h[o]od the same deceit, which Philosophers and Priests of all Ages have employed for their own selfish Purposes. We now know how their Efforts have succeeded. The old Deceivers have tryumphed over the New. Truth, must be more respected than it ever has been, before, any great Improvement can be expected in the Condition of Mankind. As Rochfaucault his Maxims drew, from history and from Practice, "I believe them true." From the whole Nature of Man, Moral intellectual and physical he did not draw them. We must come to the Principles of Jesus. But, when will all Men and all Nations do as they would be done by? Forgive all Injuries and love their Enemies as themselves? I leave those profound Phylosophers whose Sagacity perceives the Perfectibility of Humane Nature, and those illuminated Theologians who expect the Apocalyptic Reign, to enjoy their transporting hopes; provided always that they will not engage Us in Crusades and French Revolutions, nor burn Us for doubting. My Spirit of Prophecy reaches no farther than, *New England* GUESSES.

You ask, how it has happened that all Europe, has acted on the Principle "that Power was Right." I know not what Answer to give you, but this,

74. "He denies that laws were made for him; he arrogates everything to himself by force of arms."

75. See Maynard Mack, ed., *Alexander Pope, An Essay on Man* (London and New Haven, 1950 and 1951), 96.

76. Matthew Prior, "Hans Carvel," *Works* (London, 1779), 124, lines 69-70.

77. "The people wish to be deceived; then let them be deceived," Jacques-Auguste de Thou.

that Power always sincerely, conscientiously, de tres bon Foi, believes itself Right. Power always thinks it has a great Soul, and vast Views, beyond the Comprehension of the Weak; and that it is doing God Service, when it is violating all his Laws. Our Passions, Ambition, Avarice, Love, Resentment etc possess so much metaphysi[c]al Subtilty and so much overpowering Eloquence, that they insinuate themselves into the Understanding and the Conscience and convert both to their Party. And I may be deceived as much as any of them, when I say, that Power must never be trusted without a Check.

Morgan has misrepresented my Guess.[78] There is not a Word in my Letter about "a Million of human Beings." Civil Wars, of an hundred Years, throughout Europe, were guest at, and this is broad enough for your Ideas; for Eighteen or twenty Million would be a moderate Computation for a Century of civil Wars throug[h]out Europe. I still pray that a Century of civil Wars, may not desolute Europe and America too South, and North.

Your Speculations into Futurity in Europe are so probable that I can suggest no doubts to their disadvantage. All will depend on the Progress of Knowledge. But how shall Knowledge Advance? Independant of Temporal and Spiritual Power, the Course of Science and Litterature is obstructed and discouraged by so many Causes that it is to be feared, their motions will be slow. I have just finished reading four Volumes of D'Israeli, two on the Calamities and two on the Quarrels of Authors. These would be sufficient to shew that, slow rises Genius by Poverty and Envy oppressed. Even Newton and Lock and Grotius could not escape. France could furnish four other Volumes of the Woes and Wars of Authors.

My Compliments to Mrs Randolph, her Daughter Ellen and all her other Children, and believe me, as ever,

JOHN ADAMS

To which Mrs Adams adds her affectionate regards, and a wish that distance did not seperate Souls congenial.[79]

78. See JA to TJ, Nov. 13, 1815, above, 457.
79. This sentence is in AA's hand.

Adams to Jefferson

Quincy March 2. 16

DEAR SIR

I cannot be serious! I am about to write You, the most frivolous letter, you ever read.

Would you go back to your Cradle and live over again Your 70 Years? I believe You would return me a New England Answer, by asking me another question "Would you live your 80 Years over again?"

If I am prepared to give you an explicit Answer, the question involves so many considerations of Metaphysicks and Physicks, of Theology and Ethicks of Phylosophy and History, of Experience and Romance, of Tragedy Comedy and Farce; that I would not give my Opinion without writing a Volume to justify it.

I have lately lived over again, in part, from 1753, when I was junior Sophister at Colledge till 1769 when I was digging in the Mines, as a Barrister at Law, for Silver and gold, in the Town of Boston; and got as much of the shining dross for my labour as my Utmost Avarice at that time craved.

At the hazard of all the little Vision that is left me, I have read the History of that Period of 16 Years, in the six first Volumes of the Baron de Grimm. In a late Letter to you, I expressed a Wish to see an History of Quarrels and Calamities of Authors in France, like that of D'Israeli in England. I did not expect it so soon: but now I have it in a manner more masterly than I ever hoped to see it. It is not only a Narration of the incessant great Wars between the Ecclesiasticks and the Phylosophers, but of the little Skirmishes and Squabbles of Poets, Musicians, Sculptors Painters Architects Tragedians, Comediens, Opera Singers and Dancers, Chansons, Vaudevilles Epigrams, Madrigals Epitaphs, Anagrams Sonnets etc.

No man is more Sensible than I am, of the Service to Science and Letters, Humanity, Fraternity, and Liberty, that would have been rendered by the Encyclopedists and Œconomists, By Voltaire, Dalembert, Buffon Diderot, Rouseau La Lande, Frederick and Catharine, if they had possessed Common Sense. But they were all totally destitute of it. They all seemed to think that all Christendom was convinced as they were, that all Religion was "Visions Judaicques" and that their effulgent Lights had illuminated all the World. They seemed to believe, that whole Nations and Continents had been changed in their Principles Opinions Habits and Feelings by the Sovereign Grace of their Almighty Philosophy, almost as suddenly as

Catholicks and Calving[is]ts believe in instantaneous Conversion. They had not considered the force of early Education on the Millions of Minds who had never heared of their Philosophy.

And what was their Phylosophy? Atheism; pure unadulterated Atheism. Diderot, D'Alembert, Frederick, De Lalande and Grimm were indubitable Atheists. The Univer[s]e was Matter only and eternal; Spirit was a Word Without a meaning; Liberty was a Word Without a Meaning. There was no Liberty in the Universe; Liberty was a Word void of Sense. Every thought Word Passion Sentiment Feeling, all Motion and Action was necessary. All Beings and Attributes were of eternal Necessity. Conscience, Morality were all nothing but Fate.

This was their Creed and this was to perfect human Nature and convert the Earth into a Paradise of Pleasure. Who, and what is this Fate? He must be a sensible Fellow. He must be a Master of Science. He must be Master of spherical Trigonometry and Great Circle sailing. He must calculate Eclipses in his head by Intuition. He must be Master of the Science of Infinitesimal "Le Science des infiniment petits." He must involve and extract all the Roots by Intuition and be familiar with all possible or imaginable Sections of the Cone. He must be a Master of Arts Mechanical and imitative. He must have more Eloquence than Demosthenes, more Wit than Swift or Volltaire, more humour than Butler or Trumbull. And what is more comfortable than all the rest, he must be good natured, for this is upon the whole a good World. There is ten times as much pleasure as pain in it.

Why then should We abhor the Word God, and fall in Love with the Word Fate? We know there exists Energy and Intellect enough to produce such a World as this, which is a sublime and beautiful one, and a very benevolent one, notwithstanding all our snarling, and a happy one, if it is not made otherwise by our own fault.

Ask a Mite, in the Center of your Mammoth Cheese,[80] what he thinks of the "το παν." [81]

I should prefer the Philosophy of Tymæus of Locris, before that of Grimm and Diderot, Frederick and D'Alembert. I should even prefer the Shast[r]a of Indostan, or the Chaldean Egyptian, Indian, Greek, Christian Mahometan Tubonic or Celtic Theology.

---

80. "The Mammoth Cheese," made by the citizens of Cheshire, Mass., in honor of TJ and his Republicanism, was presented to him at the executive mansion in Washington on Jan. 1, 1802, by the Reverend John Leland, Baptist elder, former citizen of Virginia. He had lent valuable support toward Virginia's ratification of the Constitution in 1788 and the passage of the Bill of Rights by Congress in 1791. L. H. Butterfield, "Elder John Leland, Jeffersonian Itinerant," American Antiquarian Society, *Proceedings*, 62, pt. 2 (Oct. 1952), 214-29.

81. "The all," i.e., "totality.

Timæus and Ocellus taught that three Principles were eternal, God, Matter and Form. God was good, and had Ideas. Matter was Necessity, Fate, dead, without Ideas, without form without Feeling, perverse, untractible, capable however of being cutt into Forms of Spheres Circles, Triangles, Squares cubes Cones etc. The Ideas of the good God laboured upon matter to bring it into Form: but Matter was Fate Necessity, Dulness Obstinacy and would not always conform to the Ideas of the good God who desired to make the best of all possible Worlds but Matter, Fate Necessity resisted and would not let him compleat his Idea. Hence all the Evil and disorder, Paine Misery and Imperfection of the Universe.

We all curse Robespierre and Bonaparte; but were they not both such restless vain extravagant Animals as Diderot and Voltaire? Voltaire was the greatest Litterary Character and Bona the greatest Millitary Character of the 18 Century. There is all the difference between them. Both equally Heros and equally Cowards.

When You asked my Opinion of a University, it would have been easy to Advise Mathematicks Experimental Phylosophy, Natural History Chemistry and Astronomy Geography and the Fine Arts, to the Exclusion of Ontology Metaphysicks and Theology. But knowing the eager Impatience of the human Mind to search into Eternity and Infinity, the first Cause and last End of all Things I thought best to leave it, its Liberty to inquire till it is convinced as I have been these 50 Years that there is but one Being in the Universe, who comprehends it; and our last Resource is Resignation.

This Grimm must have been in Paris when You was there. Did You know him or hear of him?

I have this moment recd. two Volumes more, but these are from 1777 to 1782, leaving the Chaine broken from 1769 to 1777. I hope hereafter to get the two intervening Volumes. I am your old Friend

JOHN ADAMS

Jefferson to Adams

Monticello Apr. 8. 16.

DEAR SIR

I have to acknolege your two favors of Feb. 16. and Mar. 2. and to join sincerely in the sentiment of Mrs. Adams, and regret that distance separates us so widely. An hour of conversation would be worth a volume of letters. But we must take things as they come.

You ask if I would agree to live my 70. or rather 73. years over again? To which I say Yea. I think with you that it is a good world on the whole, that it has been framed on a principle of benevolence, and more pleasure than pain dealt out to us. There are indeed (who might say Nay) gloomy and hypocondriac minds, inhabitants of diseased bodies, disgusted with the present, and despairing of the future; always counting that the worst will happen, because it may happen. To these I say How much pain have cost us the evils which have never happened? My temperament is sanguine. I steer my bark with Hope in the head, leaving Fear astern. My hopes indeed sometimes fail; but not oftener than the forebodings of the gloomy. There are, I acknolege, even in the happiest life, some terrible convulsions, heavy set-offs against the opposite page of the account. I have often wondered for what good end the sensations of Grief could be intended. All our other passions, within proper bounds, have an useful object. And the perfection of the moral character is, not in a Stoical apathy, so hypocritically vaunted, and so untruly too, because impossible, but in a just equilibrium of all the passions. I wish the pathologists then would tell us what is the use of grief in the economy, and of what good it is the cause, proximate or remote.

Did I know Baron Grimm while at Paris? Yes, most intimately. He was the pleasantest, and most conversible member of the diplomatic corps while I was there: a man of good fancy, acuteness, irony, cunning, and egoism: no heart, not much of any science, yet enough of every one to speak it's language. His fort was Belles-lettres, painting and sculpture. In these he was the oracle of the society, and as such was the empress Catharine's private correspondent and factor in all things not diplomatic. It was thro' him I got her permission for poor Ledyard to go to Kamschatka, and cross over thence to the Western coast of America, in order to penetrate across our continent in the opposite direction to that afterwards adopted for Lewis and Clarke: which permission she withdrew after he had got within 200. miles of Kamschatska, had him siesed, brought back and set down in Poland. Altho' I never heard Grimm express the opinion, directly, yet I always supposed him to be of the school of Diderot, D'Alembert, D'Holbach, the first of whom committed their system of atheism to writing in 'Le bon sens,' and the last in his 'Systeme de la Nature.' It was a numerous school in the Catholic countries, while the infidelity of the Protestant took generally the form of Theism. The former always insisted that it was a mere question of definition between them, the hypostasis of which on both sides was 'Nature' or 'the Universe:' that both agreed in the order of the existing system, but the one supposed it from eternity, the other as having begun in time. And when the atheist descanted on the unceasing motion and circulation of matter thro' the animal vegetable and mineral kingdoms, never resting, never annihilated, always changing form, and under all forms gifted with the power of reproduction; the Theist pointing 'to the heavens above, and to the earth beneath, and to the waters under the earth,' asked if these did not proclaim a first cause, possessing intelligence and power; power in the production, and intelligence in the design and constant preservation of the system; urged the palpable existence of final causes, that the eye was made to see, and the ear to hear, and not that we see because we have eyes, and hear because we have ears; an answer obvious to the senses, as that of walking across the room was to the philosopher demonstrating the non-existence of motion. It was in D'Holbach's conventicles that Rousseau imagined all the machinations against him were contrived; and he left, in his Confessions the most biting anecdotes of Grimm. These appeared after I left France; but I have heard that poor Grimm was so much afflicted by them, that he kept his bed several weeks. I have never seen these Memoirs of Grimm. Their volume has kept them out of our market.

I have been lately amusing myself with Levi's book in answer to Dr. Priestley. It is a curious and tough work. His style is inelegant and incorrect, harsh and petulent to his adversary, and his reasoning flimsey enough. Some of his doctrines were new to me, particularly that of his two resurrections: the first a particular one of all the dead, in body as well as soul, who are to live over again, the Jews in a state of perfect obedience to god, the other nations in a state of corporeal punishment for the sufferings they have inflicted on the Jews. And he explains this resurrection of bodies to be only of the original stamen of Leibnitz, or the homunculus in semine masculino, considering that as a mathematical point, insusceptible of separation, or division. The second resurrection a general one of souls and bodies, eternally to enjoy divine glory in the presence of the supreme being. He alledges that the Jews alone preserve the doctrine of the unity of god. Yet their god would be deemed a very indifferent man with us: and it was to correct their Anamorphosis of the deity that Jesus preached, as well as to establish the doctrine of a future state. However Levi insists that that was taught in the old testament, and even by Moses himself and the prophets. He agrees that an anointed prince was prophecied and promised: but denies that the character and history of Jesus has any analogy with that of the person promised. He must be fearfully embarrassing to the Hierophants of fabricated Christianity; because it is their own armour in which he clothes himself for the attack. For example, he takes passages of Scripture from their context (which would give them a very different meaning) strings them together, and makes them point towards what object he pleases; he interprets them figuratively, typically, analogically, hyperbolically; he calls in the aid of emendation, transposition, ellipsis, metonymy, and every other figure of rhetoric; the name of one man is taken for another, one place for another, days and weeks for months and years; and finally avails himself of all his advantage over his adversaries by his superior knolege of the Hebrew, speaking in the very language of the divine communication, while they can only fumble on with conflicting and disputed translations. Such is this war of giants. And how can such pigmies as you and I decide between them? For myself I confess that my head is not formed tantas componere lites.[82] And as you began your Mar. 2. with a declaration that you were about to write me the most frivolous letter I had ever read, so I will close mine by saying I have written you a full match for it, and by adding my affectionate respects to Mrs. Adams, and the assurance of my constant attachment and consideration for yourself.

TH: JEFFERSON

Adams to Jefferson

Quincy May 3. 1816

DEAR SIR.

Yours Ap. 8 has long since been recd.

J. "Would you agree to live your 80 Years over again?"

A. ["]Aye! And sanse Phrases."

J. "Would You agree to live Your Eighty Years over again forever?"

A. I once heard our Acquaintance, Chew, of Philadelphia say, "He should like to go back to 25, to all Eternity": but I own my Soul would start and shrink back on itself, at the Prospect of an endless Succession of Boules de Savon ["balls of soap"], almost as much as at the Certainty of Annihilation. For what is human Life? I can speak only for one. I have had more comfort than distress, more pleasure than paine, ten to one, nay if you please an hundred to one. A pretty large Dose however of Distress and Paine. But after all, What is human Life? A Vapour, a Fog, a Dew, a Clould, a Blossom a flower, a Rose a blade of Grass, a glass Bubble, a Tale told by an Idiot, a Boule de Savon, Vanity of Vanities, an eternal succession of which would terrify me, almost as much as Annihilation.

82. "It is not for me to settle for you such great arguments." Virgil, *Eclogues*, III, 108.

J. "Would you prefer to live over again rather than Accept the Offer of a better Life in a future state?" A. Certainly not. J. "Would you live again, rather than chang[e] for the worse in a future State, for the sake of trying something new?" Certainly Yes.

J. "Would you live over again once or forever, rather than run the risque of Annihilation, or of a better or a worse State at or affter death"?
A. Most certainly I would not.

J. "How valiant you are!" A. Aye, at this moment, and at all other moments of my Life that I can recollect: but who can tell what will become of his Bravery when his Flesh and his heart shall fail him?

Bolin[g]broke said "his Philosophy was not sufficient to support him in his last hours." D'Alembert said "Happy are they who have Courage, but I have none." Voltaire the greatest Genius of them all, behaved like the greatest Coward of them all, at his death as he had like the wisest fool of them all in his Lifetime. Hume aukwardly Affect[ed] to sport away all sober thoughts. Who can answer for his last Feelings and Reflections? especially as the Priests are in possession of the Custom of making them the great Engines of their Craft. [Procul o,] Procul este Prophani ["Back, ye unhallowed"]!

J. "How shall We, how can We, estimate the real Value of human Life?" A. "I know not. I cannot weigh Sensations and Reflections, Pleasures and Pains, Hopes and Fears in Money Scales. But I can tell you how I have heard it estimated by some Phylosophers. One of my old Friends and Clients, a Mandamus Counseller against his Will, a Man of Letters and Virtues without one Vice, that I ever knew or suspected, except Garrulity, William Vassall, asserted to me, and strenuously maintained that *"pleasure is no Compensation for Pain."* "An 100 Years of the keenest delights of human Life could not atone for one hour of Billious Cholic, that he had felt." The sublimity of this Philosophy my dull Genius could not reach. I was willing to state a fair Account between Pleasure and Pain, and give Credit for the Ballance, which I found very great in my favour. Another Philosopher, who as We say, believed nothing, ridiculed the Notion of a future State. One of the Company asked "Why are you an Ennemy to a future State?" ["]Are you weary of Life?" "Do you detest existence?" "Weary of Life!—Detest Existence!["] said the Philosopher, No, "I love Life so well, and am so attached to Existence, that to be sure of Immortality I would consent, to be pitched about with forks by the Devils among flames of fire and Brimstone to all Eternity."

I find no Resources in my Courage, for this exalted Philosophy. I had rather be blotted out.

Il faut trancher Cet Mot ["One must speak out"]! What is there in Life to attach Us, to it; but the hope of a future and a better? It is a Cra[c]ker, a Rocquett a Firework, at best.

I admire your Navigation and should like to sail with you, either in your Bark or in my own, along side of yours; Hope with her gay Ensigns displayed at the Prow; fear with her Hobgoblins behind the Stern. Hope springs eternal; and Hope is all that endures. Take away hope and What remains? What pleasure? I mean. Take away Fear, and what Pain remains? 99/100ths of the Pleasures and Pains of Life are nothing but Hopes and Fears.

All Nations, known in History or in Travels have hoped, believed, an[d] expected a future and a better State. The Maker of the Universe, the Cause of all Things, whether We call it, *Fate* or *Chance* or GOD has inspired this Hope. If it is a *Fraud*, We shall never know it. We shall never resen[t] the Imposition, be grateful for the Illusion, nor grieve for the disappointment. We shall be no more. Credat Grim, Diderot, Buffon, La Lande, Condorcet, D'Holbach, Frederick Catherine; Non Ego. Arrogant as it may be, I shall take the Liberty to pronounce them all, *Idiologians*. Yet I would not persecute a hair of their Heads. The World is wide enough for them and me.

Suppose, the Cause of the Universe, should reveal to all Man kind, at once a *Certainty* that they must all die within a Century, and that death is an eternal Extinction of all living Powers, of all Sensation and Reflection. What would be the Effect? Would there be one Man Woman or Child existing on this Globe, twenty Years hence? Would not every human Being be, a Madame Deffand, Voltaires "Aveugle clairvoiante ["blind clairvoyant"]," all her Lifetime regretting her Existance, be wailing that She had ever been born; grieving that She had ever been dragged without her Consent, into being. Who would bear the Gout the Stone the Cholick, for the sake of a Boule de Savon when a Pistol a Cord, a Pond, or a Phyal of Laudanum was at hand? What would Men say to their Maker? would they thank him? No They would reproach him; they would curse him to his Face.

Voila! a sillier Letter than my last! For a Wonder, I have filled a Sheet. And a greater Wonder, I have read fifteen Volumes of Grim. Digito comesce Labellum.[83] I hope to write you more upon this and other Topicks of your Letter. I have read also a History of the Jesuits in four Volumes.[84] Can you tell me the Author or any Thing of this Work?

JOHN ADAMS

83. "Hold your tongue." Juvenal, *Satires*, I, 160.
84. See JA to TJ, Aug. 9, Nov. 4, 1816, below, 486, 494.

Adams to Jefferson

Quincy May 6 1816

DEAR SIR

Neither Eyes Fingers or Paper held out, to dispatch all the Trifles I wished to write in my last Letter.

In your favour of April 8th, You "wonder for what good End the Sensations of Grief could be intended"? You ["]wish the Pathologists would tell Us, what the Use of Grief, in Our Œconomy, and of what good it is the Cause proximate or remote." When I approach such questions as this, I consider myself, like one of those little Eels in Vinaigre, or one of those Animalcules in black or red Peper or in the Horse radish Root, that bite our Tongues so cruelly, reasoning upon the το παν ["totality"]. Of what Use is this Sting upon the Tongue? Why might We not have the Benefit of these Stimulants, without the Sting? Why might We not have the fragrance and Beauty of the Rose without the Thorn?

In the first place, however, We know not the Connections between pleasure and Pain. They seem to be mechanical and inseperable. How can We conceive a strong Passion, a Sanguine Hope suddenly disappointed without producing Pain? or Grief? Swift at 70, recollected the Fish he had angled out of Water when a Boy, which broke loose from his hoock, and said I feel the disappointment at this Moment. A Merchant plans all his fortune and all his Credit, in a single India or China Ship. She Arrives at the Viniard with a Cargo worth a Million, in Order. Sailing round the Cape for Boston a sudden Storm wrecks her, Ship Cargo and Crew all lost. Is it possible that the Merchant ruined, bankrupt sent to Prison by his Creditors, his Wife and Children starving, should not grieve? Suppose a young Couple, with every Advant[a]ge of Persons, fortunes and Connection on the Point of an indissoluble Union. A flash of Lightening or any one of those millions of Accidents which are alloted to Humanity prove fatal to one of the Lovers. Is it possible that the other, and all the Friends of both should not grieve? It should seem that Grief, as a mere Passion must necesarily be in Proportion to Sensibility.

Did you ever see a Portrait or a Statue of a great Man, without perceiving strong Traits of Paine and Anxiety? These Furrows were all ploughed in the Countenance, by Grief. Our juvenile Oracle, Sir Edward Coke, thought that none were fit for Legislators and Magistrates, but "*Sad Men.*" And Who were these sad Men? They were aged Men, who had been tossed and buffeted in the Vicissitudes of Life, forced upon profound Reflection by Grief and disappointments and taught to command their Passions and Prejudices.

But, All this, You will say, is nothing to the purpose. It is only repeating and exemplifying a Fact, which my question supposed to be well known, viz the Existence of Grief; and is no Answer to my Question, "What Are the Uses of Grief." This is very true, and you are very right: but may not the Uses of Grief be inferred, or at least suggested by such Exemplifications of known facts? Grief Compels the India Merchant to think; to reflect upon the plan of his Voyage. "Have I not been rash, to trust my Fortune, my Family, my Liberty, to the Caprices of Winds and Waves in a single Ship? I will never again give a loose to my Imagination and Avarice." ["]It had been wiser and more honest to have traded on a smaller Scale upon my own Capital." The dessolated Lover and disappointed Connections, are compelled by their Grief to reflect on the Vanity of human Wishes and Expectations; to learn the essential Lesson of Resignation; to review their own Conduct towards the deceased; to correct any Errors or faults in their future Conduct towards their remaining friends and towards all Men; to recollect the Virtues of the lost Friend and resolve to imitate them; his Follies and Vices if he had any and resolve to avoid them. Grief drives Men into habits of serious Reflection sharpens the Understanding and softens the heart; it compels them to arrouse their Reason, to assert its Empire over their Passions Propensities and Prejudices; to elevate them to a Superiority over all human Events; to give them the Felicis Annimi immotan tranquilitatem ["the imperturbable tranquillity of a happy heart"]; in short to make them Stoicks and Christians.

After all, as Grief is a Pain, it stands in the Predicament of all other Evil and the great question Occurs what is the Origin and what the final cause of Evil. This perhaps is known only to Omnicience. We poor Mortals have nothing to do with it, but to fabricate all the good We can out of all inevitable Evils, and to avoid all that are avoidable, and many such there are, among which are our own unnecessary Apprehensions and imaginary Fears. Though Stoical Apathy is impossible, Yet Patience and Resignation and tranquility may be acquired by Consideration in a great degree, very much for the hapiness of Life.

I have read Grim, in fifteen Volumes of more than five hundred pages each. I will not say, like Uncle Tobey "You shall not die till you have read him." But you ought to read him, if possible. It is the most entertaining Work I ever read. He appears exactly as you represent him. What is most of all remarkable, is his Impartiality. He spares no Characters, but Necker and Diderot. Voltaire, Buffon, D'Alembert, Helvetius Rousseau, Marmontel, Condorcet, La Harpe, Beaumarchais and all others are lashed without Ceremony. Their Portraits as faithfully drawn as possible. It is a compleat Review of French Litterature and fine Arts from 1753 to 1790. No Politicks. Criticisms very just. Anecdotes with out number, and very merry. One ineffably ridiculous I wish I could send you, but it is immeasurably long. D'Argens, a little out of health and shivering with the cold in Berlin asked leave of the King to take a ride to Gascony his Native Province. He was absent so long that Frederick concluded the Air of the South of France was like to detain his Friend and as he wanted his Society and Services he contrived a Trick to bring him back. He fabricated a Mandement in the Name of the Archbishop of Aix, commanding all the Faithful to seize The Marquis D'Argens, Author of Ocellus, Timæus and Julian, Works Atheistical, Deistical, Heretical and impious in the highest degree. This Mandement composed in a Style of Ecclesiastical Eloquence that never was exceeded by Pope, Jesuite, Inquisitor, or Sorbonite he sent in Print by a courier to D'Argens, who frightened out of his Witts fled by cross roads out of France and back to Berlin, to the greater Joy of the Philosophical Court for the laugh of Europe which they had raised at the Expence of the learned Marquis.

I do not like the late Resurrection of the Jesuits.[85] They have a General, now in Russia, in correspondence with the Jesuits in the U. S. who are more numerous than every body knows. Shall We not have Swarms of them here? In as many shapes and disguises as ever a King of the Gypsies, Bamfie[l]d More Carew himself, assumed? In the shape of Printers, Editors, Writers School masters etc. I have lately read Pascalls Letters over again, and four Volumes of the History of the Jesuits. If ever any Congregation of Men could merit, eternal Perdition on Earth and in Hell, According to these Historians though like Pascal true Catholicks, it is this Company of Loiola. Our System however of Religious Liberty must afford them an Assylum. But if they do not put the Purity of our Elections to a severe Tryal, it will be a Wonder.

J. ADAMS

85. During the 1760's the Jesuits, distasteful to monarchs and civil officials of the Enlightenment, were expelled from most Catholic countries, and in 1773 the Pope dissolved the Society of Jesus. It was not reconstituted until 1814.

12

"The advantages of education...
on the broad scale"

✳ AUGUST 1816 – DECEMBER 1819 ✳

D
URING THE EARLY YEARS of reconciliation between Adams and
Jefferson, the latter's correspondence with Mrs. Adams was resumed, but it was sparse and restrained and without any regularity.
She had terminated their exchange of 1804 and it was proper that she
make the first gesture for renewal of their friendship. At the urging
of her husband, she added a halfhearted postscript to his letter to
Jefferson in May 1812, and a year later, by the same device, she sent
"the regards of an old Friend, which are still cherished and preserved
through all the changes and vi[ci]ssitudes which have taken place
since we first became acquainted."[1] Jefferson acknowledged Mrs.
Adams's greeting politely to ask "how you do, how you have done?"
but his heart warmed as he told her that he had "10½ grandchildren,
and 2¾ great-grand-children; and these fractions will ere long become
units."[2] A few days afterward he received from Adams the sad news
of the death of their daughter Abigail on August 15 and a month later
Mrs. Adams wrote him at length about her bereavement. Jefferson's
letter had encouraged her to write, she explained. "But altho, time has
changed the outward form, and political 'Back wounding calumny'
for a period interrupted the Friendly intercourse and harmony which
subsisted, it is again renewed, purified from the dross."[3] Jefferson
directed his sincere, though brief, expression of condolence to
Adams.[4]

1. JA to TJ, May 3, 1812, July 15, 1813, above, 304, 358.
2. TJ to AA, Aug. 22, 1813, above, 367.
3. JA to TJ, Aug. [14?], 1813, and AA to TJ, Sept. 20, 1813, above, 366, 378.
4. TJ to JA, Oct. 12, 1813, above, 386.

No further word passed between Mrs. Adams and Jefferson until February 1816, when she penned another postscript to a letter from her husband; and during the last two years of her life she and Jefferson wrote each other twice. In his dreams of the future he always fancied the Adamses by his side, while she recalled the pleasure of "the continued Friendship of the phylosopher of Monticello." [5] Their last letters were cordial enough, concerning favors asked and granted and regrets that they could not enjoy a visit in Quincy or at Monticello.[6] Mrs. Adams died of typhoid fever on October 28, 1818, at the age of seventy-three, leaving her aged husband to an increasingly lonely existence during his last eight years. The news of Mrs. Adams's death moved Jefferson to write his old friend a tender note of sympathy, but even then his reticent nature dictated that "for ills so immeasurable, time and silence are the only medecines." [7]

Although Adams and Jefferson were often engrossed in philosophical questions, they were very much aware of the post-war world after the Peace of 1815. They followed closely the news of depression and social turbulence in England, as they reconsidered the common interests of Great Britain and the United States, seldom utilized as yet by both nations for their mutual gain. Jefferson, still resentful of past insults to his country and unsympathetic toward Britain's internal difficulties, anticipated dire consequences to her world position; but Adams better understood the flexibility of the British and expected them to "stick with their Constitution." Nevertheless, Adams, remembering his rebuffs as American minister in London, thought that "Britain will never be our Friend, till we are her Master." [8] But can we "preserve our Union?" he asked. If not, independence would be precarious. And the menace of the slavery controversy, exhibited in the Missouri question, compromised in 1820, made both statesmen fearful of the future.[9]

Conditions in the new South American republics also attracted the attention of the two elder statesmen. Adams was more confident than

5. JA to TJ, Feb. 2, 1816, above, 463; TJ to JA, Aug. 1, 1816; and AA to TJ, Dec. 15, 1816, below, 485, 500.

6. TJ to AA, Jan. 11, May 15, 1817, and AA to TJ, April 29, 1817, below, 503-4, 514, 511.

7. Whitney, *Abigail Adams*, 326; JA to TJ, Oct. 20, 1818, and TJ to JA, Nov. 13, 1818, below, 529.

8. TJ to JA, Oct. 14, Nov. 25, and JA to TJ, Dec. 16, 1816, below, 492, 496-99, 501-2.

9. JA to TJ, Dec. 16, 1816, Nov. 23, Dec. 21, 1819, and TJ to JA, Dec. 10, 1819, below, 502, 548, 551, 549.

Jefferson that the Latin American revolutions made independence secure, but both felt that ignorance and superstition, fostered by the Roman Catholic Church, cast a dark shadow on free government.[10] If the Latin Americans were not ready for republican government, however, they would grow up to it, freed from their colonial status. And "what a colossus shall we be when the Southern continent comes up to our mark!" exclaimed Jefferson. "What a stand will it secure as a ralliance for the reason and freedom of the globe! I like the dreams of the future better than the history of the past." [11]

One of Jefferson's favorite "dreams of the future" was educational reform. The epitaph which he composed—a memorial of his founding of the University of Virginia as well as his authorship of the Declaration of Independence and the Virginia Statute for Religious Freedom —does not suggest the years of frustration ending in only partial fulfillment of his hopes for free public education. He was thirty-five when he drafted the Bill for the More General Diffusion of Knowledge in 1778, which was never enacted. He was seventy-five when the act establishing the University was passed in 1819, and he had almost reached the age of eighty-two before the first academic session, of 1825-26, began.

Adams's and Jefferson's discussion of natural and artificial aristocracy led the latter into reflections on education. Good government and public education had long been inseparably associated in his mind. Inevitably he harked back to his Bill No. 79, for the More General Diffusion of Knowledge, which declared that laws wisely formed and honestly administered assure the greatest happiness and in turn the best laws, "whence it becomes expedient for promoting the publick happiness that those persons, whom nature hath endowed with genius and virtue, should be rendered by liberal education worthy to receive, and able to guard the sacred deposit of the rights and liberties of their fellow citizens, and that they should be called to that charge without regard to wealth, birth or other accidental condition or circumstance." [12]

The bill provided for three levels of education: elementary or ward schools for all children; district schools for the cream of the crop deserving of higher education; and the university for the élite of the

10. JA to TJ, Jan. 28, 1818, Feb. 3, 1821, Sept. 18, 1823, and TJ to JA, May 17, 1818, Jan. 22, 1821, Sept. 4, 1823, below, 523, 571, 599, 524, 570, 596.
11. TJ to JA, Aug. 1, 1816, below, 485.
12. Boyd, II, 527.

natural aristocracy. To Adams, Jefferson emphasized that he had proposed the ward, rather than the existing county, as the unit of local government, because he conceived it to be a "little republic," well governed by well-informed citizens. Having abolished primogeniture and entail and guaranteed religious freedom by legislative act, Jefferson hoped that the bill "on Education would have raised the mass of the people to the high ground of moral responsibility necessary to their own safety, and to orderly government." [13] He had stated the case in his *Notes on Virginia* a few years afterward. But even with Madison's support in the legislature, the bill, labeled by Jefferson as "the most important bill in our whole code," failed of passage. [14] He had to take cold comfort in the act of 1796, which provided for elementary schools for poor children but only on an optional basis. [15] In spite of prolonged inaction and half-measures, Jefferson wrote Adams in 1813 of his "great hope that some patriotic spirit will, at a favorable moment, call it [the original bill] up, and make it the key-stone of the arch of our government." [16]

In 1817 Jefferson drafted the Bill for Establishing a System of Public Education, his last attempt in a campaign begun almost forty years earlier. It might be said that he was giving the legislature a final opportunity to do right by the people of Virginia, but from past experience he reluctantly reached the conclusion that the members "do not generally possess information enough to perceive the important truths, that knolege is power, that knolege is safety, and that knolege is happiness." Again Jefferson's comprehensive plan met with defeat, but the real loss was suffered by the Commonwealth, which set up no bona fide public school system until the 1870's. As an alternative to his broad plan for public education, Jefferson was prepared to proceed with private funds to establish "a college of general science" near Charlottesville, on the same site where he was still hoping to locate the state university. [17]

13. TJ to JA, Oct. 28, 1813, above, 390; TJ to Governor Wilson C. Nicholas, April 2, 1816, Andrew A. Lipscomb and Albert Ellery Bergh, eds., *The Writings of Thomas Jefferson* (Washington, D.C., 1903-4), XIV, 454.

14. *Notes on Virginia*, ed. by Peden, 148-49; Boyd, II, 535*n.;* also TJ to George Wythe, Aug. 13, 1786, *ibid.*, X, 244.

15. Roy J. Honeywell, *The Educational Work of Thomas Jefferson* (Cambridge, Mass., 1931), 14.

16. TJ to JA, Oct. 28, 1813, above, 390.

17. Honeywell, *Educational Work of Jefferson*, 233-43; TJ to George Ticknor, Nov. 25, 1817, Ford, X, 95-96.

To Jefferson, who kept abreast of the rapid advancement of knowledge during the Age of the Enlightenment and responded to the spirit of scientific investigation, the higher education of youth seemed antiquated in many respects. He complained to Adams that "education is chiefly in the hands of persons who, from their profession, have an interest in the reputation and the dreams of Plato"; but the mysticism of Plato could not stand the test of reason, and Jefferson had no more respect for Platonic republicanism than he did for Platonic Christianity. "Our post-revolutionary youth," he observed sarcastically, "are born under happier stars than you and I were. They acquire all learning in their mothers' womb, and bring it into the world ready-made. The information of books is no longer necessary; and all knolege which is not innate, is in contempt, or neglect at least." Jefferson was advocating "education on the broad scale, not that of the petty *academies* ... starting up in every neighborhood," where the sum-total of knowledge consisted of some Latin and Greek, a measure of geography, and the first six books of Euclid. These pedagogues, he feared, "commit their pupils to the theatre of the world with just enough taste of learning to be alienated from industrious pursuits, and not enough to do service in the ranks of science." [18]

The real hope for reform and modernization seemed to be at the university level. During the Revolution, Jefferson had drafted Bill No. 80 for Amending the Constitution of the College of William and Mary, a companion piece to Bill No. 79. As one of the College's visitors during his governorship, Jefferson had succeeded in abolishing the professorships of divinity and oriental languages as well as the grammar school; but the legislature rejected the opportunity to convert the College into the state university.[19] By 1800 Jefferson concluded that the condition of the College, his alma mater, was hopeless and therefore outlined his ideas for a new institution, centrally located, "on a plan so broad and liberal and *modern*, as to be worth patronizing with the public support, and to be a temptation to the youth of other states." [20]

In July 1814, he requested Adams's advice on such an institution of higher learning and asked him to specify "the particular sciences of real use in human affairs" and "bring them within the views of a just

18. TJ to JA, July 5, 1814, above, 434.
19. Boyd, II, 535-42 and *nn*.
20. TJ to Joseph Priestley, Jan. 18, 1800, Ford, VII, 407-9.

but enlightened economy." [21] "Education! Oh Education!" replied Adams, who confessed he had never deliberately reflected on the subject. He would omit theology and metaphysics, but grouping the arts and sciences was beyond his capacity. What he jotted down, however, belied this statement and compared favorably with Jefferson's more studied effort.[22] For Adams had long believed that "the whole people must take upon themselves the education of the whole people, and must be willing to bear the expenses of it." [23] Massachusetts had won an enviable reputation in its early development of public education at the town level (which Jefferson had vainly hoped to emulate) and Harvard College provided society with its natural aristocracy; [24] indeed, Adams had never faced a glaring lack of education or public apathy such as Jefferson was combatting in Virginia.

But slow progress did not make the aging Jefferson apathetic. In 1814 he was elected a trustee of Albemarle Academy, a paper organization which had sought for a decade the means to become a reality. There was mutual advantage in this association, for Jefferson agreed to prepare a plan which, from his standpoint, could provide another opportunity to publicize the need for a system of public education and do so under specific auspices. Out of his letter of September 7, addressed to President Peter Carr of the Academy and first published in the Richmond *Enquirer*, developed a train of events leading to the establishment of the University of Virginia by legislative act of 1819. In accordance with his basic philosophy that every citizen should receive some education at public expense, depending upon his occupation and condition of life, Jefferson divided the population into two classes, "the laboring and the learned." Elementary schools would prepare the former for their pursuits in life, the latter for higher learning in "general schools" (college) and professional schools (the university). All branches of "useful science" ought to be taught in the general schools, arranged in three departments: (1) language: ancient and modern languages and history, history being associated with languages "on a principle of economy, because both may be attained by the same course of reading"; (2) mathematics, including the nat-

21. TJ to JA, July 5, 1814, above, 434.
22. JA to TJ, July 16, 1814, June 19, 1815, March 2, 1816, above, 438-39, 443-44, 466.
23. JA to John Jebb, Sept. 10, 1785, *Works*, IX, 540.
24. JA to John Taylor, [Dec. 26, 1814], *ibid.*, VI, 494-95.

ural sciences and the theory of medicine; (3) philosophy, including the law of nature and nations, government, and political economy.[25]

The professional schools, in which "each science is to be taught in the highest degree it has yet attained," were outlined as (1) fine arts, including civil architecture; (2) military and naval architecture; agriculture and veterinary; medicine, pharmacy, and surgery; (3) theology and ecclesiastical history, municipal and foreign law. To assure a continuing high caliber of the faculty Jefferson advised that the "sciences" "must be subdivided from time to time, as our means increase, until each professor shall have no more under his care than he can attend to with advantage to his pupils and ease to himself"—a utopian vision of the light "teaching load," still an ideal rather than an actuality in most institutions of higher learning. He hoped to begin with four professors: (1) language and history; (2) mathematics, physics, and medicine; (3) chemistry, zoology, botany, and mineralogy; and (4) philosophy.[26] The grouping of subjects suggests a professorial versatility that was taken for granted.

In 1816 the trustees of Albemarle Academy secured legislation to establish Central College, as a tactical move toward a university. The Board of Visitors of the new College included the President of the United States and two former Presidents—Monroe, Madison, and Jefferson—who were conferring at Monticello when Jefferson informed Adams of the new institution. Although Adams was in a pessimistic mood, he felt that "from such a noble Tryumvirate, the World will expect something very great and very new," but it would "not always have three such colossal reputations to support it." [27]

Jefferson proceeded to develop plans for a community of pavilions, rather than a single large building, on a tract of two hundred acres just west of Charlottesville. Anticipating their need for public funds in the near future, the Visitors petitioned the legislature in January 1818 and suggested tactfully that, if a state university were to be established, their College would provide the ideal site.[28] On February 21 the legislature authorized the founding of a university "in some

25. [Nathaniel F. Cabell, ed.], *Early History of the University of Virginia as contained in the Letters of Thomas Jefferson and Joseph C. Cabell...* (Richmond, 1856), 384-86.

26. *Ibid.*, 387-89.

27. *Ibid.*, 391-93; TJ to JA, May 5, 1817, and JA to TJ, May 18 and 26, 1817, below, 513, 516, 518.

28. Cabell, *Early History of University of Va.*, 400-4; TJ to JA, Sept. 8, 1817, below, 519.

convenient and proper part of the State, . . . wherein all the branches of useful science shall be taught." Commissioners appointed by the governor met at Rockfish Gap Tavern in the Blue Ridge on August 1 and selected Charlottesville for the location of the University of Virginia.[29] Jefferson's presence on the commission and the recent development of Central College undoubtedly strengthened their case.

The *Report of the Commissioners to fix the Scite of the University of Virginia* is a Jeffersonian document in its statement of educational principles, and it reiterates and expands his ideas on the curriculum and professorships.[30] The site, the plan of buildings, the program of education—all were Jefferson's. The act of January 25, 1819, confirmed the establishment of the University of Virginia on the site of Central College. This assurance was a relief to Jefferson, for, as he wrote in transmitting a copy of the *Report* to Adams, "Being a good piece of a century behind the age they [the legislators] live in, we are not without fear as to their conclusions." [31] Later he was pleased with the critical review of the *Report* in the *North American Review*. Although the reviewer regarded the omission of a professorship of divinity as a "hazardous experiment," he saw fit to quote at length the principle of religious freedom upon which the omission was based.[32]

Appointed to the University's Board of Visitors, Jefferson was chosen by them as rector in 1819. He thought himself fortunate to be "mounted on a Hobby, . . . whose easy amble is still sufficient to give exercise and amusement to an Octogenary rider." [33] But the pace was often more strenuous than an "easy amble." Six years intervened before the University opened its doors to the first students in February 1825. During that period he directed its architecture—he boasted that "it's plan is unique." [34] Jefferson searched for a faculty and helped raise funds. The University's curriculum was broadly conceived to provide a liberal education in the "useful sciences" as well as in the humanities, in modern languages as well as the classics, and to offer training for the professions. Unfettered by medieval tradition, the University of Virginia would set an example to be emulated haltingly

29. Cabell, *Early History of University of Va.*, 430-32.
30. *Ibid.*, 430-47.
31. *Ibid.*, 447-50; TJ to JA, Jan. 19, 1819, below, 532.
32. TJ to JA, Aug. 15, 1820, below, 565-66. *North American Review*, 10 (Jan. 1820), 130-31.
33. TJ to JA, Oct. 12, 1823, below, 599.
34. Cabell, *Early History of University of Va.*, 452; TJ to JA, Aug. 15, 1820, below, 565.

by its elder sister institutions. Following Jefferson's advice that the ablest scholars would be found abroad, the Board of Visitors sent Francis Walker Gilmer to Europe to engage professors and to buy books for the University library. In 1824 the Visitors, faced with a shortage of funds, courageously instituted eight professorships and gave priority to salaries while wrestling with financial problems.[35]

In December of that year Jefferson took his guests, Mr. and Mrs. George Ticknor and Daniel Webster, on a tour of the University buildings then nearing completion. Ticknor concluded prophetically, "Mr. Jefferson is entirely absorbed in it, and its success would make a *beau finale* indeed to his life." [36]

Jefferson to Adams

Monticello Aug. 1. 16.

DEAR SIR

Your two philosophical letters of May 4. and 6. have been too long in my carton of 'Letters to be answered.' To the question indeed on the utility of Grief, no answer remains to be given. You have exhausted the subject. I see that, with the other evils of life, it is destined to temper the cup we are to drink.

> Two urns by Jove's high throne have ever stood,
> The source of evil one, and one of good;
> From thence the cup of mortal man he fills,
> Blessings to these, to those distributes ills;
> To most he mingles both.[37]

Putting to myself your question, Would I agree to live my 73. years over again for ever? I hesitate to say. With Chew's limitations from 25. to 60., I would say Yes; and might go further back, but not come lower down. For, at the latter period, with most of us, the powers of life are sensibly on the wane, sight becomes dim, hearing dull, memory constantly enlarging it's frightful blank and parting with all we have ever seen or

35. Cabell, *Early History of University of Va.*, 222, 453, 455, 481-83; Richard Beale Davis, ed., *Correspondence of Thomas Jefferson and Francis Walker Gilmer, 1814-1826* (Columbia, S.C., 1946), 80-82.
36. Ticknor to William H. Prescott, Dec. 16, 1824, Hillard, ed., *Life of Ticknor*, I, 348; TJ to JA, Sept. 8, 1817, below, 519-20.
37. Pope's translation of the *Iliad*, XXIV, 663-67.

known, spirits evaporate, bodily debility creeps on palsying every limb, and so faculty after faculty quits us, and where then is life? If, in it's full vigor, of good as well as evil, your friend Vassall could doubt it's value, it must be purely a negative quantity when it's evils alone remain. Yet I do not go into his opinion entirely. I do not agree that an age of pleasure is no compensation for a moment of pain. I think, with you, that life is a fair matter of account, and the balance often, nay generally in it's favor. It is not indeed easy, by calculation of intensity and time, to apply a common measure, or to fix the par between pleasure and pain: yet it exists, and is measurable. On the question, for example, whether to be cut for the stone? the young, with a longer prospect of years, think these overbalance the pain of the operation. Dr. Franklin, at the age of 80., thought his residuum of life, not worth that price. I should have thought with him, even taking the stone out of the scale. There is a ripeness of time for death, regarding others as well as ourselves, when it is reasonable we should drop off, and make room for another growth. When we have lived our generation out, we should not wish to encroach on another. I enjoy good health; I am happy in what is around me. Yet I assure you I am ripe for leaving all, this year, this day, this hour. If it could be doubted whether we would go back to 25. how can it be, whether we would go forward from 73? Bodily decay is gloomy in prospect; but of all human contemplations the most abhorrent is body without mind. Perhaps however I might accept of time to read Grimm before I go. 15. volumes of anecdotes and incidents, within the compass of my own time and cognisance, written by a man of genius, of taste, of point, an acquaintance, the measure and traverses of whose mind I knew, could not fail to turn the scale in favor of life during their perusal. I must write to Ticknor to add it to my catalogue, and hold on till it comes.

There is a Mr. Vanderkemp of N.Y. a correspondent I believe of yours, with whom I have exchanged some letters, without knowing who he is. Will you tell me?

I know nothing of the history of the Jesuits you mention in 4. vols. Is it a good one? I dislike, with you, their restoration; because it marks a retrograde step from light towards darkness. We shall have our follies without doubt. Some one or more of them will always be afloat. But ours will be the follies of enthusiasm, not of bigotry, not of Jesuitism. Bigotry is the disease of ignorance, of morbid minds; enthusiasm of the free and buoyant. Education and free discussion are the antidotes of both. We are destined to be a barrier against the returns of ignorance and barbarism. Old Europe will have to lean on our shoulders, and to hobble along by our side, under the monkish trammels of priests and kings, as she can. What a Colossus shall we be when the Southern continent comes up to our mark!

What a stand will it secure as a ralliance for the reason and freedom of the globe. I like the dreams of the future better than the history of the past. So good night. I will dream on, always fancying that Mrs Adams and yourself are by my side marking the progress and the obliquities of ages and countries.

TH: JEFFERSON

Adams to Jefferson

Quincy August 9. 1816

DEAR SIR

The Biography of Mr. Vander Kemp would require a Volume which I could not write if a Milion were offered me as a Reward for the Work. After a learned and scientific Education he entered the Army in Holland and served as a Captain, with Reputation: but loving Books more than Arms he resigned his Commission and became a Preacher. My Acquaintance with him commenced at Leyden in 1780. He was then Minister of the Menonist Congregation the richest in Europe; in that City where he was celebrated as the most elegant Writer in the Dutch Langu[a]ge. He was the intimate Friend of Luzac and De Gyselaar. In 1788 when the King of Prussia threatened Holland with Invasion, his Party insisted on his taking a Command in the Army of defence and he was appointed to the Command of the most exposed and most important Post in the Seven Provinces. He was soon surrounded by the Prussian Forces. But he defended his Fortress with a Prudence Fortitude Patience and Perseverance, which were admired by all Europe, Till, abandoned by his Nation, destitute of Provisions and Amunition, still refusing to surrender, he was offered the most honourable Capitulation. He accepted it. Was offered very Advantageous Proposals, but despairing of the Liberties of his Country, he retired to Antwerp determined to emigrate to New York; wrote to me in London requesting Letters of Introduction. I sent him Letters to Governor Clinton and several others of our little great Men. His History in this Country is equally curious and affecting. He left Property in Holland, which the Revolutions there, have annihilated and I fear is now pinched with Poverty. His head is deeply learned and his heart is pure. I scarcely know a more amiable Character. A Gentleman here asked my Opinion of him. My Answer was, he is a *Mountain of Salt* of the Earth. He has written to me, occasionally and I have answered his Letters in great haste. You may well suppose that such a Man has not always been able to

Understand our American Politicks. Nor have I. Had he been as great a Master of our Langu[a]ge as he was of his own he would have been at this day one of the most conspicuous Characters in the U. S.

So much for Vanderkemp: now for your Letter of Aug. 1. Your Poet, the Ionian I suppose, ought to have told Us, whether Jove in the distribution of good and Evil from his two Urns, observes any Rule of Equity or not. Whether he thunders out flames of eternal Fire on the Many, and Power Glory and Felicity on the Few, without any consideration of Justice?

Let Us state a few Questions, sub rosâ.

1. Would you accept a Life, if offered You, of equal pleasure and Paine? E.G. one million of moments of Pleasure and one Million of Moments of Pain? 1,000,000 Pleasure = 1,000,000 Paine. Suppose the Pleasure as exquisite as any in Life and the Paine as exquisite as any. E.G. Stone, Gravel, Gout, Head Ache, Ear Ache, Tooth Ache, Cholick. etc. I would not. I would rather be blotted out.

2. Would you accept a Life of one Year of incessant Gout, Head Ache etc for Seventy two Years of such Life as you have injoyed? I would not.

1 Year of Cholic = 72. of Boule de Savon. pretty but unsubstantial. I had rather be extinguished. You may vary these Algebraical Equations at pleasure and without End. All this Ratiocination Calculation, call it what you will, is founded on the Supposition of no future State. Promise me eternal Life free from Pain, tho' in all other respects no better than our present terrestrial Existence, I know not how many thousand Years of Smithfield fires I would not endure to obtain it.

In fine, without the Supposition of a future State, Mankind and this Globe appear to me the most sublime and beautifull Bubble and Bauble that Imagination can conceive.

Let Us then wish for Immortality at all hazards and trust the Ruler with his Skies. I do: and earnestly wish for his Commands which to the Utmost of my Power shall be implicitly and piously obeyed.

It is worth while to live to read Grimm, whom I have read, And La Harpe and Mademoiselle D'Espinasse the fair Friend of D'Allembert both of whom Grimm Characterises very distinctly are I am told in Print. I have not seen them but hope soon to have them.

My History of the Jesuits is not elegantly written but is supported by unquesti[on]able Authorities, is very particular and very horrible. Their Restoration is indeed "a Step towards Darkness" Cruelty Perfidy Despotism Death and ———! I wish We were out of "danger of Bigotry and Jesuitism!" May We be "a Barrier against the Returns of Ignorance and Barbarism!" "What a Colossus shall We be?" But will it not be of Brass

Iron and Clay? Your Taste is judicious in likeing better the dreams of the Future, than the History of the Past. Upon this Principle I prophecy that you and I shall soon meet and be better Friends than ever. So wishes

JOHN ADAMS

Adams to Jefferson

Quincy Septr. 03. 1816

DEAR SIR

Dr. James Freeman, is a learned, ingenious, honest and benevolent Man, who wishes to see President Jefferson, and requests me to introduce him. If you would introduce some of Your Friends to me, I could with more confidence introduce mine to You. He is a Christian, but not a Pythagorian a Platonick or a Philonick Christian. You will ken him and he will ken You: but you may depend, he will never betray, deceive or injure You.

Without hinting to him, any Thing which had passed between You and me, I asked him, your Question *"What are the Uses of Grief?"* He stared. Said "the question was new to him." All he could say at present was that he had known in his own Parish, more than one Instance of Ladies, who had been thoughtless, modish, extravagant in a high degree; who upon the death of a Child, had become thoughtfull, modest, humble, as prudent amiable Women as any he had known. Upon this I read to him Your Letters and mine, upon this Subject of Grief, with which he seemed to be pleased. You see I was not afraid to trust him: and you need not be.

Since I am, accidentally, invited to write to You, I may add a few Words Upon Pleasures and Pains of Life. Vassall thought, an hundred Years, nay an eternity of Pleasure was no Compensation for one hour of billious Cholic. Read again Mollieres Spsyke [i.e., Psyche]. Act. 2. Scene 1st. On the Subject of Grief. And read in another place "On est payé de mille Maux Par un heureux moment." [38] Thus differently do Men speak of Pleasures and Pains.

Now, Sir, I will tease you with another Question. What have been the *Abuses* of Grief?

In Answer to this question, I doubt not, you might write an hundred volumes. A few hints may convince You that the Subject is ample.
1. The Death of Socrates excited a general Sensibility of Grief in Athens, in Attica and in all Greece. Plato and Xenophon two of his Disciples took

38. "One happy moment compensates for a thousand ills."

Advantage of that general Sentiment, by employing their enchanting Style to represent their Master to be greater and better than he probably was. And What have been the Effects of Socratic, Platonick which were Pythagorean, which was Indian Philosophy, in the World?

2. The Death of Caesar, Tyrant as he was, spread a general Compassion which always includes Grief, among the Romans. The Scoundrel, M. Anthony availed himself of this momentary Grief to destroy the Republick, to establish the Empire, and to proscribe Cicero.

3. But to skip over all Ages and Nations for the present, and descend to our own Times. The Death of Washington, diffused a general Grief. The Old Tories, the Hyperfederalists, the Speculators, sett up a general Howl. Orations Prayers Sermons Mock Funerals, were all employed, not that they loved Washington, but to keep in Countenance the Funding and Banking Systems; And to cast into the Background and the Shade all others who had been concerned in the Service of their Country in the Revolution.

4. The Death of Hamilton, under all its circumstances, produced a General Grief. His most determined Ennemies did not like to get rid of him, in that Way. They pitied too his Widow and Children. His Party seized the moment of publick Feeling to come forward with Funeral Orations and Printed Panegyricks reinforced with mock Funerals and solemn Grimaces, and all this by People who have buried Otis, Sam. Adams Handcock and Gerry in Comparitive Obscurity. And Why? Merely to disgrace the old Whiggs, and keep the Funds and Banks in Countenance.

5. The Death of Mr. Ames excited a General Regret. His long Consumption his amiable Character and respectable Talents had attracted a general Interest, and his Death a general Mourning. His Party made the most of it, by Processions Orations, and a Mock Funeral. And Why? To glorify the Torys, to abash the Whiggs, and maintain the Reputation of Funds, Banks and Speculation. And all this was done in honour of that insignificant Boy, by People who have let a Dana a Gerry and a Dexter go to their Graves without Notice.

6. I almost shudder at the thought of alluding to the most fatal Example of the Abuses of Grief, which the History of Man kind has preserved. The Cross. Consider what Calamities that Engine of Grief has produced! With the rational Respect that is due to it, knavish Priests have added Prostitutions of it, that fill or might fill the blackest and bloodiest Pages of human History. I am with ancient friendly Sentiments

JOHN ADAMS

Adams to Jefferson

Quincy Sept. 30. 16

PRESIDENT JEFFERSON.

DEAR SIR

The Seconds of Life, that remain to me, are so few and so short; (and they seem to me shorter and shorter every minute) that I cannot stand upon Epistolary Ettiquette: and though I have written two Letters, yet unnoticed I must write a third. Because I am not acquainted with any Man on this side of Montecello, who can give me any Information upon Subjects that I am now *analysing* and *investigating;* if I may be permitted to Use the pompous Words now in fashion.

When I read Dr. Priestleys Remarks upon *"Du Puis,"* I felt a Curiosity to know more about him. I wrote to Europe and engaged another to write. I had no Idea of more than one or two Volumes in 8° [octavo] or 12mo [duodecimo].

But Lo! I am overwhelmed with 8 or ten Volumes and another of Planches!

Sixteen Years of Research the Author acknowledges, and as he quotes his Authorities I would not undertake to verify them in 16 Years, If I had all his Books which surely are not to be found in America.

If you know any Thing of this "Monsieur Du Puis["] or his *"Origine de tous les Cultes";* Candidus imperti ["candidly impart it"].

I have read only the first Volume. It is learned and curious. The whole Work will afford me Business, Study and Amusement for the Winter.

Dr. Priestley pronounced him an Atheist, and his Work "The Ne Plus ultra of Infidelity." Priestley agrees with him, that the History of the Fall of Adam and Eve, is "an Alegory," a Fable, an Arabian Tale, and so does Dr. Middleton, to account for the Origin of Evil; which however it does not.

Priestly says that the Apocalypes, according to Dupuis is the most learned Work that ever was written.

With these brief Fletrissures, Priestly seems to have expected to anni[hi]late the Influence of Dupuis Labours; as Swift destroyed Blackmore with his

"Did off Creation with a Jerk

And of Redemption made damn'd Work." And as he disgraced Men as good at least as himself by his

"Wicked Will Whiston
And Good Master Ditton." [39]

But Dupuis is not to be so easily destroyed. The Controversy between Spiritualism and Materialism between Spiritualists and Materialists, will not be settled by Scurrilous Epigrams of Swift, nor by dogmatical Censures of Priestly.

You and I have as much Authority to settle these Disputes as Swift Priestley or Dupuis, or The Pope.

And if you will agree with me, We will issue our Bulls, and enjoin upon all these Gentlemen to be Silent, till they can tell Us, What Matter is and What Spirit is! And in the mean time to observe the Commandments and the Sermon on the Mount.

J. ADAMS

Jefferson to Adams

Monticello Oct. 14. 16.

Your letter, dear Sir, of May 6. had already well explained the Uses of grief, that of Sep. 3. with equal truth adduces instances of it's abuse; and when we put into the same scale these abuses, with the afflictions of soul which even the Uses of grief cost us, we may consider it's value in the economy of the human being, as equivocal at least. Those afflictions cloud too great a portion of life to find a counterpoise in any benefits derived from it's uses. For setting aside it's paroxysms on the occasions of special bereavements, all the latter years of aged men are overshadowed with it's gloom. Whither, for instance, can you and I look without seeing the graves of those we have known? And whom can we call up, of our early companions, who has not left us to regret his loss? This indeed may be one of the salutary effects of grief; inasmuch as it prepares us to lose ourselves also without repugnance. Dr. Freeman's instances of female levity cured by grief are certainly to the point, and constitute an item of credit in the account we examine.

I was much mortified by the loss of the Doctor's visit by my absence from home. To have shewn how much I feel indebted to you for making good people known to me would have been one pleasure; and to have

39. *The Works of the Rev. Jonathan Swift, D.D.*, arranged by Thomas Sheridan, A.M. . . . corrected and revised by John Nichols (London, 1803), XXIV, 39, 73. In the first ditty the first line should read: "Undid Creation with a Jerk."

enjoyed that of his conversation, and the benefits of his information so favorably reported by my family, would have been another. I returned home on the third day after his departure. The loss of such visits is among the sacrifices which my divided residence costs me.

Your undertaking the 12. volumes of Dupuis is a degree of heroism to which I could not have aspired even in my younger days. I have been contented with the humble atchievement of reading the Analysis of his work by Destutt-Tracy in 200 pages 8vo [octavo]. I believe I should have ventured on his own abridgment of the work in one 8vo. volume, had it ever come to my hands; but the marrow of it in Tracy has satisfied my appetite: and, even in that, the preliminary discourse of the Analyser himself, and his Conclusion, are worth more in my eye than the body of the work. For the object of that seems to be to smother all history under the mantle of allegory. If histories so unlike as those of Hercules and Jesus, can, by a fertile imagination, and Allegorical interpretations, be brought to the same tally, no line of distinction remains between fact and fancy. As this pithy morsel will not overburthen the mail in passing and repassing between Quincy and Monticello, I send it for your perusal. Perhaps it will satisfy you, as it has me; and may save you the labor of reading 24 times it's volume. I have said to you that it was written by Tracy; and I had so entered it on the title-page, as I usually do on Anonymous works whose authors are known to me. But Tracy had requested me not to betray his anonyme, for reasons which may not yet perhaps have ceased to weigh. I am bound then to make the same reserve with you. Destutt-Tracy is, in my judgment, the ablest writer living on intellectual subjects, or the operations of the understanding. His three 8vo. volumes on Ideology,[40] which constitute the foundation of what he has since written, I have not entirely read; because I am not fond of reading what is merely abstract, and unapplied immediately to some useful science. Bonaparte, with his repeated derisions of Ideologists (squinting at this author) has by this time felt that true wisdom does not lie in mere practice without principle. The next work Tracy wrote was the Commentary on Montesquieu, never published in the original, because not safe; but translated and published in Philadelphia [1811], yet without the author's name. He has since permitted his name to be mentioned. Although called a Commentary, it is in truth an elementary work on the principles of government, comprised in about 300. pages 8vo. He has lately published a third work on Political economy, comprising the whole subject within about the same compass; in which all it's principles are demonstrated with the severity of Euclid, and, like him, without ever using a superfluous word. I have procured this to be translated, and have been 4 years endeavoring to get it printed.

40. *Elements d'ideology* ..., 5 pts. (Paris, 1803-15).

But, as yet, without success.[41] In the mean time the author has published the original in France, which he thought unsafe while Bonaparte was in power. No printed copy, I believe, has yet reached this country. He has his 4th. and last work now in the press at Paris, closing, as he concieves, the circle of metaphysical sciences. This work which is on Ethics, I have not seen, but suspect I shall differ from it in it's foundation, altho not in it's deductions. I gather from his other works that he adopts the principle of Hobbes, that justice is founded in contract solely, and does not result from the construction of man. I believe, on the contrary, that it is instinct, and innate, that the moral sense is as much a part of our constitution as that of feeling, seeing, or hearing; as a wise creator must have seen to be necessary in an animal destined to live in society: that every human mind feels pleasure in doing good to another; that the non-existence of justice is not to be inferred from the fact that the same act is deemed virtuous and right in one society, which is held vicious and wrong in another; because as the circumstances and opinions of different societies vary, so the acts which may do them right or wrong must vary also: for virtue does not consist in the act we do, but in the end it is to effect. If it is to effect the happiness of him to whom it is directed, it is virtuous, while in a society under different circumstances and opinions the same act might produce pain, and would be vicious. The essence of virtue is in doing good to others, while what is good may be one thing in one society, and it's contrary in another. Yet, however we may differ as to the foundation of morals, (and as many foundations have been assumed as there are writers on the subject nearly) so correct a thinker as Tracy will give us a sound system of morals. And indeed it is remarkable that so many writers, setting out from so many different premises, yet meet, all, in the same conclusions. This looks as if they were guided, unconsciously, by the unerring hand of instinct.

Your history of the Jesuits, by what name of the Author, or other description is it to be enquired for?

What do you think of the present situation of England? Is not this the great and fatal crush of their funding system, which, like death, has been foreseen by all, but it's hour, like that of death, hidden from mortal prescience? It appears to me that all the circumstances now exist which render recovery desperate. The interest of the national debt is now equal to such a portion of the profits of all the land and the labor of the island, as not to leave enough for the subsistence of those who labor. Hence the owners of the land abandon it and retire to other countries, and the

41. *A Treatise on Political Economy* . . . By the Count Destutt de Tracy . . . Translated from the unpublished French original (Georgetown, D.C., 1817). The original was not published until five years later (Paris, 1822). See below, JA's and TJ's comments on this work, 493, 495-96.

laborer has not enough of his earnings left to him to cover his back, and to fill his belly. The local insurrections, now almost general,[42] are of the hungry and the naked, who cannot be quieted but by food and raiment. But where are the means of feeding and clothing them? The landholder has nothing of his own to give, he is but the fiduciary of those who have lent him money: the lender is so taxed in his meat, drink, and clothing, that he has but a bare subsistence left. The landholder then, must give up his land, or the lender his debt, or they must compromise by giving up each one half. But will either consent *peaceably* to such an abandonment of property? Or must it not be settled by civil conflict? If peaceably compromised, will they agree to risk another ruin under the same government unreformed? I think not; but I would rather know what you think; because you have lived with John Bull, and know, better than I do the character of his herd. I salute Mrs Adams and yourself with every sentiment of affectionate cordiality and respect.

TH: JEFFERSON

Adams to Jefferson

Quincy Nov. 4 1816

DR. SIR

Your Letter of Oct. 14 has greatly obliged me. Tracys Analysis, I have read once; and wish to read it a second time. It shall be returned to you. But I wish to be informed whether this Gentleman is of that Family of Tracys with which the Marquis La Fayette is connected by intermarriages?

I have read, not only the Analysis, but Eight Volumes out of 12 of The Origine de tous les Cultes, and if Life lasts will read the other four.

But, my dear Sir, I have been often obliged to stop; and talk to myself like the Reverend, Alegorical, Hierogriphical and Apocaliptical Mr. John Bunyan; and say "Sobrius esto John ["John, be sober"]!" Be not carried away by sudden blasts of Wind, by unexpected flashes of Lightening, nor terrified by the sharpest Crashes of Thunder!"

We have now, it seems a National Bible Society,[43] to propagate King

42. They resulted from the new Corn Law of 1815, raising the import duties on grains to the point of excluding them unless prices were very high. Wage earners suffered not only from exorbitant food prices but also from the post-war depression in industry, bringing low wages and unemployment.

43. The American Bible Society was organized in New York in 1816 at a convention of delegates from 31 local societies. Henry O. Dwight, *The Centennial History of the American Bible Society* (N.Y., 1916), 18-30.

James's Bible, through all Nations. Would it not be better, to apply these pious Subscriptions, to purify Christendom from the Corruptions of Christianity; than to propagate those Corruptions in Europe Asia, Africa and America!

Suppose, We should project a Society to translate Dupuis into all Languages and offer a Reward in Medals and Diamonds to any Man or Body of Men who would produce the best answer to it.

Enthusiams, Crusades, French Revolutions are Epidemical or Endemial Distempers, to which Man kind are liable. They are not tertian or Quartan Agues. Ages and Centuries are sometimes required to cure them.

It is more worth your while to live to read Dupuis than Grim. Of all the Romanc[e]s, and true Histories I ever read, it is the most entertain[in]g And instructive, though Priestley calls it "*dull*."

Conclude not from all this, that I have renounced the Christian Religion, or that I agree with Dupuis in all his Sentiments. Far from it. I see in every Page, Something to recommend Christianity in its Purity, and Something to discredit its Corruptions.

If I had Strength, I would give you my Opinion of it in a Fable of the Bees.[44]

The Ten Commandments and The Sermon on the Mount contain my Religion.

I agree perfectly with you, that "The Moral Sense is as much a part of our Constitution as that of Feeling," and in all that You say, upon this Subject.

My History of the Jesuits, is in 4. Vol. in twelves, under the Title of "Histoire Generale de la naissance et des progres, de la Compagnie de Jesus, et l'analyse de ses Constitutions et ses Privileges.["] Printed at Amsterdam in 1761. The Work is anonymous;[45] because, as I suppose, the Author was afraid as all the Monarks of Europe were at that time, of Jesuitical Assassination. The Author however supports his Facts by authentic Records and known Authorities which the Publick may consult.

This Society has been a greater Calamity to Mankind than the French Revolution or Napoleons Despotism or Idiology. It has obstructed the Progres of Reformation and the Improvement of the human Mind in Society much longer and more fatally.

44. Bernard Mandeville, *The Fable of the Bees: or, Private Vices, Public Benefits* (London, 1714; Oxford, 1924): "As to Religion, the most knowing and polite Part of a Nation have every where the least of it; ... Vice in general is no where more predominant than where Arts and Sciences flourish.... It is certain that we shall find Innocence and Honesty no where more general than among the most illiterate, the poor silly Country People"; 1924 edn., I, 269.

45. The *Histoire* was written by Christophe Coudrette, the *Analyse* by Louis-Adrien Le Paige.

The Situation of England may be learned from the enclosed Letter,[46] which I pray you to return to me.

Little reason as I have to love the old Lady, I cannot but dread that she is going after France, into a Revolution which will end like that of England in 1660 and like that of France in 1816. In all Events, our Country must rise. England cannot.

We have been long afflicted with a Report that your Books and Harvard Colledge Books, and John Q. Adams's Ouranologia were lost at Sea.[47] But lo! The Astronomy has arrived in one Ship and Colledge Books in another. We hope your Books are equally safe: but should be glad to know.

It seems that Father and Son have been employed in contemplating The Heavens. I should like to sitt down with him and compare Du Puis with his Uranologia.

I have been disappointed in the Review of Sir John Malcoms History of Persia.[48] Those cunning Edinburgh men break off, at the Point of the only Subject that excited my Curiosity the ancient modern Religion and Government of Persia. I should admire to read an Edinburg or a Quarterly Review of Du Puis 12. Volumes. They have reviewed Grim who is not of half the importance to Mankind. I suspect the Reviewers evaded the Religion of Persia for fear they should be compelled to compare it with Du Puis.

A Scrap of an English Paper in which you are honorably mentioned and I am not much abused must close this Letter from your Friend

JOHN ADAMS

Jefferson to Adams

Poplar Forest. Nov. 25. 16.

I recieve here, dear Sir, your favor of the 4th. just as I am preparing my return to Monticello for winter quarters; and I hasten to answer to some of your enquiries. The Tracy I mentioned to you is the one con-

46. See TJ to JA, Nov. 25, 1816, below, 496-99. The enclosure was probably from John Quincy Adams, American minister to Great Britain at this time.

47. All of these books, bought by George Ticknor in Europe, were shipped to Boston in care of his father; TJ's were then to be forwarded to Monticello. Elisha Ticknor to TJ, Oct. 22, 1818, "The Jefferson Papers," Mass. Hist. Soc., *Collections*, 7th ser., 1 (1900), 263-65.

48. In the *Edinburgh Review*, 26 (1816), 282-304.

nected by marriage with La Fayette's family. The mail which brought
your letter brought one also from him. He writes me that he is become
blind and so infirm that he is no longer able to compose any thing. So that
we are to consider his works as now closed. They are 3. vols. of Ideology.
1. on political economy. 1. on Ethics, and 1. containing his Commentary
on Montesquieu, and a little tract on education. Altho' his Commentary
explains his principles of government, he had intended to have substituted
for it an elementary and regular treatise on the subject: but he is prevented by his infirmities. His Analyse de Dupuys he does not avow.

My books are all arrived, some at New York, some at Boston; and I
am glad to hear that those for Harvard are safe also; and the Uranologia
you mention, without telling me what it is. It is something good, I am sure,
from the name connected with it, and if you would add to it your Fable
of the bees, we should recieve valuable instruction as to the Uranologia
both of the father and son; more valuable than the Chinese will from our
bible-societies. These Incendiaries, finding that the days of fire and faggot
are over in the Atlantic hemisphere, are now preparing to put the torch to
the Asiatic regions. What would they say were the Pope to send annually
to this country colonies of Jesuit priests with cargoes of their Missal and
translations of their Vulgate, to be put gratis into the hands of every one
who would accept them? and to act thus nationally on us as a nation?

I proceed to the letter you were so good as to inclose to me. It is an
able letter, speaks volumes in few words, presents a profound view of
awful truths, and lets us see truths more awful, which are still to follow.
George the IIId. then, and his minister Pitt, and successors, have spent the
fee-simple of the kingdom, under pretence of governing it. Their sinecures,
salaries, pensions, priests, prelates, princes and eternal wars have mortgaged
to it's full value the last foot of their soil. They are reduced to the dilemma
of a bankrupt spendthrift who, having run thro' his whole fortune, now
asks himself what he is to do? It is in vain he dismisses his coaches and
horses, his grooms, liveries, cooks and butlers. This done, he still finds he
has nothing to eat. What was his property, is now that of his creditors.
If still in his hands, it is only as their trustee. To them it belongs, and
to them every farthing of it's profits must go. The reformation of extrav-
agancies comes too late. All is gone. Nothing left for retrenchment or
frugality to go on. The debts of England however, being due from the
whole nation, to one half of it, being as much the debt of the creditor as
debtor, if it could be referred to a court of Equity, principles might be
devised to adjust it peaceably. Dismiss their parasites, ship off their paupers
to this country, let the landholders give half their lands to the moneylenders, and these last relinquish one half of their debts. They would still
have a fertile island, a sound and effective population to labor it, and

would hold that station among political powers, to which their natural resources and faculties entitle them. They would no longer indeed be the lords of the ocean, and paymasters of all the princes of the earth. They would no longer enjoy the luxuries of pyrating and plundering every thing by sea, and of bribing and corrupting every thing by land; but they might enjoy the more safe and lasting luxury of living on terms of equality, justice and good neighborhood with all nations. As it is, their first efforts will probably be to quiet things awhile by the palliatives of reformation; to nibble a little at pensions and sinecures; to bite off a bit here, and a bite there to amuse the people; and to keep the government agoing by encroachments on the interest of the public debt, 1. per cent. of which, for instance, withheld, gives them a spare revenue of 10 millions for present subsistence, and spunges in fact 200. millions of the debt. This remedy they may endeavor to administer in broken doses of a small pill at a time. The first may not occasion more than a strong Nausea in the moneylenders; but the 2d. will probably produce a revulsion of the stomach, borborisms, and spasmodic calls for fair settlement and compromise. But it is not in the character of man to come to any peaceable compromise of such a state of things. The princes and priests will hold to the flesh-pots, the empty bellies will seize on them, and these being the multitude, the issue is obvious, civil war, massacre, exile as in France, until the stage is cleared of everything but the multitude, and the lands get into their hands by such processes as the revolution will engender. They will then want peace and a government, and what will it be? certainly not a renewal of that which has already ruined them. Their habits of law and order, their ideas almost innate of the vital elements of free government, of trial by jury, habeas corpus, freedom of the press, freedom of opinion, and representative government, make them, I think, capable of bearing a considerable portion of liberty. They will probably turn their eyes to us, and be disposed to tread in our footsteps, seeing how safely these have led us into port. There is no part of our model to which they seem unequal, unless perhaps the elective presidency; and even that might possibly be rescued from the tumult of elections, by subdividing the electoral assemblages into very small parts, such as of wards or townships, and making them simultaneous. But you know them so much better than I do, that it is presumption to offer my conjectures to you.

While it is much our interest to see this power reduced from it's towering and borrowed height, to within the limits of it's natural resources, it is by no means our interest that she should be brought below that, or lose her competent place among the nations of Europe. The present exhausted state of the continent will, I hope, permit them to go through their struggle without foreign interference, and to settle their new government according to their own will. I think it will be friendly to us, as the nation itself would be were it not artfully wrought up by the hatred their government bears us. And were they once under a government which should treat us with justice and equality I should myself feel with great strength the ties which bind us together, or origin, language, laws and manners: and I am persuaded the two people would become in future, as it was with the antient Greeks, among whom it was reproachful for Greek to be found fighting against Greek in a foreign army. The individuals of the nation I have ever honored and esteemed, the basis of their character being essentially worthy: but I consider their government as the most flagitious which has existed since the days of Philip of Macedon, whom they make their model. It is not only founded in corruption itself, but insinuates the same poison into the bowels of every other, corrupts it's councils, nourishes factions, stirs up revolutions, and places it's own happiness in fomenting commotions and civil wars among others, thus rendering itself truly the hostis humani generis.[49] The effect is now coming home to itself. It's first operation will fall on the individuals who have been the chief instruments in it's corruptions, and will eradicate the families which have, from generation to generation been fattening on the blood of their brethren: and this scoria once thrown off, I am in hopes a purer nation will result, and a purer government be instituted, one which, instead of endeavoring to make us their natural enemies, will see in us, what we really are, their natural friends and brethren, and more interested in a fraternal connection with them than with any other nation on earth. I look therefore to their revolution with great interest. I wish it to be as moderate and bloodless, as will effect the desired object of an honest government, one which will permit the world to live in peace, and under the bonds of friendship and good neighborhood.

In this tremendous tempest, the distinctions of whig and tory will disappear like chaff on a troubled ocean. Indeed they have been disappearing from the day Hume first began to publish his history. This single book has done more to sap the free principles of the English constitution than the largest standing army of which their patriots have been so jealous. It is like the portraits of our countryman Wright, whose eye was so unhappy as to sieze all the ugly features of his subject, and to present them faithfully; while it was entirely insensible to every lineament of beauty. So Hume has consecrated, in his fascinating style, all the arbitrary proceedings of the English kings, as true evidences of the constitution, and glided over it's whig principles as the unfounded pretensions of factious dema-

49. I.e., Hostem generis humani, "an enemy of the human race." Pliny the Elder, *Natural History*, VII, 6.

gogues. He even boasts, in his life written by himself, that of the numerous alterations suggested by the readers of his work, he had never adopted one proposed by a whig.

But what, in this same tempest, will become of their colonies and their fleets? Will the former assume independance, and the latter resort to pyracy for subsistence, taking possession of some island as a point d'appui? A pursuit of these would add too much to the speculations on the situation and prospects of England, into which I have been led by the pithy text of the letter you so kindly sent me, and which I now return. It is worthy the pen of Tacitus. I add therefore only my affectionate and respectful souvenirs to Mrs Adams and yourself.

TH: JEFFERSON

Adams to Jefferson

Quincy Decr. 12 1816

DEAR SIR

I return the Analysis of Dupuis with my thanks for the loan of it. It is but a feignt Miniature of the original.

I have read that original in twelve Volumes, besides a 13th. of plates.

I have been a Lover and a Reader of Romances all my Life. From Don Quixotte and Gill Blas to the Scottish Chiefs and an hundred others.

For the last Year or two I have devoted my self to this kind of Study: and have read 15 Volumes of Grim, Seven Volumes of Tuckers Neddy Search and 12 Volumes of Dupuis besides a 13th of plates and Traceys Analysis, and 4. Volumes of Jesuitical History! Romances all! I have learned nothing of importance to me, for they have made no Change in my moral or religious Creed, which has for 50 or 60 Years been contained in four short Words "*Be just and good.*" In this result they all agree with me.

I must acknowledge however, that I have found in Dupuis more Ideas that were new to me, than in all the others.

My Conclusion from all of them is Universal Tolleration.

Is there any Work extant so well calculated to discredit Corruptions and Impostures in Religion as Dupuis.

I am Sir, with Friendship, as of old

JOHN ADAMS

Abigail Adams to Jefferson

Quincy December 15th 1816

DEAR SIR

My good Husband has called upon me for some Letters, written to me by my son, when he was last in paris, in 1815 in which he gives me a particular account of the Family of Count deTracy and of the circumstances which introduced him to their acquaintance.

Beleiving that it will give you pleasure to become acquainted with this happy domestic circle, I readily embrace this opportunity of transmitting them to you, with two or three other Letters which follow in succession, and are interesting, as they describe the novel and important events, to which Mr. Adams was an Eye witness.[50]

I rely upon your known care and punctuality to return them to me. I need not add, how valuable they are to me. They may also afford some entertainment to your Grandaughter Miss Ellen Randolph, whose praises are in the mouths, of all our northern Travellers, who have been so happy as to become acquainted with her. They bring us also: such delightfull accounts of Monticello and its inhabitants that I am tempted to wish myself twenty years younger, that [I might] visit them, but I am so far down Hill, that I must only think of those pleasures which are past. Amongst which, and not the least is my early acquaintance with, and the continued Friendship of the phylosopher of Monticello, to whom are offerd the respectfull attachment of Dear Sir your Friend

ABIGAIL ADAMS

Adams to Jefferson

Quincy Decr.16th. 1816

Your Letter dear Sir of Nov. 15 from Poplar Forrest, was sent to me from the Post Office the next day after I had sent "The Analysis" with my Thanks to you.

"3 Vols. of Idiology!" Pray explain to me this Neological Title! What

50. John Quincy Adams was in Paris during most of the Hundred Days of Bonaparte's return to power.

does it mean? When Bonaparte used it, I was delig[h]ted with it, upon the Common Principle of delight in every Thing We cannot understand. Does it mean Idiotism? The Science of Non compos Menticism. The Science of Lunacy? The Theory of Delerium? Or does it mean the Science of Self Love? of Amour propre? or the Elements of Vanity?

Were I in France, at this time, I could profess Blindness and Infirmity and prove it too. I suppose he does not avow the Analysis, as Hume did not avow his Essay on human Nature. That Analysis however does not show a Man of excessive Mediocrity. Had I known any of these Things two Years ago I would have written him a Letter. Of all Things, I wish to see his Idiology upon Montesquieu. If you, with all Your Influence have not been able to get your own translation of it with your own Notes upon it, published in four Years, where and What is the Freedom of The American Press.? Mr. Taylor of Hazel Wood Port Royal can have his voluminous and luminous Works published with Ease and dispatch.

The Uranologia, as I am told, is a Collection of Plates, Stamps Charts of the Heavens Upon a large Scale representing all the Constellations. The Work of some Professor in Sweeden. It is said to be the most perfect that ever has appeard. I have not seen it. Why should I ride 15 miles to see it When I can see the original every clear Evening; and esp[e]cially as Dupuis has almost made me afraid to enquire after any Thing more of it than I can see with my naked Eye in a Star light night?

That the Pope will send Jesuits to this Cou[n]try I doubt not; and the Church of England, Missionaries too. And the Methodists, and the Quakers and the Moravians, and the Sweedenburgers and the Menonists, and the Scottish Kirkers, and the Jacobites and the Jacobins and the Democrats and the Aristocrats and the Monarkists and the Despotists of all Denominations And every Emissary of every one of these Sects will find a Party here already formed, to give him a cordial R[e]ception; No Power or Intelligence less than Raphaels Moderator can reduce this Chaos to order.

I am charmed with the fluency and rapidity of your Reasoning on the State of Great Britain. I can deny none of your Premisses: but I doubt your Conclusion. After all the Convulsions that you forsee, they will return to that Constitution which You say has ruined them, and I say has been the Source of all their Power and Importance. They have as you say too much Sense and Knowledge of Liberty, ever to submit to simple Monarchy or absolute despotism on the one hand; And too much of the Devil in them ever to be governed by popular Elections of Presidents, Senators and Representatives in Congress. Instead of "turning their Eyes to Us," their innate Feelings will turn them from Us. They have been taught from their Cradles to despize scorn, insult and abuse Us. They hate Us more Vigorously, than they do the French. They would sooner adopt the simple Monarchy of France than our republican Institutions. You compliment me, with more knowledge of them than I can assume or pretend. If I should write you a Volume of Observations I made in England You would pronounce it, a Satyre. Suppose, the "Refrein" as the french call it, or the Burthen of the Song as the English express it; should be, the Religion, the Governmen[t] the Commerce the Manufactures, the Army and Navy of G. B. are all reduced to the Science of Pounds Shillings and Pence. Elections appeared to me a mere commercial Traffick; mere bargain and Sale. I have been told by sober steady Freeholders, that "they never had been and never would go to the Poll, without being paid for their Time, Travel and Expences." Now suppose an Election for a President of the British Empire. There must be a Nomination of Candidates by a National Convension, Congres, or Caucus, in which would be two Parties, Whigs and Tories. Of course two Candidates at least would be nominated. The Empire is instantly divided into two Parties at least. Every Man must be paid for his Vote, by the Candidate or his Party. The only Question would be, Which Party has the deepest Purse. The same Reasoning will apply to Elections of Senators and Representatives too. A Revolution might destroy the Burroughs and the Inequalities of Representation and might produce more toleration, and these Acquisitions might be worth all they would cost. But I dread the Experiment.

Britain will never be our Friend, till We are her Master. This will happen in less time than you and I have been struggling with her Power—provided We remain United. Aye! there's the rub! I fear there will be greater difficulties to preserve our Union, than You and I, our Fathers Brothers Friends Disciples and Sons have had to form it.

Towards G. B. I would adopt their own Maxim. An English Jocky says "If I have a wild horse to brake I begin by convincing him that I am his Master. And then I will convince him that I am his Friend." I am well assured that nothing will restrain G. B. from injuring Us, but fear.

You think that "in a revolution the distinction of Whig and Tory would disappear." I cannot believe this. That distinction arises from nature and Society; is now and ever will be time without End among Negroes Indians and Tartars as well as Federalists and Republicans. Instead of "disappearing since Hume published his History," that History has only increased the Tories and diminished the Whigs. That History has been the Bane of G. B. It has destroyed many of the best Effects of the Revolution of 1688. Style has governed the Empire. Swift, Pope and Hume have disgraced all the honest Historians. Rapin and Burnet Oldmixen and Coke, contain more honest Truth than Hume and Clarendon and all their disciples and Imitators. But Who reads any of them at this day? Every one of the fine Arts from the earliest times has been inlisted in the service of Superstition and Despotism. The whole World at this day Gazes with Astonishment at the grossest Fictions because they have been immortalized by the most exquisite Artists, Homer and Milton Phidias and Raphael. The Rabble of the Classic Skies and the Hosts of Roman Catholic Saints and Angells are still adored in Paint and Marble, and verse.

Raphael has sketched the Actors and Scenes in all Apuleus's Amours of Psyche and Cupid. Nothing is too offensive to morals delicacy or decency, for this Painter.

Raphael has painted in one of the most ostentati[o]us Churches in Italy, the Creation. And with what Genius? God Almighty is represented, as leaping into Chaos and boxing it about with his Fists and kicking it about With his feet, till he tumbles it into Order! ! ! Nothing is too impious or profane for this great Master who has painted so many inimitable Virgins and Childs.

To help me on in my career of improvement I have now read four Volumes of La Harps Correspondence with Paul and a Russian Minister.

Phylosophers! Never again think of annuling Superstition per Saltum ["by a leap"]. Festine lente ["Hasten slowly"].

JOHN ADAMS

Jefferson to Abigail Adams

Monticello Jan. 11. 17.

I owe you, dear Madam, a thousand thanks for the letters communicated in your favor of Dec. 15. and now returned. They give me more information than I possessed before of the family of Mr. Tracy, but what is infinitely interesting is the scene of the exchange of Louis XVIII for Bonaparte. What lessons of wisdom Mr. Adams must have read in that short space of time! more than fall to the lot of others in the course of a long life. Man, and the Man of Paris, under those circumstances, must have been a subject of profound speculation! It would be a singular addition to that spectacle to see the same beast in the cage of St. Helena, like a lion in the tower. That is probably the closing verse of the chapter of his crimes. But not so with Louis. He has other vicissitudes to go through.

I communicated the letters, according to your permission, to my grandaughter Ellen Randolph, who read them with pleasure and edification. She is justly sensible of, and flattered by your kind notice of her; and additionally so by the favorable recollections of our Northern visiting friends. If Monticello has anything which has merited their remembrance, it gives it a value the more in our estimation: and could I, in the spirit of your wish, count backwards a score of years, it would not be long before Ellen and myself would pay our homage personally to Quincy. But those 20. years, alas! where are they? With those beyond the flood. Our next meeting must then be in the country to which they have flown, a country, for us, not now very distant. For this journey we shall need neither gold nor silver in our purse, nor scrip, nor coats, nor staves. Nor is the provision for it more easy than the preparation has been kind. Nothing proves more than this that the being who presides over the world is essentially benevolent, stealing from us, one by one, the faculties of enjoyment, searing our sensibilities, leading us, like the horse in his mill, round and round the same beaten circle.

> to see what we have seen,
> To taste the tasted, and at each return,
> Less tasteful; o'er our palates to decant
> Another vintage.

Until satiated and fatigued with this leaden iteration, we ask our own Congé. I heard once a very old friend, who had troubled himself with neither poets nor philosophers, say the same thing in plain prose, that he was tired of pulling off his shoes and stockings at night, and putting them on again in the morning. The wish to stay here is thus gradually extinguished: but not so easily that of returning once in a while to see how things have gone on. Perhaps however one of the elements of future felicity is to be a constant and unimpassioned view of what is passing here. If so, this may well supply the wish of occasional visits. Mercier has given us a vision of the year 2440, but prophecy is one thing, history another. On the whole however, perhaps it is wise and well to be contented with the good things which the master of the feast places before us, and to be thankful for what we have, rather than thoughtful about what we have not. You and I, dear Madam, have already had more than an ordinary portion of life, and more too of health than the general measure. On this score I owe boundless thankfulness. Your health was, some time ago, not so good as it had been; and I perceive, in the letters communicated, some complaints still. I hope it is restored; and that life and health may be continued to you as many years as yourself shall wish is the sincere prayer of your affectionate and respectful friend

TH: JEFFERSON

Jefferson to Adams

Monticello Jan. 11. 17.

Forty three volumes read in one year, and 12. of them quartos! Dear Sir, how I envy you! Half a dozen 8vos. [octavos] in that space of time are as much as I am allowed. I can read by candlelight only, and stealing long hours from my rest; nor would that time be indulged to me, could I, by that light, see to write. From sun-rise to one or two aclock, and often from dinner to dark, I am drudging at the writing table. And all this to answer letters into which neither interest nor inclination on my part enters; and often for persons whose names I have never before heard. Yet, writing civilly, it is hard to refuse them civil answers. This is the burthen of my life, a very grievous one indeed, and one which I must get rid of. Delaplaine lately requested me to give him a line on the subject of his book; [51] meaning, as I well knew, to publish it. This I constantly refuse; but in this instance yielded, that, in saying a word for him, I might say two for myself. I expressed in it freely my sufferings from this source; hoping it would have the effect of an indirect appeal to the discretion of those, strangers and others, who, in the most friendly dispositions, oppress me with their concerns, their pursuits, their projects, inventions and speculations, political, moral, religious, mechanical, mathematical, historical etc. etc. etc. I hope the appeal will bring me relief, and that I shall be left to exercise and enjoy correspondence with the friends I love, and on subjects which they, or my own inclinations present. In that case your letters should not be so long on my files unanswered, as sometimes they have been to my great mortification.

To advert now to the subjects of those of Dec. 12. and 16. Tracy's Commentaries on Montesquieu have never been published in the original. Duane printed a translation from the original MS. a few years ago. It sold I believe readily, and whether a copy can now be had, I doubt. If it can, you will recieve it from my bookseller in Philadelphia, to whom I now write for that purpose. Tracy comprehends, under the word 'Ideology,' all the subjects which the French term *Morale*, as the correlative to *Physique*. His works on Logic, government, political economy, and morality, he considers as making up the circle of ideological subjects, or

51. Joseph Delaplaine's *Repository of the Lives and Portraits of Distinguished American Characters* (Philadelphia, 1815-16). Delaplaine had asked TJ for a sketch of Peyton Randolph, which TJ sent with his reply of July 26, 1816. Ford, X, 55-56 and *n.*, 56-60.

of those which are within the scope of the understanding, and not of the senses. His logic occupies exactly the ground of Locke's work on the understanding. The translation of that on Political economy is now printing; but it is no translation of mine. I have only had the correction of it; which was indeed very Laborious. Le premier jet having been by some one who understood neither French nor English, it was impossible to make it more than faithful. But it is a valuable work.

The result of your 50. or 60. years of religious reading in the four words 'be just and good' is that in which all our enquiries must end; as the riddles of all the priesthoods end in four more 'ubi panis, ibi deus ["where there is bread, there is God"].' What all agree in is probably right; what no two agree in most probably wrong. One of our fan-colouring biographers, who paints small men as very great, enquired of me lately, with real affection too, whether he might consider as authentic, the change in my religion much spoken of in some circles. Now this supposed that they knew what had been my religion before, taking for it the word of their priests, whom I certainly never made the confidants of my creed. My answer was 'say nothing of my religion. It is known to my god and myself alone. It's evidence before the world is to be sought in my life. If that has been *honest and dutiful to society*, the religion which has regulated it cannot be a bad one.' Affectionately Adieu.

TH: JEFFERSON

Adams to Jefferson

Quincy Feb. 2d. 1817

DEAR SIR

In our good old English language of Gratitude, I owe you and give you a thousand thanks for Tracy's Review of Montesquieu, which Mr. Dufief has sent me by your Order. I have read an hu[n]dred pages, and will read the rest. He is a sensible Man and is easily understood. He is not an abstruse, misterious, incomprehensi[ble] Condorcet. Though I have banished the Subject from my thoughts for many Years, yet if Tracy and I were thirty Years Younger I would ask him an hundred or two of questions. His book was written when the French Experiment was glowing in the furnace not yet blown out. He all along supposes that Men are rational and consciencious Creatures. I say so too: but I say at the same time that their passions and Interests generally prevail over their Reason and their consciences: and if Society does not contrive some means of controuling and restrain[in]g the former the World will go on as it has done.

I was tollerably well informed, fifty years ago, how it had gone on, and formed some plausible conjectures how it would go on. Grim, Dupuis and Eustace have confirmed all my former Notions and made immense Additions to them. Eustace is a Suppliment to Dupuis; and both together contain a compleat draught of the Superstition, Credulity and Despotism of our terrestrial Universe. They show how Science, Litteratur, Mechanic Arts, and those fine Arts of Architecture, Painting, Statuary, Poetry, Musick and Eloquence: which you love so well and taste so exquisitely, have been subservient to Priests and Kings Nobles and commons Monarchies and Republicks. For they have all Used them when they could, but as the rich had them oftener than the poor, in their power, the latter have always gone to the Wall.

Eustace is inestimable to a young Schollar, and a Classic Traveller: but he is a plausible, insidious Roman Catholick Priest and I doubt not Jesuit. He should have read Dupuis before he comenced his Travels. Very little, of the Religions of Nations more antient than the Greeks and Romans, appears to have been known to him.

I am glad to see, that De la plane has published a part of your Letter, and I hope it will procure You some relief. I have suffered in the same manner, though not probably in the same degree. Necessity has compelled me to resort to two expedients to avoid or escape excessive importunity. One has been, by totally neglecting to answer Letter, after Letter. But this Method has cost me very dear in the loss of many Correspondances that had been and would have been instructive and profitable to me, as well as honourable and entertain[in]g. The other has been by giving gruff, short, unintelligible, misterious, enigmatical, or pedantical Answers. This resource is out of your power, because it is not in your nature to avail Yourself of it.

The practice, however, of publishing private Letters without leave, though even as rude ones as mine, is an Abuse and must be reformed.

Theodore Lyman Esqr., Junior, will I hope, deliver you this. He is an Educated and travelled Son of one of our Richest Merchants. His Hea[l]th has been, and is precarious. I have been indebted to him for the perusal of the Baron de Grim. I find that all our Young Gentlemen who have any *Nous*, and can afford to travel, have an ardent Curiosity to visit, what shall I say? the Man of the Mountain? The Sage of Monticello? Or the celebrated Philosopher and Statesman of Virginia? They all apply to me for Introduction. In hopes of softening asperities and promoting Union, I have refused none whom I thought Men of Sense.

I forgot one thing that I intended to say. I pitty our good Brother

Madison. You and I have had Children and Grand Children and great grand Children. Though they have cost us Grief, Anxiety, often Vexation, and some times humiliation; Yet it has been cheering to have them hovering about Us; and I verily believe they have contributed largely to keep Us alive. Books cannot always expell Ennui. I therefore pitty Brother Madison and especially his Lady. I pitty him the more, because, notwithstand[ing] a thousand Faults and blunders, his Administration has acquired more glory, and established more Union, than all his three Predecessors, Washington Adams and Jefferson, put together. I am, as ever

JOHN ADAMS

Adams to Jefferson

Quincy April 19 1817

DEAR SIR

My loving and beloved Friend, Pickering, has been pleased to inform the World that I have "few Friends." I wanted to whip the rogue, and I had it in my Power, if it had been in my Will to do it, till the blood come. But all my real Friends as I thought them, with Dexter and Grey at their Head insisted "that I should not say a Word." "That nothing that such a Person could write would do me the least Injury. That it would betray the Constitution and the Government, if a President out or in should enter into a Newspaper controversy, with one of his Ministers whom he had removed from his Office, in Justification of himself for that removal or any thing else." And they talked a great deal about *"The Dignity"* of the Office of President, which I do not find that any other Persons, public or private regard very much.

Nevertheless, I fear that Mr. Pickerings Information is too true. It is impossible that any Man should run such a Gauntlet as I have been driven through, and have many Friends at last. This "all who know me know" though I cannot say "who love me tell."

I have, however, either Friends who wish to amuse and solace my old age; or Ennemies who mean to heap coals of fire on my head and kill me with kindness: for they overwhelm me with Books from all quarters, enough to offuscate all Eyes, and smother and stifle all human Understanding. Chateaubriand, Grim, Tucker, Dupuis, La Harpe, Sismondi, Eustace A new Translation of Herodotus by Belloe with more Notes than Text. What should I do, with all this lumber? I make my "Woman kind" as the

Antiquary expresses it, read to me, all the English: but as they will not read the French, I am obliged to excruciate my Eyes to read it myself. And all to what purpose? I verily believe I was as wise and good, seventy Years ago, as I am now.

At that Period Lemuel Bryant was my Parish Priest; and Joseph Cleverly my Latin School Master. Lemuel was a jolly jocular and liberal Schollar and Divine. Joseph a Scollar and Gentleman; but a biggoted episcopalian of the School of Bishop Saunders and Dr. Hicks, a down right conscientious passive Obedience Man in Church and State. The Parson and the Pedagogue lived much together, but were eternally disputing about Government and Religion. One day, when the Schoolmaster had been more than commonly fanatical, and declared "if he were a Monark, *He would have but one Religion in his Dominions*" The Parson coolly replied "Cleverly! You would be the best Man in the World, if You had no Religion."

Twenty times, in the course of my late Reading, have I been upon the point of breaking out, "This would be the best of all possible Worlds, if there were no Religion in it." ! ! ! But in this exclamati[on] I should have been as fanatical as Bryant or Cleverly. Without Religion this World would be Something not fit to be mentioned in polite Company, I mean Hell. So far from believing in the total and universal depravity of human Nature; I believe there is no Individual totally depraved. The most abandoned Scoundrel that ever existed, never Yet Wholly extinguished his Conscience, and while Conscience remains there is some Religion. Popes, Jesuits and Sorbonists and Inquisitors have some Conscience and some Religion. So had Marius and Sylla, Caesar Cataline and Anthony, and Augustus had not much more, let Virgil and Horace say what they will.

What shall We think of Virgil and Horace, Sallust Quintillian, Pliny and even Tacitus? and even Cicero, Brutus and Seneca? Pompey I leave out of the question, as a mere politician and Soldier. Every One of these great Creatures has left indelible marks of Conscience and consequently of Religion, tho' every one of them has left abundant proofs of profligate violations of their Consciences by their little and great Passions and paltry Interests.

The vast prospect of Mankind, which these Books have passed in Review before me, from the most ancient records, histories, traditions and Fables that remain to Us, to the present day, has sickened my very Soul; and almost reconciled me to Swifts Travels among The Yahoo's. Yet I never can be a Misanthrope. Homo Sum ["I am a man"]. I must hate myself before I can hate my Fellow Men: and that I cannot and will not do. No! I will not hate any of them, base, brutal and devilish as some of them have been to me.

From the bottom of my Soul, I pitty my Fellow Men. Fears and Terrors appear to have produced an univer[s]al Credulity. Fears of Calamities in Life and punishments after death, seem to have possessed the Souls of all Men. But fear of Pain and death, here, do not seem to have been so unconquerable as fear of what is to come hereafter. Priests, Hierophants, Popes, Despots Emperors, Kings, Princes Nobles, have been as credulous as Shoeblacks, Boots, and Kitchen Scullions. The former seem to have believed in their divine Rights as sincerely as the latter. Auto de fee's in Spain and Portugal have been celebrated with as good Faith as Excommunications have been practiced in Connecticutt or as Baptisms have been refused in Phyladelphia.

How it is possible than [i.e., that] Mankind should submit to be governed as they have been is to me an inscrutable Mystery. How they could bear to be taxed to build the Temple of Diana at Ephesus, the Pyramyds of Egypt, Saint Peters at Rome, Notre Dame at Paris, St. Pauls in London, with a million Etceteras; when my Navy Yards, and my quasi Army made such a popular Clamour, I know not. Yet all my Peccadillos, never excited such a rage as the late Compensation Law! ! ! [52]

I congratulate you, on the late Election in Connecticutt.[53] It is a kind of Epocha. Several causes have conspired. One which you would not suspect. Some one, no doubt instigated by the Devil, has taken it into his head to print a new Edition of "The independent Whig" even in Connecticut, and has scattered the Volumes through the State. These Volumes it is said, have produced a Burst of Indignation against Priestcraft Bigotry and Intollerance, and in conjunction with other causes have produced the late Election. When writing to you I never know when to Subscribe

JOHN ADAMS

52. In 1816 and 1817 Congress passed several invalid-pension bills for veterans of the War of 1812. Adams apparently refers to the bill enacted on March 3, 1817; *U. S. Stat. at L.*, III, 394. Also see William H. Glasson, *Federal Military Pensions in the United States* (N. Y., 1918), 108-9.

53. The campaign issue in the spring election of 1817 was "whether freemen shall be tolerated in the free exercise of their religious and political rights." Oliver Wolcott, father of the Constitution of 1818 (Connecticut's first), was elected governor. George L. Clark, *A History of Connecticut, Its People and Institutions* (N.Y., [1914]), 349.

Abigail Adams to Jefferson

Quincy, April 29th 1817

DEAR SIR

What right have I to be one of your tormentors? And amongst the numerous applicants for introductory letters?

Why I will plead, old acquaintance, old Friendship and your well known benevolence. But to the subject of my present address. Mr. Theodore Lyman, who possesses an ardent thirst for Literature, and whose Father, is one of our most respectable Characters for probity, honour, and wealth, this young Gentleman has been much out of health, occasioned by too close application to his studies. He is now going abroad with the hopes of regaining it. He is desirious of getting an introduction to some Gentlemen of Letters in France—my good Husband has furnished him, with one to the Marquis La Fayette, one to Mr. Marbois, and one to Mr. Gallatin. But as your acquaintance with men of Letters in France is of a more recent date, I thought it probable that you might give him a Letter or two, which might be of much service to him, from the weight and respectability of your Character. He understands the French language, and is a young Gentleman of most estimable Character, and acquirements, whom I am not ashamed to recommend. He is a nephew of Mr. Williams, late consul of the U S in England. He has been once in England and in France before, and knows full well that to Men of Letters he cannot be easily admitted, without honorable introduction. He has been so attentive in supplying us with such rare and valuable Books that I feel indebted to him for his kindness. And as I am not able myself to repay his civility, like other debtors, I am drawing upon my Friend's. Any Letter you may think proper to forward, you will please to send under cover to my Husband, and they will be gratifully acknowledged by your old and steady Friend

ABIGAIL ADAMS

Jefferson to Adams

Monticello. May 5. 17.

DEAR SIR

Absences and avocations had prevented my acknoleging your favor of Feb. 2. when that of Apr. 19. arrived. I had not the pleasure of recieving the former by the hands of Mr. Lyman. His business probably carried him in another direction; for I am far inland, and distant from the great line of communication between the trading cities. Your recommendations are always welcome, for indeed the subjects of them always merit that welcome, and some of them in an extraordinary degree. They make us acquainted with what there is of excellent in our ancient sister state of Massachusets, once venerated and beloved, and still hanging on our hopes, for what need we despair of after the resurrection of Connecticut to light and liberality.[54] I had believed that, the last retreat of Monkish darkness, bigotry, and abhorrence of those advances of the mind which had carried the other states a century ahead of them. They seemed still to be exactly where their forefathers were when they schismatised from the Covenant of works, and to consider, as dangerous heresies, all innovations good or bad. I join you therefore in sincere congratulations that this den of the priesthood is at length broken up, and that a protestant popedom is no longer to disgrace the American history and character. If, by *religion*, we are to understand *Sectarian dogmas*, in which no two of them agree, then your exclamation on that hypothesis is just, 'that this would be the best of all possible worlds, if there were no religion in it.' But if the moral precepts, innate in man, and made a part of his physical constitution, as necessary for a social being, if the sublime doctrines of philanthropism, and deism taught us by Jesus of Nazareth in which all agree, constitute true religion, then, without it, this would be, as you again say, 'something not fit to be named, even indeed a Hell.'

You certainly acted wisely in taking no notice of what the malice of Pickering could say of you. Were such things to be answered, our lives would be wasted in the filth of fendings and provings, instead of being employed in promoting the happiness and prosperity of our fellow citizens. The tenor of your life is the proper and sufficient answer. It is

54. Massachusetts continued the state-supported church until 1833, but in Connecticut the election of the liberal Oliver Wolcott as governor in 1817 brought about the Constitutional Convention of 1818. Article VII of the new Constitution provided for religious freedom. Clark, *History of Conn.*, 350-52.

fortunate for those in public trust that posterity will judge them by their works, and not by the malignant vituperations and invectives of the Pickerings and Gardeniers of their age. After all, men of energy of character must have enemies: because there are two sides to every question, and taking one with decision, and acting on it with effect, those who take the other will of course be hostile in proportion as they feel that effect. Thus in the revolution, Hancock and the Adamses were the rawhead and bloody bones of tories and traitors; who yet knew nothing of you personally but what was good.

I do not entertain your apprehensions for the happiness of our brother Madison in a state of retirement. Such a mind as his, fraught with information, and with matter for reflection, can never know ennui. Besides, there will always be work enough cut out for him to continue his active usefulness to his country. For example, he and Monroe (the president) are now here on the work of a collegiate institution to be established in our neighborhood, of which they and myself are three of six Visitors. This, if it succeeds, will raise up children for Mr. Madison to employ his attentions thro' life. I say, if it succeeds; for we have two very essential wants in our way 1. means to compass our views and 2dly. men qualified to fulfill them. And these you will agree are essential wants indeed.

I am glad to find you have a copy of Sismondi, because his is a field familiar to you, and on which you can judge him. His work is highly praised, but I have not yet read it. I have been occupied and delighted with reading another work, the title of which did not promise much useful information or amusement, 'l'Italia avanti il dominio dei Romani dal Micali.' It has often you know been a subject of regret that Carthage had no writer to give her side of her own history, while her wealth, power, and splendor prove she must have had a very distinguished policy and government. Micali has given the counterpart of the Roman history for the nations over which they extended their domination. For this he has gleaned up matter from every quarter, and furnished materials for reflection and digestion to those who, thinking as they read have percieved there was a great deal of matter behind the curtain, could that be fully withdrawn. He certainly gives new views of a nation whose splendor has masked and palliated their barbarous ambition.

I am now reading Botta's history of our own revolution. Bating the antient practice, which he has adopted, of putting speeches into mouths which never made them, and fancying motives of action which we never felt, he has given that history with more detail, precision and candor, than any writer I have yet met with. It is to be sure compiled from those writers; but it is a good secretion of their matter, the pure from the impure, and presented in a just sense of right in opposition to usurpation.

Accept assurances for Mrs. Adams and yourself of my affectionate esteem and respect.

TH: JEFFERSON

Jefferson to Abigail Adams

Monticello May 15. 17.

Your letters, dear Madam, are always welcome, and your requests are commands to me. I only regret that I can do so little towards obeying them. But eight and twenty years since I left France would, in the ordinary course of mortality, have swept off seven eighths of my acquaintances, and when to this lapse of time are added the knife of the Guillotine and scythe of constant and sanguinary wars, I am left without a single personal acquaintance there of the literary family; for Dupont, the only one of that day still living, is in the US. A correspondence however has since taken place with some literati not known to me personally, nor their habits of society or situations in life. Among these I have chosen M. destutt-Tracy and Say; the former great in the moral sciences, the latter particularly in that of Political economy. Mr. Tracy's connection too with M. de la Fayette will facilitate Mr. Lyman's acquaintance with him. I have selected these two the rather because, in the course of our correspondence, I owe a letter to each, and am glad to avail myself of the opportunity by Mr. Lyman of paying the debt, adding to my letters the recommendations of him which your information authorises. Should therefore any circumstance prevent Mr. Lyman's visit to France direct, I will pray him to forward the letters by the first entirely safe conveyance, under cover to Mr. Gallatin. In the letter to M. de la Fayette I have associated my sollicitations with those of Mr. Adams for the courtesies to Mr. Lyman, which he so willingly extends to all Americans. Wishing a pleasant voyage and tour to him, and to yourself and Mr. Adams long years of health and happiness, I tender you the homage of my constant respect and attachment.

TH: JEFFERSON

Adams to Jefferson

Quincy May 18. 1817

Dear Sir

Lyman was mortified that he could not visit Montecello. He is gone to Europe a second time. I regret that he did not see you, He would have executed any commision for you in the litterary line, at any pain or any expence. I have many Apprehensions for his health, which is very delicate and precarious. But he is seized with the Mania of all our young etherial Spirits, for foreign travel. I fear they will loose more than they will acquire. They will loose that unadulterated Enthusiasm for their native Country which has produced the greatest Characters among Us.

Oh! Lord! Do you think that a Protestant Popedom is annihilated in America? Do you recollect, or have you ever attended to the ecclesiastical Strifes in Maryland Pensilvania, New York, and every part of New England? What a mercy it is that these People cannot whip and crop, and pillory and roast, *as yet* in the U. S.! If they could they would.

Do you know that The General of the Jesuits and consequently all his Host have their Eyes on this Country? Do you know that the Church of England is employing more means and more Art, to propagate their demipopery among Us, than ever? Quakers, Anabaptists Moravians Swedenborgians, Methodists, Unitarians, Nothingarians in all Europe are employing understrand [underhand?] means to propagate their sectarian Systems in these States.

The multitude and diversity of them, You will say, is our Security against them all. God grant it. But if We consider that the Presbyterians and Methodists are far the most numerous and the most likely to unite; let a George Whitefield arise, with a military cast, like Mahomet, or Loyola, and what will become of all the other Sects who can never unite?

My Friends or Enemies continue to overwhelm me with Books. Whatever may be their intension, charitable or otherwise, they certainly contribute, to continue me to vegetate, much as I have done for the sixteen Years last past.

Sir John Malcoms History of Persia, and Sir William Jones's Works are now poured out upon me and a little cargo is coming from Europe. What can I do with all this learned lumber? Is it necessary to Salvation to investigate all these Cosmogonies and Mythologies? Is Bryant Gebelin, Dupuis, or Sir William Jones, right?

What a frown upon Mankind, was the premature death of Sir William

Jones? Why could not Jones and Dupuis have conversed or corresponded with each other? Had Jones read Dupuis, or Dupuis Jones, the Works of both would be immensely improved though each would probably have adhered to his System.

I should admire to see a Counsel, composed of Gebelin, Bryant Jones and Dupuis. Let them live together and compare Notes. The human race ought to contribute to furnish them with all the Books in the Universe, and the means of Subsistence.

I am not expert enough in Italian to read Botta, and I know not that he has been translated. Indeed I have been so little satisfied with Histories of the American Revolution, that I have long since, ceased to read them. The Truth is lost, in adulatory Panegyricks, and in vituperary Insolence.

I wish You, Mr. Madison and Mr. Monroe Success, in Your Collegiate institution. And I wish that Superstition in Religion exciting Superstition in Politicks, and both united in directing military Force, alias glory may never blow up all your benevolent and phylanthropic Lucubrations. But the History of all Ages is against you. It is said, that no Effort in favour of Virtue, is ever lost. I doubt whether it was ever true; whether it is now true; but hope it will be true. In the moral Government of the World, no doubt it was, is, and ever will be true: but it has not Yet appeared to be true on this Earth. I am Sir, Sincerely your friend

JOHN ADAMS

P. S. Have You seen [Buchanan's] the Phylosophy of human Nature, and [McAfee's] the History of the War, in the Western States, from Kentucky? How vigorously Science and Litterature spring up, as well as Patriotism and Heroism in transalleganian Regions? Have you seen Wilkensons History? etc. etc. etc.

J. A.

Adams to Jefferson

Quincy May 26. 1817

DEAR SIR

Mr. Leslie Combs of Kentucky has sent me "a History of the late War, in the Western Country, by Mr. Robert B. McAffee" And "The Phylosophy of Human Nature by Joseph Buchanan."

["]The History," I am glad to see: because it will preserve facts, to the honour, and immortal Glory of the Western people. Indeed I am not sorry that "the Phylosophy" has been published, because it has been a maxim with me for Sixty Years at least, Never to be afraid of a Book.

Nevertheless I cannot foresee much Utility in reviving, in this Country, the controversy between the Spiritualistes and the Materialists. Why should time be wasted in disputing about two Substances when both parties agree that neither knows any thing about either. If Spirit is an abstraction, a conjecture, a Chimera: Matter is an abstraction, a conjecture, a Chimera; for We know as much, or rather as little of one as of the other. We may read Cudworth Clerk Leibnitz, Berkley Hume Bolin[g]broke and Priestley and a million other Volumes in all Ages, and be obliged at last to confess that We have learned nothing. Spirit and matter still remain Riddles. Define the terms however, and the controversy is soon settled. If Spirit is an active Something and matter an inactive Something, it is certain that one is not the other. We can no more conceive that Extension or Solidity can think or feel, or see, or hear, or taste or smell: than We can conceive that Perception Memory Imagination or Reason can remove a mountain or blow a rock. This Enigma has puzzled Mankind from the beginning, and probably will to the End. Œconomy of time requires that We should waste no more in so idle an Amusement. In the 11th. discourse of Sir William Jones before The Asiatic Society Vol. 3. p. 229. of his Works, We find that Materialists and Immaterialists existed in India and that they accused each other of Atheism, before Berkly or Priestley, or Dupuis, or Plato, or Pythagoras were born. Indeed Neuton himself, appears to have discovered nothing that was not known to the Antient Indians. He has only furnished more ample demonstrations of the doctrines they taught. Sir John Malcomb agrees with Jones and Dupuis in the Astrological origin of Heathen mithologies.

Vain Man! Mind Your own Business! Do no Wrong! Do all the good You can! Eat Your Canvas back ducks, drink Your burgundy, sleep Your S[i]esta, when necessary, And *Trust in God.!*

What a mighty bubble! What a tremendous Waterspout has Napolion been according to his Life, written by himself? He says he was the Creature of the Principles and manners of the Age. By which no doubt he means the Age of Reason; the progress of Manilius's Ratio; of Plato's Logos etc. I believe him. A Whirlwind raised him and a Whirlwind blowed him a Way to St. Helena. He is very confident that the Age of Reason is not past; and so am I; but I hope that Reason will never again rashly and hastily create such Creatures as him. Liberty, Equality, Fraternity, and Humanity will never again, I hope blindly surrender themselves to an unbounded Ambition for national Conquests, nor implicitly commit themselves to the custody and Guardianship of Arms and Heroes. If they do, they will again end in St. Helena, Inquisitions Jesuits and Sacre Ligues ["holy leagues"].

Poor Laureate Southey, is writhing in Torments under the Laugh of the three kingdoms all Europe and America, upon the publication of his Wat Tyler.[55] I wonder whether he, or Bona suffers most.

I congratulate You and Madison and Monroe, on your noble Employment in founding a University. From such a noble Tryumvirate, the World will expect something very great and very new. But if it contains any thing quite original, and very excellent, I fear the prejudices are too deeply rooted to suffer it to last long, though it may be accepted at first. It will not always have three such colossal reputations to support it.

The Pernambuco Ambassador, his Secretary of Legation and private Secretary, respectable People, have made me a Visit. Having been some Year or two in a similar Situation I could not but sympathize with him. As Bona says the Age of Reason is not ended. Nothing can tottally extinguish or eclipse the Light which has been shed abroad by the press. I am, Sir, with hearty wishes for Your health and hapiness Your Friend and humble Servant

JOHN ADAMS

Adams to Jefferson

Quincy July 15. 1817

DEAR SIR

I am impatient to see your Plan of a University and new System of Education. To assist You in your contemplations, I send you a Pamp[h]let, "The Politicks of Connecticut." By a federal Republican in the name of Hamilton. Was there ever such a combination? Two Copies were sent me from the Post on Saturday last: I know not from whence nor by whom.

Now Sir! please to hear a modest Proposal. Let me go back to twenty. Give me a million of Revenue, a Library of a Million of Volumes, and as many more as I should want. I would devote my Life to such an Œ[u]vrage as Condorcet tells us, that Turgot had in contemplation, all

55. Robert Southey's poem, *Wat Tyler*, written in 1794, expressed strongly republican sentiments which he had later renounced. In 1817, when the poem was surreptitiously published, he was poet laureate and suffered criticism for being a traitor to his early liberalism.

his Lifetime. I would digest Bryant, Gebelin, Dupuis, Sir William Jones and above all the Acta Sanctorum of the Bolandists.

I know where the investigation would end. In Montesquieus 12 duo-decimo Pages.

Is the Biography of Democratus and Heraclitus a Fable, or History? I cannot contemplate human Affairs, without laughing or crying. I choose to laugh. When People talk of the Freedom of Writing Speaking or thinking, I cannot choose but laugh. No such thing ever existed. No such thing now exists: but I hope it will exist. But it must be hundreds of years after you and I shall write and speak no more.

JOHN ADAMS

Jefferson to Adams

Poplar Forest, near Lynchburg. Sep. 8. 17.

DEAR SIR

A month's absence from Monticello has added to the delay of acknoleg-ing your last letters; and indeed for a month before I left it our projected College gave me constant employment; for being the only Visitor in it's immediate neighborhood, all it's administrative business falls on me, and that, where building is going on, is not a little. In yours of July 15. you express a wish to see our plan. But the present visitors have sanctioned no plan as yet. Our predecessors, the first trustees, had desired me to propose one to them, and it was on that occasion I asked and recieved the benefit of your ideas on the subject. Digesting these with such other schemes as I had been able to collect, I made out a Prospectus, the looser and less satisfactory, from the uncertain amount of the funds to which it was to be adapted. This I addressed, in the form of a letter to their President Peter Carr; which going before the legislature, when a change in the constitution of the College was asked, got into the public papers, and, among others, I think you will find it in Niles's register, in the early part of 1815.[56] This, however, is to be considered but as a premiere ebauche, for the consideration and amendment of the present visitors, and to be accommodated to one of two conditions of things. If the insti-tution is to depend on private donations alone, we shall be forced to

56. TJ to Peter Carr, Sept. 7, 1814, Lipscomb and Bergh, eds., *Writings*, XIX, 211; "Jefferson on Education," *Niles' Weekly Register*, 10, no. 3 (March 16, 1816), re-printed from the Richmond *Enquirer*.

accumulate on the shoulders of 4. professors a mass of sciences which, if the legislature adopts it, should be distributed among ten. We shall be ready for a professor of languages in April next; for two others the following year, and a 4th a year after. How happy should we be if we could have a Ticknor for our first. A critical classic is scarcely to be found in the US. To this professor, a fixed salary of 500. D. with liberal tuition fees from the pupils will probably give 2000. D. a year. We are now on the look-out for a professor, meaning to accept of none but of the very first order.

You ask if I have seen Buchanan's, McAfee's, or Wilkinson's books? I have seen none of them; but have lately read with great pleasure, Reid and Eaton's life of Jackson, if life may be called what is merely a history of his campaign of 1814. Reid's part is well written; Eaton's continuation is better for it's matter than style. The whole however is valuable.

I have lately recieved a pamphlet of extreme interest from France. It is De Pradt's historical recital of the first return of Louis XVIII to Paris. It is precious for the minutiae of the proceedings which it details, and for their authenticity, as from an eye witness. Being but a pamphlet, I enclose it for your perusal, assured, if you have not seen it, that it will give you pleasure. I will ask it's return, because I value it as a morsel of genuine history, a thing so rare as to be always valuable. I have recieved some information, from an eye witness also, of what passed on the occasion of the 2d. return of Louis XVIII. The Emperor Alexander it seems was solidly opposed to this. In the consultation of the allied sovereigns and their representatives, with the Executive council at Paris, he insisted that the Bourbons were too incapable and unworthy of being placed at the head of the nation, declared he would support any other choice, they should freely make, and continued to urge most strenuously that some other choice should be made. The debates ran high and warm, and broke off after midnight, every one retaining his own opinion. He lodged, as you know, at Talleyrand's. When they returned into council the next day, his host had overcome his firmness. Louis XVIII. was accepted, and thro' the management of Talleyrand, accepted without any capitulation, altho' the sovereigns would have consented that he should be first required to subscribe and swear to the constitution prepared, before permission to enter the kingdom. It would seem as if Talleyrand had been afraid to admit the smallest interval of time, lest a change of wind would bring back Bonaparte on them. But I observe that the friends of a limited monarchy there consider the popular representation as much improved by the late alteration, and confident it will in the end produce a fixed government in which an elective body, fairly representative of the people will be an efficient element.

I congratulate Mrs. Adams and yourself on the return of your excellent and distinguished son, and our country still more on such a minister of their foreign affairs, and I renew to both the assurance of my high and friendly respect and esteem.

TH: JEFFERSON

Adams to Jefferson

Quincy Oct. 10. 1817

DEAR SIR

I thank you for your kind congratulations on the return of my little family from Europe. To receive them all in fine health and good Spirits, after so long an absence, was a greater Blessing, than at my time of Life when they went away I had any right to hope or reason to expect. If the Secretary of State can give Satisfaction to his fellow Citizens in his new Office it will be a Source of consolation to me while I live: [57] though it is not probable that I shall long be a Witness of his good Success or ill Success. I shall soon be obliged to say to him and to you and to your Country and mine, God bless you all! Fare Ye Well. Indeed I need not wait a moment. I can say all that now with as good a Will and as clear a conscience as at any time past or future.

I thank you also for the loan of Depradts narration of the Intrigues at the second restoration of the Bourbons. In this as in many other Instances is seen the influence of a Single subtel mind and a trifling Accident in deciding the fate of Mankind for Ages. De Pradt and Talleyrand were well associated. I have ventured to send the Pamphlet to Washington with a charge to return it to you. The French have a King a Chamber of Peers and a Chamber of Deputies. Voila! Les Ossemen[t]s ["The Bones"] of a constitution of a limited monarchy; and of a good one, provided the bones are united by good joints and knitted together by strong tendons. But where does the Souvereignty reside? Are the three branches sufficiently defined? A fair representation of the body of the People by Elections sufficiently frequent is essential to a free Government: but if the commons cannot make themselves respected by the Peers and the King, they can do no good nor prevent any evil. Can any Organisation of

57. John Quincy Adams, American minister to the Court of St. James, 1815-17, had returned to the United States to become secretary of state under President Monroe. Bemis, *John Quincy Adams*, 246-49.

Government secure public and private liberty without a general or universal freedom without Licence or licentiousness of thinking speaking and writing. Have the French such Freedom? Will their Religion, or Policy allow it? When I think of Liberty and a Free Government, in an ancient opulent populous and commercial empire I fear I shall always recollect a Fable of Plato.

Love is a Son of the God of Riches and the Godess of Poverty. He inherits from his father, the intrepidity of his Courage, the Enthusiasm of his thoughts, his Generosity, his prodigality, his confidence in himself, the Opinion of his own merit, his impatience to have always the preference: but he derives from his mother that indigence which makes him always a begger, that importunity with which he demands every thing, that timidity which sometimes hinders him from daring to ask any thing, that disposition which he has to Servitude, and that dread of being despised which he can never overcome.

Such is Love according to Plato, who calls him a Demon, and such is Liberty in France and England and all other great rich old corrupted commercial Nations. The Opposite qualities of the father and mother are perpetually tearing to pieces himself and his friends as well as his Enemies.

Mr. Monroe has got the un[i]versal Character among all our Common People of "A very smart Man" And verily I am of the same Mind. I know not another who could have executed so great a plan so cleverly. I wish him the same happy Success through his whole Administration. I am, Sir with respect and Frien[d]ship Your

JOHN ADAMS

Adams to Jefferson

Quincy Jan. 28 1818

DEAR SIR

Permit me to introduce to you Mr. Horace Holley, who is on his Way to Kentucky where he has been invited to undertake the Superintendance of a University. This Gentleman was settled very young at Greenfield as Successor to Dr. Dwight; but having a Mind too inquisitive for Connecticut he removed to Boston, where he has been settled nine Years and where his fame has erected one of the loftyest Temples and assembled the most numerous Congregation of Auditors in Boston.

You will find him frank enough candid enough, social enough, learned enough and eloquent enough. He is indeed an important Character; and if Superstition Bigotry, Fanaticism and Intolerance will allow him to live in Kentucky, he will contribute Somewhat to the illumination of the darkest and most dismal Swamps in the Wilderness. I shall regret his Removal from Boston because that City ought always to have one Clergyman at least who will compell them to think and enquire: but if he can be supported in Kentucky I am convinced he will be more extensively usefull. If upon conversing with him Your Conscience will allow you to give him a Line to any of your Friends in Kentucky where all are your Friends, you will do him more Service and perhaps more Service to our Country and our kind than you or I may be aware. He is one of the few who give me delight.

I am anxious for South America. They will be independent of Spain. But can they have free Governments? Can the Roman Religion and a free Government exist together? I am, dear Sir with the old Friendship your

JOHN ADAMS

Jefferson to Adams

Monticello May 17. 18.

DEAR SIR

I was so unfortunate as not to recieve from Mr. Holly's own hand your favor of Jan. 28. being then at my other home. He dined only with my family, and left them with an impression which has filled me with regret that I did not partake of the pleasure his visit gave them. I am glad he is gone to Kentucky. Rational Christianity will thrive more rapidly there than here. They are freer from prejudices than we are, and bolder in grasping at truth. The time is not distant, tho' neither you nor I shall see it, when we shall be but a secondary people to them. Our greediness for wealth, and fantastical expense has degraded and will degrade the minds of our maritime citizens. These are the peculiar vices of commerce.

I had been long without hearing *from* you, but I had heard *of* you thro' a letter from Dr. Waterhouse. He wrote to reclaim against an expression of Mr. Wirt's, as to the commencement of motion in the revolutionary ball.[58] The lawyers say that words are always to be expounded secundum

---

58. In William Wirt's laudatory *Sketches of the Life and Character of Patrick Henry* (Philadelphia, 1818), especially secs. iv-vi.

subjectam materiem ["according to the subject matter"], which in Mr. Wirt's case was Virginia. It would moreover be as difficult to say at what moment the revolution began, and what incident set it in motion, as to fix the moment that the embryo becomes an animal, or the act which gives him a beginning.

But the most agreeable part of his letter was that which informed me of your health, your activity, and strength of memory; and the most wonderful that which assured me that you retained your industry and promptness in epistolary correspondence. Here you have entire advantage over me. My repugnance to the writing table becomes daily and hourly more deadly and insurmountable. In place of this has come on a canine appetite for reading. And I indulge it: because I see in it a relief against the taedium senectutis ["weariness of old age"]; a lamp to lighten my path thro' the dreary wilderness of time before me, whose bourne I see not. Losing daily all interest in the things around us, something else is necessary to fill the void. With me it is reading, which occupies the mind without the labor of producing ideas from my own stock.

I enter into all your doubts as to the event of the revolution of S. America. They will succeed against Spain. But the dangerous enemy is within their own breasts. Ignorance and superstition will chain their minds and bodies under religious and military despotism. I do believe it would be better for them to obtain freedom by degrees only; because that would by degrees bring on light and information, and qualify them to take charge of themselves understandingly; with more certainty if in the mean time under so much controul only as may keep them at peace with one another. Surely it is our duty to wish them independance and self-government, because they wish it themselves, and they have the right, and we none, to chuse for themselves: and I wish moreover that our ideas may be erroneous, and theirs prove well founded.

But these are speculations, my friend, which we may as well deliver over to those who are to see their developement. We shall only be lookers on, from the clouds above, as now we look down on the labors, the hurry, and bustle of the ants and bees. Perhaps in that super-mundane region we may be amused with seeing the fallacy of our own guesses, and even the nothingness of those labors which have filled and agitated our own time here. En attendant, with sincere affections to Mrs. Adams and yourself, I salute you both cordially.

TH: JEFFERSON

P.S. There is now here a Mr. Coffee, a sculptor and Englishman, who has just taken my bust, and is going on to take those of Madison and

Monroe.[59] He resides at New York and promises me he will ask permission to take yours and send me one. I hope you will permit him. He is a fine artist. He takes them about half the size of life in plaster.

Adams to Jefferson

Quincy May 29. 1818

DEAR SIR

As Holly is a Diamond of a Superiour Water, it would be crushed to pouder by mountainous oppression in any other Country. Even in this, he is a light shining in a dark place. His System is founded in the hopes of Mankind: but they delight more in their Fears. When will Men have juster Notions of the Universal eternal Cause? Then will rational Christianity prevail. I regrett Hollys Misfortune in not finding you, on his Account to whom an Interview with you would have been a lasting Gratification.

Waterhouses Pen "Labitur et labetur ["overflows and will overflow"]." He has let it run on with too much fluency. I have not a tenth part of the Vivacity, Activity, Memory, or Promptitude and pun[c]tuality in Correspondence that he ascribes to me. I can answer but few of the Letters I receive, and those only with short Scratches of the Pen.

I agree with you that "it is difficult to say at what moment the Revolution began." In my Opinion it began as early as the first Plantation of the Country. Independence of Church and Parliament was a fixed Principle of our Predecessors in 1620 as it was of Sam. Adams and Chris. Gadsden in 1776. And Independence of Church and Parliament were always kept in View in this Part of the Country and I believe in most others. The Hierarchy and Parliamentary Authority were dreaded and detested even by a Majority of professed Episcopalians.

I congratulate you on your "Canine Appetite for reading." I have been equally voracious for several Years and it has kept me alive. It is policy in me to despize and abhor the "Writing Table" for it is a Bunch of Grapes out of reach. Had I Your Eyes and Fingers I should Scribble forever, such poor Stuff as you know I have been writting by fits and

59. William J. Coffee's bust of TJ has been lost, but those of other members of the family are extant. TJ commissioned Coffee to do the ornaments of cornices at the University of Virginia and at Poplar Forest. In 1822 Coffee returned to Monticello to restore the paintings in TJ's collection. Fiske Kimball, "The Life Portraits of Jefferson and Their Replicas," Amer. Philo. Soc., *Proceedings*, 88 (1944), 532.

starts for fifty or sixty Years without ever correcting or revising any thing.

Helluo ["Glutton"] as I am, I hunger and thirst after what I shall never see, Napolions Publication of the Report of his Institute of Cairo.[60] Denons Volumes have excited an inextinguishable Curiosity for an unattainable Object.

Mr. Coffee has been mentiond to me by my Son. He will be welcome. But though Robin is alive he is not alive like to be. Mr. Coffee must be very qui[c]k or Robbin may die in his hand.

Mr. Binon a French Artist from Lyons who has studied Eight Years in Italy has lately taken my Bust. He appears to be an Artist and a Man of Letters. I let them do what they please with my old head.

When We come to be cool in the future World, I think We cannot choose but smile at the gambols of Ambition Avarice Pleasure, Sport and Caprice here below. Perhaps We may laugh like the Angels in the French Fable. At a convivial repast of a Clubb of Choice Spirits of whom Gabriel and Michael were the most illustrious, after Nectar and Ambrosia had sett their hearts at Ease, they began to converse upon the Mechanique Cœleste. After discussing the Zodiack and the Constellations and the Solar System they condescended to this Speck of dirt the Earth, and remarked some of its Inhabitants, The Lyon the Elephant the Eagle and even the Fidelity Gratitude and Adroitness of the Dog. At last one of them recollected Man. What a fine Countenance! What an elegant figure! What Subtilty, Ingenuity, Versatillity Agility! And above all, *a rational Creature!* At this the whole board broke out into a broad Ha! Ha! Ha! that resounded through the Vault of Heaven: exclaiming *"Man a rational Creature!"* How could any rational Being even dream that Man was a rational Creature?

After all, I hope to meet my Wife and Friends, Ancestors and Posterity, Sages ancient and modern. I believe I could get over all my Objections to meeting Alec Hamilton and Tim Pick, if I could perceive a Symptom of sincere Penitence in either. My fatigued Eyes and Fingers command me very reluctantly to subscribe abruptly

JOHN ADAMS

60. *Memoirs relative to Egypt, Written in That Country during the Campaigns of General Bonaparte, in the Years 1798 and 1799, by the Learned and Scientific Men Who Accompanied the French Expedition* ... (London, 1800). The Institut d'Egypte, 1798-1801, established by Napoleon, was modeled after the Institut de France.

Adams to Jefferson

Quincy July 18. 1818

DEAR SIR

Will you accept a curious Piece of New England Antiquities? [61] It was a tolerable Chatechism for The Education of a Boy of 14 Years of Age, who was destined in the future Course of his Life to dabble in so many Revolutions in America, in Holland and in France.

This Doctor Mayhew had two Sisters established in Families in this Village which he often visited and where I often saw him. He was intimate with my Parson Bryant and often exchanged with him, which gave me an Opportunity often to hear him in the Pulpit. This discourse was printed, a Year before I entered Harvard Colledge and I read it, till the Substance of it was incorporated into my Nature and indelibly engraved on my Memory.

It made a greater Sensation in New England than Mr. Henrys Philippick against the Parsons did in Virginia.[62] It made a Noise in Great Britain where it was reprinted and procured the Author a Diploma of Doctor in Divinity.

That your Health and voracious Appetite for reading may long continue is the Wish of your Old Friend and humble Servant

JOHN ADAMS

61. Jonathan Mayhew, *Discourse concerning Unlimited Submission and Non-Resistance to the Higher Powers* (Boston, 1750); reprinted in Richard Barron, ed., *The Pillars of Priestcraft and Orthodoxy Shaken* (London, 1752). Mayhew, almost a Unitarian, was a staunch upholder of civil liberty and defended popular disobedience in all cases where orders contrary to God's laws were given. The University of Aberdeen conferred on him the degree of D.D. in 1751. Alice M. Baldwin, *The New England Clergy and the American Revolution* (Durham, N. C., 1928), 44-45, 69-70; John W. Thornton, ed., *The Pulpit of the American Revolution* (Boston, 1860), 46.

62. In the "Parson's Cause" the Reverend James Maury brought suit in Hanover County Court, Va., 1763, to recover on his salary (17,200 lbs. of tobacco per year) the difference between the legal rate of two pence per pound (act of 1758) and the current market price. Patrick Henry defended the parish against the clergy and attacked the royal disallowance of provincial laws necessary for the public good (the King had disallowed the act and the Hanover Court had ruled it invalid from its passage). The jury awarded Maury one penny damages. Robert D. Meade, *Patrick Henry, Patriot in the Making* (Philadelphia and N. Y., 1957), 114-38.

Jefferson to Adams

Monticello Oct. 7. 18.

It is very long, my dear friend, since I have written to you. The fact is that I was scarcely at home at all from May to September,[63] and from that time I have been severely indisposed and not yet recovered so far as to sit up to write, but in pain. Having been subject to troublesome attacks of rheumatism for some winters past, and being called by other business into the neighborhood of our Warmsprings, I thought I would avail myself of them as a preventative of future pain. I was then in good health and it ought to have occurred to me that the medecine which makes the sick well, may make the well sick. Those powerful waters produced imposthume, general eruption, fever, colliquative sweats, and extreme debility, which aggravated by the torment of a return home over 100. miles of rocks and mountains reduced me to extremity. I am getting better slowly and, when I can do it with less pain shall always have a pleasure in giving assurances to Mrs. Adams and yourself of my constant and affectionate friendship and respect.

TH: JEFFERSON

Adams to Jefferson

Quincy Octr. 20. 1815 [i.e., 1818]

MY DEAR FRIEND

One trouble never comes alone! At our Ages We may expect more and more of them every day in groups, and every day less fortitude to bear them.

When I saw in Print that You was gone to the Springs, I anxiously suspected that all was not healthy at Monticello.

You may be surprised to hear that your favour of the 7th has given me hopes. "Imposthume, general Eruptions, colliquative Sweats," sometimes and I believe often indicate Strength of Constitution and returning

63. During Aug. 1 to 4 TJ had been at Rockfish Gap as a member of the commission to select the site of the University of Virginia. Philip Alexander Bruce, *History of the University of Virginia, 1819-1919* (N.Y., [1920-22]), I, 210-21.

Vigour. I hope and believe they have given you a new Lease for Years, many Years.

Your Letter which is written with your usual neatness and firmness confirms my hopes.

Now Sir, for my Griefs! The dear Partner of my Life for fifty four Years as a Wife and for many Years more as a Lover, now lyes in extremis, forbidden to speak or be spoken to.[64]

If human Life is a Bubble, no matter how soon it breaks. If it is as I firmly believe an immortal Existence We ought patiently to wait the Instructions of the great Teacher. I am, Sir, your deeply afflicted Friend

JOHN ADAMS

Jefferson to Adams

Monticello Nov. 13. 18.

The public papers, my dear friend, announce the fatal event of which your letter of Oct. 20. had given me ominous foreboding. Tried myself, in the school of affliction, by the loss of every form of connection which can rive the human heart, I know well, and feel what you have lost, what you have suffered, are suffering, and have yet to endure. The same trials have taught me that, for ills so immeasurable, time and silence are the only medecines. I will not therefore, by useless condolances, open afresh the sluices of your grief nor, altho' mingling sincerely my tears with yours, will I say a word more, where words are vain, but that it is of some comfort to us both that the term is not very distant at which we are to deposit, in the same cerement, our sorrows and suffering bodies, and to ascend in essence to an ecstatic meeting with the friends we have loved and lost and whom we shall still love and never lose again. God bless you and support you under your heavy affliction.

TH: JEFFERSON

64. Mrs. Adams died of typhoid fever on Oct. 28, 1818, at the age of nearly seventy-four. Whitney, *Abigail Adams*, 326.

Adams to Jefferson

Quincy Dec. 8. 18.

DEAR SIR

Your Letter of Nov. 13 gave me great delight not only by the divine Consolation it Afforded me under my great Affliction: but as it gave me full Proof of your restoration to Health.

While you live, I seem to have a Bank at Montecello on which I can draw for a Letter of Friendship and entertainment when I please.

I know not how to prove physically that We shall meet and know each other in a future State; Nor does Revelation, as I can find give Us any possitive Assurance of such a felicity. My reasons for believing, it, as I do, most undoubtingly, are all moral and divine.

I believe in God and in his Wisdom and Benevolence: and I cannot conceive that such a Being could make such a Species as the human merely to live and die on this Earth. If I did not believe a future State I should believe in no God. This Un[i]verse; this all; this το παν ["totality"]; would appear with all its swelling Pomp, a boyish Fire Work.

And if there be a future State Why should the Almighty dissolve forever all the tender Ties which Unite Us so delightfully in this World and forbid Us to see each other in the next?

Trumbull with a band of Associates drew me by the Cords of old Frien[d]ships to see his Picture [65] on Saturday where I got a great Cold. The Air of Ph[an]euil Hall is changed. I have not been Used to catch Cold there.

Sick or Well the frien[d]ship is the same of your old Acquaintance

JOHN ADAMS

65. In Feb. 1816 Congress commissioned the sixty-year-old John Trumbull to paint four scenes of the Revolution for the rotunda of the Capitol, as he had conceived them a quarter-century earlier. He painted the 12′ x 18′ canvases in New York and exhibited them commercially before they were installed in the Capitol in 1824. J. Q. Adams saw the "Declaration of Independence" on exhibit in Sept. 1818. It was shown in New York, Philadelphia, and Baltimore. Was this the picture JA went to Boston to see? Theodore Sizer, "Trumbull, John," *DAB*, XIX, 14.

Adams to Jefferson

Quincy Dec 30th. 1818

DEAR SIR

Late last night I received Your Report and your translation of Tracy,[66] for both of which, tho' I have read neither, I thank You. But the full proof of your returning health has given me more Pleasure than both. I envy your Eyes and hands and Horse. Mine are too dim, too tremulous and my head is too dizzy for the Sovereign Doctor.

All is now still and tranquil. There is nothing to try Mens Souls nor to excite Men's Souls but Agriculture. And I say, God speed the Plough, and prosper stone Wall.

Had I your Eyes and Fingers, and 100 Years to live, I would write an 100 Volumes in folio; but neither myself nor the World would be the wiser or the better for any thing that could be done by your assured Friend

JOHN ADAMS

Jefferson to Adams

Monticello Jan. 19. 19.

DEAR SIR

About a week before I recieved your favor of Dec. 30. the 22d. No. of the North American review had come to hand, without my knowing from what quarter. The letter of Mr. Channing to Mr. Shaw, which you have been so good as to inclose, founds a presumption that it was from Mr. Channing, and that he is the editor. I had never before seen the work; but have read this No. with attention and great satisfaction. It may stand boldly on the shelf by the side of the Edinburg Review; and, as I find that Mr. Channing has agents in George town and Richmond, where I can readily make the necessary payments, I shall write to one of them to enter me as a subscriber. I see with pride that as we are ahead of Europe in Political science, so on other subjects we are getting along side of them.

66. *Report of the Commissioners appointed to fix the Scite of the University of Virginia, Thomas Jefferson* [*and others*], Aug. 4, 1818 [Richmond, 1818]. For Jefferson's discussion of Tracy's work, see above, 491-92 and n. 41.

I hope you have read our University Report with approbation, as I am sure you will the work of Tracy, if you trouble yourself with such subjects. We are all atiptoe here in the hourly expectation of hearing what our legislature decides on the Report.[67] Being a good piece of a century behind the age they live in, we are not without fear as to their conclusions. We have to contend with so many biasses, personal, local, fanatical, financial etc. that we cannot foresee in what their combinations will result.

God bless you, and preserve you in good health and spirits.

TH: JEFFERSON

Adams to Jefferson

Quincy January 29th. 1819

DEAR SIR

If I am not humble I ought to be, when I find myself under the necessity of borrowing a juvenile hand to acknowledge your kind favour of the 19th. I have read your university report throughout with great pleasure and hearty approbation; Of Tracy's report I have read as much as I could. The Translation appears to me an original written with all the purity, accuracy, and elegance of its author in his maturest age. If it can destroy the Parasite Institutions of our country it will merit immortal honor.

The Medici rose to the despotism of Europe, ecclesiastical and political, by the machinery of banks. Hundreds of mushrooms or Jonah's gourds have sprung up in one night in America by the strength of the same rotten manure. How has it happened that the Bank of Amsterdam has for so many years conducted all most all the commerce of Europe without making any profit to the proprietors? And how has it happened that religious liberty, fiscal science, coin and commerce, and every branch of political economy, should have been better understood and more honestly practised in that Frog land, than any other country in the world?

Your letter shall be communicated without loss of time to Mr. Shaw and consequently to Mr. Channing by your friend

JOHN ADAMS

67. The *Report* recommending Central College as the site for the University of Virginia was presented to the General Assembly in Dec. and a bill for this purpose was passed on Jan. 25. Joseph Carrington Cabell, ardent advocate of higher education in Virginia, wrote to TJ on Jan. 18, 1819: "Grateful, truly grateful, is it to my heart, to be able to announce to you the result of this day's proceedings in the House of Delegates." Cabell, *Early History of University of Va.*, 149, 152, 153, 447-50. The Senate also passed the bill on Jan. 25.

Adams to Jefferson

Quincy Feby. 13th. 1819.

DEAR SIR

As you was so well acquainted with the philosophers of France I presume the name and character of Mademoiselle De Lespinasse is not unknown to you.

I have almost put out my eyes by reading two volumes of her letters which as they were printed in 1809 I presume you have read long ago. I confess I have never read any thing with more ennui, disgust and loathing. The eternal repitition of mon dieu and mon ami—je vous aime; je vous aime eperdument; je vous aime a la follie; je suis au desespoir, je espere la mort; je suis morte; je premme l'opium etc. etc. etc.

She was constantly in love with other womens husbands, constantly violating her fidelity to her own keepers with other women's husbands constantly tormented with remords [i.e., remorse] and regrets constantly wishing for death and constantly threatning to put herself to death etc. etc. etc.

Yet this great lady was the confidential friend of Mr. Turgot the Duke De la Rochefaucault the Duchess D'anville, Mr. Condorcet; the only lady who was admitted to the dinners which Madame Geoffrim made for the litterati of France and the world and the intimate friend of Madame Boufflers and the open acknowledged mistress of the great D'allembert and much admired by Marmontel.

If these letters and the fifteen volumes of De Grimm are to give me an idea of the amelioration of society and government and manners in France I should think the age of reason has produced nothing much better than the Mahometans the Mamalukes or the Hindoos or the North American Indians have produced in different parts of the world.

Festine lente ["Hasten slowly"], my friend, in all your projects of reformation abolish polytheism however in every shape if you can, and unfrock every priest who teaches it, if you can. To compensate in some measure for this crazy letter I enclose to you Mr. Pickering's essay on the pronounciation of the Greek language [68] which very probably you have received from various quarters before now and with it I pray you to accept assurances of the unabated friendship of your humble servant

JOHN ADAMS

68. Published in the *Memoirs* of the American Academy of Arts and Sciences (Cambridge, Mass., 1818).

Adams to Jefferson

Quincy Feby. 19th. 1819

DEAR SIR

As you know I have often been ambitious of introducing to your acquaintance some of our literary characters. I now send you in the same spirit, some mathematical papers by our Mr. Bowditch, who has translated La Place's mechanique coeliste and has written commentaries upon it as voluminous as the book, which are thought by our scientific people to be one of the greatest astronomical productions of the present age: I hope the public will soon see it in print. I would write you news if I had any, but this is "the piping time of peace." I am as ever your friend and humble servant,

JOHN ADAMS

Adams to Jefferson

Quincy Feb'y. 24th. 1819

DEAR SIR

I am diligently and laboriously occupied, in reading and hearing your "political economy"—I call it yours because I do not believe that Tracys is more of an original in point of purity, perspicuity or precission. I have read as yet only to the 90th page. It is a connected chain of ideas and propositions, of which I know not which link to strike out. His philosophy appears to me to be precisely that of Dupuis—that is, the eternity, infinity, and mechanism of the universe. His philosophy appears to me to roll on in a continued stream untill it disembogues itself into the unfathomable gulph of liberty and necessity.

Is liberty a word void of sense? If it is, there [is] no merit or guilt, and there can be neither reward or punishment in the universe. His ethics appear to me in substance and essence to be those of Butlers sermons on human nature; and his preface to them of Hutchinsons writings throughout and of Tristram Shandy. At the bottom of the gulph of liberty and necessity for aught I know the key may lie which is to unlock the universe. But you know my opinion is that the key will never be found but by one being who will ever keep it in his own custody. Human understanding will never dive in this state of existence to such depths, and it is a vain and impertinent curiosity to think of it. Our duties are the charities of father, friend and brother. Fifty years ago I delighted more to see metaphysicians dance upon the point of their needles, than to see the exploits of dancers on the slack ropes or tight rope, but now my eyes are not keen enough to see the agility and capers of either. I am very glad however I have read so much and I intend to read the rest or hear it read. At present I will acknowledge one great obligation to it, that is the Chapter sixth, of money, page 2 1st: "When these denominations are admitted and employed in transactions, to diminish the quantity of metal to which they answer by an alteration of the real coins, is to steal. A theft of greater magnitude and still more ruinous is the making of paper. It is greater because in this money there is absolutely no real value. It is more ruinous because by its gradual depreciation during all the time of its existence it produces the effect which would be produced by an infinity of successive deteriorations of the coin." That is to say, an infinity of successive felonious larcenies. If this is true, as I believe it is, we Americans are the most thievish people that ever existed: we have been stealing from each other for an hundred and fifty years. If anything like health remains to me, you shall hear more upon this subject from your friend and humble servant,

JOHN ADAMS

Adams to Jefferson

Quincy March 2d. 1819

DEAR SIR

I have taxed my eyes with a very heavy impost to read the senator Tracy's Political Economy, and been amply rewarded for the expense. When I first saw the volume I thought it was impossible I should get through it, but when I had once made a beginning I found myself led on in so easy a train from proposition to proposition, every one of which appeared to me self evident, that I could not leave the book till I had finished. It is a condensation into a little globule not comparatively bigger than a nut shell of all the sound sense and solid knowledge of the grand master Quanay [i.e., Quesnay] and all the redoubtable knights his disciples and all their numerous huge volumes, and those of Sir James Stuart and Adam Smith, the Chevalier Pinto and the Enciclopedists, discarding all their mysteries, paradoxes and enigmas.

I have endeavoured and shall endeavour to draw the attention of all my acquaintances to this work. I would endeavour to get it reviewed but I should despair of success, for there is no man in this quarter who would dare to avow such sentiments; and no printer who would not think himself ruined by the publication of it for it is a magazine of gunpowder placed under the foundation of all our mercantile institutions. Yet every sensible man in the nation knows it to be founded in immutable truth though not one in a hundred would acknowledge it, and they only sub-rosa. I have never been so prudent. I have preached this doctrine thirty years in season and out of season and this heresy has been one of the principal causes of the immense unpopularity of Your old friend and humble servant

JOHN ADAMS

Jefferson to Adams

Monticello Mar. 21. 19.

DEAR SIR

I am indebted to you for Mr. Bowditch's very learned mathematical papers, the calculations of which are not for every reader, altho' their results are readily enough understood. One of these impairs the confidence I had reposed in La Place's demonstration that the excentricities of the planets of our system could oscillate only within narrow limits, and therefore could authorise no inference that the system must, by it's own laws, come one day to an end. This would have left the question of infinitude, at both ends of the line of time, clear of physical authority.

Mr. Pickering's pamphlet on the pronunciation of the Greek, for which I am indebted to you also, I have read with great pleasure. Early in life the idea occurred to me that the people now inhabiting the antient seats of the Greeks and Romans, altho' their languages in the intermediate ages had suffered great changes, and especially in the declensions of their nouns, and in the terminations of their words generally yet having preserved the body of the word radically the same, so they would preserve more of it's pronunciation. That at least it was probable that a pronunciation, handed down by tradition, would retain, as the words themselves do, more of the original than that of any other people whose language has no affinity to that original. For this reason I learnt, and have used the Italian pronunciation of the Latin. But that of the modern Greeks I had no opportunity of learning until I went to Paris. There I became acquainted with two learned Greeks, Count Carberri and Mr. Paradise, and with a lady, a native Greek, the daughter of Baron de Tott, who did not understand the ancient language. Carberri and Paradise spoke it. From these instructors I learnt the modern pronunciation, and in *general*, trusted to it's orthodoxy. I say, *in general*, because sound being more fugitive than the written letter, we must, after such a lapse of time, presume in it some degeneracies, as we see there are in the written words. We may not indeed be able to put our finger on them confidently, yet neither are they entirely beyond the reach of all indication. For example, in a language so remarkable for the euphony of it's sounds, if that euphony is preserved in particular combinations of it's letters, by an adherence to the powers ordinarily ascribed to them, and is destroyed by a change of these powers, and the sound of the word thereby rendered harsh, inharmonious and unidiomatical, here we may presume some degeneracy has taken place. While therefore I gave in to the modern pronunciation generally, I have presumed, as an instance of degeneracy, their ascribing the same sound to the six letters, or combinations of letters η, ι, υ, ει, οι, υι to all of which they give the sound of our double *e*, in the word *meet*. This useless equivalence of 3. vowels and 3. diphthongs did not probably exist among the antient Greeks; and the less probably as, while this single sound, *ee*, is overcharged by so many different representative characters, the sounds we usually give to these characters and combinations would be left witho[ut] any representative signs. This would imply either that they had not these sounds in their language, or no signs for their expression. Probability appears to me therefore against the practice of the modern Greeks of giving the same sound to all these different representatives, and to be in favor of that of foreign nations, who, adopting the Roman characters, have assimilated to them, in a considerable degree, the powers of the corresponding Greek letters. I have accordingly excepted this in my adoption of the modern pronunciation. I have been more doubtful in the use of the αυ, ευ, ηυ, ωυ, sounding the υ, upsilon, as our f. or v. because I find traces of that power of υ, or of u, in some modern languages. To go no further than our own, we have it in laugh, cough, trough, enough. The county of Louisa, adjacent to that in which I live, was, when I was a boy, universally pronounced Lo*v*isa. That it is not the *gh* which gives the sound of f. or v. in these words is proved by the orthography of *plough, through, thought, fraught, caught*. The modern Greeks themselves too, giving to υ, upsilon, in ordinary the sound of our *ee* strengthen the presumption that its anomalous soun[d] of f or v. is a corruption. The same may be inferred from the cacophony of ηλαφνε (elavne) for ηλαυγε (elawne), Αχιλλεφς (Achillefs) for Αχιλλευς (Achilluse) ηφς (eves) for ηϋς (eeuse) οφκ (ov̄k) for ουκ (ouk) ωφτος (ovetos) for ωϋτος (o-u-tos) Ζεφς (zevs) for Ζευς (zuse) of which all nations have made their Jupiter; and the uselessness of the υ in ευφωνια, which would otherwise have been spelt εφωνια. I therefore except this also from what I consider as approvable pronunciation.

Against reading Greek by accent, instead of quantity, as Mr. Ciceitira proposes, I raise both my hands. What becomes of the sublime measure of Homer, the full sounding rythm of Demosthenes, if, abandoning quantity, you chop it up by accent? What ear can hesitate in it's choice between the two following rhythms?

Τὸν δ'απαμειβόμενος προσεφὴ πόδας ωκυς Αχιλλεύς, and
τόν δ'απαμείβομενός προσεφή ποδας ὡκυς Αχίλλευς.[69]

the latter noted according to prosody, the former by accent, and dislocating our teeth in it's utterance; every syllable of it, except the first and last, being pronounced against quantity. And what becomes of the art of prosody? [70] Is that perfect coincidence of it's rules with the structure of their verse merely accidental? or was it of design, and yet for no use.

On the whole I rejoice that this subject is taken up among us, and that it is in so able hands as those of Mr. Pickering. Should he ultimately establish the modern pronunciation of the letters without any exception I shall think it a great step gained, and giving up my exceptions shall willingly rally to him; and as he has promised us another paper on the question whether we shall read by quantity or by accent, I can confidently trust it to the correctness of his learning and judgment. Of the origin of accentuation I have never seen satisfactory proofs. But I have generally supposed the accents were intended to direct the inflexions and modulation of the voice; but not to affect the quantity of the syllables.

You did not expect, I am sure, to draw on yourself so long a disquisition on letters and sounds. Nor did I intend it. But the subject run before me, and yet I have dropped much of it by the way.

I am delighted with your high approbation of Tracy's book. The evils of this deluge of paper money are not to be removed until our citizens are generally and radically instructed in their cause and consequences, and silence by their authority the interested clamors and sophistry of speculat-

69. "And answering him, swift-footed Achilles said...." Homer, *Iliad*, I, 58, 64, *et passim.*

70. In an undated letter to Chastellux, apparently written after Jefferson returned from France in 1789, TJ sent his Thoughts on English Prosody, based upon a comparative study of Greek and Latin and English verse. Lipscomb and Bergh, eds., *Writings*, XVIII, 414-51. With his letter of Oct. 30, 1798, to Herbert Croft of London, who was preparing an etymological dictionary, TJ sent his Essay on the Anglo-Saxon Language, first printed by order of the Board of Trustees, University of Virginia (N.Y., 1851); also in Lipscomb and Bergh, eds., *Writings*, XVIII, 361-411.

ing, shaving and banking institutions. Till then we must be content to return, quoad hoc, to the savage state, to recur to barter in the exchange of our property, for want of a stable, common measure of value, that now in use being less fixed than the beads and wampum of the Indian, and to deliver up our citizens, their property and their labor passive victims to the swindling tricks of bankers and mountebankers. If I had your permission to put your letter into the hands of the editor (Milligan) with or without any verbal alterations you might chuse, it would ensure the general circulation, which my prospectus and prefatory letter will less effectually recommend. There is nothing in the book of mine but these two articles, and the note on taxation in page 202. I never knew who the translator was: but I thought him some one who understood neither French nor English: and probably a Caledonian, from the number of Scotticisms I found in his MS. The innumerable corrections of that cost me more labor than would a translation of the whole de novo; and made at last but an inelegant altho' faithful version of the sense of the author. Dios guarde á V.S. muchos años [May God preserve your health for many years].

TH: JEFFERSON

Adams to Jefferson

Quincy April 2d. 1819

DEAR SIR

Your Letter of March 21st. I will communicate to Mr. Bowditch, and Pickering.

You may put my Letters upon the Subject of Tracy's Book into any hands you please, with or without any verbal alterations, as you may think fitt—"what you would have them, make them." Or as James Otis used to say to Samuel Adams—here, take it and "Quicu Wuicu" it.

I am obliged to borrow the hand of a friend to write you this Letter.

There seems to be some evil communication between Monticello and Montezillo, for at the same moment when your complaint appears to be perfectly cured, I am teazed with something very much like it. I wish you could convey to me by some Subterranean Canal or Air-Balloon as clear Eyes, and as steady hands as yours. I am as ever yours

JOHN ADAMS

Jefferson to Adams

Monticello May 15. 19.

DEAR SIR

Your letter of Apr. 2. was recieved in due time, and I have used the permission it gave me of sending a copy of that of Mar. 2. to the editor of Tracy's Political economy.

Mr. S. A. Wells of Boston, grandson of our old friend Saml. Adams, and who proposes to write the life of his grandfather,[71] has made some enquiries of me relative to revolutionary antiquities which are within your knolege as well as mine. I therefore put my answer under your cover, and open for your perusal and animadversion to him if I have committed any error. I fear none where I have taken facts from written notes. In other parts there may be error. When [rea]d, will you have the goodness to insert a wafer and send the lette[r to] the post office? Ever and affectionately yours.

TH: JEFFERSON

Adams to Jefferson

Quincy May 21st. 1819.

DEAR SIR

All the Literary Gentlemen of this part of the Country have an Ambitious Curiosity to see the Philosopher and Statesman of Monticello—and they all apply to me for Introductions—and if I had ever received one introduction from you, I should have less scruple of Conscience in granting their requests. In the Stile of our New-England, the Reverend Mr. Greenwood, the successor of Mr. Thatcher and Dr. Kirkland in the Church of Summer Street, Boston, will deliver you this letter with my affectionate respects.

Tho I cannot write I still live and enjoy Life. The World is dead. There is nothing to Communicate in Religion, Morals, Philosophy, or Politicks. I hope your Health is perfectly restored. Mine is pritty much like that of

71. The biography was written by the great-grandson: William Vincent Wells, *Life and Public Services of Samuel Adams* (Boston, 1865).

Voltaire Frankline and Samuel Adams, at my Age. But I am still unalterably your Friend,

J. Adams

Adams to Jefferson

Quincy May 27th. 1819.

Dear Sir

I have transmitted your letter to Samuel Adams Welles, Esqr. in Boston, as you desire.

This gentleman is a singular character. He is, I beleive, the only surviving male [heir] of his Grandfather, the late gove[r]nor of Massachusetts, Samuel Adams, who never had but two children, a son and a daughter; his son who bore his name died early, a surgeon in the army of the Revolution, without issue; his daughter married a Mr. Welles and her only son, as I beleive, is your correspondent, Samuel Adams Welles. He is now virtuously, amiably and laudably employed in collecting memorials of his grandfather, in which I heartily wish him success. His grandfather's character however will never be accurately known to posterity, as it never was sufficiently known to its own age: his merit in the Revolution, if there was any merit in it, was and is beyond all calculation. I know but one superior to it and that was James Otis. As your correspondent is the only representitive of him, I feel a strong interest in his favour; he was bred a merchant, has talents, industry, a taste for letters, and a fair, unspotted and irreproachable character. I wish you would speak a good word for him to Mr. Munroe. I believe him well qualified to be a commissioner under the Spanish treaty to adjust the American claims for spoliations on our commerce, and I believe the appointment would be more popular in Massachusetts than any other that could be named, except among the old tory refugees and their rancorous disciples. I am dear Sir Your friend and humble Servant

John Adams

Adams to Jefferson

Quincy June 22d. 1819

MY DEAR SIR.

May I inclose you one of the greatest curiositys and one of the deepest Mysterys that ever occoured to me. It is in the Essex Register of June the 5th. 1819. It is entitled from the Raleigh Register Declaration of Independence.[72] How is it possible that this paper should have been concealed from me to this day had it been communicated to me in the time of it, I know, if you do not know, that it would have been printed in every Whig News-paper upon this Continent. You know if I had possessed it, I would have made the Hall of Congress Echo and re-echo, with it fifteen Months before your Declaration of Independence.

What a poor ignorant, Malicious, short-sighted, Crapulous Mass, is Tom Pains Common Sense;[73] in comparision with this paper. Had I known it I would have Commented upon it from the day you entered Congress till the fourth of July 1776.

The Genuine sense of America at that Moment was never so well expressed before nor since. Richard Caswell, William Hooper, and Joseph Hughs the then Representatives of North Carolina in Congress you knew as well as I do, and you know that the Unanimity of the States finally depended on the Vote of Joseph Hughes, and was finally determined by him, and yet History is to ascribe the American Revolution to Thomas Pain—Sat verbum sapient[i] ["a word to the wise is sufficient"]. I am my dear Sir your invariable friend

JOHN ADAMS

72. The Raleigh *Register and North Carolina Gazette,* April 30, 1819, first printed the Mecklenburg Declaration of Independence, purportedly the work of a meeting of citizens at Charlotte, N.C., on May 20, 1775. According to the account they declared that "a free and independent people, are and of right ought to be a sovereign and self-governing association under the control of no other power than that of our God and the General Government of Congress." The resolutions were dispatched a few days later to the North Carolina delegates in the Continental Congress, who commended the meeting but felt that action on behalf of independence was premature. The original record of the meeting on May 20 was reported burned in 1800. While JA gave countenance to the document, TJ denounced it as spurious (TJ to JA, July 9, 1819, below, 543-44.); but its authenticity was not seriously questioned until 1847. Hoyt, *Mecklenburg Declaration,* Chap. I.

73. Paine's *Common Sense,* first printed in Philadelphia in Jan. 1776, and widely circulated in a short time, was powerful propaganda on behalf of independence; but JA always regarded Paine's influence as vastly overrated.

Jefferson to Adams

Monticello July 9. 19.

DEAR SIR

I am in debt to you for your letters of May 21. 27. and June 22. The first delivered me by Mr. Greenwood gave me the gratification of his acquaintance; and a gratification it always is to be made acquainted with gentlemen of candor, worth and information, as I found Mr. Greenwood to be. That on the subject of Mr. Samuel Adams Wells shall not be forgotten in time and place, when it can be used to his advantage. But what has attracted my peculiar notice is the paper from Mecklenburg county of N. Carolina, published in the Essex Register which you were so kind as to inclose in your last of June 22. And you seem to think it genuine. I believe it spurious. I deem it to be a very unjustifiable quiz, like that of the Volcano, so minutely related to us as having broken out in N. Carolina, some half dozen years ago, in that part of the country, and perhaps in that very county of Mecklenburg, for I do not remember it's precise locality. If this paper be really taken from the Raleigh Register, as quoted, I wonder it should have escaped Ritchie, who culls what is good from every paper, as the bee from every flower; and the National Intelligencer too, which is edited by a North Carolinian [Joseph Gales, Jr.], and that the fire should blaze out all at once in Essex, 1000. miles from where the spark is said to have fallen. But if really taken from the Raleigh Register, who is the Narrator, and is the name subscribed real, or is it as fictitious as the paper itself? It appeals too to an original book, which is burnt, to Mr. Alexander who is dead, to a joint letter from Caswell, Hughes and Hooper, all dead, to a copy sent to the dead Caswell, and another sent to Doctr. Williamson, whose memory, now probably dead, did not recollect, in the history he has written of N. Carolina, this Gigantic step of it's county of Mecklenburg. Horry too is silent in his history of Marion, whose scene of action was the country bordering on Mecklenburg. Ramsay, Marshal, Jones, Girardin, Wirt, historians of the adjacent states, all silent. When Mr. Henry's resolutions, far short of independance, flew like lightning thro' every paper, and kindled both sides of the Atlantic,[74] this flaming declaration, of the same date, of the independance of Mecklenburg county of

74. Patrick Henry's resolutions, introduced in the Virginia Convention in Richmond on March 20, 1775, and passed on March 23, provided that "this Colony be immediately put into a posture of defence." It was in his speech urging the passage of the resolutions that Henry proclaimed, "Give me liberty, or give me death." Peter Force, ed., *American Archives* . . . (Washington, 1837-53), 4th ser., II, 168.

N. Carolina, absolving it from British allegiance, and abjuring all political connection with that nation, altho' sent to Congress too, is never heard of. It is not known even a twelve month after when a similar proposition is first made in that body. Armed with this bold example, would not you have addressed our timid brethren in peals of thunder, on their tardy fears? Would not every advocate of independance have rung the glories of Mecklenburg county in N. Carolina in the ears of the doubting Dickinson and others, who hung so heavily on us? Yet the example of independant Mecklenberg county in N. Carolina, was never once quoted. The paper speaks too of the continued exertions of their delegation, (Caswell, Hooper, Hughes) 'in the cause of liberty and independance.' [75] Now you remember as well as I do, that we had not a greater tory in Congress than Hooper, that Hughes was very wavering, sometimes firm, sometimes feeble, according as the day was clear or cloudy; that Caswell indeed was a good whig, and kept these gentlemen to the notch, while he was present; but that he left us soon, and their line of conduct became then uncertain until Penn came, who fixed Hughes and the vote of the State. I must not be understood as suggesting any doubtfulness in the state of North Carolina. No state was more fixed or forward. Nor do I affirm positively that this paper is a fabrication: because the proof of a negative can only be presumptive. But I shall believe it such until positive and solemn proof of it's authenticity shall be produced. And if the name of McKnitt be real, and not a part of the fabrication, it needs a vindication by the production of such proof. For the present I must be an unbeliever in this apocryphal gospel.

I am glad to learn that Mr. Tickner has safely returned to his friends. But should have been much gladder had he accepted the Professorship in our University, which we should have offered him in form. Mr. Bowditch too refuses us. So fascinating is the vinculum of the dulce natale solum ["the bond of the sweet natal soil"]. Our wish is to procure natives where they can be found, like these gentlemen, of the first order of acquirement in their respective lines; but, preferring foreigners of the 1st. order to natives of the 2d. we shall certainly have to go, for several of our Professors, to countries more advanced in science than we are.

I set out within 3. or 4. days for my other home, the distance of which and it's cross mails, are great impediments to epistolary communications. I shall remain there about 2. months; and there, here and every where, I am and shall always be affectionately and respectfully your's.

TH: JEFFERSON

75. TJ misinterpreted the statement in the *Essex Register*. The "delegation" referred to was that of Mecklenburg County, not the three members of the North Carolina delegation in Congress. Hoyt, *Mecklenburg Declaration*, 9.

Adams to Jefferson

Quincy July 21st. 1819.

DEAR SIR,

I am greatly obliged to you for your letter of the 9th. It has entirely convinced me that the Mecklengburg Resolutions are a fiction. When I first read them in the Essex Register, I was struct with astonishment. It appeared to me utterly incredible that they should be genuine; but there were so many circumstances calculated to impose on the public, that I thought it my duty to take measures for the detection of the imposture. For this purpose I instantly inclosed the Essex Register to you, knowing that if you had either seen, or heard of these resolutions, you would have informed me of it. As they are unknown to you, they must have been unknown to all Mankind. I have sent a Copy of your letter to Salem, not to be printed but to be used as decisive authority for the Editor to correct his error in the Essex Register.[76]

But who can be the Demon to invent such a machine after five and forty years, and what could be his motive?[77] Was it to bring a charge of Plagiarism against the Congress in 76, or against you, the undoubted, acknowledged draughtsman of the Declaration of Independence? Or could it be the mere vanity of producing a jeu d'esprit, to set the world a gasp and afford a topic of Conversation in this piping time of Peace?

Had such Resolutions appeared in June 75, they would have flown through the Universe like wildfire; they would have Elevated the heads of the inhabitants of Boston and of all New England above the Stars, and they would have rung a peal in Congress, to the utter Confusion of Toryism and timidity, for a full Year before they were discomforted.

76. In an article containing the substance of TJ's letter to JA of July 9, 1819, but mentioning no names, the *Essex Register* announced on July 24 that the Mecklenburg resolutions had not been universally credited and that more information about them was desired. In reply on Aug. 6 the Raleigh *Register* explained how the resolutions had been brought to light and published. The editor claimed he could secure testimony of several persons who had been present on the occasion. Statements to this effect and other information were printed in the Raleigh *Register*, Aug. 13, 1819, Feb. 11 and 18, May 26, 1820 (reprinted as a pamphlet, 1822). These statements stood unchallenged publicly until TJ's letter to JA appeared in the first edition of his works in 1829, Randolph, ed., *Correspondence*, IV, 314-16.

77. It was rather an expression of state patriotism on the part of certain North Carolinians who were making known nationally an idea which had existed in the state since 1777. Hoyt, *Mecklenburg Declaration*, 113ff.

I wish you a pleasant tour to your second home, and remain your. friend and Humble Servant

JOHN ADAMS

Adams to Jefferson

Quincy July 28th. 1819.

DEAR SIR

I inclose you a National Register, to convince you that the Essex Register is not to blame for printing the Mecklingburg County Resolutions. On the contrary I think it to be commended, for if those Resolutions were genuine, they ought to be published in every Gazette in the World. If they are one of those tricks which our fashionable Men in England call hoax'es and boares, they ought to be printed in all American journals, exposed to public resentment, and the Author of them hunted to his dark Cavern. For altho you and I should as easily believe that a flaming Brand might be thrust into a Magazine of Powder without producing an Explosion, as that those Resolutions could have passed in 1775; [and] had not been known to any Member of Congress in 1776. And if they were not known to you, as I am very sure they were not, It is impossible they could have been known to any other Member. I am, Sir, whether at your first, or second home, always affecly. and Respectfully your Friend

JOHN ADAMS

Jefferson to Adams

Monticello Nov. 7. 19.

DEAR SIR

Three long and dangerous illnesses within the last 12. months must apologize for my long silence towards you.

The paper bubble is then burst. This is what you and I, and every reasoning man, seduced by no obliquity of mind or interest, have long foreseen. Yet it's disastrous effects are not the less for having been foreseen. We were laboring under a dropsical fulness of circulating medium.

Nearly all of it is now called in by the banks who have the regulation of the safety valves of our fortunes and who condense or explode them at their will. Lands in this state cannot now be sold for a year's rent: and unless our legislature have wisdom enough to effect a remedy by a gradual diminution only of the medium, there will be a general revolution of property in this state. Over our own paper and that of other states coming among us, they have competent powers. Over that of the bank of the US. there is doubt; not here, but elsewhere. That bank will probably conform voluntarily to such regulations as the legislature may prescribe for the others. If they do not we must shut their doors and join the other states which deny the right of Congress to establish banks, and sollicit them to agree to some mode of settling this constitutional question. They have themselves twice decided against their right, and twice for it. Many of the states have been uniform in denying it, and between such parties the constitution has provided no umpire.[78] I do not know particularly the extent of this distress in the other states, but Southwardly and Westwardly I believe all are involved in it. God bless you and preserve you many years.

TH: JEFFERSON

Adams to Jefferson

Montezillo Alias the little Hill [79]
November 23d. 1819

MY DEAR SIR

I congratulate you and myself on your recovery from the three Illnesses that have distressed you. The means that have been used to preserve you may, and I hope will have laid a foundation for good Health and many more years of an already long Life. My Health is astonishing to

78. Overexpansion of banking and credit after the War of 1812, of which the Bank of the United States as well as the state banks was guilty, precipitated the Panic of 1819. When certain state legislatures tried to tax branches of the Bank of the United States out of existence, the question was appealed to the United States Supreme Court in McCulloch v. Maryland (1819). When the Court upheld the bank as an instrument of the federal government, Kentucky found ways of circumventing the decision. Having seen the effects of the panic in Virginia, which had followed a more conservative fiscal program, TJ sympathized with the states. He felt the pinch in his personal fortunes too. Frederick J. Turner, *Rise of the New West, 1819-1829* (N.Y., [1906]), 59, Chap. IX; George T. Starnes, *Sixty Years of Branch Banking in Virginia* (N.Y., 1931), 63-67.

79. Here JA began his imitation of TJ's Monticello.

myself. I can say, like Deborah Queen Ann Dutchess of Marlbourgh, who in one of her letters, after innumerating a Multitude of her griefs and Misfortunes, says, I believe nothing but Distemper will kill me. Though I have not had three remarkable Illnesses, I have been afflicted with three times three Misfortunes, grievous enough to have shaken the philosophy of the most hardened Stoic. I ought however, to remember the saying of a Bishop with whom I dined once at Versailles who asked me many questions concerning Dr. Frankline, his Health, his Spirits, and his Mind. I answered, his Health is very robust, his Spirits very cheerful, and his Intellect as bright as ever. Monseignieur reply'd, "mais a son age il ne faut que tres peu de chose pour abbatre un colasse ["but at his age he should be careful not to grow angry"]."

What a Murrain there has been among the Governours within a few Months—Langdon, Strong, Snyder, Johnson, Lee, Raban. I hope there will not be such an other among the ex and in Presidents.

Congress are about to assemble and the Clouds look Black and thick, Assembling from all points, threatening thunder and Lightning. The Spanish Treaty, the Missouri Slavery, the encouragement of Manufactures by protecting duties or absolute prohibitions, the project of a Bankrupt Act, the plague of Banks, perhaps even the Monument for Washington, and above all the bustle of Caucuses for the approaching Election for President and Vice President, will probably produce an effervescence, though there is no doubt that the present President and Vice President will be re-elected by great Majority's,[80] as they ought to be, unless Tompkins should be chosen Governour of New York.

May God preserve you many years, Amen.

JOHN ADAMS

Jefferson to Adams

Monticello Dec. 10. 19.

DEAR SIR

I have to acknolege the reciept of your favor of Nov. 23. The banks, bankrupt law, manufactures, Spanish treaty are nothing. These are occurences which like waves in a storm will pass under the ship. But the

---

80. In the election of 1820 Monroe and Tompkins were re-elected president and vice-president following the Republican party caucus which made no recommendations for the nomination. John Bach McMaster, *A History of the People of the United States . . .* (N.Y., 1883-1913), IV, 515-18, 598-600.

Missouri question is a breaker on which we lose the Missouri country by revolt, and what more, God only knows.[81] From the battle of Bunker's hill to the treaty of Paris we never had so ominous a question. It even damps the joy with which I hear of your high health, and welcomes to me the consequences of my want of it. I thank god that I shall not live to witness it's issue. Sed haec hactenus ["But more of these things later"].

I have been amusing myself latterly with reading the voluminous letters of Cicero. They certainly breathe the purest effusions of an exalted patriot, while the parricide Caesar is left in odious contrast. When the enthusiasm however kindled by Cicero's pen and principles, subsides into cool reflection, I ask myself What was that government which the virtues of Cicero were so zealous to restore, and the ambition of Caesar to subvert? And if Caesar had been as virtuous as he was daring and sagacious, what could he, even in the plenitude of his usurped power have done to lead his fellow citizens into good government? I do not say to *restore it*, because they never had it, from the rape of the Sabines to the ravages of the Caesars. If their people indeed had been, like ours, enlightened, peaceable, and really free, the answer would be obvious. 'Restore independance to all your foreign conquests, relieve Italy from the government of the rabble of Rome, consult it as a nation entitled to self government, and do it's will.' But steeped in corruption vice and venality as the whole nation was, (and nobody had done more than Caesar to corrupt it) what could even Cicero, Cato, Brutus have done, had it been referred to them to establish a good government for their country? They had no ideas of government themselves but of their degenerate Senate, nor the people of liberty, but of the factious opposition of their tribunes. They had afterwards their Titusses, their Trajans and Antoninuses, who had the will to make them happy, and the power to mould their government into a good and permanent form. But it would seem as if they could not see their way clearly to do it. No government can continue good but under the controul of the people: and their people were so demoralised and depraved as to be incapable of exercising a wholsome controul. Their reformation then was to be taken up ab incunabulis ["from the beginning"]. Their minds were to be informed, by education, what is right and what wrong, to be encoraged in habits of virtue, and deterred from those of vice by the dread of punishments, proportioned indeed, but irremissible; in all cases, to follow

81. The question of admission of Missouri to the Union as a slave state raised the explosive issue of expansion of slavery into the territories and brought about the drawing of an artificial geographical line (36° 30′ N. Lat.) "which on an abstract principle is to become the line of separation of these States, and to render desperate the hope that man can ever enjoy the two blessings of peace and self-government. The question sleeps for the present, but is not dead." TJ to Hugh Nelson, March 12, 1820, Lipscomb and Bergh, eds., *Writings*, XV, 238.

truth as the only safe guide, and to eschew error which bewilders us in one false consequence after another in endless succession. These are the inculcations necessary to render the people a sure basis for the structure of order and good government. But this would have been an operation of a generation or two at least, within which period would have succeeded many Neros and Commoduses, who would have quashed the whole process. I confess then I can neither see what Cicero, Cato and Brutus, united and uncontrouled, could have devised to lead their people into good government, nor how this aenigma can be solved, nor how further shewn why it has been the fate of that delightful country never to have known to this day, and through a course of five and twenty hundred years, the history of which we possess one single day of free and rational government. Your intimacy with their history, antient, middle and modern, your familiarity with the improvements in the science of government at this time, will enable you, if any body, to go back with our principles and opinions to the times of Cicero, Cato, and Brutus, and tell us by what process these great and virtuous men could have led so unenlightened and vitiated a people into freedom and good government, et eris mihi magnus Apollo. Cura ut valeas, et tibi persuade carissimum te mihi esse ["and you will be great Apollo to me. Take care of your health and be assured that you are most dear to me"].

TH: JEFFERSON

Adams to Jefferson

Montezillo December 21st. 1819

DEAR SIR

I must answer your great question of the 10th. in the words of Dalembert to his Correspondent, who asked him what is Matter—"Je vous avoue que Je n'en scais rien ["I confess that I know nothing about it"]."

In some part of my Life I read a great Work of a Scotchman on the Court of Augustus, in which with much learning, hard Study, and fatiguing labour, he undertook to prove that had Brutus and Cassius been conqueror, they would have restored virtue and liberty to Rome.

Mais Je n'en crois rien ["But I don't believe it"]. Have you ever found in history one single example of a Nation th[o]roughly Corrupted, that was afterwards restored to Virtue, and without Virtue, there can be no political Liberty.

If I were a Calvinest, I might pray that God by a Miracle of Divine Grace would instantaneously convert a whole Contaminated Nation from turpitude to purity, but even in this I should be inconsistent, for the fatalism of Mahometnism Material[i]sts, Atheists, Pantheists and Calvinests, and Church of England Articles, appear to me to render all prayer futile and absurd. The French and the Dutch in our day have attempted reforms and Revolutions. We know the results, and I fear the English reformers will have no better success.

Will you tell me how to prevent riches from becoming the effects of temperance and industry? Will you tell me how to prevent riches from producing luxury? Will you tell me how to prevent luxury from producing effeminacy intoxication extravagance Vice and folly? When you will answer me these questions, I hope I may venture to answer yours. Yet all these ought not to discourage us from exertion, for with my friend Jeb, I believe no effort in favour of Virtue is lost, and all good Men ought to struggle both by their Council and Example.

The Missouri question I hope will follow the other Waves under the Ship and do no harm. I know it is high treason to express a doubt of the perpetual duration of our vast American Empire, and our free Institution[s], and I say as devoutly as Father Paul, estor [i.e., esto] perpetua ["be thou everlasting"], but I am sometimes Cassandra enough to dream that another Hamilton, another Burr might rend this mighty Fabric in twain, or perhaps into a leash, and a few more choice Spirits of the same Stamp, might produce as many Nations in North America as there are in Europe.

To return to the Romans, I never could discover that they possessed much Virtue, or real Liberty there. Patricians were in general griping Usurers and Tyrannical Creditors in all ages. Pride, Strength and Courage were all the Virtues that composed their National Characters. A few of their Nobles effecting simplicity frugality and Piety, perhaps really possessing them, acquired Popularity amongst the Plebeians and extended the power and Dominions of the Republic and advanced in Glory till Riches and Luxury come in, sat like an incubus on the Republic, victamque ulcissitur orbem.[82]

Our Winter setts in a fortnight earlier than usual, and is pretty severe. I hope you have fairer skyes and Milder Air. Wishing your health, may last as long as your Life, and your Life as long as you desire it, I am dear Sir   Respectfuly and affectionately

JOHN ADAMS

---

82. "And take vengeance on a conquered world."

13

"Calms succeeding the storm which our Argosy . . . so stoutly weathered"

ADAMS AND JEFFERSON grew old gracefully, exemplifying some of the better qualities that Cicero commended in his essay on the subject, *De Senectute*, familiar to a generation steeped in the classics. At least three reasons may be suggested for the contentment reflected in their letters. Retirement, which came in their sixties, resulted from desire, not compulsion. Adams was eager to return to Quincy in 1801 after his stormy presidential administration. He conceded that "ennui, when it rains on a man in large drops, is worse than one of our northeast storms; but the labors of agriculture and amusement of letters will shelter me." [1] When Jefferson was welcomed home in 1809 by fellow citizens of Albemarle County, he told them that the pomp and turmoil of office during "a wonderful era . . . have drawn but deeper sighs for the tranquil and irresponsible occupations of private life." [2]

In the second place, as philosophers, Adams and Jefferson were mentally active, whether in reflection on first principles and the order of the universe or in judgment on contemporary problems. The "amusement of letters" (i.e., of literature) which occupied much of their time was well mixed with the writing of letters. Keeping up with their correspondence and thus abreast of the outside world continually refreshed and stimulated the confinements of old age.

The third element conducive to happiness late in life was sound health. Except for brief illnesses, both enjoyed this good fortune until 1818, although by this time the chronic condition of palsy prevented

1. JA to Christopher Gadsden, April 16, 1801, *Works*, IX, 585.
2. TJ "to the Inhabitants of Albemarle County, in Virginia," Ford, IX, 250.

Adams from writing and Jefferson's injured wrist became stiffer with advancing age. The elder statesman fared better than the younger, for Adams's physical condition did not deteriorate seriously until he was almost ninety.[3] In the late summer and early fall of 1818 Jefferson at seventy-five suffered his first prolonged sickness, which was aggravated by the waters of Warm Springs; they proved to be enervating rather than remedial and brought on a chronic condition of discomfort.[4]

Each continued his customary exercise until sheer weakness interfered and prevailed. For Adams it was walking and riding, and, when he could no longer mount his horse, he was still able to "walk three miles over a rugged rockey Mountain" (which should be rendered "hill" for the environs of Quincy).[5] For Jefferson it was riding and walking; he was often on horseback three to four hours a day and at the age of seventy he rode ninety miles to his second home, Poplar Forest, in Bedford County. A decade later, although he could walk from the house only to the near-by garden "and that with sensible fatigue," he might be seen daily near Monticello, mounted on Eagle, who likewise had long since passed his prime.[6] From a broken left arm Jefferson recovered remarkably well at the age of seventy-eight, and his handwriting shows ample evidence of a firm right hand until the last months of his life, even though the wrist was incurably stiff and painful.[7] The two philosophers found some consolation in comparing notes on their afflictions, as octogenarians are wont to do, but these were, for the most part, passing comments by men whose mental vigor was only slightly handicapped by physical infirmities.

In characteristic fashion they harked back occasionally to the distant past of their careers—to the years of the Revolution which had made the most indelible impression on their minds. Who first favored an American navy? How soon did New York support the movement for independence? Was reconciliation with Great Britain still a possibility in 1776? The obituary of a contemporary, the historical background of a current issue, an inquiry concerning the founding of the

3. TJ to Dr. Benjamin Waterhouse, March 3, 1818, Jan. 8, 1825, Ford, X, 103, 336.

4. TJ to JA, May 17, Oct. 7, 1818, above, 524, 528; Dec. 18, 1825, below, 614.

5. JA to TJ, Feb. 3, 1812, above, 296; June 11, 1822, below, 579.

6. TJ to JA, Jan. 21, 1812, above, 292; Aug. 15, 1820, June 1, 1822, below, 565, 578; Randall, *Jefferson*, III, 538.

7. JA to TJ, Dec. 2, 1822, and TJ to JA, Feb. 25, Oct. 12, 1823, Jan. 8, 1825, below, 585-86, 589, 599, 605.

Republic—all put Adams and Jefferson in a reminiscent mood. They became increasingly the arbiters of their country's early history, not by design, but by reason of their venerable reputation and their personification of American patriotism. Although they were no longer guiding the affairs of the nation, they had retained that element of statesmanship which correlates the historical past with the present. They saw their revolution projected into the nineteenth century, not always successfully, in view of the Napoleonic regime and its aftermath, but hopefully nevertheless, as in the case of Greek independence. Despite the prevalence of reactionary governments in Europe, Jefferson maintained that "the flames kindled on the 4th. of July 1776. have spread over too much of the globe to be extinguished by the feeble engines of despotism." [8] As the fiftieth anniversary of the Declaration of Independence approached, these assertions by the last of the signers expressed not the outmoded sentiments of a forgotten generation but rather the spirit of the young Republic.

During the last ten years of his life Jefferson's chief outside concern was the planning and establishing of the University of Virginia. Adams had no comparable absorbing activity, but he never lost interest in political issues. Jefferson had eschewed politics, even restricting his newspaper reading to the Richmond *Enquirer*, edited by his good friend Thomas Ritchie.[9] To the Massachusetts Constitutional Convention of 1820, Adams lent considerable prestige as a delegate (he declined the presidency), although his amendment to the Commonwealth's Bill of Rights, guaranteeing complete religious freedom, failed of adoption. Because he had not engaged in public debate since the convention of 1779, he minimized his part in revising the old constitution: "I boggled and blundered more than a young fellow just rising to speak at the bar." [10] This was his last public appearance, but his interest in national politics continued as keen as ever, for a very good reason. Secretary of State John Quincy Adams was presidential timber and became one of the four candidates in the acrimonious election of 1824. The son was as independent and as much a man of principle as the father—an ex-Federalist, a neo-Jeffersonian, who could do best as a free lance during this period of political transition, who

8. TJ to JA, Sept. 12, 1821, June 1, 1822, and JA to TJ, Dec. 29, 1823, below, 575, 578-79; 602.

9. TJ to Macon, Jan. 12, 1819, Ford, X, 120; Hillard, ed., *Life of Ticknor*, I, 349.

10. JA to TJ, Feb. 3, 1821, Jan. 23, 1825, below, 571-72, 608; C. F. Adams, "Life of John Adams," *Works*, I, 627-28.

was too much the individualist to play well the game of party politics. Although the election had to be settled in the House of Representatives, the victory of the younger Adams must have seemed utterly appropriate and justified to his father, who wrote, "The multitude of my thoughts, and the intensity of my feelings are too much for a mind like mine, in its ninetieth year." [11] Death spared him disappointment over his son's defeat in 1828.

In that phase of history called "past politics" the friendship of Jefferson and Adams had faced its severest tests. As late as 1823 repercussions of political storms of an earlier period threatened, as Jefferson expressed it, "to draw a curtain of separation between you and myself"; [12] but he had not forgotten previous unhappy experiences in which both of them were the victims of malignancy perpetrated by others for political purposes. On a previous occasion Jefferson had been on the spot to explain his words.[13] This time the embarrassment was Adams's, but Jefferson dissolved it with kindness. When it had seemed likely that President Jefferson would be a candidate for re-election in 1804 and the Federalists were seeking every means of recovery from their disastrous defeat of 1800, William Cunningham, one of their henchmen, requested of Adams some statements concerning the President which might be used in the coming campaign. Adams, whose political wounds of 1798-1800 remained unhealed long afterward, obliged Cunningham with some harsh comments on Jefferson, with the understanding that they would not be published during the writer's lifetime. He wished the President no ill, but "I shudder at the calamities which I fear his conduct is preparing for his country: from a mean thirst of popularity, an inordinate ambition, and a want of sincerity." [14] It was a characteristic Adamsian blast with more heat than right reason, unworthy of his honest conviction and his inherent respect for Jefferson. In 1823, immediately after Cunningham's death, his son published Adams's statements to turn discredit onto Adams and refract it toward John Quincy Adams and his presidential ambitions. Jefferson, the original object of attack, would not allow his friendship with John Adams to be exposed to accusations and suspicion derived from an "outrage on private confidence" and the revival of issues long buried. The cool detachment of old age proved

11. JA to J. Q. Adams, Feb. 18, 1825, *Works*, X, 416.
12. TJ to JA, Oct. 12, 1823, below, 600; Randall, *Jefferson*, III, 493.
13. See above, Chap. 7.
14. Gilbert Chinard, *Honest John Adams* (Boston, 1933), 320-21.

to be a saving grace. "It would be strange indeed," observed the Sage of Monticello, "if, at our years, we were to go to an age back to hunt up imaginary, or forgotten facts, to disturb the repose of affections so sweetening to the evening of our lives." [15] This expression of reassurance brought great relief to Adams. In reply he praised it as noble and magnanimous. Although it called for no explanation, Adams made an ineffectual attempt, with a concluding salute of cordial esteem and affection. This letter of November 10 Jefferson endorsed as received ten days later, and he consigned it to oblivion in his files.[16]

Year after year the aging statesmen pursued the epistolary art, to the lasting benefit of posterity. Not that they thought of it as an art; it was a necessity, an integral part of their daily lives. Both complained about the heavy burden of letter writing, but they felt an obligation they could not shirk. Once, in desperation, Adams resorted to two expedients: neglecting to answer his mail and "giving gruff, short, unintelligible, misterious, enigmatical, or pedantical answers." But he could not recommend the first device to Jefferson because one could ill afford deliberately to sacrifice instructive and entertaining letters; as for the second expedient, "this resource is out of your power, because it is not in your nature to avail Yourself of it." [17] Adams was not indulging in flattery but rather bespeaking his understanding of Jefferson's habits and conscience. The latter confessed that he was "drudging at the writing table" from sunrise to one or two o'clock, often from dinner (in the late afternoon) until dark. He begrudged these long hours all the more because they reduced the time available for reading. Although he envied Adams's gratification of a voracious appetite for reading, Jefferson could not rest content with an accumulation of unanswered correspondence.[18]

In 1822, while in one of his moods for recording data, he computed his incoming letters at 1,267 for the year 1820 and many of them required "elaborate research" to answer.[19] These represented an average of twenty-four per week; his replies, often of considerable length, written in his careful, steady hand, confirm the hours of labor that had become habitual early in his career. Adams doubted that he received throughout the year the equivalent of Jefferson's mail in a month or

15. TJ to JA, Oct. 12, 1823, below, 601.
16. JA to TJ, Nov. 10, 1823, below, 601-2.
17. JA to TJ, Feb. 2, 1817, above, 507.
18. TJ to JA, Jan. 11, 1817, above, 505.
19. TJ to JA, June 27, 1822, below, 581.

that ever during his public life he had received one-fourth as many (probably an underestimate), but, he added, "there are reasons enough for the difference." [20] Among those reasons, which he did not enumerate, were the wider range of Jefferson's intellectual interests, his political connections as first head of the Republican party, and the rigid self-discipline he imposed on his time throughout most of a busy life. If this phenomenal production seems less impossible after he retired from public office, the time required for managing his plantations must not be overlooked. One can only wonder how he kept up private as well as public correspondence along with his other duties as governor, diplomat, secretary of state, vice-president, and president of the United States. When Adams reflected on the problem of retiring on a reduced income, he could only conclude that old public servants turned out, "either by legal suffrages or from complaisance to a vulgar opinion," ought to be compensated. No doubt he was thinking of himself as well as Jefferson, and deservedly so. His argument is still applicable today to our higher officials, "for by making them conspicuous, and multiplying their acquaintances, they expose them to expences heavier than when in office." [21]

Although Jefferson had ample justification for expressing hearty agreement with this opinion and for citing his own case to confirm it, his correspondence with Adams contains no mention, indeed no hint, of the indebtedness from which he found it impossible to extricate himself. Jefferson was in large part a victim of postwar inflation and depression in the Old Dominion, with credits on a long-time basis and cash usually a scarce item. His social habits were those of openhanded hospitality in the Virginia tradition. His generosity, embracing financial obligations of others, complemented his hospitality. Perhaps Adams read about the lottery authorized by the state in 1825 to salvage the homestead of Virginia's first citizen and how it was replaced by a less embarrassing private subscription on his behalf by his fellow countrymen in many states.[22] It seemed certain now that Monticello would be saved. This assumption, which proved to be erroneous, put Jefferson's mind at ease during the remaining months of his life, but the menace to his papers and other choice possessions loomed up

20. JA to TJ, July 12, 1822, below, 581-82.

21. *Ibid*. See also TJ to James Madison, May 25, 1788, Boyd, XIII, 201-3.

22. Randall, *Jefferson*, III, 535-37; TJ to Thomas Jefferson Randolph, Feb. 8, 1826, TJ to James Madison, Feb. 17, 1826, TJ to James Monroe, Feb. 22, 1826, Ford, X, 374-79.

ominously. By contrast, Adams faced no such critical circumstances. According to his grandson and biographer, he "lived free from pecuniary obligations of every kind to others, a fate which has not always attached to the incumbents of the highest executive posts in America." [23] And the Adams Papers passed safely from father to son through successive generations.

The Argonauts of the revolutionary era (to use one of Jefferson's last allusions) continued their correspondence to within three months of their deaths. It lapsed in the early spring of 1826 on a pleasant note. Jefferson's favorite grandson and namesake, Thomas Jefferson Randolph, was making a trip to Boston which he could not consider complete without meeting Mr. Adams.[24] The visit was arranged, and young Randolph, in his early thirties, of a stature that impressed the venerable patriot, delivered Jefferson's last letter. It "has been a cordial to me," wrote Adams in his last reply, especially since Randolph was accompanied by Joseph Coolidge, recently married to Jefferson's granddaughter Ellen Wayles Randolph.[25] Thus the two brothers-in-law provided a double tie between Monticello and Montezillo, as Adams several years before had renamed Peacefield, the old house in Quincy.

Adams and Jefferson in collaboration had "done for our country the good which has fallen in our way, so far as commensurate with the faculties given us." [26] They had differed politically, suffered estrangement, and derived fresh satisfaction from renewal of their friendship. More than ever before, their minds were free to express conflicting opinions and to give fair consideration to opposing points of view. They found much in common in their religious ideas but in an era which had achieved religious freedom only haltingly by law and halfheartedly in spirit, they exchanged opinions in private. It was characteristic that Adams, not Jefferson, should have expressed the valedictory: "We shall meet again, so wishes and so believes your friend, but if we are disappointed we shall never know it." [27] Too feeble to accept invitations to celebrations of the fiftieth anniversary of the Declaration of Independence, they anticipated the spirit of the forthcoming occasion, Jefferson in thanking the citizens of Washing-

23. C. F. Adams, "Life of John Adams," *Works*, I, 639.
24. TJ to JA, March 25, 1826, below, 613-14.
25. JA to TJ, April 17, 1826, below, 614.
26. TJ to JA, March 14, 1820, below, 562.
27. JA to TJ, Feb. 25, 1825, below, 610.

ton: "Let the annual return of this day forever refresh our recollections of these rights [of man], and an undiminished devotion to them";
Adams in providing the citizens of Quincy at their request with a
toast: "INDEPENDENCE FOREVER!" [28] On the day of celebration, July 4,
1826, they died, Jefferson at noon, Adams a few hours later.[29]

Adams to Jefferson

Montezillo January 20th. 1820

DEAR SIR

When Harris was returned a Member of Parliament a Friend introduced
him to Chesterfield whom he had never seen. So Mr. Harris said his Lordship you are a Member of the House of Commons. You have written upon
Universal and scientifick Grammer! You have written upon Art, upon
Musick, Painting and Poetry! And what has the House of Commons to
do with Art, or Musick, or Painting, or Poetry, or Taste? Have not you
written upon Virtue and Happiness? I have my Lord indulged myself in
Speculations upon those subjects. And what the devil has the House of
Lords to do with either Happiness or Virtue? This Idle Tale which I had
from the mouth of Sir James Harris, now Lord Malmsbury, I repeat to
you for a Preface to another idle tale which I am about to relate to you.

Viz—Too much confined by the Cold Weather, I have for a few days
past whirled away the time in reading these pieces of Harris, and another
intitled Philosophical Arrangements. The Dialogue upon happiness is one
of the first pieces of Morals I ever read; the Hermes is acknowledged a
Master piece. The others under the appearance of immense learning and
much ingenuity contain little information, and few Ideas that are new. I
have read them with the fond delight of a Young Lady reading a Romance,
on account of the investigation of the Sentiments of Ancient Philosophers,
Poets and Orators, and the quotations from them in their own Words—
such by David Williams called the beautiful rags and tatters of Antiquity.
By Philosophical Arrangements he says he means Catigories or Predica-
ments, or general or Universal Truths, or the first Philosophy. But I have
been most amused with his endeavours to find the meaning of the Ancient

28. TJ to Roger C. Weightman, June 24, 1826, Ford, X, 390-92; C. F. Adams, "Life
of John Adams," *Works*, I, 634-35.
29. Lester J. Cappon, "A Postscript from Monticello, July 4, 1826," Albemarle
County Historical Society, *Papers*, 1 (1940-41), 30; C. F. Adams, "Life of John
Adams," *Works*, I, 636.

Philosophers concerning the first Principles, or Elements of Matter which they reduce down to particles, so nice and mince as to become geometrical points, and this seems to me, to be much more Orthodox Philosophy, and Mathematics too, than Buffons Molecules Organiques or Epicurrus's Atoms.[30] With such games at push pins have the Childish Philosophers of all Ages diverted and distracted themselves, not once considering that neither human sense nor imagination nor Intellect were ever formed to comprehend all things. Harris's Dialogue on Happiness is worth all the Metaphysical researches of Philosophers from the beginning of the World into the Nature of Matter and Spirit, of Energy, of Power of Activity of Motion, or any such thing. When we say God is Spirit, we know what we mean as well as we do when we say that the Pyramids of Egypt are Matter. Let us be content therefore to believe Him to be a Spirit, that is, an Essence that we know nothing of, in which Originally and necessarily reside all energy, all Power, all Capacity, all Activity, all Wisdom, all Goodness.

Behold the Creed and Confession of Faith of your ever affectionate Friend

JOHN ADAMS

Adams to Jefferson

Montezillo February 21st. 1820.

DEAR SIR,

Was you ever acquainted with Dugald Stuart? Before I left France I received a letter from Benjamin Vaughn, Esqre. in London, Introducing and recommending in strong terms two Gentlemen from Scotland, one by the name of Dugald Stuart and the other Lord— [31] whose name and title I forget—as young Gentlemen of great talents and attainments sufficient to diminish our American prejudices against Scotland. I received the Letter, but never saw the Gentlemen, from which I conjecture that they did not reach Paris till after I went away, and that you probably had the Satisfaction to enjoy their Company. I regret very much that I missed his Visit. Can you tell me anything of his present State? I am informed that he

30. Buffon's system of organic molecules has been refuted by modern scientists. The principal theory of Epicurus in the field of physics was that all that exists is corporeal: that space is filled with innumerable indivisible atoms in perpetual motion and constantly making new worlds.

31. TJ identifies him in the following letter as Lord Dare, but the Marquis of Lansdowne had only one son in 1787 old enough to travel, John Henry (d. 1809); the title Lord Dare did not exist in the British nobility.

is dying at top, like Sir Isaac Newton and Dr. Swift. I have a prejudice against what they call Metaphysicks because they pretend to fathom deeper than the human line extends. I know not very well what e'er the *to metaphusica* [32] of Aristotle means, but I can form some idea of Investigations into the human mind, and I think Dugald in his Elements of the Philosophy of the human Mind has searched deeper and reasoned more correctly than Aristotle, Des Cartes, Locke, Berkeley, Hume, Condillac and even Reid. I would therefore propose this problem or Theorem for your consideration: whether it would not be adviseable to institute in the Universities Professorships of the Philosophy of the human Understanding, whose object should be to ascertain the Limits of human knowledge already acquired. If I was worth as much money as some of the shop Boys I left in Boston, I would give fifty thousand dollars to establish such a professorship—though I suppose you will have doubts of the propriety of setting any limits, or thinking of any limits of human Power, or human Wisdom, and human Virtue.

I wish the Missouri question may not sett too narrow limits to the Power and Respectability of the United States. Yet I hope some good natureal way or other will be found out to untie this very intricate knot, and am, dear Sir, as ever your friend,

JOHN ADAMS

Jefferson to Adams

Monticello Mar. 14. 20.

DEAR SIR

A continuation of poor health makes me an irregular correspondent. I am therefore your debtor for the two letters of Jan. 20. and Feb. 21. It was after you left Europe that Dugald Stuart, concerning whom you enquire, and L[or]d Dare, second son of the Marquis of Lansdowne came to Paris. They brought me a letter from L[or]d Wycombe whom you knew. I became immediately intimate with Stuart, calling mutually on each other and almost daily, during their stay at Paris, which was of some months. Ld. Dare was a young man of imagination, with occasional flashes indicating deep penetration, but of much caprice, and little judgment. He has been long dead, and the family title is now, I believe, in the 3d son who has shewn in parliament talents of a superior order. Stuart is a great man,

32. These two words were added in JA's hand after his scribe had written the letter.

and among the most honest living. I have heard nothing of his dying at top, as you suppose. Mr. Ticknor however can give you the best information on that subject; as he must have heard particularly of him when in Edinburgh, altho' I believe he did not see him. I have understood he was then in London superintending the publication of a new work. I consider him and Tracy as the ablest Metaphysicians living; by which I mean Investigators of the thinking faculty of man. Stuart seems to have given it's natural history, from facts and observations; Tracy it's modes of action and deducation, which he calls Logic, and Ideology; and Cabanis, in his Physique et Morale de l'homme, has investigated anatomically, and most ingeniously, the particular organs in the human structure which may most probably exercise that faculty. And they ask Why may not the mode of action called thought, have been given to a material organ of peculiar structure? as that of magnetism is to the Needle, or of elasticity to the spring by a particular manipulation of to the steel. They observe that on ignition of the needle or spring, their magnetism and elasticity cease. So on dissolution of the material organ by death it's action of thought may cease also. And that nobody supposes that the magnetism or elasticity retire to hold a substantive and distinct existence. These were qualities only of particular conformations of matter: change the conformation, and it's qualities change also. Mr. Locke, you know, and other materialists have charged with blasphemy the Spiritualists who have denied to the Creator the power of endowing certain forms of matter with the faculty of thought. These however are speculations and subtleties in which, for my own part, I have little indulged myself. When I meet with a proposition beyond finite comprehension, I abandon it as I do a weight which human strength cannot lift: [33] and I think ignorance, in these cases, is truly the softest pillow on which I can lay my head. Were it necessary however to form an opinion, I confess I should, with Mr. Locke, prefer swallowing one incomprehensibility rather than two. It requires one effort only to admit the single incomprehensibility of matter endowed with thought: and two to believe, 1st. that of an existence called Spirit, of which we have neither evidence nor idea, and then 2dly. how that spirit which has neither extension nor solidity, can put material organs into motion. These are things which you and I may perhaps know ere long. We have so lived as to fear neither horn of the dilemma. We have, willingly, done injury to no man; and have done for our country the good which has fallen in our way, so far as commensurate with the faculties given us. That we have not done more than we could cannot be imputed to us as

33. Karl Lehmann, *Thomas Jefferson, American Humanist* (N. Y., 1947), 76, discusses Jefferson's skepticism about human speculation beyond the realm of the tangible.

a crime before any tribunal. I look therefore to that crisis, as I am sure you also do, as one 'qui summum nec metuit diem nec optat.'[34] In the mean time be our last as cordial as were our first affections.

TH: JEFFERSON

Adams to Jefferson

Montezillo May 12th. 1820.

DEAR SIR

I have received with great pleasure your favour of March 14th. Mr. Ticknor informes me that Dugald Stuart was not reduced to a state of Idiocy as I had been informed, but that he was in bad Health, and by the advice of his friends and Physicians to remove to Devenshire in England, in hopes by the change of air, tranquil repose and retirement from the irritations of society, he might recover his health. But he said there was something mysterious in the business and the Gentlemen in Scotland did not love to converse upon the subject, but chose to wave as well as they could, questions concerning it—That he had not been in London superintending any work.

This account leaves ample scope for all our conjectures, but in all events it is very melancholy that so profound a genius should be obliged to retire before he had exhausted all his Speculations for the Illumination of his Species; for, indeed, all his writings are melancholy; they are humiliating; for they show us our ignorance, and the utmost limits to which the human understanding may hope to go in this Inferior World. They ought, however, to be consolatory, because they furnish us with abundance of your pillows of Ignorance—an expression that I very much admire—on which to repose our puzzeld heads.

The question between spirit and matter appears to me nugatory because we have neither evidence nor idea of either. All that we certainly know is that some substance exists, which must be the cause of all the qualitys and Attributes which we perceive: Extension, Solidity, Perception, memory, and Reason, for all these are Attributes, or adjectives, and not Essences or substantives.

Sixty years ago, at College, I read Berkley, and from that time to this I have been fully persuaded that we know nothing of Essences, that some Essence does exist, which causes our minds with all their ideas, and

34. "Who neither fears the final day nor hopes for it."

this visible World with all its wonders. I am certain that this Cause is wise, Benevolent and powerful, beyond all conception; I cannot doubt, but what it is, I cannot conjecture.

Suppose we dwell a little on this matter. The Infinite divisibility of it had long ago been demonstrated by Mathematicians—When the Marquis De L'Hospital arose and demonstrated that there were quantities and not infinitely little, but others infinitely less than those infinitely littles, and he might have gone on, for what I know, to all Eternity demonstrating that there are quantities infinitely less than the last infinitely littles; and the Phenomena of nature seemes to coincide with De L'Hospitals demonstrations. For example, Astronomers inform us that the Star draconis is distant from the Earth 38. 000, 000. 000. 000. miles. The Light that proceeds from that Star, therefore, must fill a Sphere of 78. 000, 000, 000, 000, miles in diameter, and every part of that Sphere equal to the size of the pupil of the human Eye. Light is Matter, and every ray, every pencil of that light is made up of particles very little indeed, if not infinitely little, or infinitely less than infinitely little. If this Matter is not fine enough and subtle enough to perceive, to feel and to think, it is too subtle for any human intellect or imagination to conceive, for I defy any human mind to form any idea of anything so small. However, after all, Matter is but Matter; if it is infinitely less than infinitely little, it is incapable of memory, judgement, or feeling, or pleasure or pain, as far as I can conceive. Yet for anything I know, it may be as capable of Sensation and reflection as Spirit, for I confess I know not how Spirit can think, feel or act, any more than Matter. In truth, I cannot conceive how either can move or think, so that I must repose upon your pillow of ignorance, which I find very soft and consoleing, for it absolves my conscience from all culpability in this respect. But I insist upon it that the Saint has as good a right to groan at the Philosopher for asserting that there is nothing but matter in the Universe, As the Philosopher has to laugh at the Saint for saying that there are both Matter and Spirit, Or as the Infidel has to despise Berckley for saying that we cannot prove that there is anything in the Universe but Spirit and Idea—for this indeed is all he asserted, for he never denied the Existence of Matter. After all, I agree that both the groan and the Smile is impertinent, for neither knows what he says, or what he affirms, and I will say of both, as Turgot says of Berkley in his Article of Existence in the Encyclopedia: it is easier *to despise* than to answer them.

Cabanis's Ignition can destroy nothing in the Magnet. But motion, magnetism, Electricity, Galvanism, Attraction, Repulsion, are nothing but motion, and have no more relation to, Analogy or resemblance to, memory, Perception, conception or Volition, than black has to white, or falshood to truth, or right to wrong. When two Billiard Balls meet and repell each other, we know nothing of the Cause, Contact or repulsion than we do of Spirit. We see nothing but motion in the Case, and what motion is, we know not.

Oh delightful Ignorance! When I arrive at a certainty that I am Ignorant, and that I always must be ignorant, while I live I am happy, for I know I can no longer be responsible.

We shall meet hereafter and laugh at our present botherations. So believes your old Friend,

JOHN ADAMS

Jefferson to Adams

Monticello. Aug. 15. 20.

I am a great defaulter, my dear Sir, in our correspondence, but prostrate health rarely permits me to write; and, when it does, matters of business imperiously press their claims. I am getting better however, slowly, swelled legs being now the only serious symptom, and these, I believe, proceed from extreme debility. I can walk but little; but I ride 6. or 8. miles a day without fatigue; and within a few days, I shall endeavor to visit my other home, after a twelve month's absence from it. Our University, 4. miles distant, gives me frequent exercise, and the oftener as I direct it's architecture. It's plan is unique, and it is becoming an object of curiosity for the traveller. I have lately had an opportunity of reading a critique on this institution in your North American Review of January last, having been not without anxiety to see what that able work would say of us: and I was relieved on finding in it much coincidence of opinion, and even, where criticisms were indulged, I found they would have been obviated had the developements of our plan been fuller. But these were restrained by the character of the paper reviewed, being merely a report of outlines, not a detailed treatise, and addressed to a legislative body, not to a learned academy.[35] E.g. as an inducement to introduce the Anglo-Saxon into our plan, it was said that it would reward amply the *few weeks* of attention which alone would be requisite for it's attainment; leaving both term and degree under an indefinite expression, because I know that not much time is necessary to attain it to an

35. *Proceedings and Report of the Commissioners for the University of Virginia, presented 8th of December 1818* (Richmond, 1818), reviewed in *North American Review*, 10 (Jan. 1820), 115-37.

useful degree, sufficient to give such instruction in the etymologies of our language as may satisfy ordinary students, while more time would be requisite for those who would propose to attain a critical knolege of it. In a letter which I had occasion to write to Mr. Crofts (who sent you, I believe, as well as myself, a copy of his treatise on the English and German languages, as preliminary to an Etymological dictionary he meditated) I went into explanations with him of an easy process for simplifying the study of the Anglo-Saxon, and lessening the terrors, and difficulties presented by it's rude Alphabet, and unformed orthography.[36] But this is a subject beyond the bounds of a letter, as it was beyond the bounds of a Report to the legislature. Mr. Crofts died, I believe, before any progress was made in the work he had projected.

The reviewer expresses doubt, rather than decision, on our placing Military and Naval architecture in the department of Pure Mathematics. Military architecture embraces fortification and field works, which with their bastions, curtains, hornworks, redoubts etc. are based on a technical combination of lines and angles. These are adapted to offence and defence, with and against the effects of bombs, balls, escalades etc. But lines and angles make the sum of elementary geometry, a branch of Pure Mathematics: and the direction of the bombs, balls, and other projectiles, the necessary appendages of military works, altho' no part of their architecture, belong to the conic sections, a branch of transcendental geometry. Diderot and Dalembert therefore, in their Arbor scientiae, have placed military architecture in the department of elementary geometry. Naval architecture teaches the best form and construction of vessels; for which best form it has recourse to the question of the Solid of least resistance, a problem of transcendental geometry. And it's appurtenant projectiles belong to the same branch, as in the preceding case. It is true that so far as respects the action of the water on the rudder and oars, and of the wind on the sails, it may be placed in the department of mechanics, as Diderot and Dalambert have done: but belonging quite as much to geometry, and allied in it's military character, to military architecture, it simplified our plan to place both under the same head. These views are so obvious that I am sure they would have required but a second thought to reconcile the reviewer to their *location* under the head of Pure Mathematics. For this word *Location*, see Bailey Johnson, Sheridan, Walker etc. But if Dictionaries are to be the Arbiters of language, in which of them shall we find *neologism*. No matter. It is a good word, well sounding, obvious, and expresses an idea which would otherwise require circumlocution. The Reviewer was justifiable therefore in using it; altho' he noted at the same time, as unauthoritative, *centrality, grade, sparse;*

36. See Chap. 12, n. 70.

all which have been long used in common speech and writing. I am a friend to *neology*. It is the only way to give to a language copiousness and euphony. Without it we should still be held to the vocabulary of Alfred or of Ulphilas; and held to their state of science also: for I am sure they had no words which could have conveyed the ideas of Oxigen, cotyledons, zoophytes, magnetism, electricity, hyaline, and thousands of others expressing ideas not then existing, nor of possible communication in the state of their language. What a language has the French become since the date of their revolution, by the free introduction of new words! The most copious and eloquent in the living world; and equal to the Greek, had not that been regularly modifiable almost ad infinitum. Their rule was that whenever their language furnished or adopted a root, all it's branches, in every part of speech were legitimated by giving them their appropriate terminations. αδελφος ["brother"]. αδελφη ["sister"]. αδελφιδιον ["little brother"], αδελφοτης ["brotherly affection"], αδελφιξις ["brotherhood"], αδελφιδους ["nephew"], αδελφικος ["brotherly," adj.], αδελφιζω ["to adopt as a brother"], αδελφικως ["brotherly," adv.]. And this should be the law of every language. Thus, having adopted the adjective *fraternal*, it is a root, which should legitimate fraternity, fraternation, fraternisation, fraternism, to fraternate, fraternise, fraternally. And give the word neologism to our language, as a root, and it should give us it's fellow substantives, neology, neologist, neologisation; it's adjectives neologous, neological, neologistical, it's verb neologise, and adverb neologically. Dictionaries are but the depositories of words already legitimated by usage. Society is the work-shop in which new ones are elaborated. When an individual uses a new word, if illformed it is rejected in society, if wellformed, adopted, and, after due time, laid up in the depository of dictionaries. And if, in this process of sound neologisation, our transatlantic brethren shall not choose to accompany us, we may furnish, after the Ionians, a second example of a colonial dialect improving on it's primitive.

But enough of criticism: let me turn to your puzzling letter of May 12. on matter, spirit, motion etc. It's croud of scepticisms kept me from sleep. I read it, and laid it down: read it, and laid it down, again and again: and to give rest to my mind, I was obliged to recur ultimately to my habitual anodyne, 'I feel: therefore I exist.' I feel bodies which are not myself: there are other existencies then. I call them *matter*. I feel them changing place. This gives me *motion*. Where there is an absence of matter, I call it *void*, or *nothing*, or *immaterial space*. On the basis of sensation, of matter and motion, we may erect the fabric of all the certainties we can have or need. I can concieve *thought* to be an action of a particular organisation of matter, formed for that purpose by it's creator, as well as that *attraction* is an action of matter, or *magnetism* of loadstone. When he who denies to the Creator the power of endowing matter with the mode of action called *thinking* shall shew how he could endow the Sun with the mode of action called *attraction*, which reins the planets in the tract of their orbits, or how an absence of matter can have a will, and, by that will, put matter into motion, then the materialist may be lawfully required to explain the process by which matter exercises the faculty of thinking. When once we quit the basis of sensation, all is in the wind. To talk of *immaterial* existences is to talk of *nothings*. To say that the human soul, angels, god, are immaterial, is to say they are *nothings*, or that there is no god, no angels, no soul. I cannot reason otherwise: but I believe I am supported in my creed of materialism by Locke, Tracy, and Stewart. At what age of the Christian church this heresy of *immaterialism*, this masked atheism, crept in, I do not know. But a heresy it certainly is. Jesus taught nothing of it. He told us indeed that 'God is a spirit,' but he has not defined what a spirit is, nor said that it is not *matter*. And the antient fathers generally, if not universally, held it to be matter: light and thin indeed, an etherial gas; but still matter. Origen says 'Deus reapse corporalis est; sed graviorum tantum corporum ratione, incorporeus.' Tertullian 'quid enim deus nisi corpus?' and again 'quis negabit deum esse corpus? Etsi deus spiritus, spiritus etiam corpus est, sui generis, in sua effigie.' St. Justin Martyr 'το Θειον φαμεν ειναι ασωματον· ουκ οτι ασωματον· —επειδη δε το μη κρατεισθαι ὑπο τινος, του κρατεισθαι τιμιωτερον εστι, δια τουτο καλουμεν αυτον ασωματον.' And St. Macarius, speaking of angels says 'quamvis enim subtilia sint, tamen in substantiâ, formâ et figurâ, secundum tenuitatem naturae eorum, corpora sunt tenuia.'[37] And St. Austin, St. Basil, Lactantius, Tatian, Athenagoras and others, with whose writings I pretend not a familiarity, are said by those who are, to deliver the same doctrine. Turn to your Ocellus d'Argens 97. 105. and to his Timaeus 17. for these quotations. In England these Immaterialists might have been burnt until the 29. Car. 2. when the writ de haeretico comburendo was abolished:[38]

37. Origen says, "God is in very fact corporeal, but, by reason of so much heavier bodies, incorporeal." Tertullian, "for what is God except body?" and again, "Who will deny that God is body? Although God is spirit, yet spirit is body, of his own nature, in his own image." St. Justin Martyr says, "We say that the divinity is without body, not because it is bodyless, but since the state of not being bounded by anything is a more honorable one than that of being bounded, for this reason we call him bodyless." And St. Macarius, speaking of angels, says, "For although their bodies are of light texture, nevertheless in substance, form, and figure, their bodies are rare, according to the rarity of their nature."

38. On the system of philosophy of the early Church fathers and its origins, see William Enfield, *Of the Philosophy of the Ancient Christians* (London, 1837), Bk. VI. 29. Car. 2. refers to the twenty-ninth year of Charles II's reign, 1678. The writ de haeretico had been used when a heretic was convicted, had abjured, and relapsed into heresy.

and here until the revolution, that statute not having extended to us. All heresies being now done away with us, these schismatists are merely atheists, differing from the material Atheist only in their belief that 'nothing made something,' and from the material deist who believes that matter alone can operate on matter.

Rejecting all organs of information therefore but my senses, I rid myself of the Pyrrhonisms with which an indulgence in speculations hyperphysical and antiphysical so uselessly occupy and disquiet the mind. A single sense may indeed be sometimes decieved, but rarely: and never all our senses together, with their faculty of reasoning. They evidence realities; and there are enough of these for all the purposes of life, without plunging into the fathomless abyss of dreams and phantasms. I am satisfied, and sufficiently occupied with the things which are, without tormenting or troubling myself about those which may indeed be, but of which I have no evidence. I am sure that I really know many, many, things, and none more surely than that I love you with all my heart, and pray for the continuance of your life until you shall be tired of it yourself.

Th: Jefferson

Jefferson to Adams

Monticello Jan. 22. 21.

I was quite rejoiced, dear Sir, to see that you had health and spirits enough to take part in the late convention of your state for revising it's constitution, and to bear your share in it's debates and labors. The amendments of which we have as yet heard prove the advance of liberalism in the intervening period; [39] and encourage a hope that the human mind will some day get back to the freedom it enjoyed 2000 years ago. This country, which has given to the world the example of physical liberty, owes to it that of moral emancipation also. For, as yet, it is but nominal with us. The inquisition of public opinion overwhelms in practice the freedom asserted by the laws in theory.

Our anxieties in this quarter are all concentrated in the question What does the Holy alliance, in and out of Congress, mean to do with us on the Missouri question? And this, by the bye, is but the name of the case. It is

39. JA proposed in the convention that the third article of the Massachusetts Bill of Rights be amended to abolish recognition of religious sects by the state. Chinard, *John Adams*, 340-41.

only the John Doe or Richard Roe of the ejectment. The real question, as seen in the states afflicted with this unfortunate population, is Are our slaves to be presented with freedom and a dagger? For if Congress has a power to regulate the conditions of the inhabitants of the states, within the states, it will be but another exercise of that power to declare that all shall be free. Are we then to see again Athenian and Lacedemonian confederacies? To wage another Peloponnesian war to settle the ascendancy between them? Or is this the tocsin of merely a servile war? That remains to be seen: but not I hope by you or me. Surely they will parley awhile, and give us time to get out of the way. What a Bedlamite is man!

But let us turn from our own uneasinesses to the miseries of our Southern friends. Bolivar and Morillo it seems, have come to a parley with dispositions at length to stop the useless effusions of human blood in that quarter. I feared from the beginning that these people were not yet sufficiently enlightened for self-government; and that after wading through blood and slaughter, they would end in military tyrannies, more or less numerous. Yet as they wished to try the experiment, I wished them success in it. They have now tried it, and will possibly find that their safest road will be an accomodation with the mother country, which shall hold them together by the single link of the same chief magistrate, leaving to him power enough to keep them in peace with one another, and to themselves the essential powers of selfgovernment and selfimprovement, until they shall be sufficiently trained by education and habits of freedom to walk safely by themselves. Representative government, native functionaries, a qualified negative on their laws, with a previous security by compact for freedom of commerce, freedom of the press, habeas corpus, and trial by jury, would make a good beginning. This last would be the school in which their people might begin to learn the exercise of civic duties as well as rights. For freedom of religion they are not yet prepared. The scales of bigotry are not sufficiently fallen from their eyes to accept it for themselves individually, much less to trust others with it. But that will come in time, as well as a general ripeness to break entirely from the parent stem.

You see, my dear Sir, how easily we prescribe for others a cure for their difficulties, while we cannot cure our own. We must leave both, I believe, to heaven, and wrap ourselves up in the mantle of resignation, and of that friendship of which I tender to you the most sincere assurances.

TH: JEFFERSON

Adams to Jefferson

Montezillo February 3d. 1821

DEAR SIR

I have just read a sketch of the life of Swedenborg,[40] and a larger work in two huge volumes of Memoirs of John Wesley by Southey, and your kind letter of January 22d. came to hand in the nick of time to furnish me with a very rational exclamation, "What a bedlamite is man!" They are histories of Galvanism and Mesmerism [41] thrown into hotch potch. They say that these men were honest and sincere—so were the Wors[h]ipers of the White Bull in Egypt and now in Calcutta; so were the Worshipers of Bacchus and Venus; so were the worshipers of St. Dominick and St. Bernard. Swedenborg and Westley had certainly vast memories and immaginations, and great talents for Lunaticks.

Slavery in this Country I have seen hanging over it like a black cloud for half a Century. If I were as drunk with enthusiasm as Swedenborg or Westley, I might probably say I had seen Armies of Negroes marching and countermarching in the air, shining in Armour. I have been so terrified with this Phenomenon that I constantly said in former times to the Southern Gentlemen, I cannot comprehend this object; I must leave it to you. I will vote for forceing no measure against your judgements. What we are to see, *God* knows, and I leave it to him, and his agents in posterity. I have none of the genius of Franklin, to invent a rod to draw from the cloud its Thunder and lightning. I have long been decided in opinion that a free government and the Roman Catholick religion can never exist together in any nation or Country, and consequently that all projects for reconciling them in old Spain or new are Eutopian, Platonick and Chimerical. I have seen such a prostration and prostitution of Human Nature to the Priesthood in old Spain as settled my judgment long ago, and I understand that in new Spain it is still worse, if that is possible.

My appearance in the late convention was too ludicrous to be talked of. I was a member in the Convention of 1779, and there I was loquacious enough. I have harrangued and scribbled more than my share, but from that time to the convention in 1820 I never opened my lips in a publick debate. After a total desuetude for 40 years I boggled and blundered

40. By John Clowes, who wrote three works on Baron Swedenborg, published in 1799, 1806, and 1807.
41. Luigi Galvani, Italian physiologist, developed a theory of animal electricity, disputed by Alessandro, Count Volta. Frederick Anton Mesmer believed that an occult force within himself could influence others.

more than a young fellow just rising to speak at the bar. What I said I know not; I believe the Printers have made better speeches than I made for myself. Feeling my weakness, I attempted little and that seldom. What would I give for nerves as good as yours? But as Westley said of himself at my age, "Old time has shaken me by the hand, and parallized it."

What pictures of Monarchy, even limited Monarchy, have the trials of the Duke of York and the Queen of England held up to the astonishment, contempt and scorn of mankind.[42] I should think it would do more than the French and American revolutions to bring it into discredit. Indeed, all human affairs, without your philosophical and Christian mantle of resignation, would be deeply malancholy—even that friendship which I feel for you, ardent and sincere as it is, would be over clouded by constant fears of its termination.

JOHN ADAMS

Adams to Jefferson

Montezillo May 19. 1821

MY DEAR FRIEND

Must We, before We take our departure from this grand and beautiful World, surrender all our pleasing hopes of the progres of Society? Of improvement of the intellectual and moral condition of the World? of the reformation of mankind?

The Piemontese Revolution scarcely assumed a form; and the Neapolitan bubble is burst. And what should hinder the Spanish and Portuguese Constitutions from rushing to the same ruin?[43] The Cortes is in one

42. Frederick Augustus, Duke of York, was dismissed as commander-in-chief of the army for promoting officers who bribed his mistress, Mary Anne Clarke, to use her influence on their behalf. Queen Caroline, a princess of Brunswick, was the wife of George IV. They were married in 1795 when he was prince of Wales but their early separation had resulted from George's intimacy with Mrs. Fitzherbert. Although he broke with her in 1811, George never became reconciled with Caroline, who died soon after his coronation in 1821. Ernest L. Woodward, *The Age of Reform* (Oxford, 1938), 64-66.

43. In Naples a military mutiny in July 1820 had forced promulgation of a democratic constitution, but in March 1821 an Austrian invasion ended the new regime. A similar development took place in Piedmont in 1821 which was also crushed by Austria. The Spanish democratic constitution of 1812, restored in 1820, was overthrown by a French invasion and succeeded by a reactionary monarchy. Only in Portugal was the democratic constitution of 1820 maintained, in spite of the opposition of the Roman Catholic Church and insistence by Great Britain that the king be restored. Frederick B. Artz, *Reaction and Revolution, 1814-1832* (N. Y., 1934), 152-60, 165-70; Oscar Browning, *A History of the Modern World* (N. Y., 1916), 112-17; Charles D. Hazen, *Europe Since 1815* (N. Y., 1910), 49-50, 60-63.

Assembly, vested with the legislative power. The King and his Priests Armies Navies and all other Officers are vested with the Executive Authority of Government. Are not here two Authorities Up, neither Supream? Are they not necessarily Rivals constantly contending like Law Physick and Divinity for Superiority? Are they not two Armies drawn up in battle Array just ready for civil War?

Can a free Government possibly exist with a Roman Catholic Religion?

The Art of Lawgiving is not so easy as that of Architecture or Painting. New York and Rhode Island are struggling for Conventions to reform their Constitutions [44] and I am told there is danger of making them worse. Massachusetts has had her Convention: but our Sovereign Lords The People think themselves wiser than their Representatives, and in several Articles I agree with their Lordships. Yet there never was a cooler, a more patient candid, or a wiser deliberative Body than that Convention.

I may refine too much. I may be an Enthusiast. But I think a free Government is necessarily a complicated Piece of Machinery, the nice and exact Adjustment of whose Springs Wheels and Weights are not yet well comprehended by the Artists of the Age and still less by the People.

I began this letter principally to enquire after your health and to repeat Assurances of the Affection of your Friend

JOHN ADAMS

Adams to Jefferson

Montezillo August 20 1821

DEAR SIR

There are on the Journals of Congress some early resolutions for establishing a Nursery for the education of young men in military Science discipline and tactics; but paper money was so scarce that they never could afford to carry them into execution. When the idea was revived I do not remember; but it has been cherished under Jefferson Madison and Monroe and is now brought to a considerable degree of perfection. The late Visits of the Cadets to several States seem to have made the institution popular.[45]

44. New York held a constitutional convention and adopted a new constitution in 1821, but Rhode Island continued government under her colonial charter until 1840.

45. At a meeting of President Washington's cabinet, Nov. 23, 1793, according to TJ, "It was proposed to recommend the establishmt of a military academy. I objected that none of the specified powers given by the constn to Congress would authorize this. It was therefore referred for further considn and inquiry." "Anas," Ford, I, 269-70. In 1794 Congress established a School for Artillerists and Engineers at West Point, for military training only. During TJ's presidency a superintendent of the Academy was

Would not a similar establishment for the education of naval Officers be equally Usefull.[46] The public Opinion of the nation seems now to be favourable to a Navy as the cheapest and safest Arm for our national defence. Is not this a favourable moment for proposing a naval Accademy?

Floyd is gone! You and Jay and Carrol are all who remain.[47] We shall all be asterised very soon. Sic transit Gloriola (is there such a latin Word?) mundi.

JOHN ADAMS

Jefferson to Adams

Monticello Sep. 12. 21.

DEAR SIR

I am just returned from my other home, and shall within a week go back to it for the rest of the autumn. I find here your favor of Aug. 20. and was before in arrear for that of May 19. I cannot answer, but join in, your question, of May 19. Are we to surrender the pleasing hopes of seeing improvement in the moral and intellectual condition of Man? The events of Naples and Piedmont cast a gloomy cloud over that hope: and Spain and Portugal are not beyond jeopardy. And what are we to think of this Northern triumvirate, arming their nations to dictate despotisms to the rest of the world? And the evident connivance of England, as the price of secret stipulations for continental armies, if her own should take side with her malcontent and pulverised people? And what of the poor Greeks, and their small chance of amelioration even if the hypocritical Autocrat should take them under the iron cover of his Ukazes. Would this be lighter or safer than that of the Turk? [48] These, my dear friend,

---

appointed, but the type of education for which West Point is noted today was not begun until 1814 when Sylvanus Thayer became superintendent. Edward C. Boynton, *History of West Point...* (N. Y., 1863), 186, 208, 217.

46. The United States Naval Academy was not established until 1845; George Bancroft, secretary of the navy, deserves chief credit for its founding. Russel B. Nye, *George Bancroft, Brahmin Rebel* (N. Y., 1945), 143-46.

47. William Floyd, of New York, signer of the Declaration of Independence. John Jay was not a signer. See above, TJ to JA, Jan. 21, 1812, above, 292 and n. 38.

48. The Northern Triumvirate consisted of Russia, Prussia, and Austria, authorized by the Congress of Vienna of 1815 to interfere in the internal affairs of the smaller nations to maintain the reactionary peace. The Greek war for independence against Turkey began in 1821 and was encouraged by the "hypocritical Autocrat," Tsar Alexander I of Russia, to embarrass the Turks. When war almost resulted between Russia and Turkey, Austria and Great Britain intervened to persuade the Tsar that it was bad policy to support revolutions. Nevertheless, Greek independence was proclaimed in Jan. 1822. Artz, *Reaction and Revolution*, 162-72, 207-8, 247-62, esp. 255.

are speculations for the new generation, as, before they will be resolved, you and I must join our deceased brother Floyd. Yet I will not believe our labors are lost. I shall not die without a hope that light and liberty are on steady advance. We have seen indeed once within the records of history a compleat eclipse of the human mind continuing for centuries. And this too by swarms of the same Northern barbarians, conquering and taking possession of the countries and governments of the civilized world. Should this be again attempted, should the same Northern hordes, allured again by the corn wine, and oil of the South, be able again to settle their swarms in the countries of their growth, the art of printing alone, and the vast dissemination of books, will maintain the mind where it is, and raise the conquering ruffians to the level of the conquered, instead of degrading these to that of their conquerors. And even should the cloud of barbarism and despotism again obscure the science and liberties of Europe, this country remains to preserve and restore light and liberty to them. In short, the flames kindled on the 4th. of July 1776. have spread over too much of the globe to be extinguished by the feeble engines of despotism. On the contrary they will consume those engines, and all who work them.

I think with you that there should be a school of instruction for our navy as well as artillery; and I do not see why the same establishment might not suffice for both.[49] Both require the same basis of general mathematics, adding projectiles and fortification for the artillery exclusively, and Astronomy and theory of navigation exclusively for the Naval students. Bezout conducted both schools in France, and has left us the best book extant for their joint and separate instruction. It ought not to require a separate professor.

A 4th. of July oration delivered in the town of Milford in your state gives to Samuel Chase the credit of having 'first started the cry of independance in the ears of his countrymen.' Do you remember anything of this? I do not. I have no doubt it was uttered in Massachusets even before it was by Thomas Paine. But certainly I never considered Samuel Chase as foremost, or even forward in that hallowed cry. I know that Maryland hung heavily on our backs, and that Chase, altho' first named, was not most in unison with us of that delegation, either in politics or morals, et c'est ainsi que l'on ecrit l'histoire ["and thus it is that history is written"]!

Your doubt of the legitimacy of the word *gloriola* is resolved by

49. In a special message of March 18, 1808, President Jefferson had advised Congress that the military academy was too limited in its subjects and recommended that it be transferred to Washington so that perhaps the Navy might have a part in it. Lipscomb and Bergh, eds., *Writings*, III, 471-72.

Cicero, who in his letter to Lucceius expresses a wish '*ut nos metipsi vivi gloriola nostra perfruamur* ["that we ourselves while living might enjoy our little bit of glory"].' Affectly. Adieu.

TH: JEFFERSON

Adams to Jefferson

Montizello 24 Septr. 1821.

DEAR SIR

I thank you for your favour of the 12 inst. Hope springs eternal. Eight millions of Jews hope for a Messiah more powerful and glorious than Moses, David, or Solomon, who is to make them as powerful as he pleases. Some hundreds of millions of Musslemen expect another Prophet more powerful than Mahomet who is to spread Islamism over the whole earth. Hundreds of millions of Christians expect and hope for a millenium in which Jesus is to reign for a thousand years over the whole world before it is burnt up. The Hindoos expect another and a final incarnation of Vishnu who is to do great and wonderful things, I know not what. All these hopes are founded on real or pretended revelation. The modern Greeks too it seems hope for a deliverer who is to produce them. The Themistoclese's and Demostheneses—The Plato's and Aristotle's The Solon's and Lycurgus'. On what prophecies they found their belief I know not. You and I hope for splendid improvements in human society and vast ameliorations in the condition of mankind. Our faith may be supported by more rational arguments than any of the former. I own that I am very sanguine in the belief of them as I hope and believe you are and your reasoning in your Letter confirmed me in them. As Brother Floyd has gone I am now the oldest of the little Congressional group that remain. I may therefore rationally hope to be the first to depart; and as you are the youngest and the most energetic in mind and body, you may therefore rationally hope to be the last to take your flight and to rake up the fire as father Sherman who always staid to the last and commonly two days afterwards used to say, "that it was his office to sit up and rake the ashes over the coals" and much satisfaction may you have in your office.

The Cholera Morbus has done wonders in St. Helena and in London. We shall soon hear of a Negociation for a second Wife. Whether in the body or out of the body I shall always be your friend.

The anecdote of Mr. Chase contained in the Oration delivered at Milford must be an idle rumour for neither the State of Maryland nor [any] of their Delegates were very early in their conviction of the necessity of Independence, nor very forward in promoting it. The old Speaker Tilghman, Johnson, Chase, and Paca, were steady in promoting resistance but after some of them Maryland sent one at least of the most turbulent Tory's that ever came to Congress.[50]

JOHN ADAMS

Jefferson to Adams

Monticello June 1. 22.

It is very long, my dear Sir, since I have written to you. My dislocated wrist is now become so stiff that I write slowly and with pain, and therefore write as little as I can. Yet it is due to mutual friendship to ask once in a while how we do? The papers tell us that Genl. Starke is off at the age of 93. Charles Thomson still lives at about the same age, chearful, slender as a grasshopper, and so much without memory that he scarcely recognises the members of his household. An intimate friend of his called on him not long since: it was difficult to make him recollect who he was, and, sitting one hour, he told him the same story 4. times over. Is this life?

> With lab'ring step
> To tread our former footsteps? pace the round
> Eternal?—to beat and beat
> The beaten track? to see what we have seen
> To taste the tasted? o'er our palates to decant
> Another vintage? [51]

It is at most but the life of a cabbage, surely not worth a wish. When all our faculties have left, or are leaving us, one by one, sight, hearing, memory, every avenue of pleasing sensation is closed, and athumy, debility and mal-aise left in their places, when the friends of our youth are all

50. Is TJ referring to Thomas Stone, who voted for independence but favored the peace negotiations with Lord Howe in Sept. 1776? Mary E. Fittro, "Stone, Thomas," *DAB*, XVIII, 84.

51. See Edward Young, *Night Thoughts on Life, Death and Immortality*, ed. by James Robert Boyd (N.Y., 1851), 157. TJ earlier quoted a portion of this poem in his letter to AA, Jan. 11, 1817, above, 504.

gone, and a generation is risen around us whom we know not, is death an evil?

> When one by one our ties are torn,
> And friend from friend is snatched forlorn
> When man is left alone to mourn,
> Oh! then how sweet it is to die!
> When trembling limbs refuse their weight,
> And films slow gathering dim the sight,
> When clouds obscure the mental light
> Tis nature's kindest boon to die!

I really think so. I have ever dreaded a doting old age; and my health has been generally so good, and is now so good, that I dread it still. The rapid decline of my strength during the last winter has made me hope sometimes that I see land. During summer I enjoy it's temperature, but I shudder at the approach of winter, and wish I could sleep through it with the Dormouse, and only wake with him in spring, if ever. They say that Starke could walk about his room. I am told you walk well and firmly. I can only reach my garden, and that with sensible fatigue. I ride however daily. But reading is my delight. I should wish never to put pen to paper; and the more because of the treacherous practice some people have of publishing one's letters without leave. L[or]d Mansfield declared it a breach of trust, and punishable at law. I think it should be a penitentiary felony. Yet you will have seen that they have drawn me out into the arena of the newspapers. Altho' I know it is too late for me to buckle on the armour of youth, yet my indignation would not permit me passively to receive the kick of an Ass.[52]

To turn to the news of the day, it seems that the Cannibals of Europe are going to eating one another again. A war between Russia and Turkey is like the battle of the kite and snake. Whichever destroys the other, leaves a destroyer the less for the world. This pugnacious humor of mankind seems to be the law of his nature, one of the obstacles to too great multiplication provided in the mechanism of the Universe. The cocks of the henyard kill one another up. Boars, bulls, rams do the same. And the horse, in his wild state, kills all the young males, until worn down with

---

52. TJ to Messrs. Ritchie and Gooch, May 13, 1822, thanking them for the paper "containing the arraignment of the Presidents of the United States generally, as peculators or accessories to peculation, by an informer who masks himself under the signature of a 'Native Virginian.'" The part relating to TJ was first published in the Baltimore *Federal Republican* "during the ferment of a warmly-tested election," and a copy was sent to him. He then explained to Ritchie and Gooch, editors of the Richmond *Enquirer*, how accounts owed him for his diplomatic service were still unpaid by the government after 1789 and how they were settled. Lipscomb and Bergh eds., *Writings*, XV, 365-70.

age and war, some vigorous youth kills him, and takes to himself the Haram of females. I hope we shall prove how much happier for man the Quaker policy is, and that the life of the feeder is better than that of the fighter: and it is some consolation that the desolation by these Maniacs of one part of the earth is the means of improving it in other parts. Let the latter be our office. And let us milk the cow, while the Russian holds her by the horns, and the Turk by the tail. God bless you, and give you health, strength, good spirits, and as much of life as you think worth having.

TH: JEFFERSON

Adams to Jefferson

Montezillo June 11th. 1822.

DEAR SIR,

Half an hour ago I received, and this moment have heard read for the third or fourth time, the best letter that ever was written by an Octogenearian, dated June the 1st. It is so excellent that I am almost under an invincible temptation to commit a breach of trust by lending it to a printer. My Son, Thomas Boylston, says it would be worth five hundred dollars to any newspaper in Boston, but I dare not betray your confidence.

I have not sprained my wrist, but both my Arms and hands are so over strained that I cannot write a line. Poor Starke remembered nothing, and talked of nothing, but the Battle of Bennington. Poor Thomson is not quite so reduced. I cannot mount my Horse, but I can walk three miles over a rugged rockey Mountain, and have done it within a Month. Yet I feel when setting in my chair, as if I could not rise out of it, and when risen, as if I could not walk across the room; my sight is very dim; hearing pritty good; memory poor enough.

I answer your question, Is Death an Evil? It is not an Evil. It is a blessing to the individual, and to the world. Yet we ought not to wish for it till life becomes insupportable; we must wait the pleasure and convenience of this great teacher. Winter is as terrible to me, as to you. I am almost reduced in it, to the life of a Bear or a torpid swallow. I cannot read, but my delight is to hear others read, and I tease all my friends most unmercifully and tyrannically, against their consent. The Ass has kicked in vain, all men say the dull animal has missed the mark.

This globe is a Theatre of War, its inhabitants are all heroes. I believe the little Eels in Vinegar and the animalcule in pepper water, I believe are quarrelsome. The Bees are as warlike as Romans, Russians, Britains, or Frenchmen. Ants or Caterpilars and Canker worms are the only tribes amongst whom I have not seen battles. And Heaven itself, if we believe Hindoos, Jews, and Christians, has not always been at peace. We need not trouble ourselves about these things nor fret ourselves because of Evil doers but safely trust the ruler with his skies. Nor need we dread the approach of dotage, let it come if it must. Thomson, it seems, still delights in his four stories. And Starke remembers to the last his Bennington, and exulted in his Glory. The worst of the Evil is that our friends will suffer more by our imbecility than we ourselves.

Diplomatic flickerings, it seemes, have not yet ceased. It seems as if a Council of Ambassadors could never agree.

In wishing for your health and happiness I am very selfish, for I hope for more letters; this is worth more than five hundred dollars to me, for it has already given me, and will continue to give me more pleasure than a thousand. Mr. Jay who is about your age I am told experiences more decay than you do. I am your old friend

JOHN ADAMS

Jefferson to Adams

Monticello June 27. 22.

DEAR SIR

Your kind letter of the 11th. has given me great satisfaction for altho' I could not doubt but that the hand of age was pressing heavily on you, as on myself, yet we like to know the particulars and the degree of that pressure. Much reflection too has been produced by your suggestion of lending my letter of the 1st. to a printer. I have generally great aversion to the insertion of my letters in the public papers; because of my passion for quiet retirement and never to be exhibited in scene on the public stage. Nor am I unmindful of the precept of Horace 'solvere senescentem, mature sanus equum, ne peccet ad extremum ridendus.' [53] In the present case however I see a possibility that this might aid in producing the very quiet after which I pant. I do not know how far you may suffer as I do, under the persecution of letters, of which every mail brings a fresh load. They are letters of enquiry for the most part, always of good will, sometimes from friends whom I esteem, but much oftener from persons whose names

53. "Set free an aging horse in a rational state lest he, being made sport of, make a complete fool of himself."

are unknown to me, but written kindly and civilly, and to which therefore civility requires answers. Perhaps the better known failure of your hand in it's function of writing, may shield you in greater degree from this distress, and so far qualify the misfortune of it's disability. I happened to turn to my letter-list some time ago, and a curiosity was excited to count those recieved in a single year. It was the year before the last. I found the number to be 1267. many of them requiring answers of elaborate research, and all to be answered with due attention and consideration. Take an average of this number for a week or a day, and I will repeat the question suggested by other considerations in mine of the 1st. Is this life? At best it is but the life of a mill-horse, who sees no end to his circle but in death. To such a life that of a cabbage is paradise. It occurs then that my condition of existence, truly stated in that letter, if better known, might check the kind indiscretions which are so heavily oppressing the departing hours of life. Such a relief would to me be an ineffable blessing. But yours of the 11th. equally interesting and affecting, should accompany that to which it is an answer. The two taken together would excite a joint interest, and place before our fellow-citizens the present condition of two antient servants, who having faithfully performed their 40. or 50. campaigns, stipendiis omnibus expletis [after all their military duty had been completed], have a reasonable claim to repose from all disturbance in the Sanctuary of Invalids and Superannuates. But some device should be thought of for their getting before the public otherwise than by our own publication. Your printer perhaps could frame something plausible. C. Thomson's name should be left blank, as his picture, should it meet his eye, might give him pain. I consign however the whole subject to your consideration, to do in it whatever your own judgment shall approve, and repeat always with truth the assurances of my constant and affectionate friendship and respect.

TH: JEFFERSON

Adams to Jefferson

Quincy Montezillo July 12th. 1822

DEAR SIR

Yours of the 27th June is received with pleasure, for the free air of it delights me.

Your number of 1267. letters in a year does not surprise me; I have no list of mine; and I could not make one without a weeks research, and I do not believe I ever received one quarter part of your number. And I very much doubt whether I received in the same year one twelfth part; there are reasons enough for the difference.

I hope one day your letters will be all published in volumes; they will not always appear Orthodox, or liberal in politicks; but they will exhibit a Mass of Taste, Sense, Literature and Science, presented in a sweet simplicity and a neat elegance of Stile, which will be read with delight in future ages. I think that when a people turn out their old servants, either by legal suffrages or from complaisance to a vulgar opinion, they ought to grant them, at least, an outfit; for by making them conspicuous, and multiplying their acquaintances, they expose them to expences heavier than when in office. Your stationary bill alone for paper, Quills, Ink, Wafers, Wax, Sand and Pounce, must have amounted to enough to maintain a small family. I never can forgive New York, Connecticut, or Maine for turning out Venerable Men of sixty or seventy from the seats of Judgement, when their judgement is often the best.[54] To turn out such men to eat husks with the prodigal or grass with Nebuchadnezzar ought to be tormenting to the humanity of the Nation; it is infinitely worse than sa[y]ing "go up thou bald Head." For my part, my blindness and Palsy lay me under a necessity of neglecting to answer many letters, and other kind civilities which otherwise I should delight to acknowledge. I believe it will be best to brave it out; it will be impossible to conceal anything. I am your friend of forty seven Years Standing.

JOHN ADAMS

Adams to Jefferson

Montezillo October 15th. 1822

DEAR SIR.

I have long entertained scruples about writing this letter, upon a subject of some delicacy. But old age has over-come at last.

You remember the four Ships, ordered by Congress to be built, and the four Captains appointed by Washington—Talbot and Truxton and Barry etc. to carry an Ambassador to Algiers and protect our Commerce in the

54. In the new constitutions of Connecticut (1818) and New York (1821) age was a qualification for judges of the higher courts (the maximum was seventy and sixty respectively). This was not so in Maine, which JA may have confused with New Hampshire (age seventy under the constitution of 1792). Thorpe, ed., *Federal and State Constitutions*, I, 536-555; V, 2639-51; IV, 271-90.

Mediterranean. I have always imputed this measure to you; for several reasons.[55] First, Because you frequently proposed it to me while we were at Paris, negotiating together for peace with the Barbary powers. 2dly. Because I knew that Washington and Hamilton, were not only indifferent about a Navy, but averse to it. There was no Secretary of the Navy; only four heads of Departments. You were Secretary of State; Hamilton Secretary of the Treasury, Knox Secretary of War; and I believe Bradford was Attorney General. I have always suspected that you and Knox were in favour of a Navy. If Bradford was so, the majority was clear. But Washington, I am confident was against it in his judgment. But his attachment to Knox and his deference to your opinion, for I know he had a great regard for you—might induce him to decide in favour of you and Knox, even though Bradford united with Hamilton in opposition to you. That Hamilton was averse to the measure, I have personal evidence, for while it was pending, he came in a hurry and a fit of impatience, to make a visit to me. He said he was like to be called upon for a large sum of money to build Ships of War, to fight the Algerines and he asked my opinion of the measure. I answered him that I was clearly in favour of it. For I had always been of Opinion, from the Commencement of the Revolution, that a Navy was the most powerful, the safest and the cheapest National defence for this Country. My advice therefore was that as much of the Revenue as could possibly be spared, should be applied to the building and equipping of Ships. The conversation was of some length, but it was manifest in his looks and in his air that he was disgusted at the measure as well as at my opinion, that I had expressed.

Mrs. Knox, not long since, wrote a letter to Dr. Waterhouse,[56] requesting him to procure a Commission for her Son, in the Navy; that Navy, says her Ladyship, of which his Father was the parent, for, says she, "I have frequently heard General Washington say to my husband; the Navy was your Child." I have always believed it to be Jefferson's child, though Knox may have assisted in ushering it into the world. Hamilton's hobby was the Army. That Washington was averse to a Navy, I have full proof from his own lips, in many different conversations, some of them of length, in which he always insisted that it was only building and arming Ships for the English.

55. Congress authorized six frigates in 1794, including the *Constitution, Chesapeake,* and *Constellation.* The captains of the new Navy, chosen that year, were Joshua Barney, John Barry, Richard Dale, Samuel Nicholson, Silas Talbot, and Thomas Truxton. Barney declined to serve because he was put under Talbot, his junior. Edgar S. Maclay, *A History of the United States Navy from 1775 to 1901* (N. Y., 1901), I, 158-60. JA had asked these questions about the Navy in his letter of June 11, 1813, Chap. 9, n. 70, 328.
56. See TJ to JA, May 17, 1818, above, 523.

Si quid novisti rectius istis, Candidus imperti,
Si Non, his utere mecum." [57]

If I am in error in any particular, pray correct Your Humble Servt.

JOHN ADAMS

Jefferson to Adams

Monticello Nov. 1. 22.

DEAR SIR

I have racked my memory, and ransacked my papers to enable myself to answer the enquiries of your favor of Oct. 15. but to little purpose. My papers furnish me nothing, my memory generalities only. I know that while I was in Europe, and anxious about the fate of our seafaring men, for some of whom, then in captivity in Algiers we were treating, and all were in like danger, I formed undoubtingly the opinion that our government, as soon as practicable, should provide a naval force sufficient to keep the Barbary states in order, and on this subject we communicated together as you observe. When I returned to the US. and took part in the administration under Genl. Washington I constantly maintained that opinion, and in Dec. 90. took advantage of a reference to me from the first Congress which met after I was in office to report in favor of a force sufficient for the protection of our Mediterranean commerce, and I laid before them an accurate statement of the whole Barbary force, public and private.[58] I think Genl. Washington approved of building vessels of war to that extent. Genl. Knox I know did. But what was Colo. Hamilton's opinion I do not in the least remember. Your recollections on that subject are certainly corroborated by his known anxieties for a close connection with Great Britain, for which he might apprehend danger from collisions between their vessels and ours. Randolph was then Attorney General; but his opinion on the question I also entirely forget. Some vessels of war were accordingly built and sent into the Mediterranean. The additions to these in your time I need not note to you, who are well known to have ever been an advocate for the wooden walls of Themistocles. Some of those you added were sold under an act of Congress passed while you

57. "If you know anything more correct than these, candidly share them; if not make use of these with me."
58. "Report relative to the Mediterranean Trade," Dec. 28, 1790, Washington, ed., *Writings*, VII, 519-32.

were in office. I thought afterwards that the public safety might require some additional vessels of strength to be prepared and in readiness for the first moment of a war, provided they could be preserved against the decay which is unavoidable if kept in the water, and clear of the expence of officers and men. With this view I proposed that they should be built in dry docks above the level of the tide waters, and covered with roofs. I further advised that places for these docks should be selected where there was a command of water on a higher level, as that of the Tyber at Washington, by which the vessels might be floated out, on the principle of a lock. But the majority of the legislature was against any addition to the navy, and the minority, altho' for it in judgment, voted against it on a principle of opposition. We are now, I understand building vessels to remain on the stocks under shelter until wanted, when they will be launched and finished. On my plan they could be in service at an hour's notice. On this the finishing, after launching will be a work of time. This is all I recollect about the origin and progress of our navy. That of the late war certainly raised our rank and character among nations. Yet a navy is a very expensive engine. It is admitted that in 10. or 12. years a vessel goes to entire decay; or, if kept in repair costs as much as would build a new one. And that a nation who could count on 12. or 15. years of peace would gain by burning it's navy and building a new one in time. It's extent therefore must be governed by circumstances. Since my proposition for a force adequate to the pyracies of the Mediterranean, a similar necessity has arisen in our own seas for considerable addition to that force. Indeed I wish we could have a convention with the naval powers of Europe for them to keep down the pyrates of the Mediterranean, and the slave ships on the coast of Africa, and for us to perform the same duties for the society of nations in our seas. In this way those collisions would be avoided between the vessels of war of different nations, which beget wars and constitute the weightiest objection to navies. I salute you with constant affection and respect.

TH: JEFFERSON

Adams to Jefferson

Montezillo 2d. December. 1822

DEAR SIR

I have been deeply afflicted with the account of your accident. At first your Leg was broke—I shuddered, I feared that I should have no more letters from Montecello. Next came the account that it was only a small bone in the Arm. My hopes revived. The difference between the leg and the Arm was immense. To illustrate this difference, and for your consolation and amusement, I will give you an egotistical anecdote. When one of the Comets was here in our neighborhood I went out one evening into my garden to look at the wandering Star, with four or five Gentlemen. We returned through an alley over which my Men had placed a strong stake to prevent a peach tree from breaking down with its load of fruit. In the dark I blundered against this stake, broke its fastness—it fell and I with it on the sharp edge of a knot in it. I felt a sharp cut but thought it had only broke the skin. I scampered up and returned to the house with the other Gentlemen. My Daughter Smith cryed out, Sir, what has happened to you, your Leg is all bloody. I strip[p]ed off the stocking and low[!] a gash from half an inch, to an inch deep cut by the sharp knot, bleeding profusely. My Daughter cried out, bring me some Laudanum. I knew no better. Her Mother [who] always had an Apothecarys Shop in her closet instantly brought a Bottle. They poured a quantity of it into the wound and washed the neighboring flesh with it, [and] bound a bandage around it, but it produced an inflamation which cost me a confinement for two months. Several surgeons came to see me and all agreed that neither the genius nor experience of Philosophers, Physicians nor surgeons had hitherto invented any means of preventing the humours falling down into a wound in the Leg but by holding it up. They accordingly compelled me to hold mine almost perpendicularly, oftener lieing on my back on a Sofa oftener at an angle of forty five but never lower than an horizontal line. In this manner they made me vegitate for two months suffering continual twinges on the shin. The Bathes, tents and bandages and lotions I pass over. I verily believe that if nothing had been done to it but washing in warm water it would have been well in three days. You may console yourself with the hope that your Arm will soon be well; you will not be obliged to hold your arm up pointing to the skies.

If you cannot write yourself, pray the fair lovely and accomplished Miss Hellen Randolph [59] to write a line to inform me of your recovery. Your affectionate friend,

JOHN ADAMS

59. Ellen Randolph, TJ's granddaughter, the third daughter of Thomas Mann Randolph and Martha Jefferson Randolph.

Adams to Jefferson

Quincy February 10th. 1823.

DEAR SIR

Your Virginia Ladies have always been represented to me, and I have always believed it, as among the most beautiful, virtuous, and accomplished of their Sex. One of them has given me a most luxurious entertainment in a narration of her Visit to your Domicil.[60] Her description of the Mountain, the Palace, the Gardens, the vast Prospect, The lofty Mountains at a distance, The Capacious Valley between them, The Oceans of Fogg and Vapours appearing in the morning, Their dissipation with the rising Sun, and everything else, are painted in colours so distinct and lively that I seem to have as cleare an idea of the whole scene, as if I had led her by the hand, in all her rambles. Her account of the hospitality of the Family almost gave me a jealous and envious fit, as Swift says Popes Couplet gave him.[61]

But now to the point: This Lady says she saw in your sanctum sanctorum a large folio Volume on which was written libels, on opening which she found it was a Magazine of Slips of newspapers, and pamphlets, vilifying, calumniating and defaming you. I started as from a trance, exclaiming, what a dunce have I been all my days, and what lubbers my Children, and Grand Children, were, that none of us have ever thought to make a similar collection. If we had I am confident I could have produced a more splendid Mass than yours. I could have enumerated Alexander Hamilton, and Thomas Paine,[62] The two most extraordinary Men that

60. JA may have been referring to Mrs. Margaret Bayard Smith's account of her visit to Monticello in 1809. Gaillard Hunt, ed., *The First Forty Years of Washington Society, portrayed by the Family Letters of Mrs. Samuel Harrison Smith . . .* (N. Y., 1906), 65-81.

61. "On the Death of Dr. Swift, 1731":

> In POPE, I cannot read a Line,
> But with a Sigh, I wish it mine:
> When he can in one Couplet fix
> More Sense than I can do in Six:
> It gives me such a jealous Fit,
> I cry, Pox take him, and his Wit.

Harold Williams, ed., *The Poems of Jonathan Swift* (Oxford, 1937), II, 555.

62. Hamilton printed his bitter denunciation of JA in *Letter from Alexander Hamilton, concerning the Public Conduct and Character of John Adams, Esq., President of the United States* (N. Y., 1800). Paine's attack on JA appeared in a series of articles entitled "To the Citizens of the United States and Particularly to the Leaders of Federal Faction," *National Intelligencer*, Washington, Nov. 1802, especially in Letter II (Nov. 22). Philip S. Foner, ed., *The Complete Writings of Thomas Paine* (N. Y., 1945), II, 912-18.

this Country, this Age or this World, ever produced. "Ridendo dicere verum quid vetat?" [63]

I most sincerely congratulate you on the recovery of your hand, and am your friend for this, and, I hope, and believe, for all future Worlds

J. Adams

Jefferson to Adams

Monticello Feb. 25. 23.

Dear Sir

I recieved in due time your two favors of Dec. 2. and Feb. 10. and have to acknolege for the ladies of my native state their obligations to you for the encomiums which you are so kind as to bestow on them. They certainly claim no advantages over those of their sister states, and are sensible of more favorable circumstances existing with many of them, and happily availed of, which our situation does not offer. But the paper respecting Monticello to which you allude was not written by a Virginian, but by a visitant from another state; and written by memory at least a dozen years after the visit. This has occasioned some lapses of recollection, and a confusion of some things in the mind of our friend, and particularly as to the volume of slanders supposed to have been cut out of newspapers and preserved. It would not indeed have been a single volume, but an Encyclopedia in bulk. But I never had such a volume. Indeed I rarely thought those libels worth reading, much less preserving and remembering. At the end of every year, I generally sorted all my pamphlets, and had them bound according to their subjects. One of these volumes consisted of personal altercations between individuals, and calumnies on each other. This was lettered on the back 'Personalities,' and is now in the library of Congress. I was in the habit also, while living apart from my family, of cutting out of the newspapers such morsels of poetry, or tales as I thought would please, and of sending them to my grand-children who pasted them on leaves of blank paper and formed them into a book.[64] These two volumes have been confounded into one in the recollection of

63. "What forbids me to speak the truth by joking?"
64. See Constance E. Thurlow and Francis L. Berkeley, Jr., comps., *The Jefferson Papers of the University of Virginia. A Calendar* (Charlottesville, 1950), item 759: "Scrapbook of Songs and Poems. [1801 *et seq.*] 204 pp."

our friend. Her poetical imagination too has heightened the scenes she visited, as well as the merits of the inhabitants to whom her society was a delightful gratification.

I have just finished reading O'Meara's Bonaparte.[65] It places him on a higher scale of understanding than I had allotted him. I had thought him the greatest of all military captains, but an indifferent statesman and misled by unworthy passions. The flashes however which escape from him in these conversations with O'Meara prove a mind of great expansion, altho' not of distinct developement and reasoning. He siezes results with rapidity and penetration, but never explains logically the process of reasoning by which he arrives at them. This book too makes us forget his atrocities for a moment in commiseration of his sufferings. I will not say that the authorities of the world, charged with the care of their country and people had not a right to confine him for life, as a Lyon or Tyger, on the principle of self-preservation. There was no safety to nations while he was permitted to roam at large. But the putting him to death in cold blood by lingering tortures of mind, by vexations, insults, and deprivations, was a degree of inhumanity to which the poisonings, and assassinations of the school of Borgia and the den of Marat never attained. The book proves also that nature had denied him the moral sense, the first excellence of well organised man. If he could seriously and repeatedly affirm that he had raised himself to power without ever having committed a crime, it proves that he wanted totally the sense of right and wrong. If he could consider the millions of human lives which he had destroyed or caused to be destroyed, the desolations of countries by plunderings, burnings and famine, the destitutions of lawful rulers of the world without the consent of their constituents, to place his brothers and sisters on their thrones, the cutting up of established societies of men and jumbling them discordantly together again at his caprice, the demolition of the fairest hopes of mankind for the recovery of their rights, and amelioration of their condition, and all the numberless train of his other enormities; the man, I say, who could consider all these as no crimes must have been a moral monster, against whom every hand should have been lifted to slay him.

You are so kind as to enquire after my health. The bone of my arm is well knitted, but my hand and fingers are in a discouraging condition, kept entirely useless by an oedematous swelling of slow amendment. God bless you and continue your good health of body and mind.

Th: Jefferson

65. Barry Edward O'Meara, *Napoleon in Exile; or, A Voice from St. Helena* ... (2nd edn., Philadelphia, 1822).

Adams to Jefferson

Quincy March 10th. 1823.

DEAR SIR.

The sight of your well known hand writing in your favour of 25. Feb. last, gave me great pleasure, as it proved your arm to be restored and your pen still manageable. May it continue till you shall become as perfect a calvinist as I am in one particular. Poor Calvins infirmities his rheumatism his Gouts and sciatics made him frequently cry out Mon dieu Jusque au quand. Lord how long! Prat once Chief Justice of New York always tormented with infirmities dreamt that he was situated on a single rock in the midst of the Atlantick ocean. He heard a voice—"Why mourns the bard Apollo bids thee rise, renounce the dust, and claim thy native skies."

The Ladies visit to Monticello has put my reader in requisition to read to me Simons travels in Switzerland.[66] I thought I had some knowledge of that country before, but I find I had no idea of it. How degenerated are the Swiss. They might defend their country against France, Austria, and Russia, neither of whom ought to be suffered to march armies over their Mountains. Those powers have practised as much tyrany and immorality as ever the Emperor Napoleon did over them or over the Royalists of Germany or Italy. Neither France Austria or Spain ought to have a foot of land in Italy.

All conquerors are alike. Every one of them. "Jura negat sibilata [i.e., sibi nata] nihil non arrogat armis.["] [67] We have nothing but fables concerning Theseus Bacchus and Hercules and even Sesostris, but I dare say that every one of them was as tyranical and immoral as Napoleon. Nebuchandnezzar is the first great conqueror of whom we have any thing like history and he was as great as any of them. Alexander and Cesar were more immoral than Napoleon. Zingis Kan was as great a conqueror as any of them and destroyed as many millions of lives and thought he had a right to the whole globe if he could subdue it. What are we to think of the crusades in which three millions of lives at least were probably sacreficed, and what right had St. Louis and Richard Coeur de Lion to Palestine and Syria more than Alexander to India, or Napoleon to Egypt and Italy. Right and justice have hard fare in this World, but there is a power above

66. Louis Simond, *Switzerland; or, A Journal of a Tour and Residence in that Country in the Years 1817, 1818, and 1819* ... (Boston, 1822).

67. "He denies that laws were made for him; he arrogates everything to himself by force of arms."

who is capable, and willing to put all things right in the end, et pour mettre chacun a sa place dans l'Universe and I doubt not he will.

Mr. English a Bostonian has published a volume of his expedition with Ishmael Pashaw up the river Nile.[68] He advanced above the third Cataract and opens a prospect of a resurrection from the dead of those vast and ancient Countries of Abyssinia and Etheopia. A free communication with India and the river Niger and the City of Tombuctou. This however is conjecture and speculation rather than certainty, but a free communication by land between Europe and India will e're long be opened. A few American steam boats, and our Quincy Stone Cutters would soon make the Nile as navigable as our Hudson Patomac or Mississippi. You see as my reason and intellect fails my imagination grows more wild and ungovernable, but my friendship remains the same. Adieu

JOHN ADAMS by proxy

Jefferson to Adams

Monticello. April 11. 23.

DEAR SIR

The wishes expressed, in your last favor, that I may continue in life and health until I become a Calvinist, at least in his exclamation of 'mon Dieu! jusque à quand'! would make me immortal. I can never join Calvin in addressing his god. He was indeed an Atheist, which I can never be; or rather his religion was Dæmonism. If ever man worshipped a false god, he did. The being described in his 5. points is not the God whom you and I acknolege and adore, the Creator and benevolent governor of the world; but a dæmon of malignant spirit. It would be more pardonable to believe in no god at all, than to blaspheme him by the atrocious attributes of Calvin. Indeed I think that every Christian sect gives a great handle to Atheism by their general dogma that, without a revelation, there would not be sufficient proof of the being of a god. Now one sixth of mankind only are supposed to be Christians: the other five sixths then, who do not believe

68. George Bethune English, successively theologian, newspaper editor, and U. S. marine, was ordered on a cruise to the Mediterranean. In Alexandria he resigned his commission to become an officer in the Egyptian army and a Mohammedan. During 1820-21 he accompanied the son of the Pasha of Egypt to eastern Sudan and wrote one of the first descriptions of that country by a white man: A Narrative of the Expedition to Dongola and Senaar (London, 1822; Boston, 1823). Walter L. Wright, Jr., "English, George Bethune," DAB, VI, 165.

in the Jewish and Christian revelation, are without a knolege of the existence of a god! This gives compleatly a gain de cause to the disciples of Ocellus, Timaeus, Spinosa, Diderot and D'Holbach. The argument which they rest on as triumphant and unanswerable is that, in every hypothesis of Cosmogony you must admit an eternal pre-existence of something; and according to the rule of sound philosophy, you are never to employ two principles to solve a difficulty when one will suffice. They say then that it is more simple to believe at once in the eternal pre-existence of the world, as it is now going on, and may for ever go on by the principle of reproduction which we see and witness, than to believe in the eternal pre-existence of an ulterior cause, or Creator of the world, a being whom we see not, and know not, of whose form substance and mode or place of existence, or of action no sense informs us, no power of the mind enables us to delineate or comprehend. On the contrary I hold (without appeal to revelation) that when we take a view of the Universe, in it's parts general or particular, it is impossible for the human mind not to percieve and feel a conviction of design, consummate skill, and indefinite power in every atom of it's composition. The movements of the heavenly bodies, so exactly held in their course by the balance of centrifugal and centripetal forces, the structure of our earth itself, with it's distribution of lands, waters and atmosphere, animal and vegetable bodies, examined in all their minutest particles, insects mere atoms of life, yet as perfectly organised as man or mammoth, the mineral substances, their generation and uses, it is impossible, I say, for the human mind not to believe that there is, in all this, design, cause and effect, up to an ultimate cause, a fabricator of all things from matter and motion, their preserver and regulator while permitted to exist in their present forms, and their regenerator into new and other forms. We see, too, evident proofs of the necessity of a superintending power to maintain the Universe in it's course and order. Stars, well known, have disappeared, new ones have come into view, comets, in their incalculable courses, may run foul of suns and planets and require renovation under other laws; certain races of animals are become extinct; and, were there no restoring power, all existences might extinguish successively, one by one, until all should be reduced to a shapeless chaos. So irresistible are these evidences of an intelligent and powerful Agent that, of the infinite numbers of men who have existed thro' all time, they have believed, in the proportion of a million at least to Unit, in the hypothesis of an eternal pre-existence of a creator, rather than in that of a self-existent Universe. Surely this unanimous sentiment renders this more probable than that of the few in the other hypothesis. Some early Christians indeed have believed in the coeternal pre-existance of both the Creator and the world, without changing their relation of cause and effect. That this was the opinion of St. Thomas, we are informed by Cardinal Toleto, in these words 'Deus ab æterno fuit jam omnipotens, sicut cum produxit mundum. Ab æterno potuit producere mundum.—Si sol ab æterno esset, lumen ab æterno esset; et si pes, similiter vestigium. At lumen et vestigium effectus sunt efficientis solis et pedis; potuit ergo cum causâ æterna effectus co-æterna esse. Cujus sententiæ est S. Thomas Theologorum primus.' [69] Cardinal Toleta.

Of the nature of this being we know nothing. Jesus tells us that 'God is a spirit.' 4. John 24. but without defining what a spirit is 'πνευμα ὁ Θεος.' Down to the 3d. century we know that it was still deemed material; but of a lighter subtler matter than our gross bodies. So says Origen. 'Deus igitur, cui anima similis est, juxta Originem, reapte corporalis est; sed graviorum tantum ratione corporum incorporeus.' [70] These are the words of Huet in his commentary on Origen. Origen himself says 'appelatio ἀσωματον apud nostros scriptores est inusitata et incognita.' [71] So also Tertullian 'quis autem negabit Deum esse corpus, etsi deus spiritus? Spiritus etiam corporis sui generis, in suâ effigie.' [72] Tertullian. These two fathers were of the 3d. century. Calvin's character of this supreme being seems chiefly copied from that of the Jews. But the reformation of these blasphemous attributes, and substitution of those more worthy, pure and sublime, seems to have been the chief object of Jesus in his discources to the Jews: and his doctrine of the Cosmogony of the world is very clearly laid down in the 3 first verses of the 1st. chapter of John, in these words, ἐν αρχη ἦν ὁ λόγος, καὶ ὁ λόγος ἦν πρὸς τὸν Θεόν, καὶ ἦν ὁ λόγος. Οὗτος ἦν ἐν ἀρχῃ πρὸς τὸν Θεόν. Πάντα δι' αντοῦ ἐγένετο. Καὶ κωρὶς αὐτοῦ ἐγένετο οὐδὲ ἓν, ὃ γέγονεν.

Which truly translated means 'in the beginning God existed, and reason (or mind) was with God, and that mind was God. This was in the beginning with God. All things were created by it, and without it was made not one thing which was made'. Yet this text, so plainly declaring the doctrine of Jesus that the world was created by the supreme, intelligent being, has been perverted by modern Christians to build up a second person of their tritheism by a mistranslation of the word λογος. One of it's legit-

---

69. "God has been omnipotent forever, just as when he made the world. He has had the power to make the world forever. If the sun were in existence forever, light would have been in existence forever; and if a foot then likewise a footprint. But light and footprint are the effects of an efficient sun and foot; therefore the effect has had the power to be co-eternal with the eternal cause. Of this opinion is St. Thomas, the first of the theologians."

70. "God, therefore, to whom the soul is similar, in consequences of its origin, is in reality corporeal; but He is incorporeal in comparison with so much heavier bodies."

71. "The word ἀσωματον, among our writers, is not used or known."

72. "Yet who will deny that God is body, although God is spirit? Indeed He is spirit of His own type of body, in His own image."

imate meanings indeed is 'a word.' But, in that sense, it makes an unmeaning jargon: while the other meaning 'reason', equally legitimate, explains rationally the eternal preexistence of God, and his creation of the world. Knowing how incomprehensible it was that 'a word,' the mere action or articulation of the voice and organs of speech could create a world, they undertake to make of this articulation a second preexisting being, and ascribe to him, and not to God, the creation of the universe. The Atheist here plumes himself on the uselessness of such a God, and the simpler hypothesis of a self-existent universe. The truth is that the greatest enemies to the doctrines of Jesus are those calling themselves the expositors of them, who have perverted them for the structure of a system of fancy absolutely incomprehensible, and without any foundation in his genuine words. And the day will come when the mystical generation of Jesus, by the supreme being as his father in the womb of a virgin will be classed with the fable of the generation of Minerva in the brain of Jupiter. But we may hope that the dawn of reason and freedom of thought in these United States will do away [with] all this artificial scaffolding, and restore to us the primitive and genuine doctrines of this the most venerated reformer of human errors.

So much for your quotation of Calvin's 'mon dieu! jusqu'a quand' in which, when addressed to the God of Jesus, and our God, I join you cordially, and await his time and will with more readiness than reluctance. May we meet there again, in Congress, with our antient Colleagues, and recieve with them the seal of approbation 'Well done, good and faithful servants.'

TH: JEFFERSON

Adams to Jefferson

Quincy. Aug. 15th. '23

Watchman! what of the night!? Is darkness that may be felt to prevail over the whole world? Or can you perceive any rays of a returning dawn? Is the devil to be the "Lords anointed" over the whole globe? Or do you forsee the fulfilment of the prophecies according to Dr. Priestly's interpretation of them? I know not but I have in some of my familiar and frivolous letters to you told the story four times over, but if I have I never applied it so well as now. Not long after the denouement of the tragedy of Louis 16th. when I was vice-President, my friend the Dr. came to breakfast with me alone. He was very sociable, very learned and eloquent on the subject of the French revolution. It was opening a new era in the world and pre-senting a near view of the millenium. I listened I heard with great attention and perfect sang froid. At last I asked the Dr. do you really believe the French will establish a free democratical government in France? He answered; I do firmly believe it. Will you give me leave to ask you upon what grounds you entertain this opinion? Is it from anything you ever read in history—is there any instance of a Roman Catholic monarchy of five and twenty millions at once converted into a free and rational people? No, I know of no instance like it. Is there anything in your knowledge of human nature derived from books or experience that any nation ancient or modern consisting of such multitudes of ignorant people ever were or ever can be converted suddenly into materials capable of conducting a free government especially a democratical republic? No, I know of nothing of the kind. Well then Sir what is the ground of your opinion? The answer was, my opinion is founded altogether upon revelation and the prophecies; I take it that the ten horns of the great beast in revela-tions, mean the ten crowned heads of Europe: and that the execution of the king of France is the falling off of the first of those horns; and the nine monarchies of Europe will fall one after another in the same way. Such was the enthusiasm of that great man, that reasoning machine. After all however he did recollect himself so far as to say, There is however a possibility of doubt, for I read yesterday a book put into my hands by a gentleman, a volume of travels, written by a french gentleman, in 1659,[73] in which he says he had been travelling a whole year in England, into every part of it and conversed freely with all ranks of people. He found the whole nation earnestly engaged in discussing and contriving a form of government for their future regulation. There was but one point in which they all agreed and in that they were unanimous, that monarchy nobility and prelacy never would exist in England again. The Dr. then paused, and said, Yet in the very next year the whole nation called in the King and ran mad with monarchy nobility and prelacy. I am no king killer merely because they are kings—poor creatures they know no better —they believe sincerely and conscientiously that God made them to rule the world. I would not therefore behead them or send them to St. Helena to be treated as Bonaparte was, but I would shut them up like the man in the iron mask, feed them well, give them as much finery as they pleas'd

73. This volume may have been S[amuel] de Sorbière, *Relation d'un voyage en Angleterre, où sont touchées plusieurs choses qui regardent l'état des sciences et de la religion et autres matières curieuses* (Paris, 1664), translated as *A Voyage to Eng-land containing Many Things relating to the State of Learning &c.* (London, 1709); or John Evelyn, *A Character of England as It was Lately presented in a Letter to a Noble Man of France* (London, 1659), reprinted in *Harleian Miscellany*, 10 (1813), 189-98.

until they could be converted to right reason and common sense. I have nothing to communicate from this part of the country except that you must not be surprised if you hear something wonderful in Boston before long. With my profound respects for your family and half a centurys affection for yourself I am your humble servant.

JOHN ADAMS

Jefferson to Adams

Monticello Sep. 4. 23.

DEAR SIR

Your letter of Aug. 15. was recieved in due time, and with the welcome of every thing which comes from you. With it's opinions on the difficulties of revolutions, from despotism to freedom, I very much concur. The generation which commences a revolution can rarely compleat it. Habituated from their infancy to passive submission of body and mind to their kings and priests, they are not qualified, when called on, to think and provide for themselves and their inexperience, their ignorance and bigotry make them instruments often, in the hands of the Bonapartes and Iturbides to defeat their own rights and purposes. This is the present situation of Europe and Spanish America. But it is not desperate. The light which has been shed on mankind by the art of printing has eminently changed the condition of the world. As yet that light has dawned on the midling classes only of the men of Europe. The kings and the rabble of equal ignorance, have not yet recieved it's rays; but it continues to spread. And, while printing is preserved, it can no more recede than the sun return on his course. A first attempt to recover the right of self-government may fail; so may a 2d. a 3d. etc., but as a younger, and more instructed race comes on, the sentiment becomes more and more intuitive, and a 4th. a 5th. or some subsequent one of the ever renewed attempts will ultimately succeed. In France the 1st. effort was defeated by Robespierre, the 2d. by Bonaparte, the 3d. by Louis XVIII. and his holy allies; another is yet to come, and all Europe, Russia excepted, has caught the spirit, and all will attain representative government, more or less perfect. This is now well understood to be a necessary check on kings, whom they will probably think it more prudent to chain and tame, than to exterminate. To attain all this however rivers of blood must yet flow, and years of desolation pass over. Yet the object is worth rivers of blood, and years of desolation for what inheritance so valuable can man leave to his posterity? The spirit of the Spaniard and his deadly and eternal hatred to a Frenchman, gives me much confidence that he will never submit, but finally defeat this atrocious violation of the laws of god and man under which he is suffering; and the wisdom and firmness of the Cortes afford reasonable hope that that nation will settle down in a temperate representative government, with an Executive properly subordinated to that. Portugal, Italy, Prussia, Germany, Greece will follow suit. You and I shall look down from another world on these glorious atchievements to man, which will add to the joys even of heaven.

I observe your toast of Mr. Jay on the 4th. of July, wherein you say that the omission of his signature to the Declaration of Independence was by *accident.* Our impressions as to this fact being different, I shall be glad to have mine corrected, if wrong. Jay, you know, had been in constant opposition to our laboring majority. Our estimate, at the time, was that he, Dickinson and Johnson of Maryland by their ingenuity, perseverance and partiality to our English connection, had constantly kept us a year behind where we ought to have been in our preparations and proceedings. From about the date of the Virginia instructions of May 15. 76. to declare Independance Mr. Jay absented himself from Congress, and never came there again until Dec. 78. Of course he had no part in the discussions or decision of that question. The instructions to their delegates by the Convention of New York, then sitting, to sign the Declaration, were presented to Congress on the 15th. of July only, and on that day the journals shew the absence of Mr. Jay by a letter recieved from him, as they had done as early as the 29th. of May by another letter. And, I think, he had been omitted by the Convention on a new election of Delegates when they changed their instructions.[74] Of this last fact however having no evidence but an antient impression, I shall not affirm it. But whether so or not, no agency of *accident* appears in the case. This error of fact however, whether yours or mine, is of little consequence to the public. But truth being as cheap as error, it is as well to rectify it for our own satisfaction.

I have had a fever of about three weeks during the last and preceding month, from which I am entirely recovered except as to strength. Ever and affectionately yours

TH: JEFFERSON

74. In April 1776 Jay was elected to the New York Provincial Congress which met on May 14. In June he introduced a resolution demanding that the New York delegates to the Continental Congress consult the Provincial Congress before supporting independence. Jay was chairman of the committee to consider the Declaration when the New York Congress received its copy on July 9; and the committee recommended its adoption. Jay served as chief justice of New York until 1779 and did not resume his seat in the Continental Congress until Dec. 1778. George Pellew, *John Jay* (N. Y., 1890), 53-58, Chaps. III-IV.

Adams to Jefferson

Quincy September 18th. 1823.

DEAR SIR

With much pleasure I have heard read the sure words of prophecy in your letter of Sep. 4th. It is melancholy to contemplate the cruel wars, dessolutions of Countries, and ocians of blood which must occure, before rational principles, and rational systems of Government can prevail and be established. But as these are inevitable we must content ourselves with the consolations which you from sound and sure reasons so clearly suggest. Thes[e] hopes are as well founded as our fears of the contrary evils; on the whole, the prospect is cheering; I have lately undertaken to read Algernon Sidney on Government. There is a great difference in reading a Book at four and twenty, and at Eighty Eight, as often as I have read it, and fumbled it over; it now excites fresh admiration, that this work has excited so little interest in the literary world, As splendid an Edition of it, as the art of printing can produce, as well as for the intrinsick merit of the work, as for the proof it brings of the bitter sufferings of the advocates of Liberty from that time to this; and to show the slow progress of Moral phylosophical political Illumination in the world ought to be now published in America.

It is true that Mr. Jay, Mr. Dickinson, and Mr. Johnson, contributed to retard many vigorous measures, and particularly the vote of Independence untill he left Congress, but I have reason to think he would have concured in that vote when it was taken if he had been there. His absence was accidental. Congress on the fifteenth of May preceeding, as I remember had recommended to all the States to abolish all authority under the Crown, and institute and organize a new Government under the Authority of the People. Mr. Jay had promoted this resolution in New York by adviseing them to call a Convention to frame a New Constitution; he had been chosen a Member of that Convention, and called home by his Constituents to assist in it. And as Duane told me he had gone home with his Letter to Withe in his pocket for his Model and foundation, and the same Duane after the Constitution appeared asked me if it was not sufficiently conformable to my letter to Wythe.[75] I answered him I believed it would do very well. Mr. Jay was immediately appointed Chief Justice of the State,

75. JA to George Wythe, Jan. [?] 1776, "Thoughts on Government [1776]," *Works*, IV, 191, 193-200.

and obliged to enter immediately on the duties of his Office, which occasioned his detention from Congress afterwards, but I have no doubt, had he been in Congress at the time he would have subscribed to the Declaration of Independence. He would have been neither recalled by his Constituents nor have left Congress himself, like Mr. Dickinson, Mr. Willing, Governor Livingston and several others.

Nearly as I feel for the Spanish Patriots I fear the most sensible Men among them have little confidence in their Constitution which appears to me is modeled upon that in France of the Year 1789, in which the soverignty in a single assembly was every thing and the executive nothing. The Spaniards have adopted all this, with the singular addition that the members of the Cortes can serve only two years. What rational being can have any well grounded confidence in such a Constitution?

As you write so easy, and so well, I pray you to write me as often as possible, for nothing revives my spirits so much as your letters, except the society of my Son and his Family, who are now happily with me after an absence of two Years. I am Sir, with sentiments of affection and Respect Your Ancient Friend and humble Servant

JOHN ADAMS

Jefferson to Adams

Monticello. Oct. 12. 23.

DEAR SIR

I do not write with the ease which your letter of Sep. 18. supposes. Crippled wrists and fingers make writing slow and laborious. But, while writing to you, I lose the sense of these things, in the recollection of antient times, when youth and health made happiness out of every thing. I forget for a while the hoary winter of age, when we can think of nothing but how to keep ourselves warm, and how to get rid of our heavy hours until the friendly hand of death shall rid us of all at once. Against this tedium vitae ["weariness of life"] however I am fortunately mounted on a Hobby, which indeed I should have better managed some 30. or 40. years ago, but whose easy amble is still sufficient to give exercise and amusement to an Octogenary rider. This is the establishment of an University, on a scale more comprehensive, and in a country more healthy and central than our old William and Mary, which these obstacles have long kept in a state of languor and inefficiency. But the tardiness with which such works proceed may render it doubtful whether I shall live to see it go into action.[76]

Putting aside these things however for the present, I write this letter as due to a friendship co-eval with our government, and now attempted to be poisoned, when too late in life to be replaced by new affections. I had for some time observed, in the public papers, dark hints and mysterious innuendoes of a correspondence of yours with a friend, to whom you had opened your bosom without reserve, and which was to be made public by that friend, or his representative. And now it is said to be actually published.[77] It has not yet reached us, but extracts have been given, and such as seemed most likely to draw a curtain of separation between you and myself. Were there no other motive than that of indignation against the author of this outrage on private confidence, whose shaft seems to have been aimed at yourself more particularly, this would make it the duty of every honorable mind to disappoint that aim, by opposing to it's impression a seven-fold shield of apathy and insensibility. With me however no such armour is needed. The circumstances of the times, in which we have happened to live, and the partiality of our friends, at a particular period, placed us in a state of apparent opposition, which some might suppose to be personal also; and there might not be wanting those who wish'd to make it so, by filling our ears with malignant falsehoods, by dressing up hideous phantoms of their own creation, presenting them to you under my name, to me under your's, and endeavoring to instill into our minds things concerning each other the most destitute of truth. And if there had been, at any time, a moment when we were off our guard, and in a temper to let the whispers of these people make us forget what we had known of each other for so many years, and years of so much trial, yet all men who have attended to the workings of the human mind, who have seen the false colours under which passion sometimes dresses the actions and motives of others, have seen also these passions subsiding with time and reflection, dissipating, like mists before the rising sun, and

76. The first session of the University of Virginia was held during 1825-26.

77. *Correspondence between the Hon. John Adams, Late President of the United States, and the Late Wm. Cunningham, Esq., beginning in 1803, and ending in 1813* (Boston, 1823). William Cunningham, a distant relative of JA, had requested information of him which could be used against TJ as candidate for re-election to the presidency in 1804. JA's replies, characteristically frank, were written with the proviso that Cunningham would never publish them during JA's lifetime. But Cunningham died first, a suicide in May 1823, and his son immediately published the letters. Randall, *Jefferson*, III, 493. The son's purpose was to defeat J. Q. Adams in his campaigning for the presidency by casting aspersions on the character of the Adams family. J. Q. Adams recognized the purpose of the publication and regretted that such "venomous business" should have been introduced into the campaign. Charles Francis Adams, ed., *Memoirs of John Quincy Adams* (Philadelphia, 1875), VI, 176; Chinard, *John Adams*, 320-21, 342.

restoring to us the sight of all things in their true shape and colours. It would be strange indeed if, at our years, we were to go an age back to hunt up imaginary, or forgotten facts, to disturb the repose of affections so sweetening to the evening of our lives. Be assured, my dear Sir, that I am incapable of recieving the slightest impression from the effort now made to plant thorns on the pillow of age, worth, and wisdom, and to sow tares between friends who have been such for near half a century. Beseeching you then not to suffer your mind to be disquieted by this wicked attempt to poison it's peace, and praying you to throw it by, among the things which have never happened, I add sincere assurances of my unabated, and constant attachment, friendship and respect.

TH: JEFFERSON

Adams to Jefferson

Quincy 10th. November. 1823.

DEAR SIR

Your last letter was brought to me from the Post office when at breakfast with my family. I bade one of the misses open the budget; she reported a letter from Mr. Jefferson and two or three newspapers. A letter from Mr. Jefferson, says I, I know what the substance is before I open it. There is no secrets between Mr. Jefferson and me, and I cannot read it; therefore you may open and read it When it was done, it was followed by an universal exclamation, The best letter that ever was written, and round it went through the whole table—How generous! how noble! how magnanimous! I said that it was just such a letter as I expected, only it was infinitely better expressed. A universal cry that the letter ought to be printed. No, hold, certainly not without Mr. Jefferson's express leave.

As to the blunder-buss itself which was loaded by a miserable melancholly man, out of his wits, and left by him to another to draw the trigger. The only affliction it has given me is sincere grief of the melancholly fate of both. The peevish and fretful effusions of politicians in difficult and dangerous conjunctures from the agony of their hearts are not worth remembering, much less of laying to heart.[78]

78. That the *Correspondence* between JA and Cunningham was published for political purposes directed against J. Q. Adams (a point disregarded by JA in the present letter) is borne out by the fact that several persons who put up money for the publication were later appointed as postmasters or collectors of customs by President Andrew Jackson. Adams, ed., *Memoirs of J. Q. Adams*, VI, 176n., VIII, 181.

The published correspondence is garbled. All the letters are left out that could explain the whole mystery. The vengeance against me was wholly occasioned because he could not persuade me to recommend him to the national government for a mission abroad or the government of a territory—services for which I did not think him qualified.

I salute your fire-side with cordial esteem and affection. J. A. In the 89 year of his age still too fat to last much longer

JOHN ADAMS

Adams to Jefferson

Quincy December 29th '23

DEAR SIR

I return your letter at your request signified by Gen. Dearborn, though it has been such a cordial to my heart. I feel much reluctance to release it. Since it has appeared in print it has been received with applause great and universal.[79] Our fellow citizens are determined to elect a President avec connaisance de cause, for the question has [been] in discussion in every nook in the United States for seven years. I should like to see an election for a President in the British empire or in France or in Spain or in Prussia or Russia by way of experiment. We go on pretty well, for we use no other artillery than goose quills, and our ink is not so deleterious as language and grape.

My old imagination is kindling into a kind of missionary enthusiasm for the cause of the Greeks.[80] My feelings go on with N. York, Pensylvania and Massachusetts, but after all they are feelings rather than reasonings. I confess that my information is not sufficiently extensive to forsee the result, but I comfort myself with the maxim of our friend Jebb, that no effort in favour of virtue is lost. I rely with confidence on the wisdom of our government to conduct us in the road of honour and the most probable path of safety. With the compliments of the season and with the

79. TJ to Henry Dearborn, Aug. 17, 1821, Lipscomb and Bergh, eds., *Writings*, XV, 329-30. Referring to JA, TJ wrote: "I am happy to hear of his good health. I think he will out live us all, I mean the Declaration-men. . . ."

80. In his Seventh Annual Message to Congress, Dec. 2, 1823, President Monroe spoke on behalf of "the heroic struggle of the Greeks," just before he enunciated the "Monroe Doctrine." Richardson, ed., *Messages and Papers of the Presidents*, II, 217.

best wishes for your long continuance in life and health I remain your affectionate friend

JOHN ADAMS

Jefferson to Adams

Monticello July 11. 24.

DEAR SIR

My friend and correspondent of Richmond, Colo. Bernard Peyton will have the honor of delivering you this letter. He was a worthy officer of the late war, and now an equally worthy member of the mercantile body. Proposing to visit Boston, he has the natural ambition of being presented to the first of the revolutionary characters now living. I ask, of your friendship to give him a few moments of your time, the remembrance of which will to him be a gratification thro' life. I have pleasure in availing myself of every occasion of repeating to you the assurances of my constant friendship and respectful consideration.

TH: JEFFERSON

Adams to Jefferson

Quincy July 24th 1824

DEAR SIR

Mr. Benjamin Parker Richardson, a Grandson of a neighbour of mine, who has lived in harmony with me for almost eighty nine years, is very desirous of seeing the venerable Author of the Declaration of Independence, and as this is a virtuous curiosity which I always applaud and encourage in our young men, I have ventured to give him a line of introduction to you. A freedom which I have taken too often, especially as the reciprocity has always been on my side—never having received, as I recollect, in any one instance, a similar introduction from you.

I still breathe, which will not be long, but while I do I shall breathe out wishes for the welfare of mankind, hoping that they will daily become more deserving of it.

You are quite a young gentleman in comparison with your old friend

JOHN ADAMS.

Adams to Jefferson

Quincy November 15th. 1824

DEAR SIR

Your friend Professor Ticknor is bound upon a Tour in Virginia. Though he needs no introduction to you, he has requested a letter from me, and I cannot deny him. He carries his Lady with him, who is rich enough, and handsome enough, and amiable enough, and what can one say more? [81]

Is the present calm in the Political World to continue long or not? Our controversy will all be settled in a short time, and then we shall all submit like lambs. I hope the future Administration [82] will be as wise, as prudent, and as fortunate as the present, and then we shall all set down as quietly as Lambs.

Advanced fifteen days in my ninetieth year, I salute you as cordially as ever. I envy Mrs. Ticknor the pleasure of becoming acquainted with your family of Grand Daughters—my love to Mrs. Randolph.

You and I have been favored with a visit from our old friend General La Fayette.[83] What a wonderful Man at his Age to undergo the fatigues of such long journeys and constant feasts. I was greatly delighted with the sight of him and the little conversation I had with him.

France changes her King as easily as her glove.[84] His present Majesty, it is said, has commenced his reign by some very popular acts, and very wise ones, such as more freedom to the press, and unlimited Amnesty to all political offenders. Vale—

JOHN ADAMS

81. George Ticknor had married in 1821 Anna Eliot, daughter of the prosperous Boston merchant Samuel Eliot. Mr. and Mrs. Ticknor, accompanied by Daniel Webster, visited TJ in Dec. 1824. Ticknor found Mr. Jefferson "very little altered from what he was ten years ago, very active, lively, and happy...." Ticknor to William H. Prescott, Monticello, Dec. 16, 1824, Hillard, ed., *Life of Ticknor*, I, 348.

82. This proved to be the administration of J. Q. Adams, after the final decision in the election of 1824 was made in the House of Representatives.

83. At the invitation of President Monroe, Lafayette visited the United States during Aug. 1824–Sept. 1825. Symbol of victorious America of the revolutionary period, Lafayette was received everywhere with the wildest enthusiasm. He dined with Adams in Quincy on Aug. 29 and spent ten days with Jefferson at Monticello, Nov. 4-15, 1824. Edgar E. Brandon, ed., *Lafayette, Guest of the Nation...in 1824-1825* (Oxford, Ohio, 1944-57), I, 121, 129-30; III, 126-31, 137.

84. On the death of Louis XVIII in 1824, his brother Charles X, uncompromising reactionary, became king of France. He abdicated during the July Revolution of 1830.

Jefferson to Adams

Monticello Jan. 8. 25.

DEAR SIR

It is long since I have written to you. This proceeds from the difficulty of writing with my crippled wrists, and from an unwillingness to add to your inconveniences of either reading by the eyes, or writing by the hands of others. The account I recieve of your physical situation afflicts me sincerely. But if body or mind was one of them to give way, it is a great comfort that it is the mind which remains whole, and that it's vigor, and that of memory, continues firm. Your hearing too is good as I am told. In this you have the advantage of me. The dullness of mine makes me lose much of the conversation of the world, and much a stranger to what is passing in it. Acquiescence is the only pillow, altho' not always a soft one. I have had one advantage of you. This presidential election has given me few anxieties. With you this must have been impossible, independently of the question whether we are at last to end our days under a civil or a military government? I am comforted and protected from other solicitudes by the cares of our University. In some departments of science we believed Europe to be in advance before us, and thought it would advance ourselves were we to draw thence instructors in these branches, and thus to improve our science, as we have done our manufactures, by borrowed skill. I have been much squibbed for this; perhaps by disappointed applicants for professorships to which they were deemed incompetent. We wait only the arrival of three of the professors engaged in England to open our university.[85]

I have lately been reading the most extraordinary of all books, and at the same time the most demonstrative by numerous and unequivocal facts. It is Flourens' Experiments on the functions of the Nervous system, in vertebrated animals. He takes out the cerebrum compleatly, leaving the cerebellum and other parts of the system uninjured. The animal loses all it's senses of hearing, seeing, feeling, smelling, tasting, is totally deprived of will, intelligence, memory, perception etc. yet lives for months in perfect health, with all it's powers of motion, but without moving but

85. TJ sent his friend Francis Walker Gilmer abroad in 1824 to secure professors for the new University. In England he engaged Professors George Long (ancient languages), Thomas Hewett Key (mathematics), George Blaetterman (modern languages), Charles Bonnycastle (natural philosophy), and Robley Dunglison (anatomy). Herbert B. Adams, *Thomas Jefferson and the University of Virginia* (Washington, 1888), 111-18; Davis, ed., *Correspondence of Jefferson and Gilmer*, 113.

on external excitement, starving even on a pile of grain unless crammed down it's throat; in a state, in short, of the most absolute stupidity. He takes the cerebellum out of others, leaving the cerebrum untouched. The animal retains all it's senses, faculties and understanding, but loses the power of regulated motion, and exhibits all the symptoms of drunkenness. While he makes incisions in the cerebrum and cerebellum, lengthwise and crosswise which heal and get well, a puncture in the medulla elongata is instant death, and many other most interesting things, too long for a letter. Cabanis had proved, from the anatomical structure of certain portions of the human frame, that they might be capable of recieving from the Creator the faculty of thinking.[86] Flourens proves that the cerebrum is the thinking organ, and that life and health may continue, and the animal be entirely without thought, if deprived of that organ. I wish to see what the spiritualists will say to this. Whether, in this state, the soul remains in the body deprived of it's essence of thought, or whether it leaves it as in death, and where it goes? His memoirs and experiments have been reported on with approbation by a committee of the Institute, composed of Cuvier, Bertholet, Dumeril, Portal and Pinel. But all this you and I shall know, when we meet again in another place, and at no distant period. In the mean time, that the revived powers of your frame, and the Anodyne of philosophy may preserve you from all suffering, is my sincere and affectionate prayer.

TH: JEFFERSON

Adams to Jefferson

Quincy 22d January 1825

DEAR SIR

Your letter of the 8th has revived me. It is true, that my hearing has been very good, but the last year it has decayed so much, that I am in a worse situation than you are; I cannot hear any of the common conversation of my family, without calling upon them to repeat in a louder tone.

The presidential election has given me less anxiety than I, myself could have imagined. The next administration will be a troublesom one to whomso-ever it falls. And our John has been too much worn to contend much longer with conflicting factions. I call him our John, because when you was at Cul de sac at Paris, he appeared to me to be almost as much

86. See TJ to JA, March 14, 1820, above, 562.

your boy as mine. I have often speculated upon the consequences that would have ensued from my takeing your advice, to send him to William and Mary College in Virginia for an Education.

As to the decision of your Author, though I wish to see the Book I look upon it as a mere game at push-pin. Incision knives will never discover the distinction between matter and spirit, or whether there is any or not. That there is an active principle of power in the Universe is apparent, but in what substance that active principle of power resides, is past our investigation. The faculties of our understanding are not adiquate to penetrate the Universe. Let us do our duty which is, to do as we would be done by, and that one would think, could not be difficult, if we honestly aim at it.

Your University is a noble employment in your old Age, and your ardor for its success, does you honour, but I do not approve of your sending to Europe for Tutors, and Professors. I do believe there are sufficent scholars in America to fill your Professorships and Tutorships with more active ingenuity, and independent minds, than you can bring from Europe. The Europeans are all deeply tainted with prejudices both Ecclesiastical, and Temporal which they can never get rid of; they are all infected with Episcopal and Presbyterian Creeds, and confessions of faith, They all believe that great principle, which has produced this boundless Universe. Newtons Universe, and Hershells universe, came down to this little Ball, to be spit-upon by Jews; and untill this awful blasphemy is got rid of, there never will be any liberal science in the world.

I salute your fire side, with best affection, and best wishes for their health, wealth, and prosperity Ever your friend

JOHN ADAMS

Adams to Jefferson

Quincy 23rd. January 1825.

MY DEAR SIR.

We think ourselves possessed or at least we boast that we are so of Liberty of conscience on all subjects and of the right of free inquiry and private judgment, in all cases and yet how far are we from these exalted privileges in fact. There exists I believe throughout the whole Christian world a law which makes it blasphemy to deny or to doubt the divine inspiration of all the books of the old and new Testaments from Genesis to Revelations. In most countries of Europe it is punished by fire at the stake, or the rack or the wheel: in England itself it is punished by boring through the tongue with a red hot poker: in America it is not much better, even in our Massachusetts which I believe upon the whole is as temperate and moderate in religious zeal as most of the States. A law was made in the latter end of the last century repealing the cruel punishments of the former laws but substituting fine and imprisonment upon all those blasphemers upon any book of the old Testament or new. Now what free inquiry when a writer must surely encounter the risk of fine or imprisonment for adducing any argument for investigation into the divine authority of those books? Who would run the risk of translating Volney's Recherches Nouvelles? who would run the risk of translating Dupuis? but I cannot enlarge upon this subject, though I have it much at heart. I think such laws a great embarassment, great obstructions to the improvement of the human mind. Books that cannot bear examination certainly ought not to be established as divine inspiration by penal laws. It is true few persons appear desirous to put such laws in execution and it is also true that some few persons are hardy enough to venture to depart from them; but as long as they continue in force as laws the human mind must make an awkward and clumsy progress in its investigations. I wish they were repealed. The substance and essence of Christianity as I understand it is eternal and unchangeable and will bear examination forever but it has been mixed with extraneous ingredients, which I think will not bear examination and they ought to be separated. Adieu

JOHN ADAMS

Jefferson to Adams

Monticello Feb. 15. 25.[87]

DEAR SIR

The people of Europe seem still to think that America is a mere garden plat, and that whatever is sent to one place is at home as to every other. The volume I forward you by this mail was found on Majr. Cartwright's death, to have in his own handwriting an address for you altho' mistaking your Christian name. His friends having occ[asio]n to write to me

87. This letter is a draft in TJ's hand, in Jefferson Papers, Lib. Cong. See JA to TJ. April 19, 1825, below, 610.

on another subject, and supposing we were but next door n[eigh]bors sent this vol. to N. Y. under my address, whence it has travelled post to this place, and must now travel back again and thence to the point to which it o[ugh]t to have gone at first.

I sincerely congratulate you on the high gratific[atio]n which the issue of the late election must have afforded you. It must excite ineffable feelings in the breast of a father to have lived to see a son to whose educ[atio]n and happiness his life has been devoted so eminently distinguished by the voice of his country. Nor do I see any reason to suppose the next adm[inistratio]n will be so difficult as in your favor of Jan. 22. you seemed to expect. So deeply are the principles of order, and of obedience to law impressed on the minds of our citizens generally that I am persuaded there will be as immediate an acquiescence in the will of the majority as if Mr. Adams had been the choice of every man. The scriblers in newspapers may for a while express their disapp[oint]m[en]t in angry squibs; but these will evaporate without influence[in]g the public functionaries, nor will they prevent their harmonising with their associates in the transaction of public affairs. Nights of rest to you and days of tranquility are the wishes I tender you with my affect[iona]te respects

TH: J.

Adams to Jefferson

Quincy 25th. Feby. 1825

DEAR SIR

Every line from you exhilarates my spirits and gives me a glow of pleasure, but your kind congratulations are a solid comfort to my heart. The good-natured and good-humoured acquiescence of the friends of all the candidates gives me a comfortable hope that your prediction may be fulfilled, that the ensuing administration will not be so difficult as in a former letter I had apprehended.

Here we have lost Eustace in whom the people appeared to be better united than under any former Governor, but we have a prospect now of a successor in Lincoln, in whom the people promise to be still more united; so that it is probable that this State will not be so troublesome to the National administration as it was some time ago.

I had not heard of the death of Major Cartwright. That gentleman has been an anxious and laborious writer against boroughs and borough-mongers for more than fifty years. He appears to have had an ardent love for liberty but he never understood the system necessary to secure it— One of those ardent spirits whose violent principles defeated all their benevolent purposes, of whom Horne Took was the most eminent and the great Greek scholar another.[88]

I look back with rapture to those golden days when Virginia and Massachusetts lived and acted together like a band of brothers and I hope it will not be long before they may say redeunt saturnia regna,[89] when I hope the world will hear no more of Hartford Convention or Virginian Armories.[90]

Have you read Genl. Smyth's Apocalypse? I wish he had read Dupuis. This Genl. Smyth appears to have an ardent, inquisitive head. I like him much for his curiosity. My old friend Randolph, whose fierce fire appears to have cooled down into a more moderate and dignified light and splendour, appears to have lost some of his animosity against me. He has not honoured me with a compliment for a year or two.

I wish your health may continue to the last much better than mine. The little strength of mind and the considerable strength of body that I once possessed appear to be all gone, but while I breathe I shall be your friend. We shall meet again, so wishes and so believes your friend, but if we are disappointed we shall never know it.

JOHN ADAMS

Adams to Jefferson

Quincy 19th April 1825

DEAR SIR

Mr. Charles Sigourney and lady, a respectable pair in Hartford, Connecticut, the Husband a Son of my old friend in Amsterdam, and the

88. Probably Richard Bentley (1662-1742), master of Trinity College, Cambridge, who was influential in the restoration of classical learning in Great Britain. *Dict. Nat. Biog.*, IV, 306-14.

89. "The golden age is returning."

90. The Virginian Armory was built in 1798 as a part of the regular program of state defense, but during the hysteria over the Alien and Sedition Acts the Federalists charged that Virginia had taxed its people to buy arms for use against the federal government. In the session of Congress, 1816-17, John Randolph of Roanoke made some loose remarks about Virginia's Armory in Richmond having been built "to resist, by force, the encroachments of the then Administration upon her indisputable rights." Professor Davidson has blasted the myth by pointing out that a program for defense was not new in Virginia in 1798 and that the Armory was authorized before the Alien and Sedition Acts were passed. Philip G. Davidson, "Virginia and the Alien and Sedition Acts," *Amer. Hist. Rev.*, 36 (1930-31), 336-42.

Wife a very conspicuous literary Lady,[91] have requested a line to you, as they are bound on a journey to the seat of your University and wish, I suppose, an apology for visiting Monticello.

I have lost your last letter to me, the most consolatory letter I ever received in my life.[92] What would I not give for a copy of it. Your friend to all eternity,

JOHN ADAMS

Adams to Jefferson

Quincy December 1st. 1825

DEAR SIR

I ought not to have neglected so long to write you an account of the delightful visit I received from Mr. and Mrs. Coolidge.[93] Mrs. C. deserves all the high praises I have constantly heard concerning her. She entertained me with accounts of your sentiments of human life, which accorded so perfectly with mine that it gave me great delight. In one point, however, I could not agree. She said she had heard you say that you would like to go over life again. In this I could not agree; I had rather go forward and meet whatever is to come. I have met in this life with great trials. I have had a Father, and lost him. I have had a Mother and lost her. I have had a Wife and lost her. I have had Children and lost them. I have had honorable and worthy Friends and lost them—and instead of suffering these griefs again, I had rather go forward and meet my destiny. I am, as ever, affectionately

JOHN ADAMS

91. Mrs. Lydia Howard Huntley Sigourney.
92. TJ to JA, Feb. 15, 1825, above, 608-9.
93. Joseph Coolidge, Jr., of Boston, married Eleanora Wayles Randolph, daughter of Thomas Mann Randolph and Martha Jefferson Randolph, on May 27, 1825. She was TJ's favorite granddaughter and he had the highest respect for Mr. Coolidge. TJ to Edward Everett, July 21, 1825, Lipscomb and Bergh, eds., *Writings*, XIX, 285; Zorn, *Descendants of the Presidents*, 49.

Jefferson to Adams

Monticello Dec. 18. 25.

DEAR SIR

Your letters are always welcome, the last more than all others, it's subject being one of the dearest to my heart. To my grand-daughter your commendations cannot fail to be an object of high ambition, as a certain passport to the good opinion of the world. If she does not cultivate them with assiduity and affection, she will illy fulfill my parting injunctions. I trust she will merit a continuance of your favor, and find in her new situation the general esteem she so happily possessed in the society she left.

You tell me she repeated to you an expression of mine that I should be willing to go again over the scenes of past life. I should not be unwilling, without however wishing it. And why not? I have enjoyed a greater share of health than falls to the lot of most men; my spirits have never failed me except under those paroxysms of grief which you, as well as myself, have experienced in every form: and with good health and good spirits the pleasures surely outweigh the pains of life. Why not then taste them again, fat and lean together. Were I indeed permitted to cut off from the train the last 7. years, the balance would be much in favor of treading the ground over again. Being at that period in the neighborhood of our Warm springs, and well in health, I wished to be better, and tried them. They destroyed, in a great degree, my internal organism, and I have never since had a moment of perfect health. I have now been 8 months confined almost constantly to the house, with now and then intervals of a few days on which I could get on horseback.

I presume you have recieved a copy of the life of Richd. H. Lee, from his grandson of the same name, author of the work. You and I know that he merited much during the revolution. Eloquent, bold, and ever watchful at his post, of which his biographer omits no proof. I am not certain whether the friends of George Mason, of Patrick Henry, yourself, and even of Genl Washington may not reclaim some feathers of the plumage given him, notable as was his proper and original coat. But on this subject I will not anticipate your own judgment.

I learn with sincere pleasure that you have experienced lately a great renovation of your health. That it may continue to the ultimate period of your wishes is the sincere prayer of usque ad aras amicissimi tui ["ever at the altars of your dearest friend"].

TH: JEFFERSON

Adams to Jefferson

Quincy 14th. January 1826

MY DEAR SIR

Permit me to introduce to your acquaintance a young Lawyer by the name of Josiah Quincy and with the title of Coll. being an Aid to our Governor. The name of Coll. Quincy has never I believe been extinct for over two hundred years. He is a Son of our Worthy Mayor of the City of Boston and possesses a character unstained and irreproachable. I applaud his ambition to visit Monticello and its great inhabitant, and while I have my hand in I cannot cease without giving you some account of the state of my mind. I am certainly very near the end of my life. I am far from trifling with the idea of Death which is a great and solemn event. But I contemplate it without terror or dismay, "aut transit, aut finit ["either it is a transformation, or it is the end"]," if finit, which I cannot believe, and do not believe, there is then an end of all but I shall never know it, and why should I dread it, which I do not; if transit I shall ever be under the same constitution and administration of Government in the Universe, and I am not afraid to trust and confide in it.

I have not the pleasure to see Mr. and Mrs. Coolidge as often as I wish— but I hear nothing of them but what is respectable and pleasing. I am as ever your friend

JOHN ADAMS

Jefferson to Adams

Monticello Mar. 25. 26.

DEAR SIR

My grandson Th: Jefferson Randolph, being on a visit to Boston, would think he had seen nothing were he to leave it without having seen you. Altho' I truly sympathise with you in the trouble these interruptions give, yet I must ask for him permission to pay to you his personal respects.

Like other young people, he wishes to be able, in the winter nights of old age, to recount to those around him what he has heard and learnt of the Heroic age preceding his birth, and which of the Argonauts particularly he was in time to have seen. It was the lot of our early years to witness nothing but the dull monotony of colonial subservience, and of our riper ones to breast the labors and perils of working out of it. Theirs are the Halcyon calms succeeding the storm which our Argosy had so stoutly weathered. Gratify his ambition then by recieving his best bow, and my solicitude for your health by enabling him to bring me a favorable account of it. Mine is but indifferent, but not so my friendship and respect for you.

TH: JEFFERSON

Adams to Jefferson

Quincy April 17th. 1826

MY DEAR SIR

Your letter of March 25th. has been a cordial to me, and the more consoling as it was brought by your Grandsons, Mr. Randolph and Mr. Coolidge. Everybody connected with you is snatched up, so that I cannot get any of them to dine with me—they are always engaged. How happens it that you Virginians are all sons of Anak? [94] We New Englanders are but Pygmies by the side of Mr. Randolph. I was very much gratified with Mr. Randolph, and his conversation. Your letter is one of the most beautiful and delightful I have ever received.

Public affairs go on pretty much as usual: perpetual chicanery and rather more personal abuse than there used to be. Messrs. Randolph and McDuffie have out-Heroded Herod.[95] Mr. McDuffie seems to be swallowed up in chivalry. Such institutions ought not to be suffered in a republican Government. Our American Chivalry is the worst in the World. It has no Laws, no bounds, no definitions; it seems to be all a Caprice. My love to all your family, and best wishes for your health

JOHN ADAMS.

94. Joshua 11:21.
95. Both John Randolph and George McDuffie in Congress were bitterly opposed to President J. Q. Adams's administration. McDuffie charged the President and his secretary of state, Henry Clay, with corruption in the electoral vote of 1824. Samuel F. Bemis, *John Quincy Adams and the Union* (N. Y., 1956), 41-42, 132-33.

INDEX

The index covers the introduction, text, and notes. Pages i-li, 1-282, are in Volume I; pages 283-614 are in Volume II.

A

Abdurrahman, Tripolitan ambassador to Great Britain, 121, 126, 127
Abyssinia, expedition to, 591
Academy of chirurgery, 132
Acherly, Roger, 294
Achilles, 462
Acta Sanctorum, 419, 429, 447, 450, 452, 454
Acton, Mr., naval minister of Naples, 143
Adair, James, 305, 323
Adams, Miss Abigail (JA's daughter), mentioned, 21, 30, 35, 58, 80, 81, 98, 110, 119, 120; accompanies AA to London, 14; as secretary to JA, 26; marries Col. W. S. Smith, 137. *See also* Smith, Abigail Adams
Adams, Abigail (Mrs. John), as grandmother, 184; breaks with TJ, xlii, 273-74; characterized, xl; compares European society with American, 119; correspondence with TJ evaluated, xxxviii-xxxix; death of, 476, 529; friendship with TJ, 226-27, 446, 463; kindness of, 28; meets TJ, 14; mentioned, 17, 21, 119, 137, 237; on Court of St. James, 228; on English society, 74, 145; on French society, 145; on JA's reception at Court, 29; on JA's regard for TJ, 28; on J. Q. Adams's removal, 280-81; on living allowances for diplomats, 227; on "midnight appointments," 271-72; on music, 30; on TJ and Callender, 266, 276-77; on TJ's administration, 268; on Polly Jefferson, 109, 165, 169, 178, 179, 183-84, 185, 197, 212, 213; on Polly Jefferson's death, 265, 268-69; on Republican opposition to JA, xli; on Shays's Rebellion, 165-66, 168-69; political differences with TJ, 267; renews correspondence with TJ, 378; sails Boston to London, 16; sends J. Q. Adams's letters to TJ, 500-1; shops for TJ, 70, 79, 81, 108, 120, 185, 186, 201, 213, 215

Adams, Abigail (JA's grandchild), 296
Adams, Charles (JA's son), 264, 269
Adams, George Washington (J. Q. Adams's son), 352
Adams, John, accounts as minister to Great Britain, 260-61; addresses of 1798, 288, 327; and Declaration of Independence, 2; and U.S. navy, 287, 584-85; as political philosopher, xxxiv-xxxv; breaks with TJ, 240-41, 243, 244; characterized, xxxvi, xxxvii, xliii; compares his republicanism with TJ's, xlv; confers with Lord Gordon, 30; confers with Vergennes, 18-20; correspondence of, 507, 556; death of, xxxiii, 559; defeated by Democratic-Republicans, xli, xlv; diplomatic career of, xliii, 2-4, 12-15, 72-75, 125-28, 205-8; elected president, 242; elected vice president, 236; favors ransoming American prisoners, 161; favorite at Court of St. James, 108; fondness for Polly Jefferson, 187; friendship with TJ, 250; health of, 552-53; hopes for publication of TJ's letters, 582; illness of, 84, 539; independence of, 176-77; injures his leg, 586; interests of, xlvii; invites TJ to London, 125; TJ on, 1, 13; learns Italian, 187-88; meets Queen Charlotte, 31; meets TJ, 1; member of Mass. Constitutional Convention, 3; negotiates Dutch loan, 187, 191, 206, 207, 219; negotiations with Portugal, 74-75; on administrations of TJ and Madison, 301; on appointment procedures, 107; on chance, 373; on correspondence with TJ, 163, 177; on costs of protection from Barbary pirates, 133-34; on death of his son Charles, 264; on draft treaty with England, 50-52, 74; on Dutch speculation in American debt, 224-25; on election of 1800, 283; on European political upheaval, 214-15; on favorite reading, 362; on first elections under Constitution, 234; on George III, 15, 31; on Indians, 289, 308;